BY STEVEN RINELLA

MeatEater's American History: The Long Hunters (1761–1775) (audiobook)

Catch a Crayfish, Count the Stars: Fun Projects, Skills, and Activities for Outdoor Kids

MeatEater's Campfire Stories: Narrow Escapes & More Close Calls (audiobook)

Outdoor Kids in an Inside World: Getting Your Family Out of the House and Radically Engaged with Nature

MeatEater's Campfire Stories: Close Calls (audiobook)

The MeatEater Guide to Wilderness Skills and Survival

The MeatEater Fish and Game Cookbook

The Complete Guide to Hunting, Butchering, and Cooking Wild Game, Volume 1: Big Game

The Complete Guide to Hunting, Butchering, and Cooking Wild Game, Volume 2: Small Game & Fowl

Meat Eater: Adventures from the Life of an American Hunter

American Buffalo: In Search of a Lost Icon

The Scavenger's Guide to Haute Cuisine

The MEATEATER OUTDOOR COOKBOOK

WILD GAME RECIPES FOR THE GRILL, SMOKER, CAMPSTOVE, AND CAMPFIRE

Steven Rinella
WITH KRISTA RUANE

Photography by John Hafner
Additional Photography by Seth Morris

Random House
New York

Random House
An imprint and division of Penguin Random House LLC
1745 Broadway, New York, NY 10019
randomhousebooks.com
penguinrandomhouse.com

2025 Random House Trade Paperback Edition

Originally published in hardcover in the United States by Random House, an imprint and division of Penguin Random House LLC, in 2024.

LIBRARY OF CONGRESS CATALOGING-IN-PUBLICATION DATA
Names: Rinella, Steven, author. | Ruane, Krista, author.
Title: The MeatEater outdoor cookbook: wild game recipes for the grill, smoker, campstove, and campfire / with Steven Rinella and Krista Ruane.
Description: New York: Random House, [2024] | Includes index.
Identifiers: LCCN 2023034189 (print) | LCCN 2023034190 (ebook) | ISBN 9798217154807 (box set) | ISBN 9780593449042 (ebook)
Subjects: LCSH: Outdoor cooking. | Cooking (Game) | Cooking (Wild foods) | MeatEater (Television program) | LCGFT: Cookbooks.
Classification: LCC TX823 .R46 2024 (print) | LCC TX823 (ebook) | DCC 641.5/78—dc23/eng/20230728
LC record available at https://lccn.loc.gov/2023034189
LC ebook record available at https://lccn.loc.gov/2023034190

Printed in China on acid-free paper

987654321

Book design by Debbie Glasserman

The authorized representative in the EU for product safety and compliance is Penguin Random House Ireland, Morrison Chambers, 32 Nassau Street, Dublin D02 YH68, Ireland. https://eu-contact.penguin.ie

FOR JAMES, ROSEMARY,
AND MATTHEW—
DIRT UNDER YOUR NAILS,
LOVE IN YOUR HEARTS

CONTENTS

INTRODUCTION

Recently I was reading about the Blackfoot tribe of the northern Great Plains. They would make an energy-rich food called pemmican by mixing dried and shredded buffalo meat with tallow and grease extracted from buffalo bones. They'd store this mixture inside fresh buffalo skins sewn into oblong bags. As the buffalo skin dried, it would shrink so tightly over the pemmican that the package would achieve, as one observer put it, "the solidity and weight of a rock." I may find zero inspiration in the technology and innovation that goes into something like an iPhone, but I'm routinely blown away by the amazing things that our species has figured out when it comes to feeding ourselves.

We humans have been developing innovations in outdoor cooking for a staggeringly long time. So long, in fact, that we were doing it back when we weren't the only human species. Archaeological evidence links multiple human species with at least limited use of fire dating back some eight hundred thousand years. By three hundred thousand years ago, our own distant *Homo sapiens* ancestors were using fire on a daily basis, as were Neanderthals and *Homo erectus*. Imagine for a moment that you're a time traveler visiting Spain about fifty thousand years ago. You approach a campfire at night and detect the unmistakable smell of roasting meat. Just as you might wonder what type of animal is being cooked, you'd also have to wonder what type of human is doing the cooking—or being cooked.

Since then we've made a lot of nice progress toward a civilized existence, but in our fervor to advance, we've made some terrible mistakes. Our taming of the planet brought about inestimable environmental damage as we leveled forests for building materials, drove dozens of wildlife species to extinction, gutted the earth for minerals and oil, and poisoned our lakes, rivers, and oceans with industrial pollutants. Our intimate and personal relationships with nature have suffered as well. For millions of years, hunting and fishing fueled within us a deep, visceral bond to nature. Our evolving lifeways and interests have pushed us away from these disciplines. In California, the most populous and perhaps most influential state in America, only about one-half percent of residents hold a hunting license. So in a random sampling of two hundred Californians, you'd find only one who might still know the hands-on joy and beauty of deriving their own sustenance from the breathtaking menagerie of wild birds and animals that have supported human life since our beginning.

Hunting and fishing are admittedly extreme examples of engagement with nature. When taken seriously by an individual, they tend to assume the characteristics of a discipline or lifestyle. But even our more casual relationships with nature are dying. In 2005, the author and journalist Richard Louv introduced the term *nature deficit disorder* as a description of the human costs associated with an increasing alienation from nature. He recognized that our divorce from nature began long ago, with the introduction of agriculture. However, he recognized that it accelerated greatly in recent years due to the "proliferation of electronic communications; poor urban planning and disappearing open space; increased street traffic; diminished importance of the natural world in public and private education; and parental fear magnified by news and entertainment media." Louv's writing focuses on children, but a lack of time spent outdoors is a major problem for adults as well. The average American spends 87 percent of their time inside buildings, and 7 percent inside vehicles. That leaves about one half of one day per week that's spent outside. It's an astounding statistic, especially when you consider the dozens of studies over the last several decades linking disengagement with the outdoors to everything from depression to obesity to environmental apathy. While writing about similar findings in my own book *Outdoor Kids in an Inside World* (2022), I pointed out to my readers that the results of such research shouldn't sound particularly surprising. We don't need academic studies to tell us that we feel better when we step outside.

Nor do we need someone to tell us that food tastes better when it's cooked outside. This is something I've recognized ever since I was a little kid. One summer, when I was nine or ten, my dad put me to work with a hammer and chisel removing the old mortar from a pickup-truckload of red bricks that he'd salvaged from a demolished building. I was then tasked with stirring batches of fresh mortar with a garden hoe while my dad and a friend named Eugene built a gigantic fire ring in our backyard down by the lake. For the next decade or so, that fire ring served as a sort of laboratory for adolescent experiments in outdoor cooking. Through an endless litany of burns and scalds on our hands, my neighborhood buddies and I fine-tuned the making of sassafras tea (add lots of sugar), botched multiple attempts at roasting whole chipmunks, incinerated dozens of foil-wrapped potatoes that were buried beneath the coals for too long, fried countless bluegill caught from the lake, and made so many "hobo pies" (nowadays, these are more politely referred to as iron pies) that we'd frequently drain a tub of margarine in a single cooking session and then melt the polypropylene container over the heat of the fire because we liked the crazy zipping sound that the material made when it dripped into the flames.

All of it tasted amazing! Even the burned and desiccated potatoes were a treat once you became accustomed to the grittiness of wood ash. But the actual flavors and textures of the meals had little to do with how much I loved them. Instead, I was drawn to the labor, ingenuity, and ever-so-slight danger involved with outdoor cooking. And I was inspired by the environment. While cooking outside, the walls and ceiling of a conventional indoor kitchen were replaced by the open sky and the lake. A humming exhaust fan and the background noise of TV became wind through the trees and birdsong. While cooking in that environment, with smoke in my eyes and the fire's heat on my arms, I couldn't help but feel connected to something deep and eternal about my own human experience. It drew me into the present and opened me up to the past. When roasting a raw-in-the-middle-but-burned-on-the-outside chipmunk, it was easy to imagine the exhilaration that might have come from flipping a rack of mammoth ribs. And when sharing the concoctions with friends and family, it was easy to imagine walking through the woods toward the firelight of a distant camp in order to share appetizers with that friendly band of Neanderthals that had recently moved into our territory.

Both personally and professionally, I've continued to chase those same outdoor cooking adventures and lessons that I cultivated around the fire pit of my childhood home. Early on, I was focused on the regional favorites of my home turf in western Michigan. Around there, major occasions were often celebrated by roasting a whole hog with the skin, feet, and head intact. I provided the meal for my own high school graduation party by staying up all night to cook a 125-pound pig in a fuel-oil drum that my neighbor had converted into a charcoal-fired roaster. A couple of years later, my college buddy Andy and I borrowed that roaster again in order to attempt something bigger and better. We stuffed a large hog with the bone-in quarters of a whitetail deer that had been run over by the car in front of me while I was driving home from fishing salmon on Michigan's Pere Marquette River. Years later, while living in Brooklyn, New York, I wanted to attempt an even more technically complex underground hog cooking strategy that I'd witnessed in Hawaii. I started by digging a giant hole in the backyard garden space of our apartment building. The first step was generating a deep bed of coals in the bottom of the hole. The plume of smoke that developed as I

pitched in armloads of oak firewood resembled something from an urban warfare news dispatch. I got nervous when I heard the distant scream of fire truck sirens. The nervousness blossomed into full-on panic when two ladder trucks pulled up in front of our building. Five or six firemen poured through the front door of my apartment and then out the backdoor into the garden space. When I explained what I was fixing to do, the captain said, "That's a great idea, but you're gonna need to put that out. Right now."

My adventures in hog roasting demonstrate a familiar pathway that I've taken with many other outdoor cooking strategies: Investigation leads to inspiration, which leads to experimentation, which leads to innovation. Or at least *attempted* innovation. This path of discovery has led to some of my most unique and memorable outdoor cooking experiences. Some were mighty short, such as the one initiated by the journal of a hunter who mentioned flavoring raw buffalo liver with the animal's own bile. I tried that once, in Sonora, Mexico, and once was enough. (If you like the alkaline-goodness of pressing a nine-volt battery to your tongue, you're gonna love bile.)

Another lengthier journey was prompted by a visit to an archaeological site in northern New Mexico. Known as the Folsom site, it's a location where Ice Age hunters corralled at least thirty-two bison in a box canyon and killed them using stone projectile points. A peculiarity of the site is the lack of tail bones in the bone bed that contains the butchered remains of the animals. Researchers have postulated, reasonably so, that the hunters hauled away the hides with the tails intact—which is how it's still done today. While archaeologists recovered jaw bones showing distinctive cut marks where the hunters removed the animals' tongues, there were no femurs recovered at the site. These were likely hauled away to a nearby camp to be boiled for bone grease and then smashed open for the marrow. (As I mentioned with regards to the Blackfeet, grease and marrow were used in the making of pemmican.) You might wonder, as I did, how an Ice Age hunter would go about boiling something. After all, they had no metal pots or other large vessels that would withstand the direct heat of a fire. I researched this question and found multiple references to other indigenous hunters using animal hides to line shallow pits dug in the ground that were then filled with water. They would heat rocks in a fire, then give the rocks a quick rinse before dropping them into the hide-lined cauldron. The heat from the rocks would then bring the water to a boil.

It's not that I necessarily doubted these accounts; it's just that I had such a hard time imagining what it looked like to see a rock bring water to a boil. I thought about it for a couple of years, until one day, in west Texas, I lined a head-sized hole with the stomach of a javelina (also known as a collared peccary, these small pig-like critters are fairly common in the deserts of the Southwest) and filled the makeshift pot with water and a few strips of javelina meat. I then dropped in a few porous lava rocks that I'd heated in my campfire, and voilà! The water hissed and steamed, and a profusion of bubbles spread forth from where the rocks had disappeared. That night, lying in my sleeping bag with a belly full of boiled javelina meat, I luxuriated in the knowledge that old recipes never die.

Ultimately, the cookbook in your hands represents the future of outdoor cooking more than it represents the past. You're holding a modern but timeless take on everything from preparing charcuterie to cocktails in the great outdoors. But before we get to that, I want to explain one last culinary adventure that exemplifies what I love most about the subject of outdoor cooking. This story, perhaps more than any other, is to thank for the fact that this book now exists. It begins with me reading *The Oregon Trail,* Francis Parkman's journal about his travels on America's western frontier in 1846. In what is now Wyoming, Parkman and his companion were honored by their Oglala Sioux hosts with the meat of a puppy that was plucked from a nest of its littermates in the back of a teepee and knocked over the head with a stone mallet. Parkman describes how the woman responsible for cooking the dog held it by the back foot as she waved it through the flames

of the fire in order to burn off the hair before cutting the animal into pieces and dropping them into a kettle to boil, skin and all. It was a startling passage for me, especially since I'd been raised in the constant presence of my own pet dogs. It forced me to reckon with my personal taboos. And, in a roundabout way, the passage from Parkman's book eventually led me to northern Vietnam in order to write a magazine story about the tradition of consuming dog meat during the Lunar New Year celebrations. Dog meat, thit cho, is regarded as a "warming" food that has the power to change one's fortunes.

It was on that trip, while riding a rented moped into the mountains, that I encountered a shirtless Vietnamese farmer who had just killed a small animal with an air rifle. At first I thought it was a squirrel, but it was actually some kind of arboreal marsupial—think of a small opossum. He already had a fire burning. Holding the critter by the back foot, he waved it through the flames in order to burn the hair off. I was reminded, immediately, of the passage from Parkman's book that had initially sent me on this journey.

I sat down on a stump to watch the man prepare his meal. As he scraped away the burned hair, a golden-colored skin emerged that reminded of a perfectly roasted hog. He went to his garden plot and gathered a handful of thin red peppers, a large banana leaf, a green herb that I didn't recognize, and a few stalks of lemongrass. Working with a small machete that had been forged from a vehicle's leaf spring, he prepared his collection of ingredients and layered them in the center of the banana leaf with a splash of rice wine. He laid the animal atop the ingredients and then rolled the banana leaf into an envelope-shaped package. He folded the package into an old piece of crumpled-up and blackened aluminum foil that he smoothed back out for reuse. This he set into the fire.

What emerged from the coals, an hour or so later, was the most delicious meal that I ate during my time in Vietnam. In fact, taken as a whole, it was the most memorable meal that I've eaten in my entire life. The fork-tender meat occupied a space between squirrel and chicken thighs. It was perfectly sweet and hot and exotic, with that magical bit of wildness that comes with game meat. Even better, the meal brought together every element of outdoor cooking that I've come to love. It captured the adventure of travel and the thrill of the hunt. It expressed the continuity of ancient skill sets. It contained the heat and smoke of fire and the pragmatic ingenuity and elbow grease that are integral to working outside. Yet the ruggedness was balanced with careful attention to detail and an awareness of the primacy of flavor. The meal was built with an acknowledgment that it needed to taste perfect in order to honor all of those constituent elements that went into its creation.

This book was built in the same spirit as that meal. It's my hope that this spirit flows through to you as you prepare these meals for your friends, family, and loved ones. Here's to the smoke in your eyes, the burns on your fingers, and the flavor on your plate.

« Roasting whole small mammals like this marmot on a fire is an ancient cooking technique that still persists in some cultures around the world.

USING THIS BOOK
A NOTE ON VARIABILITY

There are an estimated 20,000 species of fish in the world, 10,000 birds, and about 5,400 species of mammals. We're certainly not recommending all of them as food items, but the numbers help illustrate how hard it is to list every possible protein source that might work for the preparations found within this book. If we have a recipe that calls for halibut, what we're really saying is that it works for things that are halibut-*like*—meaning it works for larger specimens of firm, white-fleshed fish. So if you're looking at this halibut recipe and you say to yourself, "Dammit, all I have is a big redfish," you shouldn't despair. There's a good chance that these two fish species would both work for the same thing. Likewise, moose, caribou, and elk are all members of the deer family, and all of them have relatively lean red meat. Using the same recipe and method of cooking, you can expect to get the same basic results from all three species—and any other member of the deer family, for that matter.

To help you navigate the endless possibilities around ingredient selection, we use a heading called *Also works with* in our recipes. When you see this, you're looking at some of our suggestions for possible substitutions, both wild and domestic, that would work for that particular recipe. If you see a recipe for quail, we might point out that the same preparation would still be pretty damn good with chicken, pheasant, or grouse. Of course, you might have to apply a little common sense to the cooking process. You might need to adjust certain ingredient measurements to account for the increase in size, or perhaps increase the cooking time a bit, but it'll work.

On the subject of variability, we'd also like to point out that there can be as much variability within a species of game animal as there is between different species of game animals. Meaning, the meat from two whitetail deer might have greater differences in quality than there are between the meat of a particular elk and that of a particular moose. Factors such as health, age, diet, and other uncontrollable variables can greatly impact the flavor and texture of an animal's meat; a yearling whitetail doe will almost certainly be more tender than an old buck, but the buck will likely have a more robust flavor. So if a recipe doesn't turn out as planned, consider the possibility that you might get different results the next time you try that recipe with the meat from a different critter.

Likewise, fish and meat that is harvested in nature has tremendous variability in terms of size and weight. While we list ingredient weight and size in our recipes, don't get hung up on the details. A couple of 1-pound beaver thighs will work just as well for the Beaver Confit Toasts with Grilled Figs and Balsamic-Honey Glaze recipe (page 20) as the single 1½- to 2-pound thigh that's listed. And, if your protein weight is a little over what we've listed, proportionally increase the other ingredients to match.

To sum up, think of these recipes as guidelines. They have all been tested and retested in various conditions to achieve desired results. Our instructions will guide you toward a good outcome, but it's best if you meet us halfway by keeping your wits about you and trusting your instincts. This is a collaboration. We promise to uphold our end of the deal.

RECIPE ICONS

Anyone who has spent a little time camping, fishing, or hunting should be familiar with the icons on maps that identify places like campgrounds, trailheads, and boat ramps. Because these symbols are so embedded in the culture and traditions of American outdoorsmen and -women, we're using a similar icon system that will allow you to navigate the recipes in this book.

While some of the recipes in this book were developed with a very specific type of equipment and outdoor location in mind, many can be made pretty much anywhere with just a little tweaking and flexibility. You may see recipes with just a single icon or they may have more than one. For instance, smoking a wild hog ham on a wilderness backpacking trip isn't realistic, but you can cook bratwursts or burgers over a campfire just as easily as you can at home on a propane grill.

BACKYARD

Best suited for an outdoor space right outside your home, such as a backyard or deck. You may need access to a proper kitchen, an extensive ingredient list, or specialized pieces of cooking equipment.

CAR CAMPING

Designed for camping trips where you can carry a decent amount of gear. Think cars, campers, boats, and even packhorses. These may require coolers, utensils, pots and pans, and cooking systems such as two-burner campstoves, portable firepit grills, or Dutch oven tripod setups. You'll find most recipes include make-ahead sauces and rubs or components that can be cooked in a home kitchen and assembled on-site.

BACKCOUNTRY

Suitable for wilderness or backwoods cooking. While remote camping usually involves meals such as instant oatmeal and freeze-dried entrées, these recipes can help you step up your wilderness cooking game with a few packable or freshly sourced ingredients and a minimal amount of gear.

OUTDOOR COOKING APPLIANCES AND KITCHEN SETUPS

When I was in high school, a guy named Brian moved into a rental house down the road from us. We became buddies. One of the things I liked about his family was that they did more outdoor cooking than anyone I knew. Their outdoor "kitchen" consisted of a patch of gravel beneath the carport and was equipped with a simple charcoal kettle grill and a sack of Kingsford briquettes. One spatula, one set of tongs. They had that grill fired up three or four nights a week, and they knew how to use it. It was a good place to be invited for dinner. They roasted chicken, smoked pork butt, and grilled locally caught salmon from Lake Michigan—all on that same setup.

I think of that family and their simplified outdoor kitchen every time I walk into a big home and garden store and get greeted by the latest display of utensils, grills, smokers, and wood-fired pizza ovens that look like Star Wars robots and come with a user's manual as thick as your hand. All too often, I see friends splurge on these ultra-sophisticated gadgets that end up rusting away beneath the eaves of their house with a family of mice living in the pan where the wood chips are supposed to go. Meanwhile, Brian's family is probably still slinging burgers off that same grill they owned twenty-some years ago.

That's not to knock innovative outdoor cooking equipment. Now and then, they come out with stuff that is pretty damned nice, and I do like to keep abreast of the trends. I remember dismissing pellet grills when I first heard about them, because it seemed like sourcing the pellets would be a pain in the ass. And besides that, you had to have a place to plug them in. That just goes to show how wrong I can be. My pellet grill is now my second-favorite piece of outdoor cooking equipment. (My new commercial-grade deep fryer really is a sight to see.)

The point I'm trying to make here is that you should be honest with yourself about your intentions, skills, dedication, and time constraints when selecting outdoor cooking equipment. If you typically have twenty minutes to prepare dinner at night and all you want is a hamburger, don't buy a smoker that takes two hours and an engineering degree to heat up. And you can certainly take a minimalist approach to camp kitchens, too. This is something you should keep in mind as you go through this section that details some of our favorite outdoor cooking appliances and kitchen equipment. In other words, think of this section as more of a conversation starter than a shopping list. And when considering a piece of gear, look through the recipes in this book to make sure you're drawn to the sorts of preparations that the appliance can be used for. America's backyards are full of unused outdoor cooking equipment. There's no need to add to the pile.

Throughout this book, you'll see some uniquely designed DIY cooking rigs, like the rotisserie trompo grill on page 252 and the whole-hog roaster on the opposite page, that were built by friends. Though these contraptions are precious to me, the truth is they typically get used on special occasions for preparations that I like to call showstoppers. Here's a more practical list of what I'd consider to be the essential, everyday workhorses for outdoor cooking.

OUTDOOR COOKING APPLIANCES

Propane Grills

Gas grills are a fast, simple, convenient tool for outdoor cooking. And with easily controlled heat settings and add-ons like side burners, rotisseries, and wood chip containers, you can cook just about anything on them. I like a propane grill with enough surface area to cook meat and vegetables at the same time or to make a big batch of burgers for a group of neighbors and friends. Look for a grill with durable cast-iron grates. You can't go wrong with Camp Chef or Weber grills.

Charcoal Grills

The big knock against gas grills is they don't impart natural smoke flavor. That's certainly true, but charcoal grills aren't for impatient chefs or time-starved parents. A charcoal chimney starter gets you cooking faster, but charcoal grills don't heat up instantly with the turn of a knob. And controlling the temperature requires moving hot coals around. Then there's cleaning up all that burnt ash to consider. But despite all the extra work, charcoal grills are definitely worth having around. Even a simple hamburger tastes better cooked over smoldering briquettes. For my money, it's hard to beat the simplicity and functionality of the original Weber kettle grill.

No matter the brand, you can use standard machine-formed briquettes, lump hardwood charcoal mixes, or a combination of the two. The flavor and intense heat from natural hardwood charcoal surpasses manufactured briquettes; however, briquettes usually burn longer. The varieties of charcoal now available in stores have expanded significantly in the past few years. If you're into doing some experimentation, it's worth exploring how each one cooks. What we don't recommend are charcoal briquettes pre-soaked in lighter fluid. Sure, the chemicals burn off eventually, but the nasty flavor of the fuel does penetrate into your food. Plus, by using a chimney, you can skip the lighter fluid.

Fire Pits

Before I got my hands on one of the portable double-walled metal fire pits that are so popular these days, I was pretty skeptical. I didn't buy claims of smokeless wood fires, and I certainly didn't consider them a must-have piece of outdoor cooking equipment. In fact, they didn't strike me as much more than a glorified version of a chopped-down 55-gallon drum that you'd use to burn trash. Man, was I wrong. I like these things so damn much that I've got two of the Breeo models—a big one that lives on our porch and a smaller one that goes wherever our camper goes. They really do cut way down on smoke, and they put off an amazing amount of heat on cold nights. These types of fire pits also provide a safe place for a contained fire in a small backyard or at a crowded campsite. Best of all, with a few super handy attachments like a grill grate, griddle, and pothanger, it's a joy to cook directly over a wood fire.

Electric Pellet Grills

These grills burn pellets made of food-grade pulped hardwoods that add rich, smoky flavors to food. Pellet grills bridge the gap between a regular grill and a conventional smoker. Although most can't reach the extremely high searing temperatures that gas and charcoal grills can attain, some can hit 500°F and operate as low as 150°F. In other words, you can quickly grill a steak to medium-rare at high temperatures and you can precisely maintain lower temperatures for smoking salmon or ham. And pellet grills are ideal for roasting big chunks of venison backstrap and round roasts. Many pellet grills are programmable and can be run remotely with wireless controllers. Keep in mind, pellet grills do require regular maintenance and cleaning, and you have to keep a supply of wood pellets on hand. GreenMountain and Camp Chef both manufacture quality pellet grills in a variety of sizes.

Chamber Smokers

Chamber smokers smolder wood chips to create smoke. They do a great job of smoking and drying jerky, fish, and summer sausage. When I was a kid, it seemed like half the people I knew had an old Smokehouse Big Chief smoker in their garage. You'd just plug it in, put a pan of wood chips on the hot plate, and you were smoking. There are still plenty of electric smokers on the market today, including the Smokehouse Big Chief, and some are pretty slick. You can get programmable models that operate on autopilot with preset start and stop times. Despite the ease of electric smokers, I prefer propane-fired chamber smokers, such as the Camp Chef Smoke Vault. They have a wide temperature range, and you don't need a nearby power source. I also like the presence of the flame, if only for aesthetic reasons. Get a tall one (I use a smoker that's about 28 inches high) with heavy gauge metal walls to hold the temperature and plenty of shelves for smoking large batches of fish, jerky, sausages, mushrooms, and whatever else you want to cram in there. You can also remove the shelves and hang large items like hams and venison legs.

Deep Fryer

You might not think of a deep fryer as an outdoor cooking appliance, but experience has taught me that outside is the best place to use your fryer. Frying outside means you won't have to contend with grease splatters and oily smells inside your house. Just make sure you've got a covered spot where you can store and use your fryer out of the weather. There are all kinds of small deep fryers made strictly for the at-home chef, but most of them tend to be cheaply built and generally don't last very long before something breaks or the heating element burns out. I have had good luck with a Breville Smart Fryer, but your best option is a heavy-duty stainless steel commercial-grade countertop fryer. You can buy them from restaurant supply businesses online in gas or electric models. For at-home use, electric is the way to go. A good one might cost you a few hundred dollars, but over the long haul, the increased durability and added features justify the investment. With proper care, a commercial fryer should last a lifetime. Look for a double basket model from Globe or Vollrath with a 10-pound grease vat.

Outdoor Cookers

You'll see these things categorized as turkey fryers, crayfish boilers, or just plain old outdoor cookers, but most share the same basic design—a large single burner that sits on four steel legs or a pedestal and connects to a 20-pound propane tank. Many are sold as kits with a 30- to 100-quart pot, a thermometer, and a steaming/frying basket. These setups have long been a mainstay in coastal communities, and they came into wider popularity with inlanders during the deep-fried turkey craze. I find that they're a very useful and versatile part of my outdoor cooking equipment lineup. At our fish shack in southeastern Alaska, we use our outdoor cooker nearly every day to steam crabs, boil shrimp, and deep-fry large quantities of fish and sea cucumbers. They're also useful for big pots of gumbo and chili meant to serve large crowds. On a side note, outdoor cookers are also a handy tool for scalding game birds for easy plucking and cleaning up big game skulls for mounts. Companies like King Kooker and Bayou Classic produce simple, quality outdoor cookers.

Car Camping Grills

Small, portable gas grills that run off green single-use 1-pound propane canisters are super convenient for quickly cooking typical car camping fare like burgers and brats. Due to wildfire restrictions, cooking over a campfire isn't always an option. But Coleman and Camp Chef make affordable, lightweight gas grills that are often legal to use when open fires are strictly outlawed. If fire restrictions aren't a concern and you prefer grilling over briquettes, there are downsized versions of charcoal grills that work well for car camping. But no matter the fuel source, grills do have their limitations. Yes, it's possible to use one to steam some veggies in a foil pack or warm up a pot of water for instant coffee, but there are much better options for things like boiling and frying.

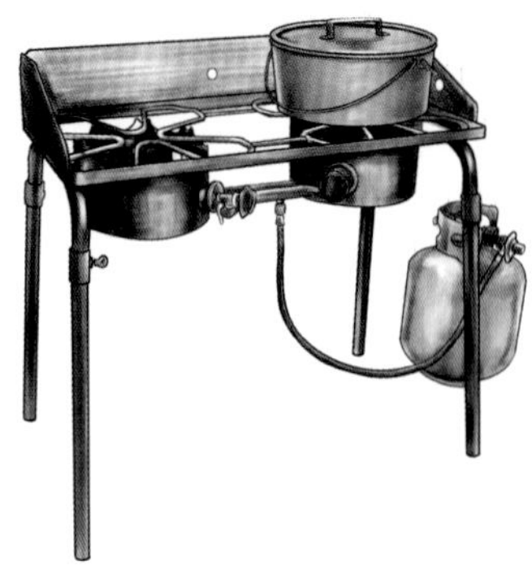

Propane Stoves

A two-burner propane stove will cover the vast majority of your cooking on a car camping trip—and again, it will be indispensable when fire restrictions forbid open flames. If you're looking for something basic, reliable, and highly portable, go with a small, lightweight stove that runs off 1-pound propane tanks like the Coleman Classic Propane Camping Stove. It won't take up much space in your vehicle, and I've even packed one along on canoeing trips. Camp Chef and other manufacturers offer models with an integrated griddle system that adds some valuable versatility. The beauty of these things lies in their simplicity, but be aware that they don't have burners with super-high Btu (British thermal unit) output. It takes time to get a big pot of water boiling, especially in cold, windy weather. Most also lack the space to accommodate two large pots or pans at the same time.

If you're willing to haul around a heavier appliance, consider one of the portable stand-up gas stoves that run off full-size 20-pound propane tanks. With an increased surface area that will accommodate full-size pots, skillets, and griddles over high-Btu burners, models like the Camp Chef Pro 16 come close to matching the convenience of cooking on your range at home. The sturdy folding legs with levelers allow you to set up anywhere, the windscreen ensures the burners don't blow out, and the side shelves provide extra working space.

Campfires

It's easy to forget that there was a time when cooking a camp meal meant making a fire. These days, a propane stove may be the best tool for the bulk of your camp cooking, but it's fun to slow down and do at least some of your cooking over a campfire. With the right equipment, there's a lot more you can do than roast marshmallows and hot dogs on a stick. Most developed campsites, and even some primitive ones, have a metal fire ring with an attached cooking grate. But you shouldn't count on it, especially if you're boondocking where there aren't any designated campsites.

At the very least, you'll want to bring a basic metal grill grate that can be rested on a base of rocks or logs. You can salvage a grate from a retired barbecue grill, but if you want a grate that's going to last and doesn't get all bent to hell, buy a heavy-duty one made out of cast iron or a similarly durable material. It should support the weight of a cast-iron skillet or Dutch oven while also allowing you to cook directly on the grate. Or go with one of the metal Breeo fire pits mentioned earlier (page xxvi). That way you don't have to worry about digging your own fire pit, and they're genuinely safer and less smoky than open fires. Sure, they're a little bulky and heavy, but the grate, griddle, and pot-hanger attachments score big points for ease of use.

Finally, you can do a lot with a Dutch oven nestled among hot campfire coals, but a cast-iron tripod makes it even more versatile; tripods are an indispensable tool for making big batches of stew, chili, and gumbo.

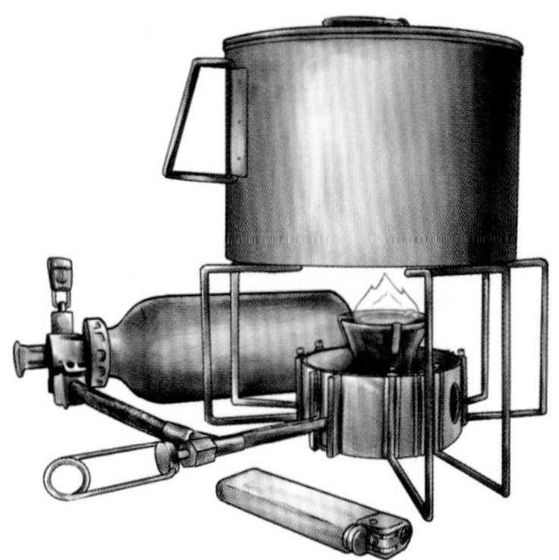

Backcountry Cooking Equipment

When you're tired and hungry after hiking all day in miserable weather, you want to be able to quickly and easily make a meal that carries a heavy payload of calories. Backcountry camping means you're limited to carrying everything you need in your backpack. So you'll want a stove that's lightweight, compact, and works reliably in wet or windy conditions. Jetboil stoves are very popular with backpackers, and they work very well, but over decades of backcountry hunting, I've experimented with all manner of backpacking stoves, and I've settled on the MSR Reactor and MSR PocketRocket as my two favorite options.

The Reactor's enclosed burner is impervious to wind and gets a pot of water boiling in about ninety seconds. It's also a very stable cooking platform, with three different pot sizes available. And the stove and fuel canister pack neatly inside the pot, which has a locking lid to keep everything secure. While there's not a better stove for quickly making coffee and rehydrating freeze-dried meals, I've used my Reactor to cook everything from Chinese hot-pot ptarmigan to hunks of bear meat fried in bear fat. If you're looking to shave a few ounces from a heavy pack wherever possible, try the MSR PocketRocket Deluxe stove kit. The ultralight stove, cooking pot, pot handle, bowl, and fuel canister all pack neatly into the pot. Be aware that the PocketRocket doesn't boil water as quickly or handle wind as well as the Reactor, but that's the price you pay for a stove that fits in the palm of your hand and weighs less than 3 ounces.

Of course, on some backcountry expeditions you may also want to do some campfire cooking. If you can find some green willows or other suitable wood, you can fashion some skewers or a makeshift grill grate with your pocket knife. But a metal grate designed specifically for backpackers can be a real time-saver. There are various sizes and iterations available, from ultralight wire mesh designs to larger, sturdier versions with folding legs that weigh a couple pounds. Your choice will ultimately rest on how much extra weight you're willing to carry and how much pack space you're willing to sacrifice.

Help Wanted
Send Resume to:
JEANNE PHILLIPS

HOCKEY
House for sale
Three Forks.
Save time
Every Day of the Week!
582-2800
SERVICE DIRECTORY

OUTDOOR KITCHEN KITS

Some of our backyard recipes require you to have access to a full at-home kitchen equipped with blenders, food processors, ovens, and occasionally a slow cooker or a pressure cooker. As you get more and more interested in backyard cooking, you may want to add a few pieces of specialty equipment that allow you to work comfortably around flames and other heat sources without needing to worry about ruining your indoor gear. When stocking up on outdoor cooking accessories, avoid the temptation to buy one of those grilling kits that pop up in home and garden stores every spring; they're usually composed of useless trash you don't need along with cheap, poorly designed tools that won't last more than a summer. Invest a little more and buy sturdy, stainless-steel tongs and spatulas. If need be, spread out the cost by buying them one at a time. We also recommend getting a quality coal rake for moving hot coals around in charcoal grills, fire pits, and campfires. And make sure to save some money for a good pair of grilling or welding gloves made from thick leather. Your hands will thank you.

BACKYARD KITCHEN KIT LIST

- Large carbon-steel or cast-iron skillet, cast-iron griddle, cast-iron Dutch oven
- Large boiling/deep-frying pot
- Long-handled metal tongs, spatula, ladle
- Wire fish basket
- Paella pan
- Metal skewers
- Charcoal chimney(s)
- Coal rake
- Spray bottle(s)
- Basting brushes
- Heat-resistant leather grilling gloves
- Wire grill brush
- Meat thermometer
- Propane tanks, wood pellets, charcoal briquettes
- Propane fire-starter torch
- Heavy-duty aluminum foil
- Cooking twine
- Baking sheets

On camping trips based out of a camper, car, or boat, you have the ability to create a functional hybrid of your indoor and backyard kitchens. My basic car-camping kitchen kit lives in a couple of Action Packer plastic totes. Prior to leaving on a trip, I usually tweak it based on the number of people in the group, how long the trip will be, and the simplicity or complexity of the meals I'm planning to make. Generally, the items in my kit are either tools that are necessary for a very specific duty or that serve as multipurpose workhorses that allow me to pack less and do more. For instance, a quart-sized water bottle can also serve as a measuring cup. A nylon cutting board works just fine as a serving tray. For cookware, seek out carbon-steel or cast-iron sets (Lodge is the king of these) that consist of a deep cast-iron pan with a lid that can be inverted to be a skillet—more tools in one. With this setup you're covered for a wide range of cooking techniques including simmering, sautéing, and frying; you can even use the bottom of a standard cast-iron skillet as a pizza pan or to bake flatbread. You'll certainly want to poach some items from your indoor and backyard kitchen, but don't forget that you'll also need plenty of things at camp that are more likely to come from your garage than your kitchen. Inevitably, you'll find you can't run an efficient camp kitchen without items like headlamps and tarps. The list below is just a guide; it may take you a few trips to get your camp kitchen system dialed in. Focus on must-have essentials first. And then, after some trial and error, you can work on customizing your kit to suit your needs.

CAR CAMPING KITCHEN KIT LIST

Plastic totes. For cooking gear and food storage, you'll need at least a couple of totes. I like those in the 25- to 30-gallon size range for general use. Stay away from the generic cheapies made out of thin, transparent plastic. For function and durability, you can't go wrong with Action Packers and Brutes from Rubbermaid.

Cooler(s). Keeping perishables cold is critical on camping trips. The size and number of coolers you'll need depends on how long you'll be camping and the amount of food and beverages you bring. At a minimum, you'll want a hard-bodied cooler in the 75-quart range for perishable food and a 20- to 40-quart soft-sided cooler for drinks. The Yeti Tundra, Flips, and Hopper coolers will last you a lifetime. There are plenty of less expensive options, but the cheapest coolers have a way of ending up in the landfill after just one or two uses.

Ice and/or ice packs. Bags of ice cubes, block ice, frozen jugs of water, and reusable hard-sided ice packs all have their pros and cons. Ice cubes are great for chilling fresh-caught fish and making cocktails. However, they melt quickly in hot weather, which can result in soggy ingredients. For a longer-lasting option that won't ruin the contents of your cooler, freeze tap water in recycled two-liter soda bottles. After the ice melts, you can drink the water or cook with it.

Water jugs. If you're boondocking where there's no potable water available, you'll either need to bring your own water or else treat water from a natural source by boiling or filtering it. Natural water sources are often silty or muddy, and finding water close to camp is never a guarantee. So, for car camping, I prefer to bring way more water than I think I'll need inside 5- or 6-gallon water jugs.

A 5-gallon bucket. You'll find a multitude of uses for a bucket. On the same camping trip you might use it as a camp stool, as a trash can, or as a receptacle for foraged foods like wild mushrooms or razor clams.

Camp table. You'll want a sturdy camp table that packs down into a lightweight package. The Camp Time Roll-a-Table and the Camp Chef Mesa are two of the best.

Large lightweight tarp. It's no fun to cook or eat in the rain or under a blazing hot sun, so pack a lightweight tarp that can serve as a cooking and eating shelter. Don't forget to bring some paracord and extra tent stakes for rigging your shelter.

Large tools. A shovel and a hatchet are required car-camping tools, but you may also need a maul, or even a chainsaw, for cutting and splitting firewood.

Small tools. Always carry a small basic tool kit, a folding EDC (everyday carry) knife, and a multi-tool for quick fixes around camp. These will come in handy when fashioning wood skewers or grill grates that might be missing from your cooking kit.

Headlamps, lanterns, and flashlights. If you're cooking before the sun comes up or after it sets, you can't get by without artificial lighting.

Utility lighters. Keep a couple of utility lighters in your kit. Their long nozzle makes lighting propane grills and campfires much easier.

Heavy-duty gloves. Standard leather work gloves are handy for all kinds of camp chores, but heat-resistant leather fireplace or welding gloves are even better for working around campfires and hot pots and pans.

Cooking fuel. Bring enough propane (and tinder, kindling, and fuel wood, if necessary) to last for your entire camping trip.

Pots, pans, and other cookware. Bring what you need based on what you'll be cooking. At a minimum, you'll want a large frying pan, a large pot, and a water kettle. Fair warning—food burns easily in cheap, thin aluminum cookware, and plastic handles have a nasty habit of melting. Cast-iron Dutch ovens, skillets, and griddles have long been considered the best option for campfire cooking, and they work great on stoves, too. But if you're looking to save on weight without giving up performance, carbon-steel pots and pans are more durable than stainless steel or aluminum. Carbon steel can also handle high temperatures very well. Other items to consider are metal skewers, steamer baskets, and iron-pie makers (see page 151).

Cooking utensils. Plastic measuring cups and spoons are fine for camping, but avoid plastic cooking utensils. Long-handled metal ladles, spatulas, and tongs won't melt on a hot skillet or if they're left too close to open flames. A full set of kitchen knives isn't necessary. Instead, you'll want at least one sharp chef's knife for chopping veggies and cutting meat. I always have a fillet knife around camp, too, in case there's a nearby opportunity for fishing. Thin, flexible plastic cutting boards are ideal for camping. Lightweight nylon boards are a good choice as well.

Plates, bowls, cups, and silverware. For all their time-saving convenience, single-use plastic silverware and paper plates create a lot of trash. You can get a nice durable set of metal camping dinnerware and silverware for not much more than you'd pay for the disposable stuff. For beverages, standard travel mugs make for excellent camp cups. And of course, you'll need a dishwashing bin, dish soap, and a couple of scrub pads. If you've got the money, collapsible silicone cups and bowls are the best option. They are lightweight, take up minimal space, and are very easy to clean.

Basic cooking ingredients. Keep a handful of basic cooking ingredients on your car-camping packing list. At a minimum, pack a bottle of oil and some salt and pepper. Other useful items include eggs, flour, milk, sugar, honey or maple syrup, butter, hot sauce, soy sauce, and all-purpose spice blends such as Cajun or Greek seasonings.

The standard kitchen kit used by backcountry hunters, anglers, and backpackers is designed for one primary purpose: boiling water for instant oatmeal and freeze-dried meals. But that type of food gets old in a hurry. Fortunately, if you add just a few extras to your pack, it is possible to cook some surprisingly delicious food on backcountry trips. With nothing more than a backpacking stove, a small nonstick pot, and a miniature bottle of cooking oil, you can fry chunks of elk meat and simmer up a huckleberry sauce to drizzle on that elk meat. A piece of aluminum foil, some seasoned salt, a small lemon, and a campfire are all you need to transform a freshly caught trout and some wild mushrooms into a meal you'll remember forever.

BACKCOUNTRY KITCHEN KIT LIST

- BIC cigarette lighter(s)
- Fire-starting aids like cotton balls slathered in Vaseline
- Small, lightweight backpacking pot like MSR Trail Lite
- Large, folded piece of aluminum foil
- Sea to Summit long-handled titanium spork
- EDC knife for carving skewers and forks
- Small bottle of cooking oil
- Small bottle of seasoned salt, hot sauce, or any of the rubs in this book (see pages 347 and 355)

COOKING OVER FIRE

A cooking fire has a life cycle comprising three stages: youth, middle age, and old age. A young fire is flashy, with lots of flames dancing about and not much in the way of history—meaning that the base of the fire is lacking a bed of embers and charcoal. A young fire might look like it's kicking ass, but looks can be deceiving. The structure of the ignited wood could tip over, a heavy wind might blow through, or a bit of rain may fall and the fire dies. It has no real staying power. Young fires are only good for a fine point of intense heat located near the flame. It's okay for blackening a hot dog, but that's about it. On the other hand, an old fire at the end of its life cycle is nothing but fading embers; the last of the fuel has been consumed and now the fire is shedding its heat. Even if you toss new wood on an old fire, it might be too late to make a difference unless you stir up the coals and blow some air on it. Otherwise, the new log will do nothing but smolder and smoke. It has some use for warming foods, but that usefulness is waning.

That leaves a middle-aged fire, which is the fire you want. It's been burning for an hour or so and has a rich bed of coals and ash. Hold your hand a few inches over the bed of coals—you shouldn't be able to leave it more than a few seconds. A fresh log thrown on this charcoal bed will combust in short order, so it's possible to keep a fire like this going for as long as you care to feed it. It gives you a lot of options. You can pile the coals together in order to throw some intense heat on a steak for a good sear, or you can spread the coals out and get some nice, slow heat that'll penetrate a turkey breast without incinerating the outside. Or, you can do a bunch of things all at once: You've got a hot place for meat grilling, a bed of embers to brew a pot of coffee, and a few scoops of charcoal to place on top of a Dutch oven full of biscuits.

Of course, building a great cooking fire is easier said (and written) than done. It shouldn't be surprising that the people who are best at cooking over fires are the people who've been doing it the longest. There are all kinds of idiosyncrasies around wood qualities and climatic conditions that will complicate your efforts. Over time, you learn how to deal with them and make the appropriate adjustments. The information you'll find below, and sprinkled throughout the book, will hopefully shorten your journey to mastering the cooking fire by many years. Take it all in and start practicing. But make sure to remember the most important thing: Let that damn thing burn for a while!

STARTING A FIRE

Matches are about as antiquated as bow drills when it comes to starting fires. They get ruined when wet, and the strike pads are equally vulnerable to moisture and overuse. The most effective tool for getting fires started is an electric or propane grill torch. I don't personally have one of these, but I'd be excited if I found one in my Christmas stocking. Till then, I remain a devoted fan of the reliable, inexpensive BIC Classic lighter.

The tinder you use will depend a lot on where you're building your fire and the current weather conditions. If it's dry, you should be fine with a handful of paper or lightweight cardboard. Natural tinder supplies abound. You can make wood shavings with a pocket knife, or use an old bird nest or dry grass. A while back, my buddy Cal stumbled across an old dried-out pine stump that was caked in resin. He packed out enough of that fat wood to supply several of his friends with a lifetime supply of highly flammable, naturally waterproof tinder.

In rainy or windy conditions, your tinder might need a little booster. Lighter fluid is a standard option for many folks, but I don't use it very often, because it creates black soot and has an unpleasant odor. I'd rather use just a bean-sized hunk of Coghlan's Fire Paste. You'll find it in most sporting goods and hardware stores; a little goes a long way, so a tube should last you months or even years. For backpacking trips, I like a chewing tobacco tin filled with cotton balls slathered in petroleum jelly, aka Vaseline. These burn great, even when wet, and the Vaseline can also treat chapped lips, prevent chafing, and act as a lubricant on everything from tent zippers to the locking mechanisms on pocket knives.

Kindling is mid-sized fuel that comes between tinder and firewood. In other words, tinder ignites kindling and kindling ignites your primary pieces of firewood. The most common mistake I see from rookie fire builders is that they transition too aggressively from tinder to big pieces of wood. They think they've got a good fire going, but as soon as the tinder is exhausted, there's nothing to show for their efforts besides a little smoke. A dozen pieces of kindling, ranging from the thickness of a pencil to the diameter of your finger, will generally do the trick. You can split these pieces off larger blocks of firewood with a hatchet, or just search around for dry sticks.

If you're building a campfire for the ambience or to stay warm, you can burn pretty much any dry wood. For a cooking fire, the type of wood you burn is a more important consideration. We'll discuss cooking with different woods in a bit. For now, suffice it to say that your firewood needs to be thoroughly dry, or seasoned. If wet wood burns at all, it'll be smoky and weak. My fish shack in southeastern Alaska sits in one of the rainiest environments on the planet. You could walk around for days without finding a piece of wood on the ground that's dry enough to burn. The yellow cedar we cut and stack for our wood stove has to be seasoned for at least a year before we can even think about getting it burning, and even then it's not always easy. Ideally, it has dried in a covered place for two years. This place is an extreme anomaly, but I'm mentioning it to illustrate the lengths I'll go to in order to have dry wood at my disposal.

1. A hatchet can be used to split large, dry pieces of firewood into kindling, tinder, and small pieces of fuelwood.

2. Used in conjunction with a loose ball of natural tinder like dry grass and small twigs, artificial fire starters like the ones pictured here can come in handy in the backcountry during inclement weather.

AN IMPORTANT NOTE ON SAFETY AND WEATHER CONDITIONS

Let's say you've got plenty of dry wood on hand and you're ready to build a fire. Before you flick that lighter, you'll need to consider the weather conditions. Rainy days will make it challenging to get the fire started. Once you've got it cranking, though, a light drizzle won't have any impact at all; you can even keep a fire burning through a steady downpour, though it's a good idea to keep your wood under a tarp or other overhead cover. (A pro tip is to use your fire to dry out the wood that you'll be burning next.) Likewise, high winds can disperse the heat from your fire enough to make cooking difficult. A stiff wind can even extinguish small campfires. But these are problems that can be overcome with a little ingenuity: Place your fire in the lee of a natural windbreak or build a windbreak with a stack of rocks. A much larger concern with fires and high winds is one of safety, especially when those winds are coupled with hot, dry conditions.

Unfortunately, we are experiencing this type of weather pattern more than ever before in many areas of the country. Wildfire seasons have grown longer, and the number of fires per season has increased. Many of these wildfires are caused by people who are being careless. Others are caused by people who blatantly disregard rules. When handling fires and other cooking setups, you have to pay attention to what you're doing, and you need to obey fire restrictions. Otherwise, you not only risk shutting down millions of acres of public land to other uses, but you also risk killing innocent people and damaging invaluable ecological resources. There's not a burger in the world worth that.

Of course, a campfire can turn into a wildfire even without hot, dry winds. All it takes is for you to walk away from a fire that isn't properly extinguished. You'd be shocked by how well a smoldering fire can travel underground by following tree roots or other organic matter in the soil. I've personally seen fires pop out of the ground and start burning twenty feet away from my fire pit. That's one of the reasons I've started using metal fire pits such as Breeo stoves when I'm camping in the arid West. Wherever you make your fire, thoroughly douse it with water in order to put it out. Make sure to stir the water around so it reaches the buried coals. If possible, shovel a few scoops of dirt or sand over the fire as a final safety measure.

COOKING WITH DIFFERENT TYPES OF WOOD

The type of firewood you select will impact how hot your fire burns, how long the coals will last, and what flavors your food will absorb from the smoke. Hardcore barbecue fanatics are as picky about the species of the wood they cook over as they are about the quality of their meat, and experts like the Argentine chef Francis Mallmann and the American grilling aficionado Steven Raichlen have devoted many pages into the minutiae of the subject. While I have a great deal of respect for folks who pour that level of dedication into their craft, this isn't that kind of book. I appreciate the smoky flavor of a pizza cooked in an oak-fired oven and subtle sweetness of a trout smoked over applewood, but I've also cooked countless backcountry meals over plain old spruce or willow coals when there wasn't an oak or apple tree within hundreds of miles. While spruce and willow are generally regarded as poor choices for cooking, they've produced some of the best and most memorable meals that I've ever eaten.

The type of firewood we have access to is generally dictated by where we live. In the Northeast and Midwest, hardwoods like hickory, maple, and oak are readily available. In much of the South, pecan is a favorite. Mesquite is synonymous with Texas barbecue. Up in Alaska, alder is the wood of choice for smoking salmon, though cottonwood is commonly used if alder can't be found. Hardwood fruit trees like apple and cherry are available throughout much of the country, but in the Rockies you're often stuck with softwoods like aspen, pine, and spruce.

The flavor profiles different woods lend to your food are best approached in general terms. If you're planning on cooking over a pine or spruce fire, wait until the smoke dies down and you've got nothing but red-hot coals. (The resin in coniferous treewood produces a bitter smoke so don't use it in your smoker.) Alder, maple, and hardwood fruit trees are all known for their mild and sweet smoke that complements fish and fowl. On the other end of the spectrum, mesquite and hickory are often used in conjunction with meats that can handle a more powerful smoky flavor like venison, beef, and pork. Species like oak and pecan fall directly in the middle ground, with smoke that's described as nutty.

Of course, there's more to a cooking fire than the flavors it might produce. If you're making a stew in a Dutch oven, you'll need wood that creates hot coals that will smolder for a long time. A lot of research has gone into what happens when different types of wood are burned, including how fast or slow they burn and how much heat they produce. In terms of energy output, this information is expressed as a fuelwood's Btu (British thermal unit) value; one Btu is the amount of energy required to raise the temperature of one pound of water by a single degree Fahrenheit. The Btu value of firewood is measured by the amount of Btus (in millions) produced by one cord of seasoned (dry) wood. Fortunately, it's unnecessary to have an advanced degree in physics and chemistry to understand which types of wood have the best thermal qualities.

Regardless of the type of wood, moisture content plays a major role in heat output. Dry wood burns hot. When unseasoned wood is burned, much of its potential energy is wasted heating and vaporizing the water trapped inside. Next, in very basic terms, high-density hardwoods burn hotter and longer than low-density softwoods. The Btu value of black locust, for instance, is almost 28 million per cord, while red cedar measures in at just 13 million. If well-aged, hickory, oak, sugar maple, and apple all produce hot fires that burn for a long time. But don't get too hung up on Btu values. Even if all you have is a lower quality firewood like cottonwood that doesn't kick out as much heat, you can still produce a great meal.

COOKING-FIRE BUILDS

In the course of making this book, we refined lifetimes of outdoor cooking experience in order to serve you the best information on fire building. What we found was that the specific type of fire you build isn't nearly as important as how you maintain that fire. After all, you can't always control what types of wood you have access to, but you can control how you arrange it when constructing a fire. At home, you might have the time and resources to pull off an all-day fire in order to roast a whole hog for thirty guests. But on a remote backpacking trip, you might have to scrounge around for twenty minutes to find enough dry twigs to keep a small campfire burning long enough to cook yourself a single trout. On a car-camping trip, a cooking fire could fall anywhere in between these two spectrums. With that said, you'll find a lot of strong opinions out there on the best way to construct a cooking fire. A quick internet search will result in several build styles specific to over-the-fire cooking, a couple of which we describe in the following pages. But in the end, pretty much any basic fire-building strategy will work as long as you're familiar with a couple of different ways to manipulate the fire and the heat it produces for different cooking purposes.

A typical campfire is burned inside a ring of stones. The stones help prevent the fire from spreading, they absorb and contain heat, and they can mitigate the effects of wind gusts. Your fire ring doesn't have to be large; smaller fires are easier to manage. A three-foot-diameter ring is about right for a family meal, but you may need a larger one for big groups, and a smaller one will work just fine for one or two people. A selection of grapefruit- to volleyball-sized rocks are about right for making a fire ring from scratch. Just make sure to gather dry rocks; wet river rocks, especially those with hairline cracks that can trap moisture, will often split apart when exposed to high temperatures. Sometimes, they crack rather violently and send out showers of heated rock that can cut or burn.

TEEPEE FIRE

Just about every wilderness skills book out there, including my own, will tell you that building a teepee fire is the simplest and most efficient way to get a fire burning. Teepee fires are also ideal for getting bigger, longer-burning fires going. As the teepee burns down, slowly add larger pieces of fuelwood to create the coals you'll need for cooking.

1. First, place an artificial fire starter between two large pieces of kindling.

2. Place a layer of small kindling over the artificial fire starter.

3. Form a loose bundle of kindling over the tinder ball and ignite it. Blow on the flame lightly to encourage the kindling to burn.

4. When the kindling is burning steadily, begin forming a teepee frame with small pieces of fuel-wood. Gradually add larger pieces of fuelwood to the teepee frame as needed.

LOG CABIN AKA HASHTAG FIRE

Rather than tending a teepee fire until it produces coals, you can speed up the process by building the frame for a "log cabin" fire around your teepee fire before you light it. The log cabin fire's stacked hashtag design creates plenty of airflow, which efficiently burns larger pieces of firewood from the inside out.

1. Build a tinder ball between two thick pieces of fuelwood.

2. Stack layers of kindling over the tinder ball in a hashtag pattern.

3. Stack layers of larger fuelwood on top of the kindling in a hashtag pattern and ignite the tinder ball.

4. Add more fuelwood as necessary.

STUMP STOVE

Stump stoves, also known as Swedish fire logs, are one worthwhile exception to the rule of keeping your fire builds simple. Frankly, before I tried one out, I was skeptical of their efficacy. You'll have to be handy with a chainsaw to build a stump stove, but out of all the fires we built, this one burned the hottest and for the longest period of time. The fact that you need only a single log for a fire that'll burn at least a couple hours is reason enough to give it a try, but they have other distinct advantages as well. For starters, stump stoves are a super-efficient cooking system because the chainsaw cuts used to create them are made to draw air upward, like a chimney, instead of outward in all directions. In fact, there's not a better way to get a big pot of water boiling over a fire. They also make for a stable cooking platform; you can throw a big, heavy cast-iron skillet full of food directly on top of a stump stove without worrying about everything tipping over. It's worth cutting a few logs for stump stoves in advance of needing them, so you'll always have one around for the backyard or camp.

To begin, you'll need a log from which you can cut several rounds between 18 and 24 inches long and about 10 to 12 inches in diameter.

1. First, cut a 4- to 6-inch square through the top that extends two-thirds the depth of the log.

2. Make two additional cuts inside the square. Next, make four cuts across the top of the log, dividing it into eight wedges that extend two-thirds of the way downward.

3. Here's what the log will look like at this point.

4. Create a vent by cutting a notch all the way through the side of the log, near the bottom.

5. Hollow out the cut at the top of the stove, removing as much wood as possible to create an open chimney.

6. Add some fire-starting gel, tinder, and kindling to the chimney and ignite it. Let the fire burn for a while, then use the top of the log as a cooking platform.

REFLECTOR FIRES

Reflector fires, which use rocks arranged to direct a fire's heat in a specific direction, are a very efficient way to keep warm when it's cold and windy. The rock wind barriers also act almost like an oven, so reflector fires excel in cooking situations, especially if you're working with a small fire that isn't producing a lot of hot coals. Build your fire right in front of a big boulder or prop up as many slabs of rock around the fire as you need to make a wall that contains and reflects heat. You can also arrange stones against the reflector wall to serve as a convenient cooking platform.

1. A reflector fire built against a stone slab to preheat the rocks.

2. The stone slab protects the cooking fire from wind and elements, while adding radiant heat to the pan.

KEYHOLE FIRES FOR COOKING

A keyhole fire is one the best setups for cooking over hot coals while maintaining an active fire at the same time. The fire (and the stone ring that surrounds it) is shaped like, you guessed it, a skeleton keyhole. The main body of the fire goes in the round part of the hole with the thin arm of the keyhole (lined with rocks) extending outward from there. It's here, away from the active flames, that you'll do your cooking. By using a shovel, coal rake, or stick, you can drag hot coals out of the main fire into the keyhole's slot. Depending on the width of the arm, you can balance a Dutch oven or grill grate directly over the narrow part. Otherwise you'll need to locate a stone slab big enough to create a platform that spans the gap.

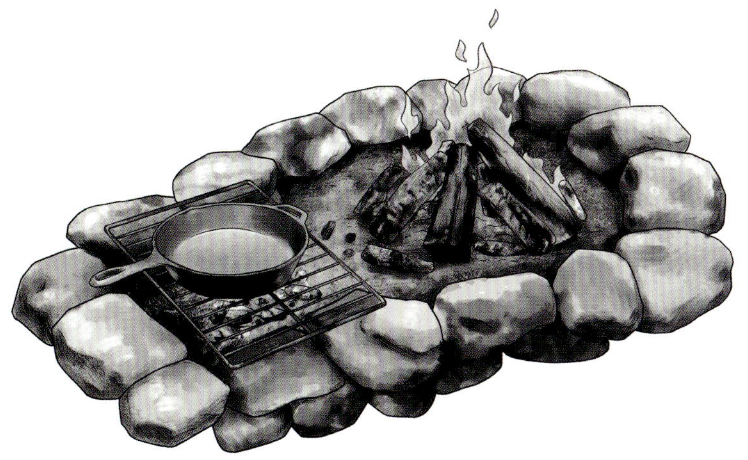

01 OVER THE FLAMES

In 2009, I was given an ambitious assignment by *Outside* magazine to find the best steak in Argentina. This was one of the most exciting assignments I'd ever gotten. The Argentineans are regarded as masters of open-flame cooking. Here was a chance to get paid while studying their techniques.

First off, the beef in Argentina is outstanding. Their cattle eat a free-range diet of grass throughout their entire life instead of spending their final months confined to a pad of concrete while they slurp up prodigious volumes of corn. The meat is a little bit chewier than typical USDA Prime beef, but it has a more robust flavor. It's prepared simply but fastidiously: a bit of salt, then careful monitoring above an open flame.

What I liked even better than Argentinean beef was the grilling contraptions upon which it was cooked. Someone who is unfamiliar with outdoor grilling might mistake an Argentinean grill, or parrilla, for one of those medieval torture devices used to stretch people out. It features a chain and sprocket system with a big wheel that can be turned by hand to make micro adjustments to the height of the welded metal

grill. The fire table is at the height of a countertop, so the grill man, or asador, is looking pretty much eye to eye with the meat. The asador keeps a fire of hardwood burning at the edge of the fire table and uses a small shovel and a set of tongs to place embers and burning wood in strategic positions beneath the grill. No matter what, they don't ever let a flame make contact with the meat. To do so would be the moral equivalent of bestiality.

When I got back to America, I was dying to make one of these setups on my own back porch. I built a big table about as high as my belly button and stacked bricks on top of it to create a bunch of little shelves that would support my grill at whatever height I wanted it. For the floor of my fire table, I had a couple friends help me carry over a huge slab of landscaping slate that I'd pried up from the mud next to my garden.

The first time I used this grill was almost the last time I ever cooked anything. When that wet slate heated up beneath a burning mound of lump charcoal, the water trapped within the sedimentary layers of rock started to expand. At first I thought someone was shooting at me with a .22 rifle, but then I realized the slate was exploding with superheated rock fragments that were zipping all over the deck. Somehow I managed to escape unharmed. Later, when everything cooled off, I put what was left of that slate right back in the mud where I found it and replaced it with a piece of quarter-inch plate steel.

That jury-rigged Argentinean contraption was just one of a bazillion or so ways that I've grilled food over an open flame. I've cooked Dall sheep ribs and black bear loins on grills made of interwoven willow limbs supported by river cobbles. On a road trip down the entire length of Mexico's Baja peninsula, my buddies and I carried a wire shelf salvaged from a discarded refrigerator in the back of our rented minivan. At night we'd prop that thing on whatever was available, ranging from bricks to truck tires, and light a fire of driftwood and coconut husks beneath it. Over the course of days, we grilled everything from onions to grouper to coconut meat on that thing. At the end of the trip, before leaving our last beach camp and heading to the airport, I hung that grill on a tree branch near our fire ring in hopes that someone else would find it and put it to good use.

Clearly, I've got as much love for grilling rigs as I do for grilled food. But if there's one thing I've learned from homemade grills, it's that store-bought grills are pretty damn nice. Turns out professional engineers know a thing or two about how to heat surfaces in a hurry with an efficient use of fuel and predictable results. My wife and I are currently raising three young kids, so this convenience means a lot to me these days. The kids often have after-school activities and we enforce bedtimes, so dinner needs to happen in an orderly and efficient fashion at night. In other words, I don't always have an hour to wander through the woods or rummage through a junk pile in search of some novelty that would hold a hunk of meat at an appropriate height above a flame. And since I'd never deny my kids or my wife and myself the pleasures and smells of outdoor grilling, we've slowly added conveniences such as a gas grill and an electric pellet grill to our outdoor cooking arsenal. It keeps us in the grilling game on a weekly basis, but without hot fragments of rock flying toward the kids' heads.

Of all the forms of outdoor cooking covered in this book, we're starting with the grilling chapter because grilling is a familiar and relatively easy way to produce great meals outside. From burgers to whole fish to spatchcocked fowl, you'll learn how to grill pretty much everything you can find from the top of the mountains to the bottom of the sea—including any grocery stores encountered along the way. Not only that, but we'll cover plenty of sauces and sides, along with strategies and recommended gear to keep you grilling great foods no matter where you might find yourself.

GRILLING: WHAT YOU NEED TO KNOW

In its simplest form, grilling is a cooking method that involves placing food on some sort of grate that sits over or near a dry heat source. Gas flames, wood fires, and charcoal briquettes can all be used as heat sources for grilling. Each will create a slightly different finished product (see page xxvi for more about this).

Cooking temperatures are typically high, often in excess of 500°F. The intense heat speeds up what's known as the Maillard reaction, which is a chemical process that breaks down proteins into amino acids that react with the sugars in your meat or veggies to produce a charred brown crust. The crust lends that complex and delicious umami flavor to grilled foods. The intense heat of a cooking grill also allows the outside of foods to be quickly seared without overcooking the inside. Although grilling is most often associated with the hot and fast cooking of foods like steaks, burgers, and fish fillets, you can also use a grill to slow roast foods such as whole birds, large cuts of meat, and even whole sheep, goats, or hogs. This is accomplished by using either a combination of direct and indirect heat or lower cooking temperatures.

When it comes to grilling (or any other method of cooking) wild game, I get asked over and over for recipes that pertain to specific species. My answer to those questions is always the same: Don't be concerned so much about the species as with the general characteristics of the flesh and the cut of meat you want to cook.

For hooved animals—including all species of deer, antelope, wild hogs, and even wild or feral sheep and goats—the cuts that work best for grilling are muscles without a lot of connective tissue. Backstraps, tenderloins, and roasts or steaks from the upper hind leg are best grilled hot and fast to medium-rare. Tough cuts like shanks and shoulders should be braised in liquid until nearly fork-tender before grilling. Another option is grinding tough cuts into burger or sausage with added beef or pork fat. A 1:10 fat-to-meat ratio works well for burger while a higher 2:10 ratio is ideal for sausage.

Much like big game animals, most upland game birds lack fat, and their legs can be tough and chewy. But the boneless breasts from just about any game bird are the equivalent of backstrap or tenderloin when it comes to grilling. It's fairly easy to get moist and tender results, especially if they've been brined or marinated in dairy first. The same goes for small whole plucked birds like quail and doves and like critters such as squirrels and rabbits. Large whole birds benefit from being spatchcocked before grilling (see page 75).

Grilling fish requires some special considerations, too. Thick chunks of firm-fleshed fish like tuna can be grilled with or without the skin, like a steak. Just be sure to oil both the grill grate and fillet to prevent sticking. When grilling more fragile fish, such as trout or bluefish, leaving the scaled skin on helps hold the fillet together. Grilling fish "on the half-shell" was popularized by Southern chefs working with unscaled, skin-on redfish fillets, but the technique works well with fish such as salmon that have sturdy skin and scales. Meanwhile, grilling whole fish without having the entire thing fall apart can be difficult. You can get around this by wrapping them in foil or banana leaves, but nothing beats a wire fish basket, especially for ultra-delicate fish such as flounder.

Direct Grilling

Direct grilling means the food is positioned directly over a heat source. When you're using a gas grill, direct heat means all of the burners are on, usually medium-high to high. For a charcoal grill or a grate over a wood fire, direct heat means the coals are spread evenly under the grate so that the food is positioned directly over the coals. With direct heat cooking, the entire area of the grill to be used for cooking is usually heated to the same approximate temperature.

Indirect Grilling

Indirect grilling involves creating two grill zones, one over medium-high or high heat, the other with no heat. This grilling setup gives you the most control over your grilling. It allows you to sear and char the outside of meats and vegetables over the direct heat and then move the food to continue cooking with indirect heat. (Think of the indirect portion of the grill like an oven—it's hot, but there's no concentrated or direct heat source below the food.) On a gas grill you can achieve this by turning off one of your burners. It can be the one in the middle on a three-burner setup, or on one side of the grill. On a charcoal grill, you can bank the hot coals off to one side or the other.

You can also set up your grill to create a single ambient grilling zone for long, slow cooks and for meat that drips a lot of fat, such as pork chops, duck, or beer-can chicken. Flare-ups from fat creates a lot of smoke and can impart nasty flavors. Ambient grilling solves this problem by allowing the fat to drip away from the heat source. It also helps to place a drip pan with an inch of water underneath the food to keep any dripping fat from running into the fire.

To set up on a gas grill, use one burner and place foods away from the heat source. On a charcoal grill, place coals to one side and offset the food to the other side; use the grill's lid to trap heat. With campfires, position your coals around the perimeter of the grill and place food in the center.

Cooking with Charcoal

The most useful accessory you can buy to simplify cooking on a charcoal grill is a charcoal chimney. In fact, we recommend getting the largest size you can find at your local home and garden store. Better yet, get two. A chimney expedites the process of getting coals hot enough for cooking, but it will still take a good 15 to 20 minutes before the coals are ready, so plan accordingly. Having plenty of coals on standby really helps when you're tackling a long grilling project or a large meal.

To light a chimney, follow these steps:

1. Fill the chimney with charcoal and set it on a heat-proof surface where you can safely light it.

2. Place a wad of newspaper or other tinder in the cavity at the bottom of the chimney reserved for tinder. Ignite the tinder.

3. The chimney is ready when the coals are smoldering, glowing orange, and showing some gray ash. This should take roughly 15 to 20 minutes.

4. Carefully pour the charcoal into the grill and arrange for direct or indirect heat.

5. Return the grate and close the lid to preheat the grill. Keep the vents open for oxygen flow.

With any grilling method, preheating is an important first step. Allow yourself adequate time to light a charcoal chimney, preheat a gas grill, or let a fire burn down to coals. When you take this step, the entire cooking process improves. A hot grill means you should be able to hold your hand a few inches from the grill for no longer than three to four seconds before having to pull it away. You'll also want to make sure your grates are very clean. Use a wire grill brush or a piece of wadded-up aluminum foil to scrape the grates.

After scraping, brush the hot grate with lightly oiled paper towels. If the food you're grilling already has oil or an oily marinade, you can skip the step of oiling the grate. The bottom line is that oil helps keep food from sticking to the grates. Just don't overdo it—if you use too much, you'll get flare-ups.

WHEN TO OIL GRILL GRATES

Should you oil your grill grates or rub down your meats and veggies? This topic is widely debated among grilling pros. But whether you oil your grates or load your grill with food that's already well greased, the bottom line is that oil helps keep food from sticking to the grates. If the food you're grilling already has oil or an oily marinade, you can skip the step of oiling the grate. If it doesn't and you're working with a steak with a dry rub or basting with a sticky glaze, oil the grate. Using tongs, brush the hot grate with lightly oiled paper towels. Don't overdo it—if you use too much oil, you'll get a flare-up.

BACKCOUNTRY GRATE

You might find yourself in a situation where you want to grill a bird, a fish, or a chunk of meat over a fire but don't have a metal grate. Fortunately, it's not all that difficult to make your own. In fact, this is something I do on a regular basis when I can carry only a limited amount of gear on backcountry hunts. Here's how to do it with just a knife or a hatchet and some green sticks:

1

2

3

4

1. Use a handsaw or hatchet to cut four sturdy green legs that end in a Y and are about 18 inches long. Arrange these legs in a square or rectangle 18 to 24 inches wide and pound them several inches into the ground.

2. Cut two more green support poles that span the gap between the leg poles. Rest them in the Ys of the legs.

3. Make a grilling grate with as many green sticks as needed.

4. Remove the sticks from the grate and light a fire. When the fire is hot, return the sticks to their position to form the grate. Add food and grill.

STICKY AND SWEET GRILLED FROG LEGS

SERVES 4 TO 6 AS AN APPETIZER

Bullfrogs are a popular food item in many rural areas of the American South, where gigging frogs at night is an age-old pastime. In many other parts of the country, the resource is hardly exploited. Where I grew up, in western Michigan, there are swamps that haven't seen a serious bullfrog hunter in decades. In terms of texture and flavor, frog legs bridge the gap between fish and fowl. The bulk of those harvested in the United States are breaded and fried, although the traditional French-style garlic-butter-and-lemon preparation is worth trying. This version is inspired in part by Chinese cuisine and delivers a sticky-sweet umami punch. It's the perfect appetizer to gnaw on while grilling up the rest of your dinner.

STICKY AND SWEET SAUCE

Yield ⅔ cup; serves 4 to 6 as an appetizer

3 tablespoons honey

2 tablespoons hoisin sauce

1 tablespoon soy sauce

1 tablespoon Shaoxing wine (see Cook's Note)

1 teaspoon toasted sesame oil

½ teaspoon five-spice powder

2 garlic cloves, grated

FROG LEGS

1¾ to 2 pounds bullfrog legs

1 tablespoon canola oil, plus more for grilling

2 teaspoons kosher salt

½ teaspoon ground white pepper

FOR THE SAUCE. In a small bowl, whisk together the honey, hoisin sauce, soy sauce, wine, sesame oil, five-spice powder, and garlic. Set aside.

FOR THE FROG LEGS. Prepare a medium-hot grill for direct and indirect grilling. Spread the coals in the center of the grill, allowing space around the edges for indirect grilling.

Rinse the frog legs and pat them dry with paper towels. Put them into a large bowl and drizzle with the oil. Sprinkle with the salt and pepper and toss to combine.

Arrange the frog legs on a well-oiled grill. Grill on one side for 4 to 5 minutes, brushing with the sauce several times. When the meat on the grill side becomes opaque, forms grill marks, and releases easily from the grill, it's time to flip. (If they stick, let them sit another minute.) Flip and move them away from the coals slightly, with the meatier sides closer to the heat. Cook, brushing occasionally with the sauce, until the legs are lacquered and cooked through, 5 to 6 more minutes. You'll know they are cooked through when the meat is fully opaque and loosens from the bone when pierced with a fork.

Serve immediately.

The sauce can be made well over a week ahead, but do not add the garlic until you're ready to use the sauce. Store in an airtight container at room temperature.

ALSO WORKS WITH. *The legs from common green frogs, though they're quite a bit smaller than the legs from bullfrogs. Plan on two or three times the quantity to get the same weight. This marinade works with parcooked rabbit or squirrel legs, as well as quail and other small game birds. It is also good for chicken wings and makes a good glaze for salmon or shrimp.*

COOK'S NOTE. *Shaoxing wine is a Chinese rice wine available online or at Asian grocers across the country. While Shaoxing does have a unique flavor, you can use Japanese rice wine or mirin as a substitute.*

STUFFIES

SERVES 8 AS AN APPETIZER

CLAMS

Kosher salt

12 topneck quahogs (about 3½ pounds), scrubbed clean

STUFFING

½ pound raw (soft) chorizo

Kosher salt

Olive oil for the pan, as needed

2 tablespoons unsalted butter

1 medium onion, finely chopped (about 1 cup)

1 celery rib, finely chopped (about ½ cup)

2 garlic cloves, minced

1 medium red bell pepper, cored and finely chopped

20 Ritz crackers, finely ground (about 1 cup)

1 cup fresh flat-leaf parsley leaves and tender stems, finely chopped

Lemon wedges and hot sauce, for serving

ALSO WORKS WITH. *Any large hard-shelled clam whose shell can be reused for stuffing—choose clams that can hold ¼ to ½ cup of filling.*

COOK'S NOTE. *Topneck clams are 3 to 4 inches in diameter and are the most widely available. If larger or smaller clams are used, adjust the yield of cooked meat; you will need ½ cup minced clam meat.*

These old-school appetizers hail from coastal New England—Rhode Island to be specific—where quahog clams are a regional favorite. Italian and Portuguese immigrants are said to have popularized this dish, but its true origins are unknown. You'll find recipes using a range of sausages that represent both of these southern European cultures. Traditionally these recipes used quahog clams, which have rich flesh and a strong briney flavor. But the recipe would work with pretty much any clam. For sausage, we're using a soft chorizo. You can use store-bought or homemade chorizo as well as Portuguese linguiça. The crackers that you use should be as basic as they come: oyster crackers, saltines, or a buttery cracker such as Ritz. (The latter option is my favorite.)

TO PURGE AND COOK THE CLAMS. Fill a large bowl with about 8 cups cold water. Add 3 tablespoons salt. Add the scrubbed clams; the water should cover them. Let sit at room temperature for 30 minutes to 1 hour to purge any sand or dirt. Remove the clams and rinse them in a colander. If the clams are exceptionally dirty or sandy, repeat the purging step.

Add 1 to 2 inches water to a saucepan and bring to a boil. Carefully add the clams, lower the heat to a simmer, and cover the pan. Cook for about 8 minutes, until all the clams open. Place the clams in a colander in the sink to drain, reserving the cooking liquid. When the clams are cool enough to handle, remove the meat. Mince the clam meat (you should have about ½ cup minced clams) and set aside. Rinse 8 of the whole clam shells and twist them apart. Lay the shells upside down on a baking sheet. Discard the remaining shells.

FOR THE STUFFING. Heat a large skillet over medium-high heat. Add the chorizo, sprinkle with ½ teaspoon salt, and break apart with a wooden spoon. If necessary, add a little olive oil to keep the chorizo from sticking to the pan. Continue to break into small pieces until cooked through, about 5 minutes, then transfer to a small bowl. Remove all but a thin layer of fat from the pan. Return the skillet to medium-high heat and melt the butter. Add the onion, celery, and garlic, stir together, and cook for 30 seconds. Add the bell pepper and ¼ teaspoon salt and cook until softened, about 8 minutes. Remove from the heat and stir in the minced clams, cracker crumbs, and parsley. Stir ¼ cup of the reserved clam broth into the stuffing. You want the stuffing to be moist and hold together. Add more broth if needed. You should have about 3 cups stuffing.

Prepare a grill for direct medium heat.

Fill each clam shell half with 3 tablespoons of the filling. Place the clams directly on the grill and cover for 2 minutes. Uncover the grill and continue to cook until the filling is bubbling and the tops are lightly crisped. Check after 5 minutes, although it could take as long as 10 minutes. If making these indoors in an oven, finish by browning the tops under a broiler.

Remove the stuffies to a platter and serve with lemon wedges, hot sauce, and a cold beer.

UNDERSTANDING QUAHOG VARIETIES

Quahogs are found on the East Coast from Canada to Florida. Most states require a license to harvest the clams, which are sold under names according to their size. Littlenecks (1½ to 2 inches) are the smallest and sweetest. Cherrystones (under 3 inches) are the second most desirable. These first two varieties are used in raw bars, steamed, and in pasta dishes. Topnecks (3 to 4 inches) are a medium-sized clam that can be sliced into strips and deep-fried or used in stuffie recipes like this one. Chowder clams (over 4 inches) are the largest and toughest of all. They're usually minced for chowders and stews.

Whether you're harvesting your own clams or buying them at a seafood market, there are plenty of suitable substitutes for the various quahog varieties. On the East Coast, Atlantic surf clams are widely available, and clam diggers on the West Coast have several options including razor clams, Pacific littlenecks, Washington clams, and Manila clams.

BEAVER CONFIT TOASTS

WITH GRILLED FIGS AND BALSAMIC-HONEY GLAZE

MAKES ABOUT 24 TOASTS

CURE

1½ to 2 pounds bone-in beaver thigh or equivalent

¼ cup kosher salt

8 fresh thyme sprigs

2 fresh rosemary sprigs

2 garlic cloves, smashed

CONFIT

10 fresh thyme sprigs

4 fresh rosemary sprigs

2 garlic cloves, smashed

2 bay leaves

1 shallot, sliced

1 teaspoon freshly ground black peppercorns

Duck fat, bear grease, beef tallow, or olive oil (see Cook's Notes)

BALSAMIC-HONEY GLAZE

¼ cup balsamic vinegar

¼ cup honey

GRILLED FIGS

12 small fresh figs, stemmed and halved (see Cook's Notes)

1 tablespoon extra-virgin olive oil

¼ teaspoon kosher salt

TOASTS

1 baguette, cut on the bias into 24 slices

Reserved duck fat (optional)

I've read pretty much everything there is to read about the Rocky Mountain beaver trappers of the early nineteenth century. It's common knowledge that these fellas, otherwise known as mountain men, were big into eating beaver tails. When I first started cooking beaver tails in an effort to mimic their preparations, the results were so bad that I figured there must be some confusion about what exactly a beaver tail is. By "tail," maybe they meant the tail end, or rump of the beaver? While I eventually realized that they were in fact eating the black, scaly tails of beavers (they were after the fat inside), the experimentations led me to discover just how good the thighs are. I've been eating them for years in simple braised dishes. I also like to corn them, similar to how you'd fix corned beef for St. Paddy's Day. However, this preparation here is my all-time favorite. It came about when I substituted beaver thighs for goose thighs in a confit recipe. Here's a slightly modified and dressed-up version of that original preparation. It's probably the classiest thing you can do with a beaver thigh. And it's definitely the best.

FOR THE CURE. Put the beaver thigh in a resealable container and rub it all over with the salt. Scatter half of the thyme, rosemary, and garlic in the bottom of the container, then top with the beaver thigh and the remaining aromatics. Cover and refrigerate for 48 hours.

FOR THE CONFIT. Preheat the oven to 250°F. Thoroughly rinse the salt off the beaver thigh and pat dry. Place the thigh in a small, narrow baking vessel (like a loaf pan) set on top of a baking sheet. Scatter the thyme, rosemary, garlic, bay leaves, shallot, and peppercorns over the thigh in the loaf pan. Pour enough fat over the beaver to completely cover it. If you don't have enough fat to cover, add olive oil or avocado oil to top it off. Cover tightly with an oven-safe lid or aluminum foil. Cook until the beaver is very tender and shreds easily, 4 to 5 hours. Let the beaver cool in the fat. Discard the aromatics, cover, and refrigerate until ready to serve.

FOR THE GLAZE. In a small bowl, combine the balsamic vinegar and honey and whisk together until blended.

TO REHEAT. Prepare a grill for medium-high heat. Remove the beaver from the fat, then shred the meat (you should have about 2 cups). Heat a cast-iron pan or other heavy grill-safe pan on the grill. Add the beaver to the pan and heat gently until just warmed. If necessary, add more fat to keep it from sticking to the pan. Set aside.

FOR THE FIGS. In a bowl, toss the halved figs with oil and salt. Place them on the grill and cook until grill marks appear, about 2 minutes. Flip and lightly grill another 1 to 2 minutes, until they soften. Transfer to a cutting board. Cut each piece into halves. (See Cook's Notes for dried figs method.)

ASSEMBLE THE TOASTS. Dab the sliced bread with fat, if desired. Grill the bread on both sides until lightly toasted but still soft in the center. Top each toast with a generous tablespoon of the confit beaver and 2 fig quarters. Drizzle with the balsamic-honey glaze and serve.

COOK'S NOTES. *You'll need about 3½ cups duck/animal fat to cover the meat in oil if you're using a 10 × 5-inch loaf pan.*

To prepare when figs are out of season, use dried figs. Rehydrate them in warm water and add to a small saucepan with warm balsamic-honey glaze.

MAKE AHEAD. *The confit can be made up to 1 month in advance and stored in the fridge submerged under its fat. Or frozen up to 6 months. The glaze can be made up to 1 week in advance and stored in the fridge.*

CHEESEBURGER POPPERS

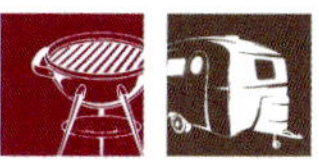

SERVES 10 TO 12 AS AN APPETIZER

Poppers are one of my favorite ways to use up smaller quantities of game meat. While I often use the breasts from quails or doves to make poppers, this version is ideal for using up the excess of ground game meat that every hunter seems to have in their freezer. This version is an ode to the cheeseburger, and boy does it nail it. It's fun for entertaining a group, and it can easily be doubled (or tripled) for a crowd. It makes a great appetizer for that first night of a car-camping trip. Whatever happens, don't skip the dipping sauce.

FILLING

1 tablespoon vegetable oil

½ red onion, diced (½ cup)

¾ pound ground game meat

Kosher salt and freshly ground black pepper

1 small plum tomato, diced (½ cup)

2 tablespoons pickle relish

12 large jalapeño peppers

12 American cheese slices, halved

DIPPING SAUCE

½ cup mayonnaise

1 tablespoon ketchup

¼ teaspoon onion powder

FOR THE FILLING. Heat the oil in a large skillet over medium-high heat. Add the onions and cook 3 to 4 minutes, stirring until softened. Push to the side of the pan, then add the ground elk and sprinkle with ¾ teaspoon salt and a few grinds of pepper. Break the meat up with a spoon and incorporate the onions into the meat. Cook the meat all the way through, 5 to 6 minutes. Stir in the tomatoes and relish and remove from the heat. Let cool.

Halve the jalapeños lengthwise and remove the seeds. Top each half with about 2 tablespoons of the meat filling. Arrange the filled jalapeños in flat layers in a storage container (use foil to separate the layers) and refrigerate until ready to grill.

FOR THE DIPPING SAUCE. In a small storage container, stir together the mayonnaise, ketchup, and onion powder. Refrigerate until ready to serve.

FOR THE POPPERS. Prepare a grill or wood fire with a grate for direct heat. Place the poppers on the grill and cook until the jalapeños are lightly charred, 7 to 10 minutes. Top each popper with half a slice of cheese. Cover the grill and cook for another minute, or until the cheese melts. Serve with the dipping sauce.

ALSO WORKS WITH. *All types of ground meat, wild or domestic. If using wild hog or bear, be sure to cook the meat to well done on the first step.*

MAKE AHEAD. *The filling can be made up to 1 week in advance or frozen for up to 2 months. The dipping sauce can be refrigerated for 2 weeks or kept in a cooler for up to 3 days.*

GRILLED TONGUE TARTINES

WITH ZUCCHINI, CORN, AND CILANTRO-LIME CREMA

Danielle Prewett

As a native Texan, I frequently eat foods that are heavily influenced by Tex-Mex cuisine. This culinary tradition really shines through with this tartine recipe. If you're new to tartines, it's just a fancy word for an open-faced sandwich. This one is layered with grilled zucchini, romaine, and sweet corn. The chile rub on the tongue adds the perfect amount of heat and vibrant red color to an otherwise unattractive piece of meat. A quick sear on the grill adds caramelization and incredible flavor. The texture reminds me of lamb shawarma from Middle Eastern cuisine, the kind that's been shaved off a vertical rotisserie. It's very tender and very delicious!

SERVES 6 TO 8 AS AN APPETIZER OR 4 AS A MAIN

CHILE RUB

2 teaspoons coarse sea salt

1½ teaspoons ancho chile powder

1 teaspoon brown sugar

½ teaspoon dried oregano

¼ teaspoon ground cumin

¼ teaspoon cayenne pepper

GARNISH

Cilantro-Lime Crema (recipe follows)

Quick Pickled Red Onion (recipe follows)

Chopped fresh cilantro leaves

TARTINES

1 elk tongue or 2 deer tongues (about 12 ounces total)

1 garlic head, halved but unpeeled

2 bay leaves

½ bunch fresh cilantro, sprigs and stems separated

Neutral-flavored oil (such as avocado or grapeseed oil)

2 medium zucchini

Kosher salt and freshly ground black pepper

2 ears of corn with husks

8 slices sourdough bread

1 cup shredded romaine lettuce

½ cup cotija cheese

FOR THE CHILE RUB. Stir together the sea salt, chile powder, brown sugar, oregano, cumin, and cayenne in a small bowl and set aside.

FOR THE TARTINES. Start by cooking the tongue in a large pot with water to cover. Add the halved garlic head, bay leaves, and cilantro stems. Bring to a boil, skim off any scum that rises to the surface, and reduce to a low simmer. Cook for about 4 hours, or until the tongue is tender when pierced with a fork. Keep in mind that tongues from older animals may take longer to braise.

Remove the tongue from the water and let it cool enough to handle. While still warm, use a knife or your fingers to peel away the outer skin. (This step can be done up to a day in advance.) Transfer the peeled tongue to a refrigerator or freezer for 15 to 20 minutes to firm up; this makes it easier to slice. Slice the chilled tongue into thin ⅛-inch pieces at a 45-degree angle to create wider pieces of meat and place it in a bowl.

Drizzle enough oil over the meat to fully coat it and season generously with the chile rub.

Using a mandoline or sharp knife, slice the zucchini lengthwise into ⅛-inch-thick pieces. Brush both sides with oil and season with kosher salt and black pepper. Set aside until ready to grill.

Recipe continues

Prepare and preheat a grill. If using propane or charcoal, make a small foil packet with wood chips to infuse a smoke flavor. Grill the whole corn, husks intact, over medium-high heat with the lid closed for 15 minutes. Remove and shuck the corn when it's cool enough to handle. Brush the corn with oil and season with kosher salt and black pepper. Increase the heat of the grill to high heat. Return the corn and lightly char it on all sides. Remove and cool to room temperature, then use a sharp knife to cut the kernels off the cob. Set aside.

Oil the grill grates. Working in batches, grill the zucchini strips over high heat for 1 to 2 minutes on each side, just until you see char marks. Don't overcook it or it will turn to mush. Remove when ready and continue with the remaining zucchini. The zucchini will soften into beautiful ribbons when it cools.

Finally, brush the sliced bread lightly with oil. Place the bread and the sliced tongue on the grill. Grill the bread on both sides until toasted. Grill the tongue for a couple minutes on each side until lightly seared. (You can also prepare this recipe in a cast-iron skillet over a campfire.)

Assemble each tartine by layering the toasted bread with tongue, romaine, zucchini, and corn. Top with crema and garnish with a spoonful of cotija cheese, some pickled onions, and cilantro.

CILANTRO-LIME CREMA

1 cup Mexican crema or sour cream

1½ limes, zested and juiced

½ jalapeno, chopped

½ bunch of cilantro, chopped

1 clove of garlic

Combine all of the ingredients for the crema together in a small food processor. Pulse until you reach a smooth consistency. Store in an airtight container in the refrigerator until ready to serve.

QUICK PICKLED RED ONION

1 red onion, sliced with the grain

1 cup white vinegar, apple cider vinegar, or lime juice

1 cup water

2 tablespoons sugar

2 teaspoons coarse sea salt

Place the sliced onion in a mason jar. Heat the vinegar, water, sugar, and salt in a small saucepan over high heat. Once it boils, remove from heat and stir to combine. Pour the hot vinegar over the onions. Once the vinegar has cooled completely, place a lid on top and store in the refrigerator. This is best done in advance and served cold.

STUFFED VENISON BURGERS, THREE WAYS

MAKES 4 BURGERS

1½ pounds ground venison, with an 80/20 ratio of meat to added fat

Neutral oil for grill

Kosher salt

Freshly ground black pepper

4 hamburger buns

Condiments and toppings of your choice

ALSO WORKS WITH. *Beef burger, or any ground big game meat mixed with added fat. If using wild hog or bear meat, bring the internal temperature of your burger to 160°F for safety.*

ADDITIONAL FLAVOR COMBINATIONS

Kalamata olives, feta, and capers

Cheddar, diced apple, and smoked ham

Shredded mozzarella, marinara, and breadcrumbs

Pimiento cheese and chopped pickle

Manchego cheese and membrillo (quince paste)

Sauerkraut, Russian dressing, and shredded Swiss cheese

Because game meat is inherently lean, it takes a bit of skill to grill a juicy game burger. Adding beef fat or pork fat certainly helps, but it's still way easier to mess up a game burger than a standard beef burger. This recipe, for stuffed burgers, is perhaps the most surefire way to grill the game burger of your dreams. The filling combos are endless, but I've outlined three of them here, along with some additional options in the sidebar below. Whatever you choose as a stuffing, the process is the same. This can be a fun project with kids, so get them involved. These recipes can also be doubled or quadrupled, depending on the crowd you're feeding.

If you're making these for car camping, fully assemble and chill the burgers overnight before transporting them to the campground. Grill and serve them on the first or second night of camp for best results.

CHILLING AND GRILLING. Form the ground venison into eight (3-ounce) balls. Then gently pat out to 3½ inches wide and ¼ inch thick. Assemble and stuff the burgers according to the specific filling recipe of your choice. Cover and chill the patties for at least an hour before grilling. This helps them hold together.

TO GRILL. Prepare a charcoal, propane, or wood fire grill for high-heat direct grilling. Grease the grill grate.

Sprinkle both sides of the patties with salt and pepper. Place on the grill and cook until the bottoms form a light brown crust, about 5 minutes. Flip the patties. Grill a few more minutes, until the other side browns and the internal temperature of the meat is 130°F to 135°F for a medium-rare burger. (If you're making the Green Chili Cheeseburger, add cheese and cover with the lid for a minute to help the cheese melt.) Remove the burgers from the grill to a platter.

Put a burger on each hamburger bun and serve with your favorite condiments and toppings.

1. *Form the ground venison into eight 3-ounce balls. Then gently pat each out to measure 3½ inches wide and ¼ inch thick.*

2. *Spread a heaping tablespoon of your filling (see recipes on following page) into the center of four of the patties.*

3. *Place plain patties on top of the filling-topped patties and press edges together to seal.*

BACON JAM AND BLUE CHEESE FILLING

MAKES ABOUT ½ CUP

FOR THE BACON JAM. Add the bacon to a medium skillet and cook over medium heat, flipping occasionally, for about 10 minutes. Add the onions and cook, stirring occasionally, until they are softened, about 10 more minutes. Add the vinegar, 2 tablespoons water, and the brown sugar and, when it starts to simmer, turn the heat to low and cook until the onions are very soft and jammy and little liquid remains, about 10 more minutes. This mixture can be made up to 1 week in advance and stored in the refrigerator.

TO ASSEMBLE. Gently smoosh a heaping teaspoon of the blue cheese in the center of 4 of the patties. Next, add 2 teaspoons of the bacon jam per patty. Place the remaining 4 patties on top and press the edges to seal. Follow the burger chilling and grilling instructions.

4 slices thick-cut bacon (4 ounces), chopped

1 medium onion, thinly sliced with the grain (about 2 cups)

2 tablespoons balsamic vinegar

1 tablespoon light brown sugar

2 ounces blue cheese, crumbled

BOURBON-GINGER MUSHROOMS WITH GRUYÈRE FILLING

MAKES A HEAPING ⅓ CUP

FOR THE MUSHROOM MIXTURE. Heat a large skillet over medium-high heat. Add the butter to melt and then add the mushrooms. Cook and stir for 5 to 6 minutes, until soft. Add the ginger, ¼ teaspoon salt, and a few grinds of pepper. Stir and cook until fragrant, about 30 seconds. Remove from the heat and add the bourbon. Return to the heat and cook until the liquid is incorporated. Set aside to cool. This mixture can be made a week in advance and stored in the refrigerator.

TO ASSEMBLE. Evenly divide the bourbon-ginger mushrooms among 4 patties (about 1 tablespoon per patty). Top with a quarter of the shredded Gruyère. Place the remaining 4 patties on top and press the edges to seal. Follow burger chilling and grilling instructions.

2 tablespoons unsalted butter

4 ounces cremini mushrooms, finely chopped

1 (1-inch) piece ginger, peeled and grated (1½ teaspoons)

Kosher salt and freshly ground black pepper

2 tablespoons bourbon

1 ounce Gruyère, shredded (about ¼ cup)

GREEN CHILE CHEESEBURGER FILLING

TO ASSEMBLE. Pile 1 tablespoon of the chiles in the center of 4 patties. Place the remaining 4 patties on top and press the edges to seal. Follow the burger chilling and grilling instructions. Add a slice of Monterey Jack cheese on top of each burger during the last minute of grilling.

4 tablespoons diced green Hatch chiles

4 slices Monterey Jack cheese

A FEW FANCY WAYS TO DRESS UP YOUR HOT DOGS

SERVES 4 TO 6

Hot dogs and bratwurst are plenty tasty with just a squirt of mustard, but the magic really happens when they're paired with the right toppings. No matter how you cook your dogs—on a grill, on a griddle, or over a fire—these tried-and-true toppings add layers of flavor and texture that turn simple dogs into a masterpiece. Use any of your favorite hot dogs, brats, or other sausages, or make the Camp Sausage recipe on page 36. All of these toppings can be made in advance of a camping trip or on-site.

4 to 6 cooked hot dogs or Camp Sausages (page 36)

4 to 6 hot dog buns or long Italian rolls

Choose a topping combination; each topping makes enough for up to 6 dogs.

KIMCHI SLAW

MAKES 1½ CUPS

DRESSING

1 tablespoon mayonnaise

2 teaspoons kimchi juice

1 teaspoon fresh lime juice

1 teaspoon toasted sesame oil

¼ teaspoon kosher salt

SLAW

⅛ head napa cabbage, finely chopped (about 1 cup or ¼ pound; see Cook's Note)

½ cup kimchi, chopped

½ cup packed fresh cilantro, chopped

2 scallions, white and green parts, thinly sliced

Stir the mayonnaise, kimchi juice, lime juice, sesame oil, and salt together in a medium bowl. Add the cabbage, kimchi, cilantro, and scallions. Toss to coat.

Put a hot dog in a bun. Spoon some kimchi slaw over top. Serve immediately.

COOK'S NOTE. *We've made this with napa cabbage, which is tender and has a flavor that is mild and sweet. You can swap with a sturdier savoy cabbage or a green cabbage if that's all that is available.*

MAKE AHEAD. *Although this slaw can be prepped ahead of time, it shouldn't be assembled until ready to serve as it gets soggy quickly. Combine the dressing ingredients, store them in a resealable container, and refrigerate; prep the slaw components, omitting the kimchi, and refrigerate. When ready to serve, combine the slaw with the dressing and kimchi.*

CHICAGO-STYLE RELISH

MAKES 1¼ CUPS

5 teaspoons sweet relish

¼ medium white onion, chopped (⅓ cup)

1 medium plum tomato, chopped (heaping ½ cup)

1 whole jarred kosher dill pickle, chopped

4 sport peppers, pickled serrano peppers, or peperoncini, finely chopped

¼ teaspoon celery salt

¼ teaspoon poppy seeds (optional)

Yellow mustard, for serving

In a small bowl, stir together the relish, onions, tomatoes, dill pickles, peppers, celery salt, and poppy seeds (if using).

Put a hot dog in a bun. Squiggle yellow mustard on top and generously spoon about 3 tablespoons of the Chicago-style relish over the top.

PEPERONATA-STYLE

MAKES 2 CUPS

2 tablespoons olive oil

2 medium red bell peppers, sliced into strips ½ inch thick

1 medium yellow bell pepper, sliced into strips ½ inch thick

1 jalapeño pepper, seeded and sliced into strips ¼ inch thick

1 medium yellow onion, halved, sliced ½ inch thick with the grain

2 garlic cloves, minced

1 teaspoon dried oregano or 1 fresh thyme sprig

1½ teaspoons kosher salt

1 tablespoon red wine vinegar

4 to 6 slices provolone cheese (roughly ¼ pound)

Hot sauce, for serving

Heat the oil in a 4-quart saucepan over medium-high heat. Add the peppers, onions, garlic, oregano, and salt. Cook, stirring occasionally, until the onions start to stick to the bottom, about 10 minutes. Splash in ½ cup of water, then reduce the heat to medium-low. Cover with a lid and continue to cook for 10 minutes, stirring occasionally, adding a little water as needed if the onions stick. Cook until the peppers are very soft. Remove the lid and raise the heat to medium-high to evaporate any excess liquid. When the mixture is stewlike and very soft, about 30 minutes total, turn off the heat. Remove from the heat. Stir in the vinegar.

Place a slice of provolone in each bun. Add a hot dog and top with peperonata. Serve with hot sauce.

CAMP SAUSAGE

MAKES 10 POUNDS LINKED OR BULK SAUSAGE

8 pounds lean game meat, cut into 1-inch cubes

2 pounds pork fatback, cut into 1-inch cubes

20 feet of natural hog casings (32 to 35 millimeters in diameter; optional)

4¼ tablespoons kosher salt

2 tablespoons ground white pepper

1 tablespoon fresh thyme leaves

1½ teaspoons caraway seeds

1½ teaspoons ground nutmeg

1½ teaspoons ground allspice

1½ teaspoons ground ginger

1½ tablespoons crushed red pepper flakes

3 tablespoons minced garlic

¾ cup white wine vinegar or champagne vinegar, chilled

½ cup ice water

SPECIAL EQUIPMENT

Meat grinder

I used to mess around with a buddy of mine trying to make traditional hot dogs from wild game. The process is a pain in the ass, and I was never entirely happy with the results. Instead, I now prefer to make a basic camp sausage that can stand in for hot dogs and still be used for a variety of other purposes. You can braise them just like a bratwurst in a mixture of beer, butter, herbs, and onion. After braising, you can grill them to finish. Or poach them in water with a splash of wine, then grill; this helps prevent them from bursting open on the grill. You can also hot-smoke these sausages if you'd like; see the Cook's Notes for instructions.

This sausage is based on an 80/20 mixture of lean game meat and pork fatback. You can raise the fat level to 70/30 for a juicier sausage that's not overly greasy. Alternatively, you can sub a pound or three of lean game meat for something like pork butt if you desire, but the 80 percent wild game version is just fine. Use natural hog casings with diameters between 32 and 35 millimeters.

TO GET STARTED. Place the cubed meat and fat in a bowl in the freezer to chill and harden, but don't freeze them all the way through. Meanwhile, set up your meat grinder according to the manufacturer's instructions and soak the natural hog casings (if using) in lukewarm water. Once the casings are pliable, change the water and soak them another 20 to 30 minutes. Then fit one end of each casing over the kitchen faucet and run a cup or two of water into the casing. Push the water all the way through to rinse the inside of the casing. Set aside in clean water until ready to use.

TO GRIND THE SAUSAGE. Combine the chilled cubed meat and pork fat with the salt, white pepper, thyme, caraway seeds, nutmeg, allspice, ginger, and red pepper flakes in a large bowl and mix well to coat evenly. Cover and marinate in the refrigerator for 24 hours for the best flavor.

Fill a tub with ice and place the bowl of chilled meat inside the tub to keep it cool. Using a medium die, grind the sausage mixture into another bowl that's also set in a tub filled with ice. Using a rubber spatula, fold in the garlic and vinegar, distributing them evenly. While it's not necessary, it wouldn't hurt to further combine the mixture in a stand mixer with the paddle attachment for a smoother consistency, or you could run it one more time through the medium die (it will still make a great sausage if you skip this extra step). The mixture should be like a wet paste. If it does not seem moist, add up to ½ cup ice water as needed. Cover and refrigerate while you set up your sausage stuffer to either case the meat in the soaked hog casings or divide it into 1-pound poly bags as bulk sausage.

STUFF THE SAUSAGES. Fill the hopper of your sausage stuffer with the sausage mixture. Crank the handle to clear all the air out of the stuffer tube and fit the tube with a clean casing. Tie a simple granny knot in the end of the casing. Working slowly, stuff the sausage into the casing. Be careful not to overstuff, and expel any large air bubbles inside the casing by pricking it multiple times with a sewing needle. When filled, tie off the casing with another granny knot.

TO CREATE LINKS. With the end of the casing tied off in a granny knot, make two creases in the casing, one 5 inches from the end and another at 10 inches from the end. Twist the sausage at these two creases about eight times. Now you have two links. Make two more creases at 5-inch intervals and spin these. Continue down the length of the casing. To separate the individual links, gently pull the links apart and snip the middle of the "twist" with a pair of scissors or knife.

COOK'S NOTES. *To hot-smoke your sausage, heat a pellet or vertical smoker to 200°F. Smoke the sausages with a mild fruitwood until the internal temperature of the meat reaches 145°F (or 160°F for bear or wild hog). You can eat them immediately or save for later and warm them up on a hot grill.*

When freezing your cased sausages in vacuum-sealed bags, make sure to orient the sausages vertically rather than horizontally. Horizontally placed sausages can form a dam in the bag that prevents the sealer from removing all of the air. I generally freeze my bulk sausage in poly burger bags, though it can also be frozen in a thin layer inside standard vacuum bags. In a hurry, you can toss a vacuum-sealed bag of sausage into a tub of cold water, and it'll thaw pretty quickly. This comes in handy when you're trying to prepare a meal in a rush, and you didn't thaw anything out beforehand.

ALSO WORKS WITH. *This sausage can be made with all kinds of big game, and it would also work with beavers or geese. Sausages made from bears, wild pigs, and javelinas should be cooked to an internal temperature of 160°F.*

BULGOGI LETTUCE WRAPS

SERVES 6

MARINADE

Makes 2 cups

6 tablespoons soy sauce

¼ cup packed dark brown sugar

2 tablespoons mirin

2 tablespoons toasted sesame oil

¼ teaspoon freshly ground black pepper

1 pear or sweet apple, or ½ Asian pear, peeled, cored, and cut into chunks

8 garlic cloves

1 small onion, cut into chunks

4 scallions, cut into 2-inch batons

1 tablespoon toasted sesame seeds

---

2 pounds elk backstrap, sliced ⅛ inch thick; partially frozen

---

SSAMJANG

Makes ⅓ cup

¼ cup miso or doenjang (see Cook's Note)

2 tablespoons seasoned gochujang sauce (see Cook's Note)

1 tablespoon honey or granulated sugar

1 teaspoon toasted sesame seeds

1 teaspoon toasted sesame oil

1 garlic clove, grated or minced

Neutral oil for grilling

FOR SERVING

Red or green leaf-lettuce leaves

Kimchi, cut into bite-sized pieces

Steamed white rice

Sliced scallions (optional)

Bulgogi is a traditional Korean dish made of thinly sliced marinated beef or pork that is grilled over fire. Its origins go back thousands of years. It's now one of the most popular Korean dishes served in the United States, and it can be scaled up to serve a crowd. The key to good bulgogi is having thinly sliced meat that's been perfectly marinated. The pear used in this recipe will release enzymes that tenderize the meat, so don't skip it. The ingredients for the Ssamjang, the dipping sauce served alongside the meat, are available in most grocery stores across the country; if not, you can find them in Korean markets or online. You can vac-seal and freeze the bulgogi sauce alone or with the meat in the marinade to use at a later date.

FOR THE MARINADE. Add the soy sauce, brown sugar, mirin, sesame oil, pepper, and pear to a food processor. Pulse until chunky. Add the garlic and onion and blend until smooth. Transfer to a large bowl and stir in the scallion batons and sesame seeds.

Add the meat to the marinade and stir to coat well. Cover and refrigerate for at least 2 hours or up to overnight.

FOR THE SSAMJANG. Combine the miso, gochujang sauce, honey, sesame seeds, toasted sesame oil, and garlic. Cover and set aside until ready to serve.

TO GRILL. Prepare a hot grill for direct grilling. Oil the grill grate. Working in batches, cook the meat for 1 minute, until lightly charred, and flip. Cook for another minute. Transfer to a platter when done. Clean the grill as necessary between batches. Repeat until all of the meat is grilled.

FOR SERVING. Cut the meat into bite-sized pieces with kitchen shears and serve with the ssamjang, lettuce leaves, kimchi, rice, and (if using) perilla leaves, garlic, and scallions to make lettuce wraps.

COOK'S NOTES. *Doenjang is a Korean fermented bean paste.*

Gochujang Sauce is a Korean condiment made from a fermented red chili paste thinned out with soy and vinegar.

ALSO WORKS WITH. *A whole muscle roast or a backstrap from any hooved big game or a wild hog, or domestic beef or pork.*

HOW TO COOK A WILD GAME STEAK

Grilling a great steak ain't as easy as you might think, and it can be especially tricky when you're dealing with wild game steaks. Here we break down the process, from butchering and seasoning to grilling and serving.

Butchering

The best steaks on big game animals come from either the backstrap or the large muscles on the upper hind leg. When I'm butchering an animal, I like to freeze these cuts as 2- to 3-pound whole muscle pieces. This gives me the option to cook an entire piece or slice it into steaks after it's thawed. You can also precut the steaks and freeze them that way, if you know that's how you're gonna use them. When you're cutting a lean wild game roast into steaks, don't skimp on the thickness; you're much more likely to overcook a thin one. A thicker steak is more forgiving on the grill and yields a juicer, tastier product. Steaks that are about 1½ to 2 inches thick are ideal. They can tolerate a hard sear on the outside and remain tender and rare to medium-rare on the inside.

Marinating

After butchering, the next step is imparting flavor with rubs or marinades. It's important to understand the role of acidity in a marinade: The acids in a marinade tenderize and flavor the steak by breaking down the long proteins in the meat. If you leave a steak in an acidic marinade for too long, however, it will begin to break down the proteins at the surface of the steak a bit too aggressively. This affects the texture, causing the meat to be mushy rather than tender. If your marinade includes wine, citrus juice, or even vinegar, it's best not to marinate it for more than 24 hours. Adding oil or some kind of insulating fat will help extend the marinating time.

A simple combination of olive oil, a few smashed garlic cloves, and some torn rosemary works great on wild game steaks. To up the ante a bit, try a splash of soy sauce, balsamic vinegar, and toasted sesame oil or sliced ginger, a bit of neutral oil, and a squeeze of lime. There are more flavor-packed marinades in this chapter and in the back of the book (page 346).

Dry Rubs

Dry rubs and dry brines are another simple way to impart flavor. You can add a rub right before cooking, but they season steaks all the way through if they're left on for 12 to 24 hours. The best ones maintain a balance of flavors with salt, sugar, something spicy, and something earthy, for example, kosher salt, a pinch of light brown sugar, a good dash of smoked paprika, and some ground cumin. Or try kosher salt, brown sugar, crushed red pepper flakes, and mushroom powder. Once the steak is seasoned, place it on a rack over a baking sheet and set the rubbed steak in the refrigerator for the desired amount of time. A bit of air circulation is good here to aid in drying out the surface of the meat, but you can also store pre-rubbed steaks in a plastic bag if you're transporting them to camp. Rubs and dry brines can also be made ahead of time and stored in an airtight container. (See a list of rubs and dry brines on pages 345 and 347.)

Grilling Steaks

1. PREHEAT the grill with the cover closed in order to make sure the grate is hot. Charcoal grills or wood fires need plenty of time to develop hot coals. The old hold-your-hand-four-inches-above-your-grill test holds true. If you can hold it there for longer than 4 seconds, it's not hot enough.

2. BRING MEAT TO ROOM TEMP. For steaks 1½ inches thick or thicker, pull it out of the refrigerator about 30 minutes before cooking. For thin steaks, you can skip this step. The colder center will help prevent overcooking.

3. DRY THE STEAK on all sides with paper towels. Moisture is the enemy when searing a steak, so you want to remove as much of it as possible.

4. SEASON THE STEAK with kosher salt and black pepper. You can skip this step if you have dry rubbed your steak, but a last-minute sprinkling of salt is not a bad thing. If you are starting with a naked steak, season with gusto.

5. DRY YOUR MEAT AGAIN. It can't be too dry.

6. DRIZZLE THE STEAK WITH A BIT OF NEUTRAL OIL. There is much debate as to whether you should oil the meat or oil the grill. To play it safe, lightly oil both. You don't want the oil to pool on the meat, just lightly coat it. If you are using a pan, a good drizzle in the pan is all you need.

7. GRILL. If your steak is very thick, it is beneficial to prepare a section of the grill for indirect heat, in case it needs to cook a bit longer (see page 8 for details).

When the heat is right and your steak is ready, wipe the grates of the grill with lightly oiled paper towels. Add your lightly oiled meat to the hot grill and cook undisturbed for 3 to 4 minutes with the cover on. Don't try to move the meat, don't press it down. It will release from the grates on its own when it is properly seared. Using tongs, flip the steak to a clean area of the grill. This ensures that the grates will be oiled and perfectly heated to sear the second side of the steak. Cook covered for another 3 to 4 minutes, or until the desired temperature is reached. I prefer to cook big game steaks rare to medium-rare. That's 125°F to 135°F on an instant-read thermometer. If you go much past that point, the meat gets dry and tough. Once the steak hits the bottom of that temperature range, remove it to a plate and allow it to rest for 10 minutes. At this point, it is beneficial to squeeze a bit of lemon juice over the steak. The juice adds a bit of fresh brightness to the richness of the steak. If served with an acidic, herby condiment like chimichurri, there's no need to add the lemon. Slice, season with a bit of coarse salt, and serve after the steak has rested.

Cooking Steaks in a Skillet

Just like grilling, the key here is to get your pan nice and hot before adding anything to it. You'll need a pan made of stainless or carbon steel or cast iron that can withstand the heat of the grill. Once hot, add a tablespoon or so of neutral oil or lard to the pan and swirl it to coat the bottom. Add the steak to the pan and let it sear for 3 to 4 minutes. It will release itself from the pan when it is ready. When a brown crust has formed on the steak, use tongs to flip it and continue to cook for about another 3 minutes, or until the internal temperature reaches 120°F to 125°F. At this point, it is nice to add a few pats of unsalted butter, a few cloves of smashed garlic, and perhaps some herbs. Toss all of those into the pan and tilt the pan toward you to allow the fatty, flavorful butter to pool near the handle. Now push the steak to the other side of the pan. Use a large spoon to baste the steak with the butter. After a minute of basting, remove the steak to a plate and pour on all of the aromatics and butter. Rest for 10 minutes before serving.

WEEKNIGHT BUTTERFLIED STEAK

SERVES 4 TO 6

This is a favorite recipe due to its simplicity and approachability. Anyone who loves a good steak is gonna love this preparation, so it's a safe bet for folks who might not be entirely adventurous eaters. This marinade is great for any steak, but we're talking here about a butterflied cut of meat; it's a technique where you can take a sizable chunk of meat, open it up with a knife, and then flatten it into a steak of uniform thickness. It's an easy way to get a delicious, healthy meal on the table in a hurry.

1 (2- to 3½-pound) piece of big game top round roast or large, thick backstrap

Neutral oil, for the grill

MARINADE

Makes 2¾ cups

4 garlic cloves, grated on a rasp

1 cup extra-virgin olive oil

¾ cup soy sauce

½ cup Worcestershire sauce

¼ cup balsamic vinegar

Juice of 1 lemon (about ¼ cup)

2 tablespoons Dijon mustard

2 fresh thyme sprigs, leaves stripped, or 1 teaspoon dried (optional)

½ teaspoon kosher salt

½ teaspoon freshly ground black pepper

TO BUTTERFLY THE STEAK. The goal of butterflying a roast is to turn a thick chunk of backstrap or roast into one big flat steak. (Following the illustrations on page 46, make a horizontal cut across the roast through the middle, stopping short of cutting all the way through. Lay the two halves open like the wings of a butterfly. Pound to tenderize and flatten if necessary to ¾ to 1¼ inches thick.

FOR THE MARINADE. Combine the garlic, olive oil, soy sauce, Worcestershire, vinegar, lemon juice, Dijon mustard, and thyme (if using) in a baking dish. Coat both sides of the steak in the marinade and put it in a large baking dish. Let it sit at room temperature for up to 30 minutes. Flip the steak halfway through the marinating time.

TO GRILL. Prepare a grill for a hot fire with both direct and indirect heat. Remove the steak from the marinade to a plate. Pat the steak dry and season with the salt and pepper. Strain the marinade into a small pot.

Oil the grill grate and place the steak over direct heat for 4 to 5 minutes. If the fire seems too hot, move the steak to the indirect side, then back to the direct side as needed. Flip the steak after 4 minutes and cook on the second side for about 3 minutes. Using a meat thermometer, check the internal temperature of the steak. When it reaches 125°F to 130°F, remove the steak from the grill to rest.

Meanwhile, boil the marinade on the grill for at least 5 minutes. Remove from heat and set aside.

Use the boiled marinade as a sauce for the steak and for grilled vegetables (see page 272). Serve with bread and a side salad (see page 300).

ALSO WORKS WITH. *Beefsteak. Also backstrap from bison, elk, or moose, and top round or other tender hindquarter roasts from deer-sized animals. You can do this with a goose breast as well.*

MAKE AHEAD. *For car camping, make the marinade ahead of time, store it separately from the steak in a sealable container, and bring it with you in a cooler. Marinate the steak in a resealable bag.*

BUTTERFLYING A ROAST

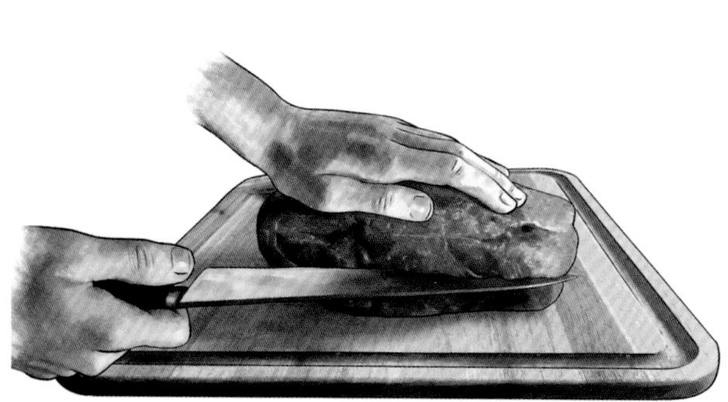

1. *Lay the roast on a cutting board and place one hand on top of the roast to keep it in place.*

2. *Use a chef's knife to make a lengthwise cut with the grain that divides the roast horizontally into an upper and lower half. Stop about 1 inch short of cutting all the way through.*

3. *Lay the two connected halves out flat on the cutting board as if you were opening a book.*

4. *Pound the whole steak to tenderize and ensure it is an even thickness of roughly ¾ to 1 inch throughout. If necessary, even out any thick spots by scoring the steak a few times with your knife (being careful not to go all the way through the steak) and pound again.*

MEATEATER

VENISON CHOPS SCOTTADITO-STYLE

SERVES 4 AS A MAIN OR 8 AS AN APPETIZER

A favorite grilled meat from the days of the Roman Empire was called *abbacchio a scottadito,* or "young lamb in the scottadito style." According to writers from the time, the dish was sold by vendors in the Roman Forum. *Scottadito* roughly translates to "scalds finger," which means these are meant to be eaten hot and with your hands—no knives and forks necessary. *Abbacchio a scottadito* is still very popular today, and it may be served at Easter or anytime throughout the summer. The dish is certified as a protected recipe of the region, meaning that its preparation is an official piece of regional cultural heritage. Here, we are cheating tradition a bit by swapping young lamb for the rack of any kind of medium-sized big game from which you can easily remove chops. (To see the butchering process, turn to page 50.) The meat is pounded lightly and then marinated in rosemary, citrus, and garlic. It's then grilled quickly over high heat.

8 to 10 rib chops from a mule deer rack, cut a rib's width wide

2 garlic cloves, minced

1 lemon, zested and cut into wedges

Kosher salt and freshly ground black pepper to taste

¼ cup extra-virgin olive oil

2 large rosemary sprigs, leaves stripped, plus more sprigs for garnish

Trim the chops of any thick tallow and silverskin. Be careful not to overdo it or the meat may fall off the bone. Lay the chops in a baking dish or baking sheet. Combine the minced garlic and lemon zest. Sprinkle each chop with the lemon zest mixture and season with salt and pepper on both sides. Massage the seasonings into the chops. Lightly drizzle the chops with some of the oil to coat evenly. Divide the rosemary leaves among the chops (on both top and bottom) and set aside to marinate at room temperature for 30 minutes or in the refrigerator for up to 1 hour. Remove before grilling.

Preheat a grill to high heat for direct and indirect heat. When the grill is hot, add the chops, let the excess oil drip off, and grill the chops for 3 to 4 minutes per side, until well seared. Don't overcook them; you're aiming for rare to medium-rare with a caramelized crust on the outside. When done, remove the chops to a plate to rest. Drizzle with more olive oil, add a squeeze of lemon juice, and garnish with the lemon wedges and additional rosemary sprigs. Eat while they're hot enough to burn your fingers, just as the Romans did.

ALSO WORKS WITH. *Rib racks from all hooved game animals, as well as lamb.*

HOW TO CUT CHOPS FROM A MULE DEER RACK

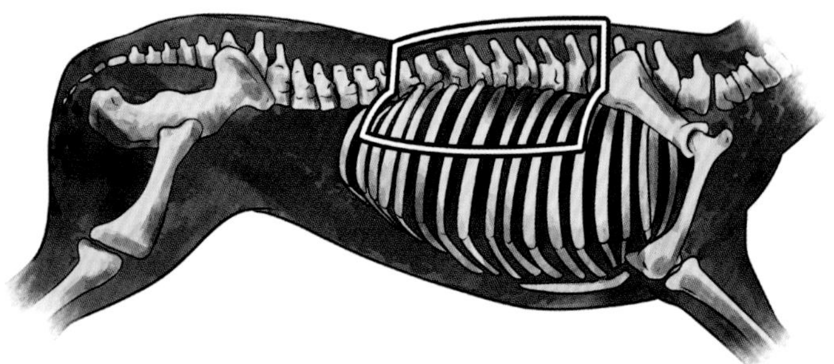

1. The chops are located in the middle, or "saddle," portion between the shoulder and the hip. Using a bone saw, make one cut through the rib cage a few inches below the backstrap and another through the rib cage between the backstrap and the spine.

2. Use a knife to free the entire bone-in section of backstrap.

3. Cut this section into individual bone-in chops by making a slice through the meat between each rib bone. Trim any large chunks of fat, silverskin, or gristle.

HOW TO GRILL FISH FILLETS

There is nothing more frustrating than putting all of the time, care, and attention into catching and cleaning a fish only to ruin it when you cook it. Using the following techniques, you'll enjoy eating your fish as much as you did catching it.

1. MARINATE IT. This a great way to bump up the flavor of otherwise mild fish. When you think about a marinade, always consider the thickness and fattiness of the fish. If it is a rich fish, such as salmon or bluefish, a touch of citrus or something bright like mustard is a smart addition. If it is a lean white fish, adding some fatty richness is a good idea; toasted sesame oil or coconut milk is a good option.

The great thing about fish is that you do not have to marinate it for long—30 minutes in a flavorful bath will give it just the lift you are looking for. Keep the sugar content low in marinades to avoid burning fish on the grill.

2. BASTE IT. Try basting fish with a glaze, flavorful sauce, or compound butter when they are just a moment from being done. Make these condiments ahead of time so you can put them on as soon as the fish is ready.

3. DRY RUB. When grilling fish it's best to keep rubs simple. A lemon pepper blend, or a mix of granulated garlic, paprika, celery seed, and cayenne pepper works well for all kinds of fish.

4. CONDIMENTS. Sometimes the simplest solution is to season the fish with kosher salt and freshly ground black pepper and pair it with a lively condiment. There are many options for these in the back of this book.

Grilling

Grilling fish doesn't take long, so have everything you need by your side before you start. This includes your basting sauce, seasonings, spatula, and a plate for the cooked fish. You'll also want a wire fish basket for grilling fillets of fish with delicate flesh. Otherwise, they'll fall apart.

1. Preheat your grill.

2. Remove fish from the refrigerator 30 minutes before cooking. This will allow for very even cooking.

3. If you are using skin-on fillets, score the skin crosswise in a few spots. This prevents the fillet from curling when cooking.

4. Dry your fish very well, even if it was marinated. You want to remove as much moisture as possible. Then season it with kosher salt and give it a good drizzle of neutral oil on all sides.

5. Get your fish on the grill. If using skin-on fillets, place the fish skin-side down on the hot grill. If you are using fillets without skin, place the side that did not originally have skin on it on the grill. This side will be your "presentation" or "good" side. Allow the fish to cook, covered, until nicely browned and you can see that the flesh is beginning to turn opaque around the edges on the top side. This should only take a few minutes. The fish will naturally release from the hot grill when ready to flip.

6. If you're not using a fish basket, carefully flip the fillet with a fish spatula or a long rectangular grilling spatula. Don't use tongs; they will likely tear the fragile flesh. Move the spatula in the direction of the grates when you flip the fish in order to avoid tearing it. If possible, flip the fish onto a clean section of the hot grill. Cover once again.

7. Depending on the thickness of the fillet, the fish only needs to cook for a couple more minutes. If you are using a glaze, brush it on and allow it to cook on the fish during the final minute of cooking. A thick fish steak will probably need additional time over indirect heat.

8. Remove the fish to a plate to rest. If you are using a compound butter, add it now so it melts and coats the fish. Serve immediately.

GRILLED MACKEREL
WITH PANCETTA-ONION JAM

SERVES 4

The various mackerel species are among those fishes that are often criticized for being too fishy. The complaint of excessive fishiness is hard for a lover of fish to argue against, because it's used in the same haphazard fashion as the complaint of "too gamey." A coho salmon that isn't particularly fresh might be described as "too fishy" by one person, while a totally fresh but improperly cleaned lemon shark might be described as "too fishy" by the next. (The white flesh on a lemon shark is good; the reddish flesh and fat that lies against the skin is admittedly heinous.) Countering claims of "too fishy" usually comes down to educating the complainer. But when it comes to arguing about the fishiness of mackerel, there's not a lot you can do. Folks who say it's too fishy are probably referring to the robust flavor of the oily flesh, to which you can only say that they're missing the point. The robust flavor of a mackerel's oily flesh is what makes it so damn good. Mackerel is especially suitable for grilling because that oil makes it a bit more forgiving. A mackerel can withstand a moment or two of neglect on the grill. And thanks to the robust flavor of the fish, you can dress it up with the Pancetta-Onion Jam in this recipe without risk of overpowering it. Go ahead and try it with bluefish or salmon as well. You're gonna love it. Just don't come complaining about fishiness.

PANCETTA-ONION JAM

Makes 1⅓ cups

4 ounces pancetta, diced (about ¾ cup)

2 tablespoons unsalted butter

3 tablespoons packed dark brown sugar

1 teaspoon kosher salt

⅛ teaspoon ground black pepper

6 fresh thyme sprigs

3 large red onions, thinly sliced (about 5½ cups)

1 bay leaf (optional)

2 tablespoons sherry vinegar

---

4 whole or portions of mackerel fillets (6 to 8 ounces each)

2 teaspoons kosher salt

¼ teaspoon freshly ground black pepper

1 teaspoon avocado or canola oil, plus more for the grill

Lemon wedges, for serving

FOR THE ONION JAM. In a medium saucepan, cook the pancetta over medium heat, stirring occasionally, for about 15 minutes, until most of the fat renders out and the pancetta is lightly browned. Add the butter and let it melt. Add the brown sugar, salt, pepper, thyme, onions, and bay leaf (if using) and toss to coat the onions evenly. Cook for 5 minutes then lower the heat to medium-low and cook, partially covered, for 20 to 25 minutes, stirring occasionally until the onions cook down and are very soft. Stir in the vinegar and continue to cook, stirring occasionally, until thick and jammy. Discard the thyme sprigs and bay leaf. Transfer the onions to an airtight container and let cool. The onion jam can be stored in the refrigerator for up to 10 days.

FOR THE FISH. Remove any pin bones with tweezers; this can be done with freshly caught fish, but it is easier if the fillets have been frozen and thawed. Season the fillets with the salt and pepper. Let sit for 20 minutes.

While you're waiting, prepare a medium-high grill. Pat the fish dry and brush with the oil. Place the fish skin-side down on a well-oiled grill and cook for about 3 minutes, until the skin is browned and blistered in spots. Carefully flip the fish over and cook for another 1 to 2 minutes. Transfer the fish to plates, skin-side up, and spread the onion jam on top of the fillets. Serve with lemon wedges and remaining onion jam.

ALSO WORKS WITH. *Atlantic, Spanish, cero, or king mackerel as well as bluefish, salmon, and trout. Cut large fish into steaks and fillets into serving-sized portions.*

COOK'S NOTE. *Onion jam can be used on basically anything—grilled meats, fish, pizzas, sandwiches, eggs, and even a piece of toast. The longer you cook it, the jammier it gets. It's worth making a double batch to keep in the fridge for other uses.*

GRILLED WHOLE FISH IN FOIL

WITH GRILLED SCALLIONS

SERVES 2

- 1 (2-pound) whole fish, gutted, scaled, fins trimmed off
- 2 teaspoons kosher salt
- ¼ teaspoon freshly ground black pepper
- 1 garlic clove, thinly sliced
- 1 small serrano or Fresno chile, with seeds, thinly sliced into rounds
- 5 thin orange wheels
- 5 thin lemon wheels
- 9 large fresh marjoram or oregano sprigs
- 1 large shallot, thinly sliced into rounds
- 1 large fennel bulb, thinly sliced crosswise
- 3 tablespoons extra-virgin olive oil
- 1 tablespoon drained capers
- 4 scallions, white and green parts, ends trimmed

ALSO WORKS WITH. *Various species of snappers and Pacific rockfish, striped bass, surf perch, Spanish mackerel, and speckled trout. You could also try this with smallmouth bass, large crappie, and even tilapia.*

The Atlantic black sea bass pictured in the photo opposite this recipe is counted among the dozens of species of fish that have been undeservedly regarded as "trash fish" by anglers. If you have ever heard someone say that about black sea bass, bonk them on the head for me. This species is one of the most flavorful and interesting fish that are readily available to fishermen along the Atlantic Seaboard. The fish has delicate flesh that is sweet and firm, and it's usually harvested in the 1- to 3-pound range, which is ideal for cooking whole. But you can use any 1 to 3 pound whole fish in this recipe, which essentially steams the fish over high heat inside its packaging of foil, large leaves, or even a salt crust. The filling can easily be simplified for the backcountry or adjusted with foraged ingredients such as wild garlic, ramps, or mushrooms.

Prepare a medium-hot grill for direct grilling.

Rinse the fish inside and out and pat it dry. Set it on a cutting board and cut three or four parallel, angled slits on both sides of the fish, cutting into the fish until you hit the bone. Rub the fish, including inside the slits and cavity, with 1 teaspoon of the salt and ⅛ teaspoon of the black pepper. Stuff the slits with the garlic and chile slices. Halve one of the orange wheels and stuff it into the cavity, along with 1 of the lemon wheels, 1 of the marjoram sprigs, and a pinch of the shallots.

In a medium bowl, toss the remaining shallots with the sliced fennel, 1 tablespoon of the oil, ½ teaspoon of the salt, and the remaining ⅛ teaspoon black pepper. Set aside.

On a large 18 × 20-inch sheet of foil, drizzle 1 tablespoon of the oil in the center where the fish will lie. Layer 3 of the orange wheels and 2 of the lemon wheels, half of the fennel-shallot mixture, half of the capers, and 4 of the marjoram sprigs over the oil. Lay the fish on top and drizzle with 2 teaspoons of the oil. Layer the remaining marjoram, capers, fennel-shallot mixture, and lemon and orange wheels on top of the fish. Fold the sides and ends of the foil together tightly and seal to close.

Place the foil packet on the grill and cook for 5 to 6 minutes. While the fish is grilling, toss or brush the scallions with the remaining 1 teaspoon oil and ½ teaspoon salt. Grill the scallions for 3 minutes until slightly charred. Transfer to a plate.

Flip the fish and cook for another 5 to 6 minutes. Carefully open the foil to see if the fish is cooked through. The flesh should be opaque, not translucent. Reseal the foil and keep cooking if needed.

Serve the fish with the filling ingredients and the grilled scallions.

GRILLED WHOLE FLOUNDER

WITH SAUCE CHIEN BEURRE MONTÉ

SERVES 4

Butter sauces pair well with light-fleshed, nonoily fish like flounder. This one is an adaptation of the French West Indies' *sauce chien,* or dog sauce, a spicy, herby, garlicky sauce used for fish and meat. *Chien* actually refers to the knife that is used to chop the ingredients for the sauce. The dog knife, or *couteau chien,* was created in 1880. It's a steel knife with a watchdog carved in the hilt and is given out as a wedding gift in the French West Indies. My adaptation on the sauce utilizes the French technique of adding butter to emulsify the sauce and give it some additional richness (see Cook's Note). You can omit the butter and go with olive oil or vegetable oil for a lighter sauce. While sauce chien pairs perfectly with flounder, it would also be a nice addition to upland game birds.

FLOUNDER

- 1 whole flounder (about 2 pounds), gutted
- 3 tablespoons kosher salt
- 2 tablespoons neutral oil, plus more for the fish basket

SAUCE CHIEN

- 8 tablespoons (1 stick) unsalted butter, cut into tablespoons
- 2 tablespoons fresh lemon juice, plus (optional) zest from one lemon
- 2 tablespoons chopped fresh chives
- 1 tablespoon chopped fresh flat-leafed parsley
- 1 teaspoon fresh thyme leaves
- 1 garlic clove, chopped (about 1 teaspoon)
- 1 or 2 habanero or Scotch bonnet chiles, seeded (optional), finely chopped (about 2 teaspoons)
- 1 shallot, finely chopped (about 3 tablespoons)
- ½ teaspoon kosher salt, plus more as needed
- ⅛ teaspoon finely ground black pepper, plus more as needed

FOR THE FLOUNDER. Scrub the flounder all over with 2 tablespoons of the salt. Rinse the fish, inside and out, and dry well with paper towels. Place the fish on a baking sheet or baking dish and chill in a cooler or refrigerator while you start the grill or prepare a campfire.

Prepare a grill or campfire with an area for direct and indirect heat. Just before grilling, gently brush the oil all over the fish and season with the remaining 1 tablespoon salt. Place in a lightly oiled fish basket. Place the basket on the hot side of the grill and cook, uncovered, until the fish chars in spots, about 4 minutes. Move the basket to indirect heat occasionally so the fish doesn't scorch.

Flip the basket and continue to grill for another 4 to 5 minutes, until the fish is cooked through at the thickest area toward the head. Use a small knife to check whether the flesh is flaky and opaque.

FOR THE SAUCE. Bring 2 tablespoons water to a boil in a small saucepan. Remove the pan from the heat and slowly whisk in the butter, 1 tablespoon at a time, until emulsified into a creamy sauce. Keep warm but do not let it boil. Stir in the lemon juice and (if using) zest, chives, parsley, thyme, garlic, habanero (if using), and shallots. Add salt and pepper and adjust the seasonings to taste.

Carefully transfer the fish to a platter. Pour half of the sauce over the fish and serve the remaining sauce on the side.

COOK'S NOTE. *Ideally, this sauce will remain in an emulsified state. Don't be too hard on yourself, however, if it breaks, especially when keeping it warm over a fire or grill outdoors. As you can see in the photo, we broke it, too. It still tasted great!*

ALSO WORKS WITH. *Other flatfish such as sole and small halibut or any light-fleshed saltwater or freshwater fish. Also shrimp, lobster, quail, grouse, and pheasant.*

GRILLED LOBSTER

WITH KELP BUTTER AND FINGERLING POTATO SALAD

SERVES 4

KELP GODDESS DRESSING

Makes ½ cup

1 (⅛-ounce) piece dried kelp

¼ cup mayonnaise

1 tablespoon sour cream

1 teaspoon fresh lemon juice

1 teaspoon red wine vinegar

1 teaspoon anchovy paste

1 small garlic clove, minced

1 ounce fresh chives, chopped (2 tablespoons)

KELP BUTTER

1 (⅛-ounce) piece dried kelp

6 tablespoons (¾ stick) unsalted butter

GRILLED FINGERLING POTATO SALAD

2 pounds fingerling potatoes, halved if large

Olive oil

Kosher salt and freshly ground black pepper

1 celery rib, cut into ¼-inch half-moons

½ cup purslane, roughly chopped (optional; see Cook's Note)

¼ cup Kelp Goddess Dressing

GRILLED LOBSTER

4 (1¼- to 1½-pound) lobsters

ALSO WORKS WITH. *Maine lobster, spiny lobster, langoustines, prawns, salmon, or clams and oysters on the half shell.*

Perhaps you're familiar with the culinary saying "What grows together, goes together." There are notable exceptions to this, of course. I love oyster mushrooms, for instance, but I would never choose to pair them with insect larvae that you find proliferating in their bases near the season's end. Other pairings make more sense. American pronghorn and sage. Mule deer and juniper. Lobster and seaweed. This recipe is based on the latter. It uses kelp to make a butter topping for lobster (or pretty much any other seafood) that is served alongside a refreshing and lively grilled potato salad. The Kelp Goddess Dressing requires a food processor, so plan ahead if you want to make this at the beach with some fresh-caught seafood. Everything else can be done in the field. Dried kelp is becoming more available in grocery stores nationwide. It's also available online from small coastal farms.

FOR THE DRESSING. Cover the kelp with water in a small saucepan and bring to a boil over high heat. Reduce to a simmer and cook for about 20 minutes, until the kelp swells, softens, and turns a lighter green. (You may need to poke it from time to time to keep it submerged.) Drain and rinse under cool water. Squeeze and discard any water from the kelp and add the kelp to a food processor. Chop coarsely. Scrape down the sides of the food processor bowl and then add the mayonnaise, sour cream, lemon juice, vinegar, anchovy paste, garlic, and chives. Process until combined.

FOR THE KELP BUTTER. Toast the dry kelp in a small skillet over medium-high heat for 6 to 7 minutes, flipping occasionally, until it dries up and crisps. Remove from the skillet and let cool. In the same skillet over medium heat, melt the butter. Crumble the dried kelp with your fingers into the melted butter and let it infuse the butter for a minute. Remove from the heat.

FOR THE GRILLED POTATO SALAD. Prepare a grill or open fire for indirect medium-high heat. If you're using charcoal or a wood fire, bank the hot coals on one side. Toss the potatoes with oil, salt, and pepper. Arrange in a pan over indirect heat, cover the grill, and cook for 20 to 25 minutes, until the potatoes are soft and you can easily pierce them with a knife. Remove to a large bowl and toss with ¼ cup of the dressing, the celery, and purslane (if using).

FOR THE GRILLED LOBSTER. Hold the lobster firmly stomach-side down. Use a very sharp knife to pierce the head portion of the shell where it meets the abdomen. Push the knife down with the heel of your hand to

Recipe continues

MAKE AHEAD. *The Kelp Goddess Dressing requires the use of a food processor, but it can be stored in a sealed container inside a chilled cooler for up to 3 days and in a refrigerator for up to 1 week.*

separate the tail. Next, cleave the tail in half lengthwise. Remove the claws. Whack the claw with back of the knife to crack them. Repeat with the remaining lobsters.

Spread out the coals (adding more if needed to keep the heat going) and put the claws and tails (flesh-side up) on the grill. Spoon the kelp butter over the tail meat. Cover and cook until the meat is no longer translucent and the shells turn bright red. This should take 8 to 10 minutes for the tail sections and 10 to 12 minutes for the claws. Remove to a platter and serve with the fingerling potato salad.

COOK'S NOTE. *To clean purslane, submerge it in water and swish it around to get rid of the little black seeds and any other detritus. The seeds are edible, so it's okay if they don't all wash off. Trim any thick stems that look woody.*

GRILLED SEAFOOD PAELLA

SERVES 6

Paella is a dish that is meant to be cooked slowly over flames and coals in a shallow paella pan. In Valencia, Spain, the region that claims ownership of this dish, a true paella is made with rabbit, snails, and chicken over a fire of orange wood from the region. The rice is cooked until it becomes a shallow layer lacquered with stock and should adhere to the bottom of the pan. This sticky, crunchy layer of rice is called the socarrat—it's the sign of a well-made paella. By virtue of Spain's proximity to the ocean, seafood variations of paella are also popular. According to local traditions, however, seafood shouldn't mix with meat, so they never put chorizo in a seafood paella. This grilled seafood paella is a campfire classic. As an angler or a hunter, you can use this base recipe to make your own wild variations. Practice the patience it takes to rotate the pan methodically to achieve that crunchy, caramelized layer of rice. The results are well worth the effort.

6 tablespoons extra-virgin olive oil

1 large onion, chopped (about 1½ cups)

1½ teaspoons kosher salt, plus more to finish

½ teaspoon freshly ground black pepper, plus more to finish

1 teaspoon smoked paprika

4 garlic cloves, grated or finely chopped

1 (15-ounce) can cherry tomatoes or whole peeled plum tomatoes in puree

1 cup dry white wine or dry sherry

2 cups short-grain Spanish rice, preferably Calasparra, Valencia, or Bomba

Pinch of saffron threads, crumbled

4 cups homemade or store-bought seafood stock or a combination of clam juice and water, plus more if needed

6 to 9 colossal (U10) head-on shrimp, peeled with heads and tails still attached, deveined (reserve shells for stock)

8 ounces cleaned squid bodies, sliced into ¾- to 1-inch-wide rings

8 ounces red snapper fillet, cut into 2- to 3-inch pieces

1¾ pounds mussels, scrubbed and beards removed

¼ cup fresh flat-leaf parsley, chopped

1 lemon, halved

For an open fire or fire pit, prepare a grate for direct and indirect grilling.

If using a charcoal grill, start a second chimney after the first is added to the grill. You'll need more coals when the first batch starts to die down.

Put a 14- to 15-inch paella pan on the grill grate. Add 4 tablespoons of the oil, the onions, ½ teaspoon of the salt, and ¼ teaspoon of the pepper. Cook and stir frequently until the onions soften, about 5 minutes, rotating the pan to the cooler part of the grill as necessary to avoid burning. Add the paprika and garlic and cook for 60 seconds, stirring constantly until fragrant. Add the tomatoes and use a spoon to smash and break them up. Cook and stir until the tomatoes have reduced into a paste, 5 to 8 minutes. Add the wine, cover, and cook until the liquid is mostly reduced, about 5 minutes.

Stir in the rice to coat it evenly. Add the saffron and the stock. Stir and spread the rice into an even layer. Let the paella simmer until most of the liquid has been absorbed, rotating the pan halfway through, 15 to 20 minutes. Taste a kernel of rice. If the rice is still partially raw and the liquid level is low, drizzle in more stock. Do not stir the rice.

Gently toss the shrimp, squid, and fish with the remaining 2 tablespoons oil, 1 teaspoon salt, and ¼ teaspoon pepper. Scatter the mussels and shrimp over the rice. Cover the pan (or close the grill lid) and continue to cook for about 5 minutes, or until the mussels just start to open up and

Recipe continues

the shrimp are almost cooked through. Add the squid and fish, cover, and cook another 3 to 5 minutes, until everything is cooked through.

Remove the pan from the grill grate. Cover the pan with the lid or foil and let the paella steam for 5 minutes. Uncover and discard any mussels that haven't opened.

While the paella is resting, grill the lemon cut-side down over direct heat until charred, 2 to 3 minutes. Uncover the paella, sprinkle it with parsley, and squeeze lemon over it. Adjust seasonings and serve.

COOK'S NOTES. *You'll find fresh tomatoes in most traditional paella recipes. Here we use canned for convenience in outdoor settings. Feel free to substitute fresh tomatoes if they are in season.*

Never mind what makes a "true" paella, because it's a free country and you can do what you want! Here's a way to take the dish in wild directions. Try this when you're feeling adventurous and the freezer is full. The proportions are as follows: Give or take 2 rabbits; 1- to 2-pound upland bird, each broken down into quarters or eighths, 1 to 2 dozen live snails; ½ pound flat green beans, trimmed; a big pinch of pimenton (smoked paprika); and a sprig of fresh rosemary. Start by parboiling the rabbit and bird legs until tender (anywhere from 1 to 2 hours). Then, in a paella pan, brown the rabbit and bird parts well in olive oil, then stir in the onion and garlic. Add the tomatoes and cook them down to a paste. Add the green beans, pimenton, rosemary, saffron, snails, and a light game stock. Season with kosher salt and black pepper. Bring to a boil, then sprinkle in the rice. Without stirring, rotate the pan until the liquid has absorbed, roughly 15 to 20 minutes.

ALSO WORKS WITH. *Octopus, scallops, and other shellfish, plus any firm white-fleshed fish such as halibut, mahi mahi, redfish, and similar freshwater substitutes. (See Cook's Notes for information about rabbit, upland birds, and snails.)*

HOW TO CATCH AN OCTOPUS

Kimi Werner

I was eleven years old the first time I caught an octopus on my own. I had grown up tagging along with my dad as he would free dive and spearfish on the north shore of Maui. I was the bag girl, just observing him and putting in my orders for my favorite dinners as I helped him bag his harvests. But one day, he spotted an octopus in its hole in about fifteen feet of water. He encouraged me to hold my breath and swim down to the bottom to try to catch it. I had watched my dad do this many times and knew his rules—he never speared them in their home. He always used his three-prong pole spear to gently tickle them out of the hole. Then he'd grab them in his hand and dispatch them. He did this so he could make sure they were a good size to take—and also to ensure that he didn't end up fatally wounding an octopus that he wouldn't be able to recover. The theory made sense, but the actual practice was trickier than it looked. By the time I got to the octopus in its hole and started to "tickle" it, I'd be out of breath and have to return to the surface. My dad kept encouraging me to relax, which is key to staying down longer. I tried over and over again, and soon my tickles resulted in long, suction-cup-covered legs jetting out and wrapping around my spear. I'd rush to grab ahold of them and pull the octopus out, only to see it retreat immediately back into its hole. Finally, after a lot of coaching about patience from my dad, I let the octopus grab my spear with all of its legs and pulled it out completely. I remember the feelings of joy and victory as I brought it to the surface. That joy immediately collided with the most painful sensations I had ever experienced. Right when I broke the surface, a Portuguese man-of-war, an organism related to a jellyfish with an insanely powerful sting that feels like fire, wrapped around my neck. I screamed in agony and splashed at the surface, and my dad yelped, too, as he pulled it off and got stung himself. Our day pivoted immediately, with Dad rushing me out of the water as my neck and chest swelled up and taking me straight to a little mom-and-pop store, where he bought meat tenderizer and applied it to my throat to reduce the swelling. I felt horrible. But I never let go of my tako, or octopus. And I'm happy to say that octopus diving only got easier for me from there on out.

Hawaii is a place of connection. The plants and animals I harvest are the same ones I want to see forever thriving. I grew up with them. They've fed me and given me so much in life: a connection to the natural world that we are a part of, my greatest adventures, my fondest memories, my most excruciating challenges. They have taught me who I am and who I want to be. So whenever I cook a meal, there's a very special sacredness I feel simply by acknowledging that I am putting nature into my body. Connecting to that idea makes me strive to turn those gifts from nature into dishes that are worthy of their components. This tako, or octopus, recipe was taught to me by my friend Justin Lee, who learned it from his friend Sam Myers. It's one of my go-to party-pleasers and is a hit every time. The dish is a vibrant celebration of the ingredients themselves!

OCTOPUS CHIMICHURRI

AN INSTANT POT METHOD

SERVES 4

1 (2-pound) octopus

3 tablespoons Hawaiian salt or coarse sea salt

Neutral oil, for grilling

CHIMICHURRI

Makes 2¼ cups

1 bunch cilantro, roughly chopped to yield 1 cup

1 medium bunch flat-leaf parsley, roughly chopped to yield 1 cup

2 fresh oregano sprigs, stems discarded, chopped fine

½ medium red onion, chopped fine

3 garlic cloves, minced

¾ teaspoon kosher salt

1 teaspoon crushed red pepper flakes or minced fresh red jalapeño

½ cup red wine vinegar

1 cup extra-virgin olive oil

FOR THE OCTOPUS. Gut the octopus by flipping the head inside out and pulling out the innards. Place the octopus in a large bowl and sprinkle it with the coarse salt. Massage it vigorously for 7 minutes, then rinse well to remove all the slime. Keep rinsing until the water runs clear and there are no more suds and bubbles. Add the cleaned octopus and 2 cups water to the Instant Pot. Pressure cook for 10 minutes. Once cooked, vent quickly using the steam release valve.

FOR THE CHIMICHURRI. Combine all the ingredients in a bowl and stir to combine. Set aside until ready to serve.

TO GRILL. Prepare a fire pit for direct heat. Remove the octopus from the Instant Pot and shake off the water. Slather it with oil and grill over high heat and open flames until charred. Smother the octopus in chimichurri sauce, cut it into bite-sized pieces, and serve.

Kimi Werner is a native Hawaiian, a steward for a sustainable global community, and one of the world's best free divers and spearfishers. She's also an avid cook with a lifetime of experience perfecting recipes that feature Hawaiian seafood. Kimi was born and raised on Maui and currently lives on Oahu with her family.

SPATCHCOCKING GAME BIRDS

One of my all-time favorite ways to handle birds such as grouse, quail, and chicken is to spatchcock them and throw 'em on a grill. Spatchcocking involves removing the backbone, snipping the breast bone, and flattening the bird into a more manageable shape that can be flipped on a grill and cooked evenly. (If you don't like the idea of tossing out the backbone, you can freeze it and save it for making game stock.) A bonus element of spatchcocking your birds is that the rib cage acts as a built-in roasting rack that protects the meat from the grill's direct heat; the crispy roasted skin on the other side helps to keep the meat moist.

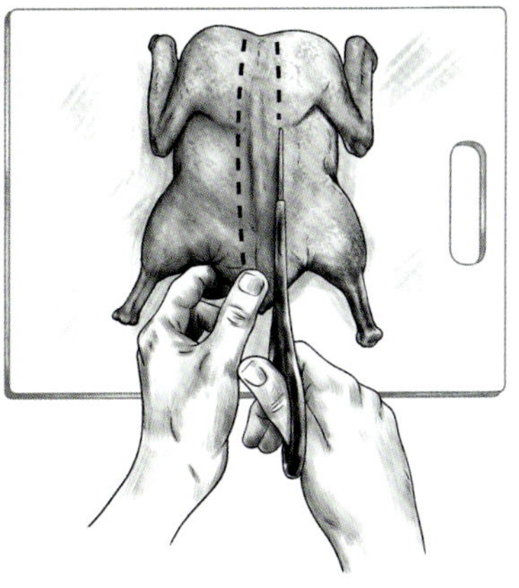

How to Spatchcock

1. Place the bird back-side up with the legs pointing toward you. Use kitchen shears to make a cut on each side of the hip, then continue the cuts along both sides of the spine until you can remove the hip, spine, and neck in one piece.

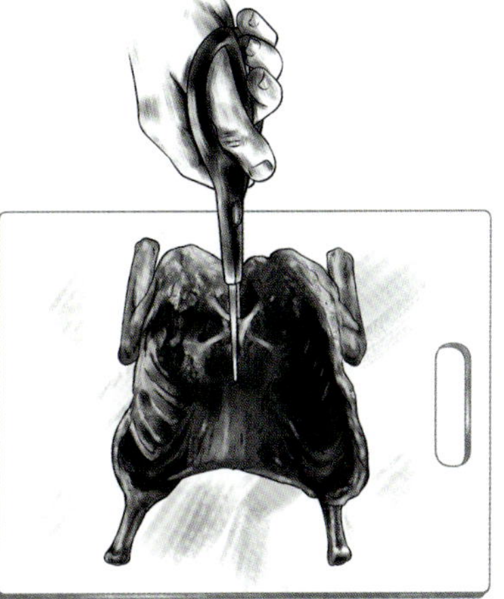

2. Starting on the other end of the bird, so that the legs are pointing away from you, use the shears to snip a notch in the thick upper part of the breastbone. Then use a knife to make a shallow slit on either side of the breastbone to disconnect the meat from the breastbone.

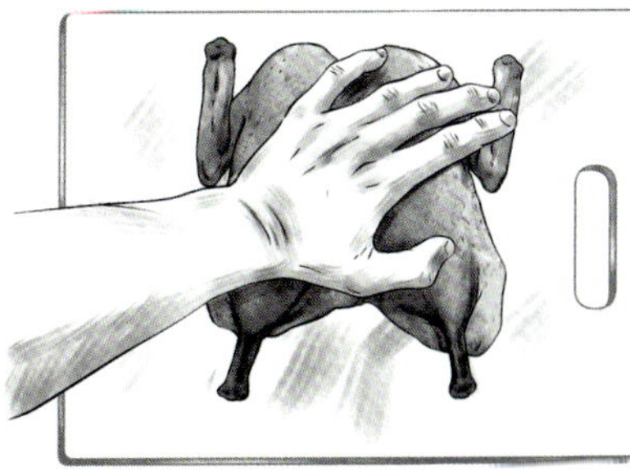

3. Flip the breast over and press gently in the center of the breast to flatten. You'll hear a little pop in the rib cage. Remove the wings and legs, if you wish to cook them separately. Save the backbone for stock.

MARINADES FOR SPATCHCOCKED BIRDS AND OTHER WILD GAME

The following three marinades are phenomenal with all kinds of birds, but they're also fantastic with big game, small game, and even vegetables. They can be made ahead of time for entertaining. Don't omit the side sauces where they appear. They're just as tasty as the marinades.

SHAWARMA-STYLE YOGURT MARINADE

(FOR SPATCHCOCKED BIRDS)

¾ cup plain full-fat Greek yogurt

¼ cup extra-virgin olive oil

3 garlic cloves, grated on a rasp

Juice of 1 lemon

1 teaspoon freshly ground black pepper

2 teaspoons kosher salt, plus more as needed

1½ teaspoons ground coriander

1½ teaspoons ground cumin

1 teaspoon ground allspice

1 teaspoon ground cinnamon

¾ teaspoon ground turmeric

The tenderizing properties of this yogurt-based marinade are helpful when cooking with game. The recipe comes from the style of marinades frequently used for shawarma in the Middle East, where it's typically paired with lamb or chicken. It gets its name from the Arabic word for "turning"—referencing primarily the vertical rotating rotisserie on which marinated meats are roasted and then shaved for sandwiches, salads, and other dishes. A similar vertical roasting pit called the trompo is used in Mexico to make tacos al pastor (see our version of that dish on page 281). But interestingly, the trompo came to the region via the Syrian and Lebanese immigrants who brought their shawarma-style of vertical roasting spit to Mexico in the late nineteenth century.

It's best to let the marinade do its work on the meat for at least an hour before grilling or smoking. This marinade is traditionally used for skewers, but it's also a natural addition to a shawarma-style cook on a rotisserie.

The marinade will cover 1 medium game bird, such as a pheasant or large grouse, or 3 to 6 small game birds such as ducks or quail. Makes about 1¼ cups.

ALSO WORKS WITH. *Upland birds, puddle ducks, and domestic chickens as well as hooved big game cuts like backstrap and roasts that have been cut into thin steaks.*

FOR THE MARINADE. In a bowl, combine all marinade ingredients and whisk to combine. Adjust salt to taste. Set aside.

TO MARINATE. Dry the meat well. Slather the marinade liberally all over the interior, exterior, and under the skin of the bird in a thick layer. Marinate for at least 1 hour. Remove most of the marinade from the surface of the meat before grilling. Any unused marinade that has not touched raw meat can be stored in an airtight container for up to 1 week in the refrigerator.

SOUR CREAM HERB MARINADE FOR GRILLED (OR SMOKED) GAME BIRDS

MAKES ABOUT 1¼ CUPS

Simple recipes like this one come down to the quality of your ingredients. It's worth it to source a decent sour cream (or a similar quality cultured dairy product like crème fraîche or Greek yogurt). If you have the time, the birds will benefit from marinating for a few hours or even overnight to let that lactic acidity do its thing and tenderize the meat. You can easily make this by hand and chop the garlic and herbs with a knife. You can also swap the specified herbs for any soft herb you have on hand. While dill and mint are fantastic, so are basil, parsley, cilantro, or a combination of them all.

6 garlic cloves

1 cup mixed fresh soft herbs, like dill and mint, roughly chopped

1 cup sour cream

2 teaspoons kosher salt, plus more as needed

½ teaspoon freshly ground black pepper, plus more as needed

Marinade will cover 1 medium game bird, such as a pheasant or large grouse, or 3 to 6 small game birds like ducks and quail.

FOR THE MARINADE. In a food processor with the motor running, drop the garlic cloves in one by one to mince them. Stop the machine and add the herbs, sour cream, salt, and pepper. Pulse until smooth (there will be visible pieces of herbs in the cream). Adjust seasonings to taste.

TO MARINATE. Dry the meat well. Slather the herb mixture all over the interior, exterior, and under the skin of the bird. Keep the marinade on while you grill. It will create a saucy, caramelized layer on the outside of the bird.

ALSO WORKS WITH. *Upland birds, small puddle ducks, wild turkey breasts, and domestic chickens as well as big game loins and tenderloins.*

COOK'S NOTE. *This marinade works for grilled, roasted, and smoked birds. It also makes an excellent dip for crudités. To make the dip, use only 3 garlic cloves and add 2 tablespoons mayonnaise and 1 tablespoon lemon juice.*

PERUVIAN-STYLE MARINADE FOR DUCK

WITH AJÍ VERDE (GREEN JALAPEÑO SAUCE)

On any given day, Peruvians fire-roast millions of chickens that are paired with ají verde. Once you try it, you'll wish this dish was part of your own routine. The warm spices complement any kind of bird and hold up exceptionally well with waterfowl. The tangy, spicy ají sauce (Peruvian green chili sauce) works as well with roasted potatoes and French fries as it does with meat, so make extra in order to experiment a bit. Serves 4 to 6, depending on the size of the ducks.

MARINADE

Makes about ¾ cup

4 garlic cloves, smashed and roughly chopped

2 teaspoons kosher salt, plus more as needed

¼ cup vegetable oil, plus more for the grill

Juice from 2 large limes (about ¼ cup)

1 tablespoon red wine vinegar

1 teaspoon sugar

1 tablespoon ground cumin

2 tablespoons paprika

1 teaspoon freshly ground black pepper, plus more as needed

2 or 3 ducks (4 to 5 pounds), spatch-cocked with legs separated (see technique illustrated on page 75)

AJÍ SAUCE

Makes about 1½ cups

4 medium jalapeño peppers, roughly chopped (see Cook's Note)

1 garlic clove

1½ cups fresh cilantro leaves

½ cup sour cream

⅓ cup cotija cheese

2 teaspoons lime juice

2 tablespoons mayonnaise

1 teaspoon red wine vinegar

2 tablespoons olive oil

Kosher salt and freshly ground black pepper

COOK'S NOTE. *If you have access to Aji Amarillo paste, use 3 to 4 tablespoons in place of the fresh chiles.*

FOR THE MARINADE. Make a garlic paste with the garlic and salt: On a cutting board, pile the salt on top of the chopped garlic and, using the side of your knife blade, press the garlic and salt together across the cutting board a few times to form a paste. In a medium bowl, mix the garlic paste with the vegetable oil, lime juice, vinegar, sugar, cumin, paprika, and black pepper.

Slather half of the marinade on the outside of the bird and underneath the skin. Season the inside of the cavity with salt and pepper. Place the bird into a resealable bag and pour the remaining marinade into the bag. Seal the bag and rub the bird with the marinade to coat. Refrigerate overnight. If car camping, bring it with you like this.

FOR THE AJÍ SAUCE. Add all ingredients into a blender except for the olive oil, salt, and black pepper. With the motor running, add the olive oil slowly through the top of the blender. When smooth, season to taste with salt. Refrigerate in an airtight container until ready to serve.

TO GRILL. The next day, bring the bird to room temperature in the bag. Meanwhile, prepare your grill or live fire with a grate for indirect heat. Oil the grill grates. Put the duck breast, skin-side up, close to the direct-heat side of the grill. Place the legs on the indirect heat side, flipping them occasionally. Flip the breast to sit over direct heat to render some of the fat and to brown the skin. Be careful not to scorch it. When it starts to brown and get crispy, flip it back over to continue cooking. Do the same with the wings and thighs, moving all of them to the indirect side after rendering and charring them a bit to finish cooking.

Cook the breast until it reads 135°F with an instant-read thermometer, then remove it from the grill to rest. Cook the legs and wings to 160°F. The whole process could take from 20 to 35 minutes depending on the heat of your fire and the ambient temperatures. Use the instant-read thermometer to let you know when it's done.

Serve with the ají sauce on the side and pair with coal-roasted potatoes and vegetables (see page 159).

WILD TURKEY AND MORTADELLA PINWHEELS

WITH SAGE BALSAMIC SAUCE

SERVES 6

SAGE BALSAMIC SAUCE

Makes 2 cups

½ cup sage leaves, stalks reserved

1 cup basil leaves

1 cup flat-leaf parsley leaves

1 medium shallot, halved

4 large garlic cloves

2 tablespoons balsamic vinegar

¼ cup freshly squeezed lemon juice (from 1 large lemon)

¼ cup freshly squeezed orange juice

¾ teaspoon kosher salt

¼ teaspoon freshly ground black pepper

1 teaspoon crushed red pepper flakes

¾ cup extra-virgin olive oil

PINWHEELS

1 skinless, boneless wild turkey breast (roughly 3 to 4 pounds)

Kosher salt and freshly ground black pepper

12 (¼-inch-thick) slices smoked mozzarella or provolone

6 to 8 (⅛-inch-thick) slices mortadella (about 5 ounces)

3 roasted red peppers (jarred)

Extra-virgin olive oil

3 fresh rosemary springs

8 tablespoons (1 stick) salted butter, melted

SPECIAL EQUIPMENT

6 wooden skewers, cut down to 5 inches and soaked overnight

Butcher's twine

This is an elegant and fun way to serve up wild game in the backyard. It takes a bit of work to pull it off, but it's well worth it. It also makes a great appetizer. You'll see that the preparation involves hammering out a turkey breast into a thin sheet. This is a trick you should have up your sleeve whether you're making pinwheels or not, because you'll find that a big, thin sheet of turkey meat lends itself to all sorts of fun preparations. You can do these pinwheels with a lot of other types of meat as well, including goose and even venison, but I think turkey is the best. The key is to butterfly it and pound it to tenderize before filling, rolling, and slicing. The more tender you make it, the better it will be. (For more information on the butterflying technique, see page 46.)

FOR THE SAUCE. Place all ingredients in a blender and pulse ten to twelve times to help break down the herbs, shallot, and garlic. Once combined, let the blender run on a medium speed for 20 to 30 seconds, until evenly pureed. The sauce can be 1 day in advance and stored in an airtight container in the refrigerator.

FOR THE PINWHEELS. Trim any sinew or extra fat from the turkey breast. Flip the breast over so the interior is facing up and carefully spread out and butterfly the breast so you have a single piece that is somewhat even in thickness. Cover with a large piece of plastic wrap and pound flat until you reach a thickness of about ⅓ inch. You don't want to pound straight down; hit the turkey in the thicker spots and push to the side as you go to prevent the mallet from tearing through the meat.

Remove the plastic wrap and trim the sides of the turkey so that you're left with one nice large rectangle roughly 12 × 8 inches (this will vary depending on the size of the bird). Season the top side with salt and pepper and spread ¾ cup of the sage balsamic sauce evenly over the surface. Place the slices of cheese on the sauce, overlapping them slightly as you go. Try to leave about 1 inch of meat uncovered on one of the long sides of the rectangle. This will be the side that tucks in and seals the roulade once it's rolled. Next, lay the mortadella on top and then the roasted red pepper, keeping the layers flat and uniform.

TO ROLL THE ROULADE. Starting with the long side of the rectangle with the fillings up to the edge and using both hands, tightly tuck and roll the turkey onto itself until you are left with one long roll. Slide skewers through the roulade every 2 inches down the entire length to secure it.

Be sure the skewers catch the end flap of meat that has no filling. Rub olive oil all over the outside and season with salt and pepper. (At this point you can roll the roulade tightly in plastic wrap and stash in the refrigerator to cook later.)

TO GRILL. Set up your grill for indirect cooking. If using charcoal, light two chimneys of coals. When hot, bank the coals on one side of the grill. Cut the turkey roulade in between each skewer so you have 6 pinwheels (see illustration). Oil the grill grates. Dry the pinwheels and drizzle olive oil onto one side of each pinwheel. Flip the pinwheels and pour 1 tablespoon of sage balsamic sauce onto each pinwheel.

Tie the sage and rosemary together in a bundle with the butcher twine. Place the melted butter in a small pot, add the herb bundle, and keep it warm on the cooler side of the grill.

Grill the pinwheels over the hottest part of the fire for 2 to 3 minutes per side, until grill marks appear, rotating often to prevent charring. Use the herb bundle to brush each side of the pinwheels with herb butter as they cook. Move the pinwheels to the cooler side of the grill and cover with a lid. Continue to cook, flipping and brushing with herb butter occasionally, for 20 to 25 minutes, until the turkey reaches an internal temperature of 160°F. Remove from the grill, transfer to a platter, and allow to rest for 3 to 5 minutes.

Remove the skewers and pour the remaining sage balsamic sauce over the pinwheels. Serve while hot.

ALSO WORKS WITH. *Goose breast, big game, and wild hog roasts (be sure to cook the wild hog roast to 160°F to kill off any trichinosis)*

Slice the rolled turkey breast between each skewer.

02 INTO THE SMOKE

YETI

Around 2010, I spent a couple of weeks on a river trip in Guyana with a Macushi friend of mine named Rovin. Macushi territory straddles the borderlands of Guyana, Brazil, and Venezuela. Rovin and his family use rivers to access scattered garden plots of cassava and chiles that are fertilized by the annual flood cycles. Along the way, they collect fish with handlines and nets, and hunt a variety of birds and mammals with archery equipment that is made with natural materials found in the jungle—right down to arrow fletching made from the wing feathers of black curassow. As a child, Rovin's primary mode of transportation was a dugout canoe. Even today, aluminum boats are a fairly novel concept. I don't care what kind of backwoods badass you are, Rovin has you (and me) beat.

Guyana's southern border sits just north of the equator. Average daytime highs are in the mid-eighties. It's so humid that when you reach into your duffel bag to get a clean T-shirt, it feels like you're pulling a wet load of laundry out of the washing machine. Food spoils almost immediately in this climate. Bunches of picked bananas will stay green for days, but their yellow phase seems to last about as long as the yellow light at a traffic stop. Meat is worse. Lay a fish on the riverbank and in a few hours you'll have a stinking mess coated with flies and bees. Typically a person would solve such a problem by burying the fish in a cooler of ice or wrapping it in plastic wrap and placing it on a shelf in the fridge. But these methods have zero relevance to a river trip in the jungles of Guyana, where there's nowhere to plug in a fridge and ice has

the same life expectancy as a wounded fish tossed into a school of piranhas.

Instead, the Makushi have a method for preserving their fish and game that is magical in its simplicity and effectiveness. Every time that we moved upriver and established a new camp, Rovin walked into the jungle with a machete and cut four wooden posts that were each about 4 feet long. The posts terminated at the top end in a Y shape. He set each of these posts vertically into an elbow-deep hole in the sand that he dug by using his machete as a trowel. Rovin then spanned each pair of vertical posts with a long horizontal pole laid into the crotch of the Ys and overlaid these poles with tightly spaced limbs that were just an inch or two in diameter. When it was all said and done, he had a grill-like structure that sat about 30 inches off the ground and covered about 25 square feet of space. Above the setup, Rovin constructed a canopy of palm fronds to help trap the smoke and shield the fire from afternoon rain showers. Beneath it we kindled a slow-burning fire that would be kept alive twenty-four hours a day for as long as we stayed in that one particular camp.

Over the course of our time together, we laid an astonishing array of protein on that wooden rack to bask in the smoke of the smoldering fire: turtles, curassows, guans, catfishes, piranhas, peacock bass, and paca (a semi-aquatic, herbivorous rodent weighing about twenty pounds). Each of these critters was processed in its own particular way before getting a light coating of salt. Large catfish were gutted and chunked up with a machete, the heads split in two lengthwise; curassows and guans were plucked and spatchcocked; the bone-in legs and neck of the turtle were parboiled in a pot made from the turtle's own shell; piranhas and peacock bass were split in half down the spine with the two halves held together by a strip of belly flesh.

From the Makushi in South America to many native Alaskan cultures, the process of preserving food with woodsmoke is still widely used around the world, either because refrigeration isn't an option or because, despite access to modern conveniences, those cultures haven't turned away from traditional preservation methods and cultural foodways that have been practiced for millennia. But even though most of us store the bulk of our meat and fish in the freezer, we cer-

tainly haven't lost our taste for smoked food. And it's easy to imagine how it all began: Some long-ago human notices that the flies aren't nearly as annoying when she stands in the smoke of the fire. At some point she hangs strips of meat there in order to keep the maggots at bay. At first, it's not so much that the smoke tastes good; it's just the flavorful by-product of a novel technique. Soon, the flavor has such positive connotations that it starts to taste pretty damn good all on its own. Someone eventually couples that smoke with another natural preservative, salt. Thousands of years go by, and you can now drive down to your local grocery store and buy a 3.5-ounce bottle of a product called liquid smoke. That's right, get that great smoky flavor without the hassle of flames!

You won't find liquid smoke in any of the smoked foods recipes in this chapter. But please don't think I'm disparaging the stuff. It's described in technical lingo as a natural aqueous condensate of woodsmoke, meaning it really is what the bottle says it is: liquid smoke. The reason that we don't typically use liquid smoke is because we prefer the real stuff. However, we're not terribly picky about how that real smoke gets made. We like pellet grills, we like foil packs full of wood chips, we like good old-fashioned firewood. Nor are we terribly picky about what we put in the smoker. Here you'll find proven and honest recipes for smoking salmon, eels, all kinds of birds, venison, wild hogs, and even eggs and moose nose. With the right strategies and preparations, you'll be surprised what you can get away with. And I've got some good news for you: The more you smoke fish and game, the more skilled you'll get. So keep at it and let these recipes be a stepping stone for you.

SMOKING: WHAT YOU NEED TO KNOW

This chapter explores a range of game and fish recipes that employ different smoking techniques and equipment. Since smoking is a very broadly defined category of outdoor cooking, the ingredients, techniques, and equipment used will have a big influence on how your finished product turns out. For example, there's no reason you can't smoke catfish—just don't expect it to turn out like salmon. On a similar note, brining wild game meat and then smoking it at lower temperatures than you'd use with fatty domestic meat ensures it won't dry out. Likewise, tough cuts need to be braised before smoking. Equipment matters, too, no matter what the provenance of your meat. For example, a hog ham smoked in a pellet grill will not be the same as one smoked in a charcoal grill. I've found that I get the best results by hot-smoking fish and eels in a big propane chamber smoker. And you'll see that I don't cover cold-smoking fish at all since it relies on air-drying fish in ambient temperatures rather than the application of heat, which means it falls outside the scope of the smoking techniques used in this book. Remember, too, that smoking is never an exact science; things won't always turn out perfectly, so make it a point to learn from your successes and your failures. And as with any kind of cooking, once you have a good understanding of the basics, then you should feel free to experiment. There's always room for substitutions and innovations. With those goals in mind, here are the primary smoking methods and the equipment used in this book.

Domestic pork and beef are generally smoked at fairly low temperatures for long periods of time, with a nearly constant stream of smoke. As we've mentioned, wild game hams and fatty sausages can be smoked for longer periods, but other types of lean game meat can present a challenge using this technique. Fortunately, lean game roasts, waterfowl and upland bird breasts, and fish that cook fairly quickly can be smoked directly on grills. It is important to note that if you've got your heart set on smoking tough, sinewy cuts like shanks or shoulders, you'll need to braise or confit them before smoking on a grill.

It's very simple to turn your grill into a smoker. On a charcoal grill, you can add a smokebox full of wood chips or just toss some chips on top of smoldering briquettes. Keep the lid on to trap the smoke that's produced. Some gas grills have an offset chamber that's specifically designed for adding wood chips, but if yours doesn't, all you need is some aluminum foil. Place a fistful of wood chips and woody herbs like rosemary in a store-bought foil tray (see the illustration on page 92). Place the tray over a burner and close the grill lid. Pretty soon the chips will start releasing smoke. If you don't have a foil tray, wrap the chips in a foil packet and poke a few holes in the top of the bundle; the smoke will release through the holes in the foil. The flavor you achieve will depend on what combinations of wood chips, herbs, and spices you use. You can also experiment with aromatic teas.

Lastly, keep in mind that the temperature of propane grills is easily adjustable with the turn of a knob. It is more difficult to maintain a steady, low smoking temperature on a charcoal grill, although barbecue-focused websites like Meathead Goldwyn's Amazing Ribs have excellent tips on how to do it. In addition to a quality meat probe thermometer, it's worth investing in a digital oven thermometer to keep track of the temperature inside your grill.

SMOKING METHODS

Smoking over a Wood Fire

The most basic and purest form of smoking happens over or adjacent to a fire. A smoky fire transmits smoky flavor into game or fish, though you'll generally have more control with other methods of smoking.

Smoking over a Charcoal Fire

Charcoal smoking can be done in a run-of-the-mill kettle grill, a Japanese kamado-style grill like the Green Egg, or a charcoal chamber or offset smoker. It's a good idea to supplement smoldering lump charcoal with a few blocks of hardwood or soaked hardwood chips for longer smokes.

Smoking with Foil Trays

A simple foil tray or packet filled with wood chips can be used to add smoky flavor to grilled foods, especially with a propane or charcoal grill. For more unique flavors, you can add dried spices, teas, and hardy fresh herbs such as rosemary, lemongrass, or thyme.

Chamber Smokers

Charcoal, electric, and propane chamber smokers come in a lot of sizes and configurations, but I prefer the tall vertical propane models for long wild game and fish smokes. They can be easily adjusted and held at a wide range of temperatures. They're also great for turning out big batches of food. One knock against them is that during long smokes, you need to keep adding wood chips to the tray. This can be partially mitigated by soaking the chips in water for 20 to 30 minutes before smoking, or using larger pieces of wood that will smoke longer.

Pellet Grills

The ease and simplicity of smoking with electric pellet grills can't be overstated. All you need to do is pour your preferred flavor of wood pellets into the hopper, set the temperature and timer, and you're off to the races. The pellets are fed automatically and continually into the grill for a steady supply of smoke. They do require regular maintenance and cleanup to keep them functioning properly.

From big offset oil-drum charcoal smokers and vertical charcoal smokers to small electric models and all the various iterations of homemade smoking contraptions in between, there are, of course, more options than what's listed above. If they're not covered in this book, don't take it to mean that we think they're in some way inferior. We feel it's only fair to focus on the methods and equipment we know well and that apply to the recipes in this book. You may already have, or will develop, a preference for a completely different kind of smoker setup. That's great—the recipes in this chapter will still work for you.

MAKE SURE TO PACK YOUR SMOKER FULL OF GOOD STUFF

If you have a large-capacity chamber smoker, it seems only logical to fill the thing up rather than use just a single shelf. For efficiency's sake, I'm a big fan of smoking multiple things at once, including nonmeat items. Mushrooms, apples, pears, butter, cheeses, and hard-boiled eggs (see recipe for Smoked and Deviled Eggs on page 117) can all benefit from a stint in the smoker. Try soaking shiitake mushrooms or pears in ponzu, soy sauce, or Worcestershire with or without a pinch of crushed red pepper flakes. The umami flavors become more intense as the food dehydrates in the smoker. The finished product can be added to soups and salads, served with goat cheese as an appetizer, or used to garnish seared steaks or duck breasts.

A NOTE ON BARBECUE

These days, it seems like there's a barbecue joint around every corner selling smoked brisket, ribs, and chicken wings. There are also hundreds of wildly popular barbecue cooking competitions held all over the country that draw thousands of hungry spectators with imposing rigs of wood-fired offset smokers. And, of course, backyard barbecuing has long been a national pastime. There's a good reason for that: There's just something uniquely appealing about the bold aromas, dripping fat, tender meat, and intense flavors of smoked foods slathered in flavorful rubs and sauces.

Obviously, smoking is an integral part of the barbecuing process. But traditional barbecue-style smoking that we associate with the American South involves long hours of smoking fatty, marbled cuts that self-baste and become fall-apart tender when they're done. With the exception of hams and sausages, it's difficult to truly "smoke" big game cuts in that tradition because of their lack of fat. As such, this is not a barbecue smoking chapter in the traditional sense. This is a chapter about using smoke for flavor and preservation.

COLA ANCHO JERKY

MAKES 1 POUND DRIED JERKY

This jerky recipe is reliable and tasty, with just a hint of heat. It's not full of ghost peppers or other gimmicks that will turn kids off or make it hard to enjoy more than a bite or two. If you do want more heat, ramp up the cayenne. Take note that this recipe uses pink curing salt, which in combination with the smoke makes this jerky extremely resistant to spoilage. If you're planning on eating the jerky pretty quickly and have concerns about the nitrates and nitrites in the curing salt, substitute with ½ cup of kosher salt.

JERKY

4 pounds frozen venison bottom round roast

2 cups cola

½ cup apple cider vinegar

½ cup soy sauce

⅓ cup brown sugar

2 tablespoons hot sauce

¼ teaspoon ground cloves

1 teaspoon pink curing salt #1 or Prague powder #1 (optional)

ANCHO DUST

2 tablespoons ground ancho chile

2 tablespoons garlic powder

1 teaspoon cayenne pepper

FOR THE MEAT. Move the meat from the freezer to the refrigerator for 3 to 6 hours, until it's just beginning to thaw. Slice while partially frozen into thin pieces, about ¼ inch thick *with* the grain. (If you slice across or against the grain, the jerky will be crumbly rather than having the ideal chew factor.) Transfer the meat to a baking sheet.

FOR THE CURING MARINADE. In a flat nonreactive baking dish, combine the cola, vinegar, soy sauce, brown sugar, hot sauce, cloves, and pink curing salt.

Submerge the meat into the marinade, toss to coat. Seal tightly. Refrigerate for at least 12 hours.

FOR THE JERKY. The next day, remove from the marinade and pat it dry between layers of paper towels. Combine the ancho chile, garlic powder, and cayenne in a small bowl. Prepare a baking sheet with several layers of freezer paper. Dust the meat lightly with the mixture on both sides and lay it out on layers of freezer paper on the baking sheet.

Set up your smoker. For wood chips, fruitwoods produce the mildest flavor, but oak will work as well.

Preheat the smoker to 165°F. Transfer the meat from the freezer paper to a rack in the smoker, being sure to leave room between the slices of meat. It's important to maintain a temperature between 165°F and 200°F when dehydrating or smoking the jerky. After 2 hours, check the texture. The goal is to smoke the jerky until the meat is pliable and leathery, but not overly dry and brittle. It should crack and bend a little but not break easily into small pieces. Continue checking the texture every 15 to 30 minutes, pulling any thinner pieces that might have finished before the thicker ones. The whole process can take up to 4 hours depending on ambient humidity, the consistency of your smoker temp, and how thinly you cut your meat. Remove finished pieces to cool and store them in a resealable or vac-sealed bag.

If you used the Prague powder, the jerky can be stored at room temperature. If you didn't, store in the refrigerator for 6 to 8 weeks or in the freezer for up to 1 year.

COOK'S NOTE. *Pink curing salt #1 or Prague powder #1 should not be confused with pink Himalayan salt. Pink salt #1 is a curing salt that is used in curing hard and semisoft sausages, bacon, ham, pastrami, and corned beef. It inhibits harmful bacteria growth and adds a pink appearance to cured meats.*

ALSO WORKS WITH. *I prefer the grain of a bottom round roast for jerky, but a top round, sirloin, or eye of round roast from any red meat big game animal also works great. Goose breasts are ideal for this recipe, too. There are cuts from the front shoulder of big game animals, like the flatiron steak, that make decent jerky as well, though they tend to yield a much chewier end product.*

SUMMER SAUSAGE

MAKES 10 POUNDS

- 8 pounds meat, cut into 1-inch cubes
- 2 pounds pork fatback
- 6 tablespoons kosher salt
- ¼ cup dextrose (see Cook's Notes)
- 2 teaspoons pink salt #1 or Prague powder #1 (see Cook's Notes, page 101)
- 1½ tablespoons mustard seeds
- 1 tablespoon dry mustard powder
- 2 teaspoons garlic powder
- 2 teaspoons freshly ground black pepper
- 2 teaspoons ground ginger
- 1 cup Fermento (see Cook's Notes)
- 4 (2½ x 18-inch) collagen casings

SPECIAL EQUIPMENT

Meat grinder

I've been making this summer sausage recipe for most of my adult life. I initially shared it in the first volume of *The Complete Guide to Hunting, Butchering, and Cooking Wild Game*. I'm sharing it again here because it's stood the test of time so well that I haven't found a reason to change anything. It's perfect for everything from a backpacking trip to a holiday appetizer. You can mess with the flavor profiles if you wish by swapping spices, but this version is a proven winner. This recipe makes a 10-pound batch. You can halve or even double it if you like. I recommend a 2-day ferment, so be sure you plan appropriately.

TO GRIND/PREPARE THE SAUSAGE MIXTURE. Keep everything ice cold (following the chilling instructions for Camp Sausage on page 36). Combine the game meat, pork fat, and all of the other ingredients except for the Fermento and casings in a large bowl. Mix to combine with your hands. Work in small batches and keep the meat cold by returning it to the fridge or freezer as needed. Using the ¼-inch (medium) plate on your grinder, grind the meat mixture into the bowl set over ice. Change to the $^{3}/_{16}$-inch (small) grinder plate and pass the mixture through the grinder again.

Meanwhile, in a bowl, dissolve the Fermento in 1 cup of water and stir with a spoon. Add to the ground meat mixture and again mix well with your hands until it's all incorporated. (You can also use a standing mixer and incorporate the Fermento and water on low speed.)

Firmly press a piece of plastic wrap over the surface of the meat, making sure there are no air bubbles. Cover the bowl with a second layer of plastic wrap and set it in the refrigerator to ferment for 2 days.

After about 48 hours of fermenting, make a test patty and cook it in a sauté pan to be sure your seasoning is what you'd like it to be. Adjust the seasonings if needed.

TO STUFF THE SAUSAGE. Using a sausage stuffer, stuff the sausage into the casings. Let the stuffed casings rest in the fridge, uncovered, for 1 to 2 hours to dry out.

PREPARE THE SMOKER. Soak a pan full of applewood chips for 20 minutes. (Alternatively, choose applewood pellets if using a pellet grill smoker.) Preheat a smoker to between 112°F and 130°F; this is lower than most pellet smokers will go, so go to the lowest setting your smoker allows if that is the case. Drain the wood chips and add them to the smoker. Throughout the smoking process, keep the applewood-chip pan full. When the temperature is between 112°F and 130°F, lay or hang the sausages in the smoker. Smoke for about 1 hour at this temperature, then raise the temperature to 180°F. Smoke until the internal temperature of the sausage reaches 150°F, which will probably take 2 to 3 hours, depending on your particular smoker and the ambient temperature outside. Refill the wood chips as needed if they get low.

When the sausages are done, let them hang at room temperature for 1 hour to cool, then wrap well or vac-seal and refrigerate. They will last 4 months in the fridge and can be frozen for 6 to 12 months.

Serve with crackers and/or cheese or simply eat with a hunting knife while taking a break on a hike.

COOK'S NOTES. *Fermento is a fermentation starter made from cultured whey protein and skim milk. It's commonly used in summer sausage and other semidry sausages. It expedites the fermentation process, eliminating longer curing times. You can find it online, at specialty butcher shops, or in sporting goods stores with a well-stocked assortment of game processing supplies.*

Dextrose powder is a sugar used in sausage making. It is a nutrient that feeds the lactic organisms and aids in the fermentation process.

ALSO WORKS WITH. *Any ground meat, ranging from whitetail deer to beef.*

BROWN SUGAR WILD HOG HAM

Kevin Gillespie

Smoking a ham that has been slathered in something sweet isn't a new idea, but sometimes it's better to refine rather than reinvent. This particular version came about as a way to stop my mom from showing up to every holiday function with a precooked honey baked ham that she ordered through the mail. To me they taste overly processed and bring zero sense of nostalgia to the table. I wanted a ham that reminded me of what my late grandmother would serve every Christmas and Easter. Something with a perfect balance of sweet, salt, and smoke that left a lasting impression. I prefer to make this preparation with feral hogs because I like smaller-sized hams, but it works just as well with domestic hogs.

SERVES 4 TO 6

CURING BRINE

1¼ cups packed light brown sugar

1 cup kosher salt

1 pound onions, peeled and quartered

½ cup garlic cloves

1 tablespoon whole cloves

1 cinnamon stick

Pink curing salt #1 or Prague powder #1

2 quarts ice cubes

1 (5- to 7-pound) bone-in ham from a feral or farm-raised pig

SUGAR COATING

1 pound light brown sugar

2 teaspoons ground cloves

2 teaspoons ground cinnamon

1 teaspoon freshly ground black pepper

FOR THE BRINE. Combine the brown sugar, salt, onions, garlic, whole cloves, cinnamon stick, and 2 quarts water in a large pot and bring to a boil over high heat. Remove from the heat and stir in the curing salt. Immediately add the ice cubes, stirring till they melt and the brine is cooled completely.

Trim all discolored pieces from the outside of the ham, paying close attention to any spongy glands or membranes, as they may cause spoilage. Cut off the meat 1 inch from the shank end of the ham, exposing the bone. Trim any meat around the hip bone as well in order to expose the bone. This will allow the brine to penetrate the meat evenly.

Place the meat in a large resealable storage bag, and pour as much brine into the bag as possible. The meat needs to be fully submerged in the brine. Force any excess air from the bag and place it into a large bowl to collect any potential leakage. Place this in the fridge to cure for 7 days, making sure to flip or rotate the bag daily to ensure even curing.

On the seventh day, remove the ham from the brine and discard the liquid. Place the ham on a rack over a sheet pan and return it, uncovered, to the refrigerator for 1 more day so the exterior can dry. Alternatively, you can dry the exterior thoroughly with paper towels and place it near a fan for an hour before moving on to the next step.

Preheat your smoker to its lowest temperature and highest smoke setting. This will vary depending on the smoker you choose to use, but the goal is to create maximum smoke without cooking the ham. This step creates flavor while also providing an extra level of preservation in the final product. Smoke the ham for 2 hours.

FOR THE COATING. While the ham is smoking, mix together all the ingredients for the sugary coating and set aside. Place three pieces of heavy-duty foil, overlapping, on a sheet tray and set aside.

Preheat the oven to 350°F.

Remove the ham from the smoker and place it on top of the foil with the fat side facing up. Pack the contents of the sugar coating on top, making sure to use the entire amount. Wrap the ham in the foil, leaving room for steam to collect; ensure that all the seams are facing up so none of the juices escape during cooking.

Bake the wrapped ham for approximately 15 minutes per pound, or until the center reaches a temperature of 155°F. (The temperature will continue to rise above 160°F after the ham is removed from the oven, so don't worry about trichinosis.)

Remove the ham from the oven and allow the meat to rest for 1 hour before unwrapping and carving it. Pour the liquid contents of the package through a fine-mesh strainer into a measuring cup and skim away the fat that collects on the top. Carve the meat into slices and serve warm with the reserved juices. Alternatively, you can chill the ham overnight before carving.

COOK'S NOTE. *For larger hams in the 11- to 15-pound range, increase the brining time to 10 days.*

Kevin Gillespie is an Atlanta-based chef and restaurateur who is a seven-time James Beard Awards finalist and has appeared on Bravo's hit TV show Top Chef. *Kevin is also a lifelong hunter who has adapted many of his recipes for wild game.*

HOT-SMOKED TROUT

(OR WHATEVER OTHER FATTY FISH YOU'VE GOT)

Brody Henderson

During the spring and summer months, my family spends a lot of our free time fishing the chain of large reservoirs along Montana's Missouri River. My two sons absolutely love hauling limits of yellow perch and walleye into the boat, but often a large, chrome-bright rainbow trout ends up as a welcome bycatch when we're targeting those other species. Most of these trout are "stockers" that spend the first several months of their lives at a fish hatchery, swimming in cement raceways, where they're fed a steady diet of pellets that resemble dog food. At about 10 inches long, they take a ride in the stocking truck and get dumped into a lake. These smaller trout are very easy to catch but admittedly are not the best table fare. So, when we catch a little one, it gets released. After a few years, though, these fish transform into something more worthwhile. As they feed on aquatic insects, freshwater shrimp, and crayfish, they develop thick and meaty fillets that are a vivid orange color. If you didn't know better, you'd be forgiven for thinking you were looking at a piece of wild salmon.

I often tell my sons there are two kinds of fish. There's the fish you fry, like perch, and there's the fish you smoke, like trout. That's not strictly true, of course, but the boys have taken to calling rainbows "smokers." When we land a nice one—say 16 to 20 inches long—it gets bonked on the head, bled out, and tossed in the cooler right alongside those fish that are destined for the deep fryer. At home, the trout get filleted, and the fillets are vac-sealed and frozen until late summer or early fall. By then, we've usually built up a pretty good supply. I'll dry-brine a batch big enough to fill up my vertical propane chamber smoker. Glazing the trout with maple syrup or honey during the smoking process isn't a necessary step, but it does make the finished product more appealing to kids. Either way, it's perfect for making smoked fish dip, mixing with scrambled eggs, tossing in pasta, or on its own as an appetizer or snack. In fact, it's one of my go-to hunting snacks. Throughout the fall, I'll eat smoked trout out in the field as an alternative to jerky, so I like a product that's been dehydrated until it's a little harder and drier than the smoked salmon you'd typically find in a grocery store. That way, it won't get smashed into a mushy consistency when it's riding around in my backpack. If you prefer a softer, moister version of smoked fish, then cut down on your smoking time a bit. The great thing about this stuff is that once it's been preserved in salt, sugar, and smoke and tightly vac-sealed, it will keep for weeks in the fridge or months in the freezer without any drop-off in flavor or texture.

You'll need fillets from trout over 16 inches long or whole trout if smaller; brown sugar; kosher salt; and honey, for basting. For fish over 16 inches long, this method works best with fillets; for anything smaller, whole fish work well. For small whole fish, leave the head on so you can hang them in the smoker using the twine harness shown for hanging eels on page 113. Or smoke them lying horizontally on your smoker's rack, making sure to flip them occasionally. You can smoke just a single fish or a couple fillets, but it's better to have a pile of 6 to 12 fillets or several smaller whole fish so you can make a big batch and save a bunch for later.

FOR PREP. This step is not necessary, but I recommend it before brining: Run the tips of your fingers over the meatiest part of the fillet. You'll feel a line of pin bones that you can remove with tweezers or needle-nose pliers. This is easiest to do after the fish has been frozen and then thawed.

BRINING. A dry brine ratio of 2 cups brown sugar to 1 cup kosher salt is standard, but you can also do a 4:1 ratio for a less salty product. Make sure to brine your fish in a nonreactive container like a Pyrex casserole dish or a big plastic Tupperware container.

FOR FILLETS. Lay the fillets skin-side down in the brining container and generously coat only the flesh side of each fillet with the dry brine mixture. If necessary, you can stack fillets in layers. I don't usually brine longer than 8 hours, and you could do as few as 4 hours with small, thin fillets. If you go over 12 hours, you're going to end up with a super-salty product. You'll know the fish has been brining long enough when the fillets are swimming around in all the moisture that the brine has drawn out of the flesh.

FOR WHOLE FISH. Cover the fish inside and outside with the dry brine mixture. Aim to keep your brining time between 8 and 10 hours, but you might need more for fish with thick bodies.

CREATE A PELLICLE. Remove the fish from the brine, rinse it thoroughly, and pat it dry. Set it on a rack to dry for a couple hours in a cool spot or place it near a fan to dry. After 30 to 60 minutes, you should notice a glossy, sticky film on the surface of the flesh. This film, called the pellicle, traps minute smoke particles, which boosts the flavor of the final product.

SMOKE. Set your smoker to 160°F. Keep an eye on it throughout, and don't let the temperature get over 180°F. If you go hotter, you'll end up with a different end product, since you're cooking the fish quickly, not drying it out slowly. (And you'll also coax the white albumen from the flesh—nasty looking but harmless if it does happen.)

While smoking, baste the fish a couple times with honey so it becomes glossy and glazed.

For small whole fish, smoke just until the skin starts to become loose. Check after about 2 hours if you like your smoked fish soft and moist. Smoke up to 3 or 4 hours if you want it drier and more preserved.

STORAGE. Vac-seal the smoked fish and store it in the fridge for a few weeks or the freezer for a few months.

After a long guiding career in Colorado, Brody Henderson joined MeatEater as a wilderness production assistant. Now a senior editor on MeatEater's publishing team, he has collaborated with Steven Rinella on several books, including The MeatEater Fish and Game Cookbook, The MeatEater Guide to Wilderness Skills and Survival, *and this book.*

SALMON JERKY

MAKES ABOUT 2 QUARTS, PACKED LOOSELY

2 pounds coho salmon fillet, skin on

CURE

1 (2-pound) bag dark brown sugar (about 6 packed cups)

1 cup Diamond Crystal kosher salt (see Cook's Note)

SEASONING

4½ teaspoons coriander seed, toasted and coarsely ground

1½ teaspoons smoked paprika

1 tablespoon orange zest

⅛ teaspoon cayenne pepper

⅓ cup maple syrup

SPECIAL EQUIPMENT

Large, wide container with a tight-fitting lid

Rimmed baking sheet with a rack

These days there are so many names for hot-smoked salmon that you can't keep them all straight. You've got salmon candy, salmon jerky, kippered salmon, hard-smoked salmon, and on and on. I dig them all, even if I'm not totally sure what makes them all different. My brother Danny calls this version salmon jerky, and as he lives in Alaska and processes dozens of the fish every year, I'll defer to his judgment. The key to this recipe is that you keep your mixture at a 6:1 ratio of brown sugar to salt. The downside is that it uses a lot of brown sugar, which ain't free. The upside is that the brown sugar makes it impossible for the fish to get too salty. It's the perfect recipe for lazy or forgetful cooks, because you can leave the salmon in this cure mixture for a week and it still won't be too salty. Bag up the finished project with a vac sealer and you've got the perfect travel snack for just about any outdoor activity.

FOR THE SALMON. Cut the salmon lengthwise (from head to tail) into 5- or 6-inch-long strips about ½ inch thick. (If using small fillets, cut the strips as long as possible, even if it's crosswise.)

FOR THE CURE. In a large bowl, thoroughly combine the brown sugar and salt. Sprinkle a thin coat of the mixture over the bottom of a large, wide container with a tight-fitting lid. Arrange one layer of salmon on top of the cure. (Try to calculate how many more layers of salmon you will have and divide the cure amount so that you have enough to cover each layer.) Sprinkle more of the cure on top of the salmon. Continue to layer until all of the salmon and brine are used up. Cover and place in the refrigerator to cure for at least 8 hours or overnight.

The next day, fit a rack into a rimmed baking sheet and set it aside. Rinse the salmon well and pat dry.

FOR THE SEASONING. In a large bowl, mix the coriander, paprika, orange zest, and cayenne until well combined. Add the salmon to the spice mixture and toss until evenly coated. Arrange the salmon in a single layer on the rack. Place in the refrigerator, uncovered, to dry out for at least 8 hours or overnight.

TO SMOKE. Set the smoker to 160°F using the wood pellets of your choice. Transfer the salmon, still on the rack, onto the smoker grate. Close the lid and let the salmon smoke for 1 hour.

Brush the salmon with the maple syrup. Continue to smoke, brushing with the syrup every 15 minutes, until the salmon is dried and stiff but still pliable, 2½ to 3 hours total.

Transfer the rack to a baking sheet and let the jerky cool to room temperature. Once cool, transfer the jerky to a container with a tight-fitting lid and store in the refrigerator for up to a month. In a vac-sealed bag it should keep about 3 months in the fridge and 6 months in the freezer.

COOK'S NOTE. *We're using Diamond Crystal kosher salt in this recipe, which has 53 percent less sodium by volume than Morton's kosher salt, so it's important that you seek it out. If you choose to use Morton's kosher salt, it will be saltier in taste; you'll want to adjust the quantity.*

ALSO WORKS WITH. *Any species of salmon, char, or trout.*

SMOKED AMERICAN EEL

When I was writing my first book, *The Scavenger's Guide to Haute Cuisine,* I spent some time with an eel trapper named Ray who lived on the Delaware River and ran his own smokehouse. Ray had a lot of philosophies about life and how to live it. As he showed me around his facility, I was mostly focused on capturing all of his musings in my notebook. This caused me to miss what was perhaps the most important thing he told me all day, which was the exact brine recipe that he uses for his eels. I didn't know how much of a mistake I'd made until that night, when I finally sampled his wares and realized how damn good they were. Later, when reviewing my notes, I found just four simple things written down: salt, brown sugar, honey, water. I couldn't remember what other ingredients he might have listed, if in fact he listed any others at all. I had written nothing about quantities. Based on these admissions of mine, you might see how I'm torn about whether to say I stole this recipe from Ray the eel trapper. Maybe "inspired" is a better way to put it. When you make it, don't worry too much about the amount of eels you're using. This recipe will handle pretty much anywhere from one to ten if you've got an appropriately shaped container to brine these snakelike critters. But since it's not really worth firing up your smoker for just a single eel, let's say it's good for four to ten.

4 to 10 American eels

Kosher salt

BRINE

1 cup kosher salt

1 cup brown sugar

¼ cup honey

8 cups lukewarm water

ALSO WORKS WITH. *Black cod (sablefish), mackerel, herring, eulachons (hooligans), bluefish, and any other oily white-fleshed flesh.*

PREPARE THE EELS. If you have live eels, pour about an inch of salt in the bottom of a cooler and put the eels in there. This will kill them quickly and helps to remove their slime layer. Rinse the eels before making an incision on the underside of the body from the anal vent to the gills. Remove the guts and gills and rinse again thoroughly.

FOR THE BRINE. Combine all ingredients in a bowl or 3-quart dish large enough to hold the eels. Chill the brine. Add the rinsed eels and submerge them. If necessary, use a plate to keep the eels beneath the surface. Soak refrigerated for 24 hours.

SMOKE THE EELS. Truss the eels (see illustrations, opposite) so they're ready to hang in your smoker.

Prepare a vertical smoker for low heat—you want it to be 165°F to 175°F. Hang the eels from the top of the smoker. Add wet wood chips. Keep the smoker as cool as possible, adding more chips as needed.

The eel skins will take on a glossy golden hue when they're close to being ready. Similar to smoking trout, cook the eels until the skin begins to peel away and the meat becomes tender enough that you can easily break it apart. Remove the eels from the smoker and allow to cool for a few minutes before eating or storing in a vac-sealed bag for about 3 months in the fridge and 12 months in the freezer.

Serve over rice with a soy-based sauce like teriyaki.

TRUSSING EELS

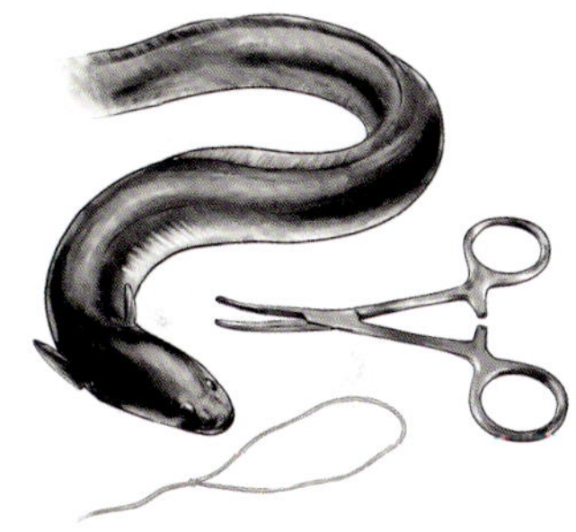

1. *Tie an 8- to 10-inch piece of kitchen twine into a loop.*

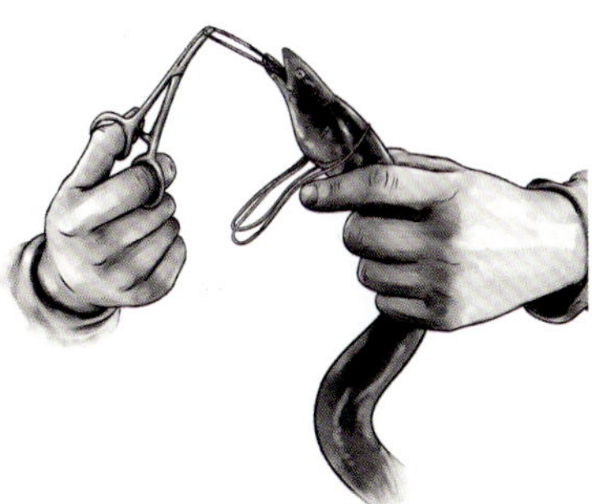

2. *Stick the eel's head through the loop and use a pair of hemostats or needle-nose pliers to feed the lower end of the loop into the gills/throat and out through the mouth.*

HOT-SMOKED FISH SAUSAGES

CHORIZO-STYLE

MAKES ABOUT 5 SAUSAGE LINKS; SERVES 12 TO 16 AS AN APPETIZER OR 4 AS A MAIN COURSE

This recipe is great for when you've got a mixed collection of fish and seafood. It's really best not to skip the scallops, as they make the texture smoother and add a richness you won't get with just fish. This sausage is made by smoking it over indirect heat on a charcoal grill. It takes less than 20 minutes, so plan to have other vegetables or bread to grill on the hot side once it comes off. It's ideal for serving as an appetizer at a backyard dinner party, but you could also prepare the sausage in advance and make it for dinner while car camping.

If you're not into smoking this sausage, you can sear it on both sides in a pan and finish it on a grill or in the oven.

FISH SAUSAGE

1½ pounds white fish fillets, such as perch, whiting, porgy, or halibut

1½ pounds salmon fillets

1½ pounds scallops

¼ cup diced guanciale (1¼ ounces)

2 tablespoons smoked paprika

1½ tablespoons kosher salt

1 teaspoon cayenne pepper

1 tablespoon granulated garlic

1 tablespoon onion powder

1 teaspoon dried oregano

1 teaspoon dry mustard powder

1 tablespoon chopped fresh flat-leaf parsley

RED PEPPER AIOLI

1 garlic clove

5 egg yolks

Pinch of kosher salt

2 roasted red bell peppers, seeded, or substitute 1½ cups drained jarred roasted peppers

2 tablespoons Dijon mustard

¾ cup neutral oil, such as canola

2 teaspoons lemon juice

Neutral oil for the grill

1 baguette, sliced into ¼-inch-thick rounds

Olive oil, for drizzling

TO PREPARE TO GRIND. Soak the hog casings in fresh water for 30 minutes. Rinse a few times to remove the salt, then run water from the faucet through the casing to remove any excess salt inside it. Chill the grinder attachments in the freezer before getting started.

FOR THE SAUSAGE. Cut the white fish, salmon, and scallops into a medium dice and combine them in a bowl with the guanciale. Add the smoked paprika, salt, cayenne, granulated garlic, onion powder, oregano, dry mustard powder, and parsley to the bowl and mix well with your hands. Cover the bowl and refrigerate for 2 hours.

Remove the grinder attachments from the freezer and set up the grinder with a medium die. Take the fish mixture from the refrigerator. If you're making a large batch (double or more of this recipe), be sure to keep the fish mixture in a metal bowl over another bowl of ice to stay chilled while you work. In that instance, you may find that you'll need to return the mixture to the refrigerator occasionally to cool off if it loses its chill. Run the fish mixture through the grinder into a bowl.

Set up the sausage stuffer according to the manufacturer's instructions. Stuff the sausage loosely in a long, large link. Twist the sausage into links at about 5-inch intervals, the first one going clockwise, then counterclockwise, and alternating until you make it through the long link. You'll want to leave a little space between the links so they can be snipped later. You will be able to make about 5 links, give or take. Once the links are formed, examine the sausages for air bubbles and prick them with a pin or the tip of a knife to release the air. This will keep the sausages from popping when they're cooked. Refrigerate the links for at least 2 hours, uncovered, on a parchment-lined baking sheet to dry the skins out a little bit. (They can be vac-sealed and frozen for up to a year at this point.)

Recipe continues

SPECIAL EQUIPMENT

Hog casings

Sausage stuffer

Meat grinder

2 wooden skewers

ALSO WORKS WITH. *You'll want to keep the scallops, but otherwise feel free to substitute with any kind of fish, lobster, crayfish, shrimp, crab, or shellfish.*

FOR THE AIOLI. Drop the garlic down the food processor chute to mince it. (If you're using a blender, mince the garlic first before adding it.) Turn off the processor, add the egg yolks and a pinch of salt. Roughly chop the roasted peppers and add them and the mustard. Pulse to puree. With the motor running, add the oil to the pepper-egg mixture in a fine drizzle to make an emulsion. Continue to blend together for 30 to 60 seconds, until a thick aioli forms. Taste and add salt if needed and the lemon juice. Process for another 30 seconds to combine. Transfer the aioli to a serving dish or refrigerate in an airtight container. The aioli should be consumed within 24 hours, or it will begin to separate and break down.

TO SMOKE THE SAUSAGE AND GRILL THE BREAD. Soak 1 quart of cherrywood (or other fruitwood) chips in a bowl of water for 20 to 30 minutes. Set up a charcoal grill for indirect high heat. Light a chimney full of coals, and when ready, pour all of the coals on one side of the grill to make two heat zones. Sprinkle the drained cherrywood chips over the glowing coals. If using a propane grill, create two heat zones by turning off one or two rows of burners, depending on the size of your grill, and add your wood chips to a foil tray or a wood-chip smoking box.

Arrange the linked sausages in a spiral and insert two intersecting skewers to secure the spiral. When the grill is ready, lightly oil the sausages and the grill grates and place them on the indirect-heat side of the grill. Close the lid and hot-smoke for 10 to 12 minutes. Open the lid, flip the sausage, and cook for an additional 5 minutes. Check the internal temperature, which should be between 135°F and 145°F. Remove from the heat.

Lay the sliced bread out on a baking sheet. Lightly drizzle olive oil over the sliced bread on both sides. Place the oiled bread on the hot side of the grill, for about 2 minutes, flipping when it has deep brown grill marks. Cook for another minute and remove from the grill.

Slice the sausages on a bias, spread aioli on each piece of grilled bread, and top with a slice of sausage. Serve warm.

SMOKED AND DEVILED EGGS

MAKES 12 HALVES; SERVES 4 TO 6

Neutral oil for the grill

6 large eggs, hard-boiled and peeled

5 tablespoons mayonnaise

2 tablespoons Dijon mustard

1 tablespoon capers, chopped

1 tablespoon dill fronds, chopped, plus more for garnish

1 tablespoon minced red onion

Pimenton or smoked paprika, for garnish (optional)

Prepare a smoker to 225°F (this also works with a pellet grill, chamber smoker, and even a charcoal grill). Choose a mild-flavored wood, like pecan apple, or another fruitwood.

Lightly oil the grill grate. Place the eggs on the grate away from the smoke source so they are not touching the sides of the smoker or each other. Cover and smoke, maintaining the temperature as needed, for 30 to 40 minutes. The eggs will turn a streaky tawny brown when finished. Remove them from the smoker and let cool.

Cut the eggs in half lengthwise and scoop the yolks into a bowl. Mash with a fork until broken up. Mix in the mayonnaise, mustard, capers, dill, and red onion and continue to mash and stir until creamy and well combined. Use two spoons to fill each egg white with some of the filling (1 heaping tablespoon per half). Garnish with a small dill frond and pimenton (if using).

COOK'S NOTE. *The night before you hard-boil the eggs, lay them on their sides in the fridge. This will center the yolks.*

SMOKED VENISON SANDWICHES

SERVES 6 TO 8

ROAST

1 (2-pound) boneless venison roast, trimmed

Kosher salt

Neutral oil, for smoking

RUB

1¼ teaspoons dry mustard powder

1 teaspoon garlic powder

½ teaspoon onion powder

½ teaspoon paprika

½ teaspoon light brown sugar

¼ teaspoon freshly ground black pepper

¼ teaspoon kosher salt

⅛ teaspoon cayenne pepper

ANCHOVY MAYO

1 cup mayonnaise

1 tablespoon Worcestershire sauce

1 teaspoon anchovy paste

½ teaspoon fresh lemon juice

SANDWICHES

6 to 8 sandwich rolls

6 to 8 slices Swiss cheese

There's a lot of tension in my house around the subject of lunch meat. I like to run a strict wild game program in my kitchen, but my wife and kids are always complaining about not having deli sliced ham and beef for sandwiches. This recipe is a good compromise for us. Sure, you can eat the roast for dinner without confining it between slices of bread, but when paired with anchovy mayo, it makes a spectacular sandwich that'll beat anything you get from a deli counter. If anchovy mayo isn't your thing, go with a horseradish mayo or a sharp and spicy mustard.

FOR THE ROAST. Generously rub the roast all over with salt. Cover and refrigerate for 2 days, turning it once a day.

FOR THE RUB. Mix the dry mustard powder, garlic powder, onion powder, paprika, brown sugar, black pepper, salt, and cayenne in a small bowl.

TO SMOKE. The day of smoking, prepare a smoker to 225°F and maintain this approximate temperature throughout. Oil the grates. Remove the roast from the fridge but do not pat it dry. Massage the spice rub onto the meat. Smoke the roast until the internal temperature reaches 125°F (for medium-rare) to 130°F (for medium), about 3½ hours.

Remove the meat from the smoker and let it rest until the meat firms up in order to thinly slice, at least 1 hour.

FOR THE ANCHOVY MAYO. Whisk the mayonnaise, Worcestershire, anchovy paste, and lemon juice until smooth in a small bowl.

FOR THE SANDWICHES. Halve the sandwich rolls and spread each side with anchovy mayo. Put a slice of cheese on the bottom roll. Very thinly slice the meat against the grain and pile onto the rolls.

MAKE AHEAD. *This is a roast you'll want to bring with you fully cooked in a cooler on a camping trip. It's great on its own, warmed up with a bit of pan gravy, and it's versatile. Use it in sandwiches like this one or the iron pies on page 170. For best flavor, keep the mayo in an airtight container in a cooler or refrigerator for up to 2 days.*

MEATEATER

GRILLED WILD BOAR RIBS WITH PEACH GLAZE

Jesse Griffiths

Feral hogs come in all shapes, sizes, and fat contents, and so do their ribs. Some are thick enough that they'll look like you bought them from a butcher. Others are so thin you can almost read a newspaper through them. Most ribs, however, fall somewhere in the middle, with a moderate amount of fat, a lot of connective tissue, and some delicious, lean meat. The dry heat of the smoker is only effective when there's enough insulating fat to keep the layers of meat underneath moist during the long cooking process, so an individual assessment of each hog—or any game animal—is imperative. To level the playing field, I like to "cheat" the leaner ribs by gently poaching them in a highly seasoned and spiced bath, then finish them on a smoky grill when it's convenient. This method works very well on other animals with meaty ribs, like mule deer and elk. By seasoning the ribs beforehand, you'll keep the broth from being too salty, and it can then be kept and used for other purposes, like cooking beans, lentils, or even rice. Here we are glazing them with a simple barbecue-esque sauce made from peach jam. Feel free to substitute most any other fruit jam to suit your preference, availability, sense of experimentation, or regional specialization. If you're feeding a family or a crowd, you might want to double this recipe.

SERVES 4 TO 6

- 1 single side of wild boar ribs, cut in half to make two racks
- Kosher salt
- Freshly ground black pepper
- 1 teaspoon fennel seed
- 2 bay leaves
- 1 medium onion, peeled
- 1 garlic head, halved crosswise
- 1 cup peach or other fruit jam
- ¾ cup apple cider vinegar
- 8 tablespoons (1 stick) unsalted butter
- Hot sauce to taste

Season the ribs with salt and pepper. Cover and refrigerate for 24 hours. Put the ribs, spices, onion, and garlic in a big pot and cover with cold water by about 6 inches. Bring to a simmer over medium-high heat and cook until tender but not falling apart, 2 to 4 hours, depending on the age of the animal. Add water as needed to keep the ribs submerged. Remove the ribs and cool them completely in the refrigerator. Strain the broth and reserve it for another use.

Soak a handful of pecan or mesquite wood chips for 30 minutes in water. Preheat a charcoal grill until you are able to hold your hand over it for no more than 4 seconds. When ready, toss the wood chips over the coals to add some smoky flavor.

Meanwhile, in a small pot over low heat, mix the jam, vinegar, butter, and hot sauce until melted.

Place the ribs on the grill and brush with the glaze. Repeat this basting process several times more, glazing the ribs well. Once nicely charred and falling apart, remove the ribs to a cutting board and cut between each rib. Serve immediately.

A frequent MeatEater collaborator, Jesse Griffiths is a hunter, fisherman, award-winning chef, and the author of the cookbooks Afield *and* The Hog Book. *He is the co-owner of Dai Due Butcher Shop and Supper Club in Austin, Texas, where he features fresh local ingredients, including wild game and fish.*

SMOKED BONE-IN HOG ROAST

WITH MOSTARDA (MUSTARD-APPLE COMPOTE)

SERVES 4 TO 6

1 bone-in wild boar loin roast (2 to 3 pounds with 9 rib bones, depending on the size of the hog)

DRY BRINE

2 teaspoons kosher salt

1 teaspoon freshly ground black pepper

1 tablespoon ground fennel seed

SAGE PASTE

4 garlic cloves, smashed and peeled

1 bunch fresh sage, leaves picked (about 15 leaves)

2 teaspoons ground fennel

2 to 3 tablespoons olive oil

MAPLE-SAGE BUTTER

8 tablespoons (1 stick) unsalted butter

2 tablespoons maple syrup

4 fresh sage leaves

Pinch of kosher salt

1 recipe Mostarda (Mustard-Apple Compote), see page 353

Pretty much any bone-in loin rack looks cool, but this one tastes as good as it looks. The wild hog loin is hit with a dry brine (you can use a wet brine if you prefer) and then paired with an apple compote that resembles mostarda, the Italian candied fruit that comes jarred in a mustard-flavored jelly. Because wild hog ribs generally have a small amount of meat on them compared to domestic pigs, limit the dry brining time to overnight. Any longer and you risk drying out the meat or making it too salty.

Truss the hog loin with twine for even cooking.

FOR THE BRINE. Combine the dry brine ingredients. Rub the dry brine all over the trussed roast. Place the roast on a baking sheet and loosely cover with plastic wrap—or better yet, leave it uncovered to air cure. Set in the refrigerator overnight.

FOR THE SAGE PASTE. The next day, pull the roast from the refrigerator and pat dry. Mince together the garlic and sage. Add the fennel seeds and olive oil to make an herby paste. Spread the paste over the hog loin on all sides and set aside for 30 minutes to come to room temperature while you set up your smoker and make the maple-sage butter and apple mostarda.

FOR THE MAPLE-SAGE BUTTER. Combine all of the ingredients in a small saucepan over medium-high heat and whisk to combine. Bring to a boil and reduce until thick, about 3 minutes. Set aside and keep warm so it doesn't congeal.

FOR THE SMOKER. Set your smoker for 225°F. Use any fruitwood chips you've got (I prefer applewood here). Add a drip tray with water to keep moisture circulating in your smoker. Place the roast in the smoker for 45 minutes, then check the internal temperature of the meat. Once it hits 100°F, raise the temperature of the smoker to 375°F or 400°F. Begin basting the roast with the maple-sage butter about every 15 minutes. Smoke the roast until the internal temperature is 160°F (as a precaution against trichinosis), 1½ to 2 hours. It could be ready earlier, so keep a close eye on it.

Serve warm with mostarda (see page 353).

FIRST LITE
SHALE TOUCH
LG

BBQ-STYLE SQUIRREL

WITH THE SCHLITZ WHITTINGTON SMALL GAME BASTING SAUCE

Kevin Murphy

Schlitz Whittington was an insurance salesman on first shift and a cattle farmer on second shift. He obtained his people and veterinary skills working as a medic over Korea way along the 54th parallel. My friend Brooks and I worked on his farm when we were kids. He was lots of fun to work for, and we were eager to learn and not afraid to tackle a roll of woven wire fencing. We worked real cheap, too, and every day except Sunday. That's where I learned how to handle wild, exotic half-breed cattle and the concept of job responsibility. It's also how I learned about this basting sauce.

My friend and mentor loved to drink Schlitz beer, which he used to baste meats as well. He also taught me the recipe for this sauce, which was meant to keep your barbecue from drying out while cooking over wood coals. I never wrote the ingredients down, but the main components stuck with me—lard, butter, vinegar, hot sauce, and black pepper. Over time I adapted the sauce to work on wild game by adding extra lard, since most game has little fat.

The sauce has always been Schlitz's to me, but recently I found what appears to be the original recipe by way of fate. It came to me in a box of cookbooks I'd bought just last summer from Uncle Joe at Trade Day (our local flea market). This particular volume was called Kentucky Hospitality, *published by the Kentucky Federation of Women's Clubs in 1976. And lo and behold, what should I find but an "Authentic Barbecue Dip" from a BBQ stand in Old Eddyville that was owned by a Mr. Charlie Robinson around 1940! The place was behind a motel gas station in the town that Schlitz grew up in. Now it's all underwater, covered by Lake Barkley after the damming of the Cumberland River. But here was the origin of the Schlitz Whittington basting sauce!*

I have been mopping big ole fox squirrels with this sauce for forty-six years and counting. Just don't go too heavy or it will jump-start your fire and burn your squirrels.

To make the sauce, combine one gallon apple cider vinegar, one bottle of hot sauce, one pound of lard or butter, and a gob each of red and black pepper in a pot and heat to a low boil. Reserve and keep warm for basting.

Now about those squirrels. I am fortunate to live in Kaintuckie, where we are blessed with white oak and hickory in abundance. But feel free to use any hardwood that will reduce to red-hot glowing coals that create a superhot cooking surface. First build a roaring fire. After the fire has burned down, transfer the red-hot coals to your cooking area with a long-handled shovel. Place a metal cooking grate 18 inches or so above the coals using rocks or any kind of stable prop. You will need to add some coals as you cook, so be careful.

Spread 4 to 8 whole squirrels, washed, cleaned, and salted to taste on top of the grate. Baste with the Schlitz Whittington Small Game Basting Sauce real good over the top of each squirrel. Repeat this every 10 minutes. Turn the squirrel over after 20 to 30 minutes and start basting all over again every 10 minutes. After 50 minutes, start checking for doneness. I do this by sliding a fork into the thigh meat at its thickest part. When it slides through easy-peasy, it's done. If you can tear a rear leg off without much twisting at all, that's a sure sign, too! Over a hot hardwood charcoal fire it will take about an hour, maybe a little longer or a little less. At the end, you can add your favorite BBQ sauce and go to town.

Kevin Murphy is better known to MeatEater fans as the World's Best Small Game Hunter. Kevin lives in the Land Between the Lakes region of Kentucky, where he hunts, fishes, and cares for a kennel full of hounds and cur dogs that he uses to pursue his favorite game animals—rabbits and squirrels.

BRINED AND SMOKED TURKEY BREAST

WITH MAPLE-CHILE GLAZE

SERVES 6 TO 8

ENRICHED BRINE

½ cup kosher salt

½ cup packed light brown sugar

4 garlic cloves, smashed

10 black peppercorns

10 juniper berries

1 bay leaf

2 quarts ice (8 cups)

TURKEY BREAST

1 skin-on boneless turkey breast (2½ to 3 pounds), tendons removed from the tenderloin

1 teaspoon kosher salt

4 tablespoons (½ stick) unsalted butter, at room temperature and very soft

MAPLE-CHILE GLAZE

1 cup real maple syrup

1 tablespoon crushed red pepper flakes

MAKE AHEAD. *For camping trips, you can brine and smoke the breast ahead of time and then freeze it, sliced, in a vacuum-sealed bag. Add the meat to sandwiches and soups, iron pies, or just eat it as a snack. The glaze can be stored in an airtight container for up to 1 month.*

ALSO WORKS WITH. *Goose or duck breasts (skin on or off), domestic turkey and chicken breasts, and whole upland birds such as pheasant and grouse (remove the legs for another use, or cook them separately until tender).*

This recipe is tailored for pellet grills, because they make it a breeze to quickly smoke-roast meats at temperatures around 350°F. The Maple-Chili Glaze is ridiculously simple as well; it has just the right sweetness and heat to counter the smoke of the grill. You can use another kind of smoker, or any of the setups described on pages 92–93. Just bear in mind that you want to keep the heat fairly consistent and baste the meat often.

FOR THE BRINE. Add all brine ingredients and 6 quarts water to a pot, bring to a boil, and stir to dissolve. Remove from the heat to cool. Transfer the brine to a heatproof container and stir in the ice. This should cool the brine sufficiently enough so that you can add the meat; it should be cold to the touch, and ice cubes should still be floating.

FOR THE TURKEY. Brine the meat, covered and refrigerated, for 2 to 3 hours in a large container. The meat should be submerged under the brine. If it is not, weigh it down with a plate or pot lid.

After the meat has brined, remove it from the brine, rinse, and pat dry. Season the skin with salt. Slather the top of the turkey breast skin on top and under the skin with the butter. Tie the roast with cooking twine for even cooking (see illustrations on the next page).

TO SMOKE. Preheat a pellet smoker to between 365°F and 375°F. Choose a mild wood; apple or another fruitwood will work well. If using a portable grill to smoke, set the grill up for indirect heat (see the illustration on page 92).

FOR THE GLAZE. Meanwhile, combine the maple syrup and red pepper flakes in a saucepan and bring to a low boil. Boil for 3 minutes, reducing the heat slightly. Remove from the heat and allow the glaze to cool completely.

Place the breast in the center of the smoker with a drip tray slightly larger than your turkey and filled with water underneath. Don't skip this step; the butter will run off the bird and make a smoky mess if you do. Roast the bird with light smoke for about 1 hour and then begin basting it with the glaze. Keep basting every 20 minutes until the internal temperature is 155°F. (Start checking the temperature after 40 minutes. The cooking time could take about 2 hours, probably less.) The skin should be crisp and caramelized when finished. Remove the turkey from the pellet grill, glaze again, and let rest for 10 to 15 minutes before serving. Slice thinly, especially if you've got an old bird.

HOW TO TIE A TURKEY BREAST (OR ROAST)

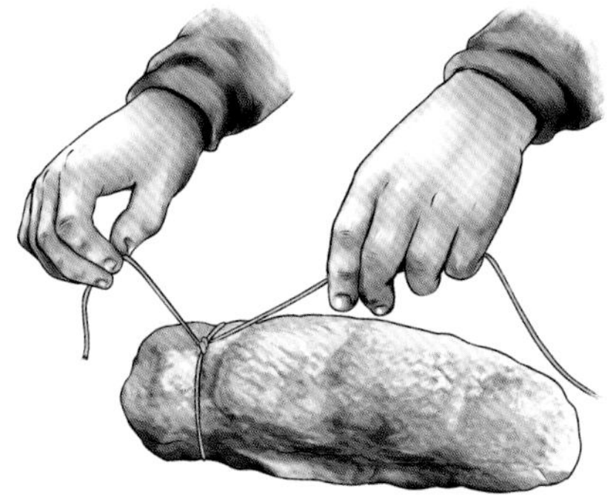

1. *Cut a length of kitchen twine about three times longer than your turkey breast or roast. Tie a basic knot around the end of the turkey breast and secure it with a second knot. Position the knot in the center of the skin-side-up turkey breast.*

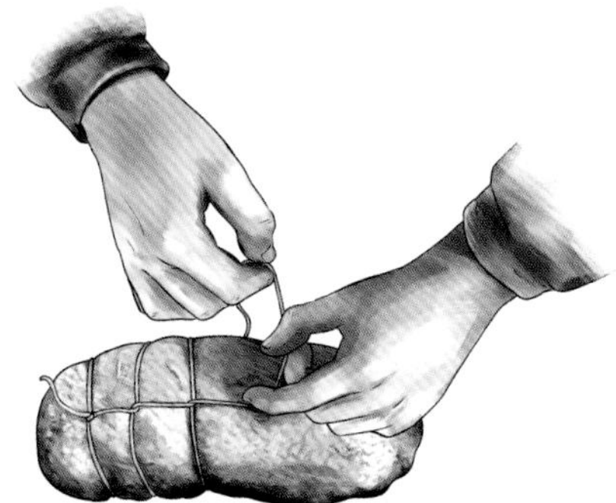

2. *Lay the string along the top of the breast and hold it down with your forefinger about 1 inch from the first knot to form an L-shaped corner. Using the other hand, wrap the string around and under the breast to meet your forefinger, and tuck the long end of the string under the L-shaped corner to form a loose knot. Repeat this step for the length of the turkey breast, making as many loops as needed.*

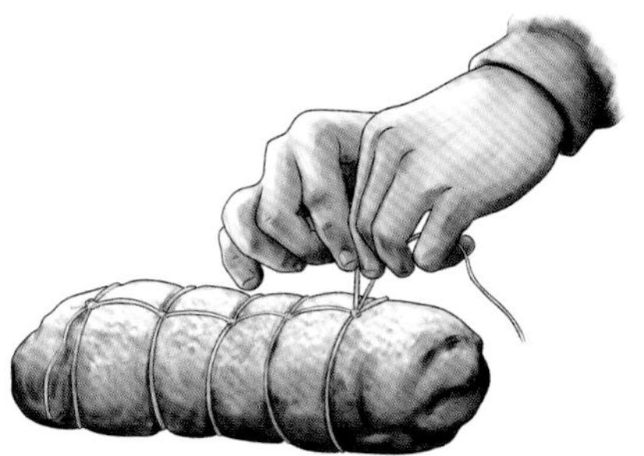

3. *When you reach the end of the turkey breast roast, secure the last knot with an additional knot. You could end here, or continue on for a tighter version (especially if using a turkey or goose breast).*

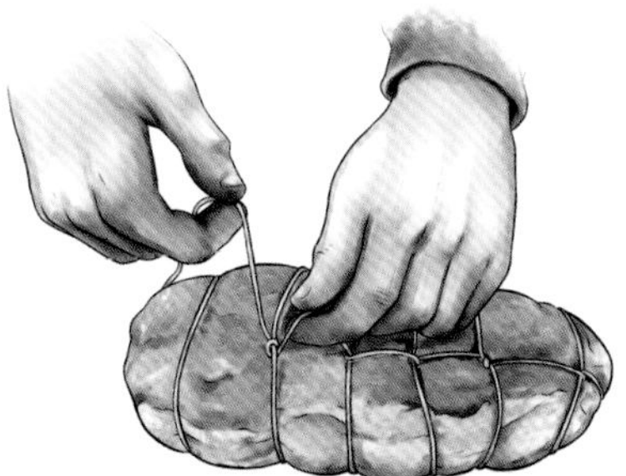

4. *Flip the roast over. Weave the remaining length of the string under and then over the cross strings to bring a uniform shape to the underside of the roast. Repeat this under all of the strings.*

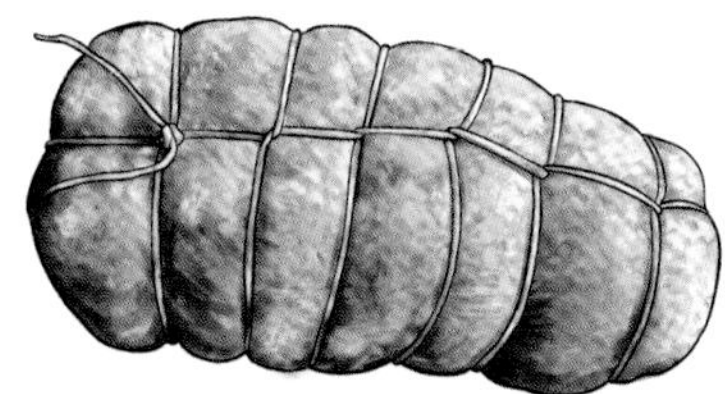

5. *After the last string on the underside, flip the roast skin-side up again. Pull the remaining loose string around the end of the roast to tie it with the original knot. You are ready to braise, roast, or smoke the turkey breast roast.*

SMOKED DUCK

WITH HONEY, BALSAMIC, AND CHIPOTLE GLAZE

SERVES 2 TO 4

BRINE

½ cup kosher salt

½ cup packed light brown sugar

5 black peppercorns

5 juniper berries

1 bay leaf

2 quarts ice (8 cups)

4 wild ducks (roughly 1½ to 3 pounds each), plucked and gutted

Kosher salt

1 garlic head, halved crosswise

6 fresh thyme sprigs

HONEY, BALSAMIC, AND CHIPOTLE GLAZE

Makes about ¾ cup

1 cup honey

1 tablespoon chipotle chile flakes

2 fresh thyme sprigs, leaves removed

¼ cup balsamic vinegar

COOK'S NOTE. *Whenever I cook with a vertical smoker, I try to make use of any available upper racks that aren't filled with meat. It's a great opportunity to dehydrate, slow roast, or smoke mushrooms, tomatoes, and even fruit (see page 94).*

ALSO WORKS WITH. *Puddle ducks such as mallards, teal, and wood ducks; domestic ducks, or upland birds and chickens as well as wild hog roasts.*

In my opinion, duck breast is always best when it's cooked hot and eaten medium-rare. I can't say the same thing about duck thighs, which I tend to prefer when they're slow-cooked to the point that the meat is ready to fall off the bone. I'll sometimes separate the thighs and breasts on my ducks for this reason, so that each portion can be handled in its own particular way. For this recipe, though, go ahead and leave your ducks whole. You'll be smoking the bird to a decent middle point, where the breast is well done and the legs will be cooked through to satisfaction. The Honey, Balsamic, and Chipotle Glaze is what makes this dish truly special.

FOR THE BRINE. Add all brine ingredients (except the ice) plus 6 quarts water to a pot, bring to a boil, and stir to dissolve. Remove from the heat to cool. Transfer the brine to a heatproof container and stir in the ice. This should cool the brine sufficiently enough so that you can add the meat.

Add the duck to the brine for 2 to 3 hours.

FOR THE GLAZE. Meanwhile, combine the honey, chipotle chile flakes, and thyme leaves in a saucepan and bring to a low boil. Boil for 3 minutes, reducing the mixture slightly. Remove the glaze from the heat and allow it to cool completely, then stir in the balsamic vinegar. Transfer to an airtight container and store in the refrigerator for up to 2 weeks.

After the duck has brined, remove it and rinse and pat dry. Season the skin with salt. Prick the skin halfway through with a fork or paring knife, making slits in several places. This helps the fat to render evenly and the smoke to permeate the meat. Fill the cavity with the garlic halves and the thyme sprigs.

TO SMOKE. Set up your vertical smoker (or another kind of smoker) with wood chips. I prefer apple- or cherrywood for this smoke, but you can use whichever wood suits you. Preheat the vertical smoker to 250°F. With a vertical smoker, you control how much smoke you want to add to your food. I usually give the bird a stronger push of smoke in the beginning, and then let the heat of the smoker finish the cooking.

Be sure to add water to the drip tray. Place the duck above the drip tray and smoke, checking the internal temperature after 1 hour to see how fast it's going, then begin basting with the glaze. Check the temperature in 30 minutes and glaze again. You're looking for an internal temp of 150°F to 155°F, which will happen between 1½ and 2 hours. At this temperature, the breast will be well done, and the legs will be tender enough to slice and serve.

SMOKED MOOSE NOSE HASH

Jessee Lawyer

Growing up in the foothills of Vermont's Jay Peak, in the small border town of East Richford, I was no stranger to catching a glimpse of a moose. The sight always left me with a sense of awe. For my Abenaki ancestors, the animal was considered one of our most important relatives for both sustenance and daily life. My first taste of moose meat was equally inspiring. My Abenaki heritage comes from my father's side, but my grandfather and two uncles on my mother's side of the family were hunters who traced their lineage back to some of the earliest settlers in Quebec. My uncle Steve always shared his moose meat with us, and those meals are some of the most memorable of my life.

It wasn't until I met Jeff, who contributed the instructions that follow this recipe, that I was able to relive those memories. Despite growing up hunting, I didn't hunt large game with any success until later in life. And although I grew up with Abenaki culture and art, my family was missing a link to our traditional food systems. I've been cooking in professional kitchens for the last fourteen years, but it wasn't until six years ago that something clicked, and I became interested in our traditional foods. Diving deep into traditional foods means reconnecting with wild game and with sometimes faint memories of northeastern delicacies such as moose nose.

This recipe for moose nose hash is based on the first moose nose that Jeff and I cooked together with fiddleheads that he foraged. This was a great addition, but any foraged or farmed greens or herbs will do.

SERVES 4

8 tablespoons (1 stick) unsalted butter, cubed

1 medium onion, diced (about 1 cup)

3 large Yukon Gold potatoes, scrubbed and cut into medium dice (about 5 cups)

½ teaspoon paprika

½ teaspoon garlic powder

¼ teaspoon freshly ground black pepper

1½ tablespoons kosher salt

¾ cup smoked moose nose fat (see page 135)

3 garlic cloves, minced

1½ cups smoked moose nose meat (see page 135)

4 large eggs

Cholula Hot Sauce, for serving

Prepare a charcoal grill. When the briquettes are completely white, place a large cast iron skillet directly on the heat. (Or use a propane camp stove set at medium high heat.) Add 2 tablespoons of butter to the pan to melt. When butter is sizzling, throw in all of your onions.

When the onions begin to brown, stir in the potatoes until they are evenly distributed. Add 4 tablespoons of the butter, the paprika, garlic powder, black pepper, and salt. Cook until the potatoes begin to soften and brown on the edges.

Add the remaining 2 tablespoons butter and the garlic and stir for a minute or two. Add the moose nose fat first, and cook for 2 minutes, then add the nose meat and let it all brown together. It's finished when the potatoes get that beautiful hash crisp and the meat and fat are all heated through.

Remove from heat. In a separate skillet or saucepan, cook your eggs over easy; if you're classy or at home, poach the eggs. You can also cook the eggs right in the hash. Runny yolks are a must for a delicious sauce that brings the hash together. Serve with your desired amount of Cholula, and enjoy.

HOW TO SMOKE A MOOSE NOSE

Jeff Stewart

I grew up in a subsistence hunting household on the Penobscot reservation in Maine, where moose hunting is embedded in the culture and identity of our people. In our family, my father did the hunting, and he hunted only moose. But he didn't actually love moose hunting—it was a job, a duty. We were dependent on the meat, but I believe the drinking and camaraderie at moose camp was what kept him going year after year. He never took me or showed me how to hunt.

We ate moose several times a week growing up, but the meat wasn't treated like something special. It was ground meat and thin, overcooked steaks. It wasn't until I became a professional chef that I started to learn nose-to-tail concepts and eating the stuff most people threw in the garbage. But it took a while before I became a hunter.

After fifteen years as a chef, I left the kitchen and took a regular nine-to-five job. I had been wanting to get back to my roots and exercise my tribal sustenance hunting rights, and I now had the time to embrace the experience. One Saturday morning in 2013, I watched a show called MeatEater *for the first time. It had a profound effect on me. Here was a hunter who was demonstrating the ideology of my indigenous culture, in terms of honoring the entire animal by cooking things like hearts and tongues. Watching Steve inspired me to use my own culinary experience to respect every animal that I harvested. Now I treat wild game like any other protein I'd encounter in a professional kitchen. If it can be done with beef, then it can be done with moose is my attitude.*

Butchering. There are a couple ways to remove the nose from an unskinned moose head. With a reciprocating saw, cut straight down all the way through the nose where bone meets the cartilage. This method gives you some bony structure to hold things together while you're cooking. Or you can use an extremely sharp boning knife with a 7- to 8-inch blade to carve the nose off. Where the bone meets cartilage on top of the nose, cut down and out along the bone to remove the nose. If you have experience with butchering animals, this part will feel intuitive, and you could also try it with a bison or bull elk. To avoid spoilage, remove the nose while field dressing or not more than 24 hours after death. Wash the nose with cold water and coarse salt to remove blood, paying special attention to rinsing the nostrils until clean.

Boiling. In a large stockpot, add the nose and a couple tablespoons of salt and cover with water. Bring to a boil over high heat, cover the pot, and reduce the heat to medium. A slow rolling boil is ideal. Cook for approximately 4 hours. If needed, add water throughout the process to make sure the nose is always submerged. Periodically skim away any floating hair, dirt, and other loose bits. To check your nose for doneness, try peeling off a small piece of the hide. If it comes off easily, the meat is ready. Remove the nose from the pot and shock it with cold water.

Peeling. It's best to peel when the nose is still warm, so don't let it sit in the cold water for more than 3 minutes. Start at the bridge of the nose and peel the thick parts first. Be careful not to get hair on the peeled parts as you're working; the fat is very tacky and makes getting hair off difficult. Use a cloth hand towel to grip the skin and help keep hair off the fat. Peeling can be a real pain in the ass, but resist the urge to put the whole thing back in the water and cook it longer. This will ruin the top layer of fat. The most difficult parts to peel will be in and around the nostrils. Use a sharp paring knife for those areas. The age of the moose is a major factor in the peeling process. The easiest nose I've ever peeled was from a young bull, and the hardest was from a very old cow.

Smoking. Get your smoking going at 225 to 250 while you're peeling the nose. I prefer to smoke with apple or maple, which are plentiful in Maine. Smoke for one hour. The cartilage in a moose nose is a maze, so removing it without wasting edible parts can be difficult. While the nose is still warm, I cut the nose in half the long way and slowly pull out the cartilage. This part, like peeling, requires some patience. A paring knife will come in handy.

Once the cartilage has been removed, you can portion out the meat. There will be some very marbled, meaty bits as well as some white fatty bits. I like to separate the meaty parts from the fatty ones. The fatty parts are incredible and can be eaten as is, but I like to cook them like bacon in a pan with some butter or bear fat. Some of the nose fat will caramelize and get crispy and other parts will melt. The meat is wonderful in sandwiches, tacos, stew, and in the hash recipe on page 133.

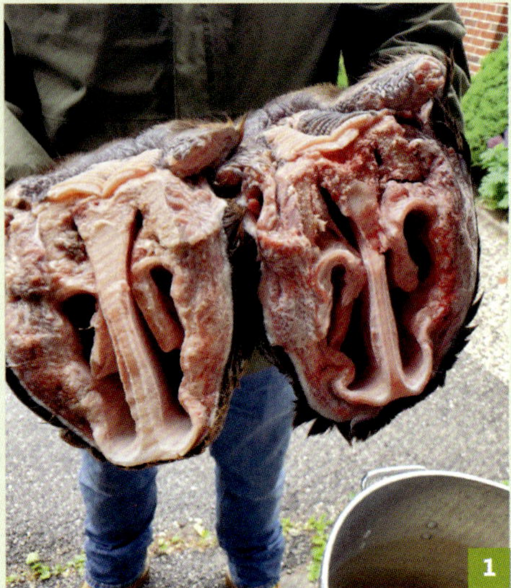

1. Moose noses removed by a reciprocating saw. They can also be removed with a boning knife.

2. Moose nose, post boil—peeling skin in preparation for smoker.

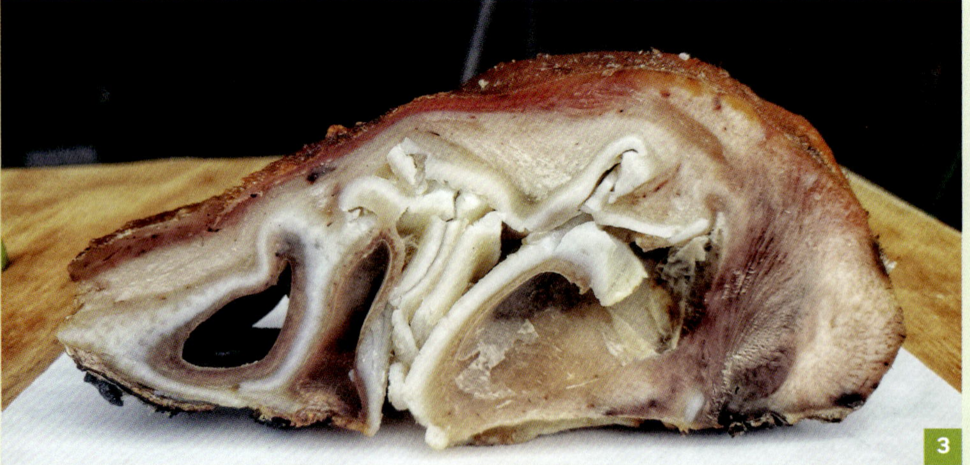

3. Fully cooked moose nose cut in half the long way. The cartilage is maze-like and very hard to remove once the nose has cooled.

4. Broken-down fully cooked and smoked nose.

5. Fatty bits separated from meaty bits.

Jessee Lawyer and Jeff Stewart are friends, hunting partners, and chefs. Jessee is a member of the Abenaki Nation in Vermont, and Jeff is a member of the Penobscot Nation in Maine. They have made it their mission to teach other hunters about the virtues of butchering and cooking moose noses. They believe it's a worthy cut of meat to be honored and eaten rather than wasted.

BRAISED AND SMOKED WILD GAME BRISKET

SERVES 4

RUB

1 tablespoon garlic powder

2 tablespoons ground black pepper

1 tablespoon paprika

BRAISE

1 large bison brisket (3 to 4 pounds), cleaned of sinew but keeping as much fat as possible

Kosher salt and freshly ground black pepper

½ cup pork lard, at room temperature

½ medium onion, sliced crosswise

1 (12-ounce) bottle light beer

ALSO WORKS WITH. *Moose, elk, or beef brisket. Or for you Texans, nilgai.*

When I go to one of those Texas BBQ joints where you get to pick your meat, I always go with beef brisket. One of the things I love about beef brisket is that it's so different from wild game. I can make an approximation of smoked ribs and sausages and even chicken with wild game, but brisket is a different story. The amount of fat and marbling in beef brisket makes it a hard thing to replicate with big game. What I've found, though, is that you can achieve the approximate results if you take an entirely different approach to get there. That approach is to braise the brisket until it's tender, and then finish the meat in a smoker. It's not the same process as Texas barbecue, nor is it the same greasy and succulent dining experience. But it is delicious nonetheless and introduces a whole new way to handle a cut of meat that usually just ends up in the grinder pile or, worse, the scrap heap. The brisket on whitetail and mule deer isn't big enough for this preparation, but bison, elk, and moose are all adequately sized. The braising liquid is a fat-laden mixture of beer and aromatics.

FOR THE RUB. In a small bowl, combine all ingredients. Set aside.

Preheat the oven to 325°F.

FOR THE BRAISE. Pat the brisket dry. Season liberally with salt and pepper on both sides. Sprinkle 1 tablespoon of the rub on the brisket, covering both sides. Slather the lard on the top of the brisket.

Measure two pieces of foil longer than a 9 x 13-inch baking dish by 6 inches on each side. Measure out a piece of parchment paper about the same length. Lay one piece of foil on the baking sheet lengthwise with the overhang even on the sides of the dish. Lay the other piece of foil perpendicular to the first piece in the middle, making a cross. Lay the parchment paper down lengthwise in the baking dish. Fold the sides of the foil up to form a loose bowl-like shape. Lay the onions down on the parchment. Add the brisket on top. Pour 8 to 12 ounces of beer into the foil—it should come halfway up the sides (make sure the foil holds in the liquid).

Carefully fold the parchment paper by joining the two short ends, then folding them over to make a somewhat airtight seal (like a tightly wrapped deli sandwich). Do the same with the two pieces of foil to enclose the meat, keeping the liquid inside the foil-parchment package.

Put the baking dish with the foil-wrapped packet into the preheated oven. Braise for 2 to 3 hours, or until tender, checking at 1½ hours. (To check, carefully open up the packet, use a knife to check tenderness, and wrap up again and return it to the oven if it's not ready.) When it is very tender with no resistance to the knife in multiple spots, remove it from the oven; the internal temperature will be over 170°F when it is ready.

Let the brisket rest at room temperature still wrapped in foil while you set up your smoker.

Remove the brisket from the foil packet, reserving the braising liquid for later use. Season with the remaining dry rub if a heavy pepper flavor is your preference.

Soak a large handful of wood chips in water, preferably a wood such as pecan or hickory. Preheat your smoker to 175°F to 200°F, and add the soaked wood chips when up to temperature. Smoke the meat aggressively for 20 to 30 minutes (the goal is to have a low cooking temperature and high smoke to impart flavor).

Slice and serve with your favorite barbecue sauce or the reserved braising liquid. Refrigerate any leftovers. To serve at a later date, reheat refrigerated slices in a sauté pan with the reserved braising liquid to warm through.

03 UNDER THE COALS

I first moved to Montana in 1997, but it took me well over a decade to learn that the state picked up its "Big Sky Country" nickname from A. B. Guthrie, Jr.'s 1947 novel, *The Big Sky*. I'd known all along about the book, which is largely set in Montana, but I wrongly assumed that it took its title from the state's nickname rather than vice versa. As it turns out, the Montana State Highway Department secured permission from Guthrie to use his novel's title for an ad campaign. Starting in 1962, tourists were baited to Montana with the enticement to "Travel Montana, the Big Sky Country, Between Yellowstone and Glacier."

Guthrie's novel tells the story of a wild and hot-tempered boy from Kentucky named Boone Caudill. In the early 1800s, Caudill flees home after nearly killing his abusive father by clocking him over the head with a piece of firewood. He winds up on a French keelboat full of traders headed up the Missouri River into what is now Montana. An ambush by Blackfoot warriors kills just about everyone on the boat. Caudill survives to become an accomplished and daring mountain man, but his hot temper never cools. Late in the novel, he puts a pistol ball through the chest of his own best friend. Alone and wayward, he's left to contemplate the death of the American West.

The novel's arc might seem like a rather gloomy foundation for a tourism ad campaign, and the treatment of Native American characters is pathetic, but

« "Panless" steaks cooked on an oiled rock

it's easy to see why the story has appealed to so many for so long. For one thing, it's an ode to outdoor cooking—not that the characters have any choice; there's no indoors available to them. You get a sense of the book's culinary sensibility early on when Caudill kills a rabbit after running away from home. He cuts it into small pieces and presses the pieces to a flat rock and then props the rock next to the fire. As an accompaniment to the rabbit, he uses creek water to moisten some cornmeal drawn from a small "poke" (that's a bag, for you folks who aren't hip to the old-timey vernacular) and rolls it into balls that he drops directly into the coals. Baked in such a way, he calls these johnnycakes. Over the course of the book, he eats a great many simple meals like this: dried corn and beans cooked with buffalo marrow, cubes of half-rotten buffalo bull meat cut with the grain to save "the blood and juice," and cubed meat boiled in a kettle with wild onions.

If Caudill has a signature dish, it's the head of a mule deer buried in the coals of a fire and left there to roast. Before reading the novel, I had experienced a similar dish in West Texas, just a few miles from the Mexico border. I was with some cowboys who shot one of their steers with a .22 rimfire and wrapped its head in chicken wire before burying it inside an underground brick oven. We used the meat to make tacos de cabeza. It was good, but not so memorable that I added it to my personal repertoire. That didn't happen until a few years later, when I was traveling with friends along the Missouri River just upstream from where Caudill first samples the deer-head-in-the-ground dish. We had the fresh head of a mule deer doe in our camp. After discussing the novel, we buried the head in the coals of a cottonwood fire and let it go for a few hours. The rich, greasy meat was textured similarly to braised spare ribs and pulled away from the bone just about as easily. The recipe that was ultimately developed from that experience is covered in detail in one of my previous books, *The Complete Guide to Hunting, Butchering, and Cooking Wild Game, Volume 1: Big Game.*

This chapter is a massive expansion on that style of cooking. Here you'll find preparations that utilize ashes and coals to cook a wide variety of dishes: roasts, veggies, game stews made in Dutch ovens, gooey sandwiches made in iron pies, next-level foil packets, and even a venison shoulder cooked in a barrel. Of all the types of outdoor cooking explored in this book, cooking beneath and among the coals is perhaps the trickiest. A lot of the action is hidden from view; cooks who like to crack open the oven or grill in order to check on the progress of their dishes are likely to have their patience tested while attempting our Towel-Wrapped Roast Beneath the Coals recipe on page 172. I realize that this might scare you off. When most folks buy a cookbook, they're not looking for an experience in trial and error. They're looking for proven methods, with all the wrinkles ironed out. Admittedly, I can't totally guarantee that you won't have any surprises or disappointments when you're messing around with this chapter. Things might get a tad burned, or things might come out a little raw. But what I can guarantee is that you'll learn a ton. Cooking food nestled in the coals is not only a way to impart a smoky sweetness to foods like potatoes and squashes, which steam in their skins; it's an efficient way to utilize a campfire: You can be grilling steaks or a whole fish on a grate over the flames while steam-roasting potatoes adjacent to the flames in the coals. Stick with it and you'll have some amazing meals. And come to think of it, there's a second guarantee that I'll make. You'll enjoy cooking under the Big Sky, wherever you find it.

COOKING WITH COALS: WHAT YOU NEED TO KNOW

Just like all of the methods discussed in this book, cooking with wood coals or charcoal briquettes is never an exact science. Although there are well-researched formulas and guidelines for coal cooking (see the sidebar on page 152), you don't have the luxury of making adjustments with the simple turn of a knob as you do when working with propane grills, smokers, or campstoves. There's also a big difference between cooking over a fire that's crackling and blazing and cooking over (or under) a bed of slowly smoldering coals. For starters, coals do throw off a predictable and consistent level of heat, so they are easier to work with than active flames, which tend to fluctuate wildly. Keep in mind, however, that over time the heat output of wood coals slowly decreases. And since we're talking about outdoor cooking, the same uncontrollable environmental factors that can affect fires (wind speed, ambient temperatures, precipitation, etc.) can also impact coals, though usually to a lesser degree.

The type of wood or charcoal you're burning is another factor to consider. Pine and other softwood coals, for example, won't crank out heat nearly as long as dense hardwoods like oak. Likewise, manufactured briquettes and lump hardwood charcoal have varying heat outputs; compressed charcoals, such as binchotan, have even more. Still, wood coals can also be manipulated in a manner that isn't possible with flames. Using shovels and coal rakes, coals can be moved around and placed precisely to allow for a variety of cooking methods ranging from searing steaks to roasting whole squash. Coals also have the staying power and high-heat output needed for all-day projects like cooking whole hogs in a caja china or drum-type roaster. The following chapter dives into several of our favorite coal cooking scenarios, along with the best equipment to use for each.

But first, it's important to understand that you're always playing the long game with coals. There are certainly times when a faster cooking method might be more practical. Even if a given recipe only takes a few minutes to cook, you'll need to plan for the additional time needed to produce coals. Charcoal chimneys and charcoal grills take a little while to heat up. It requires even more time for a fire to transform hunks of firewood into a bed of glowing orange coals. And you will need to maintain a fire or a series of charcoal chimneys in order to have a steady stream of active coals for longer cooking processes. In other words, cooking with wood coals isn't something that you can rush. In that way, it's a lot like hunting and fishing—you need to embrace the entire process, not just celebrate the end result. Approached this way, you'll get into a rhythm and get damn good at it, too.

Cooking Food Directly on Coals

Cooking food directly on coals is about as primal and basic as it gets. This can be done with lean hunks of venison, whole fish, and even sturdy hard-skinned vegetables like squash and yams. However, cooking really fatty stuff directly on coals will cause violent flare-ups. Even without fat, you're going to end up with a charred surface, but that's part of the appeal. If you want to cook something that is fatty or achieve a light sear rather than a hard char, then use a grate to suspend food away from the coals, as you would do with a charcoal grill.

Cooking in Foil Packs

The usefulness of heavy-duty aluminum foil in outdoor cooking can't be overstated. From steamed veggies to baked potatoes to roasted fish, you can season just about anything, wrap it in foil, toss the package on some hot coals, and the end result will turn out great—especially if you follow the guide on page 152. You can even turn out entire dinners packaged as individual servings this way. If you're looking for a way to keep prep and cleanup simple, foil-pack cooking is the way to go.

Dutch Ovens

Cast-iron Dutch ovens were invented for the purpose of cooking over fires and hot coals hundreds of years ago. The lids have a lip on the edge, which is meant to hold hot coals in place. Not much has changed about them since then, which ought to tell you it's worth having one around. There's really no limit to the range of cooking methods or types of recipes you can use with a Dutch oven that's hanging over, resting on, or covered up in coals. You can achieve controlled, steady temperatures that allow you to braise meat, fry fish, simmer stews, and bake desserts. (See sidebar on page 152 for Dutch oven coal ratios.)

It's hard to go wrong with a Lodge product, and when in doubt, bigger is usually better. Consider getting one with legs so you can easily shove hot coals underneath it. If yours doesn't have legs, get a pot stand, or you can make one with a few rocks. A tripod is another great accessory for hanging Dutch ovens over a fire or bed of coals.

Pie Irons

Pie irons are another cast-iron cooking implement that's designed for coal cooking. Basically a camping version of a panini press, pie irons are used to make sandwich-style dinners with multiple ingredients like ham, ground or shredded meat, onions, cheese, and/or vegetables. Whatever the ingredients, these sandwiches are regionally known as hobo pies, pudgy pies, mountain pies, or iron pies, as we like to call them. You can do a lot more with pie irons, too, from desserts to breakfast scrambles. And they're simple to use, so kids love cooking with them.

DUTCH OVENS

Counting Coals for Approximate Temperatures

The beauty of using a centuries-old cooking tool is that most of the kinks have been worked out. That's certainly the case with Dutch ovens, which have been in production since the 1700s. With a little research, you'll find plenty of charts showing how many charcoal briquettes to use around your Dutch oven in order to achieve your desired temperature. Campfire wood coals aren't an exact match to briquettes in terms of temperature, but they come close enough.

There are two common depths for Dutch ovens: a shallow or "baking oven" and a deeper Dutch oven. The baking oven's lid is closer to the food, so it can more easily brown the tops of biscuits and breads. The deeper oven is ideal for cooking large-volume stews and soups for a crowd. Whatever the size of your pot, the recipes in this book follow the coal-to-temperature guide below—if you're working with bigger or smaller pots, adjust as noted. These numbers come from the folks at Lodge Cast Iron.

We recommend starting out with these approximate quantities, knowing you may need to adjust on the fly. Learning when to add more coals is as much about gut instinct as it is following strict formulas—the more you do it, the more you will learn and feel comfortable riffing.

10-INCH-DIAMETER (4-QUART) *SHALLOW POT*
(USE 4 MORE COALS FOR A 5-QUART *DEEP POT*)

350°F—21 coals (7 underneath, 14 on top)
375°F—23 coals (7 underneath, 16 on top)
400°F—25 coals (8 underneath, 17 on top)
425°F—27 coals (9 underneath, 18 on top)

12-INCH-DIAMETER (6-QUART) *SHALLOW POT*
(USE 4 MORE COALS FOR AN 8-QUART *DEEP POT*)

350°F—25 coals (8 underneath, 17 on top)
375°F—27 coals (9 underneath, 18 on top)
400°F—29 coals (10 underneath, 19 on top)
425°F—31 coals (10 underneath, 21 on top)

COAL-ROASTED SMASHED POTATO BAR

SERVES 6

This is a fun dish to make with the family. It gives kids a nice primer on how to cook with fire using ancient techniques. Basically you're just wrapping potatoes in a protective coating—in this case, aluminum foil—and burying them in the coals until they have soft interiors and a smoky flavor from the fire. When done, you open up the foil and smash the cooked potato together with your choice of toppings. We're taking a pretty standard approach with this recipe, using sour cream, bacon, and chives. If you want some different options, check out the sidebar on this page.

6 medium Yukon Gold potatoes

Olive oil or bacon fat, for rubbing the potatoes

Kosher salt and freshly ground black pepper

6 ounces sharp cheddar cheese, shredded

6 slices cooked bacon, crumbled

Sour cream

Chopped fresh chives

Chopped pickled jalapeños

Chopped tomato

Get some briquettes going in a charcoal grill or build a wood fire in a pit or campfire circle. If using a wood fire, wait until the wood burns down into coals, or crush some charred logs with a shovel to create hot coals.

Put each potato on a double layer of heavy-duty aluminum foil. Rub the skins with oil and sprinkle with salt and pepper. Enclose the potato in the foil. Use tongs to nestle the potatoes in the coals. Don't crowd them so they're touching each other. Cover the grill and cook, turning the potatoes occasionally so all sides are exposed to the coals. If cooking on a charcoal grill, you may need to add a second chimney of prepared coals to keep the temperature high. (If using a wood fire, just keep turning the potatoes every 5 to 10 minutes and add a log to the fire to keep the coals coming.) Cook until they are very tender, 45 minutes to 1 hour. Check for tenderness with a paring knife.

Unwrap the potatoes and place them on a cutting board or serving tray. Use the lid of a small pan, the bottom of a bottle, or a sturdy spatula to press down and smash the potatoes flat (about ¾ to 1 inch thick). Sprinkle with salt and pepper. Evenly top with the cheese. Then distribute the bacon, sour cream, chives, jalapeños, and tomatoes over the top or substitute a topping from the sidebar on this page. Serve warm.

ALSO WORKS WITH. *Sweet potatoes, yams, any color or kind of potato (red, purple, or russet).*

MORE TOPPINGS

Feta, olives, chopped tomatoes

Peperonata (page 34) and mozzarella

Sausage, mushrooms, Gruyère cheese

Blue cheese, buffalo sauce, cooked game bird

Anchovy Mayo (page 118), cooked backstrap

Chili, cheddar cheese, sour cream

Arugula, prosciutto, mozzarella

MIX AND MATCH FOIL PACKS

You're not alone if the first meal that you ever cooked outdoors was a mixture of ground meat, potatoes, and onions wrapped up in a foil packet. Untold numbers of scout masters and camp counselors have trained several generations' worth of kids in this preparation. While foil packs remain a fun, simple way to make camp dinners, there's plenty that can be done to improve the experience. A shortcut to foil-pack perfection is to take a three-step mix-and-match philosophy that combines a protein, vegetable, and sauce into a hearty meal. You'll also find some more involved recipes that are worth the time and effort. For all of these recipes, we suggest using heavy-duty aluminum foil. For each serving, cut one 17 × 20-inch piece of foil.

STEP 1: CHOOSE YOUR AROMATICS AND PROTEIN

Aromatics are herbs and vegetables that add flavor and aroma to a dish. Many of the vegetables come from the allium (onion) family. You'll often see them mentioned when making stocks and stews or steaming recipes, for example, and because foil packets use a combination of steaming with a little searing against hot coals or grates, aromatics are a surefire way to add fast flavor to your meat and fish. Some of these are edible when cooked, others are too woody to eat.

Try chives and wild onions; garlic; leeks; thin slices of onion, shallots, carrots, parsnips, fennel or celery; scallions; ginger cut into coins (discard after cooking); spicy fresh chiles; bay leaves, rosemary or thyme (discard after cooking).

From a flavor perspective, the best proteins for foil packets are those that do well when poached or steamed. This brings fish and shellfish front and center, but big game and birds can be players, too. If using big game, choose ground meat or already tender cuts like backstrap, sliced thinly, and understand you may need a knife to cut them into bite-sized pieces. Whichever protein you choose, be sure to season it with kosher salt and freshly ground black pepper or a pinch of red pepper flakes before adding it to your packet.

Options include fish such as salmon or white flaky fish cut into 2- to 4-ounce pieces; small whole trout fillets; shellfish; large upland bird breasts, sliced thin and pounded, then cut into 2-ounce pieces; small whole upland bird breasts; ground game meat; thin strips of venison (this is not as palatable and my least favorite choice).

STEP 2: CHOOSE YOUR VEGETABLES

Just about any vegetable can make its way into a foil packet. Below are some of our top choices, but let your garden or the farmer's market be your guide. Heck, throw some foraged mushrooms or ramps in, too. Whatever is in season will shine when cooked this way. Keep in mind that most proteins will cook between 12 and 20 minutes, so the trick here is to cut large vegetables in a way that will allow them to cook within that time span. And remember, vegetables taste delicious with a little char. To achieve this, nestle one side of the foil packet against hot embers and flip every 5 to 10 minutes. It should also be said that vegetable-only packets are a worthwhile way to pull off a quick, healthy side while camping.

Try broccoli or cauliflower cut into ⅓ inch planks; thin strips of bell peppers, kale, bok choy, cabbage, or zucchini; green beans, wax beans, or snow peas cut lengthwise; spinach or mustard greens, potatoes or sweet potatoes cut into small rounds ¼-inch thick; cherry tomatoes.

STEP 3: CHOOSE YOUR SAUCE

Sauces for packets can be as simple as a ready-made sauce from a bottle, a drizzle of olive oil and a splash of wine, or a more elaborate concoction you make yourself. There are a few truths to keep in mind: First, fat carries flavor, so make sure you've got some in the form of olive oil, neutral oil, butter, or duck fat; second, too much acidity can burn a hole through your foil and reacts with foil in a way that creates an unpleasant taste. Insulate the acids with enough oil or other liquids. Additional flavorings like capers, olives, citrus zest, sun-dried tomatoes, wasabi, dry rubs, or seasonings can also add punch and brightness.

Great options for your sauces include citrus juice with zest; extra virgin olive oil; jarred sauces such as barbecue, Worcestershire, Thai peanut or Teriyaki; neutral oils; soy sauce; toasted sesame oil (a little goes a long way); any kind of vinegar; white or red wine—be sure to use the acidic sauces with oil so that the acidity doesn't pit the foil.

STEP 4: COOK YOUR PACKETS

Start by preparing a campfire (or charcoal or propane grill). For each foil packet: Cut your 17 × 20-inch pieces of foil. Lay your aromatics and proteins in the center of the foil and season with salt and pepper. Add your vegetables around or on top of the proteins. Add your sauce and any other additional flavorings.

Bring together the long sides of the foil up and over the food in the center. Fold the foil pieces over a few times, crimping them together securely. Seal the short sides of the foil by folding them over a few times toward the center mound.

The campfire is ready when there is a bed of glowing coals. With a coal rake or another tool, pull these coals out to the edge of the fire. Place the foil packets on and near the hot coals or on the grill grate. For fish fillets, cook about 15 minutes, flipping the packet halfway through. For other meats or all vegetable packets, cook for 20 minutes, flipping the packet halfway through. Allow the packets to rest for 5 minutes before opening and serving with a squeeze of lemon (if desired).

SOY-STEAMED GOOSE BREAST
WITH BABY BOK CHOY

Divide the scallion whites and garlic evenly between the two 17 × 20-inch pieces of aluminum foil. Drizzle each mound with 1 tablespoon of the olive oil and season evenly with ¼ teaspoon of the salt. Divide evenly and place the goose breast strips over the scallion whites and garlic and season the meat with the remaining ¼ teaspoon salt. Divide and arrange the bok choy evenly around the goose breasts. In a small bowl, stir together the soy sauce, mirin, rice vinegar, and sesame oil. Divide this mixture and pour over each portion of goose. Scatter the scallion greens on top. Seal and cook for 20 minutes. Serves 2.

ALSO WORKS WITH: *Duck or upland bird beasts, big game burgers, or thin strips of backstrap.*

COOK'S NOTE. *If you have the time, marinate the sliced goose breast for up to 4 hours in the mirin sauce mixture before placing it in the packets and steaming.*

VEGETABLE

4 small baby bok choy, halved lengthwise

AROMATICS AND PROTEIN

1 bunch scallions, white and green parts, cut into 1-inch pieces

2 garlic cloves, thinly sliced

2 tablespoons olive oil

½ teaspoon kosher salt

1 (10- to 12-ounce) goose breast, cut into ¾- to 1-inch slices (see Cook's Note)

SAUCE

1 tablespoon soy sauce or tamari

3 tablespoons mirin

1 teaspoon rice vinegar

1 teaspoon toasted sesame oil

Two 17 × 20-inch pieces of aluminum foil

MEDITERRANEAN RAINBOW TROUT

VEGETABLE

½ bunch Tuscan kale (about 5 large leaves), sliced into ribbons with thick stems removed

AROMATICS AND PROTEIN

½ red onion, thinly sliced

1 fennel bulb, trimmed and thinly sliced

1½ teaspoons kosher salt

3 tablespoons extra-virgin olive oil

4 (3-ounce) rainbow trout fillets

SAUCE

¼ cup drained and chopped sun-dried tomatoes in oil

¼ cup chopped pitted kalamata olives

½ teaspoon red wine vinegar

¼ teaspoon dried oregano

Two 17 × 20-inch pieces of foil

In a medium bowl, combine the kale, red onion, fennel, and ½ teaspoon of the salt. Drizzle with 2 tablespoons of the olive oil and toss well to coat. Divide the mixture evenly and place half in the center of each piece of foil. Score the skin of the fish fillets in three places. Season them evenly with the remaining salt. Top each mound of kale with 2 pieces of seasoned trout, skin-side down. In a separate bowl, combine the sun-dried tomatoes, olives, red wine vinegar, dried oregano, and the remaining 1 tablespoon olive oil. Stir to combine. Spoon half the mixture over the trout in each packet. Seal and cook for 15 minutes. Serves 2 (makes two packets).

COOK'S NOTE. *You can also make this recipe using a smallish whole cleaned rainbow trout wrapped in foil and use the topping as a stuffing. A whole fish usually takes a few minutes longer to cook.*

ALSO WORKS WITH. *Any fish, shrimp, or shellfish.*

SWEET CHILI-GLAZED SALMON

WITH BROCCOLINI

PROTEIN

2 tablespoons plus 2 teaspoons extra-virgin olive oil

2 (6-ounce) skinless wild salmon fillets

1 teaspoon kosher salt

VEGETABLE

1 small bunch broccolini, trimmed and cut into pieces

AROMATICS AND SAUCE

¼ cup sweet chili sauce

2 teaspoons sriracha

1 teaspoon toasted sesame oil

½ teaspoon grated fresh ginger

In this recipe, the aromatics are combined in the sauce.

Prepare a hot campfire (or charcoal grill or propane grill). Brush the inside of each foil pack with 1 teaspoon of the olive oil. Season the salmon fillets evenly with ½ teaspoon of the salt. Place a fillet in the center of each piece of foil. Divide the broccolini and place half in each packet. Drizzle each packet with another tablespoon of the olive oil. Season the packets evenly with ¼ teaspoon of the salt. In a small bowl, combine the sweet chili sauce, sriracha, sesame oil, grated ginger, and the remaining ¼ teaspoon salt. Stir until fully incorporated. Divide the sauce over the salmon and broccolini. Seal and cook for 15 minutes. Serves 2.

ALSO WORKS WITH. *Any fish, shrimp, or shellfish.*

IRON PIE SANDWICHES . . . OR WHATEVER YOU CALL THEM

We called them hobo pie makers when I was a kid growing up in Michigan, but that name has fallen out of fashion. You'll still get the right results when you type those words into a search engine, but you won't find the word *hobo* in the actual product description. Instead, you'll see terms like pudgy pie, mountain pie, campfire pie, or iron pie, which are all totally acceptable names for these classic cast-iron clamshells that can be used to make outstanding sandwiches and desserts with minimal preparation and cleanup. There aren't really any rules when it comes to iron pies—use what you've got and call them what you want.

MAKING IRON PIES

First, you've got to choose your bread. Soft, thick-cut square sandwich brioche bread is our favorite and the easiest to mold into the pie iron. Six-inch flour tortillas also work, although they require some finagling.

Next, you'll need to get some kind of grease involved. You can use softened unsalted butter, nonstick cooking spray, bear grease, duck fat, or other animal lard, or mayonnaise.

When it comes to fillings, adding meltable and oozy ingredients like cheese or peanut butter to pie iron sandwiches is our favorite way to go. These'll also help to hold the other fillings in place. Meat and cheese are an obvious pairing, but so are cooked vegetables and cheese. And don't sleep on heating up a peanut butter and jelly sandwich in a pie iron. The results are out of this world.

TO BUILD: Separate your pie iron into two pieces. Wipe out the inside of each side with a wet cloth and dry well. Liberally grease the insides of the pie iron. Or slather mayonnaise directly on both pieces of bread on the pie iron side.

Press a piece of bread snugly into each side of the pie iron as in the illustrations below. Pile your ingredients generously onto one piece of the bread. A fuller sandwich will make for a tighter press, allowing the bread to become golden brown and delicious. Place the second iron over the pile of ingredients to form a sandwich. Attach the two pieces of the pie iron and lock into place.

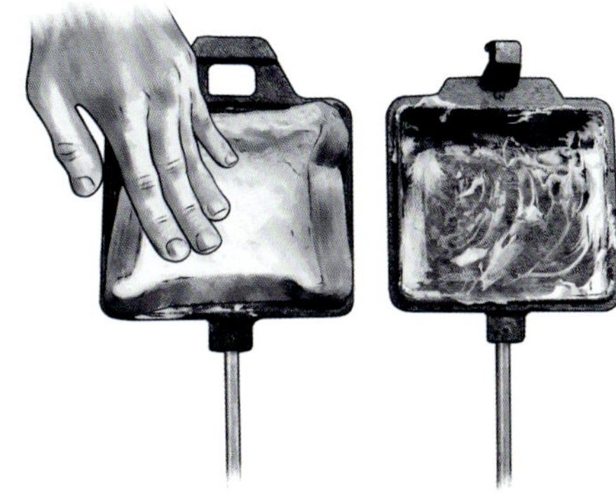

TO COOK: Prepare a campfire (or charcoal grill) for coal cooking. When you have a sufficient bed of coals, pull them out to the edge of the fire with a coal rake. Place the irons flat on the hot coals to evenly transfer the heat (if you're using a charcoal grill, bank the briquettes to one side so that you can lay the pie irons in the grill on top of the coals). A good starting point is to cook for a total of 2 to 4 minutes, then flip and cook for another 2 minutes. Pull the iron out, unlatch the handles, and carefully take a peek to see how browned it is (don't touch the actual irons—they're raging hot). If it needs more time, close it up and throw it back on the fire for a minute. If it looks good, lay the iron on a log or rock and remove the top half. Allow the sandwich to rest for a minute, then turn the iron over and deposit the sandwich onto a plate. The contents will be like molten lava, so warn any kiddos or unsuspecting adults to be careful of the hot, oozing filling when eating. Wipe out the pie iron, if necessary, add a little grease, and start your next sandwich or pie.

BIRD, CHEDDAR, AND FIG JAM SANDWICH

MAKES 1 SANDWICH

2 slices multigrain sandwich bread

1½ tablespoons softened butter

1 heaping tablespoon fig jam

3 to 4 ounces sliced cooked upland bird breast (smoked, roasted, or grilled)

4 small aged cheddar slices, or 2 precut slices (about 2 ounces)

Pinch of kosher salt

Freshly ground black pepper

Clean and dry the pie-iron interiors. Slather the insides of each pie iron with the softened butter. Press the bread slices into each half of the iron molds (see illustration on page 169). On one bread slice, spread the fig jam. Top the jam with slices of upland bird, overlapping to fill the space, then top the bird with cheese slices, also overlapping to fill the space. Sprinkle with salt and pepper. The sandwich should be piled high. If it's not, add more meat and cheese. Top with the second bread-lined pie iron and secure the fasteners to close the iron tightly.

Follow the cooking instructions on page 169.

TEN OF OUR FAVORITE IRON PIE COMBOS

We recommend using the style of breads suggested below, but feel free to experiment.

- Peanut butter and jelly or honey, country white bread
- Cooked ground-meat burger, diced onion, American cheese, ketchup, white sandwich bread or brioche
- Cooked ground burger or shredded game bird meat, taco seasoning, Mexican cheese blend, salsa, chopped onion, shredded lettuce, flour tortilla
- Sliced ham, pimiento cheese, pickles, sourdough or country white bread
- Cooked bacon or breakfast sausage, scrambled eggs, cheddar cheese, flour tortilla, brioche, or sourdough bread
- Smoked salmon or trout, cream cheese, dill, chives or pickled red onion, white or sourdough bread
- Cooked wild duck, Gorgonzola, Pancetta-Onion Jam (page 55), preserved amarena cherries, sourdough
- Peperonata (page 34), shredded mozzarella, sourdough
- Sautéed mushrooms, grilled zucchini, Gouda or cheddar, sourdough

TOWEL-WRAPPED ROAST BENEATH THE COALS

SERVES 4 TO 6

2½ pounds elk roast, exterior silverskin removed

2 pounds kosher salt (close to 2 cups)

1 dozen fresh herb sprigs (oregano, rosemary, thyme, and/or marjoram)

1 tablespoon orange zest (optional)

1 teaspoon chile-style rub, like chili powder, ancho powder, or chipotle powder (optional)

Chimichurri (see page 71), Chunky Pico de Gallo, Red Pepper Aioli (see page 115), and/or Garlic-Chipotle Faux Aioli (page 350), for serving (optional)

SPECIAL EQUIPMENT

Kitchen twine, 1 clean cotton kitchen towel, or 2 packages of cheesecloth approximately 12 x 21 inches (don't use synthetic towels). This towel will be ruined and charred in this process, so don't use the one you got for your wedding.

COOK'S NOTE. *This roast works great as a backyard recipe on a charcoal grill or fire pit and is equally simple to throw together at a campsite.*

ALSO WORKS WITH. *Deer, moose, elk, beef, and pretty much any big animal. You want a tender roast-sized hunk of meat, such as loin, tenderloin, sirloin, or round.*

This recipe uses the increasingly popular Colombian cooking technique for *lomo al trapo,* which translates to "beef tenderloin in a towel." The process is similar to baking a roast in a salt crust or a clay crust in coals, but you do it in a dampened cloth or towel instead. The result is a tasty, salt-seasoned roast that is tender and cooked to perfection. The unveiling of the meat brings a little drama and entertainment to a gathering. The traditional seasoning is salt and oregano, but, just like when you're baking with a salt crust, other aromatics work well, too. While testing this recipe, we tried it with herbs, orange zest, and even a chile-based dry rub. All were excellent.

Wet the kitchen towel or cheesecloth and wring it out so that it's dampened but not dripping wet. Lay the cloth flat on a work surface with one short side of the towel nearest to you, then follow the illustrations opposite to wrap the roast.

PREPARING AND MAINTAINING THE COALS AND FIRE. Prepare a medium fire inside a stone circle, with plenty of wood on standby. When the logs have burned and are turning into coals, use a shovel to arrange the smoldering wood around the perimeter of your fire circle (if you're using a fire pit, you'll want the logs on the edge of the pit). Move the hot coals into the opening in the center. Nestle your towel-wrapped roast on these coals (if you're cooking potatoes or other vegetables in coals also, place them on the coals now as well). You're using the direct heat of the coals and the ambient heat of the smoldering logs to cook the roast, so, if needed, add fresh logs to keep the fire going. Crush the spent logs with your shovel and toss the hot coals over the roast. Continue this process throughout the cooking time.

CHECKING FOR DONENESS. After about 20 minutes the salt on the bottom half of the roast will become hard. Do an internal temperature check with a meat thermometer through the towel. It should be around 100°F. Flip the roast at this point and add more coals under and around it. Your target internal temperature is about 130°F, so check the roast frequently, about every 10 minutes, until it reaches 100°F. It shouldn't take much longer than 30 minutes total, but keep in mind that it's nearly impossible to have perfectly even cooking from end to end, so don't be upset if there's a little variance.

Use tongs to remove the roast from the coals and let it rest for 5 to 10 minutes inside the cloth. Transfer to a serving platter, board, or baking sheet to reveal. Snip away the charred cloth and crack through the hard salt shell to reveal the roast in the interior. Slice and serve with your choice of condiments.

1. Add the salt to the towel, starting 1 inch from the short edges of the towel, and 2 inches from the long sides. You should have a rectangular layer of salt that is about ½ inch thick. Maintain a salt-free border around the edge of the towel. Lay down the herbs on top of the salt. Lay the roast in the center of the salt and herbs, parallel to the short side of the towel.

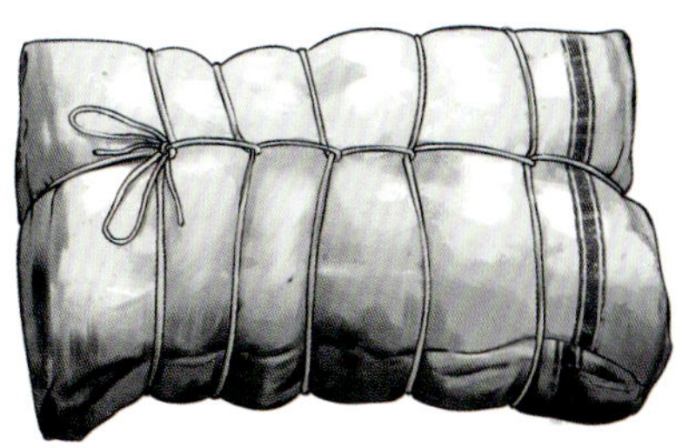

2. Roll the roast up in the towel tightly like a burrito from the short side, tucking in the sides as you go. Next, truss the wrapped roast (see page 129) securely with kitchen twine.

WHOLE VEGETABLES ROASTED IN COALS

SERVES 4 TO 6

If you've got some vegetarians running around, this is how you can introduce them to the joys of caveman cooking. In all seriousness, cooking whole vegetables in coals is a gorgeous preparation. When you dig out the finished product, it seems both elegant and ancestral. It's as though you're beholding some edible time capsule left over from humanity's earliest experiments with cooking. At home or when car camping you'll want a coal rake, long-handled tongs, and leather grilling gloves. In the backcountry, you'll have to do what our ancestors did thousands of years ago—use a stick.

Approximate weights are listed to help adjust for cooking times. Any size will do, but if they are smaller or larger than below, it will take them less or more time, respectively, to cook.

1 butternut squash, whole and scrubbed (about 1 pound)

2 acorn squashes, whole and scrubbed (about 1 pound each)

4 beets, tops removed for another use, scrubbed well (about 2 to 4 ounces each)

2 garnet yams, scrubbed well (9 to 14 ounces each)

2 large potatoes, scrubbed well (2 pounds each)

PREPARE THE VEGETABLES: Wrap the beets and potatoes in foil. You can lightly oil the vegetables before wrapping them; the foil tends to release more easily and the skins become crisper. It also works without this step—do whatever is easiest.

PREPARING AND MAINTAINING THE COALS AND FIRE. Prepare a medium fire inside a stone circle, with plenty of wood on standby. When the logs have burned and are turning into coals, use a shovel to arrange the smoldering wood around the perimeter of your fire circle (if you're using a fire pit, you'll want the logs on the edge of the pit). Move the hot coals to the opening in the center. Nestle all the vegetables among these coals, and distribute some of the coals on top of the vegetables. You're using the direct heat from the coals and the ambient heat of the smoldering logs to cook the vegetables, so, if needed, replace the latter with fresh logs to keep the fire going. Using tongs or a coal shovel, rotate the vegetables—as one side becomes charred, rotate them so the non-charred side is toward the hottest coals. Flip and turn the vegetables in foil frequently, every 10 minutes. Crush the spent logs with your shovel and toss the resulting hot coals over the vegetables. Continue this process throughout the cooking time.

CHECKING FOR DONENESS. Use a paring knife or a hunting knife to check the doneness of the vegetables. The knife should be able to go through the foil and in and out with zero resistance. The vegetables cook at the following approximate rates: acorn and butternut squash, about 30 minutes; russet potatoes, sweet potatoes, and yams, about 35 minutes; beets, about 40 minutes. Times may vary.

When done, remove the vegetables to a baking sheet using tongs. With a damp cloth, carefully wipe the ash off the skins. Carefully use a sharp knife to cut open the vegetables without foil. Watch out—they'll be hot on the inside! For the squashes, slice open and scoop out the seeds and pulp using a spoon. Peel and slice the squashes, or spoon the cooked flesh out of the charred peel and transfer it to a bowl. At this point you can eat the vegetables or mash and chop them. For the vegetables wrapped in foil, carefully unwrap them; if the skins are charred, cut away the badly charred portions. Otherwise, cut them into wedges to serve. For all of the vegetables, season with salt and pepper, drizzle with olive oil, top with crumbled cheese or a sauce or dressing of your choice.

ALSO WORKS WITH. *Any whole squash with firm skin, such as butternut, acorn, delicata, spaghetti, kabocha, sugar pumpkins, sweet dumpling, and red kuri; or root vegetables including sweet potatoes, yams, yucca, russet potatoes, beets of all sizes, carrots, and parsnips.*

COOK'S NOTE. *While campsites are the more common location for this technique, it also works great as a backyard recipe on a charcoal grill or fire pit.*

DEER SHOULDER IN A BARREL

SERVES 10 TO 15 WITH ACCOMPANIMENTS

1 small deer shoulder, roughly 6 to 8 pounds, sawed into 1-pound bone-in pieces, at room temperature.

1 cup bear grease, duck fat, beef tallow, pork lard, butter, extra-virgin olive oil, or other fat

4 potatoes, sweet potatoes, yuccas, or beets, cut in half

3 carrots, whole

2 large hard-skinned squashes, such as butternut, acorn, kabocha, halved, skin-on, seeds scooped out

2 bulbs fennel, tops removed and reserved, cut into 3 or 4 pieces

Kosher salt, freshly ground black pepper, or any dry rub for seasoning

3 shallots, peeled and halved, or a bunch of scallions, trimmed

2 heads garlic, cut in half horizontally and kept whole

3 unripe apples or pears (optional)

2 bunches cilantro, parsley, or other fragrant herb (optional)

Condiments from page 177 for serving

Cultures all around the world celebrate special occasions by burying food beneath the ground in a bed of hot coals and rocks. In Hawaii, they have kalua pig. The Peruvians of the Andes have a traditional preparation known as pachamanca, where assortments of meat and vegetables (sometimes including guinea pig) are buried in an earthen oven and covered with heated rocks. There's a traditional Mayan preparation called cochinita pibil, in which a suckling pig is wrapped in leaves and cooked underground. In southern Chile, along the Chiloé Archipelago, they have a dish of shellfish, meat, and vegetables cooked in an earthen oven. And in North America, this grouping includes traditional in-ground barbecue pits popular across the southern United States, and clambakes, constructed in fires in the sand on the shores of New England. The communal quality of these meals is easily understood. The anticipation of unveiling the food is best shared with friends and loved ones, and the methods are conducive to cooking huge batches of food that can serve a crowd.

For this recipe, you don't necessarily need a place where you can dig a big hole in the ground. All you need is a large metal drum, barrel, or even an old metal wheelbarrow. In addition to a deer shoulder, we use a lot of vegetables. Go ahead and try any combination of squashes or pumpkins, root vegetables, onions, apples, pears, cauliflower, or fennel. The veggies and fruits will soften in the heat, and the resulting meat will be fall-off-the-bone tender. As for your cooking vessel, avoid any container that once held hazardous materials—even if you've cleaned it. This whole process will take you roughly 6 to 8 hours, so start early and plan your day around it.

ALSO WORKS WITH. *Shoulders of sheep, goat, hog, or any big game animals including black bear. Remove the shank if the shoulder is too big for your barrel.*

TO BUILD THE FIRE. Add a couple of inches of soil to the bottom of the drum and arrange your rocks with even spacing on top of the soil. Kindle a fire on top of the rocks and let it rip. You want to burn as much wood as quickly as possible in the drum. (That's why smaller-diameter wood is better; it gets burning quicker.) Let the coals fill in around the rocks and keep adding wood. Periodically chop at the burning wood and coals with a shovel to create a dense layer of coals. You'll want a layer of 6 to 7 inches of live coals in the drum before you're done burning.

Meanwhile, wet the cloth and ring it out so it's damp but not soaking. Lay the cloth on a work surface. Season the meat and vegetables liberally with salt, pepper, or a seasoning rub. Slather the meat with the lard and arrange the shallots or scallions in the center of the cloth. Top with the fennel and then the meat. Surround the meat with the other vegetables and garlic, nestling them together. Add the apples or pears and herbs on top if using. Fold the cloth to make a packet enclosing the meat and vegetables. (Imagine you're folding up a burrito.)

When the coals are ready, cover them with a 2-inch layer of soil and pat it down. Lay the cloth packet containing the meat and vegetables on top of the soil, and then cover that up with more soil. Ideally, you'll fill the drum to within a couple of inches of the top. That'll give you plenty of insulation.

Kindle a small fire of coals or sticks on top of the soil. This may or may not be necessary, but I like to do it to help heat up the soil in a hurry. Keep this fire lit for about an hour or so and then allow it to die out.

Wait around 6 to 8 hours. When you're ready to serve, use a shovel and heavy leather grilling gloves to uncover the cloth package. Brush the top of the package as clean as possible before lifting it out. (It should still be hot, so be careful.) Move the package to your work surface and carefully unfold the cloth to avoid getting any dirt on the food. The squashes and potatoes should all be tender and soft. Ideally the meat should be fork tender and close to falling off the bone. If you were to check the internal temperature of the meat, you'd be looking for a temperature somewhere around 170°F or higher.

Feed a crowd and serve with condiments like Chimichurri, Salsa Verde, Red Pepper Aioli, or Harissa Aioli (pages 71, 350, 115, and 275) or the sauce of your choice.

SPECIAL EQUIPMENT

You'll want half the barrel; it doesn't matter if it has a bottom or not. It just needs to be a cylinder that's about 22 inches in diameter and 16 inches high. (You can use anything fireproof that you have with similar dimensions.) For ventilation, drill eight or nine 1-inch holes around the periphery that will become the bottom of your barrel roaster.

1 large piece of cloth, approximately 4 x 4 feet. Cotton tablecloths or untreated canvas are ideal (you can also use raw untreated burlap, or even thawed frozen banana leaves); keep in mind they will impart their flavor and aroma to the food.

A wheelbarrow load of hardwood firewood, split into small-diameter pieces. Ideally, you'd have a wheelbarrow full of firewood pieces that are 16 inches long and just 2 x 2 inches.

6 to 8 grapefruit-sized rocks. Get these from dry ground, not beneath water. Submerged rocks are dangerous because the water trapped inside will expand when heated and can send shards of rock blasting in all directions.

A few 5-gallon buckets of soil or sand. (You want it dry or semi-dry; you do not want mud.)

CLAY'S BEAR GREASE DUTCH OVEN BISCUITS

Clay Newcomb

In the South, biscuits accompany just about every meal. At my home here in the Ozarks, we make our biscuits with bear grease. Going back to Daniel Boone's frontier era, there's a long history of rural mountain folk using rendered bear fat in place of butter or pork lard since it remains shelf stable for over a year without refrigeration. I've learned that the fat from a fall black bear that has been gorging on acorns and berries is best; it renders down into a rich, golden oil that turns a pearly white when it cools. Bear grease is perfect not only for frying and especially for baking, but it's also rumored to cure baldness and forecast the weather! Folklore aside, bear grease is an important part of my heritage, and we cook with it almost every day. And there's no better way to end a long day of riding mules around in the Ozarks than with a plateful of warm, flaky bear-grease biscuits.

I usually double the recipe below. These can be baked in the coals in a Dutch oven with a lid or in a conventional oven in a baking dish or on a baking stone.

MAKES FIVE 3- TO 4-INCH BISCUITS

2 cups all-purpose flour, plus more for dusting

2½ tablespoons baking powder

1 teaspoon kosher salt

⅓ cup bear grease, chilled

5 tablespoons plus 1 teaspoon (⅓ stick) unsalted butter, chilled, plus more for greasing

½ cup milk

SPECIAL EQUIPMENT

10- or 12-inch-diameter (4- or 6-quart) shallow Dutch oven with lid for coal cooking

In a large mixing bowl, combine all the dry ingredients. Add the cold bear grease and grate the cold butter into the dry ingredients and lightly mix them in with a spoon. Then, using a pastry cutter, blend the fat into the dry ingredients until the mixture is clumpy but combined. Overall, you want to handle the dough as little as possible. Once you've reached the desired consistency, add the milk and mix together with your hands or a spoon until it becomes a dough.

Lightly flour a cold surface. Using your hands, place the dough on the surface and flatten it. Fold the dough over once (like a book), flatten it, fold it over again the opposite way, and flatten it. Repeat this three more times, making the final thickness about the height you want your biscuits to be. They won't rise much.

Cut the biscuits out with the open end of a small mason jar or circular cookie cutter. You should get 5 or 6 biscuits total. Chill the biscuits while you make your fire.

Prepare a campfire or a charcoal chimney for coal cooking in a fire pit or stone-lined fire circle. While the fire matures, prepare the Dutch oven for cooking. Using butter, thoroughly grease the Dutch oven and arrange the biscuits in the bottom. If you want soft-sided biscuits, keep the biscuits away from the sides of the Dutch oven. If you want hard, crispy sides, let them touch. Using the chart on page 152 as a guide for heat, place 10 coals in a circle on the ground and set the Dutch oven on top of the coals. Add 19 coals on top of the Dutch oven to create an oven that is approximately 425°F.

Check the biscuits after 12 minutes, but they may take as long as 20 minutes. They should be golden brown on top and browned but not scorched on the bottom. Eat them warm with butter, jam, or honey with your favorite camp meals.

BEAR
GREASE

HOW TO MAKE BEAR OIL

Clay Newcomb

At one time, making bear oil was a common practice among rural homesteads. But as a result of urbanization and industrialized food production over the last century, grain-based oils have all but eliminated the demand for this multipurpose fat in American kitchens. Today, the only place you're likely to see it is on the shelves of a few bear hunters who understand how valuable this resource is. Bear oil doesn't go rancid as quickly as pork lard and can be used for any type of cooking application. In my opinion, it's the best oil for frying, as well as making pastries, cookies, and piecrusts. Besides being a versatile cooking oil, it can also be used to lubricate guns and knives and to preserve leather.

HARVESTING THE BEAR FAT. In the fall, adult bears will have substantial amounts of whitish fat in between the hide and muscle. They usually have less fat in spring, but it's still worth harvesting. After skinning, use a sharp knife to carve off chunks of fat. You'll find most of the largest, thickest reserves of fat will be around the rump of the bear, but you'll find sizable external and internal deposits elsewhere on bears that are in exceptional condition. Remove as much fat as you can, but try not to get any meat mixed in with it.

Put all the fat in a game bag and get it cooled down immediately. Bear fat has a very low melting point, so if you can't get it to a refrigerator quickly, hang it in a cool, shady, breezy spot or put it in a cooler full of ice (keep the fat-filled game bag dry in a garbage bag). You can render the fat fresh or freeze multiple layers of big chunks together in a vac-sealed bag to reduce the potential for freezer burn. It's best to use it within 6 months of freezing.

PREPARING THE BEAR FAT. From frozen, I let the bear fat thaw about halfway before cubing it into 1-inch pieces. By cutting the fat when it's just above freezing, it slices more easily. You can render the cubes as is, but you'll get a lot more oil by grinding the fat after cubing. You'll also get better results if your grinder parts are thoroughly chilled in the freezer before grinding the fat.

RENDERING THE BEAR FAT. For rendering big batches of bear fat, I work outside with a propane outdoor cooker and a big heavy-duty aluminum cooking pot like you'd use to deep-fry a turkey. A low and slow approach with lots of stirring is the name of the game. If the fat gets too hot, it will develop a slightly burnt flavor. I prefer to cook bear fat at 225°F (use a candy thermometer to check the temperature). The slower you cook, the clearer the oil will be, and at 225°F, you can render down a pound of bear fat in about 25 minutes. It's best to work in batches, so be sure to plan your time accordingly. Stir constantly and use a wire strainer ladle to remove any large pieces of burnt cracklings that are floating on the surface. Leave the oil on the heat source until 90 percent of all solids are gone. A pound of ground bear fat should produce roughly one pint of bear oil, and slightly less if you're cubing it.

STORING THE BEAR GREASE. To store the grease, I mostly use half-pint common glass canning jars. I've found this is a convenient portion size, but pint-sized jars might be better if you have a lot of fat. Using a metal cooking funnel and triple-folded cheesecloth to strain it, carefully pour the hot oil into the jars. If you don't strain the oil, small, burnt particles of cracklings and meat will give the oil an off-flavor. I usually let the oil cool down for about 10 minutes with the lid off the jars, then put the lid on before storing it on a cool shelf in the cellar. You can also store it in the refrigerator or freezer.

Clay Newcomb is a seventh-generation Arkansan who lives on a farm in the Ouachita Mountains with his family and a whole bunch of critters. A hunter, mule skinner, curious naturalist, and student of rural culture, Clay is the host of MeatEater's Bear Grease *podcast.*

GOOSE AND DUMPLINGS

MAKES ABOUT 6 CUPS STEW AND 20 DUMPLINGS; SERVES 4 TO 6

This is a traditional-style bird-and-dumpling recipe, though we're using geese here instead of the chicken that's popular across the Midwest where many German immigrants landed. If you're intimidated by baking, don't worry. The dumplings are biscuit-like and are simply dropped onto the surface of the stew to be cooked. This is one that also works well in an oven at home if you're just trying to move through a stockpile of frozen goose breasts. The mushrooms add robust flavor to this dish.

STEW

4 tablespoons (½ stick) unsalted butter

1 tablespoon extra-virgin olive oil

2 prepared skinless goose breasts, lightly pounded with a mallet to tenderize, then cut into 1-inch cubes (about 1 pound 6 ounces total)

Kosher salt

Freshly ground black pepper

2 celery ribs, sliced ½ inch thick

1 large yellow onion, sliced ½ inch thick

3 medium carrots, sliced ½ inch thick

8 ounces cremini mushrooms (or foraged mushrooms), sliced ½ inch thick

2 bushy fresh thyme sprigs

1 fresh sage sprig

3 tablespoons all-purpose flour

4 to 6 cups blonde game stock or low-sodium chicken broth

2 tablespoons picked fresh flat-leaf parsley or celery leaves, for garnish (optional)

DUMPLINGS

2 cups (9.8 ounces) all-purpose flour, scooped and leveled

1 tablespoon baking powder

¾ teaspoon kosher salt

5 large fresh sage leaves, finely chopped (about 2 tablespoons)

1 cup milk

PREPARE THE COALS. Prepare a campfire or a charcoal chimney with briquettes in a fire pit or stone-lined fire circle. The following instructions are for a 10-inch diameter (5-quart deep) Dutch oven. Use the chart on page 152 as a guide for the number of coals needed for your pot size to reach 375°F to 400°F. For a 10-inch pot, place 25 coals in a circle on the ground and set a Dutch oven over top of the coals. Start another chimney with 25 more coals.

FOR THE STEW. In the Dutch oven, melt 3 tablespoons of the butter with the oil. Season the goose with ¾ teaspoon salt and a few grinds of pepper. Add half the goose to the hot pot and cook until deeply browned on all sides, roughly 5 to 8 minutes. Remove to a plate. Add the remaining goose and cook until browned, another 5 to 8 minutes or so. Remove to the plate. Add the celery, onion, carrot, mushrooms, thyme and sage sprigs, 2 teaspoons salt, and a few grinds of pepper. Cook, stirring often, until softened and beginning to brown, 10 to 12 minutes. Add the remaining 1 tablespoon butter to melt, and then stir in the flour to coat the vegetables. Cook for 1 minute, stirring, to cook the flour. Return the goose and any juices to the pot. Add the game stock and 1 teaspoon salt. Stir to incorporate the ingredients and any flour stuck on the bottom of the pan. Using a leather grilling glove, remove the pot to the side to refresh the coals.

Arrange 8 new hot coals in the bottom of the fire pit. Place the pot over the coals, cover with the lid, and place the remaining coals on the lid. Let the stew come up to a boil (skim any scum that rises), and cover and simmer for about 1 hour, adding more stock or water if the liquid level gets low. Once the coals have died down, replenish them and cook until the goose meat is somewhat tender, for approximately another hour.

FOR THE DUMPLINGS. Mix together the flour, baking powder, salt, and sage in a medium bowl. Add the milk and stir to combine (see Make Ahead).

Remove the lid and make sure the goose is submerged in the stew. With two spoons, drop golf-ball-sized dollops of dough on the top of the stew. Return the lid, add new coals if needed, and cook until the dumplings are tender and cooked through, 15 to 20 minutes. Serve immediately, ladled in bowls and topped with fresh parsley or celery leaves, if desired.

MAKE AHEAD. *You can make this stew at home and cook the dumplings on-site. Baking powder reacts when it comes in contact with wetness and heat, so mix the dry ingredients at home but wait to add the milk until you're on-site.*

DUTCH OVEN RABBIT BOUDIN WITH RED CABBAGE

Jean-Paul Bourgeois

Rabbit hunting with hounds is woven into the rural culture of the South. It's how I honed my shotgunning skills as a boy in Louisiana. It wasn't easy hitting a rabbit as it carved and cut through the shin-high grasses that surrounded the local sugarcane fields. I remember doing a lot of shooting, but most of the time I missed, so coming home with two or three cottontails was regarded as a big success. I was proud to contribute to the dinner table, and a couple rabbits could easily feed the whole family—if we used every edible part. This recipe honors those meals, by making boudin ("BOO-dan" as they say it in Louisiana) with the offal and leg meat, which then gets stuffed into the saddle portion of the rabbit. Boudin is a comforting staple of Cajun country; it is a cooked sausage traditionally made from pork, pork hearts and livers, and cooked rice, plus seasonings and aromatics. Boudin is often linked in hog casings, but it's also used as a stuffing for birds or, in this case, a cottontail rabbit saddle. One bite of this recipe and I'm right back in those cane fields of my youth, which is the ultimate compliment to the rich culinary traditions of my home state.

SERVES 4

RABBIT STOCK AND MEAT

2 whole skinned, cleaned rabbits, front and hind legs separated, saddles reserved

1 cup white wine

1 large yellow onion, quartered

1 carrot, cut into chunks

2 celery ribs, cut into large chunks

4 bay leaves

BOUDIN STUFFING

1 cup uncooked long-grain white rice

1 pound rabbit livers or chicken livers

Kosher salt and freshly ground black pepper

2 tablespoons bacon grease or vegetable oil

1 medium onion, diced small

2 garlic cloves, minced

1 bunch green onions (scallions), thinly sliced

½ bunch flat-leaf parsley, finely chopped

Hot sauce (I prefer Tabasco for this recipe, but Louisiana Brand and Crystal work great as well)

BRAISE

2 tablespoons bacon grease or vegetable oil

2 slices bacon, diced

¼ head shredded red cabbage (2 to 3 cups)

2 garlic cloves

½ medium onion, sliced

Hot sauce (optional)

1 tablespoon Dijon mustard (optional)

SPECIAL EQUIPMENT

Meat grinder

Butcher's twine

10- or 12-inch diameter (5- or 8-quart) deep cast-iron Dutch oven

FOR THE RABBIT STOCK. In a stockpot, place the cleaned rabbit legs, the wine, and water to cover. Add the onion, carrot, and celery (the mirepoix) and the bay leaves. Bring the liquids to a boil and then simmer for 1½ hours, or until the leg meat can be pulled from the bone. Once the rabbit is tender, allow it to cool in the broth until safe to handle with your hands.

Meanwhile, cook the rice. In a small pot, combine rice and 2 cups water over high heat. When the water boils, reduce the heat to low and cover. Cook for 20 minutes, or until fully done. Set the cooked rice aside; keep warm.

Recipe continues

FOR THE BOUDIN STUFFING. Season the rabbit livers with salt and pepper. (You can also add rabbit kidneys and hearts at this step.) In a hot skillet, add the grease and the rabbit livers and sear them on one side roughly 3 minutes. Rabbit livers should be cooked no more than medium and ideally still mid-rare when you remove them from the skillet. Set the livers aside. Add the onion, garlic, and green onions to the same skillet and sauté on medium-high heat until soft for 3 to 5 minutes.

Add 2 cups of the stock from the cooled rabbit-cooking liquid and continue to cook for 10 minutes, reducing the liquid by half. Once reduced, set aside.

Remove the rest of the rabbit pieces from the liquid and pick the meat from the bones. Reserve all of your rabbit-braising liquid (reheat and keep it hot). Roughly chop the pulled rabbit meat until it resembles coarse ground meat. Roughly chop the rabbit livers until they are a coarse mush.

ASSEMBLE THE BOUDIN SAUSAGE. In a large mixing bowl, combine the cooked hot rice, chopped rabbit livers, chopped rabbit meat, and onions with the liquid from the skillet. With a wooden spoon, begin to paddle your boudin together (mimicking the action of a standing mixer paddle). You will need to add reserved rabbit stock to the mixture as you work your boudin in the bowl. Be aggressive. The combination of starches being released from the rice, the silkiness of the livers, and hot rabbit stock is what gives boudin its iconic texture. The more stock you use, the more "wet" the mixture will be. For this recipe, you want the final product to resemble a thick rice pudding while it's still warm. Season the mixture with salt, pepper, and a couple dashes of hot sauce. Stir in the parsley and cool the mixture immediately (spread it out on a rimmed baking sheet, if needed, to expedite the process).

STUFF THE SADDLES. Once the boudin is cooled, stuff your rabbit saddles generously with the boudin, leaving enough space for the belly to overlap slightly (you'll use about 1½ cups boudin for the filling give or take). With butcher's twine, truss your saddles, tying knots every inch. (You will not use all of the boudin. See Cook's Note on uses for the remainder and how to store it.) Season the stuffed saddles with salt and pepper.

FOR THE BRAISE. Prepare a campfire with coals. Bring the Dutch oven out to the campfire and put about 10 coals underneath. Add the grease and sear the stuffed rabbit saddles until browned on all sides. Once well browned, remove the stuffed saddles to a plate and add the bacon pieces, stirring to render the fat. Add the cabbage, garlic, and onion, stirring to coat them with the fat. Add 1 cup of the rabbit stock. Place the saddles on top of your cabbage along with any juices that have collected and cover with the lid.

Add 14 coals on top of the lid (see the chart on page 152 for specifics) to approximate a 350°F oven temperature, and roast until the loin is cooked through and the filling is hot—the internal temp should register at least 135°F. Begin checking about 15 minutes in. It should be fully cooked between 25 and 35 minutes, but it could take longer.

Serve with hot sauce and Dijon mustard (if using).

COOK'S NOTE. *Should you have any extra boudin, vac-seal it as bulk sausage or patties, or throw it into a hog casing if you want to go through the effort. The sausage will keep in the fridge for up to 1 week and in the freezer for 6 months.*

Born and raised in southern Louisiana, Chef Jean-Paul Bourgeois spent his childhood surrounded by family, friends, and great Southern cooking. His mission is focused on honoring and celebrating humble beginning experiences with others.

ION R1

04 ON THE BURNER

It's a bit of an oversimplification, but I've come to think of my own camping activities as being divided into two categories. The first category is camping for the sake of camping. I do this all the time with my family and we love it. Someone will say, "Let's go camping this weekend," and everyone knows what they're thinking about: hikes, looking at the stars, campfires, reading in a hammock, maybe some casual fishing. The second category of camping is when you go camping in order to accomplish something else that happens to occur in a location that requires you to camp. Let's say you want to hunt caribou on Alaska's North Slope or run a raft down the Salmon River Gorge. The only way to pull that stuff off is to camp out, though the camping portion of the trip is secondary to the primary mission.

Each version of camping has its own culinary traditions and necessities. When you're camping for the sake of camping, there's time to luxuriate in the process of cooking. You can pack along a carful of gear—griddles, grills, propane campstoves, kettles—and make fun stuff, including most of the delicious preparations found within this book. Things like Nutella and Banana Iron Pies (see page 321), Venison Chili (page 215), Ginger Catfish Stir-Fry (page 220), and The Late Eugene Groters's Beer and Apple Pancakes (page 245). When you're camping in order to accomplish something else, cooking processes can get stripped down to their bare essentials. Just how bare depends on how much time you have to cook and how much room you have for hauling cooking gear. On that rafting trip down the Salmon River Gorge, you could live large if you've got a big raft and you pack along coolers of produce, fresh herbs, and meat; a bin of sauces and seasonings; a grill and utensils; and a spinning rod rigged for smallmouth bass. When hunting for caribou on the North Slope, you might be limited to a backpacking stove and quart-sized pot. Making dinner comes down to boiling creek water in order to rehydrate a sack of dried soup to be eaten inside a wet sleeping bag while mosquitoes and gnats maul the tops of your ears.

I picked up a lot of my outdoor skills and habits from my father, but this notion of mine about the two types of camp cooking is not one of those things. My dad had only a single mode as camp cook, and it didn't matter whether we were camping for the sake of camping or camping for the sake of hunting and fishing. As close as he could, he would replicate a home kitchen that was centered around a stovetop. He fought with the infantry in World War II and spent several summers canoeing the Boundary Waters between northern Minnesota and Canada with a troop of Eagle Scouts. Exposure to these rule-oriented, fastidious organizations led him to believe that there was one right way to do things and many wrong ways. The right way to set up a camp kitchen was to begin with the placement of a propane-powered two-burner Coleman campstove. Above this, you needed a spice rack along with a roll of paper towels suspended horizontally. Beneath the stove was a hanging rack of spoons and spatulas. Off to one side you wanted a double sink made of plastic basins mounted on a bench. To the other side were plastic milk crates stacked on their sides to form a bank of shelves for dried goods and cookware. Conveniently placed coolers functioned as a fridge, from which you'd draw butter and eggs. He'd even make a towel rack. In inclement weather, the kitchen got overhead protection from a woven poly tarp that he referred to as a "cook fly." Setting this whole thing up would take the better part of a day. Taking it down and packing it away took hours.

At home, my dad didn't do much of anything to assist my mom in the kitchen. He was in charge of fish fries, made using a deep fryer that was set up in our garage, but that was about the extent of his culinary responsibilities. In the woods, however, he was comfortable enough with pots, skillets, and griddles that you wondered why he never touched them at home. No disrespect to my mom, but he managed to cook better breakfasts in camp than my mom cared to make in the house—perhaps because cooking breakfast was a novelty to him, while my mom had long ago burned out. He made eggs-in-the-hole, beer-apple pancakes, and smoked trout hash. Standing on bare ground, with my head touching the low-slung cook fly and the morning sun shining through the trees, I loved to watch these meals take shape. I'd eat them seated in a folding chair, my plate propped on my knees.

Those early days of camping taught me to associate the use of standard cookware as much with the outdoors as indoors. Of course, there are certain things you're never gonna want to make outside. Things like soufflés or demi-glace come to mind. But other foods actually seem more fitting to the outdoors than they do the indoors, such as pan-fried trout. Looking back on my youth, I've come to see that the equipment my family used in those early days was hardly ideal. Our camp cookware consisted of thin, banged-up aluminum pots and pans that heated unevenly and were a major pain in the ass to clean. The cast-iron and nonstick camp cookware that is widely available today is so much better. You can get good results even with delicate foods, and you don't need to spend an hour trying to scrape away cooking debris with a Brillo pad. When it comes to gear, we're living in the good old days of outdoor cooking.

But don't go thinking that there's no adventure to be had while using cookware in the outdoors. A blackened cast-iron skillet laid on a bed of glowing coals is one of the most beautiful sights in the world of food. The flavors that can be achieved with this method will taste even better than they look—and it's a technique that is unique to outdoor cooking. This chapter will show how it's all done, from breakfast to dinner and from fires to the campstoves. We'll even show you how to throw the best fish fry of your life. Whether you're camping for the sake of camping or camping because you have to, you'll be slinging the finest grub ever. You won't even notice the skeeters.

LODGE

SKILLETS, GRIDDLES, AND POTS: WHAT YOU NEED TO KNOW

There's a lot more to cooking outside than just grilling and smoking. Sometimes, you want to bring the type of cooking you'd normally do on your indoor range into the outdoors, but you want it to be easy and efficient. It could be something big like a batch of chili that will feed a bunch of tailgaters or something more elaborate like making paella on the beach. No matter the specifics, you're going to need at least a basic selection of cookware, including pots, pans, and griddles. From a practical standpoint, you simply can't get by without this stuff if you want to boil, simmer, sauté, fry, or even bake foods outside. Even if all you want to do is reheat a precooked, vac-sealed meal (see page 217), you'll need to warm it up in a pot of hot water. I know plenty of people who at least partially outfit their outdoor cooking kits with pots and pans that have been retired from normal kitchen duty, and this works okay in some cases. I've also seen my fair share of meals burnt to a crisp because they were cooked in the cheap aluminum cookware you'll find in the camping aisle at discount stores.

Don't take that to mean you need to spend a fortune, but you will be way better off with a dedicated set of quality pots and pans that are built well enough to withstand the rigors of outdoor cooking. And remember that whatever specific items you ultimately end up including in your arsenal will depend a lot on what recipes you'll be preparing and for how many people. Aluminum and stainless-steel cookware with or without a nonstick coating is suitable as long as you're working with a burner that mimics an indoor stovetop. If you'll be doing some of your cooking over a campfire, carbon-steel cookware is a better choice. And, of course, the same kind of cast-iron skillets, griddles, and Dutch ovens that American settlers were using on the frontier two hundred years ago are still the most versatile choice for all types of outdoor cooking.

In some cases, however, you can't get by without a special piece of equipment that's designed for certain outdoor cooking applications. For instance, a big crayfish or seafood boil requires a pot that goes way beyond the normal stockpots you might have in your cupboard. Likewise, standard kitchen cookware won't cut it on a backcountry camping trip; at a minimum you'll want a small, ultralight, nonstick titanium or anodized aluminum pot. The following illustrations cover a range of common outdoor cooking techniques that utilize some type of pot, pan, or griddle.

Propane Stoves

Various types of two-burner propane stoves are far and away the most popular workhorse cooking appliance for most car campers. As noted earlier, fire bans make them a must-have for camp cooking in the West. You may need to account for the smaller surface area and lower Btu output of some models when choosing which size pots and pans will work best.

Outdoor Cookers

You can do a lot with these simple single propane burners and a giant pot. They have a very high Btu output, so they're great for quickly steaming crustaceans and shellfish or getting a big kettle of grease hot enough for deep-frying. The adjustable burner can also be turned down low enough to simmer stews and chilis.

Griddles

The two-burner stove shown here has a convenient built-in griddle system that makes it unnecessary to pack a separate griddle on car-camping trips. However, it's still worth owning a cast-iron skillet for other cooking setups. If nothing else, they make flipping pancakes, eggs, and burgers a lot easier.

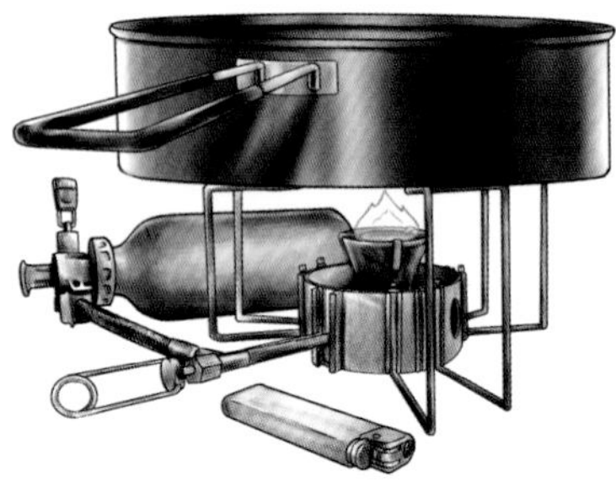

Backcountry Stoves

Prepackaged freeze-dried or dehydrated meals make up the majority of meals that are "cooked" with backpacking stoves. But don't take that to mean that fresh ingredients are off the menu. I've used my campstove to cook everything from deer tenderloins to foraged mushrooms to cubes of bear meat. Just remember, backpacking pots and pans like the one pictured here are designed specifically for use with an appropriate stove. Avoid the temptation to cook over fires or hot coals with them.

CAST-IRON PRIMER

Cast-iron cookware has been around so long that it's developed an aura of mystique and romance in the culinary space. Stories about Grandma's favorite skillet abound, and there are entire cookbooks devoted to cast iron. You'll find plenty of those kinds of recipes in this book, but we're more focused on the practical than the romantic. For starters, cast iron holds and distributes heat better than many other types of metal cookware, which makes it the ideal vessel for everything from searing steaks to simmering stews. It's also indestructible; cast iron easily withstands the abuse that would otherwise destroy more typical household cookware if it was used to cook over open fires and coals. And the great thing about cast iron is you don't have to spend a bunch of money to reap its benefits. If you're looking for something affordable, you won't be disappointed with cast iron from Lodge or Camp Chef. Garage sales and flea markets are a great place to find inexpensive cast-iron cookware, too.

For your camp kitchen, start with the basics: a skillet, a Dutch oven, and a griddle. A 10-inch skillet is big enough for just a couple people; otherwise a 12-incher is the way to go. A Dutch oven in the 5- to 7-quart range is ideal unless you regularly cook for large groups. Cast-iron griddles are available in round, rectangular, and square shapes. A rectangular model that's roughly 10 × 20 inches will rest nicely on most two-burner stoves. Go with a square 10 × 10-inch version for use on a single burner. Regardless of size, make sure to get a griddle with a raised edge that prevents grease from dripping over the side.

Most cast-iron cookware comes "seasoned" right out of the box. If your cookware didn't come preseasoned, you'll need to do it following the manufacturer's instructions. A seasoned cast-iron pan has been oiled and heated to achieve a semi-permanent, glossy nonstick coating. You may also need to re-season a well-used piece of cast iron cookware now and again. To do this, just wipe the pan with a thin layer of vegetable oil and place it upside down on a baking sheet in a 350-degree oven for an hour.

I mentioned earlier that cast iron is indestructible, but that's only the case if you take proper care with it. Cast-iron cookware's only weaknesses are moisture and neglect. If exposed to moisture for as little as a few hours, cast iron will rust, and the pan will need to be thoroughly cleaned with steel wool or a wire brush and re-seasoned.

To avoid this scenario, cast-iron cookware should be washed and dried after each use. You may have been told the harsh chemicals in dish soap will destroy cast iron's seasoned nonstick coating and impart off-putting flavors into the metal itself. While you can often get away with just wiping cast iron cookware down with paper towels or a rag, you can in fact wash it with soap if warranted. Just use the minimum amount of soap necessary, rinse thoroughly, dry, and wipe down with a lightly oiled cloth.

SIMMS

SPICY FISH CAKES

MAKES 12 CAKES; SERVES 6

I'm a big fan of crab cakes and fish cakes. One thing I like about them is that you can stretch a small amount of seafood into a much more substantial offering, thanks to the added ingredients that go into the cake. I shared one of the versions that I like, Sucker Balls with Magic Sauce, in *The MeatEater Fish and Game Cookbook*. This recipe for spicy fish cakes uses fresh fish fillets. There are also a couple of ways you can make these in advance for a camping trip (see the Make Ahead note below). While the standard practice is to top fish cakes with a squeeze of lemon and dab of tartar sauce, here I've paired them with a tomato mayo inspired by Escoffier's variation of béarnaise called "sauce choron." It's rich and tangy and works great on grilled or foil-packed fish, too.

TOMATO MAYO SAUCE

Makes ½ cup

½ cup mayonnaise

2 tablespoons tomato puree, or 1 tablespoon tomato paste (not tomato sauce)

1 small garlic clove

½ teaspoon dried tarragon

FISH CAKES

2 pounds skinless fish fillets

3 tablespoons spicy brown mustard

2 large eggs

4 scallions, minced

4 small serrano chiles, minced

2 lemons, zested and cut into wedges

4 teaspoons Creole Seasoning, homemade (page 347) or store-bought

1½ teaspoons kosher salt

3¼ cups panko

6 tablespoons vegetable oil, plus more as needed for cooking

FOR THE SAUCE. Stir together the mayo and tomato puree in a small bowl. Grate the garlic into the sauce and add the tarragon. Stir to combine. Cover and refrigerate until ready to use.

FOR THE FISH CAKES. Cut the fish fillets into 2-inch pieces (don't worry about pin bones in small fish) and place them in a food processor fitted with a metal blade. Add the eggs to the processor, lock on the lid, and pulse the machine 25 to 30 times, until the mixture resembles a slightly coarse sausage filling. Add the mustard, scallions, serranos, lemon zest, Creole Seasoning, salt, and ¾ cup of the panko, then pulse the machine another 10 to 15 times, until all the seasonings are fully distributed. If you're cooking the fish cakes right away, transfer the mixture to an airtight container and refrigerate the mixture for at least 30 minutes before making cakes and cooking them; to cook them later, see Make Ahead.

Place the remaining 2½ cups panko on a large plate. Divide the chilled fish cake mixture evenly into 12 portions. Form each into a 2½-inch-wide, 1-inch-thick cake, gently squeezing and rotating the mixture while shaping so it holds together. Pat the edges to smooth them and place the cakes on the plate of panko. Completely coat each fish cake with panko, gently pressing the panko into the cake.

Heat a large cast-iron skillet over medium-low heat on a propane campstove for about 3 minutes to warm it up. Add 3 tablespoons of the oil and tilt the skillet to coat.

Place 6 cakes in the skillet. Cook for about 6 minutes, or until browned on the bottom. Carefully flip and cook for another 5 minutes, or until browned. Remove the fish cakes from the pan and cool on a wire rack. Season with a pinch of salt. Add remaining oil and cook the rest of the cakes.

Serve with the tomato mayo sauce and lemon wedges.

MAKE AHEAD. *You can make the fish cake mixture a day in advance, but it's best not to form the cakes. Instead, store the mixture in a resealable container in the refrigerator. Transport the container to camp, well-chilled in a cooler. Form into cakes and coat with panko crumbs at the campsite and then cook. The tomato mayo sauce can be made in advance and stored for up to 4 days refrigerated or in a cold cooler. The cakes can also be formed and kept in a freezer for 3 months.*

MOROCCAN-ISH VENISON MEATBALLS

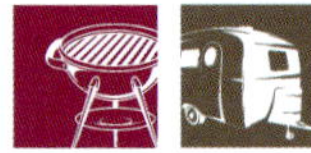

IN SPICY TOMATO SAUCE

MAKES 30 TO 32 MEATBALLS; SERVES 4 TO 6

SPICY MORROCAN-STYLE TOMATO SAUCE

Makes 3 cups

3 tablespoons extra-virgin olive oil

½ medium yellow onion, diced

1 tablespoon kosher salt

⅛ teaspoon ground black pepper

2 garlic cloves, thinly sliced

2 tablespoons harissa paste (see Cook's Note)

1 teaspoon ground cinnamon

1 teaspoon ground coriander

1 teaspoon ground cumin

1 (28-ounce) can crushed tomatoes

¼ cup cilantro leaves, coarsely chopped

MEATBALLS

½ cup panko crumbs, or 1 bread slice

½ cup whole milk

1½ pounds ground game meat

1 large egg, lightly beaten

½ medium yellow onion, grated

2 garlic cloves, grated

½ bunch cilantro, leaves finely chopped

½ bunch mint, leaves finely chopped

2 teaspoons kosher salt

1½ teaspoons ground coriander

1 teaspoon ground cinnamon

1 teaspoon ground cumin

1 teaspoon paprika, preferably smoked or hot

¼ teaspoon ground ginger

¼ teaspoon ground turmeric (optional)

⅛ teaspoon ground black pepper

¼ cup extra-virgin olive oil, for cooking

Mini-meatballs are a fun way to utilize that stash of ground game meat that you may have piled up in the freezer. Many cultures around the world share America's love of meatballs, so there are plenty of places from which to draw inspiration. This is a Moroccan-inspired meatball that is bathed in a spicy tomato sauce. It's great as an appetizer and would also make a whip-ass meatball sub. These meatballs work well with all ground big game. An 80/20 blend of meat to fat is the perfect burger ratio, but you can go richer or leaner without messing anything up.

FOR THE SAUCE. Heat the oil in a large nonstick skillet over medium heat on a propane stove. Add the onions, salt, and pepper and stir to coat with oil. Cook, stirring occasionally, until the onions are soft, about 8 minutes. Add the garlic, harissa, cinnamon, coriander, and cumin and stir to coat the onions. Let cook about 1 minute, or until fragrant. Add the tomatoes to the pan. Add ½ cup water to the empty tomato can, swirl it around, then pour it into the pan. Reduce the heat to maintain a simmer and cook, stirring occasionally, until the sauce thickens slightly, 20 to 30 minutes. Add more water if the sauce starts to get too thick. Stir in the cilantro right before adding the meatballs. (See Make Ahead tips.)

FOR THE MEATBALLS. Combine the panko and milk in a small bowl and set aside to soak about 5 minutes. Place the meat in a large bowl. Add the egg and sprinkle the onions, garlic, cilantro, mint, salt, coriander, cinnamon, cumin, paprika, ginger, turmeric (if using), and pepper over the burger. Crumble the panko paste over the meat mixture. *Gently* mix the ingredients with your hands until combined. Forming the mixture into 1½-inch balls yields about 32 balls. (See Make Ahead tips for storing and transporting.)

TO COOK. For cooking at camp, preheat a skillet with the extra-virgin olive oil, and over medium-high heat on a propane campstove cook the meatballs in batches. At home, you can cook these outside or in a propane or pellet grill with the lid down or in a 400°F oven on a greased rimmed baking sheet.

TO SERVE. Transfer the meatballs and all the juices and oil to a plate and reheat the tomato sauce. When warm, add the meatballs and juice to the sauce and stir gently to coat. Serve with sliced crusty breads that are lightly grilled or toasted over a campfire.

ALSO WORKS WITH. *Pretty much any ground meat, such as beef, sheep, wild hog, venison, goose, duck, and so on.*

Crusty bread or pita or other flatbread, lightly grilled, for serving

COOK'S NOTE. *Harissa paste comes in both spicy and mild versions. Choose a spicy one for this sauce. In a pinch, substitute ½ teaspoon cayenne pepper for the harissa.*

MAKE AHEAD. *You can precook the meatballs and freeze them in a vac bag; the sauce can also be made ahead and frozen in a sealable container. Transport both chilled in a cooler.*

TETON 2

PORTUGUESE-STYLE PANFISH AND POTATO SOUP

SERVES 4 TO 6

Believe me, I understand the temptation to fry every last perch, bluegill, crappie, or porgy that you can get your hands on. They taste great that way! But in order to develop as a cook and a husband (my wife gets burned out on fish fries), I've learned to dedicate a meaningful percentage of my panfish haul to things besides baths in hot grease. If you're in a similar position, please consider this excellent panfish and potato soup. It's perfect for a pile of small fillets. The addition of the linguiça sausage adds a lot of character and heartiness, but you can substitute any other spicy sausage. And if you're not a panfish enthusiast, don't worry. You can chunk up pretty much any firm-fleshed fish (or shellfish) and use it for this delicious preparation.

3 tablespoons olive oil

12 ounces linguiça or andouille sausage (about 4 small links), sliced into ¼-inch half-moons

1 medium onion, diced small

3 garlic cloves, minced

Kosher salt

2 celery ribs, diced small

½ red bell pepper, seeded and diced

2 bay leaves

¼ teaspoon ground allspice

Pinch of cayenne pepper

1½ pounds Yukon Gold potatoes, diced small (about a ⅓-inch dice)

5 cups homemade fish stock or a combination of chicken and clam broth

2 cups whole peeled tomatoes, crushed by hand (14.5-ounce can)

Freshly ground black pepper

1 to 1½ pounds boneless panfish fillets or other similar fish

TO SERVE

Crusty bread

Lemon wedges

Hot sauce

Fresh cilantro or flat-leaf parsley leaves, chopped

Add 1 tablespoon of the olive oil to a heavy 4-quart pot. Place over medium heat on a propane campstove. Add the sausage and cook until lightly browned and the fat has rendered out. Remove the sausage to a separate plate. Discard most of the fat from the pan.

Add the remaining 2 tablespoons olive oil, the onions, garlic, and a pinch of salt to the pot. Cook over medium heat until the onions are translucent, tender, and browned slightly at least 8 minutes. Add the celery, bell peppers, bay leaves, allspice, and cayenne. Stir to toast the seasonings and sauté the vegetables for 3 to 4 minutes.

Add the potatoes and enough of the stock to cover them (about 3 cups). Bring to a low boil and cook for about 8 minutes, or until just tender. Add the crushed tomatoes and cooked sausage and bring to a boil again. Season with salt and black pepper to taste. (You could prep the entire soup up to this point and bring it refrigerated or frozen to camp.)

Add the fillets (if the fillets are large, cut each into a few pieces) and additional broth, if needed, to cover the fillets. Cook at a low simmer for 5 minutes, stirring very gently once or twice. Remove the soup from the heat for 5 minutes (the fish will continue to cook).

Serve warm in bowls with crusty bread, lemon wedges, hot sauce, and chopped cilantro or parsley.

ALSO WORKS WITH. *Any panfish, tautog, striped bass, and other fish with light, firm flesh. Also shrimp, clams, and mussels.*

MISO UDON NOODLE SOUP WITH SALMON

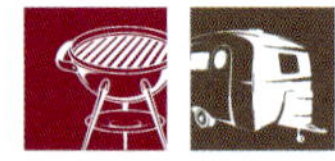

SERVES 2 GENEROUSLY

8 ounces skinless salmon fillet, cut into 1½- to 2-inch chunks

1 teaspoon kosher salt

1 scallion, thinly sliced, whites and greens kept separate

2 (9-ounce) packages frozen udon noodles (see Cook's Notes)

1 baby bok choy, quartered (1⅝ ounces)

4 tablespoons dashi-miso paste (see Cook's Notes)

Sesame oil, for drizzling (optional)

This is a versatile framework for a satisfying camp soup. It's a good option for families. It gives kids what they want, which is noodles, combined with something they should learn to love, which is fish. We're using salmon here for a few reasons. One is that my family catches a lot of salmon, so I'm always looking for good things to do with them. Another is that salmon is widely available in grocery stores, so it's impossible for landlocked cooks not to find the stuff. But you can swap out the salmon for any number of fish species, and it'll be equally good. In fact, this could be ideal to make with fresh-caught fish on a backcountry backpacking trip.

Combine the salmon, salt, and scallion whites in a bowl and set aside.

In a large pot, bring 3 quarts water to a boil over high heat on a campstove. Add the noodles and cook for 1 minute, stirring occasionally, until the noodles can be separated. Divide the noodles between two large soup bowls. Discard the water.

Add 4 cups water to the same pot and bring it to a boil. Blanch the bok choy for 60 seconds. Remove from the pot and divide it between the bowls. Reduce the heat to maintain a simmer and whisk in the dashi-miso paste.

Add the chunks of salmon to the pot. Simmer until barely cooked, about 1 minute, then remove and divide it between the bowls. It will finish cooking in the bowls. Add the soup to the bowls and top with scallion greens and a drizzle of sesame oil, if using.

Serve immediately.

COOK'S NOTES. *Udon noodles can be purchased in a variety of forms. The frozen, precooked variety is the best for camping or backpacking because preparation time is super quick. If you can't find the frozen ones, cook dry noodles according to the package instructions, drain, rinse with cold water, then drain again. Store in a zip-top bag with a splash of toasted sesame oil or neutral oil and bring to camp in a cooler.*

Dashi-miso paste is available online and in Asian grocers. Dashi (a Japanese soup base) is sold in large bags, and it's also available in tea-bag form online, which is very convenient. You can add the dashi tea bags to the miso paste that's sold in plastic tubs to achieve similar results. Otherwise, plain miso paste will work, too.

ALSO WORKS WITH. *All species of salmon, trout, char, and whitefish. Also cooked and shredded chicken, wild turkey, upland bird, rabbit, and squirrel.*

VENISON CHILI

MAKES 4 QUARTS

Growing up in Michigan, it was common for people to think of whitetail deer and chili as being inextricably linked. (I'm talking about the kind of Midwest chili that has a lot of beans and not a lot of heat.) In fact, people back home would hunt for whitetails with the stated purpose of securing their chili meat for the year. My personal love of the dish has not waned over the decades that I've been away from Michigan, though I have come to appreciate versions of the dish that would be acceptable to folks living outside of the Great Lakes region. This one uses ground meat, but it could also be made with precooked, cubed, or shredded elk or deer shoulder. It works doubled or tripled, so you can make it to handle a crowd. And with some prep work (see the Make Ahead instructions), it's a great choice for campsite cooking.

CHILI PASTE

Makes 2¾ cups

3 tablespoons canola oil

1 large white onion, chopped

4 poblano peppers, seeded and diced

4 jalapeño peppers, seeded and diced

10 garlic cloves, thinly sliced

1 teaspoon kosher salt

¼ teaspoon ground black pepper

2 tablespoons ancho chile powder

2 tablespoons dark brown sugar

2 tablespoons ground cumin

1 tablespoon dried oregano, preferably Mexican, crumbled

2 chipotle peppers in adobo sauce, plus 1 tablespoon sauce

CHILI

2 tablespoons canola oil

3 pounds ground venison (substitute some ground pork if your meat is very lean)

2 teaspoons kosher salt

½ teaspoon ground black pepper

2 (28-ounce) cans canned crushed tomatoes

2 (15-ounce) cans small red beans or kidney beans, rinsed and drained

1 (12-ounce) bottle beer

FOR SERVING

Shredded pepper Jack, or sharp cheddar

Sour cream

Chopped fresh cilantro leaves

Diced red or white onion or sliced scallions

Corn chips, tortilla chips, or cornbread

FOR THE PASTE. Heat the oil in a large skillet over medium heat. Cook the onions for about 5 minutes, stirring occasionally, until they soften slightly. Add the poblanos, jalapeños, garlic, and salt and pepper and cook 10 to 15 minutes, stirring often, until the chiles soften. Add the ancho powder, brown sugar, cumin, oregano, chipotle, and adobo sauce. Mix well. Cook for about 3 minutes, stirring often, until the paste darkens in color. Transfer to a container to cool. If saving for later, refrigerate or freeze until ready to use.

FOR THE CHILI. Heat the oil in a large Dutch oven or other heavy pot over medium-high heat on a campstove. Crumble the meat into the pot in batches and sprinkle lightly with the salt and pepper. Cook, stirring often, until the meat browns. Add the chili paste to the pot and stir to combine. Add the tomatoes, beans, and beer to the pot and bring to a simmer. Reduce the heat as low as possible while still maintaining a simmer. Cook, partially covered and stirring occasionally, until the meat is tender and the flavors have melded, about 1 hour. If using meat other than burger, such as cubed shoulder meat or turkey legs, pre-braise them in game stock to save on cook time here. Add water as needed to loosen the chili if it gets too thick.

FOR SERVING. Serve the chili with shredded cheese, sour cream, cilantro, onions, and corn chips.

MAKE AHEAD. *We've designed this recipe to be an efficient 1-hour cook on-site. For that approach, make and freeze the chili paste mixture in your home kitchen, then reheat it and add the meat and canned ingredients at camp. Or, you can prepare the whole dish as directed, then vac-seal and freeze it at home and reheat it on-site.* *For reheating instructions, see page 217.*

ALSO WORKS WITH: *Pretty much any ground meat, such as beef, sheep, wild hog, venison, goose, duck, and so on.*

CRYOVAC ME

LAYERED FISH CHOWDER -

FISH STEW -

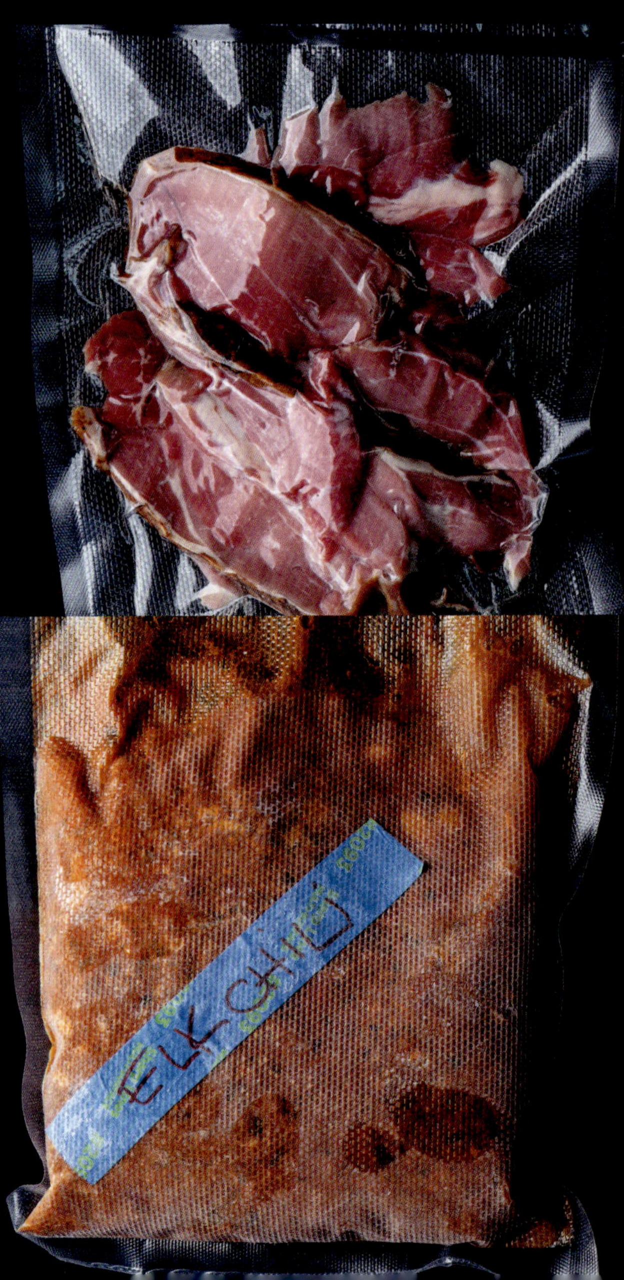
ELK CHILI

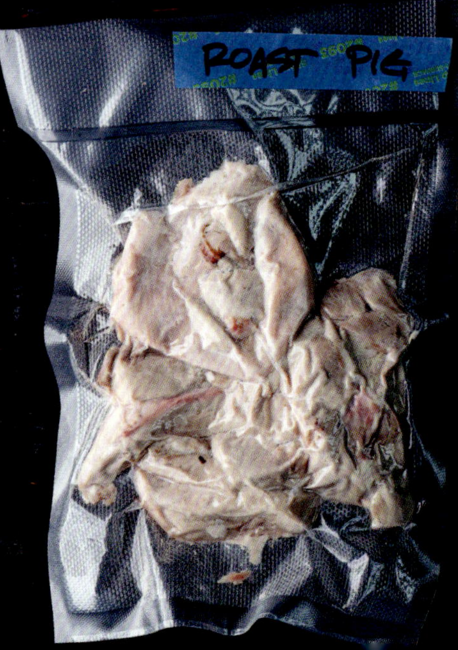
ROAST PIG

VAC-SEALING: REHEATING PRECOOKED MEALS AT CAMP

These days vacuum sealers are standard kitchen equipment for just about everyone, and like most folks, you probably use yours primarily for storing food in the freezer. But vacuum-sealed bags of premade dinners can also save you a ton of time and eliminate cleanup when you're in camp. This method of food prep does require a little advance planning, as you need to make and freeze meals (or freeze leftovers) ahead of time. While we spotlight a few meals that lend themselves to vac-sealing in the list below, this system works great for anything that is suitable for freezing ahead of time, from sloppy Joe and taco meat to all of the soup, stew, and stir-fry sauce recipes in this book.

You'll basically be doing a camping version of the sous vide process to reheat the food, which can be completely frozen or just chilled. Get a pot large enough to hold your vac-sealed meal and fill with water about halfway to two-thirds full; if it's a small bag of food for one or two people, you can reheat it in a shallow pan filled halfway with water. Bring the water to a low boil, add your bag, and cook until the interior contents are at least at 160°F to 165°F. When the food is hot, ladle it directly out of the bag and add any fresh garnishes or toppings, if needed.

The following recipes are ideal for vac-sealing. Any cooked or smoked wild game or birds will vac-seal well and keep in the freezer for 3 to 6 months, especially when in a liquid or gravy. Vac-sealing smoked fish works well, but we don't recommend vac-sealing cooked fish; in general the quality of the protein degrades and is less palatable. Below are recipes for meats, soups, stews, and complex marinades that make easy work of outdoor meals if prepared ahead and frozen.

Beaver Confit (page 20)
Boston Baked Beans (page 305)
Brined and Smoked Turkey Breast (page 128)
Brown Sugar Wild Hog Ham (page 103)
Bulgogi Marinade (Bulgogi Lettuce Wraps, page 38)
Camp Sausage (page 36)
Cooked beans (page 306)
Deer Shoulder in a Barrel (page 176)
Dutch Oven Rabbit Boudin (page 184)
Fish Sausages (page 115)
Goose and Dumplings (page 183)
Ground Venison Sauce (page 223)
Layered Fish Chowder (page 290)
Lentil Stew (page 311)
Moroccan-ish Venison Meatballs in Spicy Tomato Sauce (page 208)
Penne with Sausage and Peas (page 225)
Peruvian-Style Marinade for Duck with Ají Verde (page 78)
Portuguese-Style Panfish and Potato Soup (page 211)
Smoked Duck (page 130)
Smoked Moose Nose Hash (page 133)
Smoked Venison (page 118)
Spatchcocked birds (page 75)
Summer Sausage (page 100)
Turkey Chili Verde (page 285)
Venison Chili (page 215)
Weeknight Butterflied Steak (page 45)

CUBAN-STYLE RICE WITH RABBIT

SERVES 6 TO 8

RABBIT

5 large garlic cloves, minced (3 tablespoons)

1 tablespoon kosher salt

1½ teaspoons dried oregano

2 tablespoons apple cider vinegar

1 tablespoon olive oil, plus more as needed

2 or 3 wild rabbits (4 to 5 pounds total), each cut into 4 leg pieces and a saddle

RICE

Makes 8 cups

Olive oil

1 large red bell pepper, seeded and cut into medium dice

1 large cubanelle pepper, seeded and cut into medium dice

1 large onion, chopped

3 garlic cloves, thinly sliced

1 packed cup fresh cilantro leaves and tender stems, chopped, plus more for garnish

1½ teaspoons Sazón Coriander & Annatto Seasoning (from 1½ packets)

2 teaspoons ground cumin

2 teaspoons dried oregano

1 teaspoon paprika

3 bay leaves

Kosher salt and freshly ground black pepper

3 cups homemade game stock

1 (8-ounce) can tomato sauce

1 tablespoon drained capers

2 cups medium-grain rice, rinsed

½ cup frozen peas, thawed

½ cup pimiento-stuffed whole olives

Lime wedges, for serving

Here's a nod to the excellent chicken-and-rice dishes that abound in the Caribbean. Many of those preparations belong to that wonderful category of foods that taste better as leftovers than they do the first time around. We're making this version with cottontail rabbit, which I like to refer to as "thinking man's chicken." If you're not a rabbit hunter and you don't know any rabbit hunters, let's just hope that you're a squirrel hunter. Those work just as well here. Homemade stock makes the difference in this dish, however. Rabbit stock is even better, but you can get by with store-bought broth.

SPECIAL EQUIPMENT. Wide, heavy-bottomed 8- to 10-quart pot with a lid.

FOR THE RABBIT. Mix the minced garlic, salt, oregano, vinegar, and oil in a small bowl. Add the rabbit pieces to a zip-top bag, pour in the marinade, and seal the bag. Massage the rabbit through the bag to distribute the marinade over all the surfaces. Refrigerate for at least 1 hour but preferably overnight.

Heat a wide pot with a lid over medium heat on a camp propane burner. Add 1 tablespoon oil and swirl to coat. Pat the rabbit dry, removing the minced garlic if you can. Cook the rabbit in batches; try not to overcrowd the pot so each piece gets a good sear. Turn the meat as it browns. Each batch should take 4 to 5 minutes. Add more oil as needed between batches and lower the heat if the brown bits on the bottom of the pan start to burn. Remove the pieces to a plate as they brown.

FOR THE RICE. Once all the rabbit is browned, heat 1 tablespoon oil, or more as needed, in the pot and add the peppers, onions, sliced garlic, and cilantro. Stir to scrape up any browned bits, then add the Sazón, cumin, oregano, paprika, bay leaves, 2 teaspoons salt, and several grinds of black pepper. Cook, stirring, until softened, 5 to 8 minutes. Add the stock and bring to a simmer. Return the rabbit to the pot, nestling the pieces into the liquid. Cover and cook for about 1 hour, stirring occasionally, until the meat begins to get tender. (Older animals may need more time.)

Stir in the tomato sauce, capers, and rice. Over just enough heat to maintain a simmer, cover and cook 25 to 30 minutes, until the liquid is absorbed and the rice is tender. Remove from the heat, top with the peas and olives, cover the pan, and let sit for 10 minutes. Serve with lime wedges and garnish with cilantro.

ALSO WORKS WITH. *Wild turkey, upland birds, snowshoe hare, squirrels, nutria, or domestic rabbit and chicken. You could also try this with alligator or snapping turtle meat.*

GARLIC MISO SHRIMP

SERVES 2

I trap shrimp every summer with my family up at our fish shack in southeast Alaska. We eat them pretty much every night while we're there, usually just boiled for a quick minute and dipped in cocktail sauce. By the time we get back home to Montana, I'm usually burned out on that simple preparation, and I'm ready to make something a little more unique and exciting with the shrimp that I bring home. This marinated shrimp recipe is the perfect fix for that. It works especially well with shrimp, but the marinade can be made ahead of time for all kinds of seafood and shellfish. It's an elegant appetizer for dinner parties, and so damn good that I'm prepared to violate tradition and make a big batch the next time I'm at my shack. Those Alaskan shrimp have never had it so good.

The marinade would also work with thinly sliced big game and upland birds that will be grilled or roasted to finish. This dish can be made on a propane stove or a hot grill set up with direct and indirect heat zones.

MISO MARINADE

Makes about 2 cups

4 tablespoons white miso

3 tablespoons soy sauce

6 tablespoons mirin

2 tablespoons honey

1 tablespoon Worcestershire sauce

1 tablespoon fresh lime juice

1 tablespoon toasted sesame oil

¼ cup warm water

½ teaspoon freshly ground black pepper

1 serrano pepper, halved lengthwise

SHRIMP

1 pound large shrimp, shells on and deveined

4 tablespoons peanut oil

4 tablespoons (½ stick) unsalted butter

15 large garlic cloves, minced (about 4 tablespoons)

1 large shallot, minced (3 tablespoons)

½ teaspoon cayenne pepper

1 teaspoon rice vinegar

2 tablespoons fresh lime juice

FOR SERVING

2 tablespoons toasted sesame seeds

½ bunch cilantro, leaves picked (1 cup loosely packed)

1 bunch thinly sliced scallions, white and green parts (1 cup)

Cooked white rice (optional)

Lime wedges

SPECIAL EQUIPMENT

12-inch cast-iron skillet

FOR THE MARINADE. Place all the marinade ingredients except the serrano pepper in a container large enough to hold the shrimp and mix thoroughly. Add the shrimp and serrano pepper and marinate for 1 hour in the refrigerator.

FOR THE SHRIMP. Preheat a large cast-iron skillet over medium-high heat on a propane camp burner for 5 minutes. When the pan is hot, add the peanut oil and spread it evenly in the skillet. Remove the shrimp from the marinade, reserving the marinade. Carefully add the shrimp to the pan in a single layer, being very careful as the oil may pop and spit a little due to the moisture in the marinade. Cook the shrimp for 2 to 3 minutes on each side, until just barely cooked through. Lower the heat and transfer the shrimp to a plate.

To make the glaze, combine the butter, garlic, shallots, and cayenne in the pan and cook, stirring often, for 1 minute. Pour the marinade into the pan along with the rice vinegar and lime juice. Give everything a stir and let the sauce simmer for 2 minutes, or until it has thickened slightly.

FOR SERVING. Remove the pan from heat, place the shrimp back in the pan, and toss them thoroughly in the glaze. Sprinkle the shrimp with sesame seeds, cilantro, and scallions and serve with rice, if using, and lime wedges.

ALSO WORKS WITH. *Prawns, spiny lobster, crayfish, scallops, clams, mussels, and any firm, white, flaky fish.*

GINGER CATFISH STIR-FRY

SERVES 4 TO 6

Here's a solid option for a shore lunch or camp dinner on your next fishing trip. The recipe's combination of ginger and fish is popular in Hong Kong and the southwestern region of China. The bold ginger flavor works particularly well with a host of fish species, including catfish. You can make the marinade, broth, and vegetables in advance. Then all you need to do is procure the fish and you're ready to cook. Or drag some fish out of the freezer and use that. The marinade will help cover any off-flavors that might have come about from extended freezer times.

MARINADE

1 tablespoon Shaoxing wine or dry sherry

¼ teaspoon kosher salt

⅛ teaspoon ground white pepper

1 tablespoon cornstarch

1 to 1½ pounds skinned catfish fillets, cut into 1½-inch pieces

SAUCE

½ cup fish, chicken, or vegetable stock

1 tablespoon soy sauce

¼ teaspoon sugar

1 tablespoon cornstarch

⅛ teaspoon ground white pepper

1 tablespoon Shaoxing wine or dry sherry

3 tablespoons vegetable or neutral oil

½ cup julienned peeled ginger

1 garlic clove, finely chopped

2 scallions, trimmed and thinly sliced

2 ounces snow peas, ends trimmed, sliced into ½-inch strips on the bias

½ red bell pepper, seeded and thinly sliced

Cooked white rice, for serving

FOR THE MARINADE. Combine the wine, salt, white pepper, and cornstarch in a bowl. Add the catfish and marinate for 5 minutes.

FOR THE SAUCE. Mix the stock, soy sauce, sugar, cornstarch, white pepper, and wine.

In a large nonstick pan or wok, heat 1 tablespoon of the oil on medium-high heat on a propane campstove. When hot, add the pieces of catfish. Cook for 2 minutes, until lightly browned on the bottom, and flip. Cook for 1 to 2 more minutes until lightly browned on the other side. Remove the fish to a plate, and don't worry if it isn't cooked all the way through.

Add the remaining 2 tablespoons oil to the pan and cook the ginger, garlic, and half of the scallions for 1 minute. Then add the snow peas and bell peppers and cook for another minute. Add the sauce to the vegetables in the pan. Cook, stirring, for 30 seconds. Add the fish and continue to cook, gently stirring, for 1 minute, or until the cornstarch has thickened, the fish is cooked through, and the sauce is translucent.

Garnish with the remaining scallions and serve with white rice.

COOK'S NOTE. *Don't be put off by the amount of ginger in this dish, as it goes well with fish. Feel free to substitute broccoli, string beans, zucchini, or whatever else you like for the snow peas.*

MAKE AHEAD. *The two mixtures, the marinade and the sauce, can be made in advance, stored in separate airtight containers, and brought to camp ready to use. Use a small whisk or fork to emulsify them if they have separated.*

ALSO WORKS WITH. *When it comes to fish, you name it: walleye, northern pike, bluegill, crappie, pompano, snapper, grouper, redfish, speckled trout, and peeled shrimp. Also, upland bird breast meat cut into bite-sized pieces.*

TOSSED NOODLES WITH GROUND VENISON SAUCE

(ZHA ZHIANG MIEN)

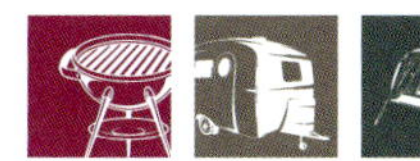

SERVES 6 TO 8

This recipe was adapted from a Chinese dish called zha zhiang mien, which translates rather clunkily to "fried sauce noodle." It's traditionally made with finely ground or chopped pork, though it works beautifully with ground game. More authentic preparations rely on a sweet bean sauce typically found in Asian specialty markets. For the sake of convenience, we built this recipe to achieve similar flavors using ingredients that are much easier to find. Big thanks to Jeannie Chen, who is friends with my collaborator, Krista Ruane. Jeannie helped us with the necessary adaptations to make this recipe achievable for folks who can't get to the big city for their ingredients.

12 ounces dried udon noodles (see Cook's Notes)

1 tablespoon toasted sesame oil

SAUCE

½ cup chicken or vegetable broth

2 tablespoons hoisin sauce

2 tablespoons oyster sauce

2 tablespoons soy sauce

1 tablespoon Shaoxing wine or dry sherry

1 teaspoon cornstarch

½ teaspoon kosher salt

¼ teaspoon sugar

3 tablespoons vegetable oil or neutral oil

6 garlic cloves, minced

2 scallions, ends trimmed, white and green parts, thinly sliced

1 pound ground venison

4 ounces white mushrooms, finely chopped (1⅓ cups)

VEGETABLE TOPPINGS

(see Cook's Notes)

1 cup unpeeled cucumber, julienned

½ cup julienned carrots

2 radishes, halved and thinly sliced

½ cup shelled and cooked edamame

In a large pot of boiling water, cook the dried noodles according to the manufacturer's instructions. Drain and toss them in a bowl with the sesame oil. (I like to blanch the edamame in this water after the noodles have cooked.)

FOR THE SAUCE. In a medium bowl, mix together the broth, hoisin, oyster sauce, soy sauce, wine, cornstarch, salt, and sugar. Set aside.

In a large cast-iron or nonstick skillet, heat the oil over medium-high heat and cook the garlic and scallions until fragrant, about 30 seconds. Add the ground meat and chopped mushrooms and cook, stirring often and breaking up the meat, until the meat is cooked through, 3 to 4 minutes. Add the sauce and stir until it thickens, 2 to 3 minutes.

To serve family-style, place the noodles in a large, wide platter, then compose the toppings over the noodles, top with all the sauce, and toss well. For individual portions, toss the noodles with the meat sauce, portion into bowls, and top with the vegetables. Eat while hot.

COOK'S NOTES. *Shaoxing wine is found in Asian markets but can be replaced with dry sherry. Dried udon noodles (look for the brand Kame) can be found in big supermarkets. The topping quantities and ingredients here are guides; use as much or as little as you like. The sauce can be tossed without the noodles with a selection of fresh vegetables for a quick, easy camp meal.*

MAKE AHEAD. *This meat sauce can be frozen to use later, which means it's an ideal sauce to keep dishes innovative on camping trips. After making the sauce, you can allow it to cool down and vac-seal to freeze the full quantity, or portion out serving-sized quantities. Either can be frozen up to 3 months. If freezing: To thaw the sauce, thaw quickly in warm water before heating thoroughly in a pan.*

ALSO WORKS WITH. *Pretty much any ground meat, such as beef, sheep, wild hog, venison, goose, duck, and so on.*

VENISON STIR-FRY WITH CABBAGE

SERVES 4

MARINADE

1 pound venison backstrap, cut into slices against the grain about ⅛ inch thick and 1½ to 2 inches long

2 tablespoons soy sauce

1 tablespoon Shaoxing wine or dry sherry

1 teaspoon toasted sesame oil

2 teaspoons cornstarch

SAUCE

1 teaspoon fennel seed

1 teaspoon cumin seed

¾ cup homemade game stock or chicken broth

1 teaspoon cornstarch

1 tablespoon soy sauce

2 teaspoons rice vinegar (optional)

---

2 tablespoons vegetable oil

2 or 3 Thai bird chiles or any chiles with heat, thinly sliced (see Cook's Note)

2 garlic cloves, finely chopped

1 teaspoon minced fresh ginger

½ head cabbage, outer leaves removed, cored, halved again, and leaves separated (about 4 cups)

⅛ teaspoon kosher salt

Cooked white rice, for serving

SPECIAL EQUIPMENT

Spice grinder or a flat stone and a rounded stone

This venison stir-fry is packed with a lot of big flavors from fennel, cumin, ginger, and garlic. It's reminiscent of the cumin lamb stir-fries that you might see on Chinese menus in the United States. In general, lamb recipes work well with venison. This one is no exception. It's especially good when combined with a sweet, hearty vegetable like cabbage. You'll see that we call for some pulverized spices in this preparation. You could be a lame-o and use a spice grinder. Or you could take the backwoods approach and grind your spices between a couple of rocks. Without getting too deep into geology, you'll want to use rocks with a lot of structural integrity for this. Crumbly rocks could give you a lot of unwanted grit in your spice. That ain't yummy.

FOR THE MARINADE. In a medium bowl, marinate the sliced meat with 2 tablespoons of the soy sauce, wine, sesame oil, and 2 teaspoons of the cornstarch.

FOR THE SAUCE. Toast the fennel and cumin seeds in the pan over medium-low heat until fragrant and slightly toasted, 2 to 3 minutes. Transfer the seeds to a spice grinder and grind into a powder. (At camp, you can put the spice seeds on a flat rock and use a rounded, rough stone to pulverize the spices as finely as you can. If some whole spices remain, it's fine). Put the ground spices into a dish and set aside.

Mix ½ cup of the stock, the remaining 1 teaspoon cornstarch, the remaining 1 tablespoon soy sauce, and vinegar (if using) in a bowl.

TO COOK. In a 12-inch pan, heat 1 tablespoon of the vegetable oil over medium-high heat on a camp burner. Add the ground fennel and cumin seeds and cook for 30 seconds, or until fragrant. Add the marinated meat in one layer. Do not move it for 1 minute to allow it to brown, then stir it around for another 30 to 45 seconds, until it's cooked to rare. Remove the meat to a bowl.

To the same pan, add the remaining 1 tablespoon vegetable oil, the chiles, garlic, and ginger and stir-fry for 30 seconds, until fragrant. Add the cabbage and stir to coat it with aromatics. Add the remaining ¼ cup stock and the salt. Stir-fry for 3 to 4 minutes, until the edges of the cabbage are a bit browned. Add the partially cooked meat back to the pan with the vegetables and stir to combine. Add the flavored broth and stir until the sauce is slightly thickened. Remove from heat and serve with rice.

MAKE AHEAD. *The marinade and sauce components can be made in advance and even frozen.*

COOK'S NOTE. *You can add more chiles if you'd like a little additional heat.*

PENNE WITH SAUSAGE AND PEAS

SERVES 4 OR 5

In my home freezer, I always keep a stash of homemade sausages packaged in vacuum-sealed bags. You can thaw these sausages with lightning speed by dropping them into a tub of cold water. They're perfect for last-minute meals when I fail to pull something out of the freezer ahead of time. In these situations, it's tempting to just slap a grilled sausage on a bun with a squirt of mustard. But that doesn't need to be your only trick. The recipe satisfies the same urgency for speed, but it hits entirely different notes. It's ideal for quick weeknight family dinners. It freezes really well, too, so it makes a good addition to your car-camping repertoire. You could even make this on a backcountry trip—just swap the frozen peas for canned.

SAUSAGE SAUCE

1 (28-ounce) can whole peeled tomatoes

4 Camp Sausages (page 36), or 1½ to 2 pounds Italian-style game sausages or bulk sausage

¼ cup plus 2 tablespoons extra-virgin olive oil

Kosher salt

1 teaspoon crushed red pepper flakes, plus more (optional) for serving

1 medium onion, chopped (about 1¼ cups)

4 large garlic cloves, thinly sliced

FOR SERVING

3 tablespoons kosher salt

1 pound penne pasta (or any other shape you like)

1½ cups frozen peas

Grated pecorino or Parmigiano-Reggiano cheese

FOR THE SAUCE. In a bowl, crush the canned tomatoes by hand. Set aside.

Cut the sausage links into ¾- to 1-inch pieces. Add 1 tablespoon of the olive oil and half of the sausage to a hot pan. Cook the sausages until they begin to brown and release from the pan. Stir or flip the sausages with tongs and continue cooking for about 8 minutes to brown the other side. Season with a pinch of salt. Remove the browned sausages from the pan and repeat with the remaining sausages, adding more oil if needed. When all the sausage is cooked, drain the fat from the bottom of the pan and move the sausage to a heatproof bowl.

Add the remaining ¼ cup oil to the pan with the red pepper flakes, onions, and garlic. Cook on high heat for 30 seconds to 1 minute, until fragrant; do not allow the garlic to brown. Add the hand-crushed tomatoes and 1½ teaspoons salt and stir. With the heat still on high, return the sausages back to the pan and bring to a simmer. Cook, simmering and stirring occasionally, for 20 minutes, until the flavors meld. Taste the sauce and add more salt if needed. Turn the heat to low to keep warm while the pasta cooks.

FOR SERVING. Meanwhile, bring a 6-quart pot of water to a boil and add the salt and the penne. Cook according to the package instructions for al dente. Add the peas and stir to thaw. Drain off the water and transfer the pasta and peas back into the pot. Add the hot tomato sauce and stir to incorporate.

Serve warm with grated cheese and additional red pepper flakes (if using).

MAKE AHEAD. *If freezing, transfer the cooled sauce to a vac-seal bag, seal, and freeze for up to 6 months. (See details on reheating on page 217.)*

ALSO WORKS WITH. *Any nonsmoked game sausage made from big game, small game, or upland birds.*

LOUISIANA-STYLE CRAYFISH, BLUE CRAB, AND SHRIMP BOIL

SERVES 8 TO 10

CRAYFISH BOIL

8 pounds live crayfish

10 live blue crabs, preferably large male crabs

2 or 3 (10-pound) bags ice

3 pounds large Gulf shrimp, shell on, split, and deveined

3½ cups Low Country Seafood Seasoning (page 348)

3¾ cups store-bought liquid seafood boil

½ cup kosher salt

6 bay leaves

2 leeks, trimmed, cut lengthwise into 4 pieces

6 medium sweet onions, quartered

6 garlic heads, halved crosswise

4 celery ribs, halved crosswise

Juice of 4 lemons

2 pounds andouille sausage, cut into 2-inch pieces

6 ears of sweet corn, halved

4 pounds new potatoes, halved

2 baguettes

SPECIAL EQUIPMENT

Propane outdoor cooker

Stainless-steel 40-quart pot with perforated steamer basket

One of the things that I love about the Atlantic Seaboard and Gulf Coast regions of the United States is how territorial everyone gets around the subject of seafood boils. On the Eastern Shore of Maryland, some cooks get so nitpicky about how to boil and eat blue crabs that they actually insist on the type of table covering to be used—brown butcher paper is standard. Some Gulf Coast Texans will tell you that the table covering has to be layers of newsprint, as though this selection will impact the flavor of the crabs. I have never seen or heard of anyone stipulating what specific publication's newsprint should be used, but I wouldn't be surprised by it. In Louisiana, I've seen otherwise laid-back people get feisty in debates regarding nuanced details of how to properly conduct the "soak" phase of a crayfish boil, even though the soak phase is literally just letting the cooked crayfish passively soak in their cooking liquid. I mention all of this because certain folks are guaranteed to receive this recipe with open hostility, as it contradicts their firmly held convictions about how seafood boils should be conducted. Our version borrows from the flavor profile of the classic Louisiana-style boil, but our combination of blue crabs and crayfish might strike some Louisianans as pure sacrilege. The only rule we insist on is that you invite a bunch of people over when you make this preparation. It's as much about camaraderie and friendly arguments as it is about the flavors.

FOR THE SEAFOOD. Place the bag of crayfish in a cooler and rinse them thoroughly with a hose or running water to remove any excess mud, grit, and debris. Repeat the rinsing process until the water runs clear; this may take four or five cycles of rinsing. Place them in a paper bag or another cooler. Rinse the blue crabs under fresh water and place them in a large paper bag. Drain any excess water from the cooler and lay down two or three bags of ice. Cover the ice with a piece of burlap or a couple large kitchen towels and place the crayfish and blue crabs on top of the burlap. Rinse the shrimp lightly in fresh water and place in a strainer to drain. Transfer the shrimp to a plastic bag and place in the cooler. Refresh the ice as needed and drain any excess water as the ice melts so the crayfish and crabs are not submerged in water.

FOR THE SEAFOOD BOIL BASE. Combine 2½ cups of the Low Country Seafood Seasoning, 3 cups of the liquid seafood boil, the kosher salt, and bay leaves in an airtight container and refrigerate. Combine the leeks, onions, garlic, celery, and lemon. Squeeze the lemons and add their juice and store in a separate airtight container.

TO COOK. Set up your propane outdoor cooker and add 5 gallons water to a 40-quart stainless-steel stockpot with a perforated steamer basket. Place the pot on the burner and add the seafood boil base ingredients. Stir the contents and cover. Light the burner and set the heat to high. Once the liquid reaches a boiling point, add the andouille sausage, corn, and potatoes to the pot. Cover the pot and cook for 5 minutes. After 5 minutes, remove the lid and put the crayfish and crabs in the pot. Bring everything back to a boil. As soon as you notice steam coming out of the sides of the lid, shut off the burner. Let the seafood steep for 10 minutes. Remove the lid, toss in the shrimp, and cover the pot for another 3 minutes. With leather grilling gloves, carefully pull the steamer basket out of the pot and rest it on the top of the pot to drain for a couple minutes.

Dump the contents of the steamer basket into a clean cooler or onto a table covered with several layers of newspaper. Cover the food with the remaining ¾ cup liquid boil, ½ to 1 cup of seafood seasoning, and 1 cup of the hot boil liquid from the pot. (If you're not a fan of spicy food, omit the last step of tossing in additional seafood spice.)

Toss everything very well until the spices are evenly distributed. Serve with large pieces of baguette.

COOK'S NOTE. *If you don't want to make your own Cajun-inspired seafood seasoning, you can substitute Zatarain's or a similar Louisiana seafood-boil spice. The Low Country Seafood Seasoning recipe makes more than needed for the recipe. It can be used as an all-purpose seasoning for any fish dish, including a fried fish fry, a fish stew, or enriched brine.*

HOW TO FRY FISH

Parker Hall

There is a weird "itchiness" that my hands get after spending half a day cleaning a cooler full of catfish. I don't know if it's a thousand micro cuts or irritation from the fish slime or a combination of the two, but I really like it. It means the freezer is getting filled up, and we are about to fire up the grease with friends and family.

Some of my earliest memories involve running trotlines. My father would operate the leaky, tiller-handled johnboat while he baited hooks, tossed fish into the cooler, and shouted at my brother and me. We were young and basically useless on the water. My dad would get so frustrated that he'd simultaneously tell us to "sit down!" and "grab the net" without realizing how confusing that was. But at the end of the day, we usually had a boatload of fish.

Back home, we helped Dad clean and process the fish. My brother and I weren't very good at it. Dad cleaned ten fish to our one, and there's no telling how many fillets we mangled. When the cleaning was done, he would then take control of cooking the fish on a double-burner propane fryer that he made himself. We weren't allowed to help, because, of course, we didn't know what we were doing. My dad still maintains that sentiment today. Whenever I cook fish, my dad always has some sort of negative comment about the amount of seasoning, temperature of the grease, or the utensil I'm using. It's all in good fun . . . I think.

Despite my dad's opinion of me, I have learned a few things over the years. Without a doubt, cleaning catfish properly is one of the most important components of having a good fry. Some folks like to claim that catfish have a muddy taste, but I've found this usually boils down to lazy preparation on the part of whoever is cleaning them. Like all fish, catfish have a bloodline that we call "red meat." I trim most of that out, particularly on larger fish. However, catfish fat is really what gives them that off-flavor. It's important to remove all of it. Catfish fat is generally light yellow in color and has a somewhat gooey consistency. Of the three species of catfish we eat—channel cats, flatheads, and blue cats—the largest and fattiest is the blue cat. No matter the species, I trim off every last bit of fat I can see, and then I give the meat a rinse with a hose using a good bit of water pressure. Soaking the fillets in ice-cold salt water for an hour or so can help, too.

For frying, I like to cut the fillets into pieces that take about two and a half bites to eat. I don't know the exact measurements, but you get the idea. If the meat is cut too small, all you will taste is fried cornmeal. If the bites are too big, they take too long to cook. The two- to three-bite size seems just about right.

If you have ever fried fish inside of your house, you are already well aware that the oily fried-fish smell will stick around for a few days. For that reason, I almost always do my frying outside. Any kind of heat source will work as long as you can get the grease up to temperature and keep it that way. I prefer a propane-powered outdoor cooker. Wind is your enemy when frying outside, as it takes the heat away rapidly. This cools the grease, and cool grease results in soggy fish. Nowadays, there are cookers with wind shields, but a pickup truck, a big tree, or a piece of plywood will also get the job done. If you are cooking anywhere other than on the grass or dirt, keep in mind that frying fish can be a messy ordeal. Consider putting down some cardboard or plywood under your fryer if you're cooking on a deck or carport.

Through the years, I have seen hundreds of combinations of pots, cookers, and stirring and dipping implements utilized while frying fish. My favorite frying container is a large cast-iron pot. Cast iron does the best job at holding heat with the least fluctuation in temperature. Granted, it takes a little longer for the grease to get up to temperature than it does with a thin steel or aluminum pot, but cast iron is more forgiving. Those other types of pots can work well, too, but attention must be paid when either adding fish (temp goes down) or when you remove a batch of fish (temp goes up). As for utensils, everyone that I know has a favorite tool for flipping, stirring, and removing fish. My dad uses a relatively short-handled wire-slotted skimmer spatula with a deer antler stuck on the end. My brother will use whatever he can find, including tongs. I like a long-handled wire-type dipping utensil called a spider strainer. I think it is also important to have a finer strainer to remove excess meal from the grease. That's especially key when cooking for a large group and running many batches of fish through the grease. If it's not removed, the meal will sink to the bottom of the pot and get scorched. This will shorten the life of the grease and give the fish a burnt taste.

Any number of kinds of grease can be utilized to fry fish, but I usually use either vegetable oil or peanut oil. Peanut is my favorite, since it has a higher smoke point than vegetable or canola oil, but it is pricier. I generally like my temperature to be somewhere right around 350°F. If I am frying large, thick pieces, like flathead belly or wild turkey strips, I like my grease just a bit cooler so the meat cooks all the way through without burning the breading. If I am doing something smaller, like a bunch of bluegill fillets, I may bring up the temperature a little as the meat is more delicate and cooks really fast. Just remember that if your temperature gets too hot, you'll end up with scorched grease and burned fish fillets. You also need to correctly match the amount of fish to the size of your pot. If you overload the grease, it will cool off and your fish will get soggy. All of your friends and family will call you horrible names if this happens. You will be pushed out of the way, and a more "experienced" fish cooker will take over. (If it's my family, they all think they are the best.)

Another important step is seasoning and breading the fish. Everyone likes it a little different, but for seasoning, I use three ingredients: black pepper, garlic powder, and Cajun seasoning, which has added salt. For breading, some folks like to add commercially produced fish-fry breading or a little flour to their meal. I do not. I use just plain yellow cornmeal. It is important to season the fish itself, not the cornmeal. Some people give in to the devil's temptation of adding spices to the cornmeal. This can be referred to as a faux pas, a vocabulary word I learned in school thirty years ago. The definition of the term is "grave social error." In this case, it means that you will find out your first batch of fish doesn't have enough seasoning, and your last batch has way too much.

Start by firing up the grease. Then lay out all the fish that you plan to cook on a cutting board, a piece of cardboard, or even newspaper. If the fish is wet, take a paper towel and soak up the excess water off the fillets. If you don't, the cornmeal will get "clumpy," and the moisture will cool your grease, popping and splattering all the while. After the fillets are mostly dry, season both sides with the three spices. Don't overdo it with the Cajun seasoning. Remember, you can always hit it again after it comes out of the grease if you need to. Once you have put on the black pepper, add a little more. It is hard to overdo it with the black pepper. The same can be said for the garlic powder.

I season the fillets while the grease is coming up to temperature. Next, I empty a bag of yellow cornmeal into a large foil pan. These work great for seasoning fish as well as for serving them. When the thermometer says the oil is about 340°F, I put six to eight pieces into the meal and coat them well, then I gently ease the fillets into the grease by hand. Don't drop them in or you will splash hot oil onto yourself, and a grease burn is the gift that keeps on giving. While this first batch is in, pay attention to your temperature and adjust accordingly. You want it to maintain that 340°F to 350°F range. While the fish are cooking, throw your next batch into the cornmeal for coating. Then take a look at the fish in the fryer. When they are close to being done, which should take only a few minutes, they will begin to float. I like to

turn them over a time or two and leave them in for another minute or so.

The first batch of fish is usually the worst for me. The oil is still new, and your pieces won't be really golden brown. It's a good time to hand a piece to your friend and have them test your seasoning to see if you need to add anything. Do that as soon as it comes out of the fryer, so you can watch your friend instantly spit the fish out because they burned their lips. The frying usually gets better after a couple of batches, but you will want to start to collect the excess meal that is in the oil to prevent it from becoming scorched, all the while watching your temperature. Another good tip is to keep a rag or towel in your back pocket in case you need to remove the pot from the burner for a minute if the oil is getting too hot. Repeat the process until you are done. As the cook, you'll probably end up eating the last batch because the rest will have already been devoured by everyone else. If you like, squeeze some lemon on and dip it in tartar sauce, cocktail sauce, or whatever other kind of sauce you like.

Remember, you can reuse your grease. I can usually get several cookings out of one potful. Just let it cool and pour it back into the original container.

I live in Florida now and don't eat as much catfish as I used to. However, my intake of what my friends and relatives call "saltfish" has increased exponentially. "Saltfish" is anything that comes out of the ocean that is foreign to my family or friends. They have no idea what it is, except that it is fish that came out of the ocean, not off a trotline or jug. That said, the process for saltfish is the same. Black pepper, garlic salt, Cajun seasoning, cornmeal, 350°F. Heck, I do the same for wild turkey, shrimp, ducks, and squirrels. You can't go wrong with anything cooked this way.

Parker Hall is the state director for the USDA/APHIS Wildlife Services Program in Florida.

MILANESA TORTA WITH WILD TURKEY

MAKES 6 SANDWICHES

Tortas are commonly known as "Mexican sandwiches" in the United States. What really sets tortas apart is the bread. Traditionally, they are served on a soft, oval roll called a telera. In Mexico City, you can find torta vendors who are regionally famous for their craft. While the rolls they use are fairly standard, the sandwiches themselves can be stuffed with all manner of different fried or grilled fillings. For this sandwich here, a Milanese-style torta, you'd normally use a pounded chicken cutlet. We're going with wild turkey instead.

TURKEY CUTLETS

1 skinless, boneless wild turkey breast (about 1½ pounds), cut into six 4-ounce pieces

1½ cups plain breadcrumbs

3½ tablespoons store-bought taco spice or Taco-Style Seasoning (page 348)

3 large eggs

1 tablespoon hot sauce, like Cholula

½ cup cornstarch

Canola oil (about 1½ cups for a ½-inch depth in a 12-inch cast-iron pan)

TORTAS

1 (16-ounce) can refried black beans, or 2 cups homemade Refried Black Beans (page 307)

2 (8-ounce) cans chipotles in adobo sauce

6 telera rolls or oval-shaped soft rolls

6 tablespoons Mexican crema

12 ounces Oaxaca cheese, shredded

1½ cups salsa verde, store-bought or homemade (see page 350)

2 tomatoes, sliced

¾ cup pickled jalapeños

1 head iceberg lettuce, shredded

1 large avocado, sliced

SPECIAL EQUIPMENT

12-inch cast-iron skillet

FOR THE CUTLETS. Cut the turkey breast crosswise against the grain into 6 pieces. (Cut out any large pieces of silverskin or connective tissue.) Place between two sheets of plastic wrap and pound them flat into ¼- to ⅓-inch-thick cutlets. The flattened cutlets should be well-tenderized and slightly larger than your torta roll.

TO SET UP THE FRY STATION. Gather three large, deep plates. Place breadcrumbs in the first large plate and stir in the taco spice. Crack the eggs into the second plate and whisk in the hot sauce. Distribute the cornstarch on the third plate.

Dip the cutlets, one by one, first in the cornstarch, shaking to remove any excess, then in the egg, and then finally into the breadcrumbs. Try to cover the entire surface of the cutlet with breadcrumbs by pressing them into any exposed areas.

TO FRY. Place a 12-inch cast-iron skillet over medium-high heat on a propane campstove and add ½ inch canola oil to the pan. Heat the oil until it hits 350°F. Test the temperature with a pinch of breadcrumbs: If they sizzle, pop, and begin to brown, the oil is hot enough.

Working in batches of 2 pieces, fry the turkey cutlets for 3 to 4 minutes on each side, until golden brown and crispy. Remove the cooked turkey, set it on a draining rack or paper towels, and season each piece with a pinch of salt. Repeat with remaining 4 pieces.

FOR THE TORTAS. Slice open the chipotle peppers and scrape out the seeds. On each roll, spread the crema on the top half and a ¼ cup refried beans on the bottom half of each roll. Place turkey on top of the beans and then shredded cheese, 2 or 3 chipotle pepper pieces, salsa verde, tomato slices, pickled jalapeños, shredded lettuce, and lastly a couple avocado slices.

Eat immediately or save the tortas for later, wrapping them tightly in parchment paper and then in foil.

THERMOS RAMEN

MAKES ENOUGH FOR ONE 18-OUNCE THERMOS; SERVES 1

½ (3.5-ounce) package dried ramen noodles (1.75 ounces), broken in half lengthwise

½ of the flavor packet from dried ramen noodles (see Cook's Note)

¼ cup frozen shelled edamame or any leftover vegetables from camp (see list below)

¼ cup sliced, shredded, or dehydrated leftover cooked protein

1¾ cups boiling water

SPECIAL EQUIPMENT

18-ounce wide-mouthed food thermos

COOK'S NOTE. *You can substitute 1 bouillon cube for the half ramen flavor packet.*

ALSO WORKS WITH. *Dehydrated mushrooms and scallions, fresh herbs, thinly sliced vegetables, any cooked and shredded big game or small game meat, or dehydrated meat like hard sausage, jerky, or dried smoked fish.*

Here's a quick and easy (and highly transportable) backcountry meal that'll have you thanking yourself on cold days in the field. You can use this recipe as inspiration and then substitute the ingredients with whatever you happen to have on hand. One package of dried ramen is good for two of these meals. Assemble the soup at home or camp in the morning and then throw it in your backpack. At lunchtime, the noodles are soft, all the ingredients are rehydrated, and the soup is still hot.

Use your backcountry stove to boil 2 cups water. Pour the boiling water into the thermos and add the half package of ramen noodles. Put the lid on for 1 to 2 minutes to soften the noodles, then add half the flavor pack, vegetables, and leftover protein and tightly close the thermos.

Allow to sit for at least 10 to 13 minutes (or the duration of your hike) before eating and then open and stir everything together.

ANODISED

CAMP BREAKFASTS, LUNCHES, AND SNACKS

SOUPED-UP TOAD IN A HOLE

SERVES 4

There are dozens of names for this dish. Egg in a hole, bird in a nest, and the far less appetizing name that I grew up with—toad in a hole—are just a few. Apparently, in some parts of the country it's referred to by the equally unappetizing moniker "spit in a hole." Some say it was made famous by the 1987 romantic comedy *Moonstruck* (where it's called *ouvo in cestino,* or "egg in a basket"), but my dad was cooking it on his camp-stove griddle way the hell before that.

This version does play with the Italian American flavors of the *Moonstruck* version. You can strip this one down as much as you'd like, but if you want something really special, you should follow through on this preparation in its entirety.

4 thin slices pancetta or bacon (4 ounces)

4 slices sandwich bread

6 tablespoons (¾ stick) unsalted butter

4 canned artichoke hearts, drained, dried, and quartered lengthwise

4 large eggs

Kosher salt and freshly ground black pepper

3 tablespoons giardiniera, any large pieces coarsely chopped

Preheat a two-burner griddle over medium-low heat on a campfire stove. Add the pancetta to one side and crisp it while the griddle heats up, flipping halfway through, about 2 minutes. Set aside when done.

Meanwhile, using a 2½-inch round cookie cutter or biscuit cutter, cut a hole in the center of each slice of bread. Set aside.

Melt 2 tablespoons of the butter on the unused side of the griddle. Put both the bread and rounds on the buttered area. Place ½ tablespoon of the butter in each hole, then set an artichoke heart, cut-side down, in the hole and press down so it splays. Crack an egg into each hole, top each with some of the giardiniera, and season with salt and pepper. Let the bread toast until golden, about 1 minute.

Move the bread slices to the side of the griddle and melt the remaining 2 tablespoons butter where the bread was. Carefully flip the bread slices and rounds over. Cook until the bread is golden on the bottom and egg is cooked to the desired doneness, about 1 minute for a runny yolk.

Transfer the egg in a nest and bread rounds to four plates and serve with a side of the pancetta.

COOK'S NOTES. *All giardinieras are not made equal. If you can get your hands on the giardiniera in oil that hails from Chicago delis, get it. It's superior to all others.*

You can invert foil pie tins over two pieces of toast to help the eggs cook faster.

ALSO WORKS WITH. *Smoked ham, game bacon, domestic duck eggs.*

HOW TO MAKE GOOD COFFEE IN THE OUTDOORS

Just like food, coffee tastes better outside. I've been drinking it daily since I was a teenager, and I'm a hopeless addict. We keep things simple at home by using a standard electric coffee maker that requires very little thought or planning. I could get that thing up and running with a blindfold on. In the outdoors, getting a coffee fix requires a little more effort. It's not that big of a deal if I'm using the kitchen stove in my camper or a two-burner stove on a car-camping trip, where I have the space to pack my French press (I love the shatterproof GSI JavaPress). But things can get a tad more specialized on backpacking trips. Back in the old days, I'd carry a zip-top baggie of Folgers instant coffee that I'd premix with powdered creamer. While I wouldn't go so far as to say I'm a coffee snob, these days I'd say I'm something close to it. Which means that I get burned out pretty quickly on Folgers instant coffee. Day one of that stuff is not so bad. But day seven is pretty awful.

Thankfully, outdoor coffee has come a long way over the years. Now you can find instant coffee that's at least 70 percent as good as the real stuff. Alpine Start and Starbucks both produce pretty tasty instant coffee that comes in single-serving packets. For coffee snobs who might balk at the weaker flavor of freeze-dried stuff like Alpine Start, the Starbucks Via packets are a mixture of freeze-dried and micro-ground coffee that are available in a range of popular blends. Either way, you just dump the packet into hot water and stir to dissolve the powder. Another simple, and arguably better, option for car camping and backpacking trips is the single servings of real ground coffee packaged in tea bags that are made by Black Rifle Coffee Company and others. To make a cup of coffee, just steep the bag in a mug of hot water for several minutes. I've yet to find a brand that will do the trick with a single packet. Instead I always start with two. Speaking of mugs, there are plenty of ultralight backpacking models to choose from. I use a GSI mug while backpacking, but I stick to a double-walled, vacuum-insulated mug with a spill-proof lid for everything else. They keep hot coffee hot for a long time without scalding your hands, and you don't have to worry about your buddy's boot kicking your mug over and spilling the goods.

If you really can't get by without brewed coffee, then you'll want to head to REI or another bougie camping retailer and you'll be blown away by the options for packable coffee presses and pour-over devices. The MSR MugMate weighs less than an ounce and filters a single serving of brewed coffee. If you've got a really big backpack, the GSI JavaPress that I mentioned can handle 30 ounces of coffee.

Finally, if you're patient and don't mind a little grit in your morning cup of joe, there's always cowboy coffee. For those of us who tend to rely on quick-and-easy outdoor coffee, making the cowboy version is something of a lost art. But all you need to do is bring a metal coffee kettle or pot of water to a boil. (Some people throw in a pinch of salt.) Historically, this was done over a campfire, but feel free to use a stove. After it reaches a boil, take the kettle off the heat to cool for a minute before adding the appropriate amount of coffee grounds. (Don't add the grounds while the pot is boiling over the flames or you risk burning the grounds and making a horrible-tasting pot of coffee.) Stir the grounds in, put the lid back on, and wait for a couple minutes. Stir again and wait a couple more minutes. Sprinkle a little cold water into the pot and tilt the pot slightly so it's resting at a bit of an angle. This will allow the grounds to settle in one corner of the pot. To serve, pour the coffee slowly without disturbing the grounds on the bottom of the kettle. Chances are there will be a few grounds floating around in your mug anyway, but I guarantee you, it'll taste a helluva lot better than instant Folgers crystals. When it's time to clean up, dump out the used grounds and rinse the pot in a creek. If you're anything like me, that'll get you wondering if trout are easier to catch when they're jacked up on coffee.

MSR

THE LATE EUGENE GROTERS'S BEER AND APPLE PANCAKES

MAKES 6 TO 8 MEDIUM PANCAKES

When I was growing up, one of my dad's fishing buddies was an eccentric junk collector and hobbyist inventor named Eugene Groters. Into his seventies, Groters kept a large mirror fastened over the bed in his log cabin that he shared with his wife, Beatrice. He kept a wild collection of oddities in the living room, including a pair of whitetail fawns stored inside a glass jar filled with what must have been formaldehyde. Overhead racks stored his gun collection, which included a gun for every year he'd been alive. He once told me that he'd made a mistake and had accumulated one more gun than he had birthdays. He then pulled a Winchester Model 94 down from the rack and gave it to me. I used to love waking up in the mornings at Groters's cabin, because he made the best pancakes in the world. He was an avid beer drinker and that's what he used to make his pancakes. He added apple slices, too. When you try these, you'll understand why he made them that way. This recipe can be doubled or tripled, depending on how many people you're feeding.

1 recipe (about 1¼ cups) Modular Pancake Dry Mix (see Cook's Note)

¾ cup American-style pale lager beer

2 tablespoons vegetable oil or melted unsalted butter

1 large egg

1 apple, peeled, cored, and sliced

Unsalted butter, as needed for cooking and (optional) serving

Maple syrup, for serving

In a medium bowl, combine the pancake mix, beer, oil, and egg, stirring until no flour is visible—don't overmix the batter. Allow it to sit for 5 minutes while you preheat a camp-stove griddle or nonstick pan over medium-low heat. (Alternatively you can use a greased cast-iron pan over a keyhole fire; see page lv.)

Melt a pat of butter on the griddle and distribute it evenly. Pour ¼ cup of the batter for each pancake on the griddle and arrange a few apple slices on top. Cook the first side until bubbles appear on top, 3 to 4 minutes, then flip with a spatula and cook the second side for 2 to 3 more minutes until golden brown on the bottom. Remove to a plate and keep warm. Repeat with remaining batter.

Serve warm topped with more butter (if using) and maple syrup.

COOK'S NOTE. *This recipe utilizes a make-ahead dry pancake mix that is featured on page 326. The mix can be used to make all sorts of batters, pancakes, and desserts, so it's a handy item to bring on camping trips.*

MONTE CRISTO SANDWICH

SERVES 4

3 large eggs

½ cup milk

¼ cup Dijon mustard

¼ teaspoon kosher salt

¼ pound Gruyère cheese

2 tablespoons unsalted butter

½ pound sliced smoked ham or Brown Sugar Wild Hog Ham (page 103)

8 slices sturdy white sandwich bread

Confectioners' sugar, for dusting (optional)

Apricot jam, for serving (optional)

Maple syrup, for serving (optional)

ALSO WORKS WITH. *Any smoked game or domestic ham or slices of Summer Sausage (page 100).*

This sandwich has a hell of a lot going for it, as it's made with good ingredients and then battered and fried. What more could you ask for? It's great for breakfast, lunch, or dinner. You can get fancy and French up the top with confectioners' sugar or apricot jam. For breakfast, go with a splash of maple syrup. This one is easy to prep in advance, so you can have it ready in a hurry when it's time to cook.

TO PREP. Up to 24 hours ahead, whisk the eggs, milk, mustard, and salt in a large bowl. Pour into a pint storage container. Refrigerate until ready to use. Grate the cheese and store in a resealable bag.

TO ASSEMBLE AND COOK. Melt 1 tablespoon of the butter in a large cast-iron skillet over medium heat on a propane campstove or keyhole fire (see page lv). Pour the batter into a shallow dish. Place half of the ham on 4 of the bread slices. Evenly top with the shredded cheese. Then place the remaining ham on the cheese. Top with the remaining 4 bread slices. Holding the sandwich closed, carefully submerge it in the batter and let it soak for at least a minute to evenly soak the bread. Place 2 sandwiches at a time in the skillet and cook until golden brown, 3 to 4 minutes per side. Wipe out the skillet and repeat with the remaining ingredients.

Dust with confectioners' sugar (if using) and top with a dollop of jam or douse with maple syrup (if using) before serving.

FIRST LITE

05 ON THE SPIT

As soon as I finished college, my brother Danny and I went down to Mexico's Yucatán Peninsula to spend a month fly-fishing for bonefish in the shallow lagoons south of Tulum. We'd camp on the beaches for three or four nights and then hitchhike our way back north to get resupplied with food and water. Sometimes we'd just hitch to Tulum, which was a hell of a lot emptier and grimier in the mid-1990s than it is today. Other times we'd get on a bus in Tulum and ride even farther north to Playa del Carmen.

We had pretty good fishing on that trip—actually much better than I thought we would—but the thing that really surprised me was the eating. There were a few places near the bus stop in Tulum that served these beautiful and muscular little chickens that they'd marinate in a garbage can. The chicken was grilled over an open flame, slowly and carefully, and then they'd dice the spatchcocked bird into small pieces using a tree stump for a chopping block and a machete. This was the best grilled chicken in the world, and I'm not just saying that because I was half starved every time I ate it. I'm saying that because it was the best grilled chicken in the world.

When we continued north to the town of Playa del Carmen, we were motivated in part by the nightlife there, which was great. But the tacos al pastor in Playa del Carmen were even better. These were small tacos made with corn tortillas and thinly sliced pork shoulder that had been marinated in citrus juices and herbs. The tacos were topped with onions and cilantro. What blew me away about the tacos was more than just the taste; I was mesmerized by the visual display of the cooking contraption, known as a trompo. A mountain of thinly sliced pork was layered on the trompo's vertically mounted rotisserie spit. The meat formed a roughly cylindrical shape about the size of a big raccoon. The cylinder was capped with a skinned-out pineapple. The rotisserie turned in front of a vertical burner. They added achiote paste to the marinade, so that the roasted meat turned a reddish pink. The rough edges of the cylinder became lightly charred in the burner's heat, and the pineapple juice running down the meat made it glisten. For maximum visual display, taco vendors positioned their trompo at chest height. They'd use long knives to whack off slices of the meat and pineapple that they'd catch in a tortilla held in their hand like a baseball mitt. Then they'd top it with cilantro and diced onion. Like I said, mesmerizing.

After eating several dozen tacos al pastor over the course of that month in Mexico, I was committed to the idea of someday owning my own trompo. I finally got around to it as I was planning the day of my wedding. I wanted to host an all-day volleyball tournament in my home state of Michigan to entertain my friends before the evening ceremony. It seemed like tacos al pastor would be the perfect thing to serve at lunch. If you hated volleyball and didn't know what to do with yourself, you could at least watch that glorious cylinder of meat spin round and round.

My buddy Ronny, who's a fabricator, welded me a beautiful trompo from stainless-steel scraps that he pilfered from a plant in Virginia that makes and packages the ultra-pasteurized single-serving half-and-half containers you see in gas stations. Instead of a propane burner, he fitted it with a rectangular charcoal box. The meat-facing side of the box was expanded

metal grating. The day before my wedding, we sliced a pile of venison roasts and added them to a marinade. The next morning, we layered the slices on the spit, topped it with a pineapple, and set that thing to turning in front of the charcoal box. Of my whole wedding day, that's pretty much the only thing I remember with any level of detail: spiking volleyballs and hammering tacos al pastor.

You can't argue against the pageantry of anything that's cooked on a spit. It's fun and it looks cool. Most of us get our first experience with this form of cooking when we're kids. Thread a hot dog or a marshmallow on a stick and then let it burn to a black mess over a campfire. My kids love cooking like this. I made them each custom marshmallow sticks with a steel rod set into a deer antler handle as Easter presents. These got zero traction. The kids much prefer taking a machete over to a stand of aspens in our backyard and whacking down their own.

If roasting marshmallows is the elementary school of cooking on a spit, the shish kebab is junior high. Linguists believe that the word *kebab* comes from an Arabic word for roasted meat. If you do things right, you can get perfectly cooked bites of meat, seafood, and veggies on a kebab without a whole lot of hassle. The presentation of a classic kebab can be beautiful, with those contrasting colors of intermixed green and yellow peppers, purple onions, and white mushrooms. But eventually you figure out that keeping the meat separate from the veggies allows you to tailor cooking times to the particular needs of each ingredient. That gives you the magic of having buttery, cooked-through mushrooms alongside rare cubes of steak on your picnic table at the same time.

This chapter will take you on a journey that goes way beyond the classic kebab, into a huge and wild world full of spit-cooking possibilities. You'll go from skewered hearts to the showstopping trompo to caveman-style ducks spatchcocked on sharpened saplings. You'll even take a detour into tripod cooking, where you'll use various contraptions to suspend cookware in the heat of a fire. Some of this might seem like a lot of work, but it's well worth it. It's certainly a lot easier than backpacking up and down the Yucatán coast for a month in search of your next fix of tacos al pastor. Besides, I've heard that part of Mexico has gotten really built up. They say it's not what it used to be.

SPITS AND SKEWERS: WHAT YOU NEED TO KNOW

Spits and skewers come in many forms, from hot dog sticks carved out of twigs to the asado crosses used in Argentina to roast whole lambs. No matter the design or material, their function is basically the same: Spits and skewers allow food of varying sizes to be easily rotated or flipped during cooking. Entire hogs, whole game birds, piles of thinly sliced or chunked meat, and all manner of vegetables can be impaled and roasted this way. In this next section, you'll find examples of the different types of spits and skewers used for the recipes in this chapter.

When you think of a skewer, you're probably envisioning a typical combination of meat and vegetables threaded in an alternating pattern onto a thin piece of metal or wood. Building skewers that way is a great idea in theory, but a better plan is to follow the rule of keeping like with like. In other words, your veggies all go together on one set of skewers and the meat goes on another. Taking this approach means no more mediocre skewers with one ingredient that's undercooked, the next that's overcooked, and some that are burnt to a crisp. Instead, each singular ingredient will be cooked to perfection before being combined on your serving platter. Although they're usually cooked on a grill (or coals) over direct heat, skewers need to be rotated, much like a miniature spit, to achieve the desired results of meat with a tender interior and a crispy, caramelized exterior.

Skewers

You can make your own skewers with the same simple tools and materials used to make a DIY spit like the one above, or you can buy them. For a few dollars, you can get a hundred throwaway spits made out of bamboo, but you have to soak them for 30 minutes in water prior to use or they tend to catch fire on the grill. Skip the hassle and get a set of reusable metal skewers; they aren't much more expensive and they'll last forever. For backyard grilling, 8- to 12-inch skewers work well, but you may want some longer skewers in the 16- to 24-inch range for campfire cooking. Flat skewers, which are most commonly used across the Mediterranean and Middle East, are intended for ground meat; you'll find a recipe using those on page 276.

Backcountry Campfire Spits

As long as there's some green, live wood nearby (willow and alder are ideal), you can fashion a sturdy campfire spit system with just a pocketknife and maybe a hatchet or small handsaw. Look for limbs at least an inch in diameter for the support poles—anything smaller may burn up and collapse, dumping your meal into the ashes. And size up your spit sticks as needed to support whatever you're cooking. This setup is ideal for cooking whole squirrels, rabbits, and small game birds in the backcountry.

Rotisserie Devices

From small electric attachments that integrate with propane grills to whole-hog charcoal spit roasters or homemade devices like the trompo pictured above, there's no shortage of innovative rotisserie options out there. Some rotisseries must be turned manually, while others are motorized. What they all have in common is allowing the user to constantly rotate roasting meat, often for a long period of time, so it cooks evenly throughout or can be shaved off as it cooks, in the style of a trompo or shawarma.

HOW TO MAKE A DIY SPIT FOR MALLARDS AND OTHER GAME BIRDS

All you need to cook game birds or small game animals over a campfire is a pocket knife and access to some green wood. First, build the support frame for the Backcountry Grate on page 12 over a bed of hot coals. Then cut your sharpened spits long enough so they can rest in the frame and hold the bird or critter while it roasts.

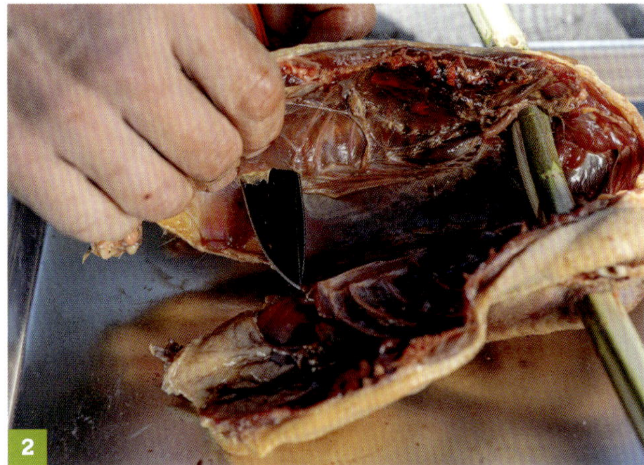

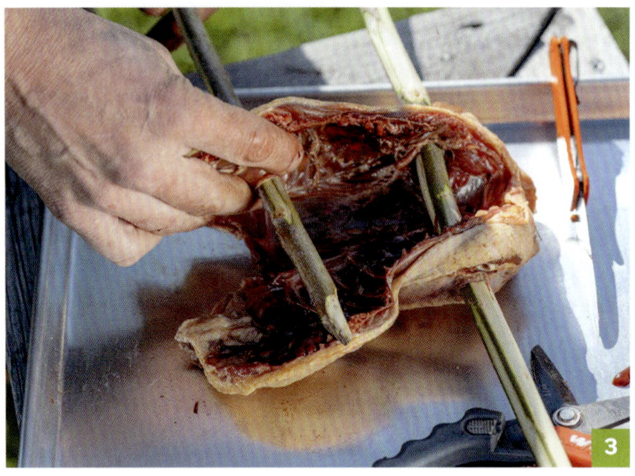

1. Spatchcock your bird (see instructions on page 75).

2. Use a sharp knife to make two slits through the back of each side of the bird. (Use the same technique for rabbits or squirrels.)

3. Insert the spits through the slits.

4. Using two spits keeps larger birds in position while they are suspended over the fire.

5. If the cavity is tight, use a third spit to open the bottom of the bird wider for more even cooking.

6. Suspend your birds on spits over an outdoor spit frame skin-side down to start.

7. Baste the birds as you cook, rotating them skin-side down and skin-side up as needed to ensure even cooking.

8. When the meat is cooked through and skin is golden, it's ready.

SICHUAN SKEWERS

MAKES 8 TO 10 SKEWERS; SERVES 2 TO 4 AS A MAIN OR 6 AS AN APPETIZER

This method is inspired by Sichuan street vendors who start by dipping skewers into hot fat before throwing them on the grill for a few minutes. After that, they repeat the dipping and grilling process, and then finally they hit the skewers with an array of aromatic spices. Often prepared with beef or lamb, this dish can be made with all kinds of big game meat. The skewers are addictive, and they're a great way to use up all of your odds and ends. You do need to plan ahead to have the right vessel for the hot fat. And it should go without saying that you need to be attentive when you have hot grease near a flaming grill. A splatter of grease can catch fire fast and easy, so be careful.

SPICE-INFUSED FAT

Depending on the size of your pot, you may want to double this infused fat so that it's deeper in the pot (see the Cook's Note).

Makes about 2 cups

14 to 16 ounces rendered fat (preferably bear, goose, or duck)

5 whole star anise

3 bay leaves

3 cinnamon sticks

5 whole cloves

½ teaspoon Sichuan peppercorns

½ teaspoon fennel seeds

SICHUAN SPICE MIX

2 teaspoons cumin seeds

2 teaspoons Sichuan peppercorns

1 tablespoon crushed red pepper flakes

2 teaspoons fennel seeds

2 teaspoons granulated garlic

2 teaspoons kosher salt

---

1 pound big game round, cut into ½- to 1-inch cubes

SPECIAL EQUIPMENT

1½-quart metal bain-marie or tall, narrow pot (see Cook's Note)

10 (8- to 10-inch) metal skewers

FOR THE INFUSED FAT. Put the fat, star anise, bay leaves, cinnamon sticks, cloves, Sichuan peppercorns, and fennel seeds into a small, heavy-bottomed saucepan that is tall and narrow. You want the fat to reach at least halfway up the pot. Heat the fat and spices over medium-low heat. Let the spices steep in the fat for 1 hour. Reduce the heat to low if the fat is bubbling. Carefully strain through a fine-mesh sieve into a heatproof bowl. If you're not using it immediately, let it cool, then cover and refrigerate. Otherwise, wipe out the pot with a dry paper towel and return the fat to the pot.

FOR THE SPICE MIX. In a small, dry cast-iron or other heavy-bottomed skillet, toast the cumin seeds over medium heat, shaking occasionally, until they are fragrant and turn a darker shade of brown. This should take only a minute. Transfer the cumin to a plate. Add the Sichuan peppercorns to the same skillet and toast for 30 seconds, again shaking occasionally, or until fragrant. Transfer to a plate and let both spices cool. Add the toasted cumin seeds and peppercorns to a spice or coffee grinder or a mortar and pestle and pulverize them. Add 2 teaspoons of the red pepper flakes and the fennel. Pulse or grind the spices until coarsely ground. Stir in the remaining 1 teaspoon red pepper flakes, the granulated garlic, and salt and transfer to a small bowl.

Prepare a grill at medium-high heat for two-thirds direct and one-third indirect grilling.

Thread the meat onto metal skewers, pushing the meat to the tip of the skewer. Set aside on a plate.

SAFETY TIPS BEFORE GETTING STARTED. Pour the fat into the tall and narrow pot. Be sure you have a towel or leather grilling gloves handy. It is

Recipe continues

COOK'S NOTE. *A narrow (4 to 6 inches in diameter), tall (6 to 8 inches high) pot or bain-marie is ideal for preparing the fat and dipping the skewers in this recipe. (If you have an asparagus pot, this might be your chance to use it.) If you're lacking a pot with the right dimensions, the best option is to use a small 1- to 1½-quart pot and baste the skewers with a brush or a spoon; you'll get approximately the same results. Make sure to use a pot with metal handles that are safe for the grill.*

ALSO WORKS WITH. *All hooved big game animals, wild turkey, geese, and ducks.*

best if you can warm the pot of fat on a grill side burner. If this isn't possible, use the grill itself, making sure the grill is level and stable. Heat the fat until hot but not smoking, then move it to the indirect side of the grill.

TO GRILL. Use a brush to coat the meat lightly with the seasoned fat. Grill very lightly on all sides, less than 30 seconds per side. Working with about four skewers at a time, carefully plunge them into the pot of fat, at an angle if necessary, to cover as much of the meat with the fat. If the fat does not completely cover the meat, spoon or brush the hot fat over the meat several times to baste it. Carefully pull the skewers from the fat and let the fat drip back into the pot.

Return the skewers to the grill and sprinkle generously with the spice mix. Cook until lightly charred in spots and to the desired doneness. Remove the skewers from the grill and sprinkle with more spice mix. Transfer to a platter and serve.

SHEEP SKEWERS (ARROSTICINI)

SERVES 6

Arrosticini are a traditional skewered dish from the Italian province of Abruzzo. Sheepherding goes back untold centuries in the Abruzzese mountains, so naturally skewers from the region are made with lamb. They're cooked on a narrow, channel-shaped grill called a canala or furnacella by street vendors who pack cubes of meat and fat closely together. The high heat sears and caramelizes the meaty bits as the fat melts and bastes the meat. The skewers are simply seasoned with sea salt and sometimes rosemary after grilling.

Wild sheep and feral sheep are an excellent wild game substitution for lamb, but be sure to choose tender cuts. Here we're substituting pancetta in place of lamb fat.

1½ pounds sheep top round, trimmed and cut into ¾-inch cubes

1 tablespoon fresh rosemary leaves, coarsely chopped (from 1 sprig)

1 tablespoon kosher salt, plus more for sprinkling

4 garlic cloves, smashed

2 tablespoon extra-virgin olive oil

1 tablespoon fresh lemon juice

6 (¼-inch-thick) slices pancetta, cut into ¾-inch chunks

Crusty bread, lightly grilled, for serving

SPECIAL EQUIPMENT

Metal or wooden skewers (see Cook's Note)

In a medium bowl, combine the meat, rosemary, salt, garlic, and oil until well coated. Cover and refrigerate for at least 5 hours or up to 24 hours. Bring to room temperature 1 hour before cooking. Toss with the lemon juice right before skewering. Prepare a medium-hot grill for direct grilling. Discard the garlic. Thread the cubes of meat onto skewers, with small pieces of pancetta between every 2 pieces of meat. Be sure to pack the skewer tightly without any space between the chunks of meat.

Grill the skewers, turning often, until they are slightly charred on the outside and medium-rare on the inside. This may take only 3 to 4 minutes total. Try to avoid flare-ups.

Sprinkle the skewers with additional salt as they come off of the grill. Serve immediately with crusty bread.

ALSO WORKS WITH. *Wild hog, antelope, deer, domestic lamb, feral sheep, and goats.*

COOK'S NOTE. *If you're using wooden skewers, soak them in water for at least 30 minutes to prevent them from burning on the grill.*

BIG GAME HEART SKEWERS

SERVES 6 TO 8

1 (2-pound) big game heart

1 tablespoon extra-virgin olive oil

2 teaspoons flaky sea salt, such as Maldon

6 fresh bay leaves, snipped crosswise into ¾-inch-wide strips

5 garlic cloves, smashed

Crusty bread, lightly grilled, for serving

ALSO WORKS WITH. *Deer, elk, moose, or pronghorn heart, cleaned and sliced, or whole rabbit, turkey, and upland bird hearts.*

Hearts are one of the finest-tasting parts of game animals—my oldest boy will say the very best part—and they're the perfect medium for grilled skewers. This simple Portuguese preparation with bay leaves and garlic lets the mild flavor and tender texture of hearts shine through. Be careful not to overcook them—they are at their very best medium-rare. This recipe uses thin slices of big game hearts. Slicing them thin makes them easier to fold on the skewer and helps the meat stay tender. Smaller hearts from ducks or rabbits can be cooked whole. If you're not familiar with how to clean a big game heart, see the sidebar below.

PREP THE HEART. Clean and prep the heart according to the instructions below, and cut it into ¼-inch-thick slices. Put the slices into a large bowl and toss with the oil, sea salt, bay leaves, and garlic. Cook immediately or marinate for up to 2 hours.

TO ASSEMBLE. Thread the slices of heart onto the skewers in a tight folding S or accordion pattern. Occasionally insert the bay leaves and garlic in between the slices of meat. Push the meat together tightly.

TO GRILL. Prepare a medium-hot grill for direct grilling. Place the skewers on a well-oiled grill grate. Grill, turning occasionally, for 6 to 8 minutes, until the meat is slightly charred on all sides but not overcooked.

Transfer to a plate and serve with crusty bread. Discard the bay leaves before eating.

HOW TO PREPARE A HEART FOR SKEWERS

Rinse the heart, pat dry, and place it on a cutting board. First trim the hard, white fat off the outside of the heart. Next, slice off the gristly top "cap" of the heart to expose the interior chambers. Butterfly the heart by making a lengthwise incision from top to bottom, but don't cut all the way through. Lay the heart out flat on the cutting board—this may require a couple more additional cuts. Now trim all interior fat, arteries, and fibrous connective tissue until you're left with clean muscle. Lastly, cut the heart into lengthwise slices about ⅛ to ¼ inch thick.

CRYING TIGER SKEWERS

WITH HEARTS OF DUCK OR UPLAND BIRD

SERVES 4

These skewers are influenced by "crying tiger," a grilled beef dish from Thailand. They're served with a spicy dipping sauce called *jaew* (see Cook's Note) that's made with dried Thai chile flakes. While it is customary to finish the sauce with ground toasted rice, it's also delicious without it. The sauce pairs well with most grilled foods and would be a welcome accompaniment to a simple seared steak.

My strategy for bird hearts is to keep storing the hearts in my freezer until I've got enough to make a dish with them.

MARINADE

2 tablespoons soy sauce

2 tablespoons oyster sauce

1 tablespoon fish sauce

1 tablespoon neutral oil, plus more for grilling

2 tablespoons granulated sugar

¼ teaspoon freshly ground black pepper

---

1 pound duck hearts

DIPPING SAUCE (JAEW)

Makes ⅔ cup

1 tablespoon uncooked jasmine or glutinous rice (optional but highly recommended)

¼ cup fish sauce

3 tablespoons fresh lime juice (about 2 limes)

3 tablespoons packed dark brown sugar

1 to 2 tablespoons crushed red pepper flakes or gochugaru, plus more as needed

1 tablespoon finely chopped fresh cilantro

1 scallion, white and green parts, finely chopped

1 medium shallot, thinly sliced crosswise (about 2 generous tablespoons)

FOR THE MARINADE. In a wide, shallow container, stir together the soy sauce, oyster sauce, fish sauce, oil, granulated sugar, and black pepper until the sugar dissolves.

Add the duck hearts to the marinade, stirring to coat them well. Cover and marinate in the refrigerator for at least 3 hours, or keep them refrigerated in a storage bag with the marinade for up to a day.

FOR THE DIPPING SAUCE. Toast the rice (if using) in a small, dry cast-iron skillet over medium heat, swirling often, until golden brown, 5 to 7 minutes. Transfer the rice to a plate to cool. Using a spice or coffee grinder or a mortar and pestle, grind the rice into a powder. Set aside until ready to use.

Mix the fish sauce and lime juice with the brown sugar until the brown sugar dissolves. Add the red pepper flakes, cilantro, scallions, and shallots. Add more red pepper flakes for spicy skewers, if desired. Cover and refrigerate until ready to use. This sauce can also be made in advance and stored in the fridge. Stir in the rice powder (if using) just before serving.

GRILL. Prepare a medium-high hot grill or campfire for direct grilling. Thread the hearts onto the skewers. Lightly brush the hearts with oil. Grill on a well-oiled grate, turning often, until seared on all sides, 3 to 4 minutes for rare.

Transfer to a platter and serve with the dipping sauce.

MAKE AHEAD. *The marinade can be made in advance and stored in a leakproof container at room temperature for up to a month.*

ALSO WORKS WITH. *Hearts from hooved big game animals, upland birds, waterfowl, and small game. If using big game, see How to Prepare a Heart for Skewers on page 268.*

COOK'S NOTE. *Jaew is a spicy dipping sauce. Start with 1 teaspoon of red pepper flakes and then add more to taste. Stir the ground rice into the sauce to thicken right before serving.*

VEGETABLE SKEWERS

SERVES 4 TO 6 AS A SIDE

- 1 pint cherry tomatoes
- 10 ounces medium mushrooms, cleaned and trimmed
- 2 small onions, peeled and cut lengthwise into 6 wedges each
- 2 zucchini, cut in half lengthwise, then cut into ½-inch half moons
- Extra-virgin olive oil, for drizzling
- Kosher salt and freshly ground black pepper

SPECIAL EQUIPMENT

10 (8- to 12-inch) metal skewers

Mushrooms don't cook at the same rate as cherry tomatoes, and cherry tomatoes don't cook at the same rate as onions. Which is to say, you'll get the best results if you don't mix different types of vegetables on the same skewer. Go ahead and mix aromatics for flavor if you want to combine a vegetable with citrus slices or a hearty flavor enhancer (such as sage, thyme, rosemary, or even scallions) that can stand up to the heat of the grill. You can make simple vegetable skewers by brushing them with a touch of olive oil and then sprinkling them with a bit of salt and pepper. For a little variety, try hitting them with a seasoned mushroom or garlic salt or one of the many spice rubs on page 355. You can also brush on one of the glazes from page 355 just before removing the vegetables from the grill. And, of course, grilled vegetables will pair well with many of the condiments in this book (see pages 349 to 355). Here's an easy recipe to get you started.

Skewer the vegetables, using 4 skewers for the tomatoes and 2 each for the mushrooms, onion wedges, and zucchini. Dress with a drizzle of olive oil and season with salt and pepper. Prepare a grill for direct heat. When hot, lay down the skewers with space in between them. Cook each to your desired doneness. Char and caramelization add flavor; it should take 3 to 5 minutes per side for the tomatoes and zucchini, and 6 to 8 minutes per side for the onions to get some color and cook through. Rotate the mushrooms as they cook. They will steam a little and then begin to crisp in parts after 10 to 12 minutes.

Remove the skewers to a plate and serve warm or at room temperature, with or without a condiment of your choice.

TUNA AND/OR YELLOWTAIL SKEWERS

AND SALAD WITH CARROT-MISO DRESSING

SERVES 2 TO 4

This dish will be familiar to anyone who's explored the menus at Japanese American restaurants across the United States. The glaze is magical and doesn't need to be used exclusively on skewered foods. It'd be just as good brushed across a grilled or baked fillet of fish. Here, I'm using a couple of my favorite ocean residents—yellowfin tuna and yellowtail (known on sushi menus as ahi and hamachi, respectively)—but you could replace these with any number of fish species. And you can put just about any vegetable under that carrot-miso dressing and it'll disappear just as quickly. Be aware of issues consuming raw fish. Always keep fish chilled until it's ready to eat, and eat fresh raw fish that has never been frozen at your own risk. Flash freezing kills off any parasites that might be lurking within.

GINGER-SOY GLAZE

Makes about 1 cup

½ cup soy sauce

¼ cup packed dark brown sugar

¼ cup honey

2 tablespoons unseasoned rice vinegar

1 (3-inch) piece fresh ginger, peeled and grated (about 5 teaspoons)

2 garlic cloves, grated

2 teaspoons cornstarch

SKEWERS

9 ounces sushi-quality skinless tuna fillet, cut into 1-inch cubes

2 or 3 scallions, white and green parts, cut into 1-inch pieces

5 ounces sushi-quality skinless yellowtail fillet, cut into ¾- to 1-inch cubes

Canola oil or other neutral oil, for brushing

1 serrano chile, thinly sliced, for garnish

SALAD

3 cups iceberg lettuce cut into bite-sized pieces

3 Persian cucumbers, cut into thick half-moons

2 (3½-ounce) medium carrots, julienned or shredded on the large holes of a box grater

½ pint grape tomatoes (about 6 ounces), quartered

1 recipe Carrot-Miso Dressing (page 302)

FOR THE GLAZE. In a small saucepan, combine the soy sauce, brown sugar, honey, vinegar, ginger, and garlic. Simmer over medium-low heat, stirring occasionally, for 15 minutes, or until the sauce reduces slightly. While the sauce is simmering, in a small bowl whisk together the cornstarch and 1 tablespoon water until smooth. Whisk the cornstarch mixture into the sauce and continue to cook, stirring, until the sauce thickens. Set aside. The sauce will continue to thicken as it cools.

FOR THE SKEWERS. Prepare a medium-hot grill. Thread two skewers, alternating with the tuna and scallions; set aside. Repeat with the yellowtail. Lightly brush the skewers with neutral oil and place them on a well-oiled grill grate. Grill on each side until grill marks appear, 5 to 10 seconds per side. Generously brush with the glaze, then return to the grill for another 5 to 10 seconds per side. Remove the skewers from the grill, brush again with the glaze, and transfer to a platter or tray. Scatter serrano slices over the skewers.

FOR THE SALAD. In a large bowl, mix the lettuce, cucumbers, carrots, and tomatoes. Drizzle with ¼ cup dressing and toss to evenly coat. Add more dressing to taste. Divide the salad between two bowls and serve each salad with one skewer of tuna and one skewer of yellowtail.

WOVEN CALAMARI SKEWERS

WITH HARISSA AIOLI

SERVES 4 TO 6

One of my earliest magazine stories was about the nocturnal culture of squid jiggers in Seattle who come to the downtown piers on winter nights to fish for *Loligo opalescens,* otherwise known as the market squid. Many years after writing the article, I ended up living in Seattle, where my kids and I joined the ranks of the nighttime squid jiggers on a regular basis. The squidding season runs pretty much from Thanksgiving to Valentine's Day, during that period of long, dark nights and short days. On a bad night we wouldn't get any, but on a good night we might get fifty or sixty squid measuring anywhere from four to eight inches, not counting the tentacles. During the few years that I lived in Seattle, we made many mounds of fried calamari, as well as various versions of stuffed squid and braised squid. I wish I had figured out this preparation back then, because it would have been a welcome way to switch things up even more. Crowding the squid rings together means they get seared quickly on the outside and steamed to cook through to the center. Done properly, you'll get squid that is tender but not overcooked. It looks really cool, too. You can use any size of squid for this, as long as you adjust the recipe for the weight. You'll see our recipe calls for larger pieces, while the photograph shows smaller squid. Both options are more than fine.

HARISSA AIOLI

Makes 1 cup

3 garlic cloves

2 tablespoons fresh lemon juice

½ teaspoon kosher salt, plus more as needed

1 large egg

¾ cup extra-virgin olive oil

2 tablespoons prepared harissa paste (see Cook's Note)

SQUID

1 pound cleaned squid tubes and tentacles, patted dry

1 tablespoon extra-virgin olive oil

1 tablespoon fresh lemon juice

¾ teaspoon kosher salt, plus more as needed

⅛ teaspoon freshly ground black pepper

Neutral oil, for greasing

FOR THE AIOLI. In a mini food chopper, pulse the garlic until minced. Add the lemon juice, salt, and egg and pulse to combine. With the motor running, slowly drizzle in the oil until the mixture is emulsified and thickened. Add the harissa and pulse to mix thoroughly. Adjust salt if needed. Cover and refrigerate until ready to serve or chill in a cooler for car camping. The aioli will keep for up to 4 days; it's best when enjoyed within a day or two.

FOR THE SQUID. Cut the calamari tubes crosswise into 1-inch-wide rings. Cut the tentacles in half. In a large bowl, toss the calamari rings and tentacles, oil, lemon juice, salt, and pepper until well coated. Fold a calamari ring in half to make a small bundle, roughly 1 inch in size, and thread it onto a skewer. Repeat and thread all the rings of calamari onto a skewer, stacking them tightly so no bare skewer appears between the pieces. Next, fold and skewer the tentacles.

Prepare a medium-hot grill for direct grilling. Place the calamari skewers onto well-oiled grates of the grill. Grill, turning occasionally, until the calamari are charred on all sides, 4 to 5 minutes. Transfer to a plate, sprinkle with a little more salt, and serve with harissa aioli.

COOK'S NOTE. *Harissa paste is a flavorful, rich hot chile–based paste that comes from the Maghreb region of North Africa. It has roasted red peppers and an array of aromatics and spices including garlic, caraway, cumin, and coriander. It is now widely available at most grocery stores, but if you have difficulty finding it, check a high-end grocery store or order it online.*

ALSO WORKS WITH. *Octopus, scallops.*

VENISON KOFTA KEBABS

WITH SALAD, YOGURT SAUCE, AND PITA BREAD

SERVES 4 (2 KEBABS AND 1 PITA PER PERSON)

KEBABS

1 small yellow onion, cut into chunks

1½ pounds finely ground big game meat (see Cook's Note)

1 teaspoon ground cinnamon

1 teaspoon ground coriander

1 teaspoon ground cumin

1 teaspoon paprika

½ teaspoon ground nutmeg

½ teaspoon ground black pepper

½ teaspoon ground white pepper

1½ teaspoons kosher salt

YOGURT SAUCE

½ cup plain whole-milk yogurt (not Greek)

1 small garlic clove, minced or grated

1 teaspoon fresh lemon juice

2 teaspoons olive oil

¼ teaspoon kosher salt

10 fresh mint leaves, finely chopped

SALAD

1 small yellow onion, halved crosswise and thinly sliced with the grain

½ bunch fresh flat-leaf parsley, leaves torn (about 1 cup)

1 tablespoon fresh lemon juice

1 tablespoon olive oil

¼ teaspoon kosher salt

---

1 recipe homemade Pita (page 314)

Neutral oil, for grilling

SPECIAL EQUIPMENT

8 flat metal 12-inch skewers

This kebab is made from ground meat that gets formed into a tight tube around a skewer. It's based on kofta, a preparation that is credited to the ancient Arabs and today is a staple of the Middle East, Turkey, and North Africa. Traditional kofta is made of finely chopped meat (it's called kofta whether it's placed on a skewer or formed into meatballs), but we're using ground meat, or burger, instead. These skewers are best enjoyed with all of the components, so make an event of it. Store-bought pita will do if there's no time to make it yourself. If you have access to a Middle Eastern market and can find the seasoning mix called Lebanese seven spices, go for it. Pick up some sumac while you're at it—it'll add extra zing to the salad. Both sumac and the spice mix are available online, but we've worked a homemade version of it into our kebab mixture below.

FOR THE KEBABS. Blitz the onion in a food processor. Put the ground meat in a large bowl. Add the onion, spices, and salt. Mix thoroughly. Using about 3 ounces of the meat per skewer, form tight tubes 7 to 9 inches long around each skewer. You need to squeeze the meat to make sure it sticks to itself and to the skewer. Be sure to seal it well so it doesn't fall off. Keep it well chilled until grilling, which will also help it stay on the skewer during cooking.

FOR THE YOGURT SAUCE. Stir together the yogurt, garlic, lemon juice, oil, salt, and mint in a small bowl.

FOR THE SALAD. If desired, soak the onions in water to cover for 5 minutes to make it less pungent. Drain, then toss the onions with the parsley, lemon juice, oil, and salt.

TO GRILL. Prepare a campfire or grill for direct heat with a grate fitted over the top. If making the pitas, follow the instructions on page 314 to make and cook the pitas before grilling the kebabs.

Clean and oil the grates. Place the kebabs over the coals and grill, turning occasionally with the help of a metal spatula to keep them from sticking, until nicely browned, juicy, and cooked to 160°F, 15 to 20 minutes.

For each serving, hold a pita in your hand and grab the kebab to slide it off the skewer. Repeat with a second kebab. Drizzle the kebabs with some yogurt sauce and top with salad.

COOK'S NOTE. *The meat should be finely ground for this kebab.*

SPIKED FOWL

This preparation is more of a technique than a recipe. It'll gather curious onlookers, for sure, who'll want to stand around debating whether or not it'll actually work out. The answer is yes, it will, if you have the patience to let the meat cook in the ambient and reflected heat from the fire rather than crowding it too close to the flames and scorching it. Variations on the technique are more commonly used for roasting lambs in Argentina or cooking batches of whole salmon that are opened like books and fixed to vertically mounted stakes set in the ground. But we're doing it here with whole game birds, which is a lot of fun and tastes really special. Make sure that your birds are plucked and not skinned, as the intact skin will help prevent the meat from drying out and a steady spritz of a salty brine will keep it moist and flavorful.

FOR EACH BIRD

1 green stake from a willow or other pliable tree, 3 to 4 feet long and 1 to 2 inches in diameter

1 nail

Length of string

Mallet or a rock

1 bird, backbone removed with game shears

SALINE SOLUTION

In a spray bottle, combine:

1¾ cups water

¼ cup kosher salt

FOR THE FIRE

10 to 16 logs of firewood

Pieces of flexible metal such as corrugated steel or sheet metal (non-galvanized), 4 feet tall and approximately 15 to 21 feet in length

Shovel to dig a trench

FOR THE BIRDS. We found that whole plucked game birds like quail, ducks, pheasant, and grouse are the perfect size for this technique. The skin shields the meat from drying out, and birds of this size don't need to cook too long, relatively speaking. You can absolutely try larger portions of big game meat that demand a longer roast; just keep in mind that the lack of fat can lead to a dry, chewy eating experience.

You can add other flavors like apple cider vinegar or citrus zest and juice, even herbs, to this solution. Just let the solution sit for at least 2 hours to absorb some of the flavors.

STAKE THE BIRDS. Whittle the bottom tip of the stake so you can pound it into the ground. Hammer a nail about 2 feet above the bottom. This will be the "stop" for your bird, should it slide. Wipe the stake down with a clean, wet rag to remove any dirt or bugs. Insert the stake into the cavity of the bird and nestle it just above the nail. Using the twine, truss each bird tightly around a stake. The back ribs will likely overlap on the stake as it's wrapped.

PLAN THE FIRE. It's a good idea to plan this out before you truss the birds or start the fire. Make sure you've got enough stakes, metal, and room to make it work. The key to this cooking setup, which essentially functions like a large oven, is the heat reflector, which is a metal perimeter that wraps around the fire. Use a flexible metal 3 to 4 feet wide that comes in sheets or rolls, like corrugated steel. Avoid galvanized steel, as it can

Recipe continues

release toxins at high temperatures. You'll need several yards, depending on the circumference of your fire pit. Arrange your firewood in an oval shape. Dig a short trench that will lead under the metal from the outside of the reflector to the edge of the fire to draw in oxygen.

Use a mallet to pound the stakes into the ground with the birds breast-side toward the fire in a semicircle about 2 feet from the fire's edge and about 1 foot from where you'll place the metal reflector. Wrap the reflector around the fire, about 1 foot behind the semicircle of birds on stakes and 3 feet from the fire. Leave a small gap in the metal perimeter where you can enter and exit. You can wedge the metal into soft ground or use makeshift exterior supports to hold it up.

ROAST THE BIRDS. Cook until the birds become golden brown, periodically spraying them with the saline solution throughout the process, about every 5 to 10 minutes. Total cooking time will vary depending on the size of the birds, the heat from your fire, and the ambient temperature. Lean the stake closer to the fire if needed. For a grouse or pheasant, the internal temperature should register 155°F deep in the breast and at the thigh joint. Expect an hour or more for birds of this size and much less for a quail. Duck breast is excellent medium-rare to medium, so don't overcook and pull the duck at 140°F. Keep in mind the legs and wings won't cook at the same rate as the breasts, so they might end up a little tough—but they're still tasty and fun to gnaw on.

Serve with any of the condiments and sauces on pages 349 to 355.

HOG ON THE TROMPO

SERVES 12 TO 16

If you want the full story behind this recipe's inspiration, you can read about my experiences on the Yucatán Peninsula back in the mid-1990s on page 253. If you're short on time, here's a truncated version: I came to love tacos al pastor while traveling in Mexico in search of bonefish. About ten years later, I pestered my buddy Ronny into welding me a trompo so that I could produce my own version for friends on my wedding day. An even shorter version of the story would simply be this: Trompos are badass. This recipe is scaled up for throwing big ol' taco parties where you might want to put 5 pounds of marinated meat on the spit. You'll find a scaled-down version with a smaller yield for 1½ pounds of meat on page 346. As for how to make friends with a welder, you're on your own.

MARINADE

Makes 5¼ cups

12 dried guajillo chiles, stems and seeds removed (21 ounces total)

3 large white onions

12 garlic cloves

3 chipotle chiles in adobo sauce

½ cup plus 1 tablespoon apple cider vinegar

⅓ cup achiote paste (3 ounces; optional but recommended)

⅓ cup plus 1 tablespoon sugar

2 to 3 tablespoons kosher salt

1 tablespoon dried oregano, preferably Mexican

1½ teaspoons ground cumin

½ teaspoon freshly ground black pepper

MEAT

5 pounds wild hog backstrap and roasts, thinly cut into ¼-inch slices

1 whole fresh pineapple, peeled with top still on

FOR SERVING

32 corn tortillas, warmed

Fresh cilantro leaves

Lime wedges

ALSO WORKS WITH. *Domestic pork and tender venison cuts from the backstrap and hindquarter. I'd be curious to try turkey breast, but haven't done it yet.*

FOR THE MARINADE. Heat a heavy, dry skillet over medium heat until hot but not smoking. Toast the guajillo chiles until they blister slightly, about 15 seconds per side. Transfer the chiles to a large bowl. Pour hot water over the chiles to cover. If necessary, place a small plate into the bowl to keep the chiles submerged. Soak the chiles 30 minutes to 1 hour, until soft. The longer they soak, the easier they will be to blend smoothly. Pour ¼ cup of the soaking liquid into a blender. Drain the chiles and add them to the blender. Wipe the bowl dry and set aside.

Chop half of the onions, transfer them to a bowl, cover, and refrigerate until ready to serve. Coarsely chop the remaining onions and add them to the blender. Add the garlic, chipotles, vinegar, achiote paste (if using), sugar, 2 tablespoons of the salt, oregano, cumin, and black pepper. Blend until a smooth thick paste forms.

Transfer the marinade to a large bowl and add the hog slices. Massage to coat them well. Cover and let marinate, refrigerated, for at least 8 hours or up to 48 hours.

FOR THE MEAT. You don't need a custom-made trompo for this recipe. Any electric rotisserie setup will work. Stack the slices of meat in layers on the skewers. Depending on the size of each slice, you may need to pierce a corner so that the bulk of the piece extends away from the skewer. Continue this process, creating a wide circular base. The meat should be packed tightly. Repeat until all the meat is stacked tightly on the rotisserie, leaving enough room to add the pineapple on top.

Recipe continues

If you're using an electric rotisserie, add the skewered meat and turn on the device. For a propane grill rotisserie, add the skewered meat, fire up the grill, and turn on the rotisserie. If your trompo uses charcoal like mine, heat up a chimney and add the hot coals to the coal chamber. Start the motor and cook. Keep the meat spinning until the outside is charred a bit and the internal temperature about 2 inches in reaches 160°F for wild hog meat (this is important as it is a precaution against trichinosis). This could take 1 to 2 hours, depending on the heat output of your contraption. With mine, I often add a reflector with foil wrapped around the front to create some additional ambient heat and keep the heat closer to the meat. This helps to speed things up.

Once your thermometer reads 160°F in multiple places at a 2-inch depth, you can shave off the outer edges of the meat directly into corn tortillas. Carve a slice of the pineapple and serve with the cilantro, lime wedges, and the reserved chopped onions.

Repeat this process of checking the internal temp and carving meat from the outside. Keep in mind that it is not necessary or even desirable to bring venison like deer or elk to 160°F; feel free to start eating as soon as it hits rare or medium-rare (about 135°F).

TURKEY CHILI VERDE

MAKES ABOUT 8 CUPS; SERVES 4 TO 6

The time-honored Mexican combination of stewed birds (usually chickens) and tomatillos makes for a hearty and exciting meal that is perfect for Dutch oven campfire cooking. In my previous book, *The MeatEater Fish and Game Cookbook*, I shared a slow cooker turkey posole with hominy grits that is similar to this dish. But this version is more of a thicker, stewier, stick-to-your-ribs recipe that you'll truly appreciate on a cold night. Be sure to consider the age of your turkey; an old tom will likely need a bit more time on the fire than a young jake (adolescent male). We give the legs a head start by par-braising them before adding them to the dish. If you're a frugal butcher, throw the wings in as well.

2 skinned turkey legs

1 tablespoon vegetable oil, plus more for grilling

Kosher salt and freshly ground black pepper

2 (12-ounce) bottles lager beer

4 cups homemade game stock or store-bought chicken stock

2 (4.5-ounce) cans chopped green chiles

1 tablespoon dried Mexican oregano

1 tablespoon ground cumin

1½ pounds skinless, boneless wild turkey breast, cut into 4 or 5 pieces

1½ pounds tomatillos, husked and rinsed

1 large white onion, quartered

1 or 2 jalapeño peppers or serrano chiles, halved

6 garlic cloves, unpeeled

3 poblano chiles

1 small bunch fresh cilantro

OPTIONAL GARNISHES

Thinly sliced radishes

Sliced jalapeños or serranos

Sour cream or crema

Cotija cheese

Fresh cilantro leaves

SPECIAL EQUIPMENT

Tripod with chain and hook

10-inch-diameter deep Dutch oven with bailing handle (about 5 quarts). (A bailing handle is a handle designed to keep the pot from slipping on the hook. Without it, be careful to keep the pot balanced when stirring.)

Manual food mill (if camping without electricity) or blender

TO BRAISE THE TURKEY. Pat the turkey legs dry. Add 1 tablespoon of the oil in the bottom of a large stock pot. Season the turkey legs with salt and pepper and cook until browned, turning every 3 to 4 minutes. Remove to a plate. In the stockpot, combine the beer, stock, green chiles, oregano, cumin, and 1 tablespoon salt over high heat and bring to a simmer. Carefully lower the turkey legs into the liquid (the liquid should almost cover the legs; if not, add more stock or water). Cover the pot and maintain a gentle simmer over low to medium-low heat for 2 to 4 hours. Check for the tenderness and add more broth and water as needed to keep the liquid level barely covering the meat. Once the legs are close to tender, add the breast pieces and remove the lid. Keep the pot over the lowest heat possible to maintain a low simmer and continue to cook until the leg meat pulls apart easily with a fork.

Remove the breast meat and turkey legs from the liquid and let cool until you can comfortably shred the meat with your hands. Discard the bones. Strain the cooking liquid (about 4 cups) through a fine-mesh strainer. Transfer the cooking liquid and the shredded turkey to two separate airtight containers and refrigerate for up to 1 week or freeze until ready to use.

PREPARE A CAMPFIRE. In a campfire stone circle, build a fire and set up a grate for high direct heat. When hot, heat a cast-iron griddle on the grate for at least 10 minutes. Lightly brush with oil. Place the tomatillos, onions, jalapeños, garlic, and poblanos on the griddle and cook, turning frequently, until charred all over. Remove to a bowl and let cool until you can easily handle them. Remove the seeds from the poblanos and jalapeños and the skins from the garlic.

If you have access to electricity, add the charred vegetables to a large blender in two batches and puree. If not, use a manual food mill to puree

Recipe continues

MAKE AHEAD. *Braise the turkey legs and shred the meat in advance for camping trips. The step of charring and pureeing the tomatillo-poblano mixture can also be done in advance, then vac-seal the puree or store it refrigerated in an airtight container for 2 weeks or in the freezer until ready to use. You can also make the entire meal ahead of time, vac-seal, and reheat it in a pot of water at camp.*

ALSO WORKS WITH. *Thighs and drumsticks from goose, duck, and various upland birds. Also shoulders or shanks from deer, elk, and wild hog.*

or chop them finely with a knife. (Make sure someone is watching your fire if you step away.)

FOR TRIPOD COOKING. Set a tripod over the campfire circle. Lower the chain so that the pot hovers 6 to 12 inches above the flames or hot coals. Suspend the Dutch oven and let sit for a few minutes to make sure the heat is penetrating the pot (add a splash of water into the pot; if it sizzles and evaporates, it's hot). Lower the pot closer to the fire or build the fire up, if necessary.

Add the puree to the pot and stir in 2 teaspoons salt. Cover and bring to a simmer, stirring occasionally, and cook until the puree thickens a bit and turns a duller green color, about 5 minutes. Add the shredded turkey and 2 cups of the reserved cooking liquid and simmer for about 20 minutes until it comes to a boil and is bubbly and hot. Stir to avoid scorching on the bottom. Add more cooking liquid as needed to reach the desired consistency.

Ladle the chili into bowls. Garnish with toppings as desired.

LATVIAN SOĻANKA SOUP

Janis Putelis

I was awestruck by the gigantic black, straight-out-of-Harry-Potter witches' cauldron that was emanating lovely smells to our hungry group of hunters. The cauldron was being heated by a wood fire, and inside was a very simple dish called soļanka (pronounced sol-YAN-kah), which is not thick enough to be called stew, but too thick and hearty to be considered soup. It was a cool, rainy October afternoon on my first day of a driven hunt in Latvia, one of the three Baltic countries in eastern Europe. Latvia borders Russia to the east and sits across the Baltic Sea from the southern tip of Sweden. My family all came from Latvia, and I grew up speaking the language, but this was my first time visiting. Our group of forty had already finished two drives, harvesting two moose and one red deer. The hunters, and especially the drivers who walk all day to push the game to the hunters, were famished.

All of us were gathered around the warm pot of soļanka, and while bowls were being passed around, I asked the cook for a recipe. In less than two minutes, she explained how to make it, though she didn't offer any strict guidelines on how much of any one ingredient to use. It's one of those preparations that's made based on intuition, experience, and how many people you'll be feeding.

Here's what she told me: Brown bite-sized venison chunks in a pan and add them to a big pot of boiling water. When the meat is tender after an hour or two, add chopped and browned smoked sausages, chopped carrots, chopped onions (one onion for every pound of meat), and one cup of ketchup for every gallon of water. Next, add chopped potatoes. When the potatoes are soft, toss in a couple handfuls of chopped pickles and season with salt, pepper, a bay leaf, and any general-purpose seasoning you like. Garnish the soup with olives, lemons, and sour cream and serve with a slice of buttered bread.

This soup has the familiar tastes of a traditional hearty "American" game stew, but the sour cream and pickled garnishes are a regional touch that make it a uniquely Latvian dish.

After a decade of guiding fly fishermen and elk hunters in Colorado and Arizona, Janis Putelis started with MeatEater as a wilderness production assistant. He went on to become the director and producer of the MeatEater *television show and* The MeatEater Podcast. *Today Janis hosts his own show,* MeatEater Hunts, *along with the* Gear Talk *podcast.*

LAYERED FISH CHOWDER

MAKES 4 TO 5 CUPS; SERVES 4 TO 6

¼ pound thick-cut bacon, cut crosswise into ¼-inch strips

1 large yellow onion, chopped

3 small, bushy fresh thyme sprigs

2 bay leaves

2 russet potatoes (about 1¼ pounds), peeled and sliced ⅛ to ¼ inch thick

Kosher salt

Freshly ground black pepper

1½ pounds thin, flaky white fish, such as flounder

1¾ cups oyster crackers

2 tablespoons unsalted butter

4 cups fish stock or bottled clam juice, plus more as needed

¼ cup heavy cream

½ bunch fresh flat-leaf parsley, chopped, for garnish (optional)

SPECIAL EQUIPMENT

10-inch-diameter (5-quart) deep Dutch oven

Leather grilling gloves

This is my take on one of the oldest chowder recipes ever printed in the United States—going back to 1751 in the *Boston Evening Post*. The technique of layering ingredients (almost like a gratin) was popular back then, and we're using it here. It's a unique way to pull the comforting flavors of a New England–style chowder into a casserole-like dish.

It's best to cook this over a bed of coals rather than flames; since there is so little liquid, you don't want to risk scorching it with intense heat. But it still works hanging from a tripod.

FOR THE FIRE. Set up a tripod over a fire pit or campfire. When there is a bed of glowing coals, suspend a cast-iron Dutch oven 3 to 6 inches over the coals. Maintain the coals and fire for the duration of the cooking process.

FOR THE CHOWDER. Cook the bacon in the pot until it begins to crisp and brown, 10 to 12 minutes. Add the onions, thyme, and bay leaves and cook about 10 minutes, or until the onions soften and the bacon gets crispier. Remove the pot from the fire. Scoop half of the onion-bacon mixture into a bowl.

TO LAYER. Arrange the onion-bacon mixture in an even layer (see illustration) in the bottom of the pot. Lay half of the potato slices over the onions and sprinkle with ½ teaspoon salt and a few grinds of pepper. Lay half of the fish over the potatoes and sprinkle with ¼ teaspoon salt and a few grinds of pepper. Scatter half of the oyster crackers over the fish. Scatter half of the onions over top. Lay the remaining potatoes and ½ teaspoon salt on top and a few grinds of pepper. Lay the remaining fish and ¼ teaspoon salt and a few grinds of pepper on top. Scatter the remaining oyster crackers and then the remaining onions on top. Dot with the butter. Pour in enough stock to just cover everything, roughly 2 to 3 cups. (If you need more than 4 cups of stock to cover, add water.) Do not stir.

Cover the pot, return it to the fire, and suspend it 3 to 6 inches over the glowing coals—adding more as needed—and simmer until the potatoes are tender and the fish is cooked through, about 30 minutes. (Check periodically and raise the pot as needed to avoid burning.) Remove the pot from the fire. Pour in the cream and gently push it into the chowder with a spoon or ladle. Cover the pot and let it stand for 5 to 10 minutes to warm and distribute the cream. Discard the thyme sprigs and bay leaves and garnish with parsley (if using).

4x4

SOL
CERVEZA
35 3235N

06 ON THE SIDE

SALADS, SIDES,
DESSERTS, AND DRINKS

Our current home has a covered deck with a fireplace at the east end. We like to sit out there on summer evenings, especially when friends are over. A few summers ago, we decided to buy a couple of outdoor couches that could sit next to the fireplace. My wife and I argued about what color to get. I thought that brown made sense. It would hide a lot of the grime that is inevitable to outdoor furniture, I figured. My wife felt that white "would be easier to clean," whatever that means. She happened to win that particular debate, and so we went with white. Since then, the kids and the dog have managed to get ridiculous amounts of soot and mud and goo on those couches. While I still don't know about "easier to clean," I'd definitely agree with the statement that they need to be cleaned way more frequently.

It's so bad that it's funny, literally. For a while I had on my phone a video that was taken while various kids from around the neighborhood were all roasting marshmallows in the fireplace. I can't even remember what was actually being filmed in the video, because one's attention focused strictly on what was happening in the background. You could see our youngest boy, Matthew, trying to figure out what to do with the gobs of melted marshmallow that were hanging off his fingertips. You see him consider the couch's fabric as a familiar napkin. He even extends his hands in that direction. But then he catches himself and pauses, perhaps contemplating the dire warnings that he's received from his mother and father about not trashing the furniture so badly. He then pauses in a moment of indecision before committing himself wholeheartedly to wiping his hands down the front of his T-shirt. Satisfied with the results, he runs off.

I watched that video a dozen times and laughed. My kids even laughed at it. It captured, beautifully, the fun and mess of outdoor cooking as well as the beauty and sticky sweetness of summer. For reasons that are hard to explain, this chapter makes me think of that video. The recipes here aren't all summertime preparations, and they're admittedly light on marshmallows, but you will find here the lighter and funner (and yes, sweeter) side of outdoor cooking. It's a trove of drinks (boozy and otherwise), desserts, salads, sides, and breads. It's the stuff that rounds out and completes any great outdoor meal, though much of it would be just as at home indoors as outdoors. I'm sure you'll enjoy it all. Just try to keep it off the furniture, okay?

SALADS AND SIDES

HOW TO MAKE A KILLER SALAD

Every summer, I grow some combination of lettuce, kale, herbs, radishes, onions, peas, and tomatoes in my garden. Just as fish taste better when you catch them yourself, veggies taste better when you grow them. I like to build salads with the stuff from my garden; it's all the better when you can eat them outside with friends and family.

Making a killer salad isn't complex. In fact, the beauty of a salad lies in its simplicity. There's no need to overwork it. If you go by this tried-and-true method, you'll make a killer salad every time without a lot of fuss.

There are three elements every salad needs: greens, some zip, and a dressing. Here's what I mean.

1. Base of Greens

I'm a fan of combining varieties of lettuces. It makes for a visually appealing salad, and you'll add texture and interest without too much effort.

Try combining soft lettuces like Bibb with a few leaves of crunchy romaine, or green or red leaf lettuces with oak leaf or iceberg. Any combination will work.

- Crunchy: romaine, iceberg, red and green leaf
- Soft: Little Gem, Bibb, oak leaf
- Baby/mixed: mesclun, baby mizuna, spinach

2. Add Some Zip

Add punch to your salad with color, texture, and/or flavor. Fresh herbs, bitter greens, and onions (added sparingly) give zip and spice to any salad. This element doesn't always have to be a plant—a handful of nuts or pickled things, even crushed corn chips, can be a game-changer. Keep it simple, though. One or two items from the below list is all you need.

- Herbs and leaves: mint, dill, parsley, basil, or celery leaves
- Chicories: radicchio, endive, or frisée
- Bitter greens and vegetables: arugula, watercress, purslane, radishes, or young mustard greens
- Alliums: chives, scallions, red onions, or yellow onions
- Crunchy: nuts, pickles, or even corn chips
- Leftover anything: cooked beans, grilled vegetables, roasted peppers, or potatoes

3. The Dressing

Choose something that lets the naturally bright flavors of the lettuces and herbs shine through. My go-to dressing is simple—olive oil and red wine vinegar (usually sherry wine vinegar) or olive oil and lemon juice—but I've also included in the pages that follow some of my favorite ways to dress things up. It goes without saying that a store-bought salad dressing is equally acceptable.

4. Add a Star Ingredient

If you've done steps 1 through 3 above, you've already got a fantastic salad. But if you have a star tomato, cucumber, avocado, some foraged mushrooms, or a wedge of noteworthy cheese, slice it up and add it in.

THE DRESSINGS

OLIVE OIL AND VINEGAR

MAKES ABOUT ¼ CUP

Quality counts here, so don't skimp on the oil. You can do a 3:1 or 2:1 ratio of oil to acid, depending on your preference for acidity. If you're doing this like Krista's Italian mother, you'd mix the components of the dressing directly into the salad with your hands. You'd start with the olive oil, mixing it gently together with your greens to coat, then add salt, mix gently again, and finally add your vinegar and toss with serving spoons. She prefers a salad on the zippier side, so use a 2:1 ratio for full authenticity.

3 tablespoons extra-virgin olive oil

½ teaspoon kosher salt

1½ tablespoons sherry wine vinegar, lemon juice, or a combination of red wine vinegar and balsamic vinegar

BASIC VINAIGRETTE

MAKES ABOUT ¼ CUP

This basic vinaigrette is a standard for any salad. Bump it up with herbs or swap out the vinegar for a different kind. It's one to commit to memory.

1 to 2 tablespoons red wine vinegar

½ teaspoon kosher salt

½ teaspoon freshly ground black pepper

½ teaspoon Dijon mustard

3 tablespoons extra-virgin olive oil

Whisk the red wine vinegar (use 1 tablespoon vinegar for a standard vinaigrette, 2 tablespoons if you like yours a little more acidic), salt, pepper, and Dijon in a small bowl. Slowly drizzle in the extra-virgin olive oil to emulsify. Taste and adjust seasonings.

SOY VINAIGRETTE

MAKES ¾ CUP

1 tablespoon rice vinegar

1 tablespoon freshly squeezed lime juice

2 teaspoons prepared wasabi

1 small shallot, finely chopped (about 1 tablespoon)

½ teaspoon sugar

¼ teaspoon kosher salt

2 tablespoons soy sauce

1 tablespoon toasted sesame oil

½ cup canola oil or other neutral oil

Whisk together the vinegar, lime juice, wasabi, shallots, sugar, salt, and soy sauce. Add the sesame oil and 1 tablespoon water, then slowly whisk in the canola oil.

CARROT-MISO DRESSING

MAKES 1¼ CUPS

2 carrots, coarsely chopped

1 (2½-inch) piece fresh ginger, peeled and coarsely chopped (1½ tablespoons)

5 tablespoons rice vinegar

2 tablespoons canola oil or other neutral oil

2 tablespoons white miso paste

1 teaspoon toasted sesame oil

1 teaspoon granulated sugar

This dressing pairs with the salad in the Tuna and/or Yellowtail Skewers recipe on page 273, but you can put it on just about any vegetable and it will be consumed with lightning speed.

In a food processor or blender (for a smoother texture, choose the blender), combine the carrots and ginger and pulse until finely ground. Add the vinegar, miso, sesame oil, and granulated sugar, and process until smooth. Cover and refrigerate until ready to use; the dressing will keep for up to 1 week in the refrigerator.

FRESH RANCH DRESSING

MAKES ABOUT 2¼ CUPS

¾ cup mayonnaise

½ cup sour cream

1 tablespoon distilled white vinegar

1 teaspoon Worcestershire sauce

4 dashes hot sauce

1 tablespoon garlic powder

2 teaspoons onion powder

1 teaspoon kosher salt

½ teaspoon freshly ground black pepper

2 tablespoons finely chopped fresh parsley

1 tablespoon finely chopped fresh dill

1 tablespoon finely chopped fresh chives

½ cup buttermilk, plus more as needed

Stir together all of the ingredients except the buttermilk. Add enough buttermilk to thin the dressing so that it's pourable. Cover and refrigerate.

TWO MORE DRESSINGS

Kelp Goddess Dressing (page 60)

Marjoram-Mint Dressing (page 308)

COLESLAW

SERVES 8

There are endless variations on coleslaw. It's good to have at least a couple favorites in your repertoire, because slaw is a quick and easy side dish for outdoor gatherings. Feel free to personalize this recipe. You can give it extra zip with the addition of jalapeños or serranos or by dousing it with sriracha at the end. If you like more color, julienne one or two bell peppers or use a mix of purple and green cabbages.

1 medium head green cabbage, shredded

8 scallions, white and green parts, sliced on a bias

2 carrots, grated

2 julienned jalapeño peppers or serrano chiles (optional)

DRESSING

1 cup mayo

½ cup apple cider vinegar

2 tablespoons Dijon mustard

2 tablespoons granulated garlic

1 tablespoon kosher salt, plus more as needed

2 teaspoons onion powder

2 teaspoons freshly ground black pepper

Combine the cabbage, scallions, carrots, and jalapeños (if using) in a bowl. In another bowl, mix the dressing ingredients until smooth. Dress the cabbage mixture and toss completely to combine; season to taste. Refrigerate for at least an hour before serving to cut down on the cabbage's crunch (see Cook's Note). Store, covered, in the refrigerator or cooler until ready to serve.

COOK'S NOTE. *To speed up the wilting process, don't add the salt to the dressing—instead, add the salt to the vegetables and massage it into the leaves. Let sit for 10 minutes, then add the dressing (and more salt to taste, if needed).*

MAKE AHEAD. *If prepping for a long camping trip, the dressing and vegetables can be prepped and stored separately until ready to use to avoid getting watery.*

BOSTON BAKED BEANS

MAKES 6 TO 7 CUPS COOKED BEANS (MORE INCLUDING LIQUID); SERVES 6 TO 8

This is a New England–style baked bean preparation, rich with animal fat and sweetened with molasses. (If you're looking for cowboy-style beans that taste more like a chili, this ain't that.) It's possible that the technique of sweetening baked beans was shown to colonists in the Northeast by Native Americans, who used maple syrup instead of molasses as their sweetener. The molasses came later, as it was a surplus by-product of sugar production from southern sugarcane plantations.

Precooking your beans saves time when you're trying to feed a group of hungry campers, so this recipe calls for cooking your beans ahead of time in an Instant Pot. But you can cook them however you please (see our stovetop method on page 306) or even use canned beans in a pinch. Keep in mind, though, that home-cooked beans really raise the level of flavor and texture, so for this dish I'd urge you to take the extra step.

1 pound dried navy beans, rinsed

1 medium onion, quartered, plus 1 large onion, chopped (about 1¾ cups)

1 medium carrot, cut into large pieces

1 celery rib, cut into large pieces

3 bay leaves

3 fresh thyme and/or rosemary sprigs

1 tablespoon kosher salt, plus more as needed

⅓ pound salt pork or fatback, rind removed, cut into ¼-inch dice (see Cook's Notes)

½ cup molasses (not blackstrap; see Cook's Notes)

2 tablespoons spicy brown mustard

Freshly ground black pepper

SPECIAL EQUIPMENT

10- or 12-inch-diameter (5- or 8-quart) deep Dutch oven with a lid for coal cooking

PRECOOK THE BEANS. Put the beans into a large saucepot and cover with water by 2 inches. Turn the heat to high and bring to a boil. Once at a boil, remove from the heat, cover the pot, and let stand for 1 hour. Drain and rinse the beans.

Put the beans in a 6-quart Instant Pot and add fresh water to cover by 2 inches (about 8 cups water). Add the quartered onion, carrot, celery, bay leaves, thyme, and salt. Secure the lid and set at manual high pressure for 4 minutes. When the cooking time is up, let the pressure naturally release for 10 minutes, then manually release the remaining pressure. You should have 6 cups cooked beans and 5 cups cooking liquid.

Discard the aromatics and let the beans cool. Then store the beans in their cooking liquid in the refrigerator until ready to use.

FOR FINISHING. Prepare a charcoal chimney with briquettes (or a hardwood campfire) in a fire pit or stone-lined fire circle. Use the chart on page 152 as a guide for the number of coals needed for your size pot to reach 350°F. (For a 10-inch Lodge pot, place roughly 21 coals in the chimney.)

Strain the beans from their cooking liquid (reserve the liquid) and put them into the Dutch oven. Add the salt pork and chopped onions to the pot. In a small bowl, whisk together the molasses, mustard, and ½ cup of the cooking liquid, and then stir this into the beans. Pour enough of the remaining cooking liquid to just barely cover the beans (roughly 1 cup) and stir together to combine. Put on the lid.

Recipe continues

COOK'S NOTES. *If your salt pork is super fatty without much meat, use ⅓ pound, as above. If it's meatier, feel free to up it to ½ pound. You can also use a slab bacon from any animal, which will add a smokier flavor.*

We recommend regular molasses here, not blackstrap, because we're using it for sweetening. Blackstrap molasses is excellent for many applications; it's high in iron and calcium but contains very little sucrose and thus has a bitter flavor and won't sweeten the beans without added brown sugar or another sweetener.

Once the coals are ready and hot, arrange 7 coals in the campfire pit, put the Dutch oven on top, and arrange the remaining coals on the lid. (Or break up coals from a spent log and gather the equivalent coals. Keep the wood fire going as you'll need more coals later). After 30 minutes, light a new chimney with 21 briquettes. Let the beans cook at a low simmer, adding new coals as needed, for 45 minutes to 1 hour. Move the pot, remove the lid, and lay down a fresh hot set of coals from the chimney or fire coals. Place the Dutch oven on top and cook the beans uncovered for 1 to 1½ hours, until a thick, stewy liquid has developed. Remove from the heat, taste the beans, and season with salt and pepper as needed. Serve warm.

COOKING DRIED BEANS ON THE STOVE

If you don't have an Instant Pot on hand, here's our preferred method for cooking dried beans on the stovetop. We're using Italian ingredients for flavoring, but you can add alternate aromatics—jalapeños and tomatoes for Mexican-style beans or smoked bacon for a rustic kick. Double or triple as desired.

Step 1: Choose your soaking method

Overnight soak: Add 1 pound of beans to a large bowl, cover with water by 2 inches, and lightly cover with plastic wrap. Let soak overnight on the countertop in a cool place. (Note: If it's very hot where you are, soak for only 4 to 6 hours, or use the quick soak method below so the beans don't sprout overnight.) Drain and rinse the beans, picking out any stones or odd-shaped beans.

Quick soak method: Put 1 pound of beans into a large saucepot and cover with water by 2 inches. Turn the heat to high and bring to a boil. Once at a boil, remove from the heat, cover the pot, and let stand for 1 hour. Drain and rinse the soaked beans, picking out any stones or odd-shaped beans.

Step 2: Cook

Put the beans in a 12-inch-diameter (8-quart) deep Dutch oven and cover the beans with fresh water by 2 inches (about 8 cups water). Add a halved head of unpeeled garlic and 1 halved, peeled white onion. Bring the beans to a boil, stirring occasionally and skimming off any scum that arises. Add 2 teaspoons kosher salt and more water, if needed, to keep the liquid level 2 inches above the beans. Cook the beans at a bare simmer for 45 minutes to 1½ hours more, checking for tenderness at 30 to 40 minutes. Check the beans more frequently at the end—every 10 minutes or so—they should be tender but not mushy. Once tender and just cooked, remove from the heat and add 1 cup olive oil to the pot and 2 fresh rosemary sprigs. Season the beans and cooking liquid to taste with additional salt and stir to combine. Let stand for 1 hour in the pot while they cool to finish cooking.

Step 3: Store

Ladle the cooled beans into vac-seal bags or resealable freezable containers, covering the beans with the liquid. If you're freezing the cooked beans, leave 1 inch of headroom to allow for expansion. Freeze the beans for up to 8 months. If you're refrigerating the beans, use within 1 week.

REFRIED BLACK BEANS

MAKES 1¾ CUPS

You can reheat a store-bought can of refried beans or make this extra-delicious version.

Put a small saucepan over low heat. Allow the pan to heat up for 3 minutes and then add the lard, onions, garlic, spices, and salt. Cook, stirring often, for 3 minutes, or until the onions and garlic soften. Stir in the beans, cover the pan, and lower the heat to maintain a simmer. Cook for another 5 minutes, then remove the lid and stir in the lime juice. Remove the pan from the heat and let the beans cool before using.

1 tablespoon lard

3 tablespoons finely chopped white onion

3 garlic cloves, finely chopped

½ teaspoon Mexican oregano

½ teaspoon ground cumin

¼ teaspoon kosher salt

1 (16-ounce) can refried black beans

Juice of ½ lime

CAMPSTOVE RICE

MAKES 6 CUPS; SERVES 4 TO 6

Wash the rice in a sieve until the water is slightly more clear and place it in a 3-quart pot with a lid. Add the cold water and cover. Bring to a boil and then reduce the heat to a low simmer. Cook for 15 minutes, or until the water is absorbed. Leave it covered for another 5 minutes, then fluff with a fork and serve hot with your choice of dish.

2 cups basmati or long-grain rice

3 cups cold water

COOK'S NOTE. *Cooking fluffy, dry rice comes down to a ratio. If you don't have an actual measuring cup, simply use the same vessel (like a thermos cup or a ladle) to measure your rice and water. Use the ratio above—2 cups rice to 3 cups water, or about 1:1.5 rice to water. For a wetter rice, the ratio can go up to 1:2 rice to water. Another method that works well is to eyeball it: Fill your pot with enough water to come up to your first knuckle when the tip of your finger is touching the rice.*

GRILLED EGGPLANT, CHICKPEAS, AND MARJORAM-MINT DRESSING

SERVES 2

Here's a good one for when the vegetarians come to dinner. It's hearty enough to serve as a main dish, or it can be a substantial side dish. It's especially good for folks who raise eggplants in their gardens and then struggle to find interesting ways to use them.

MARJORAM-MINT DRESSING

Makes ⅓ cup

1 tablespoon sherry vinegar

2 teaspoons Dijon mustard

½ teaspoon kosher salt

⅛ teaspoon freshly ground black pepper

1 garlic clove, grated

¼ cup extra-virgin olive oil

1½ teaspoons chopped fresh mint

1 teaspoon chopped fresh marjoram leaves

CHICKPEAS AND VEG

1 (15-ounce) can chickpeas, drained

1 tablespoon extra-virgin olive oil

1 teaspoon kosher salt

⅛ teaspoon ground black pepper

2 ripe but still firm Campari tomatoes, cored and quartered

2 large fresh marjoram sprigs

1 small red onion, cut into 6 wedges, core attached

EGGPLANT

1 (1¼-pound) medium eggplant with stem attached, halved lengthwise

2 tablespoons extra-virgin olive oil

1 teaspoon kosher salt

⅛ teaspoon freshly ground black pepper

Neutral oil, for the grill

Prepare a medium-hot grill, allowing three-quarters of the grill for direct grilling and the remaining quarter for indirect grilling.

FOR THE DRESSING. In a large bowl, combine the vinegar, mustard, salt, pepper, and garlic. Whisk in the oil until combined. Stir in the mint and marjoram and adjust the seasonings. Set aside.

FOR THE CHICKPEAS. In a 10-inch cast-iron skillet, combine the chickpeas, oil, salt, pepper, tomatoes, marjoram, and onions. Place the pan on the grill and cook, stirring occasionally, until the chickpeas are browned, about 5 minutes. Remove from the heat. Discard the marjoram. Add the chickpea mixture to the bowl of dressing and toss to coat well. Set aside.

FOR THE EGGPLANT. While the chickpeas are cooking, deeply score the flesh of the eggplant halves in a crosshatch pattern without cutting through the skin. Brush the eggplant flesh with the olive oil, allowing the oil to be fully absorbed. Sprinkle with salt and pepper.

Place the eggplant halves, flesh-side down, on well-oiled grill grates and grill until lightly browned, 2½ to 3 minutes. Flip the eggplant flesh-side up and continue to grill, moving it to the cooler side of the grill if the skin starts to scorch, about 8 minutes. You'll need to move the eggplant around as the stem ends and blossom ends take longer to cook. Squeeze gently with tongs to see if it's soft enough. Transfer the eggplants to two plates, top with the chickpea mixture, and serve.

COOK'S NOTE. *Marjoram is widely available. If you can't find fresh marjoram, young oregano or thyme can be substituted for a different yet still aromatic flavor.*

ALSO WORKS WITH. *Zucchini or summer squash, portobello mushrooms. This is meant to be a vegetarian dish, but the eggplant can be swapped with big game steak or hearts, meaty fish like tuna or halibut, or small spatchcocked game birds like doves or quail.*

LENTIL STEW

MAKES 10 CUPS (2½ QUARTS)

Dried lentil soups are quick and easy to pull together on a campstove, over a campfire, or to make ahead and then vacuum-seal for later use. If making a soup, add some smoked ham or smoked upland bird wings to bump the flavor and meatiness. Or lower the liquid ratio and use the lentils as a side. They can form a bed for fried or poached eggs. They can be stirred in with white rice. Or they can be chilled and added to salads for a protein boost.

1 (1-pound) bag brown lentils or green French lentils

3 tablespoons extra-virgin olive oil

1 medium onion, diced small

2 medium carrots, sliced into thin quarter rounds

3 celery ribs, diced small

2 teaspoons kosher salt

3 garlic cloves, smashed and peeled

2 quarts water or light game stock, or a combination, plus more as needed

3 fresh thyme sprigs

3 bay leaves

Freshly ground black pepper

Juice of ½ lemon

Crusty bread, for serving

In a bowl, rinse and drain the lentils two or three times, picking through them to remove any stones or discolored pieces.

In a 4- to 6-quart pot, heat the oil over medium heat until it shimmers. Add the diced onion and cook until translucent, about 6 minutes. Add the carrots, celery, and salt and cook until the vegetables are tender, 8 to 10 minutes. Stir in the drained lentils and garlic and cook for 60 seconds. Add the water or stock so that the liquid sits at least ½ inch above the surface of the lentils. Bring to a boil over high heat. Skim off any scum that rises to the surface. Add the thyme, bay leaves, and pepper to taste. Lower the heat and simmer, uncovered and stirring occasionally, for about 40 minutes, until the lentils are tender; if the liquid level lowers below the lentils before they are tender, add more water. (See Cook's Note on adjusting liquid levels.) Once tender, taste and adjust the seasonings with salt and lemon juice.

Ladle the lentils into bowls and serve hot with crusty bread.

COOK'S NOTE. *If you're making a soup, add stock or water (or a mix) to keep the liquid level at your preferred consistency. If you're making lentils as a side, they can be on the drier side: Cook with just enough liquid to keep them submerged and cook the lentils through. Try not to add too much toward the end after they have rehydrated. Use a slotted spoon to remove cooked lentils to a serving dish.*

KAINTUCKIE BUTTERMILK CORNBREAD

SERVES 8 TO 10

8 handfuls yellow self-rising cornmeal mix (3 cups)

2 big pinches kosher salt (¾ teaspoon)

½ handful sugar, plus sugar to taste after the batter is made! (2 tablespoons measurement)

3 large eggs

2 big gobs of butter, melted (2 tablespoons)

4 to 6 big splashes of warm buttermilk (1¼ cups)

Lard, for cooking

SPECIAL EQUIPMENT

12-inch cast-iron skillet

This recipe comes to us via Kevin Murphy, the World's Greatest Small Game Hunter, straight from Kentucky—or Kaintuckie as he reverently calls it. This is a quick-style cornbread that uses a cornbread mix with the baking powder and baking soda included in the base. If it's good enough for Kevin Murphy, it's good enough for you. It makes an ideal accompaniment to his BBQ-Style Squirrel recipe on page 127.

Kevin likes to use a natural "yellow" variety of corn-bread mix best, so look for that kind.

Preheat the oven to 425°F. When at temperature, place a 12-inch (man-track-sized) skillet in the oven to heat up.

In a large bowl, combine all the dry ingredients. Then, while stirring with a wooden spoon, add all the wet ingredients. The mix should be like a thick-flowing batter! Add more wet (buttermilk) or dry (cornbread mix or all-purpose flour) if it's not!

Remove the skillet from the oven and add a gob of lard to melt. It should sizzle when you drop a bit of batter in it! Pour the batter into the skillet.

Bake for about 20 minutes, until the crust is crispy. A note from Kevin: "Stick a 'coon baculum in the center to check for doneness—it's just right to eat when it pulls out shiny. You can use a wooden skewer or a toothpick if you don't have a raccoon's pecker bone layin' around."

SAVORY CHEESE BISCUITS

MAKES 8 BISCUITS

These are basic biscuits that can be made in a Dutch oven or even a skillet with a tight-fitting lid that's been placed over coals or inside an oven. They freeze well when raw, so they're also a good make-ahead staple to keep on hand for when you need them. These are flavored with black pepper and Parmigiano-Reggiano cheese, but you can tailor them to your own liking by adding herbs and/or cheddar cheese.

2 cups all-purpose flour, plus more for dusting

1 tablespoon baking powder

1 teaspoon fine salt

1 teaspoon freshly ground black pepper

2 tablespoons grated Parmigiano-Reggiano

8 tablespoons (1 stick) unsalted butter, chilled and cubed, plus more for greasing the pan and serving

¾ cup milk, plus more for brushing

Preheat your grill or oven to 425°F. If cooking over live coals, prepare a campfire or a charcoal chimney for coal cooking in a fire pit or stone-lined fire circle. Lightly grease a cast-iron skillet with a lid or shallow 10-inch-diameter (4-quart) Dutch oven with a lid and set aside.

In a large bowl, whisk together the flour, baking powder, salt, and pepper. Add the cheese and toss gently with your fingers. Cut in the chilled butter with two butter knives. When the butter is pea-sized and somewhat incorporated, form a well in the shaggy dough and pour the milk into the center. Pull the sides of the well in and knead together lightly until the mixture forms a solid mass.

Sprinkle some flour onto a cutting board. Pat the dough into a ½-inch-thick rectangle. Fold the dough into thirds, like a letter. Pat the dough out again into a rectangle about 1 inch high. Lightly flour the top; cut biscuits with a 2¾-inch round cutter (or a glass of similar diameter), pressing the scraps together and patting them down to 1 inch, to get 8 biscuits. Place the biscuits in the greased skillet or Dutch oven. Brush the tops with milk.

In the grill or preheated oven, bake the biscuits until lightly browned on the top and bottom, about 14 minutes. In a campfire, using the chart on page 152 as a guide for heat, add coals under and on top of the lid of the Dutch oven or covered skillet, whichever you're using, to create an oven that is approximately 425°F. The biscuits are done when the bottoms are browned and the tops are lightly browned, anywhere from 14 to 18 minutes; this can vary with campfire cooking. Serve warm, with butter.

PITA

MAKES 4 PITAS

1 teaspoon active dry yeast

⅛ teaspoon sugar

½ cup lukewarm water

1½ cups all-purpose flour, plus more as needed

½ teaspoon kosher salt

4 teaspoons olive oil, plus more for coating and cooking

This pita recipe is an accompaniment for the Venison Kofta Kebabs on page 276. If you're curious about making your own flatbread, this is a great place to start.

In a small bowl, combine the yeast, sugar, and warm water. Let stand until foamy, about 5 minutes.

In a large bowl whisk the flour and salt together. Pour in the oil, then stir in the yeast mixture with your fingers until a shaggy dough forms. Knead the dough in the bowl, grabbing up the stray bits as the dough forms a ball, until the dough is smooth and a finger indent slightly pushes back, about 8 minutes. If the dough is too sticky, add more flour, a little at a time, until it no longer sticks to your hands. Drizzle the dough with a little oil and turn to coat. Cover with plastic wrap and let rest for about 30 minutes to give the yeast a chance to start working. Transfer to a storage container or large plastic bag and refrigerate overnight to rise and double in size.

To cook, heat a cast-iron skillet on the grill grate over a medium-high fire for 5 to 10 minutes. Divide the dough into 4 even-sized balls. Lightly dust a work surface and roll the dough into roughly 7-inch rounds and cover with a kitchen towel. Once a flick of water on the skillet sizzles immediately, lightly oil the skillet and place a pita in it. Cook until you see bubbles forming, about 30 seconds. Flip and then cook until the pita puffs and the bottom has brown spots, 1 to 2 minutes. Wrap in a clean kitchen towel to keep the pita warm when it comes off the grill. Continue with the remaining dough.

MAKE AHEAD. *You can make dough and let it rise in the fridge overnight in a storage container, then bring it to the campsite already risen. Cook as directed above.*

HOUN

SWEET TREATS

PEANUT BUTTER S'MORES

MAKES 8 S'MORES

S'mores have long reigned supreme as the number one dessert for outdoor meals. If you ever want to add a little depth to your s'mores, try slathering on some peanut butter. It's as simple as it sounds, so don't be insulted by the fact that we're actually gonna explain how to do it below. You never know, there could be someone out there who's never made a s'more and they've been too embarrassed to ask.

8 to 16 large marshmallows

8 whole rectangular graham crackers

2½ (1.5-ounce) bars milk chocolate

A heaping ⅓ cup peanut butter

SPECIAL EQUIPMENT

Green sticks with a whittled end for roasting marshmallows

Break each of the 8 rectangular graham crackers horizontally into two squares. On half of the squares, spread 2 teaspoons peanut butter; reserve the other 8 squares as the lids for the s'mores. Divide the chocolate into 8 equal portions (about 4 squares of chocolate) and top each of the 8 peanut butter–covered squares with the chocolate.

Thread the marshmallows onto the sticks, one or two at a time, whichever you prefer. Over a campfire or hot coals, gently brown—or scorch and blister—your marshmallows. Again this is a personal preference. When done to your liking, lay the marshmallows on top of the chocolate and use the "lid" to help coax it off of the stick. Press the lid down to secure your s'more. Eat warm.

NUTELLA AND BANANA IRON PIE

MAKES 1 SANDWICH

I love iron-pie makers and the sandwiches they produce. You can see some savory concoctions on page 170, but iron pies really shine when they're put to use for desserts. It's fun to have a few options when you're camping with a group. Peanut butter and jelly is a classic, and an iron pie full of cherry pie filling is spectacular. But nothing is as good as an iron pie made with Nutella and bananas.

1½ tablespoons softened butter

2 slices sandwich bread (see Cook's Note)

1 to 2 heaping tablespoons Nutella

1 medium banana, cut into ⅓-inch slices (use as much as you can fit)

1½ tablespoons peanut butter (optional)

Pinch of kosher salt

TO ASSEMBLE. Separate your pie irons into two pieces, if attached. Wipe the inside of each pie iron with a wet cloth and dry well. Liberally coat the insides of the pie iron with the softened butter.

Press one piece of bread into each side of the pie irons (see illustration on page 169). Spread the Nutella onto one of the bread slices. Generously top the Nutella with overlapping slices of banana. On the remaining slice of bread, spread the peanut butter, if using. A fuller sandwich will make for a tighter press, allowing the bread to grill and become golden brown and delicious. Place the second piece of bread over the first, attach the two pieces of the pie iron, and lock them into place.

TO COOK. Prepare a hot campfire (or charcoal grill) for coal cooking. The campfire is ready when you have a sufficient bed of coals. With a coal rake, pull the coals out to the edge of the fire. Place the irons flat on the hot coals for an even transfer of heat (if using a charcoal grill, bank the briquettes to one side so that you can lay the pie irons in the grill on top of the coals). A good starting point is to cook for 2 to 4 minutes and then flip the iron and nestle it in the coals for another 2 minutes. Similar to cooking pancakes, you might burn or undercook the first one, but you'll know better how long to cook the second one. Pull the iron back from the fire, unlatch the handles, and carefully take a peek to see how browned it is (don't touch the actual irons as they're raging hot). If it needs more cooking time, close it up and throw it back on the fire. If it looks good, lay the iron on a log or board and remove the top half of the iron. Allow the sandwich to rest for a minute, then turn the iron holding the sandwich over and deposit it onto a plate. If it sticks, pry it out with a fork or metal spatula. The contents of the sandwich will be like molten lava, so warn any kiddos or unsuspecting adults to let the hot, oozing filling cool down some before eating. Eat whole as is or cut in half, if desired. Wipe out the pie iron if necessary, add a little softened butter, and start your next sandwich or pie.

COOK'S NOTE. *We like the consistency and ease of standard sliced bread, but to get fancy you can use sliced brioche bread or even biscuit dough in a tube. Half the fun of this dish is to play with variations and see which ones you and your family enjoy most.*

TWO MORE IRON PIES

We also like to mess around with various pie fillings. Keep in mind that these things are MOLTEN hot when they come out of the fire and really need to sit for a minute or two to cool off, especially if kids are involved.

Apple pie filling + slices of cheddar cheese: Use ½ to ¾ cup pie filling per iron pie and about 2 slices of cheese.

Cherry pie filling + cream cheese: Use about ¾ cup pie filling and 2 to 3 ounces of cream cheese per iron pie.

COAL-ROASTED BANANAS

WITH SWEET, DECADENT, OR BOOZY TOPPINGS

SERVES 4

4 bananas in their peels

DULCE DE LECHE OR CARAMEL

Makes 4 toppings

1 (4-ounce) can dulce de leche or a squeeze bottle of caramel, for drizzling

½ cup chopped salted pecans

Pinch of kosher salt or a flaky salt, such as Maldon sea salt

Splash of bourbon or whiskey (for adults if you've got it; optional)

SWEETENED CONDENSED MILK

Makes 4 toppings

1 (4-ounce) can sweetened condensed milk

1 fresh mango, seeded and diced (about 1 cup)

½ cup toasted coconut shavings (see Cook's Note)

Pinch of kosher salt or a flaky salt such as Maldon sea salt

Splash of dark rum (for adults if you've got it; optional)

COOK'S NOTE. *Here we're calling for the chunkier coconut shavings you can find in the grocery store. They come pre-toasted or you can toast your own. If you can't find them, shredded coconut or even roasted peanuts will work.*

I never knew about this preparation when I was a kid, but it seems like half the people that I hang out with have been making it their whole lives. In its most basic form, you split a banana down the center, jam it with M&M's or chocolate chips, and then wrap it in foil and chuck it onto the coals to get all roasted and gooey. This is a riff on that concept—with two versions of toppings that are a little more sophisticated but just as messy. There are also boozy variations for those who like bourbon, whiskey, or rum. Use our suggestions here, or come up with your own toppings.

PREPARE THE COALS. Make a campfire, a fire in a fire pit, or a chimney for a charcoal grill and burn until you have hot coals.

ROAST THE BANANAS. Place the bananas in their peels directly into the coals or just adjacent to them if the coals are crazy hot. (Bananas can also be wrapped in foil; both methods work.) Roast, turning a few times until the peels are charred, 6 to 12 minutes, depending on their proximity to the coals. Remove the bananas from the heat carefully with tongs and set them on a baking sheet or a rock to cool slightly.

Set each of the slightly cooled bananas onto plates. Using a knife, split the bananas lengthwise down the middle and spread the charred peels away from the interior roasted banana meat. Drizzle and spoon on your desired toppings. This is how we built ours: Spoon about 2 tablespoons of your gooey sauce of choice (either dulce de leche or sweetened condensed milk) onto the bananas and sprinkle with the crunchy toppings (either pecans or mango and coconut) and a sprinkling of salt. Splash with booze if you're into that (and of legal age).

Dive in with a spoon while it's warm.

COAL-BAKED FALL FRUIT

WITH GORGONZOLA AND WALNUTS

SERVES 4

This dessert featuring baked fruit is the antithesis of a marshmallow. It is on the savory side and has a much more sophisticated appeal. It makes a great finale to a meal around the fire, but it could just as readily start things off as an appetizer if you paired it with summer sausage or ham.

2 apples, halved lengthwise and cored with a spoon or knife

2 pears, halved lengthwise and cored with a spoon or knife

6 to 8 ounces crumbled Gorgonzola cheese, plus more as needed

¼ cup toasted and chopped walnuts, plus more as needed

½ bunch fresh chives, scallions, or wild garlic, chopped, for garnish

Crusty bread or breadsticks, for serving

SPECIAL EQUIPMENT

12- to 14-inch cast-iron skillet with lid (or heavy-duty foil) for cooking

Prepare a fire to create coals. Once the coals are hot and glowing, quickly assemble the dish.

TO ASSEMBLE. In a cast-iron skillet, arrange the fruit, cut-side up. Distribute the cheese among the halved fruit and top all with chopped walnuts. Pour ½ cup water in the bottom of the skillet.

Cover the skillet with the lid or tightly with aluminum foil. Set the skillet among the coals and top the lid with coals; if you're using aluminum foil, don't top it with coals. Bake the fruit for 35 to 40 minutes, until soft when poked with a knife, checking after 20 minutes to be sure there is still some water in the bottom of the pan. Once the fruit is tender and the cheese has melted, allow it to rest for 10 minutes. Sprinkle with chopped chives and serve with crusty bread or breadsticks.

MODULAR PANCAKE DRY MIX

MAKES 1 HEAPING CUP

1 cup all-purpose flour
2 tablespoons sugar
1 teaspoon baking powder
½ teaspoon baking soda
¼ teaspoon kosher salt

This dry mix was designed to be a flexible and versatile tool for making baked desserts and sweets when camping. Starting with a simple pancake mix (which we use for The Late Eugene Groters's Beer and Apple Pancakes on page 245), you can add cocoa, sugar, and an egg to make a chocolate cake (Steamed Moist Chocolate Cake, page 330) or you can use the batter to make a buckle, by loosening it up with milk and pouring it over assorted fruit (Peach and Raspberry Buckle, page 329).

We recommend making a few batches of this dry mix to keep in your RV or camping tote. Keep the instructions for these recipes handy—write them down or snap a photo. And break the recipes out to surprise your crew.

COOK'S NOTE. *We recommend using new baking powder and baking soda so there's no risk of keeping the dry mix past its expiration date.*

Whisk all the ingredients together thoroughly and place the mix into a resealable bag or an airtight container. Store at room temperature until ready to use.

RAINIER 2

PEACH AND RASPBERRY BUCKLE

MAKES ONE 10-INCH CAKE

This is a traditional buckle cake batter that is topped with fruit and a crumble topping. As the buckle cooks, the batter rises up around the fruit. The sugary almond crumble topping adds extra crunch and is a pleasing counterpoint to the gooey, tart flavors of the cooked fruit. You can substitute the type of fruit to suit the season.

TOPPING

4 tablespoons (½ stick) unsalted butter, diced

⅓ cup flour

½ cup granulated sugar

½ cup sliced almonds

¼ teaspoon kosher salt

BATTER

6 tablespoons (¾ stick) unsalted butter, melted or well softened, plus extra for greasing the pan

⅔ cup packed light brown sugar

1 large egg

1 teaspoon almond extract

1 recipe Modular Pancake Dry Mix (page 326), (1 heaping cup)

½ cup whole milk

2 medium peaches, peeled, pitted, and chopped into ½-inch cubes (about 2 cups)

1 cup raspberries

SPECIAL EQUIPMENT

10-inch cast-iron skillet

Preheat the grill to 350°F or make a medium-hot reflector campfire (see page liv).

Grease the bottom and sides of the cast-iron skillet well with the extra butter.

FOR THE TOPPING. In a medium bowl, combine all the topping ingredients. Cut in the butter with your fingers or two knives until well distributed among the ingredients. You will still want to see some whole pieces of butter (larger than pea size). Set aside.

FOR THE BATTER. Whisk together the melted butter with the brown sugar until well combined. Add the egg and almond extract and whisk together thoroughly. Whisk in the pancake mix, then the milk, alternating dry and wet ingredients, beginning and ending with the dry, until the batter is smooth and well combined.

Pour the batter into the buttered cast-iron skillet. Top with the peaches and raspberries. Evenly layer the crumble topping over the fruit.

TO BAKE. Bake uncovered in the grill for 50 minutes (if using the reflector fire, cover with another cast-iron skillet or lid—you may want to top the lid with a few hot coals if conditions are cool or windy and the heat isn't steady; keep rotating the position so it cooks as evenly as possible.) Bake until it's slightly browned on top and a toothpick comes out clean when inserted into the center. Cool for at least 30 minutes or more before cutting into it or spooning it onto plates for serving.

STEAMED MOIST CHOCOLATE CAKE

MAKES ONE 9-INCH-WIDE, 2-INCH-HIGH CAKE

¾ cup semisweet chocolate chips (about 4 ounces), melted and cooled slightly

6 tablespoons (¾ stick) unsalted butter, melted or well softened, plus extra for greasing the pan

¾ cup granulated sugar

1 large egg, at room temperature

1 teaspoon vanilla extract

½ cup unsweetened cocoa powder

1 recipe Modular Pancake Dry Mix (page 326)

1 cup whole milk

Confectioners' sugar, for dusting (optional)

SPECIAL EQUIPMENT

12-inch cast-iron skillet

9-inch cake pan

Large metal bowl or pot big enough (9¼- to 9½-inch diameter) to cover the cake pan snugly when inverted (see Cook's Note on finding a cover)

COOK'S NOTE. *Finding a cover for your skillet is key to this technique. I found a metal bowl with a diameter just larger than the edge of my 9-inch cake pan. It served as an ideal cover. If you aren't so lucky, you'll have to get creative; heavy-duty foil and a large bowl or an inverted pot could work. Use the foil to seal any gaps. You want a snug seal, but it doesn't have to be precise.*

This is an unusual but super-fun way to bake a cake outdoors. By steaming the cake, you get a very light and airy cake with a lavalike center. Cooking it seems almost like a magic trick, and the taste is just as good. You can bake this cake in an oven if you have access to one or would prefer the texture of a baked cake. Follow the mixing instructions and bake at 350 degrees for 40 minutes. This works well in a 10-inch cast-iron pan or a 9-inch cake pan.

Place the chocolate in a heatproof bowl and set it over a pot with an inch or two of boiling water. Do not let the water touch the bottom of the bowl. Stir once or twice to keep it from getting too hot. When the chocolate is about 75 percent melted, take it off the heat; the residual heat will melt the remaining chocolate.

TO PREP THE SKILLET. Pour 2 cups water in the bottom of a 12-inch cast-iron skillet. Place a round wire rack in the bottom of the skillet to raise the cake pan above the surface of the water; alternatively, find three flattish rocks to do the same. Grease the bottom and sides of the cake pan with the extra butter and set aside. Turn on the heat under the skillet and bring the water to a bare simmer while you make the batter.

FOR THE BATTER. In a bowl, whisk together the melted butter with the sugar until well combined. Add the egg and vanilla and mix well. In a separate container, whisk the cocoa powder and pancake mix together. Beginning and ending with dry ingredients, alternate adding the cocoa–pancake mix and the milk until smooth, then fold in the melted chocolate until well combined.

Pour the batter into the buttered cake pan. Place the pan on the rack (or stones) over the barely simmering water in the skillet. Cover and steam on medium-low heat for 30 to 35 minutes, until a toothpick comes out almost clean when inserted in the center. At this point, it will have a soft, light cake exterior and be slightly like a lava cake in the center. If you'd like it to be fully cooked throughout, steam it 5 to 10 more minutes, until the toothpick comes out clean when inserted in the center. Also check the water amount in the skillet about 20 minutes in; if there is very little remaining, add 1 more cup water to the bottom and continue cooking. When the cake is done, cool, covered, for 5 minutes before cutting into it.

Serve with a dusting of confectioners' sugar, if desired. The cake can also be frosted if desired with canned whipped cream, a soft store-bought frosting, or a homemade pourable glaze. The texture is delicate, so I don't recommend using a stiff frosting.

COCKTAILS AND DRINKS

FIRE PIT MULLED CIDER

MAKES ABOUT 18 CUPS

This is the perfect cool-weather drink to be warmed over a fire or campstove. "Mulling spices" are considered warming spices and include cloves, star anise, orange zest, and cinnamon sticks. It's a fun one for kids, without the booze, of course. To make it a cocktail, add a glug or two of bourbon or whiskey.

1 crisp apple, such as Gala or Granny Smith

1 gallon good-quality apple cider

1 cup orange juice

3 tablespoons real maple syrup

8 (¼-inch-thick) slices fresh ginger, unpeeled but washed

24 whole cloves

4 whole star anise

3 cinnamon sticks

Bourbon or whiskey, for serving (optional)

Slice the apple into rounds crosswise about ¼ to ⅓ inch thick.

Pour the cider, orange juice, and maple syrup into a large Dutch oven. Add the sliced apple, ginger, cloves, star anise, and cinnamon sticks. Cover and bring to a strong simmer over a medium fire for 30 minutes to infuse the cider with the spices. The apples will soften but not fall apart. They are delicious to eat. Ladle into mugs and add 1 to 2 ounces of bourbon, if desired.

COOK'S NOTE. *This recipe can be doubled or tripled if you've got a large enough pot.*

PITCHER O' RED BEER

MAKES 8 CUPS; SERVES 8

BASE

1 (46-ounce) bottle tomato juice

½ cup orange juice

½ cup olive brine

¼ cup prepared horseradish

1 tablespoon Worcestershire sauce

1 teaspoon hot sauce, or to taste

¾ teaspoon celery salt

FOR SERVING

Ice

4 (12-ounce) beers

Large stuffed Spanish olives, for garnish

COOK'S NOTE. *To make these as Bloody Marys, mix the base as directed and add 1 to 2 ounces vodka to the glass. For "virgin" Marys, just serve the base over ice and garnish with skewered olives or celery sticks.*

This is one of my favorite cocktails. For some odd reason, I get mighty thirsty for these when I'm ice fishing. Especially on a nice sunny day when the fish are biting. It's similar to a michelada. You could use just tomato juice or Clamato, but this here is a fancier (and much better) version using a homemade Bloody Mary base. It's just as good with nonalcoholic beer—if that's your thing.

FOR THE BASE. Mix the tomato juice, orange juice, olive brine, horseradish, Worcestershire sauce, hot sauce, and celery salt in a large pitcher. Let it sit in the fridge covered for 4 hours, if you have time. It's still delicious if you want to drink it straight away.

FOR SERVING. Fill eight tall glasses with ice. Add 1 cup of the base mix to each glass, top with 6 ounces beer, and garnish with an olive.

CHARRED LEMON G&T

MAKES 10 CUPS; SERVES 10

It may seem absurd to grill a couple dozen lemons for a cocktail—but it's worth it. The grilled citrus creates a smoky, lemony, sour counterpoint to the simple syrup and gin. It's a unique, refreshing take on a summer cocktail—built for a crowd.

ROSEMARY SIMPLE SYRUP

1 cup sugar

3 fresh rosemary sprigs, plus more for garnish

4 pounds small lemons (about 24), halved

FOR SERVING

20 ounces good-quality gin

5 ounces Rosemary Simple Syrup

40 ounces tonic water

Ice

FOR THE ROSEMARY SIMPLE SYRUP. Combine the sugar, 1 cup water, and the rosemary sprigs in a small saucepan. Bring to a simmer over medium-high heat and stir until the sugar dissolves, about 5 minutes. Let the syrup cool with the rosemary to room temperature. Discard the rosemary before using. (This will make more than you need. Store any excess in the fridge for 2 to 4 weeks.)

CHAR THE LEMONS. Heat a grill to high heat. Place the lemons cut-side down and grill until charred, 5 to 10 minutes. Let cool slightly until cool enough to handle. Juice the lemons and reserve; discard the seeds and pulp. You're aiming for 15 ounces of juice. If you have more or a little less after squeezing all of those lemons, proceed with what you have.

FOR SERVING. Pour the gin, 15 ounces charred lemon juice, and the simple syrup into a large pitcher. Add the tonic water and gently stir. Fill glasses with ice, top with the cocktail, and garnish with a rosemary sprig.

CAMP COCOA

MAKES 32 OUNCES; SERVES 4

4 cups whole milk (to make it richer use 3½ cups milk and ½ cup half-and-half)

¼ cup sugar

¼ cup unsweetened cocoa

½ cup semisweet chocolate chips or chopped semisweet chocolate

Marshmallows, for garnish

Ready-made whipped cream, for garnish

COOK'S NOTE. *To make this into a cocktail for adults, you can add a splash of rum, Kahlúa, Bailey's, or crème de menthe to the hot chocolate.*

Hot chocolate can cheer up just about anybody, especially when fingers get cold. This recipe can be doubled or tripled, depending on the crew you're serving. The flavors can be adapted for kicks: Swirl a cinnamon stick to impart a fall flavor or a peppermint candy cane to make it a mint hot chocolate. Top it with marshmallows or whipped cream from a can.

Pour the milk into a 2-quart pot and warm the milk over medium heat on a camp burner, not allowing it to boil. Once hot, remove it from the heat and whisk in the sugar, cocoa powder, and chocolate chips until smooth. Pour into individual mugs and garnish as desired.

mont

EXTRAS

BRINES, MARINADES, DRY BRINES, AND RUBS

BASIC BRINE

A variation of this recipe is used in the Brined and Smoked Turkey Breast with Maple-Chile Glaze (page 128) and the Smoked Duck with Honey, Balsamic, and Chipotle Glaze (page 130) recipes. It's good for waterfowl, upland birds, and wild hog roasts.

1 cup kosher salt
1 cup brown sugar
10 peppercorns
3 bay leaves
8 pounds ice, plus more as needed

Combine 1 gallon water, the salt, brown sugar, peppercorns, and bay leaves in a large pot over high heat and bring to a boil. Remove from the heat and let cool almost to room temperature. Transfer the liquid to a medium cooler and add the ice; there should still be ice floating in the water, but if there isn't, add more ice. Once cooled, add the meat to the brine, close the lid tightly, and brine for 8 to 24 hours.

BASIC WET BRINE FOR SMOKING FISH

This brine will work for just about any fish or small-sized bird you plan to smoke.

¾ cup kosher salt
½ cup granulated sugar
¼ cup brown sugar
¼ cup honey
8 cups lukewarm water

In a nonmetallic container big enough to hold the fish, combine the salt, both sugars, honey, and water and whisk vigorously to dissolve the ingredients. Chill the brine. Thoroughly rinse the fish and submerge them in the brine, using a plate to weigh them down beneath the surface. Brine for 6 to 8 hours in the fridge.

STEVE'S BASIC BRINE FOR CURING A HAM

This is my go-to basic brine for curing a ham. Kevin Gillespie has another version on page 103 that is excellent for a bone-in hog leg.

3 cups kosher salt
2 cups packed brown sugar
1 tablespoon Prague powder #1
2 teaspoons mustard seeds
20 black peppercorns
8 juniper berries
6 bay leaves
8 garlic cloves

In a large pot over high heat, combine 2 gallons water, the salt, brown sugar, Prague powder, mustard seeds, peppercorns, juniper berries, bay leaves, and garlic and bring to a boil. Remove from heat and let cool to room temperature. Strain the liquid into a container with a lid, discard the solids, and chill in the refrigerator until well cooled.

If you're brining a boneless ham, you can butterfly it and submerge it in the brine. You may consider injecting additional brine into thick portions of the muscle if you are brining a leg upward of 6 pounds. If you're brining a bone-in ham, take a quart of the brine and inject it into the muscle as deep as the bone. It's sufficiently saturated when the brine seeps from the injection and perforation holes. Then submerge the ham in the brine. Injecting the leg shortens the brining time to about 4 or 5 days for a 5- to 10-pound ham. If you're brining a bone-in leg without injecting, anything under 10 pounds should brine for 7 days, anything 11 to 15 pounds should brine for 10 days.

RED WINE MARINADE

1½ (750 ml) bottles dry red wine (Cabernet, Chianti, or even a Syrah will work)

4 garlic cloves, smashed, or 2 shallots, sliced

2 fresh rosemary sprigs

3 whole star anise

10 black peppercorns

2 bay leaves

2 teaspoons kosher salt

Combine the ingredients in a medium to large bowl. Add the meat you are marinating; make sure the meat is submerged or transfer to a narrower container. Cover and let marinate for at least 6 hours or up to overnight.

AL PASTOR MARINADE

This is the same marinade used in chapter 5 in the scaled-up Hog on the Trompo (page 281). That recipe, built to feed a crowd, is made for 5 pounds of meat. Here is a smaller version for 1 to 2 pounds of meat, ideal for skewers or tacos serving about 4 people. Makes 1¾ cups.

4 dried guajillo chiles, stems and seeds removed

½ large white onion, chopped

4 garlic cloves

1 chipotle chile in adobo sauce

3 tablespoons apple cider vinegar

2 tablespoons achiote paste (optional, but recommended)

2 tablespoons sugar

1 tablespoon kosher salt

1 teaspoon dried oregano, preferably Mexican

½ teaspoon ground cumin

⅛ teaspoon freshly ground black pepper

Heat a heavy, dry skillet over medium heat until hot but not smoking. Toast the guajillo chiles until they blister slightly, about 15 seconds per side. Transfer the chiles to a large bowl and pour hot water over them to cover by 1 inch. If necessary, place a small plate into the bowl to keep the chiles submerged. Soak the chiles until soft, 30 minutes to 1 hour. The longer they soak, the easier they will be to blend smoothly. Pour ¼ cup of the soaking liquid into a blender jar. Drain the chiles and add them to the blender jar. Wipe the bowl dry and set aside.

Add the onions, garlic, chipotle, vinegar, achiote (if using), sugar, salt, oregano, cumin, and black pepper. Blend until a smooth, thick paste forms.

Transfer the marinade to a bowl and add your meat. Massage to coat it well. Cover and let marinate at least 8 hours or up to 48 hours.

JESSE GRIFFITH'S COFFEE CURE AND RUB

Jesse Griffith shared this dry brine/cure recipe with us. He uses it to confit game meat (see Cook's Note). But it's so good you could use it as a dry brine for any cut of big or small game or as a rub for grilling steaks. Makes ¾ cup.

Mix all ingredients together in a small bowl. Store in an airtight container for up to 1 year.

3 tablespoons kosher salt

3 tablespoons ground coffee

2 tablespoons brown sugar

2 tablespoons smoked paprika

2 tablespoons freshly ground black pepper

COOK'S NOTE. *For more information on how to confit, see the Beaver Confit Toasts recipe on page 20.*

ALL-PURPOSE BBQ RUB

Mix all ingredients together in a bowl. Store in an airtight container for up to 1 year. Makes 3 cups.

½ cup chili powder

½ cup kosher salt

½ cup brown sugar

2 tablespoons ground cumin

2 tablespoons granulated garlic

2 tablespoons dried oregano

2 tablespoons Hungarian paprika

1 tablespoon dry mustard powder

1 tablespoon smoked paprika

1 tablespoon freshly ground black pepper

2 teaspoons onion powder

1 teaspoon cayenne pepper

CREOLE SEASONING

This recipe is used in the Spicy Fish Cakes on page 207. Makes ⅓ cup.

Mix all ingredients together in a small bowl. Store in an airtight container for up to 1 year.

2 tablespoons paprika

1 tablespoon dried basil

1 tablespoon dried oregano

1 teaspoon cayenne pepper

1 teaspoon garlic powder

1 teaspoon onion powder

1 teaspoon dried thyme

1 teaspoon kosher salt

½ teaspoon freshly ground black pepper

LOW COUNTRY SEAFOOD SEASONING

4 tablespoons celery seeds
4 tablespoons black peppercorns
3 tablespoons coriander seeds
2 tablespoons whole cloves
2 tablespoons whole allspice
2 bay leaves
½ cup kosher salt
⅔ cup packed light brown sugar
5 tablespoons cayenne pepper
6 tablespoons garlic powder
4 tablespoons onion powder
6 tablespoons paprika
1 tablespoon dry mustard powder
4 tablespoons dried thyme
4 tablespoons dried oregano
4 tablespoons dried dill

Makes 4½ cups.

Place the whole spices and the bay leaves in a spice grinder and grind for 20 seconds, or until finely ground. Place these freshly ground spices in a medium bowl and whisk in the salt, brown sugar, and remaining spices. Store in an airtight container at room temperature.

TACO-STYLE SEASONING

2 teaspoons kosher salt
1 teaspoon black pepper
2 tablespoons oregano, preferably Mexican
1 tablespoon plus 1 teaspoon chipotle chile powder
1 tablespoon plus 1 teaspoon ground cumin
2 teaspoons ground coriander
1 tablespoon plus 1 teaspoon garlic powder
1 tablespoon plus 1 teaspoon onion powder

This recipe can be used in the Milanesa Torta with Wild Turkey (page 235) in place of the store-bought taco seasoning or in any ground game meat taco, iron pie, or foil packet combination you're cooking up at camp. Makes ½ cup.

Mix all ingredients together in a small bowl. Store in an airtight container for up to 1 year.

SAUCES, MOPS, GLAZES, AND CONDIMENTS

BBQ SAUCE

Whisk together the ketchup, vinegar, BBQ rub, brown sugar, molasses, lemon juice, Worcestershire, liquid smoke, mustard, salt, and pepper in a bowl. Store in an airtight container in the refrigerator, where it will last for about 1 week (or longer if you omit the lemon juice). Makes 3 cups.

2 cups ketchup

½ cup apple cider vinegar

¼ cup All-Purpose BBQ Rub (page 347)

¼ cup brown sugar

⅓ cup molasses

2 tablespoons fresh lemon juice

2 tablespoons Worcestershire sauce

1½ tablespoons liquid smoke

1 tablespoon Dijon mustard

1 tablespoon kosher salt

1 tablespoon black pepper

ALABAMA WHITE BBQ SAUCE

Whisk together all ingredients. Let sit for a few hours or overnight in the refrigerator before using for the flavors to marry. The sauce will keep stored in the refrigerator for up to 1 week. Makes 1¾ cups.

1 cup mayonnaise

½ cup apple cider vinegar

2 tablespoons prepared horseradish

2 tablespoons yellow mustard

4 dashes hot sauce, plus more to taste

2 tablespoons sugar

1 teaspoon kosher salt

1 teaspoon black pepper

PLUM GINGER GLAZE

If you can get your hands on plum preserves, make this glaze. Blackberry preserves will work in a pinch and are more readily available. Makes a little over 1 cup.

Combine all ingredients in a medium saucepan and simmer gently over medium heat, stirring frequently, until the mixture has reduced a bit, 3 to 5 minutes. Watch carefully so it doesn't scorch. Cool completely and store in the refrigerator for up to 1 week.

1 cup plum or blackberry preserves

1 (2-inch) piece ginger, peeled and grated

1 small shallot, finely grated

2 tablespoons soy sauce

1 tablespoon rice vinegar

6 dashes hot sauce

2 tablespoons sugar

¼ teaspoon five-spice powder

Large pinch of kosher salt

3 grinds of black pepper

GARLIC-CHIPOTLE FAUX AIOLI

1 garlic clove, plus more to taste

1 cup mayonnaise

1 chipotle chile in adobo sauce, chopped

1 teaspoon adobo sauce

½ teaspoon orange zest

Pinch of kosher salt

This is a "cheater" chipotle aioli, great to make at the last minute. If you don't have chipotle, substitute hot sauce to keep it spicy. Makes about 1 cup.

Finely mince the garlic in the bowl of a mini processor. Add the remaining ingredients and process until smooth. (Alternatively you can finely chop the garlic and chipotle and stir everything together.) Cover and store in the refrigerator for up to 1 week.

SALSA VERDE

4 large tomatillos, halved

2 serrano chiles, halved

3 garlic cloves

1 small white onion, halved

½ small avocado

½ bunch fresh cilantro

Juice of 1 lime, plus more as needed

Kosher salt, to taste

This would be excellent with the Milanesa Torta with Wild Turkey on page 235 or the Hog on the Trompo tacos on page 281. It's also fantastic with chips or smoked upland birds. Makes 1¾ cups.

Preheat the oven or grill to 400°F and place the tomatillos, serranos, garlic, and white onion on a baking sheet. Char and roast the veggies for 5 minutes to soften slightly and then transfer them to a blender. Add the avocado, cilantro, lime juice, ½ cup water, and ½ teaspoon salt. Pulse the blender five to ten times, until everything is broken down but not super smooth. Taste and adjust seasoning with more salt or lime, if desired. It will keep for about 1 week in the refrigerator.

CHUNKY PICO DE GALLO

Put the tomatoes into a bowl. Add the remaining ingredients to the tomatoes and mix thoroughly. Taste and adjust seasoning with more salt and lime juice, if desired. Enjoy within 24 hours for best flavor. Makes 3 cups.

1 pint cherry or grape tomatoes, quartered (2 cups)

½ large or 1 small white onion, chopped into ½-inch dice (about 1 cup)

1 serrano chile or jalapeño pepper, quartered lengthwise, seeded, and chopped

About ½ cup roughly chopped cilantro leaves

Juice of 1 lime (about 1 tablespoon), plus more as needed

½ teaspoon kosher salt, plus more as needed

GRILLED TOMATO SALSA

Grill, broil, or char in a cast-iron pan the tomatoes, onions, jalapeño, and scallions until they are well charred but not collapsed. Split the jalapeño and remove the seeds and ribs if you don't want the salsa too spicy. Chop grilled vegetables roughly and then pulse them in a food processor or blender with the lime juice and salt. Make this as chunky as you like. Makes 4 cups.

6 Roma tomatoes (about 1 pound)

1 large white onion, halved

1 medium jalapeño pepper

4 scallions, white and green parts, trimmed

¼ cup finely chopped cilantro stems and leaves

Juice from 1 lime, plus more to taste

1 teaspoon kosher salt

CLASSIC GREMOLATA

2 lemons

2 garlic cloves

⅓ cup finely chopped fresh flat-leaf parsley

Freshly ground black pepper

Flaky sea salt, such as Maldon

This is an excellent condiment for wild game and fish. I like to use either orange zest or lemon zest, and you can play with the herbs, too—parsley, mint, oregano, and basil are all possibilities. It's fantastic on grilled steaks and birds or even grilled fish. Use flaky sea salt for best results. Makes about ⅓ cup.

Using a Microplane, finely grate the zest of the lemons into a small bowl. Grate in the garlic. Stir in the chopped parsley and pepper and flaky sea salt to taste. This is best if used within 24 hours; store in an airtight container in the refrigerator.

CLASSIC BASIL PESTO

2 cups packed fresh basil leaves

⅓ cup pine nuts

1 garlic clove

¾ cup extra-virgin olive oil, plus more to cover

2 tablespoons fresh lemon juice

1½ teaspoons kosher salt

1 teaspoon freshly ground black pepper

Pinch of ascorbic acid (optional)

½ cup grated (optional) Parmigiano-Reggiano

Homemade pesto is another go-to condiment for me. This is the basic ratio you'll need. Feel free to swap some of the basil for other soft herbs and greens like mint, parsley, spinach, or kale, and likewise the pine nuts can be swapped for less costly walnut halves or even raw almonds. A pinch of ascorbic acid or smashed vitamin C tablet will help preserve the green color of the pesto; this step is recommended if you're making a large batch. Makes 1 cup.

Combine basil, pine nuts, and garlic in a food processor and pulse until coarsely chopped. Add 2 tablespoons of the oil and the lemon juice and process until smooth. Add salt, pepper, and ascorbic acid (if using) and, with the motor running, slowly pour in the remaining oil through the hole in the lid. Add cheese and pulse a few more times to incorporate.

Transfer the pesto to a container with a tight-fitting lid and add a thin layer of oil to cover the top of the pesto. Store refrigerated for up to 2 weeks or freeze for up to 3 months.

ITALIAN SALSA VERDE

This can be used in the same way you'd use a condiment like pesto or chimichurri. Italians use it for cooked seafood and on grilled or roasted poultry. Sometimes a soft-boiled egg is added to help emulsify it; go for it if you've got the time. Makes 1¼ cup.

- 1 tablespoon breadcrumbs
- 3 tablespoons red wine vinegar
- 1 garlic clove
- 1 to 2 bunches parsley, roughly chopped
- ¾ cup extra-virgin olive oil, plus more as needed
- 4 anchovy fillets
- 1 tablespoon drained capers
- ½ teaspoon black pepper
- 1 soft-boiled egg (boiled 6 to 8 minutes), peeled (optional)
- ¼ teaspoon kosher salt, plus more to taste

Soak the breadcrumbs in the vinegar to plump them. In the bowl of a mini food processor, with the motor running, add the garlic through the chute to mince. Stop the motor, open the lid, and add the parsley, oil, anchovies, capers, black pepper, egg (if using), and salt and blend together. Taste and add salt or additional oil to get a pesto-like consistency as needed.

RED WINE MUSTARD

This vibrant-hued mustard is delicious with the Brown Sugar Wild Hog Ham on page 103. It's ideal for sandwiches, roasts, and even fish dishes. Make some extra—it holds for about a month in the fridge. This recipe can be doubled or tripled as desired. Makes a scant ⅔ cup.

- 1⅓ cups dry red wine
- 4 teaspoons sugar
- ¼ cup Dijon mustard

In a small saucepan, combine the wine and sugar over high heat. Stir to dissolve the sugar and bring the mixture to a fast simmer. Reduce the heat and simmer until syrupy and reduced by three-quarters to about ⅓ cup. Remove from the heat and let cool, then stir in the mustard. Store in an airtight container.

MOSTARDA (MUSTARD-APPLE COMPOTE)

The traditional method of making mostarda involves a lengthy process of cooking fresh and dried fruit in syrup, but this version takes on the sweet-and-sour spirit of the original without the long cooking time. Makes 4½ cups.

- 2 Golden Delicious, Fuji, or other semi-firm apples, cored and diced (about 3 cups)
- 1 red onion, sliced crosswise into half-moons (about 1½ cups)
- ¾ cup chopped dried fruit (such as dried apples, cranberries, and/or figs)
- ¾ cup dry red wine
- ¼ cup maple syrup
- 2 teaspoons kosher salt
- 2 tablespoons Dijon mustard
- 2 teaspoons mustard seeds

In a 4-quart pot, combine all of the ingredients and set the pot over medium-high heat. Stir frequently but gently until the fruit and onions begin to soften, about 5 minutes. Lower the heat to medium-low and partially cover. Stir occasionally to ensure even cooking. When the apples have softened, about 10 more minutes, remove from heat. Serve at room temperature with smoked hog loin.

MAKE AHEAD. *The mostarda can be made in advance and stored in the refrigerator for up to 1 week.*

CAYENNE COMPOUND BUTTER

2 small garlic cloves

1 cup (2 sticks) unsalted butter, softened

1½ teaspoons cayenne pepper

½ teaspoon kosher salt

Zest of 1 small lemon

Juice of ½ small lemon

2 tablespoons chopped parsley or cilantro

This compound butter is in *The MeatEater Fish and Game Cookbook* and remains a go-to for me on any kind of grilled wild game or fish preparation. A simply grilled steak topped with a pat of this butter turns into a five-star meal. I've added a fresh herb (parsley or cilantro) to the recipe for this book. Makes 2 logs.

In the bowl of a mini food processor, chop the garlic. Add the butter. Add remaining ingredients and process until smooth. Scrape out and evenly divide the butter onto two pieces of parchment paper, roll it into logs with about a 2-inch diameter, and refrigerate until firm. Refrigerate for up to 1 week or freeze for up to 3 months.

BERRY COMPOTE

1 cup sweet red vermouth

½ red onion, finely chopped

¼ cup sugar

3 (¼-inch-thick) fresh ginger coins

1 cinnamon stick

Pinch of kosher salt

1 (6-ounce) container raspberries

1 (6-ounce) container blackberries

1 (6-ounce) container blueberries

1 thyme sprig

This is a classy accompaniment for any kind of grilled or smoked upland bird or big game. Its tangy, sweet flavors complement the complexity of game meat. It's also delicious on pancakes or waffles. Makes 1⅔ cups.

Add the vermouth, onions, sugar, ginger, cinnamon, salt, and ¼ cup water to a medium saucepan. Bring to a boil over medium-high heat, 4 to 5 minutes. Reduce to a simmer and cook until the liquid has reduced by half, 10 to 15 minutes. Add the berries and thyme and simmer for another 10 minutes. Let cool to thicken. Remove the ginger, cinnamon, and thyme. The compote will set up a little when cooled and will have the consistency of a loose relish. Cover and refrigerate for up to 1 month.

A FEW MORE BRINES, RUBS, SAUCES, AND CONDIMENTS

MORE BRINES

MORE MARINADES

MORE DRY BRINES AND RUBS

MORE SAUCES, MOPS, AND GLAZES

MORE AIOLIS, MAYONNAISES, AND DIPPING SAUCES

MORE CONDIMENTS AND SAUCES

ACKNOWLEDGMENTS

Producing a cookbook is a massive undertaking with many moving parts. Without the talents of a small army of folks, you'd be holding a notebook with some half-written recipes in your hands.

First off, thank you to my publishing team at Random House: my editor, Ben Greenberg, for giving me the encouragement and room to do the best work that I can pull off; Leila Tejani, Azraf Khan, and Ted Allen for their help steering this project; and Debbie Glasserman, who designed this book, for her talent and her patience. And to the rest of our fine-tuned publishing team at Random House—Andy Ward, Tom Perry, Alison Rich, Windy Dorresteyn, and Steven Boriack—for their work in getting this book out into the world.

As always, thanks to Marc Gerald, my agent, who tracked me down twenty years ago and made me get to work.

Thanks to Krista Ruane, my collaborator on this project, who also served as the creative director, recipe developer, art director, and food stylist. Krista would take a bullet for her projects, and I'm constantly inspired by her passion and attention to detail. And a huge thanks to our internal publishing team here at *MeatEater*—Brody Henderson, Savannah Ashour, and Katie Finch. You guys do amazing work, but it's just as important that you make me laugh so much. Here's to a few thousand more pages. Together, the four of us owe a thanks to the generous and unflappable Kylee Archer for being a scheduling magician, an eel rustler, a party planner, and everyone's favorite person.

Much of the standout photography in this book is the work of John Hafner, with whom I've collaborated on three previous books. *MeatEater*'s own Seth Morris also contributed many terrific photos and was a huge help on the production of this book from start to finish. Thanks to Dave Gardner for his assistance on photo shoots. And thanks also to Brittany Brothers, Janis Putelis, and Brody Henderson for their producing skills on photo shoots. Additional photos (some plucked from the *MeatEater* archives) come by way of Garrett Smith, Justin Turkowski, Dave Gardner, Michael Mauro, Christopher Gill, and Jeff Stewart. For the top-notch illustrations, thanks to Ryan Frost.

Recipes take shape in all sorts of ways, ranging from mistakes to experiments to inspired creations. Thanks to the following folks for helping to get these into executable and replaceable form: Krista Ruane, Vivian Jao, Liz Tarpy, Jeannie Chen, Jon Heindemause, Koren Grieveson, Lish Steiling, and David Domedion. Thanks also to the professional chefs and home cooks who generously contributed completed versions of their own favorites and standbys for inclusion in this book, including my colleagues Danielle Prewett, Janis Putelis, Brody Henderson, Clay Newcomb, and fellow hunters and anglers Jean-Paul Bourgeois, Jessee Lawyer, Jeff Stewart, Jesse Griffiths, Kimi Werner, Parker Hall, and Kevin Murphy.

We could not have prepared these dishes for photography without the help of lead chefs Pancho Gatchalian and Koren Grieveson, as well as Austin "Chilly" Chleborad, Cory Calkins, Nicole Smith, David Braun, Austin Brown, Jasmine Lilly, Wyatt Hungate, Beau Linnell, Travis Barton from Barton Fabrication, and the hardworking firefighters Troy Brown and Dillon Smith. Also, thanks to Bodhi Farms, the Steiner family, and Sue Doss for help with shooting locations. And thanks to my colleagues Tracy Crane, Annie Raser, Valerie Ross, and Kristen McKellin for their behind-the-scenes support. And to Hunter Spencer for being such an incredible genius. If you want to know what something good would look like, ask him.

For your beautiful faces, thanks to Katie Finch, Jimmy, Rosy, Matty Meatball, Jennifer Jones, Aina, Mabel, Carrie Henderson, Hayden, Conley, Brett Archer, Kylee Archer, Mike Kmon, Christine Sawicki, Andre Brown, Brianna Stroebe, Corinne Schneider, Tressa Croaker, and Samantha Gilligan. I also appreciate the cameo photo appearances made by Rovin Alvin, Richard Martinez, Cameron Kirkconnell, Errol "T" Thurston Jr., Jesse Griffiths, Parker Hall, and Kevin Murphy.

ILLUSTRATION AND PHOTO CREDITS

RYAN FROST All illustrations

DAVE GARDNER 72

CHRISTOPHER GILL 248

JOHN HAFNER Cover, i, iv, vi, viii, x, xiii, xv, xvi, xviii, xx, xxiii, xxiv, xxx, xxxii, xxxiv, xxxviii, xlii, xliv, xlvi, 1, 2, 3, 5, 6, 9, 10, 14, 16, 21, 24, 27, 28, 39, 40, 43, 44, 47, 48, 52, 58, 61, 62, 64, 74, 79, 82, 84, 90, 95, 98, 102, 105, 108, 109, 111, 112, 114, 115, 119, 120, 125, 131, 132, 140, 141, 142, 145, 147, 154, 158, 160, 173, 174, 179, 180, 185, 194, 198, 204, 206, 209, 210, 213, 214, 216, 221, 222, 227, 231, 232, 234, 238, 240, 244, 247, 250, 252, 256, 260, 261, 264, 269, 270, 274, 277, 278, 280, 282, 283, 284, 292, 294, 296, 298, 304, 306, 310, 315, 316, 318, 323, 324, 327, 328, 331, 332, 334, 336, 338, 339, 340, 342, 344, 347, 351, 356, 358–59, 372–73

SETH MORRIS xxxvii, xli, xlviii, xlix, l, li, lii, liii, liv, lv, lvi, 12, 13, 22, 32, 35, 51, 53, 54, 57, 96–97, 122, 126, 134, 144, 148, 153, 165, 166, 168, 171, 177, 182, 187, 188, 190, 191, 192, 197, 202, 205, 228, 243, 254, 255, 262, 287, 291, 297, 320, 337, 348, 360, 371, 374

GARRET SMITH 86, 87, 88, 89

JEFF STEWART 136–37

JUSTIN TURKOWSKI 66–67, 69, 70

INDEX

Page numbers of illustrations appear in italics.

ABOUT THE AUTHOR

STEVEN RINELLA is an outdoorsman, writer, wild foods enthusiast, and television and podcast personality who is a passionate advocate for conservation and the protection of public lands. Rinella is the host of the television show and podcast *MeatEater;* his most recent book is the *New York Times* bestseller *The Meateater Outdoor Cookbook*. His other titles include *American Buffalo: In Search of a Lost Icon* and *Outdoor Kids in an Inside World*. Rinella lives in Bozeman, Montana, with his wife and their three kids..

themeateater.com
Facebook.com/StevenRinellaMeateater
Instagram: @stevenrinella and @meateater

BY STEVEN RINELLA

The MeatEater Fish and Game Cookbook

The Complete Guide to Hunting, Butchering, and Cooking Wild Game: Volume 2, Small Game and Fowl

The Complete Guide to Hunting, Butchering, and Cooking Wild Game: Volume 1, Big Game

Meat Eater: Adventures from the Life of an American Hunter

American Buffalo: In Search of a Lost Icon

The Scavenger's Guide to Haute Cuisine

The MEATEATER FISH & GAME COOKBOOK

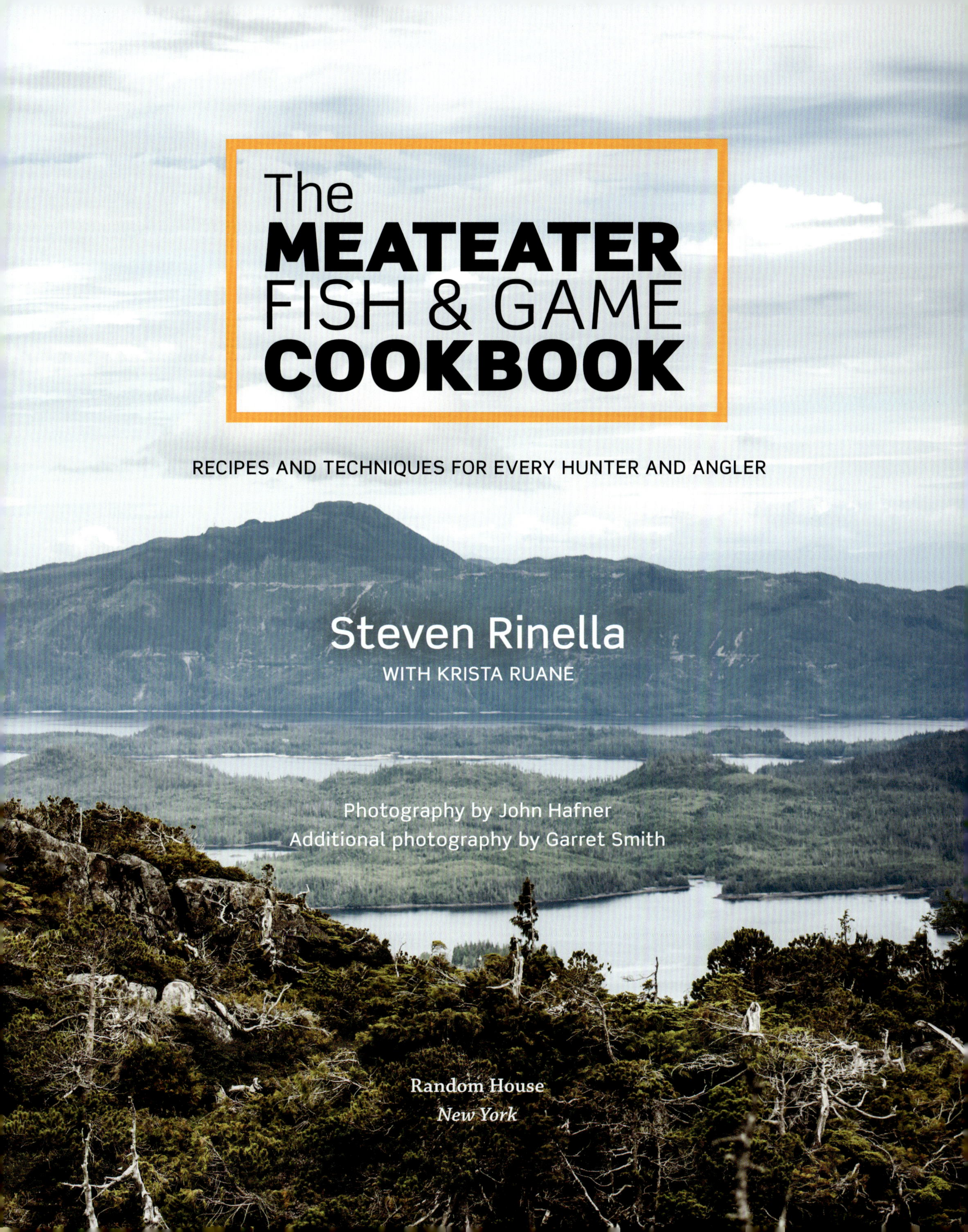

The MEATEATER FISH & GAME COOKBOOK

RECIPES AND TECHNIQUES FOR EVERY HUNTER AND ANGLER

Steven Rinella

WITH KRISTA RUANE

Photography by John Hafner

Additional photography by Garret Smith

Random House

New York

Random House
An imprint and division of Penguin Random House LLC
1745 Broadway, New York, NY 10019
randomhousebooks.com
penguinrandomhouse.com

2025 Random House Trade Paperback Edition

Originally published in hardcover in the United States by Random House, an imprint and division of Penguin Random House LLC, in 2018.

LIBRARY OF CONGRESS CATALOGING-IN-PUBLICATION DATA
Names: Rinella, Steven, author.
Title: The MeatEater fish and game cookbook: recipes and techniques for every hunter and angler / by Steven Rinella.
Description: New York: Spiegel & Grau, [2018] | Includes index.
Identifiers: LCCN 2023034189 (print) | LCCN 2023034190 (ebook) | ISBN 9798217154807 (box set) | ISBN 9780399590085 (ebook)
Subjects: LCSH: Cooking (Meat) | Cooking (Game) | MeatEater (Television program) | LCGFT: Cookbooks.
Classification: LCC TX749 .R624 2018 (print) | DCC 641.6/6—dc23
LC record available at https://lccn.loc.gov/2018002015

Printed in China on acid-free paper

987654321

Project editor and producer: Krista Ruane
Food styling: Krista Ruane
Prop styling: Krista Ruane

Book design by Debbie Glasserman

The authorized representative in the EU for product safety and compliance is Penguin Random House Ireland, Morrison Chambers, 32 Nassau Street, Dublin D02 YH68, Ireland. https://eu-contact.penguin.ie

FOR JAMES,
ROSEMARY,
AND MATTHEW.
MAY YOU LIVE IN A
WORLD FULL OF
WILD PLACES.

CONTENTS

INTRODUCTION

Wild game represents both the first and final frontier in cooking. While scholars like to argue over exactly how long anatomically modern humans have been here on Earth, there's no denying that we were eating strict wild game diets for well over 90 percent of the time. From our earliest days our dietary habits have fallen a long ways, to a point where in many circles the consumption of wild game is perceived as exotic, anachronistic, or even cruel. But in recent years, we've witnessed a great awakening around the subject of wild game in popular culture. Across the spectrum, from our most celebrated chefs to our most innovative tech executives to some of our most admired actors, athletes, and comedians, we've seen an enthusiasm for wild game that hasn't been witnessed since Daniel Boone extolled the virtues of bear meat and elk liver. It's an exciting time to be living a wild game lifestyle.

What is it about wild game that's getting people so excited? At the top of the list, certainly, is a desire to forge a deeper and more hands-on relationship to food. Going to the local farmers' market doesn't cut it. At best, you're still an arm's reach away from a truly intimate food experience. If you want to close that gap and get downright cozy with your protein, you need to pick up farming or else learn to hunt and fish. And believe me, hunting and fishing are way more exciting. What's more, hunting and fishing for food can inspire an empowering sense of self-reliance. So many of the processes that support our daily life occur out of sight and, unfortunately, out of mind. It's refreshing to take responsibility for such an elemental function of one's existence.

There's also the matter of variety. While most folks will eat dozens of types of fruits, vegetables, and grains throughout the year, many consume just three or four kinds of meat and only a small handful of fish species. Meanwhile, a skilled hunter and angler, no matter where he or she lives, has access to literally dozens of species of wild game, including many that would be impossible to obtain through commercial transactions. Pursuing these food resources will radically transform your perspective on life and the world you live in. When you open your eyes to the bloody, beautiful, sharp-toothed, and sometimes scary world of wild game, nothing will ever be the same.

It's helpful for a wild game cook to stop and think about the term *wild game*. In this context, I consider the word *wild* to have two meanings. The first is obvious, in that the meat is coming from untamed creatures that have not been corrupted through domestication by man. The other, less obvious meaning pertains to the quality of the meat itself. Dictionaries describe wild as "unrestrained" and "out of control," and those are pretty fitting descriptors for flesh that's been harvested from the natural world. Imagine for a moment the last time you were in a grocery store and saw a package of "Certified Angus Beef." Whether you saw that package in Tallahassee, Toledo, or Tacoma, you were looking at basically identical products. The animal was sent to a feedlot when it was about twelve months old, weighing about 700 pounds. It was then medicated and fed a diet of grain that added about 3.5 pounds of weight to its body every day. Ten to twelve months later, it was slaughtered at about 1,200 to 1,400 pounds in a mechanized, tightly regulated environment. The system is almost unerring in its consistency.

Wild game doesn't work that way. A pair of whitetail bucks coming at you on a trail in the woods could have two radically different histories. One might be a robust eighteen-month-old deer weighing 110 pounds that's been fattened beautifully on acorns. The other might be an emaciated six-year-old that recently lost thirty pounds while recovering from injuries sustained from coyotes when it got hung up on a barbed wire fence. That's an extreme example, but you get the point. Wild game is wildly variable. It's variable when it's alive, and variabilities are added on as you go through the processes of killing, butchering, and storing the meat. A salmon fillet taken from the left side of the fish and eaten raw on the day you caught it will be different from the right-hand fillet after it's been frozen for six months. Not that there's something wrong with a frozen salmon fillet. Handled properly, it will be a delicious reminder of your time spent on the water. But it might require some additional steps, such as the application of a dry brine followed by some applewood smoke, in order for it to reach its full and glorious potential. Such is the know-how that you'll find inside *The MeatEater Game and Fish Cookbook*.

The book is broken into eight chapters: Big Game, Small Game, Waterfowl, Upland Birds, Freshwater Fish, Saltwater Fish, Reptiles and Amphibians, and Shellfish and Crustaceans. The chapter breakdown is essential for imposing some discipline on the book and making it easy to use. But don't just hang out in whatever chapter seems to be the most relevant to the type of hunting or fishing you happen to do. No matter your personal interests, you'll find usable information in each and every chapter. For instance, a smallmouth bass fisherman who lives a thousand miles away from the nearest body of saltwater would be wise to check out the yelloweye rockfish processing photos in the saltwater chapter. (Hint: The pinbone removal cuts are the same on a smallmouth.) Also, pay close attention to the "Nature of the Beast" sections, where I share some general thoughts and guidelines about the relative qualities of a wide host of wild game species, and the "Also Works With" sections that are built into each individual recipe. At the back of the book (in the Basic and Not-So-Basic section), I have included a collection of some of my go-to recipes for stocks, sauces, sides, and accompaniments that you can use alongside the main recipes in the book or in other preparations you're making at home. The combined information from these portions of the book will prove invaluable for finding suitable substitutions for the wild game cook. A successful deer hunter who's interested in making some goose pastrami will be pleased to learn that their freezer already contains a reasonable facsimile of the necessary protein.

The recipes that follow are meant to encourage a nose-to-tail approach to wild game cooking. It's my personal belief that our wild game resources should be utilized to the fullest extent possible. I encourage deer hunters to experiment with tongue and liver; I encourage waterfowl hunters to grill their duck hearts; I encourage anglers to eat the cheeks and collars from their fish. There are practical implications to this approach—more food!—as well as benefits of a slightly more spiritual nature. To eat is to feed both your body *and* mind. Responsible use is a way of paying proper homage to the fish and animals you pursue, and it makes you a better, more thoughtful outdoorsman and wild game cook.

No matter how you rank yourself—newbie, awful, locally famous—I promise that your skill sets will grow as you apply these techniques and cook these recipes. I've been hunting and cooking for my entire life. Considering my own experiences and those of everyone else who aided in the production of this book, either directly through the contribution of recipes or indirectly by sharing with me their hard-earned tips and tricks, I can confidently say that it contains centuries' worth of wild game knowledge. It's with joy that I pass it along to you.

01 BIG GAME

INTRODUCTION

The big game section is in the front of this book because it is a fitting position for what I consider to be the pinnacle of the wild game world. While I regard myself as a hunting generalist (I'll chase anything that's good to eat, and at times my definition of good has been elastic enough to include everything from common carp to porcupines), big game hunting is my deepest passion. I killed my first deer when I was thirteen, after two unsuccessful seasons of misses and mistakes. I've kept at it, without ever missing a season, for the past thirty-three years. Every fall and winter, I put fifty days or more into pursuing big game. I believe that it's the most challenging form of hunting, both physically and mentally, and it pays off in the biggest way. Long ago, I committed to feeding my family a diet of wild meat. Big game is how I'm able to stay true to that commitment.

Most hunters share my fondness. According to statistics from the U.S. Fish and Wildlife Service, 80 percent of all hunters chase big game at some point during the year. Each of those hunters has his or her own particular set of motivations, but you can't argue with the seductive size of big game animals. A mature whitetail deer can yield anywhere from forty to eighty pounds of boneless, recipe-ready meat. An elk can yield well over two hundred pounds. A moose, well over three hundred pounds. In addition to abundance, big game also gives you variety. I break my deer down into a dozen different cuts, ranging from short ribs to sirloins to tongue. Each cut is suitable for an endless array of recipes and preparations. With just a single deer in your freezer, you can have months' worth of eating with no fear of redundancy or boredom.

This cut-based approach is the key to big game cooking. It remedies a problem that I have with wild game cookbooks in general, which tend to draw unnecessary distinctions among various species of antlered and horned game. To me, there is no fundamental difference between a recipe for a pronghorn antelope shank and a recipe for a whitetail deer shank beyond some minor adjustments in cooking times. In fact, I'd argue that it's more important to understand what part of the animal you're cooking than it is to understand what kind of big game animal it came from.

Keep this approach in mind as you work through this section. Virtually every recipe here is interchange-

able from one big game species to the next. Admittedly, the recipe for Kimchi Tacos with Wild Pig or Javelina shoulder on page 54 is especially suitable for the stringier meat and sometimes stronger flavors of those particular animals. But it could easily be applied to a venison shoulder or bear shoulder, as all three of these pieces of meat share in common a lot of sinews and connective tissue that will break down during the cooking process and yield a finished product that is rich, moist, and silky. This is just one example where substitutions are appropriate; I have called out many others in the following recipes. I'm hopeful that you'll make additional discoveries on your own as you apply these methods to whatever big game happens to turn up in your freezer over the coming years.

Finally, I'd like to throw in a few thoughts on the subject of big game meat that tastes "gamey," a term that drives me a little bit insane every time I hear it. As best as I can tell, *gamey* has no fixed definition. I've heard it used to describe a dozen or more different things. It's used to describe meat that was spoiled, meaning rotten, from improper handling in the field. I've heard it used to describe meat that hadn't been trimmed of tallow and blood clots. I've heard it used to describe meat that had been tainted by secretions from the tarsal gland on a deer's back leg. And I've heard it used by people who are trying to say that game meat doesn't taste like the flavorless beef that they're used to buying from fast-food restaurants.

Whatever it actually means to you or the people you're cooking for, most causes of gamey meat can be eliminated by taking a careful approach to your hunting techniques and field care. First off, don't let fly with an arrow or bullet unless you know exactly what's going to happen when you do it. There is no place for guesswork or surprises when it comes to marksmanship. You need to put your projectile cleanly through the lungs and/or heart of the animal for a quick, clean kill. Poor shot placement can lead to an animal being heavily stressed before it eventually dies. When that happens, there's a chance that the animal could indeed have tough meat with strong, off-putting flavors.

Gut the animal immediately. Big game animals have an internal body temperature of over one hundred degrees. Once the animal is dead, that heat will quickly spoil the meat. The area around the ball joints, at the base of the rear legs, is the first to go. Removing the guts helps cool things down. In this chapter you'll see how to properly do the job. After gutting, pack the chest cavity with ice or snow. If need be, quarter the animal and get the quarters into a walk-in meat locker, a household fridge, or even a cooler loaded with ice. Whatever it takes, keep the animal cold and dry until you're ready to butcher it. And when it comes to butchering, keep things cold and clean and follow the directions that are laid out here. You'll eliminate the majority of your gamey situations.

But no amount of careful shooting and trimming is going to change the minds of squeamish folks who think that anything other than domestically produced meat tastes different and, therefore, gamey. What will change their minds is repeated exposure to what real meat actually tastes like. It only helps when it's properly prepared and served. Getting a deer—or an elk, moose, caribou, or bear—in your freezer is the first step of the process. This chapter is the second step. Enjoy.

THE BIG BUCK/LITTLE BUCK MYTH

A lot of hunters have this idea that big bucks aren't that good to eat. This is nonsense. There are myriad factors that influence the palatability of a deer; age is hardly the defining one. We put this idea to the test on a Colorado mule deer hunt when we killed two bucks. The first was a three- to four-year-old giant; the second was a year-and-a-half-old forky. Served raw, the unanimous consensus was that the bigger and older ham was a better piece of meat. In all fairness, the older buck had been aged a day or so longer—which goes to show that factors beyond the animal's age are at play when it comes to quality meat.

American Pronghorn (Antelope)

The meat of the American pronghorn, or antelope, tends to be rather polarizing. Critics often say that it tastes gamey or musky, while fans of antelope will say that the faint hint of sage is a welcome attribute that brings to mind the open landscapes of the American West. Unpleasant experiences with antelope meat can be avoided if the hunter practices good marksmanship and field care. If you follow all of the advice within this book, you'll find that antelope have an excellent flavor on par with the finest big game animals.

Black Bear

During the time of Daniel Boone, black bear was the preferred meat on the American frontier. Deer were good for buckskin clothes, bear was good for eating. There's no reason to think any differently about black bear meat today. Trimmed of fat, the meat is excellent and can be used for a wide variety of purposes. When slow-cooked or braised it resembles beef pot roast in texture and flavor. The quality of the meat does vary according to the animal's diet. Bears that have been feeding on fish or marine mammals can have an off-putting fishy taste. A bear that's been feeding heavily on rotten carrion can also taste bad. These occasions are rare, however, as most black bears derive the bulk of their diet from plant matter. Some of the best bear meat comes from animals feeding on berries or hardwood mast. When baiting bears, avoid using animal or fish matter so that you don't taint the flesh of the animals that you're hunting. Trichinosis is another consideration with bear meat. Unless you've had your animal tested, it's safe to assume that all bears are infected by microscopic Trichinella larvae—the same larvae that used to commonly infect domestic pork and is still present in wild hogs. Destroying the threat is simple: cook all bear meat to 160°F and you're safe.

Caribou

Complaints about the gamey qualities of caribou meat can often be attributed to bulls killed during the rut. Caribou flesh seems to be affected by the hormonal changes of the breeding season in a more dramatic way than any other big game animal. For most hunters, this isn't an issue, because caribou are typically hunted between late August and early October, before the rut begins. People accustomed to eating beef are likely to recognize caribou meat as being "different," though it is highly prized by hunters who live in caribou country. The meat is often more tender than other antlered game, to the point that some people have described it as "pasty." Its coloration is sometimes lighter, too, and it can lack the deep mahogany color that characterizes the flesh of other members of the deer family. Caribou meat can be used in any recipe calling for venison.

Elk

Elk are widely regarded as the best of the best among wild game meats and are often compared to grass-fed beef. There is no such thing as a bad-tasting elk, and rarely does anyone complain about gamey elk. Older animals can be tough, but aging and proper cooking methods can take care of that. Elk meat can be used for any recipe calling for venison.

Moose

In the north, moose meat is as popular among hunters as elk meat is in the Rockies. While it doesn't prompt as many comparisons to grass-fed beef, it is mild and easily approachable. The flesh is heavily grained and colored a deep, rich red. It is generally a tougher, chewier meat than whitetail deer. It's a good practice to age your moose meat for a week or so before butchering. If you can't do that, you can let your butchered cuts rest in the freezer for a few months. You'll find that the meat gets better and better as time goes by. Moose can be used in any preparation calling for venison.

Mule Deer

Most people would have a hard time distinguishing mule deer meat from the meat of a whitetail deer. Occasionally you'll encounter a mature mule deer that has a ruttier and muskier taste than you'd find on a whitetail, but generally they are excellent. The best meat comes off the animals that are in the best condition, regardless of age or gender. If it's killed quickly and handled properly, a well-fed mule deer buck with a good layer of fat on its rump is going to provide some of the most tender and pleasantly flavored meat that you'll ever encounter.

Whitetail Deer

Whitetail deer are by far the most widely consumed game meat in the United States. If care is taken to avoid contamination by the fluids produced by the tarsal glands on the animal's rear legs, the meat is exceptionally mild and usually quite tender. Most people who have a familiarity with both whitetails and elk will choose elk as their favorite, though whitetail meat is highly regarded by most hunters.

Wild Pigs

Wild pigs, or feral hogs, are the exact same species as the farm-raised varieties of pigs that you can find in a butcher shop or grocery store: *Sus scrofa*. The difference is that wild pigs are far leaner than domestic pigs, as they eat a lot less food and get a lot more exercise. For perspective, consider that it's virtually unheard of to find a wild pig that can be used to make a slab of bacon. Because of their leanness, wild pig flesh has more in common with venison than it does with commercially produced pork. It is generally regarded as more flavorful and complex than domestic pork. When cooking with it, you usually need to add fat and take measures to prevent it from drying out. Younger pigs generally have better meat than older pigs. Many hunters prefer the flesh of a pregnant sow above all others, as they have a lot of stored body fat. Most hunters regard sexually mature boars as the least desirable when it comes to eating. At times, their meat can be very tough, with an off-putting odor. Diet matters with wild pigs. Animals feeding on green grass or acorns, for instance, will likely have much better meat than animals that are ingesting lower-quality foods or animal matter. Wild pigs often carry microscopic Trichinella larvae in their flesh, which can cause the disease trichinosis. (The larvae used to be carried by domestic pigs as well, though it's been virtually eradicated from pigs raised in accordance to USDA guidelines.) Cook all wild pork to 160°F and you're safe.

GUTTING BIG GAME ANIMALS

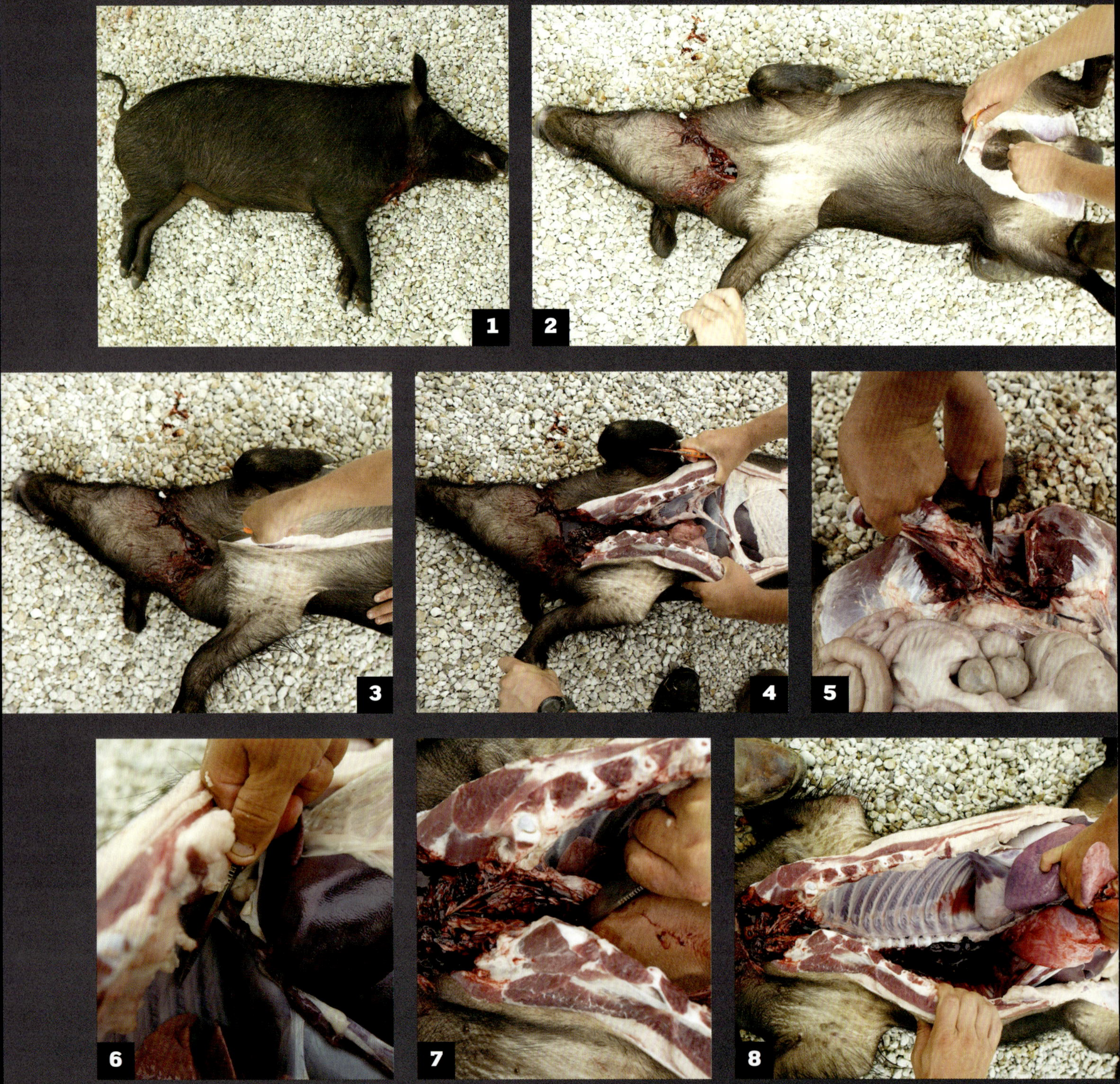

1

2

3

4

5

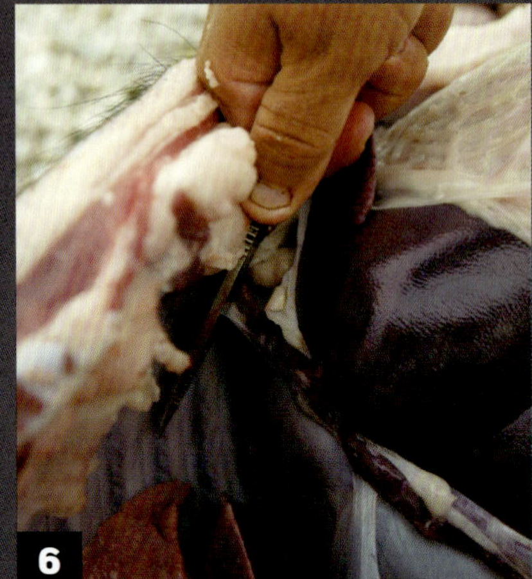

6

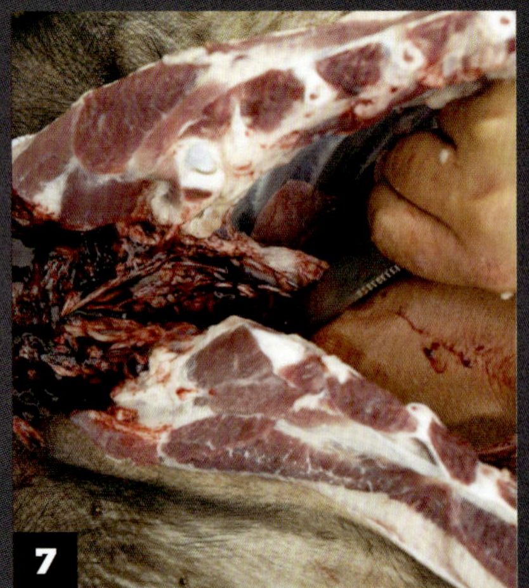

7

8

Wild hogs, like the one pictured here, share the same basic anatomy with all hooved big game animals. The process of skinning, gutting, and butchering any big game animal is basically the same, whether it's a wild pig or a whitetail deer. But there are different approaches to big game field care. Here Ben Binnion, a commercial wild hog trapper who has handled thousands of wild hogs, demonstrates a clean and efficient way to go about this process. For additional information on butchering big game animals check out *The Complete Guide to Hunting, Butchering, and Cooking Wild Game, Volume 1: Big Game.*

How to Gut Big Game Animals

1. Because this hog was trapped and shot in the head, it was necessary to bleed it out by cutting its throat immediately after the shot. Bleeding out a big game animal can give the meat a cleaner taste and better appearance, but it is unnecessary if the animal was shot in the vital heart/lung area with a rifle or bow.

2. Start by cutting through the skin around the genitals and down to the anus. Be extremely careful to cut only the hide without puncturing the gut cavity. Once this cut is made, use your knife to separate the skin and genitals from the carcass. This hog was trapped in Texas, where leaving evidence of sex on the carcass is not a legal requirement. However, some state game agencies do require that you leave evidence of sex naturally attached to the carcass of big game animals. (Read more on page 18.)

3. From the spot where the hide and genitals have been removed, make an incision through the skin extending forward to the throat. (Again, make adjustments if you need to leave evidence of sex attached.)

4. To open up the gut cavity, start at the anus and cut forward to the sternum. Point your knife toward the head of the animal with the blade facing up for this cut. With your fingers behind the knife, use them to spread and lift the abdominal wall as you cut. Make very shallow cuts through just the abdominal wall without touching the guts. On smaller big game animals, it's possible to extend this cut alongside the sternum all the way to the throat with just a knife. Bigger critters like elk may require the use of a bone saw.

5. Next, use a bone saw or stout knife to split the pelvis bone between the rear quarters just above the anus. Once the pelvis bone has been cut, the lower intestine will be exposed where it meets the anus. Make a circular cut around the anus and lower intestine to free it from the carcass.

6. Now look for the diaphragm, which divides the heart and lung area (the thoracic cavity) from the liver and digestive system (the peritoneal cavity). This thin wall of muscle needs to be cut free from the interior of the rib cage on both sides of the animal.

7. Reach forward into the chest cavity to locate the esophagus and the trachea. The trachea is a rigid tube above the heart and lungs in the throat of the animal. Hold the trachea with your nondominant hand while you use your knife to sever it. You may be working by feel here, so be extremely careful not to cut yourself.

8. Now get a good grip on the trachea with both hands and pull up and back. If you've done things right up until this point, the whole works will come out in one piece. This is the time to remove the heart, liver, kidneys, and caul fat from the rest of the gut pile. Before moving on to skinning, wash the interior of the animal to remove any blood, dirt, or digestive matter.

GAMBREL SKINNING BIG GAME

1

2

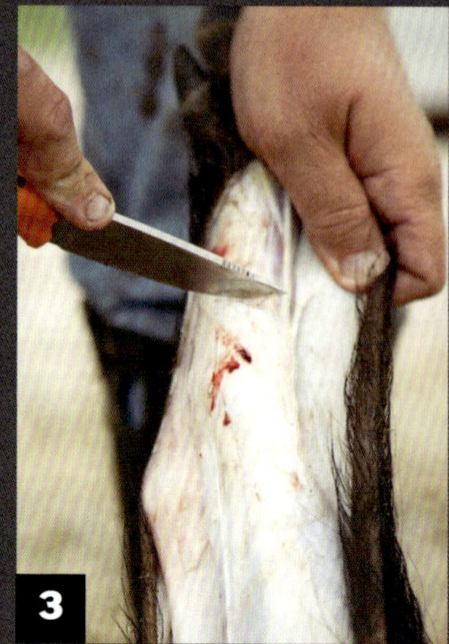
3

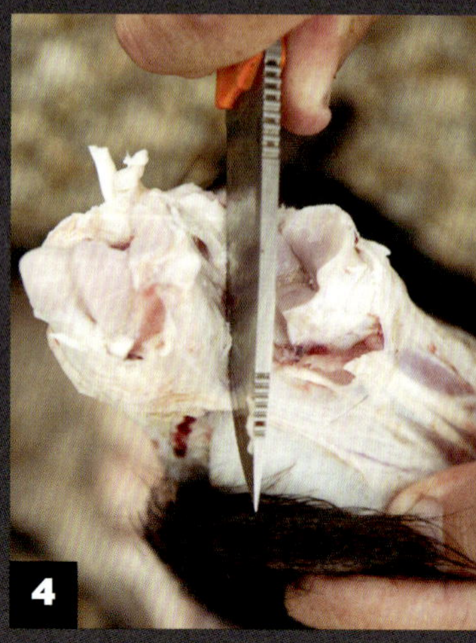
4

5

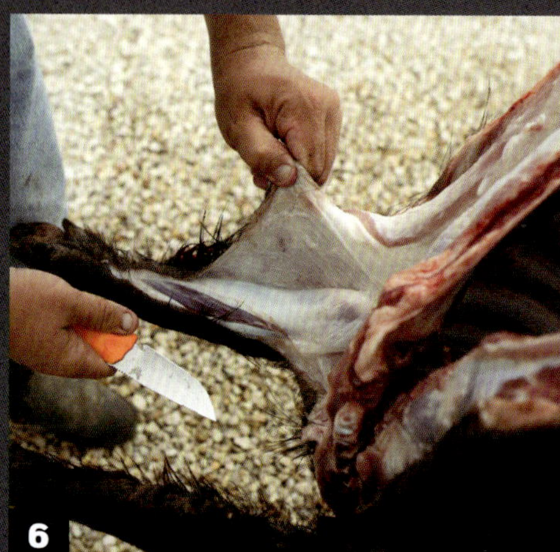
6

7

Once a big game animal has been gutted, the next butchering step is skinning. The easiest way to skin an animal is while it is hanging from a gambrel, which looks like a heavy-duty coat hanger. It is much easier to work on an animal that is suspended above the ground, and gambrels are ideal for deer-size game that hunters are able to get out of the woods in one piece.

Skinning

1. Begin by making an incision through the hide on the lower rear leg near the foot.

2. Extend this cut down along the inside of the ham until it meets your original gutting cut at the abdomen. Now begin skinning the rear leg by slicing between hide and flesh. Do your best to keep the meat clean and free of hair and dirt.

3. Skin around the ankle joint.

4. Next, you'll need to separate the meatless shin bones from the rear quarters. Find the knee joint at the top of the shin. Use your knife to cut the tendons around this joint. Continue cutting these tendons until the joint loosens enough to twist it. Twist the shin bone in a circular motion until it "pops." At this point, one or two more cuts will completely free the lower leg.

5. Each rear leg has a heavy tendon behind the knee. Cut a slit through the skin in the gap between the tendon and the leg. Lower the gambrel, or with the help of a buddy, lift your animal in order to place the hooks on each side of the gambrel through these slits. Try to hang the animal at a height that allows you to work comfortably.

6. On each front leg, make a cut from the foot to the gutting incision at the chest cavity. Now skin each front leg until the hide is hanging freely.

7. Next, move up to the rear legs. Continue skinning each rear leg downward to the rump. You should be able to separate portions of the hide from the carcass just by pulling on it. In other places, you'll need to use your knife.

8. Once each rear leg is completely skinned, continue skinning down and around the back, flank, and belly of the animal.

9. Skin the animal downward past the shoulder and front legs. At the neck, keep skinning until you reach the animal's head.

10. Now separate the head and hide from the carcass where the spine meets the base of the skull. Use a knife to do this the same way you popped the leg joints or you can quickly sever the spine with a bone saw.

11. Finally, take the time to pick any hair off the meat and then wash the carcass before moving on to breaking the animal down into individual cuts of meat.

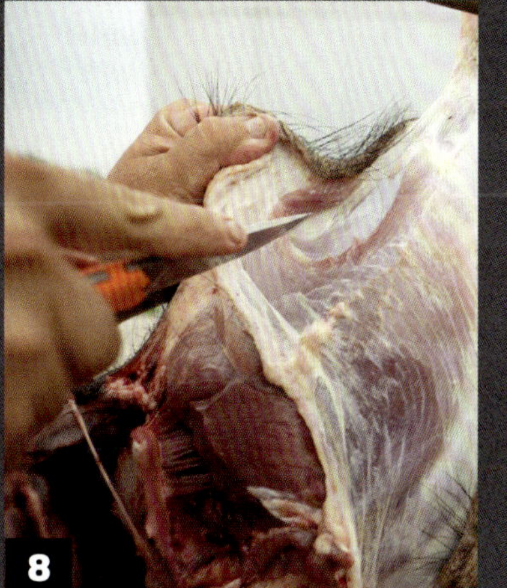
8

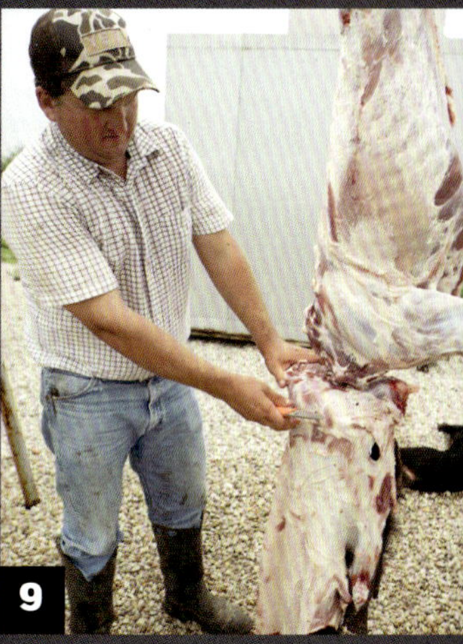
9

10

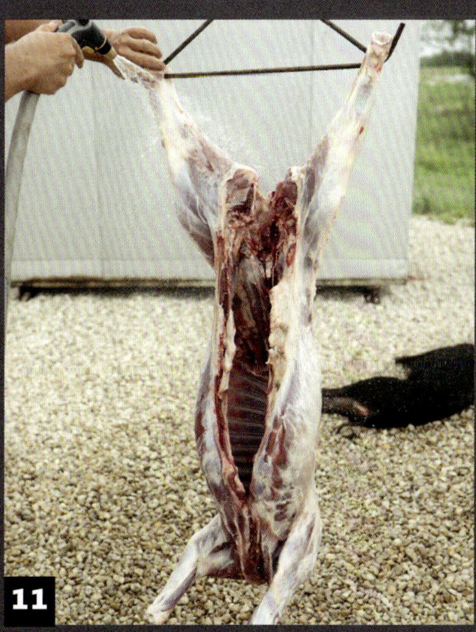
11

BUTCHERING BIG GAME ON THE GROUND

Some big game animals are much bigger than others. Bull moose can weigh more than 1,500 pounds. That's ten times the weight of the average whitetail deer. Hunters who kill large animals like elk and moose in the backcountry, or even a deer in a remote location, often use a field butchering method commonly referred to as the "gutless method." This means that the animal is butchered without removing the guts from the body cavity as a first step. It's particularly well suited for large animals that are difficult to maneuver. After butchering a large animal in the field, it's possible to pack manageable loads of meat back to camp or your vehicle.

Field Butchering Big Game

1. Field butchering large animals is a big job. If possible, it's good to have help from some friends.

2. Start by opening up the hide along the back from the neck to the tail. Then begin skinning the hide toward the belly and legs.

3. Skin one entire side of the animal first. Once the hide is removed, lay it out flat, hair-side down on the ground. This provides a relatively clean spot to place meat as it is removed from the animal.

4. The easiest piece of meat to remove is the backstrap. This tender, boneless piece of meat extends from the base of the neck to the hip bones.

5. Now remove the upward-facing rear and front legs.

6. Move your meat to the shade, where it can cool off. Hanging meat in a game bag from a tree limb is ideal, but you may need to lay large, heavy quarters on a bed of branches so they stay clean.

7. Bone saws are handy for large butchering jobs. Here, a saw is used to remove the entire rib rack in a single piece. You can reduce weight by deboning the rib meat, but you'll be missing out on grilled bone-in moose ribs.

8. With the ribs removed, you'll have easy access to all the good stuff inside the animal. The inner tenderloins rest along the spine, above the intestines, just in front of the hips. You'll also want to save the heart, liver, tongue, and perhaps the web of caul fat that surrounds the digestive system. See recipes using the heart (Skewered and Grilled Duck Hearts, page 124), liver (Venison Liver Mousse, page 30), and tongue (Seared Tongue Sandwich, page 36).

9. Here you have one side of a moose (front and rear quarters, rib rack, and backstrap) removed from the carcass. You'll also need to remove the brisket, neck meat, and other meat left on the upward side of the carcass. Now roll the animal over and repeat the process on the other side. (See pages 20–27 for information on breaking down an animal into individual cuts.)

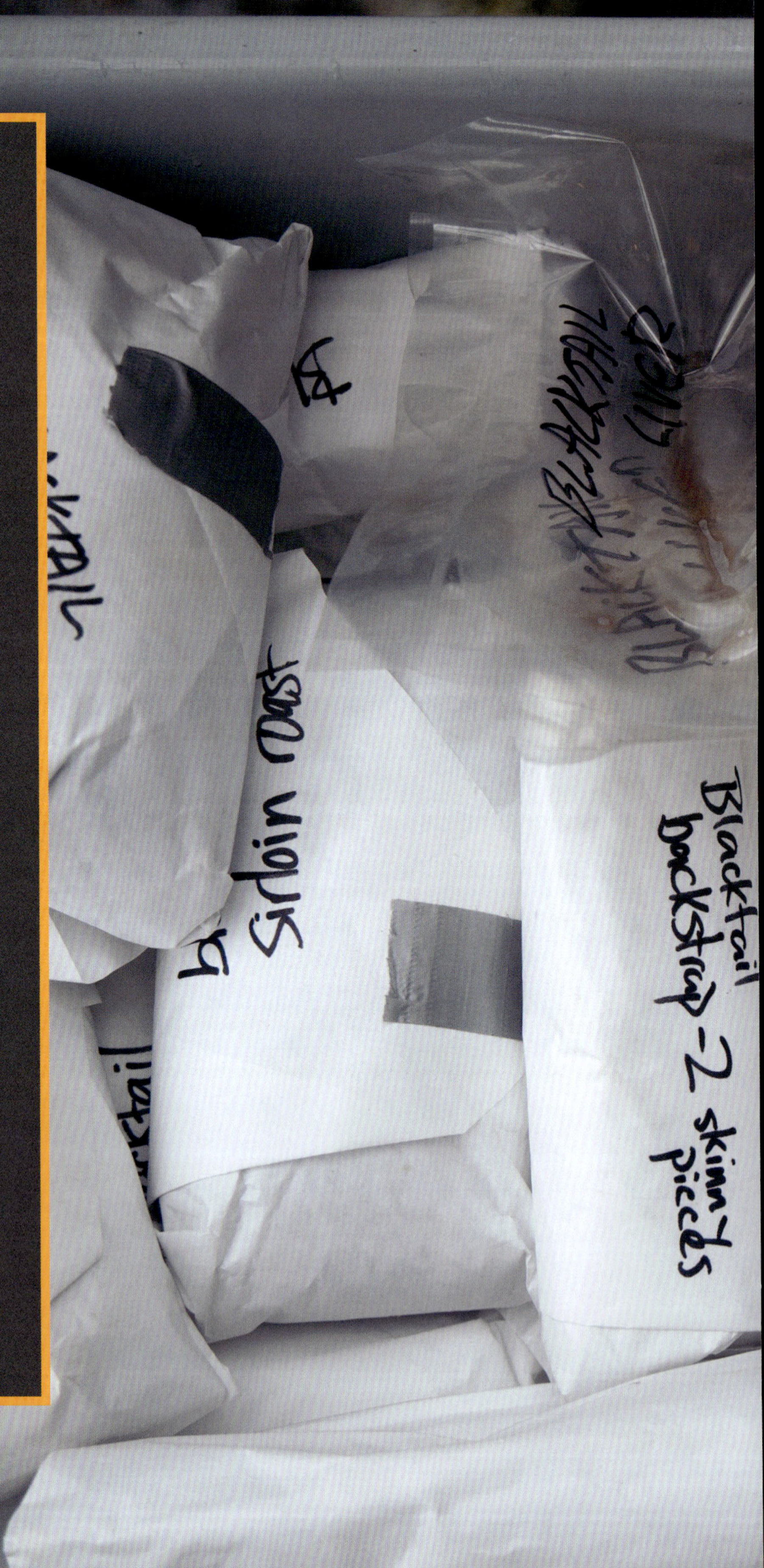

EVIDENCE OF SEX

Most states require hunters to provide evidence of sex on big game animals until the animal has been processed and packaged. For horned or antlered big game, evidence of sex can include the head of the animal as long as it remains naturally attached to the carcass. Otherwise the reproductive organs must remain naturally attached to one or both hindquarters in order for a hunter to meet evidence of sex requirements.

Proof of Sex, Male

Carefully skin the penis and testicles during the gutting process. The skinned penis can then be cut and removed at its base near the anus. Each testicle is attached to the muscle of the corresponding hindquarter with a small amount of connective tissue. Leave the testicles attached, being careful while working in this area during field butchering.

Proof of Sex, Female

Where you see the teats, skin the hide away from the mammary glands during the gutting process. Under the skin is the actual mammary gland. Like the testicles, the mammary gland is attached only by fragile connective tissue. Leave the gland attached to the muscle of each hindquarter and cut carefully around this area during field butchering.

WANTON WASTE

Hunters who are interested in filling the freezer shouldn't need to be convinced that it's worth saving neck roasts, briskets, or flank meat. But hunters should be aware that most states have various laws mandating what portions of an animal must be retained. In Alaska, where the bull moose on page 16 was killed, strict wanton waste laws require hunters to pack out all edible meat.

1

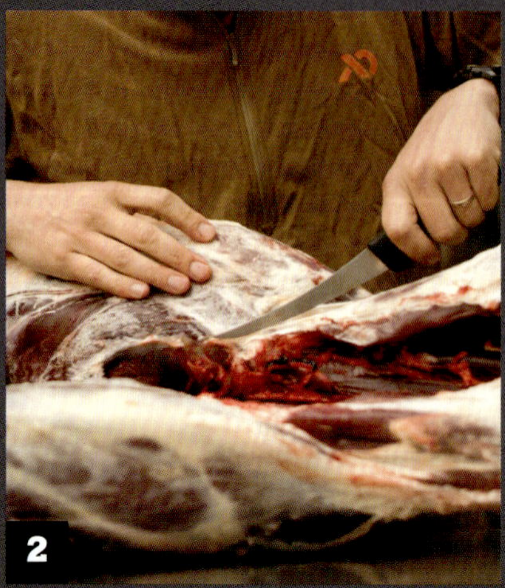
2

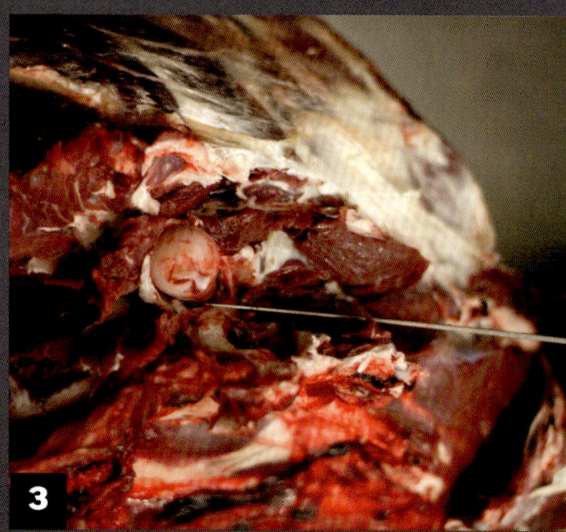
3

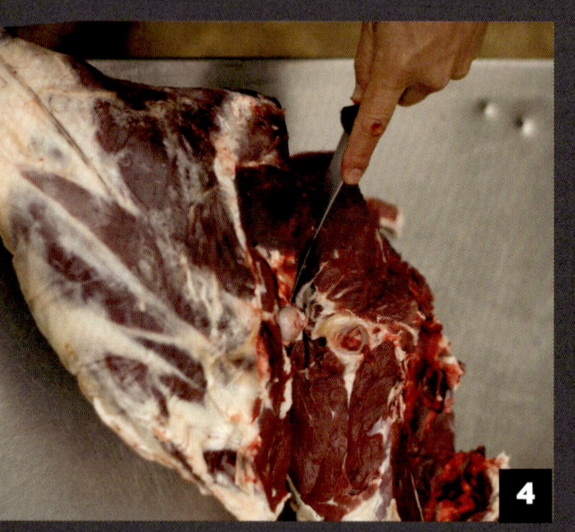
4

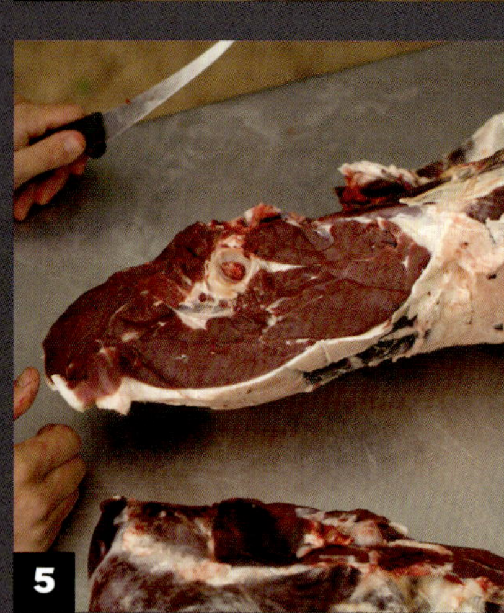
5

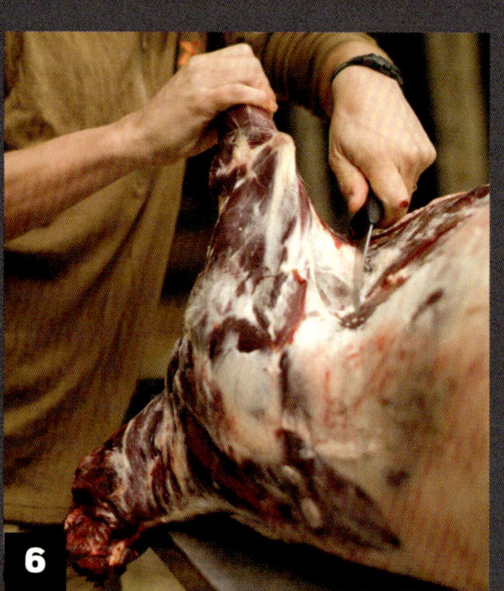
6

7

8

Breaking down a big game animal is easy with a few simple tools and some know-how. A stainless steel table makes for a clean workspace, but you can also use a kitchen counter or garage workbench. Just make sure you're starting out with a sanitized surface and sharp knives.

Removing Legs

1. Start out by inspecting the skinned and gutted carcass for hair, dirt, or blood-shot meat. Take the time to clean up the carcass before you begin cutting.

2. Begin with separating a rear leg. You'll want to start by cutting into the seam on the inner part of the hindquarter where the ham rests against the abdomen.

3. As you cut, try to run your knife between the hip bones and the meat. You'll run into bone at the hip's ball-and-socket joint. Separate this joint by cutting the tendons that surround it.

4. With the ball-and-socket joint separated, continue cutting the meat down to and around the pelvis bones.

5. After the hind leg is free, go back and trim up the hip bones around the socket. These small pieces of meat should be saved for grinding into burger or sausage.

6. Now move to the front leg. Pull the leg away from the body and begin cutting the muscle around the shoulder.

7. There are no bones or joints to worry about. Just cut between the shoulder muscle and the rib cage to separate the front leg from the carcass.

8. Next, flip the carcass over and remove the front and rear legs from the other side.

CHRONIC WASTING DISEASE

Chronic wasting disease (CWD) is a fatal degenerative disease similar to mad cow disease, which afflicts members of the deer family. CWD was first discovered in mule deer in Colorado and can also infect whitetails, elk, and moose. While there have been no known cases of humans developing CWD, there may be risks, however small, with eating CWD-infected animals. In states where CWD outbreaks have occurred, such as Colorado, Minnesota, and Missouri, hunters in certain parts of the state may be required to have their animals tested for CWD. Even where testing is not mandatory, if you kill an animal in an area where CWD is known to be present, it's a good idea to have that animal tested before consuming its meat. State fish and game agencies often conduct these tests free of charge. The prions that cause CWD are known to concentrate in the brain, spinal cord, spleen, and lymph nodes of infected deer, so it is recommended that hunters avoid cutting through the spine. Still, we enjoy bone-in neck roasts and we're comfortable preparing this meal from deer that have tested negative for CWD.

TABLETOP BUTCHERING

REMOVING PAUNCH, TENDERLOIN, AND BACKSTRAP

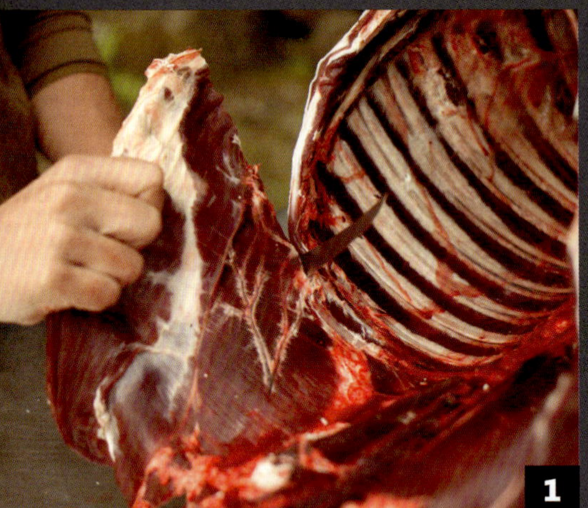
1

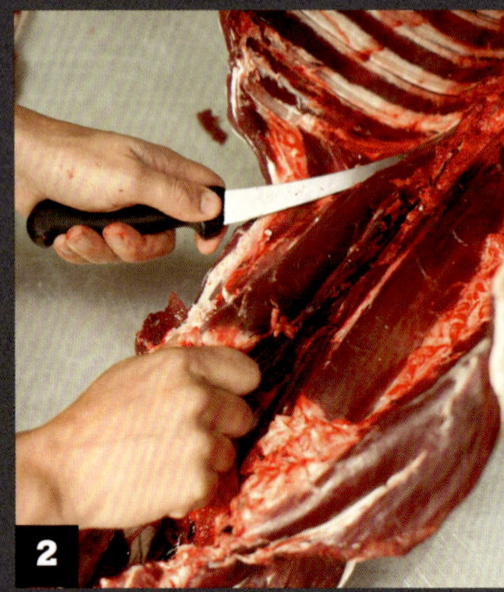
2

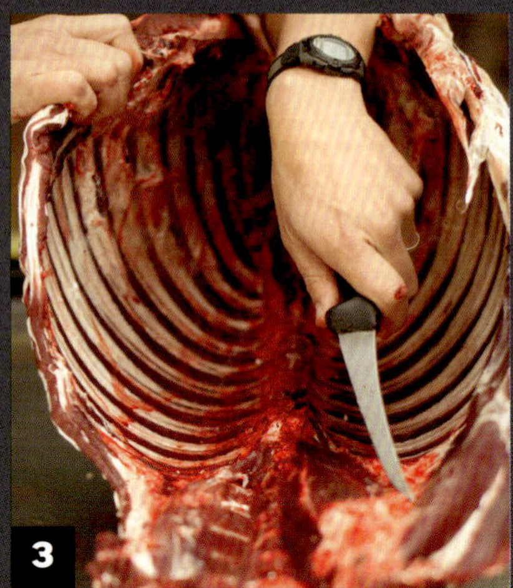
3

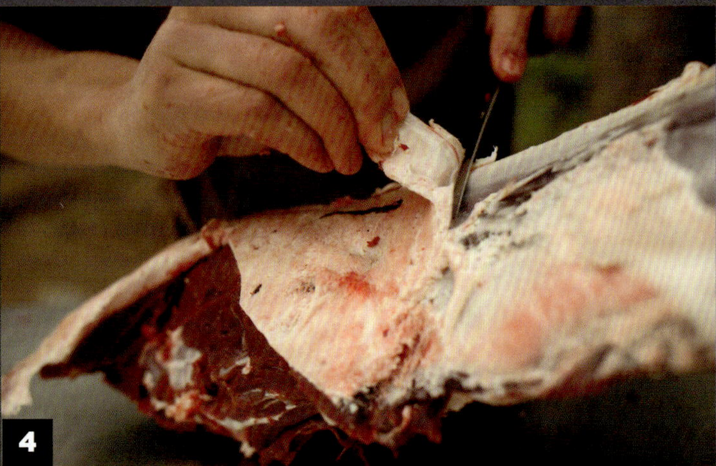
4

5

1. Start by removing the thin, flat section of belly muscle, commonly known as the paunch, which hangs behind the ribs.

2. The inner loins, or tenderloins, rest on either side of the spine just behind the ribs. Remove any fat and make a cut along each side of the tenderloin. Lift it up and cut the ends free.

3. Next, remove the paunch and tenderloin from the opposite side of the animal.

4. Position the carcass so the back faces up. Along either side of the spine are the two backstraps. Trim the tough, outer layer of fat away from the backstrap.

5. The long, tubular backstrap muscle rests between the bones of the spine and the ribs. To remove it cleanly without wasting meat, your knife should periodically scrape bone as you cut.

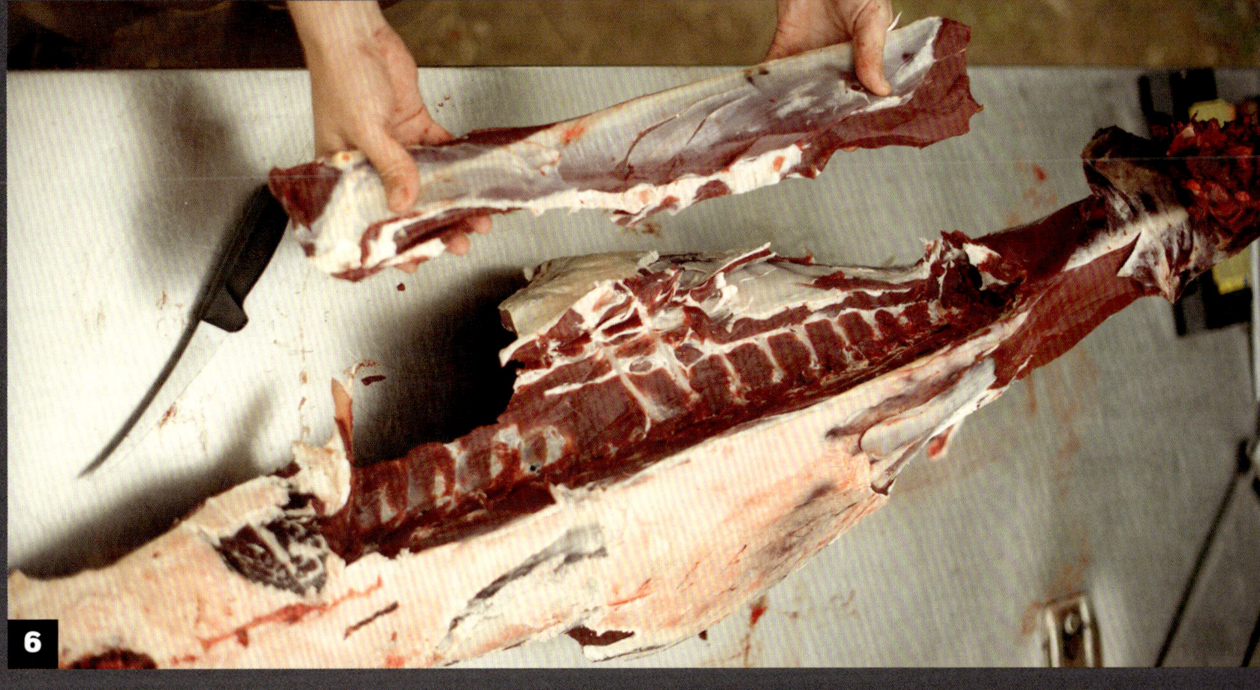

6. Here, the backstrap is completely removed. Repeat the process with the second one.

7. Each backstrap has a thick layer of tough silver skin and tendons on one side. Carefully cut it away from the meat. You can also freeze the backstrap without doing this and remove the silver skin later. It helps protect the meat from freezer burn.

8. Take the time to remove any meat attached to the silver skin. Little pieces of trimmed meat add up to a big pile of burger meat later.

REMOVING NECK ROAST AND RIBS

1

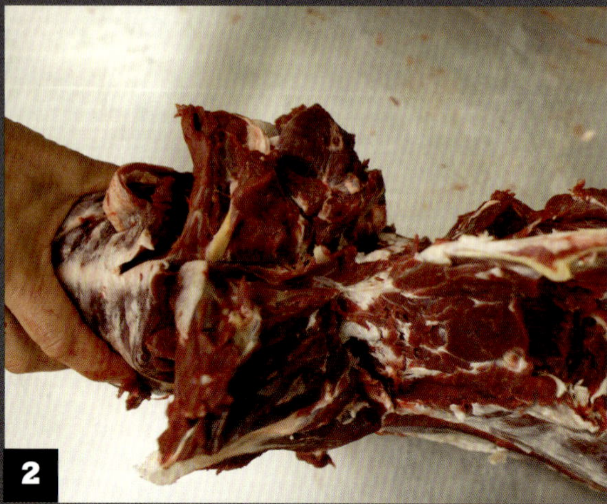
2

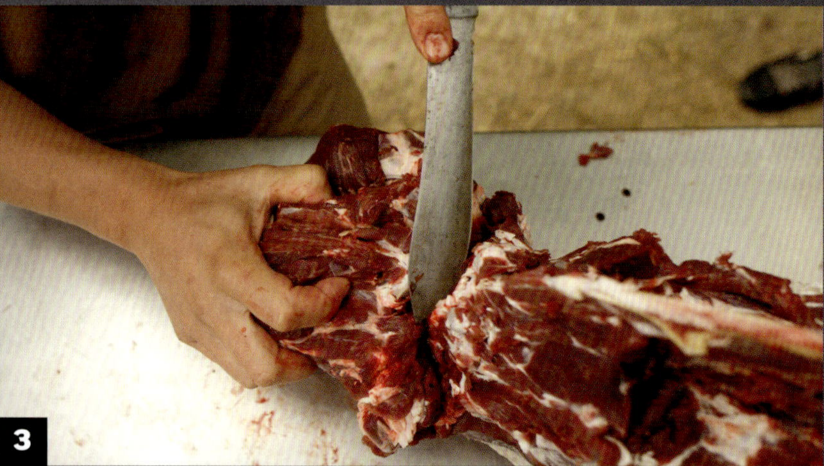
3

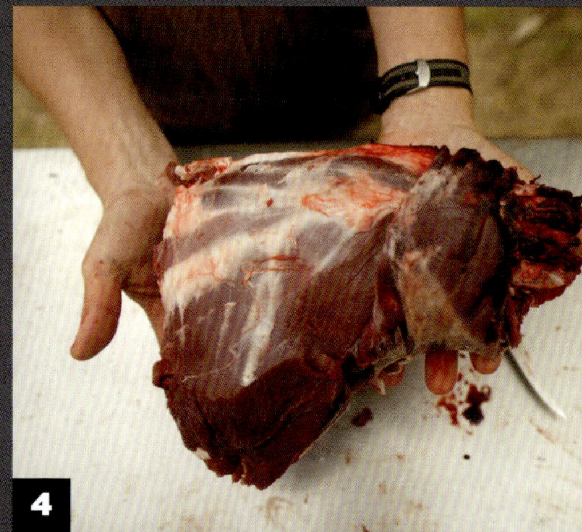
4

Neck Roast

1. To remove a bone-in neck roast, start at the base of the neck where it meets the chest.

2. Cut the lower neck muscles down to the spine around the entire circumference of the neck.

3. With the spine exposed, you'll be able to make a cut between the vertebrae at the base of the neck to separate it from the carcass. You can also use a bone saw to do the job. Before cutting or sawing through a deer's spine, make sure to consider the potential risks of chronic wasting disease (see sidebar on page 21).

4. Here you have a whole bone-in neck roast, which is great for slow-cooking recipes. The neck meat can also be cut away from the spine for boneless neck roasts or grinding into burger meat.

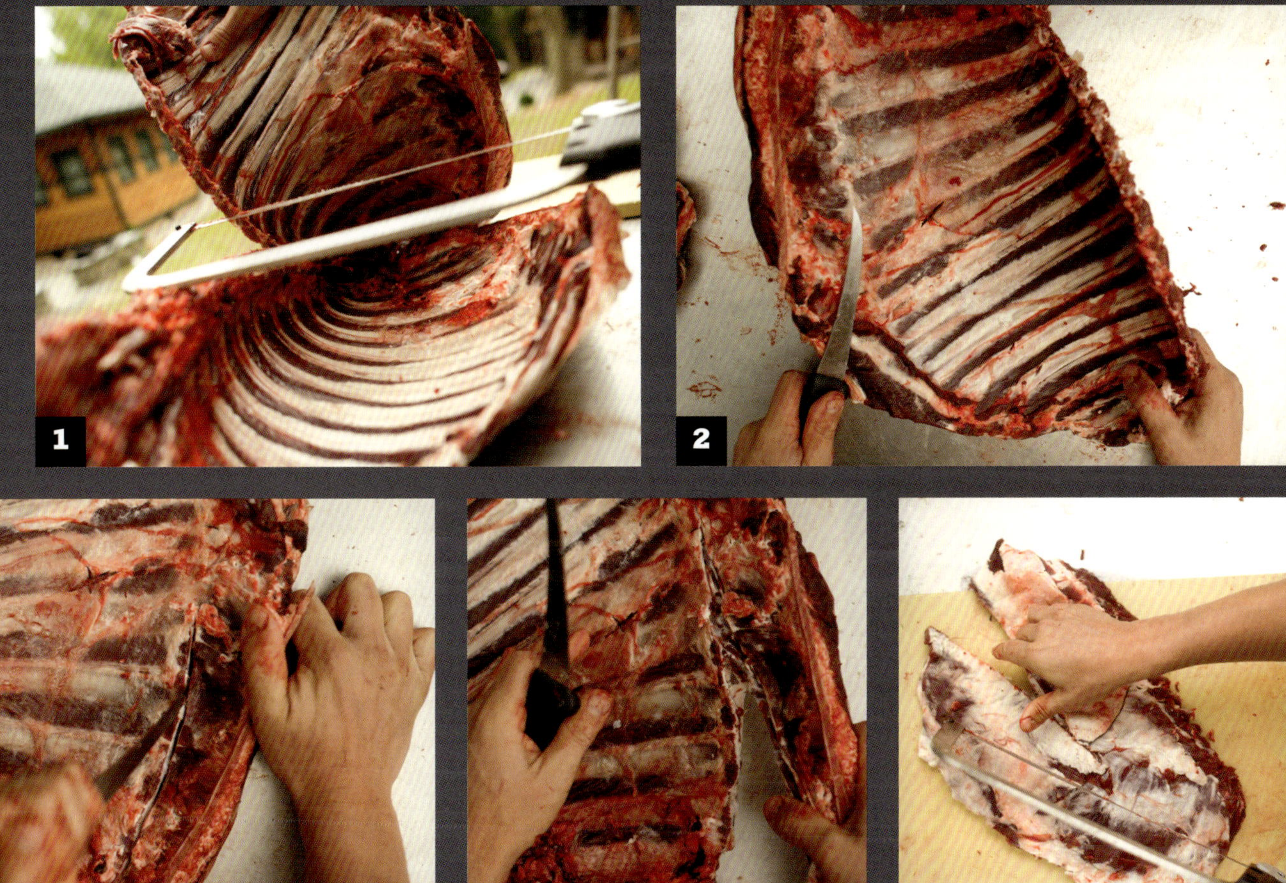

Ribs

1. Use a bone saw to separate each rib rack.

2. Now the rib rack is ready to be broken down into smaller pieces.

3. There's very little edible meat along the sternum bone of a deer. (On larger game, such as elk or moose, there's enough to warrant your attention.) Cut between the ends of the rib bones and the sternum to separate it from the rib rack.

4. Continue this cut until the sternum is removed. Trim any meat remaining on the sternum for making burgers and reserve the bone for making stock.

5. Now use your bone saw to cut the rib rack lengthwise into sections. You can then use a knife to divide these long sections into shorter, serving-size pieces of three or four ribs.

TABLETOP BUTCHERING

BONE-IN BLADE ROAST, DEBONED SHOULDER, BONELESS HAM

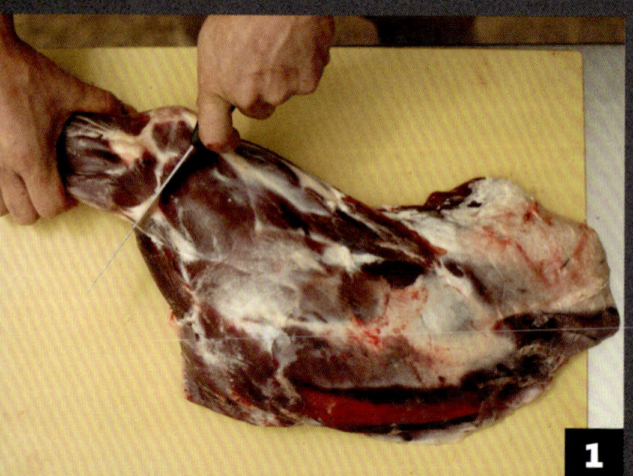

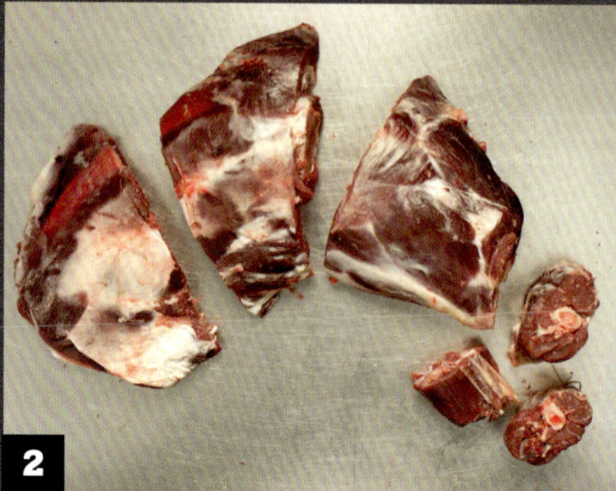

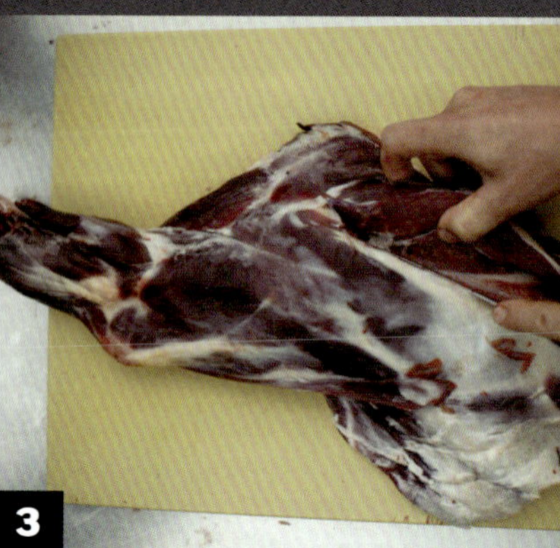

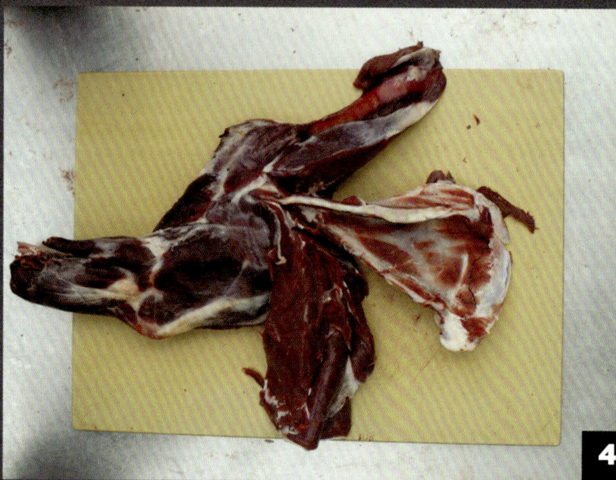

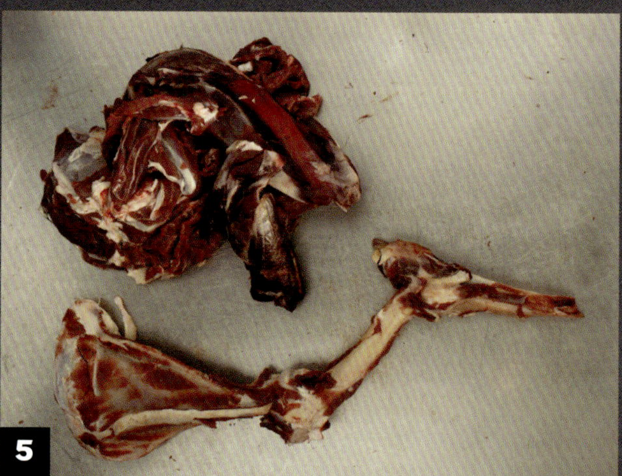

1. The front leg of a deer can be broken down into several bone-in roasts, all of which are great for braising recipes. Start by removing the shank at the joint where it joins the lower shoulder.

2. Next, use a bone saw to divide the shoulder into three bone-in blade roasts. Then saw the shank into three thick discs for making osso bucco. Check out the blade roast recipe in *The Complete Guide to Hunting, Butchering, and Cooking Wild Game, Volume 1*, and see page 60 for the Osso Bucco recipe.

3. You can also debone the front leg. Start by removing the roast along the rearward side of the narrow, raised piece of bone that divides the shoulder blade. This roast is good for jerky and slow-cooking.

4. Next, remove the roast from the other side of the shoulder blade.

5. Continue deboning the entire shoulder and shank. You can use the larger deboned roasts and shank for the same bone-in recipes mentioned above. Use the smaller pieces for burgers and sausage. Reserve the leg bones for the stock recipe on page 305.

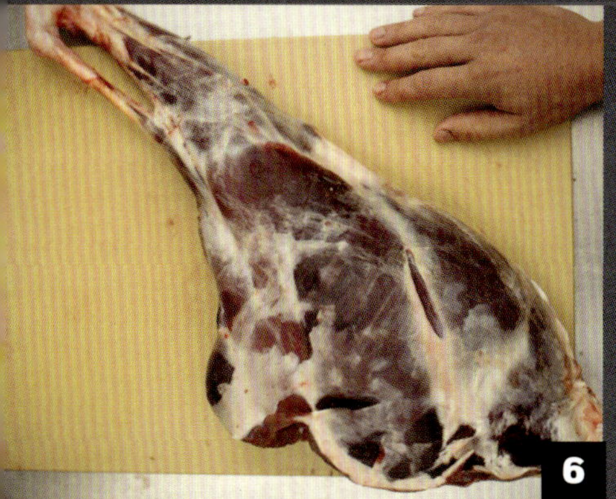

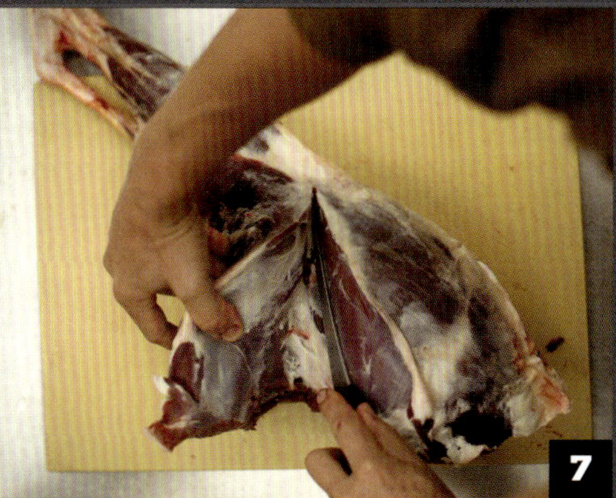

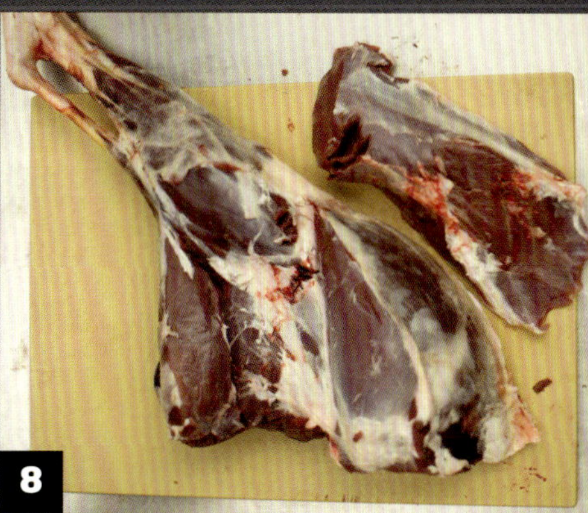

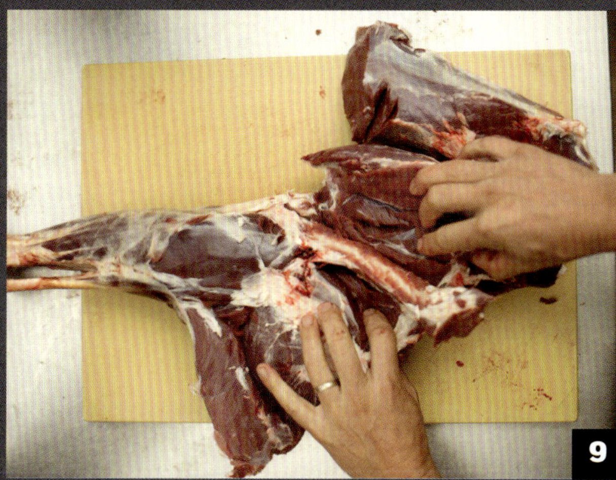

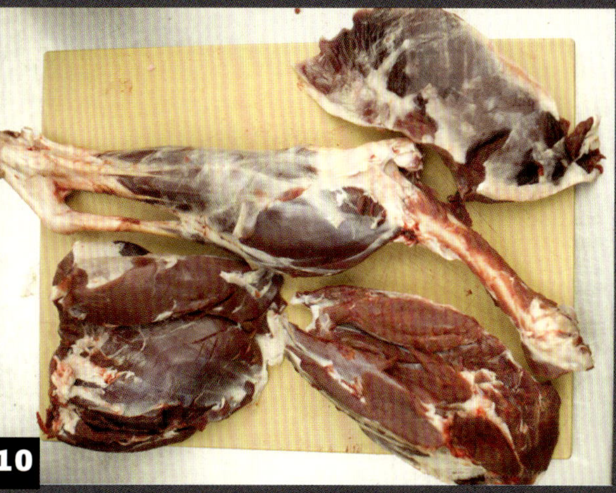

6. The rear leg can be deboned and divided into large roasts that are suitable for grilling whole or cutting into steaks.

7. Start by removing the lower, rear roast from the ham. It will separate easily if you cut between muscles rather than cutting through meat.

8. From here, it's easy to debone the rest of the rear leg.

9. Cut the large muscle groups above the shank away from the femur.

10. You'll be left with three large boneless roasts and the shank. They can be left whole or cut into smaller pieces.

Birchwood Casey
Target Spots

APRIL BLOOMFIELD'S SCOTCH EGGS

SERVES 6

Chef April Bloomfield is always doing exciting stuff with meat and fish, and I've used her food as inspiration for my own experiments with wild game. The thing about April's Scotch egg, though, is that it's too perfect to mess with on my own. So I went straight to April and asked her what she'd do differently if she were working with wild venison rather than domestic pork. She suggested some tweaks to her original recipe, including the addition of nutmeg and juniper. The next time you have guests and want to do something truly memorable, try this. It's well worth the effort.

SAGE PASTE

½ ounce fresh sage, finely chopped

½ teaspoon flaky salt

½ teaspoon extra virgin olive oil

VENISON MIXTURE

1 pound ground venison

7 ounces ground salted fatback

⅓ cup coarse filone breadcrumbs (see page 324)

⅓ cup milk

2 teaspoons kosher salt, or to taste

¼ teaspoon chopped fresh rosemary

⅛ teaspoon freshly grated nutmeg

2 juniper berries, grated on a Microplane

6 large eggs

BREADING

¼ cup all-purpose flour

2 large eggs, beaten

½ cup fine filone breadcrumbs (see page 324)

½ cup coarse filone breadcrumbs (see page 324)

5 cups peanut oil, for frying

Chopped parsley, for serving (optional)

FOR THE SAGE PASTE: Mince the sage with the salt and oil on a cutting board using the side of a chef's knife until it's a uniform pesto-like paste. Alternately, use a mortar and pestle.

FOR THE VENISON MIXTURE: Combine the venison, fatback, sage paste, breadcrumbs, milk, salt, rosemary, nutmeg, and juniper in a medium bowl. Using your hands, portion the meat mixture into six 4-ounce balls. Carefully flatten out each portion into a pancake, making sure the thickness is even all around.

Fill a large bowl with ice and water and set aside. Bring a large saucepan of water to a boil. Slowly add the eggs to the water and cook for 5½ minutes, then remove the eggs with a slotted spoon and shock them in the ice-water bath. Remove the eggs from the ice-water bath and peel them.

Place one of the soft-boiled eggs on top of the sausage and wrap it around the egg. Repeat with the remaining eggs and sausage and refrigerate until cold, 30 minutes to 2 hours.

FOR THE BREADING: Place the breading ingredients in separate shallow bowls. Remove the meat-covered eggs from the refrigerator. Dredge them first in the flour, then coat them with the egg wash, then cover with a layer of the fine breadcrumbs. Repeat the egg wash and coat a second time with a layer of coarse breadcrumbs. Repeat with the remaining eggs.

FOR FRYING: Heat the oil in a large pot until it reaches 350°F on a deep-fry thermometer. Fry the eggs, two or three at a time, depending on your pot size, for 9 minutes, then let them rest for 1 minute. You're looking for the yolk to be runny but warm inside. Repeat with the remaining eggs. Serve immediately garnished with chopped parsley (if using).

ALSO WORKS WITH: Go ahead and make the venison mix with any ground meat. As mentioned above, April usually makes her Scotch eggs with pork, so this is particularly well suited to wild pigs. But I'd feel comfortable making it with anything from bear to caribou to javelina.

Tip: Filone is a rustic, crusty Italian bread. Any crusty rustic bread will work.

VENISON LIVER MOUSSE

MAKES ABOUT 3 CUPS

3 large eggs

1 pound wild game liver, fresh

¼ cup (½ stick) unsalted butter

1 large onion, finely chopped

1 clove garlic, minced

¼ cup red wine

2 tablespoons extra virgin olive oil, plus more as needed

2 tablespoons honey mustard

1 teaspoon kosher salt, plus more as needed

Freshly ground black pepper

French bread slices, rye toast points, or crackers, for serving

---

ALSO WORKS WITH: The age of the animal is more important than the species. The liver from any young specimen of horned or antlered game will work.

Most hunters who enjoy venison liver like to eat it as simply as possible: gently sautéed in butter or bacon grease alongside a sliced onion. There's no denying how delicious that preparation is, but it's helpful to have a few more tricks on hand for those years when you're lucky enough to kill multiple deer, or just when you're looking to try something fresh and new. This liver mousse recipe is based on one that was passed along by my friend Tim Collins, a Manhattan-based lawyer and avid deer hunter whose farm happens to produce some excellent honey and maple syrup along with a fair bit of wild venison. Be aware that the best and mildest livers come from young animals. It's really hard to beat a liver from a yearling whitetail, mule deer, or elk. All livers are best when eaten fresh. While it's possible to freeze liver, the quality quickly goes downhill.

Fill a large bowl with ice and water and set aside. Place the eggs in a small pot, add water to cover, and bring to a boil. Reduce the heat to maintain a simmer and simmer for 10 minutes. Remove the eggs with a slotted spoon and shock them in the ice-water bath. Remove the eggs from the ice-water bath and peel them, then coarsely chop them.

Slice the liver into ½-inch-thick strips. Melt the butter in a large skillet over medium-low heat. Working in two batches, gently fry the liver slices on each side for 4 to 5 minutes. Do not overcook the liver and avoid searing the surfaces. It should remain a little pinkish on the inside. Remove to a plate.

Add the onion and garlic to the same skillet, increase the heat to medium, and cook until the onion begins to caramelize. Cut the liver into ½-inch cubes and add them to the pan along with the wine, oil, honey mustard, salt, and 8 or 9 twists of black pepper. Stir to combine, bring to a simmer, and then remove the pan from the heat.

Once the mixture is cooled to a safe handling temperature, transfer to the bowl of a food processor along with the chopped eggs and process until smooth. Taste and adjust the seasoning with salt and pepper. Chill and serve with bread, toast, or crackers.

MARROW BONES
WITH CELERY AND PICKLED RAISINS

SERVES 2 TO 4

I first became interested in bone marrow while researching a writing project about a Paleo-Indian archaeological culture known as the Folsom Complex. There are a lot of mysteries surrounding the lifeways of these Ice Age hunters, but there's little doubt that they enjoyed bone marrow. Femurs and shin bones that have been shattered by stone tools are a common find during archaeological excavations of their encampments and kill-sites on the high plains of the American West. Nowadays, thanks to bandsaws and hacksaws, we don't need to bust our marrow bones apart in order to get at the meaty and buttery goods that lie inside. I like to cut mine into discs and then serve the marrow right inside these all-natural and visually stunning bowls of bone.

CELERY AND PICKLED RAISIN SALAD

1 cup white wine vinegar

¼ cup sugar

1 cup golden raisins

Pinch of red chile flakes

2 ribs celery, thinly sliced

⅓ cup celery leaves

2 tablespoons thinly sliced red onion

1 tablespoon extra virgin olive oil

Kosher salt

Freshly ground black pepper

MARROW BONES

1 (or more) femur or shin bone from large-bodied game (see list below)

Coarse sea salt

3 to 6 sprigs fresh thyme, separated into pieces (optional)

Baguette or toasted sliced bread, for serving

ALSO WORKS WITH: Femurs or shin bones from elk, moose, caribou, buffalo, or other large-bodied game. If using whitetail deer or mule deer, get bones from the biggest deer you can find.

SPECIAL EQUIPMENT: band saw or hacksaw fitted with a metal cutting blade

FOR THE CELERY AND PICKLED RAISIN SALAD: Combine the vinegar and sugar in a small saucepan and bring to a boil over high heat. Turn off the heat, add the raisins, steep for 10 minutes, and then stir in the red chile flakes. Let cool. Remove the raisins from the pickling liquid using a slotted spoon. Combine the celery, celery leaves, pickled raisins, onions, and oil in a small bowl, and season to taste with salt and black pepper.

FOR THE MARROW BONES: Saw the bones into 2-inch discs. (It works well to freeze them first, but it's not necessary.) A butcher's band saw is the easiest way to cut the bones, but a basic hacksaw fitted with a metal cutting blade will do the trick. Inspect each disc to make sure there's a usable amount of marrow inside. It will look like frozen butter. Discs cut from the ends of the bones might be partially or mostly filled with a honeycombed bone structure. Use these instead for making stock or bone broth.

Preheat the oven to 400°F. Line a baking sheet or any kind of ovenproof skillet or baking dish with foil.

Stand the discs upright on the prepared pan. Roast until the marrow is soft throughout and begins to pull away from the bone. Allow the surface to bubble and crisp a bit, but don't let the marrow spill over the top. Cooking time varies according to the size of bone, but they are typically ready within 10 to 12 minutes.

Sprinkle each bone with a pinch of coarse sea salt and garnish with a small sprig of thyme placed into the marrow. Serve with the celery salad alongside. Invite your guests to spread their hot marrow on top of toasted bread slices or a warmed baguette. While there is such a thing as an actual marrow spoon, meant for digging the marrow from the bones, the handle end of a small teaspoon works really well.

VENISON CARPACCIO
WITH BITTER GREENS SALAD

SERVES 4 AS AN APPETIZER

A traditional practice among some indigenous caribou hunters in the Arctic was to open the hide on a freshly killed caribou in the center of the family's lodge and then devour the entire thing raw. I've enjoyed enough raw game meat that this tradition doesn't seem entirely foreign to me, though I've met plenty of other hunters who are afraid to try wild game carpaccio. None have cited specific fears; rather, it's just a general apprehension about picking up some sort of unknown ailment. If you share these fears, by all means, do your own research and don't just take my word for it. But I have eaten many pounds of carpaccio from horned and antlered game with no ill effect. I should point out, too, that I'm very careful about proper field care and storage. I make sure that my meat is clean and well-trimmed, and I typically freeze it beforehand as an added precaution. I also recommend that you eat carpaccio in moderation, at least at first. If your system isn't used to raw or rare meat, a large meal of it can give you a stomachache, so start out with just a few slices. After some practice, you might end up craving that whole caribou.

ALSO WORKS WITH: You could theoretically prepare carpaccio using the loin or round roast from any horned or antlered game (deer, elk, and moose are all perfect), but if you want a truly positive experience, you need to be a bit pickier than that. There's little here to mask any strong flavors, and the lack of cooking means that a tough cut of meat is going to remain tough. I try to use only the highest-grade animals for my carpaccio, meaning that I select healthy, well-fed animals for this preparation. You don't need to be a wild game expert to make such a judgment call. When butchering an animal, just take a thin slice of the backstrap or round roast and give it a quick sear on a hot skillet. Add a touch of salt and pop it into your mouth. If it tastes great and it's tender, it'll be good carpaccio. If it's tough and doesn't taste good, move on to other recipes in this book. (Warning: wild pigs, bears, javelinas, or any other carnivores or omnivores are not suitable for carpaccio.)

¼ cup black peppercorns

8- to 10-ounce portion elk loin or round roast

8 ounces fresh bitter salad greens, such as mustard, dandelion, or arugula

Spicy Citrus Dressing (page 315)

Maldon or other flaky sea salt

FOR THE VENISON: Toast the peppercorns in a small dry skillet over medium-high heat until wisps of smoke start to rise, 3 to 4 minutes. Cool, then grind in a spice grinder.

Make sure all the silver skin is carefully trimmed away and the meat is clean and dry. On a large plate or baking sheet, sprinkle the pepper in a thin even layer. Roll the loin in the pepper to completely coat. Wrap tightly in plastic wrap and freeze until the loin firms, about 1 hour. When you are ready to serve it, remove the loin from the freezer and, using a sharp slicing knife, slice the meat as thinly as possible. Arrange the slices on a platter.

FOR THE SALAD: Place the greens in a large bowl and lightly toss with the dressing right before serving.

Sprinkle the carpaccio with the flaky salt and garnish with the dressed bitter salad. Serve immediately.

SEARED TONGUE SANDWICH
WITH SPICY PICKLED RED ONIONS

SERVES 4 TO 8, DEPENDING ON THE SIZE OF THE TONGUE

12 cups cold water, plus more as needed

1 cup kosher salt

1 cup brown sugar

1 tablespoon allspice berries

1 tablespoon black peppercorns

1 teaspoon coriander seeds

1 teaspoon yellow mustard seeds

2 whole cloves

1 bay leaf

2 carrots, cut into large pieces

2 ribs celery, cut into large pieces

1 head garlic, halved through the middle horizontally

1 large onion, quartered

1 game tongue, rinsed well

1 tablespoon olive oil

Sliced country bread or split rolls, lightly toasted

Grainy mustard (optional)

Spicy Pickled Red Onions (page 318)

ALSO WORKS WITH: I've eaten tongues from black bear, whitetail deer, mule deer, elk, buffalo, caribou, muskox, wild pigs, and moose. They're all good, and they're all worthwhile, but the bigger tongues from the bigger animals are a lot more exciting because you have a lot more to work with.

I became interested in cooking wild game tongue when I was researching my book *American Buffalo*. In the 1800s, pickled and smoked buffalo tongues were a popular food item in places like Chicago, Boston, and New York. The historic record is full of tales of Euro-American and Native American hunters killing herds of buffalo just to get some quick cash, or a quick meal, from the tongues. They are just as tasty today. I've served game tongue to dozens of people who'd never had it, and the typical response is a shocked disbelief that a tongue could be so damn good.

This preparation is a great addition to any wild game charcuterie platter. (See page 122 for mine.) For a wonderful sandwich combination, serve the tongue with the Walnut and Mint Pesto on page 320.

Combine 4 cups of the water, the salt, brown sugar, allspice, peppercorns, coriander seeds, mustard seeds, cloves, and bay leaf in a medium saucepan. Bring to a boil over high heat. Reduce the heat to maintain a simmer and simmer for about 5 minutes, stirring until the sugar and salt dissolve. Transfer the brine to a large heatproof bowl or pot. Add the carrots, celery, garlic, and onion and the remaining 8 cups water and let cool completely.

Add the tongue to the brine, putting a plate on top if necessary to keep it submerged, and cover. Alternatively, put it all into an extra-large resealable plastic bag. Refrigerate for 5 days.

Preheat the oven to 300°F. Strain the tongue, reserving the solids, and put the tongue and the solids into a medium heavy-bottomed saucepan or Dutch oven. Add enough cold water to cover. Bring to a boil over high heat, then reduce the heat to maintain a simmer, partially cover, and cook until the tongue is very tender, 4 to 5 hours. Transfer the tongue to a colander and rinse with cold water. Let it rest until it's cool enough to comfortably handle, then peel off the tongue's outer skin. The tongue can be used immediately, or wrapped tightly in plastic wrap and stored for a week in the refrigerator.

When ready to serve, thinly slice the tongue. Heat a large skillet over high heat. Add the oil and sear the bread slices until golden brown on both sides, 3 to 5 minutes. Assemble the sandwiches with a smear of the grainy mustard and some spicy pickled red onions.

HOW TO ROAST A HUNK OF MEAT TO PERFECTION

SERVES 4 OR MORE

The name of this recipe is not hyperbolic. If I had to choose one way to handle wild game meat for the rest of my life, this would be it. It doesn't matter if you're making roast venison sandwiches, a simple appetizer, steak salads (my wife's favorite), or a full-on centerpiece to anchor a spread of roast vegetables and mashed potatoes, this is the single best way to go about it. This preparation works with whole or partial backstraps and tenderloins, plus any of the major muscles—sirloins, top and bottom rounds, eye rounds—from the back legs on horned or antlered game. I prefer to work with a two- to four-pound hunk of meat. When pulling a roast from your freezer, it's best if you can take it out a few days ahead of time and let it thaw gradually in your fridge. Once thawed, give it a very quick rinse under cold water and immediately pat it dry with paper towels. Then let it sit on a rack in your fridge, uncovered, for a day or so. Before cooking, pull the roast out of the fridge and let it come to room temperature. Finally, make sure you've got an accurate meat thermometer. A difference of ten degrees can be the difference between perfection and meat-flavored cardboard.

ALSO WORKS WITH: This works with all horned and antlered game. If the meat is safe to eat rare, this is a good way to cook it. When dealing with stronger-flavored game such as antelope, finicky folks who are unaccustomed to game might appreciate a sauce or other accompaniment. It's totally unnecessary, in my opinion, but then everyone has their own tastes and preferences. See opposite for serving suggestions including sauces and compound butters from the Extras section of this book.

Position a rack in the middle of the oven and preheat the oven to 375°F.

Coat the roast with 1 tablespoon of the oil and sprinkle liberally with salt and pepper. Remember, you're seasoning the outside of the roast, which is a small percentage of the total meat. When you go to put a piece in your mouth, only a small portion of the outside seasoning will accompany each bite. The salt and pepper should be a visible coating on the meat.

Heat 1 tablespoon of the oil in a large heavy-bottomed pan, preferably cast-iron, over medium-high heat. When the oil shimmers, add the roast and sear for 4 minutes per side on all sides. If the pan begins to smoke, reduce the heat. Note: With a skinny roast like a tenderloin, eye round, or the skinny end of a backstrap, the pan searing might be all you need to reach the desired doneness. Once the meat is seared, check the internal temperature of the roast with a meat thermometer. I aim for 120 to 125°F in the middle, or fattest part, of the roast, to achieve a finished product that's medium-rare (130 to 135°F) in the middle, and getting toward medium on the ends. (Most of these roasts will be oblong in shape, making for uneven temperatures from end to middle.) When the roast has reached the desired internal temperature, remove it to a grooved cutting board and allow it to rest for 5 to 10 minutes. Then proceed to the serving instructions below.

If the roast has not reached 120 to 125°F, place the pan in the preheated oven. Roast for 10 minutes and then check the roast's internal temperature again. (This is the single most important step in the process: yanking the meat from the oven at a precise temperature produces a delicious, consistent, and repeatable product.) If it still hasn't reached the desired temperature, continue roasting for another 5 minutes and check again. Repeat as necessary, but be careful: once the internal temperature is over, it's over. When the desired temperature is reached, remove the roast from the pan and place it on a grooved cutting board to rest.

Let a 2-pound roast rest for 5 minutes; a 4-pounder for 10 minutes. The roast's internal temperature will rise 5 to 8°F while it rests.

TO SERVE: With a carving knife or sharp chef's knife, slice the roast across the grain. The thinner the slice is, the easier it is to chew. A young cow elk's backstrap can be cut 1 inch thick and still melt in your mouth; a bottom round roast from a five-year-old buck should be sliced ¼ inch thick. Fan the slices onto a serving platter, drizzle the meat juices from the cutting board over the slices, sprinkle with salt, and serve immediately.

Serve with the sauces in the serving suggestions and your favorite sides, or try my Cobb Salad (see photo on page 38): Chop 2 small heads romaine lettuce into bite-size pieces and place on a platter. Add the sliced roasted game meat, with any or all of the following: sliced avocado, crumbled blue cheese, crispy bacon pieces, sliced onions, sliced cucumber, chopped tomato, sliced hard-boiled egg. Dress with Basic Vinaigrette (page 315) or Spicy Citrus Dressing (page 315). Top the salad with toasted pepitas or pumpkin seeds.

1 (2- to 4-pound) whole muscle game roast, thawed (see headnote)

2 tablespoons olive oil or vegetable oil

2 tablespoons kosher salt, plus more as needed

1 tablespoon freshly ground black pepper, plus more as needed

SERVING SUGGESTIONS

With Basic Brown Gravy (page 310)

With Balsamic Reduction (page 316)

With red currant, port, and red wine sauce (page 173)

With any one of the compound butters (pages 323) or Green Sauces (pages 320 and 321)

GRILLED VENISON LOIN
WITH CAULIFLOWER PUREE AND BALSAMIC REDUCTION

SERVES 6 (FOR 2 LOINS)

2 venison loins/backstraps, 1 to 2 pounds each, trimmed

Kosher salt

Freshly ground black pepper

Cauliflower Puree (page 333)

1 recipe Balsamic Reduction (page 316)

1 tablespoon chopped fresh chives, for garnish

This is one of several memorable wild game recipes that I cooked alongside my buddy Chef Andrew Radzialowski for a wild game dinner that we did as a fund-raiser for the Theodore Roosevelt Conservation Partnership. (If you like to hunt and fish and care about the future of wildlife in America you should support this group too!) It was the biggest hit of the night, and I begged Andy to let me use it for this book. You'll be glad he said yes. The cauliflower is a perfect accompaniment, especially when a dribble or two of the juices from the meat mixes in with the puree like a drop of blood on snow. It's beautiful.

Remove the loins from the refrigerator about 1 hour before cooking to allow them to come to room temperature. Make sure all the silver skin is carefully trimmed away and the meat is clean and dry.

Prepare a grill (gas or charcoal) for both indirect and direct heat. Smear the loins with oil and sprinkle with a generous amount of salt and pepper, making sure to get all sides. Place the loins on the hot portion of the grill and let a nice sear or crust develop on all sides, 3 to 4 minutes per side. Move to indirect heat and let the meat roast to an internal temperature of 130°F. Pull the loins off the grill and let rest on a cutting board for 10 to 12 minutes to allow the juices to redistribute through the meat. Slice the loins across the grain to your desired thickness.

Place the warm puree down the center of a platter or large plate and place the sliced venison loin fanned out on top. With a spoon, drizzle the balsamic reduction over the meat. Garnish with the chives.

ALSO WORKS WITH: I've prepared this dish successfully using whitetail deer, mule deer, and elk. Go ahead and use any horned or antlered game.

WILD HOG MILANESE
(OR FRIED HOG CUTLET WITH SALAD)

SERVES 5

Every wild game cook should learn the trick of hammering down a cutlet of meat until it's as thin as window glass before coating it in breadcrumbs and frying it in oil. While the dish is most closely associated with Austrian cuisine, where it's known as schnitzel, many cultures have their own version: the French have escalope, and some South American countries have a unique take, Milanese, that was carried to the New World by Italian immigrants. I've eaten it a few times in Argentina and Chile, where it's served in a variety of ways, including on a sandwich. But the best way I've had it, by far, is a stripped-down version where the fried cutlet is plated with a simple salad of spicy greens with a vinaigrette dressing. This is one of those versatile meals that fits just about any occasion. Try it once and you'll be schnitzeling just about anything you can get your hands on.

HOG CUTLET

1 pound roast from the rear leg of a wild hog, cut into 5 (3-ounce) slices

1 cup all-purpose flour

3 large eggs, beaten with 2 tablespoons water or milk

2 cups breadcrumbs (panko or coarse Homemade Breadcrumbs, page 324)

Kosher salt

¼ cup grated Parmigiano-Reggiano cheese

About 2 cups olive oil or peanut oil, for frying

Freshly ground black pepper

SALAD

5 cups mixed peppery greens, such as escarole, mizuna, arugula, or watercress

¼ red onion, thinly sliced

3 tablespoons extra virgin olive oil

Kosher salt

1 lemon

ALSO WORKS WITH: I've done this with everything ranging from halibut to wild turkey, so use your imagination.

FOR THE HOG CUTLET: Place the meat between two pieces of parchment paper or plastic wrap. Using a meat mallet, pound the meat really thin (about 3⁄16 inch).

Put the flour, egg wash, and breadcrumbs in three separate trays or shallow bowls. Season the flour with 1 teaspoon salt. Add 2 teaspoons salt and the cheese to the breadcrumbs.

Add oil to a large cast-iron pan or high-sided skillet so it's ¾ to 1 inch deep. Heat over medium-high heat until it reaches 365°F on a deep-fry thermometer. Line a baking sheet with paper towels.

Sprinkle the meat slices with salt and pepper. One at a time, dredge first in the flour, then the egg, and, finally, the breadcrumbs. Carefully slide the breaded cutlet into the hot oil. Fry until golden brown, flipping after 3 minutes to brown the other side. Remove to the prepared baking sheet and sprinkle with salt. Repeat with the remaining cutlets. (If your pan is large enough to cook two at a time, go ahead, but it's important not to crowd them.)

FOR THE SALAD: Combine the greens with the onion, drizzle with the oil, and toss to lightly coat. Sprinkle salt over the greens and toss to coat. Squeeze the juice of half the lemon over the salad. Taste and adjust the seasonings. Cut the other half of the lemon into wedges.

Lay the cutlets on a plate and top with a pile of salad. Serve immediately, with the lemon wedges.

THREE SPICY BULK GAME SAUSAGE RECIPES

MAKES 10 POUNDS OF SAUSAGE

There are almost as many types of sausages as there are types of people. You've got your gregarious and easygoing varieties that aim to please, such as sweet Italian and bratwurst, and then you've got your blends that are a bit more divisive, like boudin noir and leberwurst. I'll open my door to as wide a variety of these sausages as possible, though the following preparations fall well within the "friendly" category. They're all a bit spicy, but not *too* spicy, and it's easy to turn the heat up or down according to your own tastes. They can be cased in natural hog casings (my preference are casings with diameters between 32 and 35 millimeters) or left uncased as bulk sausage for use in other recipes like soups, stews, tacos, pastas, and patties. Like the big game sausages in my previous book, *The Complete Guide to Hunting, Butchering, and Cooking Wild Game,* Volume 1, these are based on an 80/20 mixture of lean game meat and pork fatback. You can raise the fat level if you prefer, all the way to 70/30, but 80/20 is a flavorful, juicy sausage that's not overly greasy. By the way, a quick tip for any javelina hunters out there: make some chorizo.

ALSO WORKS WITH: You can get away with using any and all big game in these blends. Keep in mind, though, that sausages made from bears, wild pigs, javelinas, and other carnivores or omnivores need to be cooked to a temperature of 160°F to destroy any parasites that might be lurking.

CHORIZO SAUSAGE

BASIC MEAT MIXTURE

8 pounds lean game meat (such as deer, elk, wild hog, etc.), cut into 1-inch cubes

2 pounds pork fatback, cut into 1-inch cubes

20 feet natural hog casings (32 to 35 millimeters in diameter; optional)

CHORIZO SAUSAGE

⅓ cup paprika

3 tablespoons kosher salt

3 tablespoons ground ancho chile powder

2 tablespoon ground árbol chile powder

2 teaspoons dried oregano (preferably Mexican oregano)

1½ teaspoons ground cinnamon

1½ teaspoons freshly ground black pepper

1 teaspoon ground cumin

12 cloves garlic, minced

½ cup white wine vinegar or cider vinegar, chilled

½ cup ice water, as needed

See The Sausage-Making Process (page 47) for basic sausage-making instructions.

SPECIAL EQUIPMENT NEEDED: meat grinder, sausage stuffer, natural hog casings

MERGUEZ SAUSAGE

BASIC MEAT MIXTURE

8 pounds lean game meat (such as deer, elk, or wild hog), cut into 1-inch cubes

2 pounds pork fatback, cut into 1-inch cubes

20 feet natural hog casings (32 to 35 millimeters in diameter; optional) or

20 feet natural lamb's intestine casings (18 to 22 millimeters in diameter; optional)

MERGUEZ SAUSAGE

1½ tablespoons coriander seeds

1½ tablespoons cumin seeds

1½ tablespoons fennel seeds

⅓ cup kosher salt

¼ cup paprika

1 tablespoon ground cinnamon

2 teaspoons cayenne pepper (or more, as desired)

1 cup harissa sauce, chilled

10 cloves garlic, minced

⅔ cup red wine vinegar or apple cider vinegar, chilled

¼ cup ice water, as needed

For Merguez Sausage: see page 47 for sausage-making instructions, with these notes: To bring out the flavors of the coriander, cumin, and fennel, toast them in a small skillet over medium-high heat until fragrant. Cool, then grind in a spice grinder to a coarse powder. Add the salt, paprika, cinnamon, and cayenne to the spice mixture. Fold the harissa sauce into the sausage along with the minced garlic, vinegar, and ice water after the meat has been ground. Merguez is traditionally cased in lamb casings and left as spirals rather than twisted into links. You can certainly get away with using hog casings, and you can twist them into links, but the traditional methods are a nice touch.

ANDOUILLE SAUSAGE (SMOKED, CREOLE STYLE)

BASIC MEAT MIXTURE

8 pounds lean game meat (such as deer, elk, wild hog, etc.), cut into 1-inch cubes

2 pounds pork fatback, cut into 1-inch cubes

(Alternative mixture: 7 pounds lean game meat and 3 pounds pork belly, cut into 1-inch cubes)

20 feet natural hog casings (32 to 35 millimeters in diameter; optional)

ANDOUILLE SAUSAGE (SMOKED, CREOLE STYLE)

2 onions, finely diced

3 tablespoons vegetable oil

½ cup paprika

12 cloves garlic, minced

3 tablespoons cayenne pepper

3 tablespoons kosher salt

1½ tablespoons garlic powder

1½ tablespoons onion powder

1 tablespoon ancho chile powder

1 tablespoon red chile flakes

2 teaspoons ground allspice

2 teaspoons dry thyme leaves

⅓ cup white wine vinegar or apple cider vinegar, chilled

¼ cup ice water, as needed

See page 47 for sausage-making instructions, with these notes: Cook the diced onions in vegetable oil over medium-high heat until translucent, about 3 minutes. Let cool before mixing into the meat mixture along with the spices. After casing the sausages, heat a smoker to 200°F. Smoke the sausages until the internal temperature of the meat reaches 140°F. If using wild hog, javelina, or bear meat to make this sausage, be sure to test that each sausage has gotten up to 160°F to kill off any parasites. Note: This is not a cured and smoked sausage, so fully hot-smoking is important for safety reasons, and the sausage should be consumed or frozen within a week of smoking.

THE SAUSAGE-MAKING PROCESS

Here's the basic rundown for making the sausages. Any exceptions to this process will be noted in the particular recipes.

1. TO GET STARTED: Place the cubed fat on a large plate or baking sheet in your freezer until it begins to harden, but don't let it freeze all the way through. Put the cubed meat in your fridge to cool it off. You want everything nice and cold, so that it's on the verge of painful to handle it. Meanwhile, set up your meat grinder according to the manufacturer's instructions and soak the natural hog casings (if using) in lukewarm water. Once the casings are pliable, change the water and give them another soak for 20 to 30 minutes. Then fit one end of each casing over the kitchen faucet and run a cup or two of water into the casing. Push the water all the way through, to rinse the inside of the casing. Set aside in clean water until ready to use.

2. TO GRIND THE SAUSAGE: Combine the chilled cubed meat and pork fat with the dry spices and any herbs or garlic in a large bowl. Mix well so that the meat is evenly coated with spices. Place in the fridge to marinate for 8 to 24 hours. When you're ready to grind the sausage, fill a tub with ice and place the bowl of meat inside the tub to keep it cool. Using a 3⁄16-inch (4.5-mm) grinder plate, grind the meat mixture into another bowl that's set over ice. (One pass through the grinder will give the meat a nice texture that's appropriate for most sausages. You can get a coarser texture by using a ¼-inch grinder plate; to get a finer texture, pass the meat through the grinder two times. When double grinding, be extra careful about keeping everything cold. Grinders create friction, and friction equals heat.) Using a rubber spatula or large wooden spoon, fold in the liquids and mix well. The mixture should be wet and sticky (like pizza dough), but it should not be sitting in liquid. Cover and refrigerate while you set up your sausage stuffer. Either pack the bulk sausage into 1-pound poly bags or make links using natural hog-middle casings.

3. STUFFING SAUSAGES: Fill the hopper of your sausage stuffer with the sausage mixture and fit the stuffer tube with a cleaned casing. Start pushing meat through the stuffer to clear any air in the stuffer tube. Before meat enters the casing, tie the end with a simple granny knot. Working slowly, stuff the sausage into the casings. Be careful not to overstuff, and expel any large air bubbles inside the casing by pricking it with a sewing needle. When filled, tie off the casing with another granny knot. To create links: make two creases in the casing, one 5 inches from the end and another at 10 inches from the end. Twist the sausage at these two creases about eight times. Now you have two links. Make two more creases at 5-inch intervals and spin these. Continue down the length of the casing. To separate the individual links, gently pull the links apart and snip the middle of the "twist" with a pair of scissors or a knife.

Tip: If possible, freeze your cased sausages in vacuum-sealed bags. Make sure to orient the sausages vertically rather than horizontally in the vacuum bag. Horizontally placed sausages can form a dam in the bag that prevents the sealer from expelling all of the air during the vacuum process. I generally freeze my bulk sausage in poly meat bags, though I like to freeze some bulk sausage in a thin layer inside standard vacuum bags as well. In a hurry, you can toss a vacuum-sealed bag of sausage into a tub of cold water and it'll thaw very quickly.

THE PERFECT VENISON BURGER

SERVES 4

1 pound venison, trimmed

¼ pound fatty bacon ends, pork fat, or beef fat

Kosher salt

Freshly ground black pepper

3 tablespoons olive oil or vegetable oil (to coat the skillet, if needed)

4 slices Cheddar cheese

4 hamburger rolls

Toppings: lettuce, tomato, pickle, mustard, and ketchup

ALSO WORKS WITH: You can use any big game to make burgers. But remember that hamburger made from bears, wild pigs, javelinas, and other carnivores or omnivores needs to be cooked to a temperature of 160°F to destroy any parasites that might be lurking.

SPECIAL EQUIPMENT NEEDED: meat grinder

I might question your judgment if you ground up your venison backstraps to make a cheeseburger. Those tender muscles really are better when they're cooked whole to a medium-rare temperature and then sliced thin. And I might also raise an eyebrow if you ground up all of your venison shanks, as those are pretty damn good after six hours of braising in a 325°F oven. But beyond that, I'm open to the idea of grinding just about any cut of big game as long as it's being prepared with love. Every year, I go through well over one hundred pounds of ground meat. (That might sound like a lot, but keep in mind that I provide protein for a lot of backyard barbecues.) The amount of fat that I use ranges from 10 percent to 20 percent depending on my mood, but if I had to choose a single ratio for the rest of my life, I'd go with around 20 percent. That makes a juicy hamburger that holds together and crisps nicely around the edges. With all the lean meat I eat in the form of roasts and steaks, I don't feel bad at all about having a little grease dripping down my chin when I eat a burger. Beef suet and pork fat can be used interchangeably, depending on personal tastes, and fatty bacon ends can be a nice way to mix things up now and then. Toppings can be what you like: it's about the meat. If you want to get fancy, though, sautéed onions with American cheese is well worth a try.

Slice the venison into 1- to 2-inch cubes. For best grinding, the meat should be extremely cold, almost freezing. Add the bacon ends to the pile and mix together. (This makes a 3:1 meat-to-fat ratio, 25 percent fat). You can spread the pile of meat over a baking sheet and put it in the freezer for 20 to 30 minutes to ensure that it's cold. Run the meat through a meat grinder using a ¼-inch (7-mm) grinder plate. You can stop here, or you can run the meat through the grinder a second time. The twice-ground meat will form a denser patty that holds together better; personally, I prefer a single pass through the grinder.

Prepare a grill (gas or charcoal) for direct high heat. Divide the ground meat into four parts and form patties. Make the patties as loose as you can without risking them falling apart. Be gentle. Salt and pepper the patties; depending on your affinity for salt, you might not need to add any at all, as the bacon ends are plenty salty. Place the patties on the grill (or you can use a cast-iron skillet with the oil) with the grill lid open. Cook for 3 to 4 minutes, flip, cook another 2 to 3 minutes, add a slice of cheese to each patty, close the lid or cover the skillet, and turn off the heat. As the cheese is melting (a minute or two), prep your rolls with the condiments and toppings. Serve immediately.

VENISON STEW
WITH RED WINE AND ROOT VEGETABLES

MAKES 8 1-CUP SERVINGS

I love making stews for my family. For one thing, the kids will eagerly devour them. (Giving them a sliced baguette with some butter on the side always helps.) The other thing is that I cherish the leftovers as a quick, convenient lunch. The fact that it seems to taste better and better over the next few days has me thinking that I should cook it a couple of days ahead of time and let it relax in the fridge before the initial serving. This recipe calls for a few cups of red wine. I'm sure there are some parents who might worry about serving their kids a dish prepared with such a high amount of an adult beverage. But alcohol evaporates out of cooking foods at a temperature of 172°F. Once the stew has simmered for a few minutes, the booze is long gone.

3 pounds venison stew meat, shoulder or rump cuts, cut into 1½-inch cubes

2 tablespoons kosher salt

2 teaspoons freshly ground black pepper

¼ cup extra virgin olive oil, plus more as needed

2 large carrots, diced

2 ribs celery, diced

1 large onion, diced

5 cloves garlic, chopped

½ cup all-purpose flour

3 cups red wine

4 cups Brown Game Stock (page 305) or low-sodium, store-bought beef or chicken stock

2 tablespoons chopped fresh flat-leaf parsley

3 juniper berries

1 bay leaf

Leaves from 1 sprig fresh rosemary, chopped

2 russet potatoes, diced

1 small turnip, diced

Sprinkle the meat with the salt and pepper. Heat the oil in a large Dutch oven over medium-high heat. Once the oil shimmers, add the meat and brown on all sides, 8 to 10 minutes. (Do this in batches if necessary to avoid crowding.) Remove the meat to a plate.

Add the carrots, celery, and onion to the pot and cook until softened, 5 to 8 minutes, adding more oil as needed. Add the garlic and cook for 30 seconds. Return the meat to the pot along with any juices that may have collected on the plate. Sprinkle the flour evenly over the meat and vegetables and cook, stirring, for 2 to 3 minutes. Pour in the red wine and whisk to get any clumps out. Add the stock, raise the heat, and bring to a boil. Skim and discard any scum that rises to the top. Add the parsley, juniper berries, bay leaf, and rosemary. Cover the pot, reduce the heat, and simmer for 1 hour.

Add the potatoes and turnips and simmer until the meat is very tender and the turnips and potatoes have no resistance when pierced with a fork, 15 to 20 minutes. Discard the bay leaf. Serve immediately.

ALSO WORKS WITH: Make this with pretty much any big game. I find that the texture of bear meat is especially well suited for stews.

Note: For potpies, make the recipe as directed and let cool to room temperature. Ladle the stew into a 9 x 13-inch ceramic baking dish or 6 to 8 ramekins (8 to 10 ounces each). Roll out thawed puff pastry dough or Basic Pie Dough (page 324) to 10 x 14 inches. Fit and adhere to either the large baking dish, or cut out circles slightly larger than the diameter of the ramekins, then fit individually to adhere. Make a small slit in the top of the pastry. Chill in the refrigerator for 10 minutes. Preheat the oven to 400°F. Make an egg wash by beating 1 egg with a splash of water. Brush lightly onto the pastry. Bake the potpie(s) until the pastry is golden and the stew is bubbling, about 25 minutes.

VENISON BOLOGNESE

SERVES 6 (SAUCE MAKES ABOUT 8 CUPS)

¼ cup extra virgin olive oil, plus more as needed

1 onion, finely chopped

Kosher salt

3 ribs celery, finely chopped

2 carrots, finely grated

6 cloves garlic, thinly sliced

1½ pounds ground venison (80/20 mix)

1 pound ground pork

8 ounces ground pork fat or pancetta

1 (8-ounce) can tomato paste

Freshly ground black pepper

1½ cups dry white wine

1½ cups milk

3 sprigs fresh thyme

1 bay leaf

1 (6-ounce) bunch kale or other leafy green, thinly sliced (optional)

1½ pounds linguine

½ cup grated Parmigiano-Reggiano cheese, plus more for serving

---

ALSO WORKS WITH: Anything goes, really. It'd be great with bear meat.

Note: If a saucier Bolognese is your preference, cut the tomato paste by half and add 2 cups of canned tomato sauce (or more if you wish) after you add the tomato paste. Omit the milk entirely. Continue to cook for 1 to 2 hours.

This is a pretty traditional Italian-style Bolognese recipe, except that it uses wild game. You'll want to add a good amount of fat for best results. I sometimes grind my wild game as a 90/10 mix of game meat and pork fat or beef suet, though this recipe works well with an 80/20 mix using pork fat. If the ground meat in your freezer is too lean, you can bolster the fat content by mixing in some finely chopped pancetta or bacon. The resulting ground meat mixture will work well for lasagna or any other kind of pasta dish. You'll notice that this recipe uses tomato paste and not tomato sauce. See the Note to learn how to make it saucier if that's your preference. You'll also see that the addition of greens is optional. I like them, because it's a great way to hide some added nutrients into meals that you're serving to kids.

Heat the oil in a heavy-bottomed saucepan over medium heat until it shimmers. Add the onion, season lightly with salt, and cook until softened, translucent, and lightly caramelized, 8 to 10 minutes. Add the celery and carrots, season with salt again, and cook until softened, adding more oil if needed. Add the garlic and cook, stirring, for 30 seconds. Raise the heat to medium-high, add the venison, pork, and pork fat, and brown very well, breaking it up with a wooden spoon, about 15 minutes. When the meat has browned and is audibly frying in its own fat (you should hear a popping sound), push the meat to one side, creating a "hot spot" on the bottom of the pot. Add the tomato paste to the hot spot and caramelize it lightly (being careful not to burn it). Stir to incorporate into the meat and vegetables. Season liberally with salt and pepper. Add the wine and scrape the bottom of the pot with a spoon to release the flavorful browned bits that have accumulated. Add the milk and bring to a bare simmer over medium-low heat. Drop in the thyme and bay leaf and cover. Reduce the heat to low and cook until the flavors come together, 1½ to 2 hours, stirring occasionally to prevent sticking. If using the greens, add after the first hour, along with ½ cup water. After about 2 hours, adjust the seasonings and remove from the heat. Discard the thyme sprigs and bay leaf. Refrigerate if not serving right away. The sauce can be frozen for up to 6 months.

To serve over pasta, reheat 3 cups of the sauce in a large skillet. Bring 6 quarts of water with 3 tablespoons of salt to a rapid boil. Add the linguine and cook until al dente. Add ½ cup of the pasta water to the sauce. Add the pasta to the sauce and stir to incorporate. Remove from the heat, add the grated cheese, and gently mix together. Serve immediately.

VENISON CHILI

SERVES 8

I'd be willing to bet that more pounds of ground venison go into chili than any other type of recipe. I know that I've eaten my fair share. My mom used to make what I think of as a mild "Midwest chili" using whitetail deer and kidney beans on an almost weekly basis in the winter, and I loved every bowl of it. (Thanks, Mom!) This is a more sophisticated version, with poblanos, chipotles, and whole tomatoes. A lot of the magic lies in the toppings, so don't skimp on those. It's fun to let everyone get in there and customize their own bowl.

ALSO WORKS WITH: It's wide open. Use any ground meat.

CHILI

¼ cup plus 2 tablespoons vegetable oil

2¼ pounds ground venison

Kosher salt and freshly ground black pepper

3 large poblano chiles, stemmed and diced

1 large onion, chopped

6 cloves garlic, thinly sliced

2 tablespoons ancho chile powder, or to taste

1½ tablespoons ground cumin

1 teaspoon dried oregano

3 (14.5-ounce) cans whole tomatoes, preferably in tomato puree

3 tablespoons minced chipotle chiles in adobo

2 (15-ounce) cans kidney beans or pinto beans, rinsed and drained

3 cups Blonde Game Stock (page 306) or chicken broth

TO SERVE

Corn chips or Cornbread (page 326)

Shredded sharp Cheddar or Pepper Jack cheese

Sour cream

Diced red onions or sliced scallions

Sliced jalapeño or serrano chiles

FOR THE CHILI: Heat a large Dutch oven or other wide, heavy saucepan over medium-high heat. Add 2 tablespoons of the oil. Sprinkle the venison generously with salt and pepper. Working in batches, crumble the venison into the pot in large chunks and sear until browned, 6 to 8 minutes per batch, transferring to a large bowl as each batch is done and adding more oil as needed. Reduce the heat to medium. Add the remaining 2 tablespoons oil, the poblanos, and the onion, scraping up the browned bits at the bottom of the pot. Raise the heat to medium-high heat and cook, stirring often, until softened, 8 to 10 minutes. Stir in the garlic, ancho chile powder, cumin, and oregano and cook, stirring constantly, for 1 minute. Add the tomatoes, crushing them with your hands or mashing them with a potato masher. Add the chipotles, half of the beans, the stock, and the venison with any juices that have accumulated in the bowl. Stir to combine, then bring to a simmer. Cook, partially covered, stirring occasionally, until the venison is tender, about 2 hours.

Add the remaining beans and warm through. Taste and adjust the seasonings.

FOR SERVING: Serve the chili with corn chips or cornbread, cheese, sour cream, onions or scallions, and chiles.

KIMCHI TACOS
WITH WILD PIG OR JAVELINA

SERVES 4 TO 6

2 pounds bone-in javelina thigh or shoulder, or wild hog shoulder

1 cup soju (Korean rice wine)

⅔ cup gochujang (Korean chile paste)

1 cup soy sauce

1 cup sugar

½ cup grated garlic

½ cup grated ginger

1 to 2 tablespoons toasted sesame oil

1 medium onion, sliced

Corn tortillas

2 cups kimchi

Shredded Oaxaca, Monterey Jack, or other white cheese

4 scallions, thinly sliced on a bias

Some years ago I ended up with about twenty pounds of braised wild hog and a huge jar of homemade kimchi (a spicy pickled cabbage—Korea's national dish) in my refrigerator. It was purely coincidental, but what came out of that situation was a deep respect for a crispy-fried mound of braised pork lying next to a handful of kimchi on a warm tortilla. Since then I've placed everything from javelina thighs to blacktail deer shanks in a similar context, and all of it's great. But there's something about the flavor and texture of white-fleshed hogs and javelina that really lends itself to this preparation.

ALSO WORKS WITH: If you don't have access to wild pigs or javelina but you're dying to try this, do it with a venison shank. Adjust the cooking time so that the meat can be easily pulled away from the bone with your fingers.

Put the meat in a slow cooker and add the soju, gochujang, soy sauce, sugar, garlic, ginger, and just enough water to cover the meat. Cook on low for 5 hours.

Remove the meat, transfer the liquid to a pot, and heat over high heat until reduced by half. Allow the meat to cool to comfortable handling temperature and then pick the meat from the bone. Break the meat up into pieces the size of a ballpoint pen cap and crush them slightly with your fingers. Place the pieces back into the braising liquid.

Heat the oil (enough to coat the bottom) in a medium skillet over medium-high heat. Add the onion and stir until it's translucent and begins to brown, about 10 minutes. Remove the onion from the skillet. Lift the braised meat from the liquid, shaking the pieces off, and then lay them in a single layer in the skillet. Once the meat starts to crisp and the braising liquid begins to caramelize, scrape the bottom of the skillet with a spatula and flip the meat. Don't allow it to burn, but keep frying and scraping until the meat is crispy around the edges. Toss the onions back into the skillet, stir together with the meat, and then remove from the heat.

Warm the tortillas. Arrange rows of meat and kimchi down the center of the tortillas and top with cheese and scallions.

SLOW-COOKED AND GRILLED VENISON RIBS

SERVES 4

I think of this rib recipe, or at least a version of it, as being one of the most important wild game discoveries of my life. Before my brothers and I figured this out, we always deboned the rib meat on our big game animals and used it in hamburger blends. That's because we regarded rib meat on big game as being too tough and stringy for use in standard recipes designed for pork and beef ribs. But then my older brother Matt started experimenting by putting big game ribs in his pressure cooker in order to tenderize them first. Pretty soon that developed into one of my favorite all-time wild game recipes. From then on, I've never looked at a rib cage in the same way—and I've never again deboned rib meat for making hamburgers without feeling at least a little guilty. If you're dealing with an animal that has a lot of fat over the ribs, trim away as much as possible before cooking. It's waxy and not too pleasant to eat. But don't worry if you can't get it all. Most of the remainder will render out during the initial cooking process. There is a lot of guesswork when it comes to pressure cooking ribs, as you can't visually monitor their progress inside the sealed cooker. If you let them go just ten minutes too long, the meat can become so tender that it falls away from the bone. A safer, albeit longer method is using a slow cooker.

1 slab game ribs, cut in half, then cut into 2 or 3 rib bone chunks (see image page 58)

1 teaspoon kosher salt

¼ teaspoon freshly ground fresh black pepper

About 4 cups Blonde Game Stock (page 306) or water (or substitute low-sodium chicken or vegetable broth)

1 recipe BBQ Rub (page 313), or a store-bought rub

1 recipe BBQ Sauce (page 314), or a store-bought sauce

SPECIAL EQUIPMENT:

slow cooker, hacksaw or butcher's saw

ALSO WORKS WITH: Anything goes, as long as there's enough meat to bother with. Smaller whitetails and mule deer, as well as antelope, sometimes have so little meat over and between their ribs that it doesn't warrant the effort of cooking them. In these cases, bone out whatever you can get from the ribs and add it to the trim pile for making burger. In the case of larger animals such as big deer, elk, moose (like the photo shown here), and caribou, it's possible to actually have too much meat. If there's a heavy layer of muscle over the rib cage, fillet it away for the burger pile. On these big critters, there's enough meat between the ribs that you don't need the overlayers to make it worthwhile. See page 16 for how-to on removing the ribs from the animal.

Using a hacksaw or bone saw, cut the ribs perpendicular to the bones to get a 4- to 6-inch strip of connected rib bones. Then cut these strips into pieces containing 3 or 4 ribs apiece. (See the image on page 56.)

Place the ribs, salt, and pepper in a slow cooker and add just enough stock or water to cover them. Cook on high for 2 to 3 hours or on low for 6 to 8 hours. By then the ribs should be fairly tender. The measure of a perfectly cooked venison rib is that the meat clings to the bone but it can be easily pulled away with your teeth, leaving a clean white bone behind. A little resistance when you're chewing is not a bad thing.

Prepare a grill (gas or charcoal) for medium-high direct heat.

Remove the ribs from the slow cooker and then give them a generous rub-down with the rub. Place the ribs on the grill. Since they're already cooked, you're simply reheating the meat and charring the outside a bit. Once the ribs have crisped, about 10 minutes, coat them generously with the BBQ sauce and continue cooking for 1 to 2 minutes to allow the sauce to caramelize and thicken. Serve hot.

WHOLE BRAISED VENISON SHANK ADOBADA

SERVES 6 TO 8

One of my long-standing career goals has been to get hunters excited about cooking and eating shanks. Unaware of the quality of the flesh surrounding the shin bones, too many folks are content to just bone them out for the grind pile or else discard them entirely. My guess is that some folks are intimidated by the cooking process. It can take several hours or more in a 300°F oven to soften the meat. That's a fair bit of pre-planning, but the payoff is heavenly. If you're accustomed to the flavors and textures of traditional wild game roasts, steaks, burgers, etc., you're going to be really surprised by a properly cooked shank. The meat turns rich and silky as the connective tissues and tendons soften during the cooking process. In this case, you're cooking the shanks in a flavorful adobada sauce until they're soft enough to be picked apart with your fingers. It's like magic. Cook this once and you'll never again disrespect a shank. The full-flavored meat can be served with a side of rice and a salad, as suggested here, or with mashed potatoes. Another good option is to make tacos by filling soft corn tortillas (two to four per person) with the meat and garnishing with cilantro leaves, crumbled cheese, and a squeeze of lime.

6 pounds whole venison shanks

Kosher salt

Freshly ground black pepper

¼ cup vegetable or canola oil

1 large white onion, chopped

2 bay leaves

1 recipe Adobada (page 314)

Cooked rice, for serving

Green salad, for serving

ALSO WORKS WITH: Anything goes. I haven't yet met a shank that I don't like. When dealing with big shanks from critters like elk and moose, you'll want to saw them down into pieces first. It's easiest if you freeze the whole shank and then saw it like a piece of firewood using a clean hacksaw, butcher's saw, or even a standard carpenter's saw. I've done it quite a few times with an electric reciprocating saw.

Pat the shanks dry, then sprinkle with salt and pepper. Heat 2 tablespoons of the oil in a large skillet over medium-high heat. Working in batches, sear the shanks until browned, about 4 minutes per side, adding the remaining 2 tablespoons oil for the second batch. As they are done, transfer to a large container with a lid. Reduce the heat to medium, add the onion, and cook until softened, 6 to 8 minutes. Add to the shanks along with the bay leaves. Pour the adobada over the shanks and turn to coat evenly. Let cool, then cover and refrigerate for 8 hours.

Preheat the oven to 300°F. Transfer the shanks and adobada to a large Dutch oven or small roasting pan. Cover and braise, turning occasionally, until the meat is falling off the bone, 4 to 5 hours. Discard the bay leaves. Transfer the shanks to a platter and set aside until cool enough to handle. Remove the meat from the bones and coarsely shred, discarding any gelatinous chunks. Moisten the meat with some adobada and adjust the seasonings.

Serve hot with warm rice and a simply dressed salad. (For dressing suggestions, see the Basic Vinaigrette on page 315.)

OSSO BUCCO
WITH POLENTA AND GREMOLATA

SERVES 4

2 deer shanks, cut into 3 discs measuring 3 inches long (see opposite for more portioning information)

Kosher salt

Freshly ground black pepper

All-purpose flour, for dredging

3 tablespoons extra virgin olive oil

2 carrots, cut into ⅓-inch rounds

2 medium red onions, thinly sliced

1 rib celery, cut into ⅓-inch rounds

4 cloves garlic, thinly sliced

2 tablespoons tomato paste

1 cup dry red or white wine

2 sprigs fresh thyme

1 sprig fresh rosemary

1 bay leaf

1 recipe Polenta (page 330)

1 recipe Classic Gremolata (page 316) (optional)

Freshly grated Parmigiano-Reggiano cheese, for serving

Osso bucco is an Italian dish traditionally prepared with veal shanks. The name translates as "bone with a hole," a reference to the medullary cavity at the center of a bone that is exposed as a round hole when the bone is cut in cross-section. On wild game, the shank is one of the toughest—probably *the* toughest—cuts of meat. It's so packed with sinew and connective tissue that it can clog up an otherwise trusty meat grinder even when cut into small boneless cubes. That's what makes osso bucco such a special recipe. Once the bones are cut into discs, they are braised in a thick broth containing wine and vegetables until the meat becomes so tender and silky that it can be mashed with a fork. The transformation is so stunning that it seems more like magic than science, though the actual explanation has to do with the slow process of collagen being broken down into gelatin through the application of moist heat. The meat is served, nestled around its circle of bone and marrow, over a bed of polenta and under a blanket of rich sauce. Make this once and you'll never again want to jam up your grinder with shank meat. The easiest way to cut the shanks is to saw them with a hacksaw or meat saw while they're still frozen. You can use a reciprocating saw as well.

Tie the shanks around the middle with butcher's twine to hold them in place as they cook. Heat an 8- to 10-quart Dutch oven over medium-high heat. Sprinkle the shank discs well with salt and pepper and lightly dredge them in flour. Add the oil to the pot and swirl to coat. When the oil shimmers, sear the shank discs in batches (avoid overcrowding the pan, as this will steam the meat), 4 to 6 minutes per side. When the meat is well browned on all sides, remove to a plate. Be careful not to let the bits on the bottom of the pan burn, as it will impart a bitter flavor.

Add the carrots, onions, and celery and cook until the onions are browned, 8 to 10 minutes. Add the garlic and cook until fragrant, about 30 seconds. Push the vegetables to one side, creating a "hot spot" on the bottom of the pot. Add the tomato paste to the hot spot and caramelize it lightly, about 1 to 2 minutes, being careful not to let it burn. Stir to incorporate the sauce into the vegetables. Add the wine to the pot and scrape up any browned bits from the bottom of the pan. Allow the wine to reduce slightly.

Return the meat to the pot. Add about 2 quarts water, enough to just cover the meat. Bring to a boil, then reduce the heat to low. Skim off and discard any scum that accumulates on the surface. Add the thyme and rosemary sprigs and bay leaf. Cover the pot and cook at a bare simmer until the meat is very tender but not falling off the bone, 3½ to 4 hours.

Check halfway through to make sure there is still enough liquid covering the meat; add more if needed. Discard the thyme and rosemary sprigs and the bay leaf.

When the shanks are fork tender, remove them from the pot and carefully remove the twine with kitchen shears.

Divide the polenta among dinner plates. Top each puddle of polenta with a shank piece. Spoon the sauce and the vegetables over the meat. Garnish with gremolata, if desired, and some cheese.

ALSO WORKS WITH: Use the shanks of any big game animal, including bears, wild hogs, and mountain lions. A shank from a mature whitetail or mule deer will yield a quantity of three 3-inch discs. Six of these discs should be enough for three or four people, depending on the size of the deer. A single elk shank cut into 3-inch discs will feed four people. With antelope shanks (or a yearling whitetail) you might need a whole shank per person, depending on appetites. Note that the rear shanks of antlered game animals are bigger and meatier than the fronts. On a particular mature female Shiras moose, for instance, the rear shanks weighed 6.5 pounds and the front shanks weighed 5.5 pounds.

SPECIAL EQUIPMENT: hacksaw, butcher's saw, or reciprocating saw; butcher's twine

THE QUEEN MOTHER OF ALL JERKIES

1 (3-pound) roast, frozen for 2 hours

1 cup soy sauce

½ cup pineapple juice

½ cup Worcestershire sauce

¼ cup packed brown sugar

2 tablespoons honey

1 tablespoon red chile flakes

2 tablespoons coarsely ground black pepper

1 tablespoon onion powder

3 cloves garlic, peeled

1 (1-inch) piece fresh ginger, peeled

ALSO WORKS WITH: Any horned or antlered game is suitable for jerky making. I've made jerky with black bear meat as well, but then you've got to cook the finished product to destroy parasites, which diminishes the quality of your end product. It's better to stick with meat that doesn't require the extra hassle. And while it's easier to work with large whole muscles, you can make jerky from just about any little scrap of meat. The end product will lack uniformity of size, and there might be a little more connective tissue to deal with, but that shouldn't dissuade you.

SPECIAL EQUIPMENT: dehydrator, though not necessary

One of the best pieces of jerky I ever ate was from an axis deer I killed on the Hawaiian island of Molokai. My Hawaiian hunting partners marinated thin slices in a peppery homemade teriyaki sauce and then air-dried them out in the sun under a piece of window screen to keep the flies away. This recipe is inspired by that experience, though it takes into account that most of us do not live in a climate that's suitable for air-drying jerky—especially in the fall and winter months. Still, this recipe stays true to the same mixture of salt, sweet, and spice. For the meat, I prefer to work with whole roasts from the ham or shoulder that have been trimmed of fat and silver skin. Before slicing the meat, place it in the freezer for a couple of hours. You want it icy and firm, but not so frozen that a knife can't easily pass through it. This helps you get perfect slices and saves you a lot of aggravation. There are different opinions on whether you should slice with the grain or cross-grain. Slicing with the grain gives you chewier jerky that's hard to bite, but some folks like that. A cross-grain slice gives you more tender jerky that's easy to chew.

Cut the meat into ⅜-inch-thick slices. (See above regarding cross-grain or with-the-grain slices.) Keep the slices as uniform in thickness as possible. If the meat starts to thaw, pop it back into the freezer.

Combine the soy sauce, pineapple juice, Worcestershire sauce, brown sugar, honey, red chile flakes, black pepper, and onion powder. Using a Microplane, finely grate the garlic and ginger into the bowl. Discard the fibrous bits of ginger that don't pass through the Microplane. (If you don't have a Microplane, mince the garlic and ginger with a knife as finely as you possibly can.) Add the meat, mix thoroughly, cover, and marinate in the refrigerator for about 24 hours.

Remove the meat from the marinade and drain. Lay the meat out on the dehydrator trays, leaving space between the slices. Set the dehydrator to 145°F. Depending on the idiosyncrasies of your climate and dehydrator, it probably will take between 2 and 4 hours to finish the job. Start checking the meat at 2 hours and remove pieces as they finish. They should be firm throughout, with no sponginess, and will not break when you bend them. Rather, the fold will reveal a network of thin white lines.

Tip: You can make jerky in a conventional oven by setting it to the lowest possible setting and cracking the door to adjust the temperature. Use an oven thermometer rather than relying on your oven's thermostat, and keep the temperature between 140 and 150°F.

CANNING MEAT

MAKES 1 QUART CANNED MEAT

When I was a kid, a portion of our basement was designated as the "canning room." My dad had installed wooden shelves on either side of a passageway leading to the washer and dryer. My mom kept these shelves stocked with a wide array of home-canned goods. There were a lot of vegetable products from our garden, including tomato sauces and salsa, plus a variety of fruits purchased at a large farmers' market in nearby Muskegon. But the thing that I remember most fondly were the jars of venison all lined up in neat rows. We ate some of it in stews over the winter, but we'd eat the bulk of it the following fall. My dad kept a milk crate of the jars in the back of his truck, and we'd use them for tailgate sandwiches whenever we were out in the woods hunting. There's an image that's burned into my mind of my dad holding back the meat in the jar with his folding knife while he poured off some of the excess stock. Then he'd dig the knife into the jar and pull out a few squares of meat and crush them onto rye bread. A bit of mustard and a slice of onion, and that was it. Then you went back into the woods and started looking for the deer that would make next year's sandwich.

2 pounds game meat

1 tablespoon vegetable oil

3 cups Brown Game Stock (page 305), Blonde Game Stock (page 306), or low-sodium chicken broth

1 teaspoon kosher salt

Trim the meat of tallow and heavy tendons or connective tissue, but don't be too persnickety. A little connective tissue or silver skin isn't a problem with this preparation. Cut the meat into approximately 1-inch cubes. Heat the oil in a large saucepan over medium-high heat and brown the cubes on all sides; the meat should still be rare, or undercooked. Remove from the heat. In a medium saucepan, bring the stock to a boil and boil for 5 minutes. Remove from the heat.

Add the salt to a quart jar (or ½ teaspoon per jar if you're using 2 pint jars). Pack the browned meat into the jar, leaving room for stock to cover. Pour the hot stock into the jar, leaving 1 inch of headspace—3 cups (24 ounces) for a quart jar (1½ cups or 12 ounces for a pint jar). Tap the jar gently on the counter and tap the sides with a wooden spoon to release all air bubbles. Follow the recommendations of the manufacturer using 2-piece lids. Process the quart jars at 10 pounds pressure for 90 minutes for a quart jar (10 pounds pressure for 75 minutes for a pint jar). Store the meat in a dark place at room temperature for up to 1 year for optimal quality. This is great for last-minute stews or as a protein source on car or camping trips.

ALSO WORKS WITH: Use this for virtually any big game, from wild hogs to moose. My brother Matt used to use the same recipe for jackrabbit, and my brother Danny has prepared yet another version with green-winged teal. You're looking for about 2 pound of meat per quart jar, but you can get away with a bit more or less depending on how tightly you pack the meat.

SPECIAL EQUIPMENT: pressure canner and glass canning jars with 2-piece lids (one 1-quart canning jar or two 1-pint canning jars)

Tip: For more information on canning meat or processing at high altitudes, go to the USDA home canning website, http://nchfp.uga.edu/, and search for the guide on preparing and canning meats.

SOUTH TEXAS WILD HOG SHOULDER

SERVES A CROWD

SOP

1 cup white vinegar (I've been using apple cider vinegar with good results)

1 cup water

½ cup (1 stick) unsalted butter

1 cup ketchup

1 cup Worcestershire sauce

2 to 4 lemons, sliced

1 onion, sliced

Kosher salt

Freshly ground black pepper

HOG

1 whole wild hog shoulder, a section of shoulder, whole hindquarter, or section of large hindquarter (also known as barbecue cuts; bone-in is preferred)

Kosher salt

Freshly ground black pepper

ALSO WORKS WITH: Stick with wild pork on this one.

SPECIAL EQUIPMENT: DH smoker, pellet grill, gas grill, charcoal grill, or Dutch oven. Hardwood chips, chunks, or logs. Pecan, cherry, or apple wood work well.

A few years ago I was hanging around with a wild hog trapper outside of Devine, Texas, who does damage control work on the nonnative species. We butchered a few of our hogs on our own and then dropped a few off for processing at Devine Meat Company. We ended up spending the better part of the day there, as the proprietor, Clayton Saunders, slow roasted one of our pork shoulders over his "pit," a large barrel roaster fueled by a live fire of pecan wood. Over the course of four or five hours, he brushed the meat intermittently with a special sop of vinegar, lemon juice, Worcestershire sauce, and other tasty additives. It was the best wild pork I've ever eaten, hands down. Since that day, I've had great luck replicating his recipe on my pellet grill at home. But if you want the full experience of an authentic South Texas barbecue, you should probably stick with the real hardwood fire. That'd make Clayton happy.

FOR THE SOP: Combine the vinegar, water, butter, ketchup, Worcestershire sauce, lemons, onion, and some salt and pepper in a medium saucepan and bring to a simmer. It is now ready to be applied to the cooking meat using a pastry brush or clean kitchen rag.

FOR THE HOG: This is traditionally cooked in a pit barbecue, where the heat source is offset/indirect. The fire, typically made from flavorful hardwoods, is kept up in a firebox and the smoke and heat are funneled to the pit. If you don't own a pit barbecue, you can make do with a pellet grill, a conventional gas or charcoal grill, or even a Dutch oven. Alternate cooking methods are described at the end of this recipe.

If you want to go low and slow, keep the temperature between 200 and 250°F. For a shorter cooking time, start at 300 to 350°F for an hour, and then back it down to 250°F to finish. The internal temperature of the meat must reach 160°F to destroy any parasites.

Start by liberally applying salt and pepper to all sides of the meat. Then place the meat in the preheated pit. It is important to allow a crust, or bark, to form on the meat before starting to sop the meat. The crust should be crisp and firm but not burnt and will take at least 30 minutes to an hour to form. Once the crust is formed, apply the sop every 20 minutes or so. The meat is tenderized by the long low-temperature cooking; it is much more common to undercook it and have a tough product than to overcook it and possibly dry it out. The point here is: give yourself plenty of time. Last, flipping the meat is not necessary. Let the smoke and heat do the work. The meat is ready when you can pull it away from the bone with a fork.

This will usually take between 4 and 6 hours for a medium (100-pound on the hoof) hog's shoulder.

Let the meat rest for 20 to 30 minutes after pulling it from the heat to relax the muscle and allow the juices to flow throughout the meat. The meat can be cut into ⅜-inch-thick slices, or, if it's cooked long enough, picked apart for a pulled pork presentation.

Note: This method could be used to cook a whole hog simply by lengthening the cooking time and having an adequate size pit or grill.

Note: The remaining sop makes for a great tangy barbecue sauce. Simply strain the solids from the liquid, bring the remaining liquid to a simmer, and reduce until the desired consistency is reached. More ketchup can be added to thicken the sauce faster. This will also sweeten the sauce. If you like a sweeter barbecue sauce, try adding a few tablespoons of brown sugar.

ALTERNATE COOKING METHODS

PELLET GRILL: same as above.

GAS GRILL: If possible, light only a single burner element and place the meat so that it's receiving only indirect heat. You can use wood chips to add some smoke. Soak a handful of hardwood chips in water for twenty minutes, then drain and wrap in heavy duty aluminum foil. Place the foil packet over the heat to create smoke. Refill as necessary.

CHARCOAL GRILL: Soak a handful of hardwood chips in water for 20 minutes, drain, and set aside. You can also use a few chunks of pecan or apple wood (unsoaked) instead. Make coals, set them off to one side of the grill, and then add the meat on the opposite side. Distribute soaked chips among the coals. If using hardwood chunks, add one at a time as needed to maintain a light plume of smoke. Care must be taken to keep the temperature low: even a small pile of charcoal briquettes can raise the temperature beyond what's necessary, overcooking and consequently drying out the meat. Because of the long cooking time, you'll need to replenish the charcoal. It's a good idea to keep another pile of briquettes going in a separate location just for this reason.

DUTCH OVEN: Sear the meat in a Dutch oven. This substitutes for the creation of the bark. Place the lid on the Dutch oven and cook in a 300°F oven for approximately 4 hours, applying sop periodically. This method forfeits the smoking flavor but achieves very tender meat.

SMOKED HAM

SERVES A CROWD

1 bone-in venison ham, 7 to 20 pounds, depending on the size of the animal

BRINE

2 gallons water

2½ cups kosher salt

2 cups packed brown sugar

2 teaspoons yellow mustard seeds

20 black peppercorns

8 juniper berries

6 bay leaves

8 cloves garlic

1 tablespoon Prague Powder #1

SPECIAL EQUIPMENT: large stockpot or other container for brining; heavy-duty brine injector; kitchen twine (if using an upright smoker with enough room to hang the ham); smoker; hardwood chips, pecan, apple, or cherry work well

Every time I smoke a ham, be it black bear, wild hog, or venison, I'm a little torn about whether or not to remove the femur. With the bone removed, you can truss the ham back together with kitchen twine or food-grade elastic mesh. The advantages of deboning have to do with convenience. A deboned ham brines faster, it's compact, and it's easy to slice. The advantages of leaving the femur in place are more aesthetic, which does not mean less important. A bone-in wild game ham is a bad-ass creation with an undeniably rustic elegance. It's satisfying in a primal way to haul one out of the smoker and plunk it down on a large carving board in front of guests. If you want to see the process for a deboned ham, refer back to *The Complete Guide to Hunting, Butchering, and Cooking Wild Game, Volume 1: Big Game*. If you're willing to move ahead with the bone in place, read on.

It takes a big container and a lot of refrigerator space to brine a whole ham with the shank intact. If you lack the proper container and fridge space, remove the shank at the knee. Don't worry if you have to do this. The bulk of the meat, and the best portions, are all above the knee.

ALSO WORKS WITH: Works best with deer, antelope, black bears, and wild hogs. Anything bigger than a large deer is simply too massive. It would be hard to properly brine and cook, let alone lift up. (A big moose ham will weigh well over 100 pounds; I love smoked hams, but not quite that much.) If you're working with hams from bears or wild pigs, make sure to hit that safe internal temperature of 160°F to destroy any parasites.

PREPARE THE HAM FOR BRINING: Clean the ham, trimming away as much fat as possible. Pierce and perforate the ham all over with a fillet knife. This will allow the brine to penetrate throughout the muscles faster.

FOR THE BRINE: In a large stockpot, combine the water, salt, brown sugar, mustard seeds, peppercorns, juniper berries, bay leaves, garlic, and Prague Powder #1 and bring to a boil. Remove from the heat and let cool to room temperature, then let it chill in the refrigerator.

Remove 1 quart of the liquid and inject it into the meat all over, deep in the muscles—as deep as the bone. It is sufficiently saturated when liquid begins to seep from the injection and perforation holes.

Submerge the ham in the brine. If necessary, use a plate to weight it down so that it stays submerged. Brine for 4 or 5 days in the refrigerator. Inject the meat daily (this helps shorten the overall brining time).

Prepare your smoker according to the manufacturer's instructions using a mild wood such as apple, cherry, or pecan. Adjust the temperature to 180°F, or as close as possible without falling under 180°F. Remove the meat from the brine. Discard the brining liquid. Rinse the meat well and pat dry. If you're working with an upright smoker, use kitchen twine to create a strong loop tied to the bone. Hang the ham in the smoker. If using an offset smoker, or a stack smoker, lay the ham down on the rack as you would a brisket, pork butt, or other large roast.

Smoke consistently for 8 to 10 hours, until the internal temperature reaches 150°F when checked with an instant-read thermometer. (If curing a hog or a bear ham, the internal temperature of the meat has to reach 160°F. To reach this higher temperature, you may need to raise the heat of the smoker to 200°F after 8 hours.)

Serve warm, or let cool to room temperature and wrap well. The ham will keep for up to 2 weeks in the refrigerator. The ham can be sliced and frozen in vacuum-sealed bags at this point as well.

SANDWICHES WITH CHEDDAR CHIVE BISCUITS

For this you'll need leftover smoked ham slices and a batch of Cheddar Chive Biscuits (page 325). Use freshly baked biscuits, or warm them if they're premade. Slather the cut side of the biscuits with your condiment of choice: spicy mayo or grainy mustard work, or you could even try Herbed Tartar Sauce (page 318). Top the bottom biscuit half with sliced ham and pickles, if you like, cover with the top half of the biscuit, and serve.

02 SMALL GAME

INTRODUCTION

The term *small game* is a surprisingly slippery classification. Some hunters use it as a catch-all to describe everything with feathers or fur ranging from a one-pound gray squirrel to a twenty-five-pound wild turkey. That's a little too broad for my tastes. While I tend to think of turkeys as turkeys, I'm willing to lump them in with upland birds for the sake of organizational convenience. But my willingness to lump things together finds its limits when it comes to upland birds and waterfowl, which I view as entirely distinct categories of wild game. So that narrows "small game" down to squirrels, rabbits, and hares—at least if we're speaking of conventional game species that are commonly hunted around the country. This includes gray squirrels, fox squirrels, cottontail rabbits, snowshoe hares, and a couple of jackrabbit species. Nonconventional small game species—unadventurous folks might classify them as oddball, weird, or worse—include muskrat, beaver, nutria, raccoon, porcupine, and opossum, all of which are legal to harvest according to specific regulations set forth by the state where you happen to do your hunting. While we do give a nod or two to these rogue outliers of the small game world, a full treatment on these species falls outside the scope of this book.

Once upon a time, small game was a universal gateway drug into hunting. Most hunters got their start on squirrels and rabbits and then graduated, years later, into the big leagues of deer and turkey hunting. That has changed over the past couple of decades, partly because of ecology, partly because of shifting trends, and partly because of regulatory changes. From the ecology end of things, there are simply a lot more deer and turkeys in a lot more places than there were thirty years ago. For deer and turkey hunters, right now is the good ol' days. Seasons are long, bag limits are high. The widespread availability of deer and turkeys has, in turn, affected what hunters are interested in. People want to pursue these bigger and more glamorous species, and interest in small game has waned proportionately. What's more, the legal age at which a person can begin hunting has generally gone down. For instance, you had to be fourteen to hunt deer with a firearm in Michigan when I was a kid. Now there is no minimum age requirement as long as the kid is accompanied by an adult mentor. Gone are the days when you had to hunt squirrels while dreaming of chasing deer.

Regardless, I still feel that small game hunting is the best place to begin for someone who's eager to start hunting. First off, small game seasons are generally very liberal. While big game seasons for deer or elk might run for just a few weeks or even a few days, in many states you can hunt squirrels and rabbits more days out of the year than you can't. In New York, squirrel season runs from September 1 to February 28. In Kentucky, you can hunt squirrels from the third Saturday in August through to the end of February, and again for a monthlong spring season. In California, the season for rabbits and snowshoe hares runs from July 1 to January 29, and it never closes for jackrabbits. In Montana, where squirrels and rabbits are administered as nongame species, you can hunt year-round. And the cost of a small game license is hardly a hindrance. In most states, a resident hunter can get permitted for around twenty dollars.

It's also helpful that small game weapons restrictions are not very restrictive. No matter what you're hunting, your "method of take" is going to be limited to some extent. Many states have separate big game seasons for firearms and archery equipment, and each of these methods can be further regulated with regard to calibers, broadhead types, technological enhancements, ammo types, shot sizes, and so on. Small game restrictions are relatively lax. In most states you can hunt squirrels and rabbits with air rifles, archery equipment, small-caliber rifles such as the .22 LR and .17 HMR, and even crossbows and slingshots in some states.

Finally, squirrel and rabbit populations are generally abundant and readily accessible. Of course, this depends somewhat on natural population cycles that are dictated by weather, predation, and availability of food resources. But still, it's a rare year when you can't find good numbers of small game if you're looking in the right places. And "right places" abound. Small game populations can thrive on small, isolated parcels of land that are often overlooked by other hunters. Getting permission to hunt private land is far easier when the ask involves squirrels and rabbits rather than the more coveted deer and turkey. Furthermore, the high fecundity of small game species translates to high bag limits. In most states, you'll find that you're allowed around five squirrels and five rabbits every day. When you imagine those liberal daily bag limits spread out over a six-month-long season, with a hunting license that costs half as much as a tank of gas, you'll begin to see the seductiveness of small game hunting.

And let's not forget the meat, which is tasty, versatile, and relatively easy to deal with. From barbecue to tacos to stews to buffalo-style squirrel "wings," small game will get you cooking wild. In the big game section of this book, I voiced my belief that successful big game cooking requires you to consider the particular cut of meat that you're dealing with. A great recipe for venison shanks is certainly not a great recipe for a venison sirloin, and vice versa. I would never say the same thing about small game. When it comes to squirrels, rabbits, and hares (and raccoons, for that matter), I use the

whole animal in my recipes with little or no regard to what particular "cut" it is.

There are a couple of different reasons for this. First, the cooking methods that are necessary to tenderize small game are usually aggressive enough to limit or altogether negate the very subtle distinctions that differentiate the front shoulders from, say, the loins. Second, you need to consider the small size of the animals. In all my years of hunting, I've never been in a position to eat half a squirrel and then freeze the other half for later. The small size of the animals pretty much dictates that you're going to be using several of the whole animals all at once in order to have serving-size portions for your family or a group of friends.

Almost all small game animals benefit from long and slow braises, be they recipes from this chapter or those in Big Game, Waterfowl, or Upland Birds. You'll see that most of these recipes can be used interchangeably with squirrels and rabbits, with some adjustments. In fact, I'll often mix squirrels and rabbits together in a single recipe. When I'm hunting rabbits, I'll usually get a squirrel or two, and when I'm hunting squirrels, I'll sometimes get a rabbit. Besides the similarities in the quality of flesh, it makes sense to lump them together sometimes just for the sake of having enough meat to feed your family. But don't despair about quantities if an outing to the woods yields only a single squirrel or rabbit. With a little thinking, you can reduce these recipes by half or a quarter in order to produce appetizers.

Or, better yet, save up your small game in a freezer. Take an empty gallon-size milk jug or a two-liter soda bottle, cut off the top, and wash it out. When you get a squirrel or rabbit, place the meat in the bottom and add just enough water to cover it up. Pop it into the freezer. Next week or next month, when you get another critter or two, place the meat atop the layer of ice and add just enough water to cover that. Refreeze and repeat, until some midwinter afternoon when you decide to make a giant batch of Kevin Murphy's Kentucky-Style Squirrel Gravy with Cathead Biscuits (page 92). Then you can revel in the glory of a being a small game hunter.

VORTEX

THE NATURE OF THE BEAST

Squirrels

When most people talk about squirrel hunting, they're talking about hunting for **gray squirrels** and **fox squirrels**. There are two species of gray squirrel, eastern and western, which are indistinguishable from the perspective of someone eating a prepared dish of squirrel meat. Black squirrels are common in many areas, though those are just a melanistic color phase of the eastern gray squirrel and there's no difference in the quality of meat. For that matter, the meat of a fox squirrel is basically the same as a gray squirrel's, just in bigger portions. The meat is similar in color to a dark chicken thigh, though more packed with flavor. You can grill squirrel legs if you tenderize them with a strong marinade, and they can be fried and baked. They work especially well in slow-cooked dishes.

Most squirrel hunters who live in the vicinity of gray and fox squirrels will pay no attention to pine squirrels, of which there are a handful of species. The most widely distributed is the **American red squirrel,** which is very common in the northern United States and the boreal forests of Canada. Squirrel hunters ignore them because of their diminutive size and their bad reputation as table fare. The size issue is warranted, as they weigh only about a fourth of what a fox squirrel does. The quality of flesh issue isn't quite so fair. While they do feed heavily on conifer cones, which makes people think they taste "piney," the meat is actually quite comparable to gray and fox squirrel.

Rabbits

The true rabbits of North America that attract hunter interest are variants of the cottontail rabbit. There are many, and they all look quite similar to the common **eastern cottontail**. However, they do range in size wildly. The **swamp rabbit** runs up to 6 pounds, while the **mountain cottontail** is only around 2½ pounds. All are excellent. The color is much like chicken breast, and it is mild. As with other small game, you can use everything on a cottontail all in the same recipe. The differences between "cuts" aren't enough to warrant separating the pieces out for different uses. Cottontail can be baked, grilled, fried, slow-cooked—you can do just about anything with it that you'd do with chicken.

Hares

The **snowshoe hare** of the northern United States is the most commonly hunted hare of North America. The flesh is leaner and darker than cottontail and can be a bit tougher. It's particularly suitable for any kind of slow-cooking, which allows the meat to tenderize. The addition of fat is a good idea, as snowshoe hares are very lean. Don't let this frighten you away from snowshoe hares. With the proper methods and recipes, it's a worthwhile quarry to pursue.

Despite the name, **jackrabbits** are actually hares. While not as popular as snowshoe hares, jackrabbits are certainly edible and can be quite delicious. Their meat is darker still than snowshoe hare, and also tougher. The loins can be fried, or else marinated and grilled, but you'll want to remove the silver skin on the outside of the loin first. The legs should be cooked for a long time at a low heat, which is the secret of success with jackrabbits.

Aquatic Rodents

Part of the reason that hunters don't pursue **muskrats** and **beavers** as sources of meat is because these animals have valuable pelts that are sought after by the garment industry. They are generally regulated as furbearers rather than as game animals, meaning that you need a special fur harvester license to pursue them. (These licenses are not hard to get.) Always check your state's regulations before pursuing muskrat or beaver. In many states, it's illegal to shoot them; they must be trapped. Beavers and muskrats both have excellent meat. Beaver is dark, almost like beef, and muskrat is red with a purplish tint. There are areas in the country where they are regarded as delicacies. For each, slow-cooking methods are the way to go. That includes slow-roasting in a barbecue.

Some Rogue Outliers

Just about every animal is edible, but this quick listing of alternative small game animals will focus on those species that are widely available and generally open to hunting no matter where you live. **Raccoon** is a tad greasy, though not necessarily in a bad way; people often soak them in vinegar-based marinades before cooking them. **Porcupines** are good to eat, and surprisingly mild in flavor, though you have got to be careful when skinning them; the quills can give you nasty infections. **Opossums** are stronger flavored and a tad musky; in the old days, folks would catch opossums and put them in a cage in order to fatten them on a diet of grain before butchering them. I'm told they're quite good that way.

BUTCHERING SMALL GAME ANIMALS

RABBIT AND SQUIRREL SHIRT AND PANTS SKINNING AND GUTTING

1

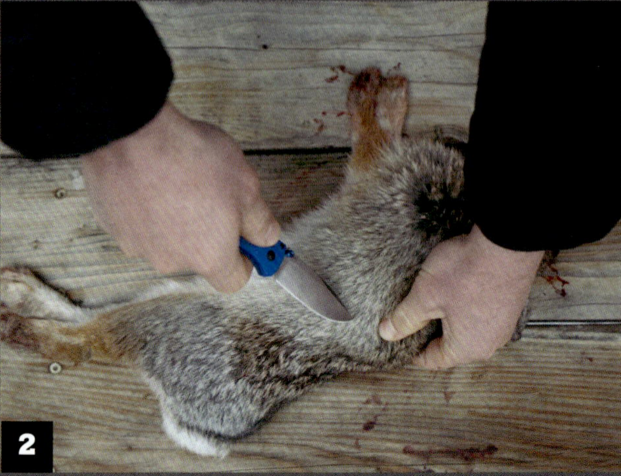

2

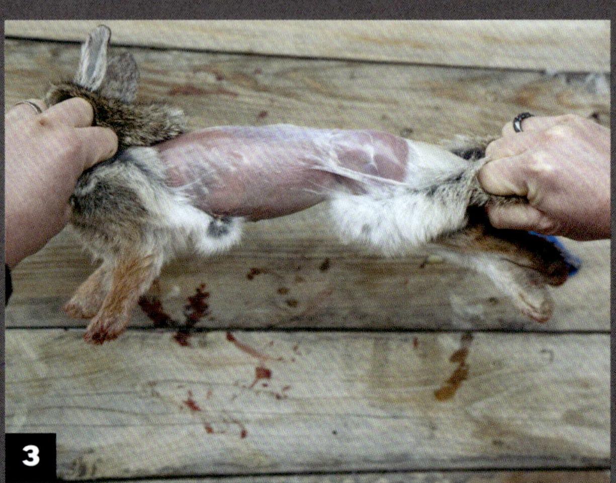

3

4

1. Cottontail rabbits used to be one of America's most popular game animals. It's a shame more people don't get after them, since they are widely available, easy to hunt, and a crowd pleaser on the dinner table. The shirt and pants method of skinning works well for rabbits and squirrels.

2. Make an incision through the skin at the top of the back. Now cut completely around the middle of the rabbit. Be sure to cut just the hide and not into the flesh or gut cavity.

3. At the cut, grab the hide along the back with each hand. Pull the hide toward the front and back legs at the same time. Rabbits peel easily, but squirrels will take a little more effort.

4. Pull the hide free on the pants half of the rabbit until you reach the bony shins on the back legs. On the shirt half of the rabbit, peel the hide free from the legs to the ankle, and off the shoulders to the neck.

5. Next, use game shears to remove the head and feet.

6. At the anus, cut through the pelvis bone with game shears.

7. Continue cutting through the upper paunch and rib cage, just below the back. With one side of the belly and ribs removed, the guts can be easily discarded. Save the heart and liver, as they can be used in many recipes.

8. Cut the paunch and ribs free from the opposite side of the rabbit. Wash the carcass and remove any bloodshot meat or shotgun pellets.

Squirrels are among the tastiest small game animals available to hunters, and they are an underutilized resource throughout America. Once you get the hang of it, the tail skinning method is a fast, simple way to cleanly remove a squirrel's tough pelt.

Tail Skinning

1. You'll need a sharp knife, a pair of game shears, and a cinder block or tree stump.

2. Start by making a cut through the underside of the tail, through the tailbone just above the anus. Stop short of completely removing the tail, leaving the hide attached to the carcass.

3. Next, lay the squirrel on its back and step firmly on the tail where you made the first cut. Get a good grip on the rear legs and slowly lift.

4. The hide will separate cleanly from the carcass as you lift.

5. When you reach the front legs, insert a finger into the gap between the hide and legs and continue to lift and pull the hide free of the forelegs.

6. The squirrel will still have some remaining hide on the lower belly and rear legs. Hold the squirrel firmly behind the front legs, and with the other hand pull the hide from the belly and rear legs down to the feet.

7. Pull the hide past all four ankles, and then use a game shear to remove the feet by cutting at the ankle joints. Remove the head and innards and, if needed, remove any hair or dirt and wash the carcass.

DISASSEMBLING RABBIT OR SQUIRREL

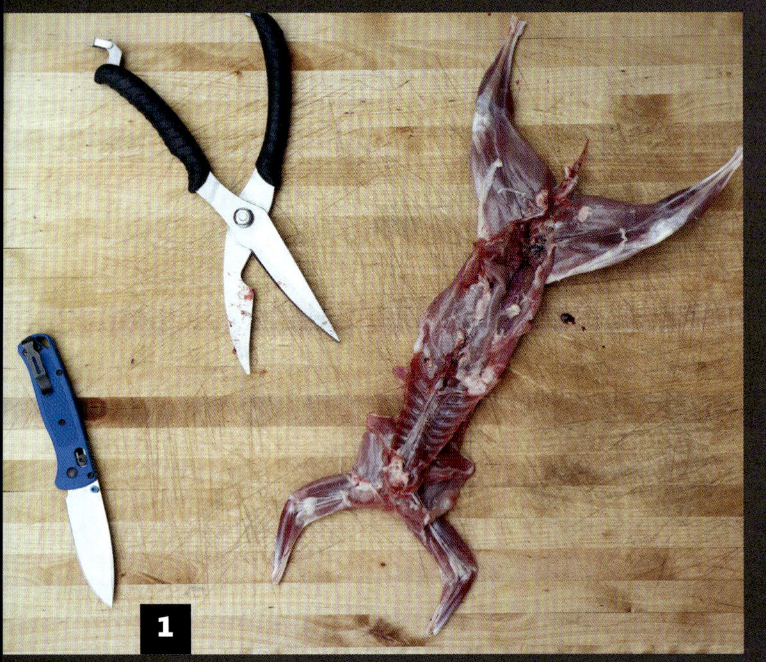
1

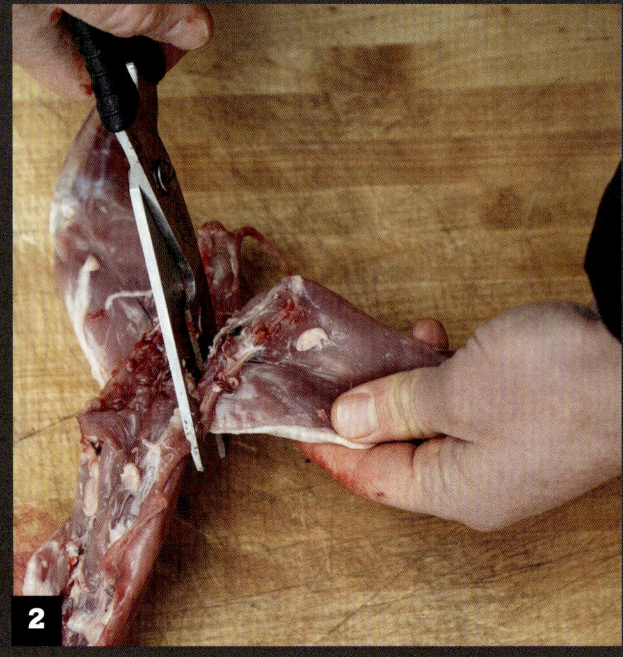
2

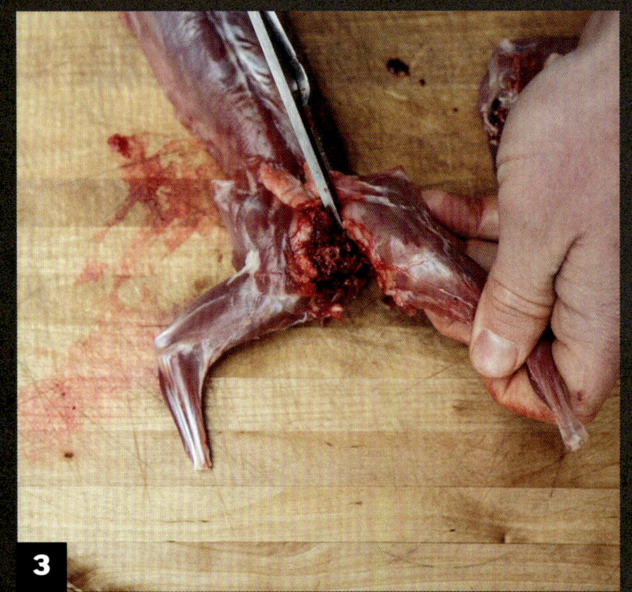
3

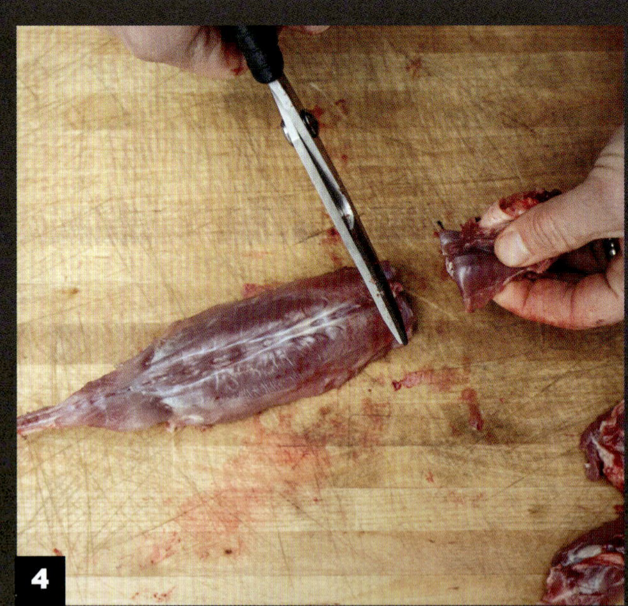
4

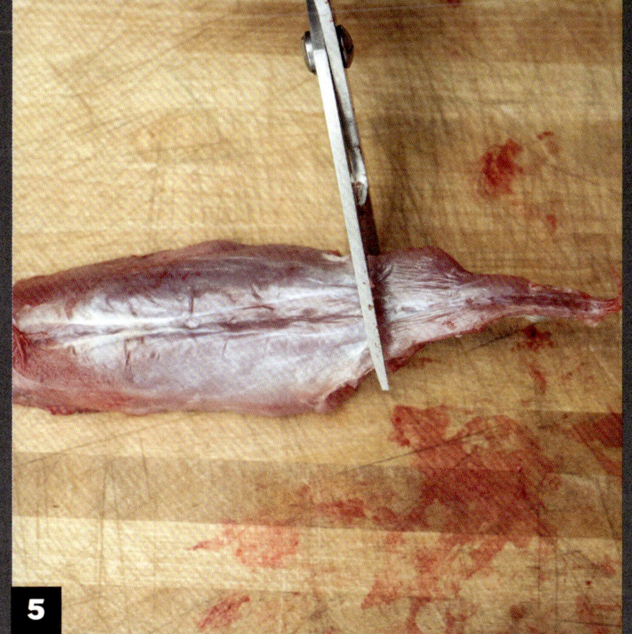
5

6

Rabbits and squirrels can be left whole after skinning and gutting or they can be broken down into pieces. It all depends on how you'll be cooking them. You can braise whole rabbits or squirrels, but if you're going to fry them, they will need to be disassembled.

1. You can do the job with a game shear or small knife.

2. Remove each back leg by cutting along the pelvis and through the hip's ball and socket joint.

3. Next, cut the front legs free.

4. Cut through the spine just forward of the loins to remove the shoulder area from the carcass.

5. Now separate the hips and tail from the back end of the carcass with a cut through the spine just behind the loins.

6. The four leg quarters and the back loins, or saddle, are ready to be cooked. Use the bony shoulder and hip pieces to make a small batch of stock for gravy.

UL Bend NWR
Crooked Creek Recreation Area
PHILLIPS COUNTY
GARFIELD COUNTY
PETROLEUM COUNTY
Second Creek School
To Sand Springs 25 miles
To Winnett 32 miles
To Malta 41 miles
To Harlem 48 miles
Upper Missouri National Wild and Scenic River
Sand Creek Wildlife Station
Bohemian Corner
To Winifred 25 miles
To Winifred 31 miles
To Lewistown 37 miles
To Grass Range 17 miles
DRINK 'TIL

BUFFALO HOT LEGS

SERVES 4

One of my older brothers did a semester or two of college at Ferris State University in Mecosta County, Michigan. I would visit him often, and we'd always do a lot of squirrel and cottontail rabbit hunting in the surrounding country. We'd find cottontails around the beaver ponds and squirrels up in the hardwoods. At night, after hunting, we would head to a bar that offered a happy hour deal of ten-cent draft beers and five-cent Buffalo chicken wings. Ever since then I've associated small game hunting with Buffalo wings. This recipe formally unites those two things in the perfect appetizer to be served with cold beer. Squirrels and cottontail rabbits can be used interchangeably here, though I do have a subtle preference for squirrel meat. It's darker and more flavorful, though rabbit does have a coloration and texture more in line with the traditional barroom buffalo chicken wings that many of us have spent our whole lives eating.

2 to 3 squirrels and/or cottontail rabbits

2¼ teaspoons kosher salt

¾ teaspoon freshly ground black pepper

2 quarts peanut oil

1½ cups Frank's Red Hot Original Cayenne Pepper Sauce

5 tablespoons maple syrup

3 tablespoons distilled white vinegar

¾ cup (1½ sticks) unsalted butter

Celery and carrot sticks, for serving

Blue cheese dressing, for serving

ALSO WORKS WITH: See above comments. Works with both squirrels and cottontail rabbits.

Cut the squirrels into 4 leg pieces and 2 back pieces. Cut the rear legs of cottontails into 2 pieces and the back into 3 or 4 pieces.

Sprinkle all the pieces with 1½ teaspoons of the salt and the pepper. Heat the oil in a medium pot or Dutch oven until it registers 300°F on a deep-fry thermometer. Group the pieces of meat by size—front legs together, rear legs together, back pieces together. Carefully lower 6 to 8 small pieces into the hot oil and cook until light golden brown in color, moving the pieces around occasionally to ensure they don't stick to the bottom, about 6 minutes. Drain on paper towels and repeat with the remaining smaller pieces. Fry the larger pieces for a total of 8 minutes.

While you're frying, prepare the buffalo sauce by warming the hot sauce, maple syrup, vinegar, and the remaining ¾ teaspoon salt in a small saucepan over low heat. Slowly stir in the butter until it has fully melted, then remove from the heat.

Raise the heat of the oil to 375°F and fry the squirrel or rabbit pieces for a second time to finish crisping the exterior, about 3 minutes per batch. Transfer the pieces to a large draining rack.

Toss half of the piping hot pieces in a bowl with half of the buffalo sauce, coating them thoroughly. Repeat with the remaining meat and sauce. Serve immediately—so you maintain that double fried crunch—as you would traditional Buffalo wings, with celery, carrots, and blue cheese dressing.

FIRE-ROASTED BEAVER TAIL

SERVES UP TO 10 PEOPLE AS A NOVELTY APPETIZER

ALSO WORKS WITH: Nothing else comes even close; a beaver tail is its own special thing.

Food is capable of doing a lot more than just tasting good. In this case, it can bring you back in time to the heyday of the mountain man era, when badasses such as Jed Smith, Jim Bridger, and Hugh Glass were working the wild Rockies for beaver pelts while dodging perils such as grizzly bears, frozen rivers, and scalping knives belonging to the rival indigenous hunters upon whose land they trespassed. Even the most casual history buff who reads about the mountain men will find references to beaver tail, which is usually described as the official favorite food of these bygone trappers. You'd never guess it from looking at one, but the interior of a beaver tail is almost pure fat and gristle, making it an essential food item for men who were living on a diet comprised almost exclusively of lean red meat. My brothers and I had several failed attempts at cooking beaver tail, which led us to believe that the history books were lying to us. But then, through trial and error, I finally figured out how mountain men were probably preparing this dish. Once I got it right, I was blown away by the visual qualities and pleasantly surprised by the taste. If possible, use a beaver killed in the fall for this preparation. A beaver's tail serves as the animal's fat reserve. After a hard winter, the tail can be too thin to bother messing with it.

1 beaver tail

Kosher salt

Build a small cooking fire. Try to use dry wood from deciduous trees. Due to the nature of a beaver's habitat, it's safe to assume that more beaver tails have been roasted over fires made of aspen, willow, and cottonwood than any other fuel source. You're looking for more than just a bed of coals, as a few flames are necessary to complete the cooking process.

As the fire builds up a hot bed of coals, pierce the base of the beaver tail with a knife and insert the sharpened end of the skewer into the slit. Now, position the beaver tail so that it's close to the fire but not too close—look for a place where you can hold your hand for about 2 seconds before you have to pull it away. The tail can get licked by a flame or two but should not be engulfed. Imagine that you're trying to roast a marshmallow without letting it burn. You can use rocks and a forked stick to support the skewer, but don't wander off.

SPECIAL EQUIPMENT: a stout skewer, as thick as your thumb, cut from a green tree or shrub, sharpened on one end

Within 5 or 6 minutes, the scaly skin of the beaver tail will begin to bubble and lift away from the fatty interior. Adjust the tail's position so that the blistering occurs evenly across the side of the tail that's facing the fire. Use the blade of a knife to test whether or not you can lift or scrape the skin away from the fat. Once that's done, rotate the tail on the skewer and repeat the process on the opposite side. Keep in mind that you're trying to cook the inside of the tail at the same time that you're bubbling the skin away, so don't rush it. If the entire process takes 15 minutes, you're in good shape.

Lay the cooked tail on a stump, rock, or platter and let it cool enough so that you can begin peeling the skin away. What remains should look like fatty gristle from a beef steak with a tailbone running down the middle. That's mountain man's gold. Slice as thin as possible, either lengthwise or crosswise, and sprinkle each slice with a bit of salt. Enjoy the taste of history.

KENTUCKY-STYLE SQUIRREL GRAVY
WITH CATHEAD BISCUITS, STRAIGHT FROM KEVIN MURPHY

SERVES 6

2 fox squirrels or 4 gray squirrels
Kosher salt
Freshly ground black pepper
All-purpose or self-rising flour
Vegetable or peanut oil, for frying
Dollop or two of melted lard
2 to 3 cups milk, or a little more if needed
Cathead Biscuits (page 95)
Curly leafed parsley (optional garnish)

ALSO WORKS WITH: This might annoy Kevin, but I'd feel comfortable using cottontail rabbits or snowshoe hares to make this recipe.

My buddies and I have dubbed our friend Kevin Murphy "the world's greatest small game hunter" without a lick of irony. While most hunters cut their teeth on small game and then move along to larger quarry, Kevin has stayed true to his foundational pursuits. He hunts the same patches of public land in Kentucky that he hunted with his dad when he was just a kid, and his primary passion is chasing squirrels with his small pack of squirrel hounds. If he's not doing that, he prefers to be chasing marsh rabbits and eastern cottontails with his small pack of rabbit hounds. If not that, he likes chasing grouse and quail with his bird dogs. You get the point. Kevin is also faithful to his culinary roots. He still likes to prepare the same dishes that his mother made for him as a kid when he brought home squirrels and rabbits for the family dinner table. He's prepared his squirrel gravy and cathead biscuits a number of times for me, and I like them so much that I asked him to give me the recipes exactly in his own words so that nothing is lost in translation. (If you're wondering, it's called a cathead biscuit because that's how big they ought to be.)

Cut the squirrels into 4 leg pieces and 2 back pieces; if you have larger squirrels, cut the rear legs into 2 pieces and then cut the back into 3 or 4 pieces.

Season and flour your squirrel pieces. Heat the oil in a seasoned cast-iron skillet over medium heat, then add the lard, cover, and steam for at least 20 minutes, until cooked through. Squirrels for the most part have very little fat reserves, unless you catch them in the fall of the year, just before winter. With a limited food source, they will consume just about everything available in the woods, from black gum berries to pine cones; in my opinion, squirrels feeding on pine cones do not taste like pine trees. (I have not seen them actually eat locusts, but in the years they emerge from the ground, which is about every seven years for a major hatch, the squirrels are mud-ball fat, and I have always assumed this was from eating locusts.) In times of food shortages, squirrels try to put on and retain weight so they can make it through the winter until the trees start budding in late winter or early spring. Water maple is the first to bud, followed by elm. Once this occurs, squirrels will become more active and spend more time out of their den or nest!

OK, back to our gravy. After the squirrel has been cooked, remove it from the skillet.

You should have a couple of tablespoons of rendered squirrel drippings and flavored fried squirrel-seasoned crispies. Scrape the bottom of the skillet clean and mix with the drippings. If you don't have 2 tablespoons, add enough lard to make up the difference. Add about 2 tablespoons flour. Adjust the heat level to medium to medium-high. Work the flour into the drippings until the flour browns and add ¼ teaspoon salt and ¼ teaspoon pepper. You can season again after the gravy is made.

Next is the tricky part of the process. Have on hand 2 to 3 cups of whole milk, maybe a little more just in case your gravy is too thick. (It's much easier to make thick gravy thin than to make thin gravy thick!) Raise the heat to high and, with a whisk in one hand, start incorporating the milk while working the edge of the browned flour. It will start to rise, bubble, and expand immediately. Keep whisking away and adding milk until all the lumps are dissolved and you have a velvety thin gravy. Now is a good time to season with salt and pepper again. Reduce the heat to medium and cook, constantly stirring, for 3 to 5 minutes, maybe a little longer. You don't want the gravy to stick to the bottom of the skillet. Remove it at a thinner stage than you like to eat it because it will thicken as it cools. Gravy making is a skill that will develop with time just like any outdoor skill. Serve over cathead biscuits.

CATHEAD BISCUITS

MAKES 5 BISCUITS

2 cups self-rising flour, plus more for sprinkling

¼ teaspoon kosher salt

½ to 1 tablespoon sugar (depending on how sweet you like them)

2 tablespoons lard, shortening, or unsalted butter (cut into small pieces), chilled, plus more for the pan

1 cup buttermilk

1 tablespoon unsalted butter, melted (optional)

SPECIAL EQUIPMENT: 1 mason jar (diameter of a cat head, 3 inches)

Preheat the oven to 425°F.

Mix the flour, salt, and sugar in a large mixing bowl. Rub the lard or shortening (or cut the butter) into the flour. When you're done it should look like coarse cornmeal.

Pour in the buttermilk and gently mix it into the flour with your hands to where it feels and looks like brick mortar (firm, but wet enough that it can still flow). Sprinkle in more flour as needed; the dough will be wet and sticky, but not so wet and sticky that it clings to your fingers or won't scrape off the counter. Place on a hard floured surface. Pat out into a rectangle about 7 by 9 inches. Fold into thirds like a letter. Pat the dough out again into a rectangle about 1 inch high. Lightly flour the top, then cut 3 biscuits with the mason jar. Then re-form to cut out 1 more, and re-form one more time for the last biscuit. Grease up a 10-inch cast-iron skillet with lard, shortening, or butter. Arrange the biscuits around each other, leaving about a ½-inch gap between them. Brush a little melted butter on top of the biscuits, if desired (it will help with the browning).

Bake until puffed and lightly golden brown on top, 13 to 15 minutes. Turn the oven light on to check the biscuits (don't open the door or you'll lose your heat). If you think the bottoms of the biscuits are done, you can turn your broiler on for 30 seconds or more to brown the tops of your biscuits.

RABBIT CURRY

SERVES 4 TO 6

I get a kick out of cooking regional foods with meats that would be totally out of place in the dish's place of origin. Such is the case with this curry recipe, so long as you're using any of the rabbits or hares available to American hunters. Making this dish with native wild game is its own strange form of fusion cuisine, a global melding of tastes and ideas.

ALSO WORKS WITH: You could get away with using 3 squirrels instead of 2 cottontails, but you'd want to increase the cooking time in order to tenderize the squirrels. It would also work with snowshoe hares or even jackrabbits.

2 cottontail rabbits

1 cup plain yogurt

2 teaspoons curry powder

1½ teaspoons kosher salt, plus more as needed

1 teaspoon chili powder

½ teaspoon ground turmeric

¼ teaspoon ground cardamom

¼ teaspoon cayenne pepper

3 cloves garlic, grated

¾-inch knob ginger, peeled and grated

2 tablespoons canola oil, plus more as needed

1 large onion, cut into ¼-inch slices

1 tablespoon tomato paste

1 teaspoon tamarind concentrate or fresh lime juice

½ butternut squash, peeled, seeded, and diced

1 large red bell pepper, cut into ¼-inch slices

1 large yellow squash, cut into ¼-inch half-rounds

Freshly ground black pepper

Steamed white rice, for serving

Fresh cilantro leaves, for garnish

Remove the ribs and lower spine from the rabbits. Cut into 6 pieces each (2 sets of legs and two back pieces, with the loins still attached to the backbone).

Mix the yogurt, curry powder, salt, chili powder, turmeric, cardamom, cayenne, garlic, and ginger in a large bowl. Add the rabbit, stir to coat, cover, and refrigerate for at least 2 hours or up to overnight.

Pour enough oil into a heavy soup pot to cover the bottom and heat over medium-high heat. Add the onion and cook, stirring occasionally, until golden brown, about 15 minutes. Push the onion to the side and add the tomato paste to the middle. Cook, stirring, until it browns, about 3 minutes. Add the rabbit, reserving the yogurt marinade. Working in batches if necessary and adding more oil if needed, cook the rabbit on each side until the meat browns a bit, about 3 minutes per side. Return all the rabbit to the pot. Stir in the reserved yogurt marinade, the tamarind, butternut squash, and enough water to cover. Bring to a boil, then reduce the heat to low, cover, and simmer until the rabbit is very tender and nearly falling off the bone, 1 to 1½ hours. By this time, the butternut squash should be beginning to fall apart. (Use your spoon to mash it against the side of the pot if it isn't.) The butternut squash acts as a thickener here. If the liquid appears curdled or broken, whisk vigorously to emulsify. Raise the heat to medium, add the bell pepper and yellow squash, and cook, uncovered, until the vegetables are softened and the curry has thickened into a stew, about 10 minutes. Season with salt and pepper.

Serve over steamed white rice and garnish with cilantro leaves. Each person gets a leg or two plus a piece of the back.

SMALL GAME AND SAUSAGE GUMBO

SERVES 10 TO 12 (MAKES 15 CUPS)

About 3 pounds squirrel and/or rabbit

1½ cups plus 2 tablespoons vegetable oil

3 tablespoons Creole Seasoning (page 312), or use store-bought

1½ cups all-purpose flour

12 to 16 ounces Andouille Sausage (page 45) or other smoked sausage, cut into ½-inch-thick half moons

1 medium onion, diced

1 large green bell pepper, diced

1¼ cups diced celery

1 tablespoon chopped garlic

2 bay leaves

2½ to 3 quarts Blonde Game Stock (page 306), Brown Game Stock (page 305), or low-sodium chicken broth

ACCOMPANIMENTS

Hot cooked white rice

Thinly sliced scallions and/or chopped fresh parsley

Gumbo filé (aka filé powder)

Hot sauce

ALSO WORKS WITH: Just about any combination of small game, upland birds, and waterfowl.

Gumbo is the hunter's best friend, especially if the hunter is a generalist who likes to do it all. What other dish can accommodate such a disparate array of ingredients? The last batch I made—and I'm not kidding here—had two species of ducks, three species of upland bird, a goose breast, some marsh rabbit, and one gray squirrel. It was a little bit of Noah's Ark in every bowl. This version calls for rabbit and/or squirrel, along with sausage, but no one's going to complain if you dig through your freezer and add in a few surprises. The trickiest part is making the roux. The old-fashioned way of doing this is to whisk the fat and flour over low heat until your arm's ready to fall off. If you're attentive, you can do as some Southern chefs do and make a speedier version over medium-high heat. Just be sure not to get distracted and walk away. If you do, you could quickly end up with a burned and bitter mess.

If you made your own andouille (see page 45) back in the fall, break it out for this recipe. If not, a store-bought version will do.

Cut the squirrels or rabbits into 4 leg pieces and 2 back pieces. On larger rabbits, cut the back legs into two pieces.

Heat 2 tablespoons of the oil in a large skillet over medium-high heat. Sprinkle the rabbit with 1 tablespoon of the Creole Seasoning. Working in batches if necessary, sear the rabbit until golden brown, about 2 minutes per side. Transfer the rabbit to a platter.

Heat the remaining 1½ cups oil in a Dutch oven over medium-high heat. Gradually add the flour, whisking until smooth. Cook, whisking constantly, until the roux thickens and turns dark, like coffee with a splash of cream, 8 to 10 minutes. Reduce the heat to medium. Carefully add the sausage, onion, bell pepper, celery, and garlic (it may splash and splutter) and cook, stirring constantly, until the vegetables soften, about 5 minutes. Add the remaining 2 tablespoons Creole Seasoning and the bay leaves. Slowly whisk in the stock to desired thickness. Add the rabbit and bring to a boil. Reduce the heat to maintain a simmer and cook, uncovered, until the rabbit is tender, 1 to 1½ hours. Skim off and discard any oil or scum that rises to the surface.

Transfer the rabbit to a shallow pan or platter and set aside until cool enough to handle. Remove the meat from the bones, discarding the bones, and shred into large pieces. Discard the bay leaves. If necessary, whisk the gumbo to emulsify. Return the rabbit meat to the gumbo and adjust the seasonings. Serve over rice and garnish with scallions and/or parsley, filé, and hot sauce.

ELK
SEX
Either Sex
Antlered Bulls
Branch Antlered
DEER
AREA NO. DATE
SEX
COUNTY
1 Oct. 1—Oct. 31
Bucks Only
Ravalli
IDAHO

RABBIT OR SQUIRREL IN CREAMY MUSTARD SAUCE

SERVES 4

- 2 cottontail rabbits
- Kosher salt
- Freshly ground black pepper
- 2 tablespoons vegetable oil
- 3 tablespoons unsalted butter
- ¼ cup finely chopped shallots
- 1 large clove garlic, minced
- 1 cup dry vermouth or white wine
- 1 cup Blonde Game Stock (page 306) or low-sodium chicken broth
- 3 tablespoons grainy Dijon or country-style mustard
- 1 large sprig fresh tarragon
- ¼ cup heavy cream
- 1 tablespoon chopped fresh tarragon or thyme
- 3 tablespoons chopped fresh flat-leaf parsley
- 1 pound hot freshly cooked egg noodles

This recipe is well suited for folks who enjoy sophisticated food but might not be totally comfortable with the idea of wild game. It's a dish with deep traditions in Europe, where rabbit is a much more common menu item than it is in the United States, so it's got a nice cosmopolitan pedigree. And there's enough going on with the creamy mustard sauce and buttered noodles to distract people away from the idea that you shotgunned the thing out of some nearby woodlot. However, any guise of true refinement will be lost when someone finds a bit of shattered bone and a shotgun pellet. That's why I always like to introduce a fun game to my guests before I serve small game: whoever finds the first shotgun pellet gets to kiss the cook.

ALSO WORKS WITH: Squirrels and snowshoe hares are a good idea, though remember that you might need an extra 20 or 30 minutes of cooking to fully tenderize the meat.

Cut the cottontails into 4 leg pieces and 2 back pieces. Sprinkle the pieces generously with salt and pepper. Heat the oil in a large, heavy skillet over medium-high heat. Working in batches if necessary, sear the rabbit until nicely browned on both sides, 3 to 4 minutes per side. Transfer to a plate when done.

Remove the skillet from the burner for a couple of minutes to let it cool a little. Reduce the heat to medium and melt in 1 tablespoon of the butter. Add the shallots and cook, scraping up the browned bits at the bottom of the skillet, until softened, 3 to 5 minutes. Add the garlic and cook for about 30 seconds. Add the vermouth and bring to a boil. Let it reduce by half, about 5 minutes. Add the stock, mustard, tarragon sprig, all of the browned rabbit, and any accumulated juices to the skillet. Bring to a boil, then reduce the heat to maintain a simmer. Cook, covered, until the meat is tender, about 1 hour. Transfer to a platter and discard the tarragon sprig.

Bring the sauce to a boil and cook until reduced by half, about 5 minutes. Stir in the cream, tarragon, and parsley. Taste and adjust the seasonings. Simmer for 3 to 5 minutes, then add the rabbit and turn each piece to coat. Toss the hot noodles with the remaining 2 tablespoons butter and serve with the rabbit.

BBQ SMOKED BEAVER SANDWICHES

SERVES 6

When you serve someone a good dish that features beaver meat, you're probably going to have to argue with them about whether or not it's really beaver. For some reason, people have a hard time believing that the flesh from an aquatic rodent with a scaly tail can taste so similar to beef pot roast. When cleaning a beaver, it's important to work carefully around the castor glands. Remove the glands quickly, and then wash your hands and knife to make sure you're not spreading the oils to the meat with your fingers or knife.

BEAVER

2 bone-in beaver thighs

½ cup BBQ Rub (page 313)

2 cups Blonde Game Stock (page 306) or low-sodium chicken broth

1½ cups BBQ Sauce (page 314)

SLAW

½ cup mayonnaise

¼ cup apple cider vinegar

3 tablespoons sugar

1 tablespoon Dijon mustard

1 tablespoon granulated garlic

1 tablespoon kosher salt

1 teaspoon onion powder

1 teaspoon freshly ground black pepper

½ head green cabbage, cored and thinly sliced

4 scallions, thinly sliced

1 carrot, grated

6 burger buns

Sweet bread-and-butter pickles

FOR THE BEAVER: Rinse the thighs under cold running water and vigorously scrub them with your hand. This helps ensure that there's no castor oil on the meat. Pat dry with paper towels and completely cover the meat with 6 tablespoons of the rub, working it into all areas of the thigh.

Prepare your smoker according to the manufacturer's instructions at 225°F and smoke the beaver with your favorite hardwood chips (I love the smell of hickory and mesquite) for 2½ hours. Remove the thighs and place them in a roasting pan or Dutch oven.

Preheat the oven to 300°F.

Add the stock to the pan, cover tightly with aluminum foil, place in the oven, and braise for 1½ hours, or until the meat is very tender and easily pulls away from the bone with a fork. Put the meat aside until it's cool enough to work with. Meanwhile, strain the braising liquid into a shallow pan and refrigerate to allow the fat layer to solidify on top. Once you can handle the meat, shred it into small pieces. This can be done up to a day ahead of time.

FOR THE SLAW: Whisk the mayonnaise, vinegar, sugar, mustard, granulated garlic, salt, onion powder, and pepper in a medium bowl until smooth. Combine the cabbage, scallions, and carrots in a large bowl. Add the dressing to the cabbage and toss until it is completely coated.

TO SERVE: Preheat the oven to 375°F. Skim the fat off of the braising liquid. Whisk ½ cup of the liquid with ½ cup of the BBQ sauce in a small bowl. Place the shredded meat in a large bowl and pour the BBQ sauce over the meat, tossing well. This will make the meat moist but not very saucy. Spread the meat out on a baking sheet and sprinkle with the remaining rub. Place the meat in the oven and heat until hot, 8 to 10 minutes. Serve on buns with coleslaw, the remaining BBQ sauce, and pickles.

ALSO WORKS WITH: I'd like to try this with a javelina thigh, but haven't done it yet.

RABBIT CACCIATORE

SERVES 4 TO 6

One of the things that makes this dish so good is that it's served over a bed of Italian-style polenta with grated Parmigiano-Reggiano cheese. There are a number of small game dishes in my personal repertoire that involve sauces and polenta. It's a brilliant combination, in my opinion, and almost guaranteed to please (but it's equally tasty over pasta or a hunk of crusty bread). What's especially cool about cacciatore is that it's an Italian word that translates as "hunter." In Italy, when a dish is described as *alla cacciatore,* or "hunter's style," it means braised with traditional ingredients of tomatoes, herbs, onion, and wine. You'll see that this dish calls for a bit of game stock. You can always substitute low-sodium chicken broth, but making game stock is a lot of fun and it puts to good use the bones and trimmings from your kill.

2 rabbits

Kosher salt

Freshly ground black pepper

Extra virgin olive oil, as needed to cover the bottom of the pan

1 onion, finely chopped

2 ribs celery, thinly sliced

10 ounces cremini mushrooms, sliced

5 cloves garlic, sliced

Pinch of red chile flakes

1¼ cups dry white wine

1 (28-ounce) can whole peeled tomatoes, drained

1 cup Blonde Game Stock (page 306) or low-sodium chicken broth

2 sprigs fresh rosemary

1 bay leaf

Leaves from 1 bunch fresh flat-leaf parsley, chopped

Freshly grated Parmigiano-Reggiano cheese

1 recipe Polenta (page 330)

FOR THE RABBIT: Cut the rabbits (or squirrels) into 4 leg pieces and 2 back pieces. On larger rabbits, cut each back leg into 2 pieces and the backs into 3 pieces. Sprinkle the meat liberally on all sides with salt and pepper. Heat the oil in a heavy-bottomed saucepan over medium-high heat until it shimmers. Brown the meat on all sides, about 10 minutes. Remove to a plate. Add the onion and cook until translucent, about 8 minutes. Add the celery and mushrooms and cook until softened, about 8 minutes. Add the garlic and red chile flakes and cook, stirring, for 30 seconds, or until fragrant. Add the wine, scraping any browned bits from the bottom of the pot. Put the tomatoes in a bowl, crush them with your hands, and add them to the pot. Pour in the stock and season with a pinch of salt. Add the meat back to the pot and bring to a simmer. Add the rosemary sprigs and bay leaf. Reduce the heat and cook at a low simmer until the meat is tender and just beginning to release from the bone, up to 1½ hours or more for a wild rabbit, depending on its size. Discard the rosemary sprigs and bay leaf.

Spoon the rabbit onto a platter. Top with the sauce and garnish with the parsley and cheese. Serve over polenta, freshly cooked pasta, or with a hunk of crusty bread.

ALSO WORKS WITH: Squirrel and snowshoe hare, even a younger jackrabbit.

03 **WATERFOWL**

INTRODUCTION

When I was a teenager, we hunted a local marsh that offered dynamite action on wood ducks in mid-October. It was hardly bigger than a basketball court and full of dead trees. The local woodies used it as a roosting pond. They'd come bombing into the marsh just five or ten minutes before the end of legal shooting light. Because of all the timber and the waning light, you could never actually see the ducks coming until they were right on top of you. They'd all of a sudden materialize, already in range, flying low and fast and then cupping their wings as they whizzed past your face. A few nights a year, for just a few minutes per night, that pond provided an exhilarating place to miss a bunch of ducks and maybe, if you were lucky, hit a few.

What amazed me about those ducks, beyond their speed and agility as they maneuvered through the trees, was how well fed they were. They'd spend their days down in the deep ravines of the aptly named Mosquito Creek, gorging themselves on beechnuts. Their crops would be so packed full of the nuts that their necks would feel like marble bags when you picked them up. After we cleaned the ducks, my mom would stuff them with chopped apples and raisins and roast them under a sheet of aluminum foil in a hot oven. Just before removing the birds, she'd pull off the foil and let them brown under the broiler. They tasted magical, moist and almost steak-like. Served alongside acorn squash from our garden, it was the perfect fall meal.

With those birds as my foundational experience, as I grew up it would surprise me when I'd meet other hunters who didn't really like eating waterfowl. I'd hear hunters tell me that ducks and geese were "pasty" or "livery" or "dry" or whatever, and it honestly was hard for me to relate to what they were saying. At least, that is, until I had the opportunity to eat a few birds that were poorly handled in the field and then grossly overcooked on a grill or pan. The fact that many of these low-grade meals were prepared by otherwise proficient wild game cooks eventually led me to the realization that ducks and geese present the most vexing challenges of all wild game categories.

To understand those challenges, it's helpful to understand just how many types of waterfowl are out there. An American waterfowl hunter who's not afraid to travel around the country might in his or her lifetime encounter around forty species. These birds are organized in a confusing fashion that will puzzle just about anyone. While some folks are familiar with the straightforward method of grouping that places waterfowl into two categories—ducks and geese—avid waterfowl hunters go a bit deeper and categorize their waterfowl into dabbling ducks, diving ducks, sea ducks, dark-colored geese, and light-colored geese.

Dabbling ducks, often called puddle ducks, primarily reside in shallow freshwater ponds, lakes, and rivers. There are about a dozen species. The classification includes some of our most popular and easily recognizable ducks, including the ubiquitous mallard, the beautifully colored wood duck, and the diminutive green wing and blue wing teals. They generally feed by tipping forward in the water, submerging their heads while leaving their tails up in the air. They are surefooted and can walk on land. If you see a duck walking in a crop field, that's a puddle duck. Another indicator is a bright, iridescent speculum, or wing patch. Puddle ducks are largely herbivorous. Most people who eat a

lot of ducks will tell you that puddle ducks taste better than diver ducks, which tend to feed below the water's surface and eat a lot more animal matter.

Diving ducks reside primarily on deep lakes, big rivers, and coastal bays and inlets. They do most of their feeding underwater. When taking flight, they can't jump off the water's surface and get airborne as quickly as a dabbling duck. Instead, they have to "run" along the water's surface before taking flight. Another reliable distinguisher is that they lack the iridescent speculum, or colored wing patch, that typifies dabbling ducks. In addition to aquatic vegetation (more or less, or none, depending on the species), they feed on fish and a wide variety of invertebrates such as mollusks, aquatic insects, marine worms, and freshwater shrimp.

There are about twenty species of diving ducks in North America, and many hunters are content to use that single classification for all of them. But guys who really geek out on waterfowl will readily draw a distinction between diving ducks and sea ducks. They'll tell you that the "diving duck" classification should be limited to a tribe of birds known as the pochards. These include the most popular of the diving ducks: canvasbacks, redheads, ringnecks, and scaups (both greater and lesser). The sea duck category contains a lot of birds that most hunters will never encounter, such as king eiders, harlequins, and long-tailed ducks. Some other sea ducks such as buffleheads and goldeneyes are quite common on interior freshwater waterways.

And then there are the geese. For convenience's sake, these are broken into classifications of light-colored and dark-colored. Dark-colored geese include brants, white-fronted geese, and the lookalike Canada geese and cackling geese. (If you really want to get confused, you might investigate the process by which taxonomists condensed dozens of species of "white-cheeked geese" down into a handful of Canada and cackling subspecies.) The light-colored geese include greater snow geese, lesser snow geese, and Ross's geese. These vary in size, but it takes a trained eye to tell them apart.

Finally, you've got a handful of birds that are considered to be waterfowl species, which aren't actually ducks or geese. These range from the sandhill crane, which has the most highly esteemed meat of all waterfowl, down to the American coot, which has perhaps the lowest.

In addition to the huge variety of waterfowl species out there, there's a lot of variability within species. The quality of a duck has a lot to do with where it's from and what it's been up to. A mallard that's been fattening itself in the grain fields of southern Illinois for two months is going to be one of the very best ducks you'll ever eat. A mallard that was born and raised on the tidal flats of southeast Alaska, where it eats crustaceans and salmon eggs, will seem like an entirely different creature. Anyone who takes up the challenge of hunting and cooking waterfowl in its many forms will encounter tastes and textures known only to a very small fraction of the world's citizens. There is no commercially available product that comes anywhere close to, say, a bufflehead or a sandhill crane, so a wild game cook who wants to get serious about cooking such birds is headed into unfamiliar territory.

Thankfully, you don't need to head into this strange land without a map. There are countless little secrets when it comes to handling waterfowl—how to remove tendons from the legs, how to burn off pin feathers, how to get a nice crispy skin on roasted ducks, what to do with the hearts and livers, how to perfectly butcher a puddle duck—that can add up to make the difference between merely acceptable dishes and dishes you'd serve to impress your future in-laws. Get out on the water with your shotgun and have a good day. Then come back inside and open this book.

THE NATURE OF THE BEAST

Dabbling Ducks

In general, this is the best category of ducks with regard to tablefare. Dabbling ducks are mild and tender. The fat and skin on dabbling ducks is usually very good. Exceptions occur when they are feeding heavily on animal matter, such as when mallards feed on salmon eggs or aquatic invertebrates, but cases like that occur only in isolated situations.

Teal (green wing, blue wing, and cinnamon teal) are small birds, but some of the best. They have delicate, relatively light-colored flesh and are suitable for many applications.

Wood ducks sometimes eat a diet similar to deer and squirrels, as they like to walk from the water into hardwood forests to feed on acorns, beechnuts, and other mast crops. They'll even eat berries. These ducks are superb.

Mallards, pintails, and **black ducks** are large and excellent, especially when fat. If you don't like these, you don't like ducks. They are good for anything that can be done with ducks.

American wigeons and **gadwalls** are not as highly esteemed as mallards and pintails, though most people would be hard-pressed to distinguish a nice fat wigeon from a nice fat mallard. They are mild, flavorful, with good fat.

Northern shovelers are the least tasty of the dabbling ducks. They eat a higher proportion of animal matter (mollusks, insects, crustaceans) than other dabblers. Their flesh suffers because of it. This is the one puddle duck whose skin you'll probably want to discard before cooking.

Diving Ducks

A common complaint about some species of diving ducks is that they have a powerful, sometimes "fishy" taste. When present, these off-putting flavors are concentrated largely in the skin and fat. A good rule of thumb when preparing diving ducks is to discard the skin and fat and use only the meat. The pochards (canvasbacks, redheads, ring-necked ducks, and scaup) are usually an exception to this rule. Their fat can be delicious.

Canvasbacks, redheads, ring-necked ducks, and **scaup** (both greater and lesser) are the best-tasting of the diving ducks. These are sizable birds with mild flesh that can be used for many applications, though you still might want to discard the skin and fat. Taxonomically, these species are classified as pochards. You'll notice that the skin of pochards peels away much more easily than it does with other diving ducks, though it's not always necessary to skin them. Try one with the skin first; if it's fishy, discard the skin on the rest of your haul.

Scoters (black, surf, and white-winged) stand out as another exception among the diving ducks, though not as remarkable an exception as the pochards. My friend Brandt has eaten more diving ducks than most people have seen, and he's insistent that their flesh is milder and more tender than most divers. Discard the skin and fat.

Buffleheads and **goldeneyes** (both common and Barrow's) are representative of diving ducks as a whole. You're not going to throw a breast on the grill and serve it rare with a pinch of salt, as you would with a fattened mallard, but there are still plenty of things that you can do with them: curries, stir-fries, jerky, slow-cooked recipes. Just make sure that you're adding some flavor and avoiding the use of the skin and fat.

Mergansers, both common and hooded, are hotly debated birds. Hunters like to argue about whether or not they're actually edible. If you peel away the skin and use them for a heavily seasoned dish like gumbo, you probably won't be able to tell them apart from many species of diving ducks.

Geese

Goose meat has as much in common with red meat as it does with duck. It's beefy, deep red, and very good if properly handled. Geese are best when they're well fed and fatty. A goose that's been migrating long distances in harsh conditions, with little food, might be poor in quality with lean breasts.

Canada geese are by far the most widely hunted species of geese. Fattened on green grass and agricultural crops, a Canada goose breast is on par with a quality steak. Geese that are feeding in saltwater estuaries sometimes consume enough animal matter (aquatic invertebrates, fish eggs, and so on) to give their meat a strong, sometimes fishy flavor. Discarding the skin and fat on these geese is helpful.

White-fronted geese, or specklebelly geese, are regarded by many as the finest-tasting of all geese.

Snow geese are not as highly esteemed as Canada geese and white-fronted geese. Many are killed along migration routes when the birds have exhausted their fat reserves and their flesh is a bit lean and tough. However, a fat snow goose is as good as a fat Canada goose, only smaller, so don't let the negative hype fool you. Any snow goose is worth your effort and deserves to be handled properly.

Cranes

Sandhill cranes are the best of the best. A crane breast is like some kind of magical fork-tender steak; if you get your hands on one, cherish it.

NO GUTS, NO GLORY: PUTTING BIRD ORGANS TO USE

You're depriving yourself if you're not retaining giblets from your waterfowl and upland birds. You can make a number of tasty concoctions from these gems, including rich pâtés, aesthetically pleasing heart skewers, and crowd-pleasing jars of what my brother and I lovingly refer to as "gib pickles." By giblets, or course, we're referring to three internal organs that you'll find when you gut your birds: the liver, heart, and gizzard. (See photograph on this page of cleaned wild turkey liver, heart, and gizzard.) These occupy the extremes on a spectrum of hardiness. The liver is so fragile that a hasty gutting job can mash it to smithereens, while the gizzard, or gastric mill, is tough enough that it would seem appropriate for industrial applications. A gizzard's toughness makes sense when you consider the job that it performs. It's part of the bird's digestive tract. The bird swallows gravel, or "grit," and this goes into the gizzard. When food passes into the gizzard, the muscle churns it together with the grit and pulverizes it into a digestible mush. Think of it as what happens when you chew, except that the gizzard acts as your jaw muscle and the grit acts as your teeth.

Because of the anatomy of a bird, the gutting incision is made down near the vent, while the organs are hidden behind the breastbone—you never actually see the organs *in situ*. Everything must be done by feel. After making your cut, which runs from the vent up to the point of the breastbone, slip your fingers inside and feel around for the smooth and silky liver. Draw this out first, or else you'll end up with a mashed and segmented mess. (You might end up pulverizing it later for a pâté or mousse, but it's easier to handle and it's much prettier in its pristine state.)

Once you get the liver free, you can reach all way up into the cavity and pull out the heart and gizzard. All you need to do is give the heart a light rinse to wash away any coagulated blood. Any bird from a dove up to a mallard has a small enough heart that you can prepare it as one bite-size piece. Bigger than a mallard and you'll probably want to halve it. Bigger than a goose and you'll want to quarter it.

Gizzards take a bit more work. Start out by using ternal pouch containing the gravel and food has a tough, slightly abrasive liner. Depending on the bird species, you can either peel this liner away by hand or else you'll have to slice it away. On smaller birds, that's all that needs to happen. The gizzard is now recipe-ready. On larger birds, say anything from a Canada goose up to a turkey, you'll want to slice away the outer wall that the abrasive liner is connected to. You'll end up with four matching quarters that are rubbery, beautiful, and rich with promise.

I generally eat my bird livers fresh, either sautéed in butter and splashed with a bit of brandy, tossed into stuffing, or whipped into a mousse. Hearts and gizzards are more resilient and can be stored away for later use. I freeze mine in water. At the beginning of hunting season, when I kill my first birds, I'll take a two-liter soda bottle and cut away the upper, tapered portion. I toss whatever giblets I've got into the bottle, cover them with water, and place it in the freezer. Then, as the season progresses, I'll keep adding layers of giblets and water

GUTTING A DUCK AND CLEANING GIZZARD

7

8

9

It is always a good idea to gut upland game birds and waterfowl in the field, soon after they've been killed. This allows the carcass to begin cooling and the hunter to properly clean out the gut cavity. The gutting process is the same whether you're dealing with a small quail or a large goose.

1. Start by making a small incision below the lower end of the breastbone—you can pluck the feathers here to make this area more visible. Continue making a shallow cut through the skin of the gut cavity down to the cloaca (anus).

2. Use your finger to open up this cut to expose the innards. Reach into the gut cavity with your fingers. You want to reach past the digestive organs until you feel the top of the chest cavity.

3. Now begin scooping downward and outward. You will feel the organs in the chest cavity pull free. Continue pulling. All of the guts should come out in one package.

4. Separate the heart, liver, and gizzard from the rest of the guts. The gizzard is a large, purplish, oval-shaped, muscular organ that pulverizes a game bird's food.

5. You'll need to cut the gizzard from the digestive system.

6. Slice down the middle of the gizzard lengthwise.

7. Now open up the gizzard and remove any bits of food and grit. You'll see a thin, light-colored layer of tissue that lines the interior of the gizzard.

8. Peel away the interior lining of the gizzard.

9. Take the time to wash the gut cavity and edible organs.

PLUCKING A DUCK

1

2

3

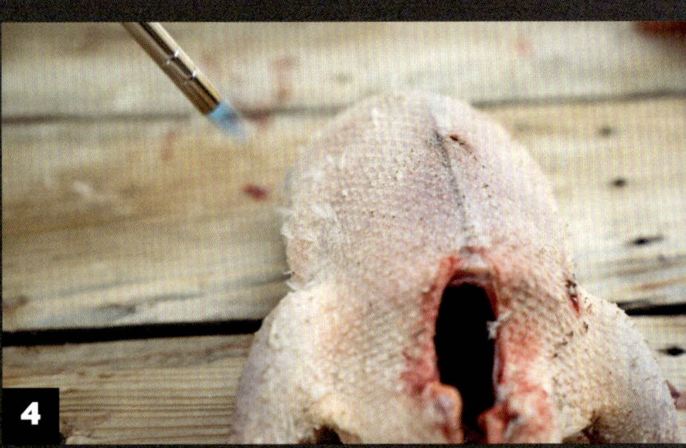

4

Too many hunters don't take the time to pluck waterfowl and upland game birds. This is a huge mistake and a mortal sin according to author Jim Harrison. Plucking is a somewhat tedious job, but eating a whole, plucked bird with crispy skin and moist, tender meat makes it worth the time and effort involved.

1. Start by plucking the larger breast feathers just below the neck. Work with grain methodically downward and be careful to avoid tearing the skin. Once you have the larger feathers plucked, go back and pluck the smaller, downy feathers that remain attached to the skin. Also pluck any small replacement feathers that are still embedded in the skin.

2. After you've plucked the breast, move on to the wings, legs, and back. These feathers are well-anchored and easier to pluck against the grain. Use a pair of game shears to cut the lower legs and wings from the carcass.

3. Now you have a plucked bird with only small, hair-like pin feathers remaining attached to the skin.

4. The easiest way to quickly remove these tiny feathers is with a handheld propane torch. Pass the flame lightly over the skin without burning it. This will quickly singe the remaining feathers away. You may need to use a toothpick to remove any shot or feathers stuck under the skin. The end result should be able to pass for a store-bought chicken, albeit one sporting a few pellet holes.

HOW TO PULL TENDONS OUT OF A DUCK LEG

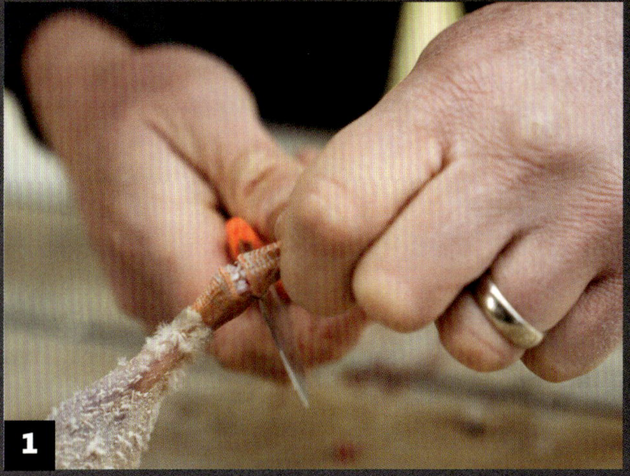

1

2

3

1. Removing the leg tendons from ducks and other game birds makes an otherwise tough piece of meat more tender. Start by making a shallow cut around the circumference of the lower leg joint.

2. Now bend the leg joint backward in the opposite direction it would normally move until it pops.

3. Slowly twist and pull the lower leg away from the upper leg. With a little effort, the tendons will slide out of the muscle. With the stringy tendons removed, you won't wear out your jaw muscles chewing on tough game bird legs.

REMOVING BREAST WITH LEG ATTACHED (SKIN-ON)

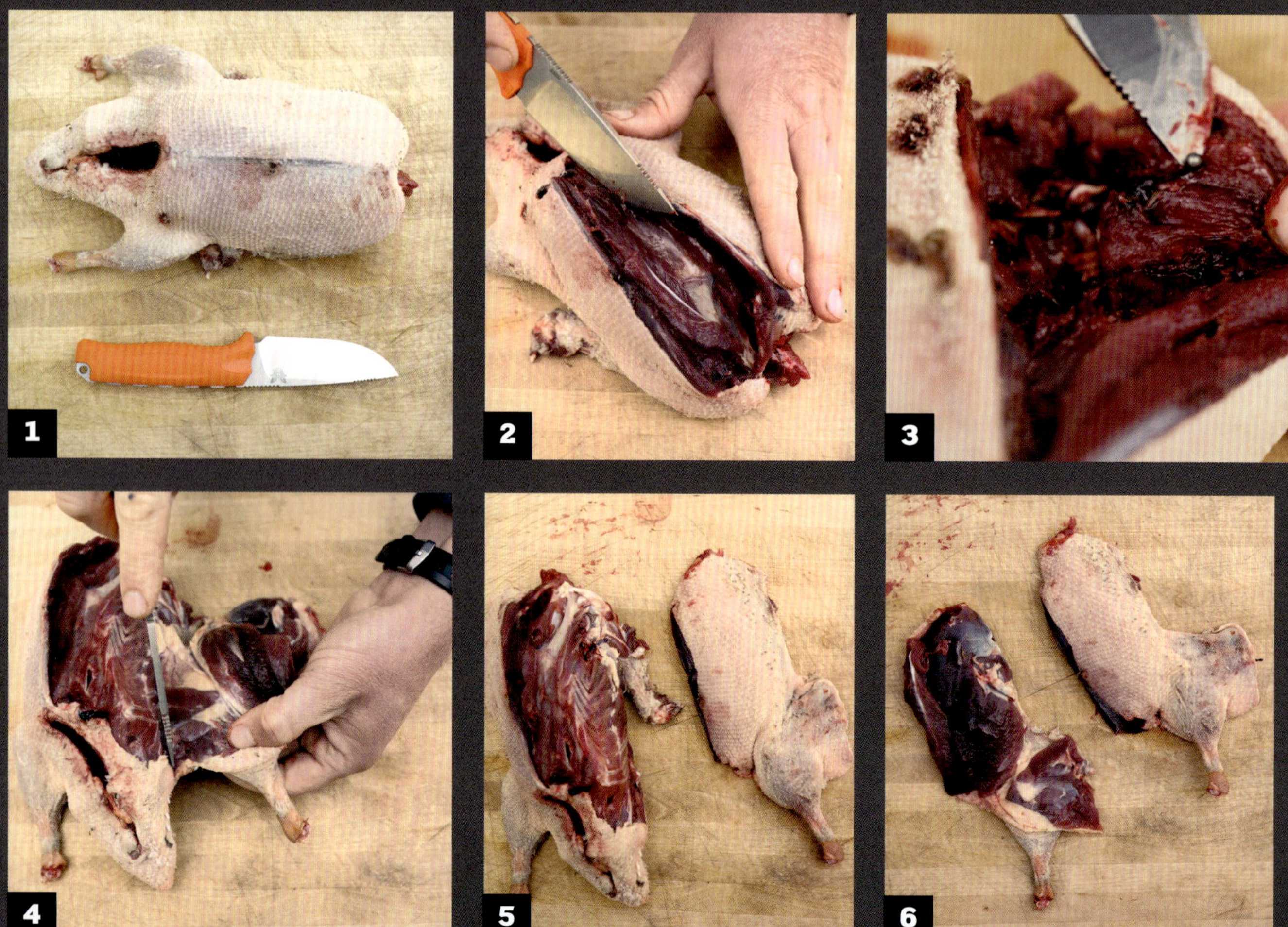

1. Leaving skin-on breasts and legs attached to each other makes for a great presentation, and the fatty skin keeps the meat moist during cooking. Start with a clean gutted and plucked duck.

2. Make your first cut through the skin and muscle parallel to the breastbone.

3. As you cut, watch for pellets or feathers embedded in the meat and remove them along with any bloodshot meat.

4. Continue to separate the breast from the chest cavity, stopping short of removing it completely from the carcass. Where the thigh muscle joins the body, find the hip's ball joint. Cut through this and the upper thigh muscle to separate the leg from the carcass.

5. Now cut through the skin along the rear and back to remove the breast and leg in one piece.

6. Next, repeat the process on the other side of the duck. This cut is ideal for grilling or searing and then finishing in the oven.

REMOVING SKINLESS BREAST FILLETS

1

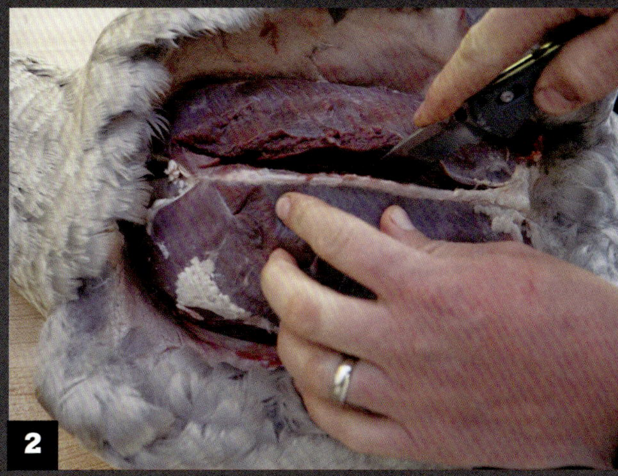
2

3

4

Removing skinless, boneless breasts from most geese, puddle ducks, and upland game birds is quick and easy.

1. Start by making a shallow cut through the skin on top of the breast. Now use your hands to peel the skin completely back from both sides of the breast. Birds that have been allowed to freeze are much harder to skin once they've been thawed out. The skin from some diver and sea duck species can be difficult to peel away, but since the skin can have a strong, fishy taste, it should be removed before cooking.

2. Cut along the bone that runs down the center of the breast to begin removing one side.

3. Now fillet the entire boneless breast off the underlying bones of the breast plate.

4. Repeat the process on the other side, and don't forget to save the legs.

WATERFOWL
LIVER PÂTÉ
PAGE 123
WILD GOOSE PASTRAMI
PAGE 128
BRANDIED CHERRIES
PAGE 318
GAME BIRD TERRINE
PAGE 159
VENISON
LIVER MOUSSE
PAGE 30
TEA-SMOKED
DUCK BREASTS
PAGE 134
SPICY PICKLED
RED ONIONS
PAGE 318
SEARED TONGUE
PAGE 36

WATERFOWL LIVER PÂTÉ

SERVES 6 TO 8 AS AN APPETIZER (MAKES 2 CUPS)

While I do freeze waterfowl livers, I'll admit that it comes at a cost. They are delicate organs, and freezing them changes the texture and consistency in a noticeable way. However, freezing livers is often necessary if you're trying to save up enough to do something major with them. By major, I'm talking about preparation like this waterfowl pâté, which requires a pound of livers. You and your buddies might get enough livers in a single day of hunting if everything falls into place, but it's more likely that you'll have to accumulate the livers over the course of a few outings. This recipe is similar to the Venison Liver Mousse (page 30) in that it uses the classic French technique of hard-boiled eggs as an emulsifier. But the flavor profile here is decidedly different. The orange, anchovies, and thyme make it lively and zesty.

ALSO WORKS WITH: Try this with livers from any upland birds or waterfowl. If you don't have a full pint in your freezer, substitute the remainder with chicken livers.

---

1 orange

¼ cup (½ stick) unsalted butter

1 large shallot, thinly sliced (about ⅓ cup)

1 pound goose livers (about 1 pint)

2 fresh thyme sprigs

2 anchovy fillets

2 cloves garlic, smashed

1 bay leaf

Pinch of red chile flakes (optional)

1 large hard-boiled egg, peeled

Kosher salt

Freshly ground black pepper

¼ cup brandy or bourbon

Baguette slices or saltines, for serving

Capers, for serving

SPECIAL EQUIPMENT NEEDED:
food processor

Remove 3 strips of zest from the orange with a peeler. Save the partially zested orange for another use.

Heat the butter in a large sauté pan over medium heat. Add the shallot and cook until translucent, 3 to 5 minutes. Add the livers, orange zest, thyme, anchovies, garlic, bay leaf, red chile flakes, and the whole hard-boiled egg. Sprinkle with a generous pinch of salt and pepper and cook until the livers are just cooked through (you will notice that blood will begin to appear on the surface of the liver), about 4 minutes. It's OK if they are a little pink in the middle. Remove the pan from the heat and pour in the brandy. Return the pan to the heat, step back, and carefully tip it away from you slightly so the brandy ignites. Let the alcohol cook off for about 1 minute, gently shaking the pan every few seconds. Toss to coat well. Remove from the heat. Discard the orange zest, garlic, bay leaf, and thyme. Cut the hard-boiled egg into quarters.

Transfer the livers, egg, and shallot to a food processor and process until smooth. Taste and season with salt and pepper as needed.

Serve on baguette slices or saltines with capers as an accompaniment.

See the photograph of pâté on charcuterie spread on page 122.

SKEWERED AND GRILLED DUCK HEARTS
AND GRAPES AND WALNUT PESTO

MAKES 6 HEARTS

2 tablespoons balsamic vinegar

2 tablespoons extra virgin olive oil

Leaves from 2 small sprigs fresh rosemary

Leaves from 2 sprigs fresh thyme

2 bay leaves

1 clove garlic, smashed

½ pound duck hearts, cleaned (about 6 hearts)

Small bunch of grapes (on stem)

Kosher salt

Freshly ground black pepper

Lightly grilled baguette slices

Walnut and Mint Pesto (page 320)

SPECIAL EQUIPMENT:
wooden skewers (optional)

First off, this dish is visually stunning. The grilled hearts and grapes come together like a work of art. There are interesting flavors and textures here as well. The hearts are little firecrackers of meaty flavor, and the experience of having a warm, smoke-flavored grape burst inside your mouth will forever change your impressions of this fruit. You can make this dish on a gas or charcoal grill, but I highly recommend an open fire. Start the blaze an hour or so ahead of time. When you're ready to cook, use a small shovel to build an off-to-the-side bed of embers and position your grilling rack above it. Keep the fire burning and add additional embers as needed. Plan on at least two or three hearts per person.

ALSO WORKS WITH: Try this with hearts from any upland game birds or waterfowl. If you're using Canada geese hearts, cut them in half lengthwise. For a wild turkey's heart, you'll want to quarter it. This recipe also works well with hearts from big game animals, though you'll have to treat them like kabobs, cubing a larger heart into 1-inch pieces then skewering as directed in the recipe.

If using wooden skewers, soak them in water to cover for at least 30 minutes to prevent them from burning.

Combine the vinegar, oil, rosemary, thyme, bay leaves, and garlic in a wide shallow bowl. Transfer half of the marinade to a resealable plastic bag, add the duck hearts, toss around to coat, then marinate in the refrigerator for 2 to 3 hours.

Heat a grill over high heat. Gently toss the bunch of grapes in the bowl of reserved marinade to coat. Sprinkle the grapes with salt and pepper, then grill, covered, turning occasionally, until slightly charred in spots, about 5 minutes. Return to the bowl of marinade until ready to serve.

Remove the duck hearts from the marinade, place them on skewers, if using, then sprinkle generously with salt and pepper. Grill the hearts, covered, until desired doneness, 4 to 5 minutes for medium-rare, turning halfway through. Serve with the grapes, baguette, and walnut pesto.

Note: You can skewer the grapes as well, as in this image. If they are clinging tightly to their bunch, try to grill them whole; it makes for a dramatic presentation.

GRILLED DUCK NACHOS

MAKES ONE 9 X 13-INCH PAN (SERVES A CROWD AS APPETIZERS)

Like most Americans, I spent the better part of my life making nachos with ground meat. I did it that way because . . . well, it's just the way that people always did it. This preparation gets away from that by using grilled, thinly sliced duck breast for the protein. I almost hate to mention this, because I don't want to dissuade you from making this recipe, but you might end up liking the grilled duck so much that you skip the tortilla chips on your next go-around and just use the duck as a main course with some grilled veggies on the side. When cooking with duck breasts, make sure not to forget about the rest of the bird. Use the legs and the wing bones to make a stock, or you can braise them down and shred the meat for all manner of uses (see the Red Curry Duck recipe on page 132). You can even take the shredded meat and toss it in some oil, then fry it until it's crispy and add it to your nachos.

DUCK

2 pounds duck breasts

1 tablespoon finely ground coffee beans

2 teaspoons kosher salt

2 teaspoons packed brown sugar

½ teaspoon garlic powder

½ teaspoon onion powder

¼ teaspoon cayenne pepper

¼ teaspoon ground cinnamon

NACHOS

Zest and juice of 1 large lime

16 ounces sour cream

6 ounces restaurant-style tortilla chips

1 (15-ounce) can black beans, rinsed well and drained

1 pound shredded Monterey Jack or Mexican-style blend cheese

2 large jalapeños or red Fresno chiles, thinly sliced

Thinly sliced scallions, for garnish

Fresh cilantro leaves, for garnish

Salsa, for serving (pico de gallo shown in photograph)

Prepare a gas grill over medium heat.

FOR THE DUCK: Score the skin of the breasts in a crosshatch pattern without cutting into the meat. Combine the coffee, salt, brown sugar, garlic powder, onion powder, cayenne, and cinnamon in a small bowl. Rub the coffee mixture all over the duck. Grill the duck skin-side down, covered, until the skin has rendered its fat and is charred in spots. (The more fat your duck has, the longer this will take, but a thin-skinned duck should only take about 4 minutes.) Flip the breasts over and grill until desired doneness (127°F on an instant-read thermometer for medium-rare, 130 to 135°F for medium). Transfer to a cutting board skin-side up and let rest for 5 to 10 minutes. Cut in half lengthwise, then thinly slice crosswise into short strips.

FOR THE NACHOS: Mix the lime zest into the sour cream in a small bowl. Spread half of the chips on the bottom of double layered 9½ x 13½-inch disposable foil lasagna tray, or a metal cake pan of similar dimensions. Top with half of the duck, beans, cheese, and jalapeños. Repeat the layering with the remaining chips, duck, beans, and cheese, holding back the remaining jalapeños. Grill, covered, until the cheese is melted, 10 to 15 minutes. Remove from the grill and top with the remaining jalapeños, scallions, and cilantro. Serve with the lime sour cream and salsa.

ALSO WORKS WITH: As is, this recipe is intended for dabbler duck species such as mallards, wood ducks, pintails, and teal, which are largely vegetarian. If you intend to use a diver duck species, which eats a lot more fish and invertebrates, make sure to discard the skin.

WILD GOOSE PASTRAMI

SERVES 4 TO 6

CURE

¼ cup Morton's Tender Quick

¼ cup freshly ground black pepper

¼ cup packed dark brown sugar

2 tablespoons granulated garlic

2 teaspoons ground coriander

2 teaspoons onion powder

2 teaspoons dried thyme

RUB

3 tablespoons freshly ground black pepper

1 teaspoon ground coriander

1 teaspoon granulated garlic

½ teaspoon onion powder

½ teaspoon smoked paprika

½ teaspoon dried thyme

GOOSE

2 goose breasts (about 1 pound each)

Mustard and pickles, for serving

SPECIAL EQUIPMENT NEEDED:
smoker or grill outfitted for smoking

With populations of snow geese and Canada geese at near record-high levels, pastrami is a goose hunter's best friend. This is a great way to get through a big haul of birds and turn them into something that your friends and family will be begging you to share. We've done as many as ten geese like this in a single batch. They're best served fresh out of the smoker alongside some good seedy mustard, bread-and-butter pickles, and maybe a handful of mixed greens tossed with a vinaigrette. After that initial serving, you can start piling leftovers into sandwiches. Keep in mind, too, that you can freeze your finished product. Just slip a breast or two into a vacuum-sealed bag and freeze it for up to a few months. The frozen pastramis are a good option for overnight hunting and fishing trips when you need a simple meal plan. Even if you don't have the time or gear needed to warm them up, you can just thaw them out and eat 'em at room temperature. If "room temperature" is below freezing, tuck one into the pocket of your down jacket for a few hours. For a photograph of the finished goose pastrami, see the charcuterie spread on page 122.

ALSO WORKS WITH: This recipe is tailored for wild geese, though sandhill cranes are going to taste even better if you have access to them. You can also make pastrami out of your big game animals. Elk and moose briskets work great, or you can use whole muscle roasts from deer or bear. Start with a 1- to 2-pound roast and go from there. See the note opposite for alternate curing/smoking times for big game.

FOR THE CURE: Mix the Morton's Tender Quick, pepper, brown sugar, granulated garlic, coriander, onion powder, and thyme in a small bowl.

FOR THE RUB: Mix the pepper, coriander, granulated garlic, onion powder, paprika, and thyme in a small bowl.

FOR THE GOOSE: Rub the goose breasts heavily with the cure, making sure to cover the whole piece of meat. Place in a resealable bag and add the remaining cure on top of the meat. Remove as much air as possible from the bag and refrigerate for 3 days. Flip the bag once each day. After 3 days, remove the meat from the bag and rinse it thoroughly. Soak the goose breasts in cold water for 30 to 45 minutes to remove all the cure. Remove the goose from the water and pat dry with paper towels.

Rub the goose breasts with the spice rub on all sides. Prepare a smoker with fruit wood to 225°F and place the breasts skin-side down on the smoker racks. Smoke until the internal temperature reaches 150°F, 1½ to 3 hours. Rest for 10 minutes. Slice the meat against the grain. Serve with your favorite mustard and pickles.

The pastrami will keep in the refrigerator for up to 2 weeks, or freeze in vacuum-sealed bags for up to 6 months. To reheat after refrigerating, slice very thinly across the grain and put the meat into a very hot sauté pan. Toss a few times to start to release the fat, about 1 minute, and then add ¼ cup water and cover for another minute to minute and a half, tossing a few times. This steam method keeps the meat moist and allows the flavors of the crust to coat the entire slice of meat.

Note: To make the pastrami with a venison roast or large brisket, rub the meat heavily with the cure, making sure to cover the entire brisket. Place the brisket in a resealable bag and add the remaining rub on top of the meat. Refrigerate for 4 days. Flip the bag once every day. After 4 days, remove the meat from the bag and rinse it thoroughly. Soak the brisket in cold water for 30 to 45 minutes to remove all the cure. Remove the brisket from the water and pat dry with paper towels. Rub the entire brisket with the spice rub. Prepare a smoker to 225°F and smoke the meat until fork tender, or to an internal temperature of 170°F, about 5 hours. Let the meat rest for 10 minutes. Slice the meat against the grain. Serve with your favorite mustard and pickles.

SOY SAUCE DUCK

SERVES 2

I love the look of a wild duck that's been cooked whole. It has a primal beauty, and every time I see one I want to rush for my carving knife. The problem is that they aren't always as good as they look. There are big differences between the breast meat and the leg meat on a wild duck. While the breasts are tender, moist, and best served rare, the legs can be rubbery and require a lot of cooking in order to tenderize them. Because of this discrepancy, you often end up with perfect legs and a breast that's dry and overdone or else a perfect breast and legs that are nearly impossible to eat. This recipe helps address that conundrum because the bird is submerged in liquid and simmered at a relatively low temperature. This prevents the breast from getting dried out too quickly while still allowing the legs plenty of time to get the heat that they deserve. The finished product is sweet and salty. Try this on folks who say they don't like wild ducks. This will change them for the better.

Remove the duck from the refrigerator about 1 hour before cooking.

Heat the oil in a tall 10-quart stockpot over medium heat. Add the ginger slices and cook, stirring, for 30 seconds. Add the garlic and scallions and cook, stirring, for another 30 seconds. Carefully add the wine, then the star anise and cinnamon. Bring to a simmer and cook for about 1 minute. Add both soy sauces, the brown sugar, orange zest, and water. Bring to a boil, then reduce the heat and simmer for about 30 minutes.

Add the duck to the pot breast-side down. Maneuver the duck so that the soy sauce mixture enters the cavity of the duck. Bring to a simmer and cook for 25 minutes, basting the top of the duck that is not submerged. (It can help to weight down the bird with a plate or small pot lid.) Immediately remove from the heat, cover, and steep the duck in the soy sauce basting liquid for 1 hour.

Remove the duck and transfer to a cutting board. When cool to the touch, proceed to carve. Serve with the ginger-scallion oil, additional sauce from the pot, and a side of rice.

1 whole mallard, pintail, or other large wild duck

1 tablespoon vegetable oil

7 thin slices ginger

2 cloves garlic, smashed

2 scallions, cut into 2-inch pieces

1½ cups Shaoxing wine

5 star anise pods

2 cinnamon sticks

1½ cups dark soy sauce

1½ cups light soy sauce

1 cup packed dark brown sugar

5 strips orange zest

10 cups water

Ginger-Scallion Oil (recipe follows)

Cooked rice, for serving

ALSO WORKS WITH: Stick with dabbler ducks on this one. Diver ducks usually need to be skinned before cooking them, and you want the skin intact for this. See page 112 for more information. Getting your portions right with wild ducks can be tricky. A large dabbler such as a mallard is plenty of meat for two people. Wood ducks, which run a bit smaller, fall in the middle; bigger appetites will eat the whole bird, smaller appetites will want to share. With teal, a single person might want one or two birds for themselves. This recipe is intended for ducks on the larger end of the spectrum, such as mallards, though it should be little problem for you to make adjustments to accommodate smaller birds.

Tip: The soy sauce basting liquid can be stored in the freezer and used over again; it's considered a master sauce that turns richer with each use. When the liquid has cooled, strain and transfer to airtight containers and store in the freezer. Add a fresh batch of ingredients when using again, plus more water if necessary.

GINGER-SCALLION OIL

MAKES ⅓ CUP

Heat the oil in a small saucepan or skillet over low heat. Add the ginger, scallion, and salt and cook for 5 minutes. Transfer to a heatproof dish and allow to cool before serving. The oil can be made a day ahead and stored in the refrigerator.

½ cup vegetable oil

1-inch piece ginger, finely chopped (about 1 tablespoon)

1 large scallion, finely chopped (about ¼ cup)

1 teaspoon kosher salt

RED CURRY DUCK

SERVES 4 TO 6

Admittedly, wild duck legs are a lot harder to deal with than the breasts. There's a lot of tendon and bone inside a leg, so the ratio of edible to non-edible meat is pretty low. And the meat that is there, at least on a roasted bird, can be tough enough to resist your best efforts at chewing. That's why many of my favorite recipes for duck legs begin with slow-cooking them until the meat is tender enough to be picked off the bone. Once that's taken care of, you have something magical on your hands. There are a hundred things that you can do with it, though this red curry recipe belongs at the top of the list.

BRAISED LEGS

1½ pounds duck and/or goose legs (roughly 18 to 22 legs), skin removed

1 onion, halved

4 cloves garlic

1-inch piece ginger, peeled, sliced into coins, and smashed

5 fresh cilantro stems

1 quart Blonde Game Stock (page 306) or low-sodium chicken broth

RED CURRY

2 tablespoons vegetable oil

2 cups fresh pineapple chunks

1 cup grape or cherry tomatoes

2 (14-ounce) cans unstirred full-fat coconut milk, chilled

4 to 6 tablespoons red curry paste

2 tablespoons fish sauce, plus more for serving

1 tablespoon brown sugar

1 medium eggplant, cut into 1-inch pieces

1 cup fresh Thai basil leaves, plus more for garnish

Hot steamed white rice, for serving

Lime wedges, for serving

Sliced Thai or serrano chiles, for garnish (optional)

Fresh cilantro leaves, for garnish

ALSO WORKS WITH: Use the skinless legs from any waterfowl, including geese. After cooking, finely mince the skin and add it back into the shredded meat. When using diver ducks, discard the skin before cooking. Use already cooked, leftover duck.

FOR THE BRAISED LEGS: Combine the duck and/or goose legs, onion, garlic, ginger, and cilantro stems in 6-quart saucepan. Add enough stock to just barely cover the meat. Bring to a boil over high heat, skimming and discarding any foam that may rise to the top. Reduce the heat to low, cover, and simmer until the leg meat is very tender but not yet falling off the bone, about 2 hours and 40 minutes.

Remove the meat to a plate. Strain the cooking liquid and discard the solids. Measure out 1½ cups of the liquid and discard the rest or reserve for another use.

FOR THE RED CURRY: Place an empty pot over medium-high heat and add the oil. Add the pineapple. Cook, stirring once or twice, until browned in some spots, about 3 minutes. Transfer the pineapple to a separate plate. Add the tomatoes and cook, stirring occasionally, until the skins start to split, about 2 minutes. Add the tomatoes to the pineapple.

Skim the thick coconut cream from the tops of the coconut milk and add to the pot along with the curry paste. Bring to a simmer, stirring often and scraping the browned bits from the bottom, about 2 minutes. Add the remaining coconut milk, the reserved braising liquid, the fish sauce, and the brown sugar. If the curry broth is too thin, reduce at a simmer to thicken it slightly. Add the eggplant and continue to simmer until the eggplant is tender, 10 to 15 minutes.

Shred the duck into bite-size pieces. Stir in the duck, pineapple, tomatoes, and basil and cook until warmed through, 3 to 5 minutes. Adjust the seasonings by adding a little extra fish sauce or salt as needed.

Serve over rice, with lime wedges and a garnish of chiles, if using, cilantro, and torn basil leaves.

ROAST DUCK
WITH POMEGRANATE GLAZE

SERVES 2

I mention in the introduction to this chapter that my love affair with eating wild ducks began with the oven-roasted woodies that my mom prepared when I was a kid. She stuffed the birds with raisins and chopped apples and cooked them hot and fast. They were simple and nearly perfect. The one drawback was that the fruit stuffing was locked up inside the chest cavity and the flavors never fully integrated with the meat. This recipe helps correct that, because here the fruit is paired more aggressively with the meat as a glaze of pomegranate molasses. The carved meat is then garnished with pomegranate seeds as a fun and surprising accompaniment. The key here, as with all roasted ducks, is not to overcook the bird. You want to hit that sweet spot where the legs are cooked through and the breast is still moist. Have a meat thermometer on hand in order to hit your preferred temperature without going over.

1 whole duck

½ cup extra virgin olive oil, if needed

Kosher salt

Freshly ground black pepper

1 small onion, quartered

1 bay leaf

¼ cup pomegranate molasses (see Tip below on making your own corn syrup)

Pomegranate seeds, for garnish

Rinse the duck inside and out with cold water, then pat dry with paper towels. Place the duck on a wire rack and refrigerate, uncovered, for 8 to 24 hours (this air-drying helps to crisp the skin but can be skipped).

Preheat the oven to 425°F. Line a roasting pan with foil. Bring the duck to room temperature.

If your duck strikes you as being a fatty specimen, do not bother brushing it with oil. But if the layer of fat looks thin (I know, this requires some guesswork, but do your best), then you'll want to rub it with a thin layer of oil. Sprinkle the duck generously with salt and pepper, including the cavity. Stuff the cavity with the onion and bay leaf. Put the duck on a wire rack and place over the prepared roasting pan.

Roast until an instant-read thermometer inserted lengthwise along the breastbone (the thickest part of the breast) registers 127°F for medium-rare or 130 to 135°F for medium.

Raise the oven temperature to 450°F. If fat has accumulated on the bottom of your pan, carefully pour it off and reserve it for another use, if you like. Baste the duck with oil. Return to the oven and roast until the skin is crisp and golden, 5 to 10 minutes. Brush the pomegranate molasses all over the duck several times while the duck rests, about 10 minutes. Discard the onion and bay leaf. Carve the duck and transfer to a platter. Sprinkle pomegranate seeds over the top.

ALSO WORKS WITH: Whole roasted geese (Canada, speckled, brants, etc.) are great. You'll have to adjust your cooking time (longer, obviously) and you'll likely have to pour off some rendered oil mid-process if it's a fatty goose. As for ducks, stick with dabblers or the pochard species. See page 112 for more information. Getting your portions right with wild ducks can be tricky. A large dabbler such as a mallard is plenty of meat for two people. Wood ducks, which run a bit smaller, fall in the middle; bigger appetites will eat the whole bird, smaller appetites will want to share. With teal, a single person might want one or two birds for themselves. This recipe is intended for ducks on the larger end of the spectrum, such as mallards, though you should be able to make adjustments to easily accommodate smaller birds.

Tip: You can make your own pomegranate glaze by reducing (simmering) pomegranate juice down to a syrup, adding sugar if necessary.

TEA-SMOKED DUCK BREASTS
WITH BLUEBERRY PORT COMPOTE

SERVES 3 TO 4

The genius of this recipe is that it brings together three things that combine into something magical: duck breasts, smoke, and chutney. Instead of traditional smoking fuels of fruitwood or hardwood, the breasts are treated to a gentler and more aromatic smoke from tea, cinnamon, and star anise. Don't worry, you do not need an outdoor smoker or smokehouse to pull this recipe off. You can do it on a conventional stovetop burner right in your kitchen, or else on a simple outdoor barbecue grill. The compote here captures some of the same flavors as the smoke, along with a bit of zip from crushed red pepper. I recommended making a double batch or more. Keep the remainder in your fridge for up to a couple of weeks or up to six months in your freezer. It's an excellent accompaniment to pretty much any roast meat, from wild hog to venison to pheasant. The Shaoxing wine and Sichuan peppercorns are available in Asian grocers or online if you can't find them at your local stores.

If you can't get everything on the list, riffing on the smoking spices and marinade ingredients is totally acceptable. As long as you use a black tea and soy sauce, you'll be onto something good. See page 122 for a photograph of my finished charcuterie platter.

- 1½ tablespoons kosher salt
- 2 teaspoons Sichuan peppercorns
- 2 pounds duck breasts (4 breasts)
- 3 tablespoons soy sauce
- 3 tablespoons Shaoxing wine
- 3 (⅓-inch) slices unpeeled ginger, smashed
- 3 star anise pods
- 2 cinnamon sticks
- 2 scallions, cut into 2-inch pieces
- ½ cup packed brown sugar
- ½ cup loose black tea leaves (such as pu-erh or Lapsang souchong)
- ½ cup uncooked rice
- Blueberry Port Compote (page 317)

Toast the salt and peppercorns in a small, dry, heavy skillet over medium-low heat, shaking the pan occasionally until the salt begins to color slightly, about 5 minutes. Set aside to cool, then grind in a mortar and pestle.

Score the duck skin in a crosshatch pattern. Rub the duck all over with the salt mixture.

Combine the soy sauce, wine, ginger, star anise, cinnamon, and scallions in a resealable plastic bag. Add the duck breasts, close securely, and refrigerate for at least 8 hours or overnight.

Bring the duck to room temperature, about 30 minutes. Remove the duck from the marinade, reserving the star anise and cinnamon. Line a wok (with a lid) with 2 long sheets of wide heavy-duty foil, crossing them in the center like a "t." They should drape over the edges of the wok by a couple of inches (see photo).

Combine the brown sugar, tea leaves, rice, and reserved star anise and cinnamon and spread out over the foil. Place a round cake rack about an inch above the smoking mixture. If necessary, use balls of aluminum foil to raise the rack (see photo). Turn the exhaust fan on. Heat the wok, uncovered, over high heat until the smoking ingredients start to let off smoke, 3 to 4 minutes. Place the duck, skin-side up, in a single layer on the rack. Cover the wok and crimp up the foil around the lid so it's tightly sealed. Reduce the heat to medium and let smoke for 8 minutes. Remove the wok from the heat, but leave covered and undisturbed for another 10 minutes, or until the internal temperature is 125 to 130°F.

Cut a slice to check for desired doneness; it should be rarer than you really want to eat it.

Uncrimp the foil and carefully uncover the wok—it will be smoky. Pat the skin dry, then place it skin-side down in a large heavy skillet over medium heat. Sear until the skin is golden and crisp, 2 to 3 minutes, or to desired doneness (135°F for medium-rare/medium). Let rest for 5 to 10 minutes before slicing on the bias. Serve as part of a charcuterie plate (see photo on page 122) with the blueberry port compote.

ALSO WORKS WITH: Any waterfowl. With cranes and geese, cooking times will need to be adjusted. If you're using diver ducks, make sure to remove the skin.

SPECIAL EQUIPMENT NEEDED: mortar and pestle; wok with lid, or, alternatively, a gas or electric grill outfitted with an aluminum tray directly over the heat to hold the aromatics

SEARED GOOSE BREAST
WITH APPLE, CHERRY, AND SAGE CHUTNEY

SERVES 4 AS AN ENTRÉE, 8 AS AN APPETIZER

CHUTNEY

1½ pounds Granny Smith apples or other tart apples, skin on, cored and cut into medium dice

½ cup apple juice

⅓ cup packed brown sugar

¼ cup apple cider vinegar

½ cup dried cherries

¼ cup golden raisins

2 tablespoons honey

2 tablespoons finely chopped fresh sage

1 tablespoon finely chopped fresh rosemary

1 tablespoon minced garlic

Juice of 1 lemon

Kosher salt

Freshly ground black pepper

GOOSE

4 boneless goose breasts, skin on

Kosher salt

Freshly ground black pepper

Olive oil, to coat the pan

1 tablespoon unsalted butter

ALSO WORKS WITH: Cranes, or any large dabbler ducks with a good layer of fat. A crane breast or a large Canada goose breast will easily feed two. Smaller goose breasts are good for one to two people, depending on appetites. With larger dabbler ducks, plan on a breast for each person.

I've cooked countless ducks and geese (and a handful of sandhill cranes) using this method. It's perhaps my favorite waterfowl recipe because it showcases the main ingredient in its pure form; the bird really gets to speak for itself. It's best when you're working with a bird that has a nice layer of fat beneath the skin. That way, the breasts do a bit of self-basting as the fat renders out, and the skin turns a beautiful golden brown. When you slice the finished breasts, you've got a piece of medium-rare meat crowned with a halo of crispy fat and skin. Put a dollop of the chutney on there and your trigger finger will start getting itchy in anticipation of your next goose hunt.

FOR THE CHUTNEY: Combine the apples, apple juice, brown sugar, vinegar, dried cherries, raisins, honey, sage, rosemary, garlic, lemon juice, and salt and pepper to taste in a medium saucepan and cook over medium heat until the mixture starts to bubble. Reduce the heat to low and simmer, stirring occasionally to prevent sticking, until the fruit is soft and pulpy, the liquid is mostly absorbed, and the chutney is fairly thick, 25 to 35 minutes. Remove the chutney from the pot and let cool.

FOR THE GOOSE BREASTS: Remove the breasts from the refrigerator about an hour before you're ready to cook and let them come up to room temperature. Preheat the oven to 400°F.

Sprinkle a liberal amount of salt and pepper on the breasts. Place a cast-iron pan big enough to hold both breasts over high heat and add enough oil to just coat the bottom of the pan. Once the oil begins to shimmer, carefully place the breasts in the pan skin-side down. Let the meat develop a nice brown sear, but be careful not to let it burn. Once the skin side is golden, flip the breasts over in the pan and place the entire pan in the oven. Cook for 4 minutes, then open the oven and put the pat of butter in the pan. After another 3 minutes, quickly remove the pan from the oven, tilt the pan to one side so all the juices and butter pool on the edge of the pan, and use a spoon to baste the breasts several times. Place the pan back in the oven and finish cooking until it achieves an internal temperature of 125°F for rare (or cook to desired doneness); this may take 5 to 7 more minutes depending on the size of the breasts. Remove the pan from the oven, baste the breasts a few more times, then let rest on a cutting board for 10 minutes. Place the chutney in the hot pan and let the residual heat gently warm it up. Thinly slice the breasts and serve with the chutney.

RED WINE-BRAISED WATERFOWL

SERVES 4 TO 6

Here's a recipe that's good for virtually any specimen of waterfowl, regardless of size or condition. I recommend using this with legs and thighs, though there's no reason you can't add some breasts as well in order to get the right amount of meat. This recipe works as a stand-alone dish, with the braised meat served atop rice, polenta, or pasta, or with mashed or roasted potatoes and vegetables. The boneless meat can also double as a base or additive for other dishes such as soups or pasta sauces. In the recipe on page 138, it's used to build the filling for the Duck Ravioli with Port and Red Wine Sauce. In following this recipe, you're going to be cooking the bone-in legs until the meat can easily be picked free of the bones. But be careful not to overdo it. You want to stop the cooking once the meat can be picked, not after it falls away from the bones on its own.

ALSO WORKS WITH: As mentioned above, it's good for any and all waterfowl.

2 pounds skinless, bone-in waterfowl legs

Kosher salt

Freshly ground black pepper

1 tablespoon vegetable oil

4 cloves garlic, smashed

2 carrots, cut into 2-inch pieces

2 ribs celery, cut into 2-inch pieces

1 onion, cut into wedges

4 sprigs fresh thyme

2 bay leaves

2 cups red wine (such as cabernet, pinot noir, or malbec)

3 cups Brown Game Stock (page 305) or low-sodium chicken broth

SPECIAL EQUIPMENT:
large Dutch oven

Preheat the oven to 325°F.

Sprinkle the legs with salt and pepper. Heat the oil in a large Dutch oven over medium-high heat. Working in batches, sear the waterfowl until golden all over, about 8 minutes per batch. Transfer to a platter as done.

Pour off all but 2 tablespoons of the rendered fat from the pot and reserve. Add the garlic, carrots, celery, onion, thyme, and bay leaves to the pot and cook until the vegetables begin to brown, 3 to 4 minutes. Add the wine, bring to a simmer, and simmer, scraping the bottom of the pot, until the wine reduces by half. Pour in the stock. Return the waterfowl and any accumulated juices to the pot. Cover and braise in the oven until the meat is very tender, 1½ to 2 hours.

Transfer the waterfowl to a platter and let cool. Strain the braising liquid, discarding the solids and any fat that rises to the top.

If making the Duck Ravioli with Port and Red Wine Sauce on page 138: reserve the liquid for Duck Ravioli and shred the duck meat, discarding the skin and bones. Or serve over pasta, polenta, or rice or with mashed or roasted potatoes and vegetables.

DUCK RAVIOLI
WITH PORT AND RED WINE SAUCE

SERVES 6 (MAKES ABOUT 48 RAVIOLI)

If I were in urgent need of help, you can bet your ass that I'd call a hunting buddy way before I'd call a drinking buddy. There's a bond that forms among hunting partners that is hard to replicate among any other group of friends. If you're wondering why I'm mentioning this in an introduction to a ravioli recipe, it's because making ravioli is the kind of thing that's best accomplished while working hand-in-hand with your most trusted buddies. A little bit of camaraderie goes a long way when you're doing the arduous work of assembling dozens of tasty little pasta packets. But don't fret if you can't get your hunting buddies together to make this dish. Your spouse will work just as well; better still if you can get a couple of kids involved. The group effort will add a fresh and welcome dimension to mealtime.

ALSO WORKS WITH: We're using the Red Wine–Braised Waterfowl from page 137 as a filling for this recipe, but any wild game–based ravioli filling will work as a substitution.

SPECIAL EQUIPMENT NEEDED: food processor

FOR THE FILLING: Melt 1 tablespoon of duck fat in a large heavy skillet over medium heat. Add the onions, season with salt, add the sugar, and toss to coat. Cut a round of parchment paper just slightly smaller than the diameter of the pan, then cut a ½-inch hole in the center. Place the parchment paper on top of the onions. Cook, lifting the parchment paper occasionally to stir, about 20 minutes. Remove the parchment paper and discard it. Continue to cook, stirring often, until the onions are jammy, sweet, and browned, 45 to 55 minutes. Transfer to a food processor.

Raise the heat to medium-high. Add remaining tablespoon of duck fat or butter if the pan is dry. Sprinkle the livers with salt and pepper, then sear quickly, about 2 minutes per side. Transfer the livers to the food processor. Add the thyme and parsley and process until smooth. Let cool.

Add the shredded waterfowl and pulse (4 or 5 short pulses) until a chunky paste forms. Transfer to a wide, shallow bowl, fold in the chestnuts, and season with salt and pepper.

FOR ASSEMBLY: Sprinkle 2 baking sheets with flour. Keep the dumpling wrappers loosely covered with plastic wrap while you're working to prevent them from drying out. Set a small bowl of water next to the work surface. Spoon 2 teaspoons of filling onto a wrapper. With your finger, swipe the perimeter of the wrapper with water. Fold the wrapper in half. Starting at the mound of filling, press outward to push air out of the ravioli and seal. Repeat forming raviolis with the remaining filling and wrappers, laying them on the prepared baking sheets in a single layer as they are done. If not cooking immediately, refrigerate until ready to use or freeze the ravioli until hard, then transfer to freezer bags or a container with a tight-fitting lid and freeze for up to 3 months.

FOR THE PORT AND RED WINE SAUCE: Melt the duck fat in a wide, heavy pan over medium-high heat, add the garlic and mushrooms, and toss to coat. Cook undisturbed until the mushrooms release their moisture and the liquid mostly evaporates, 5 to 6 minutes. Stir, then continue to cook, stirring occasionally, until golden, 3 to 5 minutes. Season with salt and pepper and transfer to a plate.

Deglaze the pan with the red wine and port, then simmer, scraping up the browned bits on the bottom of the pan, until reduced by half. Add the reserved braising liquid and stock and cook until reduced and it coats the back of a spoon, about 25 minutes.

Meanwhile, add 2 tablespoons salt to a large saucepan of water and bring to a boil. Working in batches if necessary, cook the ravioli in the boiling water until they float to the top of the pot. Drain, reserving 1½ cups of the cooking water.

Add the butter and ¾ cup of the cooking water to the mushroom mixture and simmer until the butter is melted. Stir in 1 tablespoon of the chives. Gently add the ravioli to the pot and toss gingerly to coat well, adding more cooking water as necessary to create a silky sauce.

Divide the ravioli and mushrooms among 6 pasta bowls. Garnish with the remaining 1 tablespoon chives and grated cheese. Serve immediately.

FILLING

2 tablespoons duck fat or unsalted butter

1½ pounds yellow onions, thinly sliced

Kosher salt

Pinch of sugar

4 ounces duck livers, trimmed and patted dry

Freshly ground black pepper

1 tablespoon fresh thyme leaves

3 tablespoons chopped fresh flat-leaf parsley

3 cups shredded, cooked duck meat, from Red Wine-Braised Waterfowl (page 137)

1 (4¼-ounce) package peeled roasted chestnuts, coarsely chopped

ASSEMBLY

All-purpose or semolina flour, for sprinkling

48 round dumpling wrappers, plus some extra as backup

PORT AND RED WINE SAUCE

1 to 2 tablespoons duck fat or unsalted butter

1 clove garlic, smashed

10 ounces cremini mushrooms, stems trimmed, sliced

Kosher salt

Freshly ground black pepper

¾ cup red wine (such as cabernet, pinot noir, or malbec)

¾ cup tawny port

Reserved strained braising liquid from Red Wine-Braised Waterfowl (page 137), plus enough Brown Game Stock (page 305) or low-sodium chicken broth to yield 3 cups total

5 tablespoons unsalted butter

2 tablespoons chopped fresh chives

Freshly grated Parmigiano-Reggiano cheese, for serving

04 UPLAND BIRDS

INTRODUCTION

My early exposure to upland birds was pretty limited. We had almost zero pheasants in the area of Michigan where I grew up and there was no dove season. I never ran into any quail, sharptail grouse, or chukar. The few turkeys in the state at that time were managed through a lottery-draw system, and even those were located well north of my home. (The place is now crawling with turkeys, one of the great conservation success stories of our time.)

What we did have available were ruffed grouse and woodcock, the woodcock being more sporadically available than the ruffed grouse. They'd migrate through in October, usually in small numbers but now and then in impressive groupings. I remember one time when I was running my trapline for fox and flushed a dozen or so woodcocks out of a single stand of poplars. I ran back to my truck and grabbed my Savage Model 24C, a break-open combination gun with a .22 rifle barrel mounted over a 20-gauge shotgun barrel. I went back into the poplar grove and kicked up another half-dozen birds. I downed two of them, making that my single best year for woodcocks. As for the ruffed grouse, I can't remember my brothers and I ever killing more than five or six in any given season. The ones we did get were shot incidentally while chasing more favored quarry such as cottontail rabbits, squirrels, and waterfowl. Those few upland birds that did come into our kitchen were treated as casually as store-bought chickens. They ended up in stir-fries, or else cut into leg and breast pieces that were browned in a skillet and then tossed into an oven. That I never developed any strong, well-informed opinions about cooking and eating upland birds should go without saying.

Then Montana happened. I moved out there in the mid-nineties to attend graduate school. Suddenly I was hunting for upland birds that I barely knew existed a year or two earlier. In the mountains I had access to not only the familiar ruffed grouse, but also spruce grouse and dusky grouse. Turkeys were available to the east and northwest of where I lived. Pheasants were scattered throughout the larger valley bottoms. Out on the Great Plains, less than a day's drive away, I could find sharptail grouse, sage grouse, and Hungarian partridge. In a normal hunting season I'd be dealing with five or six species of birds; I encountered even more in my out-of-state travels, which were increasing in frequency. Several species of ptarmigan in Alaska; bobwhite quail in southern Illinois; chukar in Wyoming. At some point thereabouts, I went from being naive to experienced in the ways of upland birds.

The most important thing that I learned about cooking them is that they can't be treated like domestic chickens and turkeys. This might seem perfectly obvious to many folks, but it's something that begs to be pointed out in any discussion around cooking upland birds. Many home cooks treat store-bought chicken as a blank slate upon which to add additional layers of flavor in the form of sauces and accompaniments with little consideration for the actual meat. The flesh is regarded as bland and relatively fail-safe—it's almost hard to mess it up. That's because store-bought birds are usually just a few months old, they are grossly overfed, and they've never flown or walked more than a handful of steps in any one direction. They are fatty blobs of nothingness. Upland birds, on the other hand, have qualities that are far more nuanced. They are lean and vigorous creatures that are powerful fliers. Some of them grow to be several years old, or even older.

They are far more flavorful and richly textured than domestic fowl, and also far less forgiving. Instead of using these birds as a characterless base upon which you build your dish, you need to use a gentler approach that highlights their idiosyncratic flesh and wild beauty. Half-assed attempts at cooking them can result in meat that is tough and dry. Believe me, I have eaten my way through enough mess-ups to know how true that is. It's my hope that by following the procedures and recipes laid out in this chapter, you'll avoid similar mistakes and produce meal upon memorable meal with your hard-earned birds. Anyone who has been startled and then thrilled by the explosion of a pheasant rising up suddenly from the brush beneath your boots, or by the silence-shattering gobble of a wild turkey in the spring woods, will agree that these birds deserve every bit of love that a cook can muster.

FIRST LITE

THE NATURE OF THE BEAST

Dove

Mourning doves are the most prolific and heavily harvested game animal in the United States. Hunters typically harvest well over ten million a year. The meat is dark, almost a deep purple, and excellent. Most of the meat is in the breast fillets, which are bite-size, but the legs can and should be cooked as well. Care must be taken to keep them from drying out. Add a fat, such as bacon, butter, or oil, and don't overcook. **White-winged doves** are a bit bigger, though the flesh is hard to distinguish from mourning doves.

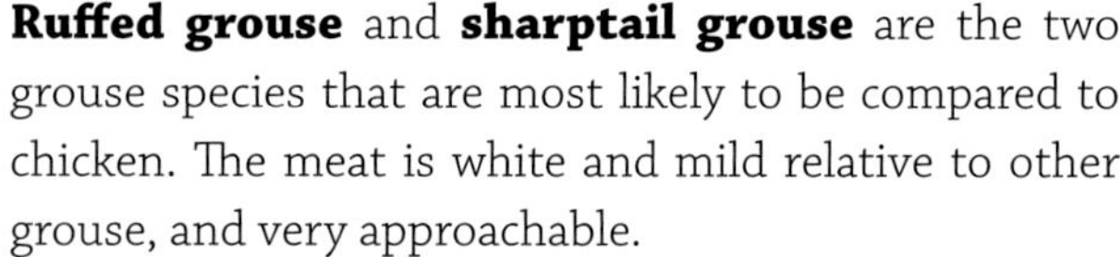

Grouse

Ruffed grouse and **sharptail grouse** are the two grouse species that are most likely to be compared to chicken. The meat is white and mild relative to other grouse, and very approachable.

Blue grouse (often known as dusky and sooty grouse, depending on location) have a slightly worse reputation than ruffed grouse. This is totally undeserved. They are excellent, one of the best game birds.

Spruce grouse have a reputation for being "piney" or "gamey," which isn't entirely unwarranted. It's better to use them as an additive to dishes than the main show. They are great for dishes such as stir-fries, pâtés, and gumbo.

Sage grouse are the meatiest of the grouse species, both in terms of size and the color of the flesh. They have dark breasts; the legs are lighter colored. Some might think of the meat as strong-flavored, but it is good when properly handled.

Pheasant

Light colored and mild, the **ring-necked pheasant** is very approachable. Young birds, hatched in the spring of the year, are especially good. Birds over a year old can be tough; generally, it's a good idea to slow-cook or braise them.

Pigeon

The **common street pigeon,** a nonnative species in North America, is edible as an adult, though not really that great; the flesh can be dryish and gray. The young, when killed before they begin to fly, are called squabs. Their meat is pinkish, tender, and superb. The **band-tailed pigeon,** a pigeon that's native to the United States, is similar in taste and texture to doves.

Ptarmigan

Hunters either love or hate **willow ptarmigan, rock ptarmigan,** and **white-tailed ptarmigan**. The three species are nearly identical in taste and texture—tender, but with hints of liver. Some ptarmigan enthusiasts say they taste better in the late summer, when feeding on berries, than they do in the winter when their diet switches to willow buds and alder catkins. Put your ptarmigan into pâtés or a Chinese hot pot and you'll hopefully become a lover rather than a hater.

Wild Turkey

Wild turkeys are truly excellent when properly prepared. You can do just about anything with a wild turkey that can be done with domestic varieties. If handled carelessly, they can be tough and dry. The birds benefit from the addition of fat when cooking. Mild brines are helpful.

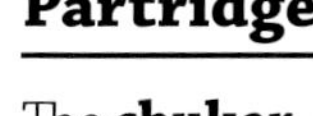

Partridge

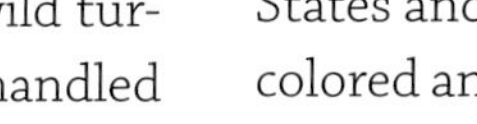

The **chukar,** a nonnative bird introduced to the United States and Canada, is one of our best game birds. Light colored and with flavorful flesh, they are comparable to sharptail grouse and are highly versatile. **Hungarian partridge,** another nonnative, are a bit darker and also excellent.

Woodcock

Woodcock are a connoisseur's item. They are renowned as a delicacy, but those who expect all birds to taste like chicken will be disappointed. These birds have a wild flavor and fairly dark meat. They are best when roasted simply with some basting or a piece of bacon laid over the breasts.

Quail

All six species of quail—**bobwhite, Gambel's, valley, Mearn's, scaled,** and **mountain**—are exceptional. The meat is tender and well-flavored. The less you do to a quail, the better. They are best when plucked, brushed with seasoned butter, and grilled over a hot flame.

PLUCKING AND GUTTING A TURKEY

Just like plucking waterfowl and smaller upland game birds, it's worth taking the time to pluck wild turkeys. You'll appreciate the culinary rewards that result from this job, which goes a lot faster with help from your hunting buddies.

1. Start by suspending your bird by the neck at a comfortable height for plucking.

2. Pluck the breast first, then work on the legs, neck, and back.

3. Now pluck the wings out to the first joint. Beyond that point, there is very little meat, and the wing feathers are extremely hard to remove.

4. Next, cut each wing free at the elbow joint.

5. Now cut the lower legs free at the joint below the drumstick.

6. Remove the head. You can save the neck for making stock if it is not too shot up.

7. Remove the tail fan by cutting below the base of the feathers just above the vent.

8. Make a gutting incision from the end of the breastbone down to the vent. See page 116 on gutting birds.

9. Remove the innards, reserving the heart, liver, and gizzard. See "No Guts, No Glory" on page 114.

10. In the pocket where the two sides of the breast split on the upper chest, you'll find the bird's crop. The crop is a pouch where game birds store food before it is ground up by the gizzard and digested. Cut the skin around the crop to expose it.

11. Pull the crop free by hand. Around and underneath the crop, you'll find a layer of fatty material called the sponge. The sponge is foul-tasting and should be cut away from the breast. Next, wash the gut cavity, inspect the bird, and remove any pellets, embedded feathers, or bloodshot areas. See page 118 for information on singeing pin feathers.

HALVING A TURKEY

Halving large game birds like wild turkeys or geese makes packaging and transporting them home easier, especially for traveling hunters. One half of a turkey is more than enough to feed several people. By splitting your birds, you can spread out the meals and try more than one preparation.

1. You'll be cutting bone, so you'll need a sharp, sturdy pair of game shears. Start at the rear and begin cutting through the back alongside the spine toward the neck. At the base of the neck, change the angle of your cut so it runs above the shoulder and wing.

2. Now flip the bird over so the breast side is facing up. Make a cut with a knife through the breast meat along one side of the breastbone. Now, use game shears to split the bony part of the chest cavity underneath the breast meat. You may need to make a couple more small cuts to completely separate the bird into two halves. One side of the bird will still have the plate-like breastbone attached to the breast meat.

3. This bone is easily removed by filleting it away from the breast muscle.

4. Now you have two bone-in, skin-on halves ready for the oven, grill, or smoker.

SEPARATING TURKEY PIECES

Breaking a turkey (or any sizable game bird) down into individual cuts gives a wild game chef the ability to prepare many different types of meals. With just a single turkey, it's possible to make everything from fried turkey nuggets to brined and smoked thighs to breakfast sausage.

1. Starting with a whole plucked and gutted bird, remove the two breasts (1) first. A small "tender" (2) is connected to each breast by a membrane. You can separate the tender by pulling it away with your fingers. See page 120 for instructions on removing breasts.

2. Next, remove the legs by cutting through the upper thigh and separating the ball joint at the hip.

3. Now separate the thigh (3) and drumsticks (4) by cutting through the knee joint.

4. Remove the wings (5) by cutting through the shoulder joint.

5. The carcass will have remaining pockets of meat that can be trimmed away or left on for making soup or stock.

SPATCHCOCKING

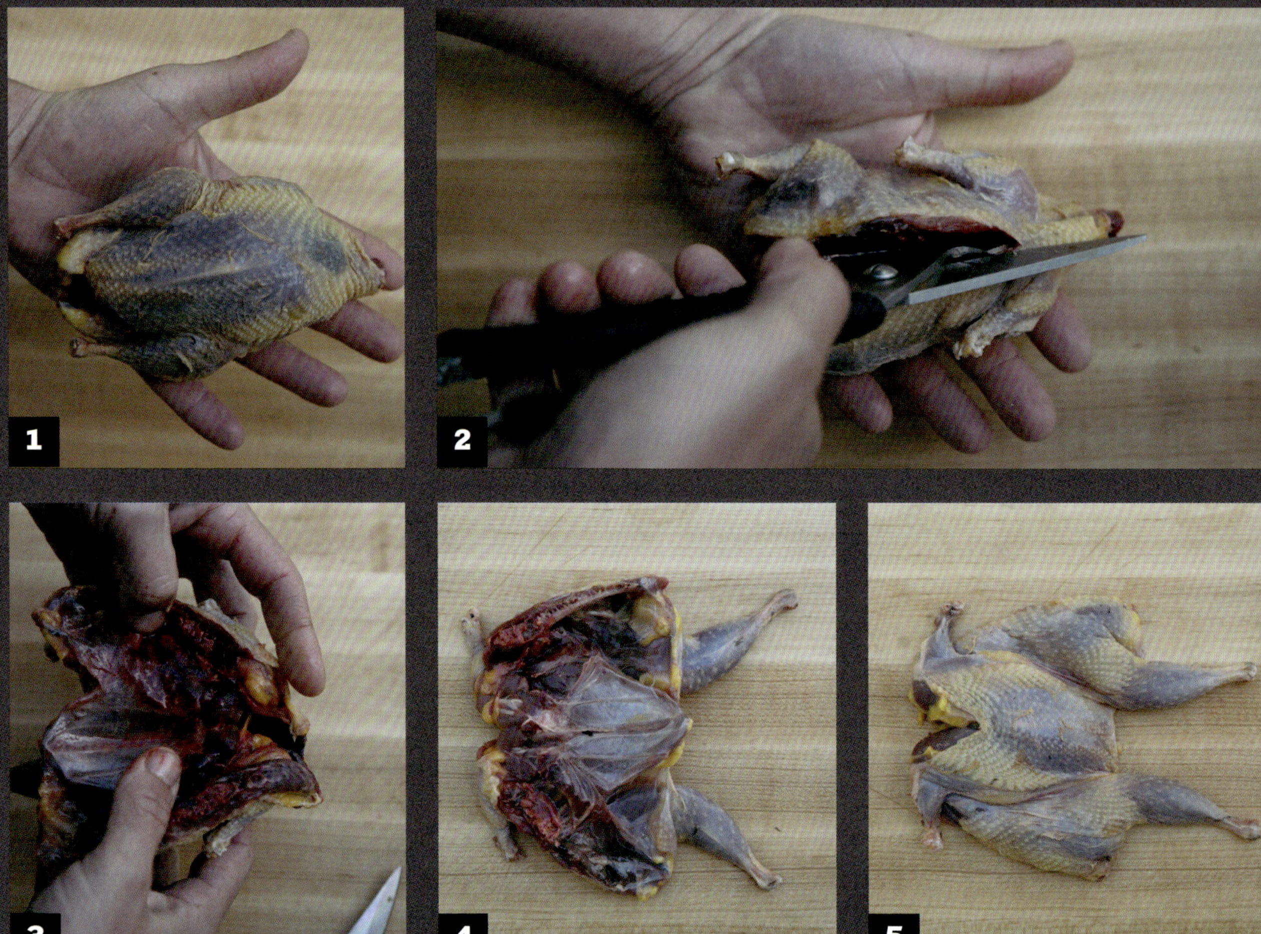

Spatchcocking is a butchering process used on game birds to butterfly, or split them open, in preparation for grilling. Spatchcocking allows the meat to cook faster and more evenly. Small birds like doves and quail lend themselves well to spatchcocking, as do medium-size birds like grouse and ducks.

1. Start with a whole gutted and plucked game bird.

2. Use a pair of game shears to split the back of the bird open from the rump to the neck.

3. Gently pull the bird apart so it can be laid out flat.

4. Wash the interior of the bird and remove any pellets, bone fragments, or damaged meat.

5. Now the bird is ready for the grill, skillet, or oven.

DOVE (OR QUAIL) JALAPEÑO POPPERS
WITH BACON-SCALLION CREAM CHEESE

SERVES 4 AS AN APPETIZER

Quail and dove hunting tend to be social affairs, and this is a social kind of recipe. Ideally, you'll pull this off with your hunting buddies within a few hours of the hunt, while you're still pumped up and excited with the thrill of being alive and well in the great outdoors. Make the bacon-scallion cream cheese ahead of time and you'll have this dish ready in a flash. If you get skunked, you can always throw it in your fridge overnight and spread it on some bagels in the morning.

4 ounces cream cheese, softened

1 tablespoon yellow mustard

¼ teaspoon garlic powder

3 slices cooked bacon, chopped

2 scallions, chopped

12 to 16 jalapeño chiles, stemmed, halved lengthwise, seeds removed

12 to 16 dove breast fillets, or 6 to 8 quail breast fillets (if using quail, slice the breasts lengthwise in half as if opening a burger bun)

Kosher salt

Prepare a charcoal grill for direct heat.

Mix the cream cheese, mustard, garlic powder, bacon, and half of the scallions in a small bowl. Evenly stuff the jalapeños with the cream cheese. Place a strip of dove or quail on top. Sprinkle with a little salt. Place on the grill meat-side up, cover, and roast until the meat is cooked through, the peppers are lightly charred, and the cream cheese is soft, about 10 minutes. Garnish with the remaining scallions.

ALSO WORKS WITH: You could use the breast meat from any upland game bird, though I'd avoid wild turkeys. Slice the breasts into sushi-size pieces and go from there.

GRILLED QUAIL LEGS WITH RANCH DRESSING

If you're wondering what to do with the quail or dove legs left from making jalapeño poppers, try this on the same grill. Take 12 to 16 dove legs (or 6 to 8 quail legs), ½ cup ranch dressing (I suggest Hidden Valley Ranch), plus more for dipping, and some vegetable oil to rub on the grates of the grill to keep the meat from sticking. Prepare a grill for direct heat. Combine the quail and ranch dressing while the grill heats. When ready, oil the grates, place the quail on the grill, and cover. Grill until lightly charred, about 2 minutes. Flip, then grill until charred and cooked through on the other side, about another 2 minutes. Serve garnished with sliced chives or scallions with additional ranch dressing for dipping.

FRIED WHOLE MOURNING DOVES

SERVES 4 AS AN APPETIZER

Peanut or vegetable oil for deep frying

1 cup fine- or medium-grind cornmeal

½ cup all-purpose flour

3 tablespoons Creole Seasoning (see page 312, or use a prepared blend such as Tony Chachere's)

8 whole mourning doves

Kosher or fine salt

1 bunch fresh curly parsley

ALSO WORKS WITH: quail

SPECIAL EQUIPMENT NEEDED:
electric deep-fryer or Dutch oven

This is the kind of recipe that prompts everyone to bust out their phones and start taking pictures. They can't help but comment on how the birds look like miniature Thanksgiving turkeys. The word *cute* gets thrown around a bunch, too. What I like about this preparation, beyond the mini-turkeyness and the cuteness, is that it utilizes the whole plucked dove so that there's no waste or leftovers. When you pull the birds out of the fryer, just give them a few minutes to cool and then you can break them apart with your fingers and devour the meat. All that remains are a few picked-clean bones.

Pour oil into an electric deep-fryer or a Dutch oven to a depth of about 3 inches, enough to submerge the doves.

Combine the cornmeal, flour, and 2 tablespoons of the Creole seasoning in a large bowl. Sprinkle each dove with a small pinch of the remaining Creole seasoning and rub it into the breast and legs. Working with one or two at a time, toss the doves into the cornmeal mixture and coat thoroughly on all surfaces. Working in two batches, fry the doves in the oil for about 4 minutes, rolling them around a few times as they cook, until all sides are browned and crispy. Remove from the oil and place them on a platter lined with paper towels to cool and immediately sprinkle with salt.

After the last batch of doves is cooked, divide the bunch of parsley into several bundles containing a few sprigs each. Drop the bundles into the hot oil and fry for 1 minute. Garnish the platter with the crispy bundles of parsley and serve as soon as the doves are cool enough to handle.

GAME BIRD TERRINE

MAKES 1 TERRINE (SERVES 18 TO 20 AS AN APPETIZER)

You could spend a week studying the distinctions between terrines and pâtés and still not fully understand it all, but here's a good primer: a terrine is a type of pâté that's cooked in a particular type of loaf-shaped pan, commonly called a terrine mold. Making a terrine is a lot of work, but it's well worth the effort when you want to make a lasting impression on your guests. See a photograph of the terrine with my charcuterie spread on page 122.

8 ounces whole boneless upland bird breast

1 pound boneless upland bird meat (which can include a mix of legs and breasts and, if available, the hearts and livers)

Kosher salt

Freshly ground black pepper

6 juniper berries, lightly crushed

4 cloves garlic, crushed

4 sprigs fresh thyme

1 small bay leaf, torn in half

½ cup brandy or cognac

1 tablespoon extra virgin olive oil

6 ounces skinless pork belly, cut into chunks, chilled

8 ounces ground pork

¼ cup chopped fresh flat-leaf parsley

1 tablespoon chopped fresh tarragon

1 teaspoon fresh thyme leaves

½ cup heavy cream

¼ cup shelled pistachios

12 (4-inch round) slices pancetta

Cut the 8 ounces of breast meat into ½-inch cubes and place them in a small container that has a tight-fitting lid. Place the 1 pound of mixed boneless breast, leg, and organ meat in a separate container. Sprinkle the mixed meat with salt and pepper. Divide the juniper berries, garlic, thyme, bay leaf, brandy, and oil between the two containers and toss everything to coat. Cover and refrigerate for at least 8 hours and up to 48 hours.

Preheat the oven to 350°F. Grind the mixed meat and pork belly through a 3⁄16-inch grinder plate into a large bowl. Add the ground pork, 1 tablespoon salt, a generous amount of pepper, the parsley, tarragon, and thyme and mix well again. Add the cubed breast meat, cream, and pistachios and mix well.

Line the bottom and sides of a 5-cup ceramic terrine mold or loaf pan with overlapping pancetta slices, allowing the pancetta to hang over the sides of the mold. Reserve 2 slices of the pancetta. Pack the mold with the pâté mixture. Arrange the remaining pancetta slices on top of the mixture, then fold the hanging ends of the pancetta over the pâté. Cover the mold with a sheet of heavy-duty foil and crimp tightly to seal.

Place the mold in a roasting pan and fill with boiling water to come halfway up the sides of the mold. Bake until an instant-read thermometer inserted into the center of the pâté reads 160°F, 1 to 1½ hours.

Remove the terrine from the water bath and remove the foil. Cover the top with plastic wrap, then place a terrine board or another board with 2 or 3 heavy cans on top to weight the pâté down. Let the terrine cool on a wire rack, then chill in the refrigerator overnight to let the flavors meld.

To serve, put the mold in a roasting pan of hot water for several minutes to melt the fat surrounding the pâté. Invert the pâté onto a plate and bring to room temperature. Transfer to a clean platter, then slice and serve with crusty bread and Brandied Cherries (page 318) or Spicy Pickled Red Onions (page 318).

ALSO WORKS WITH: Virtually any combination of small game or upland birds, including hare, ptarmigan, or dove. When cooking with hare or rabbit, substitute loins for the cubed bird breast.

SPECIAL EQUIPMENT NEEDED: meat grinder with a 3⁄16-inch grinder plate; 5-cup ceramic terrine mold or loaf pan; a small board or a terrine board (¾-inch board that is the precise area of the inside dimensions of your terrine), plus 2 or 3 cans of food to use as weights

WILD BIRD HOT POT

SERVES 4

MEAT

Around 4 ounces of raw meat per person (see headnote). Could be a single ingredient, such as ptarmigan or venison loin, or a combination of fish, birds, and various red meats.

SOUP STOCK

1 tablespoon vegetable oil

6 thin slices ginger

2 scallions, cut into 2-inch sections

2 to 3 dried árbol chiles (omit if you prefer less heat)

3 whole cloves

2 star anise pods

1 cinnamon stick

8 cups Blonde Game Stock (page 306) or low-sodium chicken broth

Kosher salt

DIPPING SAUCE

½ cup reduced-sodium soy sauce

2 tablespoons toasted sesame oil

4 scallions, finely chopped

Chile oil or hot sauce (optional)

SOUP INGREDIENTS

2 small carrots, cut into thin rounds

1 potato, peeled and cut into cubes

4 ounces shiitake mushrooms, stems removed

3 ounces enoki mushrooms (optional)

4 cups spinach leaves

5 to 6 napa cabbage leaves, cut into pieces

1½ pounds fresh udon noodles

The premise of hot pot, a dish said to have originated in Mongolia or Northern China during the Yuan dynasty, is simple and fun. Place a simmering pot of heavily seasoned soup broth in the center of your table and let everyone dunk in all manner of raw ingredients, from seafood and sliced red meat to leafy vegetables. It's a dream for the generalist hunter and angler who has a lot of good things in her freezer to bring to the table. Karl Malcolm, a wildlife biologist with the U.S. Forest Service, once had me over for a hot pot that featured about a dozen vegetables and fungi along with raw slices of walleye, elk, mule deer, turkey heart, turkey gizzard, and pronghorn heart arranged around a double-burner Coleman camp stove that supported twin pots of broth—one spicy with Sichuan peppers and the other kid-friendly. You can do this recipe with endless variations of wild game, though I implore you to include a sampling of upland birds in the mix if at all possible. Trust me, it's a radical departure from anything you've made before. You'll be struggling to rethink your vocabulary around the taste of game birds.

ALSO WORKS WITH: Just about anything (see headnote). To date, a thinly sliced ptarmigan breast was the best thing that I've ever added to a hot pot. The scalded yet still rare meat seemed to dissolve in my mouth like some sort of culinary magic trick. If you live in ptarmigan country, or know someone who does, I highly recommend that you try it.

FOR THE MEAT: Place pieces of meat in the freezer for 15 or 20 minutes until firm but not frozen. Slice as thin as possible and arrange on a plate. When using game birds, the skinless legs can be left whole.

FOR THE SOUP STOCK: Use a large open pot that can also be used to cook at the table. Heat it over medium heat, and then add the oil, ginger, scallions, chiles, cloves, star anise, and cinnamon and cook until fragrant, 1 to 2 minutes. Add the broth and the ptarmigan legs and wings. Bring to a boil, then reduce the heat to maintain a simmer and cook for 30 minutes, lightly skimming the surface if necessary. Season with salt, if needed; it shouldn't be too salty.

FOR THE DIPPING SAUCE: Whisk together the soy sauce, sesame oil, and scallions in a small bowl.

FOR THE SOUP INGREDIENTS: Arrange the raw ingredients on platters, keeping the vegetables, meats, and noodles separate. Have a portable stove on the dining table along with small ladles, small slotted spoons, or sieves. Divide the dipping sauce into individual bowls and have plates for each person. Allow guests to adjust the heat of their personal dipping sauce with chile oil, to their liking.

Transfer the soup stock onto the portable stove, keeping it at a simmer. Cook the bird legs, carrots, and potato first, 15 to 20 minutes, until tender. Mushrooms take about 3 minutes. Spinach and cabbage cook in 1 to 2 minutes. Thin breast meat cooks in about 1 minute. Thin slices of red meat, such as venison, can be cooked for less than a minute. The noodles take 3 to 4 minutes. Remove the cooked ingredients with a ladle or sieve and place on individual plates. Dip in the sauce and eat.

The broth at the end can be enjoyed as a soup, flavored with any remaining dipping sauce, if needed.

SPECIAL EQUIPMENT NEEDED: a large open pot that can also be used to cook at the table; portable tabletop stove

SLOW COOKER TURKEY POSOLE

SERVES 8 TO 10 (MAKES ABOUT 18 CUPS)

2 tablespoons vegetable oil

About 4 pounds turkey legs and wings, with the legs broken down into thighs and drumsticks

Kosher salt

Freshly ground black pepper

1 large white onion, finely chopped

5 cloves garlic, thinly sliced

1 to 2 quarts Blonde Game Stock (page 306) or low-sodium chicken broth

2 (16-ounce) jars salsa verde

2 (15-ounce) cans hominy, rinsed and drained

2 (4-ounce) cans diced green chiles

2 tablespoons ground cumin

1 tablespoon dried oregano

2 bay leaves

ACCOMPANIMENTS (OPTIONAL)

Chopped avocado

Thinly sliced radishes

Fresh cilantro leaves

Lime wedges

Sour cream

Tortilla chips

SPECIAL EQUIPMENT NEEDED:
slow cooker

Most turkey hunters would agree that wild turkey breasts are one of the best things to ever come from a bird. They are flavorful, versatile, easy to handle, and plenty big enough to feed a gathering of friends and family. The legs and wings of wild turkey are not as universally appreciated. The complaint is that they are prohibitively chewy. There's some merit to this, but the problem is easily remedied with the application of low and steady heat. If you're skeptical, this recipe will make you a believer. As for the accompaniments, don't worry about getting everything on the list, but do make sure to get more than a few of them. And have extra broth on hand, because the shredded turkey soaks it up like a sponge.

ALSO WORKS WITH: You could absolutely do this with pheasant legs, but it'd take several birds to get enough meat. This recipe can be halved to cook smaller meat quantities.

Heat the oil in a large skillet over medium-high heat. Sprinkle the turkey generously with salt and pepper. Working in batches, brown the turkey on all sides, 6 to 8 minutes per batch. Transfer to a platter as done. Add the onion to the skillet and cook, scraping up the browned bits from the bottom of the skillet and stirring occasionally, until the onion is softened, about 6 minutes. Add the garlic and cook for another minute. Transfer the onion and garlic to a slow cooker.

Stir in 1 quart of the stock, the salsa, hominy, chiles, cumin, oregano, bay leaves,1 teaspoon salt, and pepper to taste. Add the turkey and any accumulated juices to the slow cooker. Cover and cook on low until the turkey is very tender, about 6 hours.

Transfer the turkey to a platter and set aside until cool enough to handle. Shred the meat and discard the skin and bones. Discard the bay leaves. Return the turkey to the slow cooker and stir to combine. Taste and adjust the seasonings. If you like your posole brothier, add more hot stock and adjust the seasonings. Serve with your choice of accompaniments.

TURKEY APPLE SAUSAGE

MAKES 14 (4-OUNCE, 3-INCH-WIDE) SAUSAGES

A batch of wild turkey sausage is the best way to stretch out a bird for the maximum amount of enjoyment over the maximum amount of time. Frozen in half-pound quantities, you can get more than twenty meals out of a single bird. Turkey sausage is also a nice break for anyone who generally just makes their sausage from big game animals. The white-colored meat and radically different flavor of a turkey will get you excited about sausage making all over again. With apple, nutmeg, cinnamon, and bacon, this is a perfect blend for breakfast patties.

ALSO WORKS WITH: Bone out the carcasses of any white-fleshed upland birds to make this sausage.

---

2 pounds skinless, boneless turkey legs (or a mix of legs and breast), cut into 1½-inch cubes

14 ounces thick-sliced bacon, cut into large pieces

2 tablespoons olive oil, plus more as needed

1 large onion, diced

2 medium sweet-tart apples, such as Honeycrisp, peeled, cored, and cut into ¼-inch cubes

2 to 2½ tablespoons packed brown sugar

2 tablespoons fresh thyme leaves

2 tablespoons kosher salt

1½ tablespoons freshly ground black pepper

¼ teaspoon ground cinnamon

¼ teaspoon ground nutmeg

Zest of 1 lemon

SPECIAL EQUIPMENT NEEDED:
meat grinder

Place the turkey meat and bacon on a baking sheet and place in the freezer for 30 to 45 minutes so that it becomes firm but not frozen.

Meanwhile, heat the oil in a large nonstick skillet over medium heat. Add the onion and cook, stirring, until softened, about 8 minutes. Stir in the apples and continue to cook until softened, 6 to 8 minutes. Transfer to a large plate, spread in a thin layer, and let cool in the refrigerator.

Grind the turkey and bacon into a large bowl set over a large bowl of ice. Add the cooled onions and apples, the brown sugar, thyme, salt, pepper, cinnamon, nutmeg, and lemon zest. Mix well with your hands. Pinch off a small bit of the sausage mixture and cook in a little oil in a skillet to test for seasoning. Adjust the seasonings and sweetness as necessary. Cover and refrigerate until ready to use.

Form patties with a slightly wet hand. I like to make them 3 inches in diameter because they're easy to throw on the grill or in a pan, but you can make them any size you want.

Preheat a cast-iron pan over medium heat and put a little oil in the pan. Working in batches, sear the sausage patties until browned on both sides and cooked throughout, 4 to 5 minutes per side.

Note: To freeze, stuff the bulk sausage meat into poly meat bags in ½-pound or 1-pound quantities, depending on how many people you typically serve.

GRILLED GROUSE
WITH CAYENNE BUTTER

SERVES 2 TO 4

CAYENNE BUTTER

2 small cloves garlic

1 cup (2 sticks) unsalted butter, softened

1½ teaspoons cayenne pepper

¼ teaspoon kosher salt

Zest of 1 small lemon (about 2 teaspoons)

Juice of ½ small lemon (about 1 tablespoon)

GROUSE

2 spatchcocked grouse (ruffed or sharptail)

Kosher salt

Vegetable oil

ALSO WORKS WITH: Any white-fleshed game bird up to the size of a pheasant, and also squab. (In case you're wondering, a squab is a baby street pigeon. Check out my book *The Scavenger's Guide to Haute Cuisine* if you want to get the full scoop on that subject.) If you're using quail for this recipe, plan on 2 to 4 birds per person. A ruffed or sharptail grouse can feed 1 to 2 people; a mature pheasant is plenty for 2 people.

SPECIAL EQUIPMENT NEEDED:
food processor

This is a flexible preparation that can be used on a wide variety of game birds. It's mind-blowingly good for ruffed and sharptail grouse (also sooty and dusky grouse), and I've used it with great success on everything ranging from squab to quail to pheasant. You'll want your birds to be plucked and spatchcocked. The skin on a grouse is thin and delicate, so do the plucking as gently as possible so you don't tear it. As for spatchcocking, I recognize that it might seem like a complicated process. But it's really very easy, I promise, and you'll get the hang of it quickly. (See page 154 for spatchcocking instructions.) The cayenne butter that's described here is meant to be friendly and approachable in terms of heat. Feel free to crank it up to your liking.

FOR THE CAYENNE BUTTER: Put the garlic in a mini food processor and process until chopped. Break the butter up into chunks and add to the bowl of the processor. Add the cayenne, salt, lemon zest, and lemon juice and process until smooth. Scrape onto 2 pieces of parchment paper, roll into logs, and refrigerate until firm.

FOR THE GROUSE: Rinse the birds in cold water and pat them thoroughly dry with paper towels. Give the birds a sprinkling of salt on both sides and then brush them with a light coating of oil. Place them breast-side down on a medium flame grill and close the lid. Cook for 6 to 7 minutes, periodically checking the birds. A light bit of charring on the underside is good, but adjust the flame if you see any burning or blackening. Flip the birds over, baste the charred underside with the cayenne butter, and cook breast-side down for an additional 3 or 4 minutes. Flip the birds again, so that they're breast-side up, and baste the breasts with cayenne butter. Go sparingly so that you're not creating oil fires from the dripping butter. Let them cook for another 2 to 3 minutes, basting every minute or so. Be careful not to overcook. When you can prick the thickest part of the breast and the juices bubble up as a clear oily liquid, it's time to pull them. Another indicator that they're done is that the breast feels firm, like a cooked chicken breast. Baste them one last time while they're still piping hot. Serve with a simple side salad dressed with Basic Vinaigrette on page 315.

SPLIT AND SMOKED TURKEY
WITH BBQ SAUCE

SERVES A CROWD

Over the past few years I've been splitting most of my wild turkeys in half by cutting them down the spine. (See page 152 for instructions.) This particular recipe is well suited for a bird butchered in such a way, as it fits handily inside a pellet grill or on the rack of a smoker. The brine makes the bird juicy with a bit of salty sweetness, and the smoke adds a rustic woodsiness. When you're making this, you could cover the bird in strips of bacon if you're a bacon kind of person. A pound should be plenty. Yet another option is to make one of the compound butters on page 323. Chill the butter and slice it thin, then place a liberal scattering between the breast meat and the skin.

BRINE

1 gallon water

1 cup kosher salt

1 cup packed brown sugar

10 black peppercorns

3 bay leaves

8 pounds ice (1 gallon water)

TURKEY

1 turkey, split in half down the spine with breast plates removed

Olive oil

Kosher salt

Freshly ground black pepper

¼ cup BBQ Rub (optional; page 313)

1 cup (2 sticks) salted butter, melted

1 recipe BBQ Sauce (page 314)

1 recipe Cornbread (optional; page 326)

1 recipe Coleslaw (optional; page 333)

FOR THE BRINE: Combine the water, salt, brown sugar, peppercorns, and bay leaves in a large pot and bring to a boil. Remove from the heat and let cool to room temperature, then place the brine in the fridge to cool. Add the split turkey to the brine and brine for 12 to 24 hours.

Remove the split bird from the brine and rinse under cold water. Set on baking sheets and pat dry. Discard the brining liquid. Rub the outside of the bird well with oil and sprinkle generously with salt and pepper. Rub the BBQ rub, if using, evenly all over the bird.

Prepare a smoker to 275°F following the manufacturer's instructions. Use any mild flavored wood (such as cherry, apple, or pecan). It's smart to fill a foil roasting pan with an inch of water to act as a drip pan beneath the bird.

Set the turkey halves cut-side down on the smoker rack(s). After about 1 hour of smoking, begin basting with the melted butter (or substitute Clayton Saunders's BBQ Sop; page 313). Smoke the turkey to an internal temperature of 150 to 155°F (about 30 minutes per pound). The turkey can be carved and served right away, finished with BBQ sauce, or stored as described below.

To finish with BBQ sauce: If using a combination grill/smoker, raise the heat to high and baste the turkey halves with the BBQ sauce, flipping occasionally to caramelize the sauce and acquire a little char. If you just have a straight-up smoker, begin basting the turkey when the internal temperature reaches 150 to 155°F.

Serve warm with your favorite sides. Store cooled leftovers in vacuum-sealed bags in the refrigerator for up to 10 days or in the freezer for up to 6 months.

ALSO WORKS WITH: Try the same preparation with pheasants and grouse, though it's better to spatchcock those smaller birds rather than split them in half so that you're cooking the whole thing all at once.

SPECIAL EQUIPMENT NEEDED: smoker

ROASTED WILD TURKEY

SERVES 6 TO 8

1 whole wild turkey

2 heads garlic

4 sticks (1 pound) unsalted butter, at room temperature

1½ tablespoons dried thyme

Zest and juice of 2 lemons (reserve the rinds)

Kosher salt

Freshly ground black pepper

2 carrots, cut into large chunks

1 Vidalia onion, quartered

4 sprigs fresh rosemary

4 sprigs fresh sage

6 thick-cut slices smoked bacon (optional)

ALSO WORKS WITH: Use this same method for roasting whole upland birds such as pheasants and grouse. Cooking times will need to be adjusted accordingly.

I like to point out to people that there's no solid evidence suggesting that the pilgrims actually ate wild turkeys for the first Thanksgiving meal. They used the word *turkey* as a catchall for large edible birds, and some historians suggest that it's more likely they were eating waterfowl. Either way, the tradition of roasting a whole turkey for Thanksgiving is here to stay. The trouble for turkey hunters is that roasting whole wild birds can be tricky. If you don't take the necessary precautions, you can end up with a dry, leathery mess. My brother Matt has long recognized this problem, and he began searching for a solution by providing wild turkeys to his friend Shannon Harper, a private chef at a Montana dude ranch. With a little trial and error, Shannon hit upon the ultimate roasted wild turkey recipe. This is your best path to the perfect Thanksgiving.

Bring the bird to room temperature 1 hour before roasting. Rinse the bird with cold water, inside and out. Then dry it well—inside and out—with a clean kitchen towel. (Ideally, let the bird sit in your fridge uncovered overnight to fully dry. This helps to get crispier, caramelized, and more flavorful skin.)

Preheat the oven to 350°F.

Peel and mince 2 cloves garlic, then mash into the butter along with the thyme, lemon zest, and lemon juice. Sprinkle the bird inside and out with salt and pepper. Cut the remaining garlic heads in half horizontally and stuff them into the turkey's cavity along with the lemon rinds, carrots, onion, rosemary, and sage. Smear about half of the herbed butter all over the exterior of the bird. Leave no part uncovered—even the pope's nose. Put the remaining butter in a saucepan or bowl on top of the stove to melt so you can baste the turkey while it roasts. If you choose to use the bacon, drape it over the turkey's breast with each slice slightly overlapping the next. Put the turkey in the oven. After 45 minutes, baste with the melted herb butter. After 30 more minutes, crank the oven to 375°F and baste again. Baste with the butter every 20 minutes until the butter is used up or the internal temperature of the turkey reaches 160°F. To test the internal temperature of the bird, insert the thermometer into the fattest part of the thigh. For accurate measurement, be sure that the probe is not touching the bone.

After the turkey is fully cooked, place it on a cutting board or platter, cover loosely with foil, and let it rest for 20 minutes before carving.

Chefmate

ROAST PHEASANT

WITH ROOT VEGETABLES AND RED CURRANT, PORT, AND RED WINE SAUCE

SERVES 4

When roasting whole pheasants, it's best if you're working with young birds that were born in the spring of the same year that you killed them. These are more tender than older birds and easier to cook to perfection. (They are also more abundant; typically, young birds will far outnumber older birds.) Thankfully, it's easy to age a pheasant by looking at its wing feathers. Stretch the bird's wing away from the body and look at the primary feathers. If the three outermost primaries are shorter than the rest, it's a bird-of-the-year. If the outer primaries are fully grown, it's probably gonna take some time in a slow cooker in order for that bird to reach its full potential as tablefare. You'll see that this recipe calls for some brining, which, in my opinion, is generally a good idea when it comes to roasting upland birds. The challenge is to fight dryness, and brines help you win that battle.

ALSO WORKS WITH: Try this with grouse or chukars. These smaller birds will require shorter cooking times to hit a temperature of 160°F.

PHEASANTS

2 young pheasants

1 recipe Enriched Brine (page 311)

2 small lemon wedges

2 small onion wedges (can be taken from the roasted veggies below)

4 sprigs fresh thyme

1 tablespoon olive oil or 2 tablespoons softened butter

Kosher salt

Freshly ground black pepper

1 cup Blonde Game Stock (page 306) or low-sodium chicken broth

VEGETABLES

8 ounces cremini mushrooms, halved, or wild mushrooms, cut into large pieces

8 ounces micro potatoes, scrubbed and patted dry

2 parsnips, cut into 1½- to 2-inch pieces, fatter ends quartered

1 red onion, cut into wedges with the core end intact

¼ cup extra virgin olive oil

Kosher salt

Freshly ground black pepper

SAUCE

1 tablespoon unsalted butter

3 sprigs fresh thyme

1 clove garlic, crushed

1 shallot, halved

½ cup tawny port

½ cup red wine

¾ cup Blonde Game Stock (page 306), Brown Game Stock (page 305), or store-bought low-sodium chicken broth

2 tablespoons red currant or lingonberry preserves or jelly

Kosher salt and freshly ground black pepper

FOR THE PHEASANTS: Add the pheasants to the brine and brine for 4 to 8 hours. Remove the pheasants from the brine and pat dry. Bring the birds to room temperature for 30 minutes. Preheat the oven to 450°F.

Stuff each pheasant with a lemon wedge, onion wedge, and 2 thyme sprigs. Rub oil or butter all over the birds, then sprinkle with salt and pepper. Place the pheasants in a large, heavy oven-safe skillet.

FOR THE VEGETABLES: Arrange the mushrooms, potatoes, parsnips, and onion on a baking sheet and drizzle all over with the oil. Sprinkle generously with salt and pepper. Gently toss the vegetables, then spread out in a single layer.

Roast the pheasant and the vegetables for 15 minutes.

Add the stock to the pheasant pan. Reduce the heat to 350°F and roast until the juices run clear and an instant-read thermometer inserted into the thickest part of the thigh reads 155°F, about 20 more minutes. Continue to roast the vegetables until tender. Remove from the oven and tent with foil. Remove the pheasants from the skillet and transfer to a platter. Tent loosely with foil.

FOR THE SAUCE: Place a medium skillet over medium-high heat. Add the butter and any juices accumulated from the roasting pan, the thyme, garlic, and shallot to the skillet and cook, stirring, for 3 minutes. Add the port and red wine, scraping up the browned bits from the bottom of the pan, and cook until the liquid is reduced by half, about 10 minutes. Add the stock to the pan and continue to reduce until thickened, 8 to 10 more minutes. Discard the thyme, garlic, and shallot. Stir in the preserves and season with salt and pepper. (This sauce can be used for any roasted meat recipe.)

Carve the pheasants and serve with the vegetables and sauce.

Tip: Try pairing this recipe with the rich and elegant Cauliflower Puree (page 333).

WHITE WINE GROUSE OR PHEASANT
WITH BACON AND POTATOES

SERVES 4 TO 6

About 4 pounds grouse or pheasant, separated into legs and breast fillets

Kosher salt

Freshly ground black pepper

3 tablespoons extra virgin olive oil

2 tablespoons unsalted butter

3 medium carrots, sliced into ⅓-inch-thick rounds

1 onion, sliced into thin wedges

1 head garlic, cloves separated, peeled, and smashed

2 sprigs fresh thyme

1 pound waxy baby potatoes (about twelve 1-inch potatoes)

8 ounces mixed wild mushrooms, tough stems trimmed, halved if large

2 pieces thick-cut bacon, halved lengthwise, cut into ¾-inch pieces

¾ cup dry white wine

2 cups Brown Game Stock (page 305) or low-sodium chicken broth

5 sprigs fresh flat-leaf parsley, plus ¼ cup chopped, for serving

1 tablespoon fresh lemon juice

Crusty bread for serving

This recipe turns pretty much any collection of game birds into a delicious and hearty meal that's perfect for cold winter days. The thing to keep in mind here is that not all game birds were created equal when it comes to tenderness. Here we're calling for an hour of cooking time in addition to the searing process, but for something like the thighs of an older pheasant or the thighs of sage grouse, you might find that it takes up to ninety minutes or so of cooking to get the results you want. The only drawback to a longer cooking time is that your potatoes might get a little too soft while you wait for the bird to become just right. But I'm telling you, I'd rather eat soft taters than tough bird.

ALSO WORKS WITH: Any large, white-fleshed upland game bird will work here. Also a good way to prepare cottontail rabbit or squirrel, though be mindful of cooking times. It might take some extra time to tenderize a rabbit.

Preheat the oven to 375°F.

Sprinkle the grouse well on all sides with salt and pepper.

Heat the oil in a heavy-bottomed low-sided braiser or roasting pan over medium-high heat. Sear the pieces of bird in 3 batches until well browned on all sides, 8 to 10 minutes per batch, reducing the heat slightly if the oil starts to get too brown. Remove the browned pieces to a plate.

Drain and discard all but 2 tablespoons of the oil in the pan, or add more oil to equal 2 tablespoons. Add the butter, carrots, onion, garlic, and thyme and cook, stirring, until the carrots and onion begin to soften and brown, about 5 minutes. Add the potatoes, mushrooms, and bacon pieces and sprinkle with a pinch of salt. Reduce the heat to medium, cook for about 3 minutes, until the bacon starts to render, then cover the pan and cook, stirring occasionally, to crisp the bacon, 8 to 10 minutes.

Pour the wine into the pan, raise the heat to medium-high, scrape the browned bits, and let simmer to reduce by half, 2 to 3 minutes. Return the grouse and any accumulated juices to the pan. Pour in the stock and bring to a boil. Add the parsley sprigs and transfer to the oven. Bake uncovered until the meat is tender and the potatoes are cooked through. It'll take an hour, maybe a bit more, depending on the bird. Halfway through the cooking time, stir to submerge the exposed meat into the sauce. If there isn't enough liquid to come halfway up the sides of the meat, add more stock. When the meat is tender and the potatoes are cooked, remove and discard the thyme and parsley sprigs. Taste the sauce and add more salt or pepper if needed. Finish with the lemon juice.

Transfer to a platter or shallow soup dishes, spoon the sauce and vegetables over the meat, and garnish with the chopped parsley. Serve with crusty bread on the side.

POTPIES AND TURNOVERS

Turn leftovers into mini potpies or turnovers with one batch of the Basic Pie Dough (page 324) or thawed, store-bought puff pastry. To prepare, shred leftover meat and discard the bones. Separate an egg and beat both parts separately with a splash of water. Preheat the oven to 425°F. **For Potpies:** Spoon the shredded meat, vegetables, and sauce into individual ramekins. Roll out the dough and cut rounds 1 inch larger than the diameter of the ramekins. Brush the tops of the ramekins with egg-white wash, top with dough rounds, pinch to adhere, and make a half slit in the dough to release steam. Brush with egg-yolk wash. Bake until golden brown, about 20 minutes. **For Turnovers:** Roll the dough into a large rectangle. Cut into 4 or 6 even squares. Brush two adjacent edges of each square with egg-white wash. Spoon 2 tablespoons of shredded meat, vegetables, and sauce mixture off-center in each square. Fold the dough in half, folding the egg-washed corner over the filling to meet the diagonally opposite corner. Seal with a fork. Make a half slit in the dough to release steam. Brush with egg-yolk wash. Bake on a parchment paper–lined baking sheet until golden brown on top and bottom, about 20 minutes.

05 FRESHWATER FISH

INTRODUCTION

One of my earliest fishing memories is of catching a largemouth bass off my neighbor's dock on Middle Lake in Michigan when I was four years old. I was all alone and unsure how to handle the fish, so I grabbed it by the bottom lip and ran down the beach toward home. We had a holding pen in the water next to our own dock, and I wanted to drop my fish in it and then go find my dad so that he could help me clean it. While I fumbled with the lid of the holding pen, the fish slipped out of my grasp and splashed safely back into the lake. It vanished with a thrust of its tail, and I screamed with all my might. The sense of loss is burned into my memory. I was still crying about it later that night while taking my bath. In an effort to make me feel better, my dad told me that there are anglers who actually catch fish and then let them go on purpose, just for the hell of it. This was the first I'd ever heard about catch-and-release fishing. I am only slightly less suspicious of it now as I was then.

Not that I actually disagree with catch-and-release. In overexploited fisheries, it can be a way for people to continue to enjoy the sport of fishing without having a deleterious effect on the resource. But my personal take is this: why bother catching fish that you don't want to eat when there are so many great-tasting and underutilized fish resources swimming around out there? After all, that's what makes fishing so much better than silly games like golf. Not only is it more fun, it rewards you with dinner.

Of all the classifications of wild game discussed in this book, freshwater fish are the most readily available. In the United States, I don't think it's really possible to be much more than an hour's drive away from some sort of worthwhile freshwater fishing opportunity. I've spent at least six months or more living in Michigan, Rhode Island, New York, Wyoming, Montana, California, Alaska, and Washington, and in each place I've uncovered freshwater fishing opportunities close to home that paid off with more than a few memorable meals. That several of these places lie just outside of New York City—one of them is actually *in* New York City—testifies to just how abundant the resources really are. As for proximity, I once rented a house where I could catch American eels from my living room couch. That's not a joke.

As a nomadic and food-obsessed freshwater angler, I've adopted the strategies of a generalist. While some guys have a passion for a specific species of fish, say smallmouth bass or even carp, I have a passion for catching the best-tasting fish that happens to be most catchable at the moment. If that turns out to be giant eight-pound walleyes that would make the cover of a fishing magazine, that's great. If it happens to be some dinky five-inch bluegills that most anglers wouldn't even be bothered to bait a hook for, that's also great. My openness has rewarded me with a vast amount of food experiences. So far I've caught and eaten more than sixty species of freshwater fish in the United States alone. I'm happy to be passing along so much of what I've learned.

Some fishermen might be surprised or outraged to see that I've included salmon here in the freshwater section. There are a few reasons for this. First off, Atlantic salmon and several species of Pacific salmon have been established to varying degrees of success in entirely freshwater ecosystems such as the Great Lakes. There are also populations of salmon that have become separated from the ocean through naturally occurring events, and they manage quite nicely without ever touching the sea. What's more, the ocean-based populations of salmon cannot complete their life cycles without freshwater. They might build their bodies through the utilization of marine resources, but they begin their lives in freshwater and they end their lives in freshwater. Thinking of that, I can't help but see parallels with my own life. I was born on the freshwater of Middle Lake, but nowadays I can look out my bedroom window and see the Pacific. If I were to grow old and die back where I started, on that same beach where I caught and accidentally released my first bass, I'd feel pretty damn good about things.

Salmon

King salmon, or **chinook,** are the most highly prized of all salmon. They are big fish with excellent fat and beautiful red flesh that flakes easily. They can be used for any salmon recipe, including sushi, and are perfect for grilling. As with all salmon, kings that live their entire life cycle in freshwater, such as those from the Great Lakes, are not nearly as good as saltwater specimens. They are colored more like trout, are less fatty, and have a flatter, weaker taste.

Sockeye salmon, or **reds,** are excellent. Their flesh is firm and deep red. They can be quite fatty ahead of their spawning runs, especially populations that spawn in large rivers where they need to fuel a long migratory journey with stored fat reserves. They are good for any salmon preparation, though not nearly as popular as king salmon for sushi. They are widely used as a canning fish, which is a reflection of their abundance.

Coho salmon, or **silvers,** are comparable to kings; they are smaller and a bit dryer (less fatty) but still excellent. Use them for anything you'd use a king for, though they're not widely utilized for sushi. As with all salmon, the roe is excellent.

Pink salmon, or **humpies,** are not nearly as popular among anglers as kings, sockeyes, or silvers. Their flesh is not as firm, it doesn't flake quite the same way, and the color is more pinkish than red. They also have a reputation for turning mushy in the freezer. Because they generally spawn close to the coast, they do not pack on as much fat as the long-range migrators. Despite all that, pink salmon are still good. If you like trout, you'll love pinks. They're great for frying, smoking, and canning, and fresh fish are perfectly good when baked or on the grill.

Chum salmon, or **dog salmon,** have the lowest reputation of them all. The flesh is less vibrantly colored and they have low fat reserves. An exception would be chum salmon from Alaska's Yukon River, which have a better reputation thanks to a higher fat content. They're great for smoking, but don't be afraid to throw one on the grill to see what you think. There are plenty of people who love eating chums.

Wild **Atlantic salmon** are hard to come by (the stuff in stores comes from aquaculture facilities), but they are excellent. They're good for everything, including raw preparations.

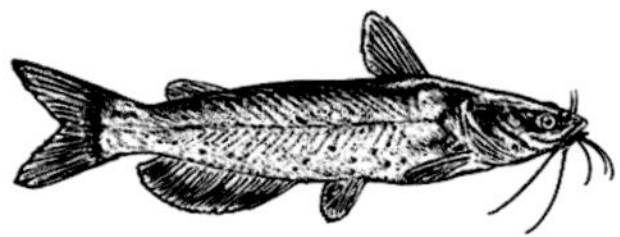

Catfish

Channel catfish are the most widely eaten catfish. They are readily available to anglers and are raised in great abundance by aquaculture facilities. They are as good as anything that swims in freshwater.

Flathead catfish are also excellent. People who are most familiar with the fish sometimes prefer it over channel catfish. The belly meat on flatheads is highly prized; it has a denser texture than the rest of the fish. With flatheads, careful trimming is essential. The fat has to go.

While rare, **blue catfish** are regarded by some as the best of all catfish. Their flesh is beautifully white, firm, and very mild. Get rid of all the fat; it has an off-putting flavor.

The various **bullheads** (**brown, black,** and **yellow**) are generally smaller than catfish but all of them are good when trimmed.

Trout

The ubiquitous **rainbow trout** is the benchmark that all other trout are compared to. It's not that they're the best tasting, it's just that they're the most familiar. The best specimens are around fourteen inches or under; they can be used for any trout preparation. Bigger fish can be filleted and smoked.

Steelhead are an anadromous species of rainbow trout. Saltwater specimens are excellent, on par with good salmon.

Cutthroat trout are excellent, comparable to rainbow trout.

Brown trout have the weakest reputation as food. The flavor can be flatter and muddier, and the texture is a bit mushier. Still, small specimens can be used for anything that you do with trout. Smoke the bigger ones, though it certainly won't hurt you to bake or grill them.

Brook trout (actually a species of char) have beautiful pink flesh and are quite good. Many anglers regard them as the best trout. They are good for anything that can be done with trout.

Lake trout, another species of char, are not universally appreciated. They are an oily fish, but the oil is not as good as salmon oil. The flesh has a pale color, and the meat may strike you as tasting "fishy" or with a subtle hint of fish oil. However, they should be treated seriously by cooks. They are excellent when smoked; the finished product is similar to smoked salmon. They are also good when baked, especially with sauces and a good squeeze of lemon. **Arctic grayling** have delicate white flesh that is prone to quick spoilage. Fish should be chilled upon catching and eaten as fresh as possible. They do not freeze well.

Whitefish are closely related to trout and they have many similar attributes. Like trout, their flesh is mild, a bit oily (in a good way), and flakes easily. **Lake whitefish** are the best, hands down. They can be baked, broiled, grilled, you name it. They are truly exceptional. **Sheefish** are not widely available, but they are also superb. **Mountain whitefish** and **round whitefish** are not as versatile but still deserve respect. They are great when smoked. Same with **bloater chubs,** which are actually a small species of whitefish. When smoked, these fish are extremely popular and demand a high price in commercial markets.

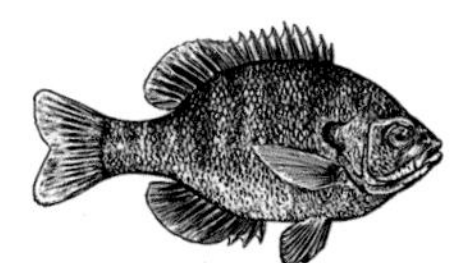

Panfish

Many panfish, including **yellow perch, crappies,** and the various **sunfish (bluegills, pumpkinseeds, redears, redbreasts,** and so on) can all be treated pretty much the same way. They are excellent. The fillets are boneless, and the white flesh is mild and flakes easily. Scale them rather than skin them, as much of their flavor lies in the skin. Soak for a few hours in ice water and then fillet.

Rock bass are a less desirable type of panfish. Still edible, but their flesh tends to be mushy and the flavor isn't as good.

While not aligned through taxonomy, there are a number of large, popular game fish with fairly similar flesh that can be used in similar ways—with a few caveats.

Pike, Bass, and Walleye

Walleye are one of the best freshwater fish. Mild, firm, and with white flesh, they can be used for almost everything and rival many saltwater fish in quality. **Sauger,** a close relative to the walleye, are a bit mushier. They are still good, but not as good as walleye.

Northern pike and **pickerel** have excellent flesh—white, firm, and well-flavored. The problem is the bones, which can be dealt with through careful filleting, or you can get rid of the bones by pickling or canning the fish.

Smallmouth bass, especially smaller fish in the range of twelve to fifteen inches, are as good as walleye when pulled from cold water. **Largemouth bass** are not nearly as good as smallmouth bass. They taste muddier, some call it "weedy," and the flesh isn't as firm. It helps if you soak the skinned fillets overnight in milk.

Sturgeon and Paddlefish

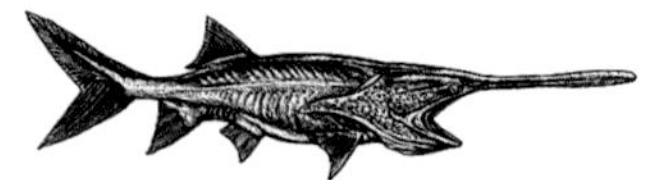

Paddlefish and sturgeon have enough similarities in life history and food quality that they can be treated almost interchangeably by a cook. **White sturgeon** of the western United States and **lake sturgeon** from the eastern half of the country are both highly regarded. Thanks to its dense, meaty quality, sturgeon steaks are often described as a combination of pork chops and fish. Their caviar is highly prized.

Shovelnose sturgeon are smaller, with a lower yield per pound of body weight. The meat is good, though it has to be carefully trimmed. Use a small, sharp fillet knife to trim away all fat and red tissue. You want the glistening white meat and nothing else.

Paddlefish can be compared to sturgeon; their flesh is firm, white, and meaty, though it must be carefully trimmed of fat and red tissue. The caviar is superb. Sturgeon and paddlefish can all be smoked.

Rough Fish

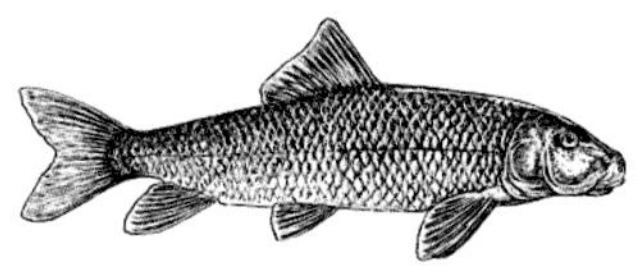

Rough fish is a big, broad category. Sometimes known as non-game fish, these are all species that are commonly hunted with bowfishing equipment.

Common carp are more or less despised by American sportsman, though in other countries they are a staple source of protein. It all depends on what you're used to. If you're used to bluegills and walleye, carp aren't that good. They are edible, however, and maybe even decent, if properly handled. Try pickling and smoking them, or better, make fish cakes.

The many species of suckers commonly encountered by anglers and bowfishers—**longnose, white,** the various **redhorse** and **buffalo** species—are all decent. The trouble is that they're bony, so you have to deal with that. The best specimens come from cold water during the winter and spring months.

Gar are one of the best rough fish. **Shortnose gar** are too small to mess with, but **longnose gar** are worth the effort. You need a pair of tinsnips to get through the skin; the backstraps hold all the meat. **Alligator gar,** which grow to enormous sizes, are a popular food item when prepared as a type of fish cake known as a gar balls.

While **bowfin,** or **dogfish,** are edible, it's a challenging meal. They are seldom eaten. The flesh has a strong taste and a poor texture. Folks who can tolerate them claim that they have to be eaten immediately after they die, as the flesh turns to mush very quickly.

Baitfish

Herrings, shads, smelts, and mooneyes can justifiably be lumped together thanks to their collective status as "baitfish" that can also be eaten. The rainbow smelt is extremely popular everywhere it can be found. It can be fried whole and eaten, bones and all. Same with longfin smelt. Candlefish, or eulachons (sometimes spelled hooligans), are a much oilier species of smelt; their flesh is less firm and has hints of fish oil. It's best if you render them out before eating.

The **American shad** and **hickory shad** are both edible, and both are very bony. The American shad has a much better reputation, because it's a bigger, meatier fish and it's easier to deal with the bones. The roe of an American shad is a true delicacy.

Mooneyes and **goldeyes** are both good smoked, though they are bony and a bit mushy. Mooneyes, being a bit bigger, are better.

Eels and Eel-like fish

Despite appearances that might be unappetizing to many people, the eels and eel-like freshwater fish are actually very good. The **American eel** is phenomenal as a smoked fish; there's a thriving commercial market for the product. It's also good pickled.

Burbot, or **lawyer,** are one of the finest freshwater fish. People call them poor man's lobster, as a popular preparation is to boil the fish and eat it with drawn butter. The **snakehead,** a nonnative species in the United States, is also highly esteemed. The flesh is firm, white, and mild.

G8918
ARCTIC CAT

SCALING AND FILLETING PANFISH

1

2

3

The term *panfish* encompasses a wide range of small freshwater fish such as yellow perch, crappie, and various sunfish species. They're usually easy to catch, bag limits are liberal, and there's no better choice for a fish fry. All panfish can be scaled using the same method. You can skip the scaling step if you'd rather remove the skin, but the skin contains much of the fish's flavor and it crisps nicely when cooked.

1. Commercially produced fish scalers work well, as do homemade scalers made from bottle caps or spoons with a hand-sharpened edge.

2. Scale both sides of the fish with a scraping motion from the tail to the gill plate. Move the tool in the opposite direction of the scales on the fish, so they are lifted from the fish's skin. Thorough scaling makes for a more palatable meal.

3. Fillet panfish as you would any other round fish, using a small fillet knife with a flexible blade. (See coho salmon on page 190 or mahimahi on page 228.) Use the carcass and head (minus the gills) for fish stock (page 309).

FILLETING SALMON

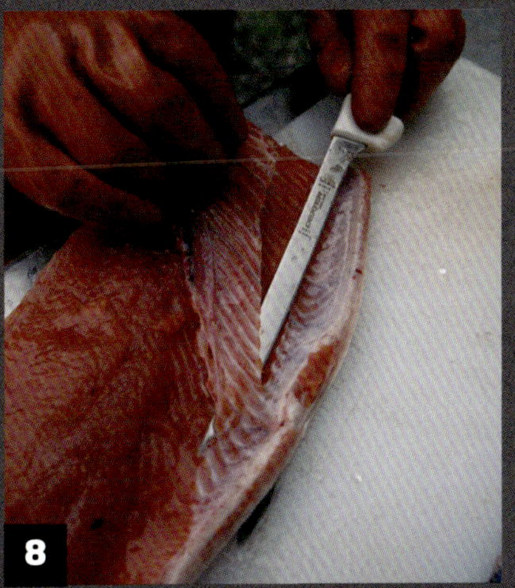
8

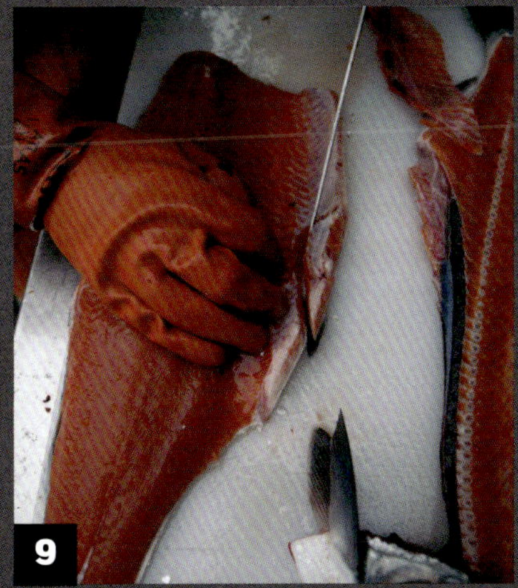
9

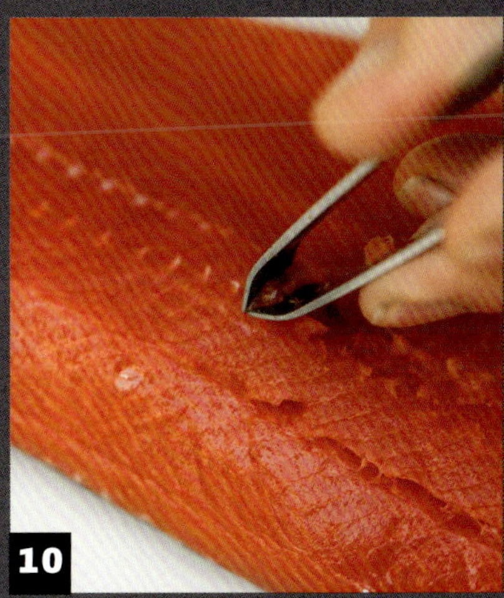
10

Coho, or silver salmon, spend most of their lives in the ocean, but they begin and end their lives in freshwater, just like all species of Pacific salmon. The process of filleting any salmon is the same for trout, walleye, and many other species of freshwater and saltwater fish. You'll be cutting through skin, bone, and flesh, so use a sharp fillet knife.

1. Start by making an incision through the belly from the anal vent up to the gills.

2. Next, make a cut behind the head and around the pectoral fin that meets your first incision through the belly. The depth of this cut should reach, but not sever, the spine.

3. At the cut behind the head, orient your knife blade toward the tail. Hold the head with one hand, and with the other, begin removing the fillet. Keep your knife running along the spine and just above the centerline of the back and dorsal fin.

4. Continue this cut all the way to the tail until the fillet is removed.

5. With one fillet removed, the guts can now be pulled out of the way. Consider saving the eggs, or roe, for making salt-cured salmon caviar. Now, flip the fish over and remove the second fillet.

6. With both fillets removed, there is very little meat left on the carcass. You can use the carcass for stock and save the collars on large salmon. See how to remove fish collars on page 231.

7. The rib bones in the belly portion of each fillet need to be removed. In the thick, middle part of the fillet, slide your fillet knife just under the ribs.

8. Make very shallow cuts downward toward the belly of the fillet to slice the ribs free.

9. Cut away the ventral fin on the belly of each fillet.

10. Next, you'll need to remove the line of pin bones. They are hard to see, but you can find them by running your fingers over the upper half of the fillet. Pull them free with fish tweezers or needle-nose pliers. Rinse and leave the skin on the fillets. The skin adds a layer of protection in the freezer and holds the fillet together on the grill.

FILLETING AND TRIMMING CATFISH

From one-pound bullheads to five-pound channels to blues and flatheads weighing well over fifty pounds, catfish are available to just about every fisherman in the country. They are also a universal favorite when it comes to fried fish platters. When dealing with catfish, it's absolutely necessary to remove dark meat and fat from your fillets.

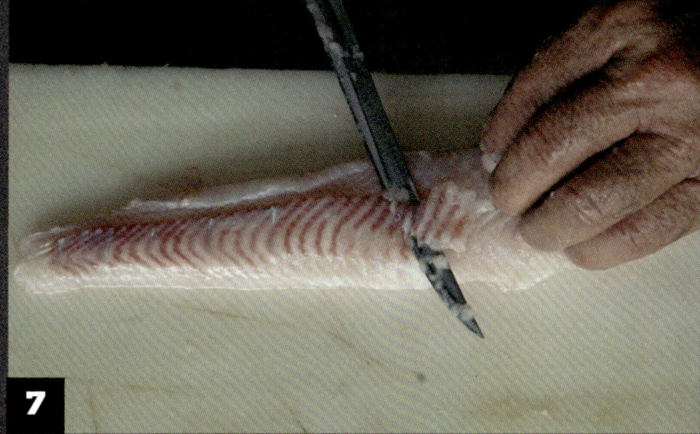

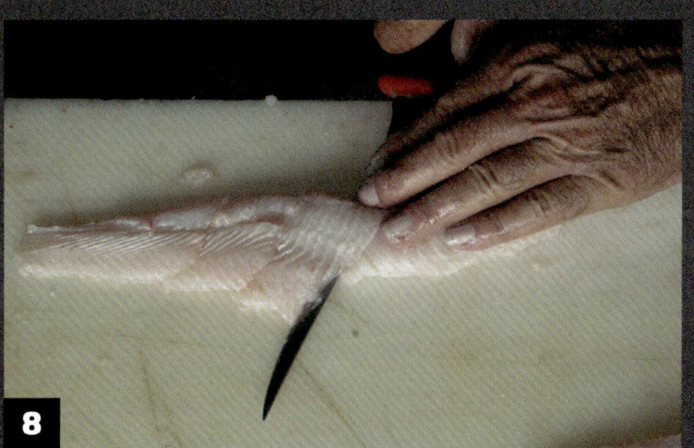

1. Start at the tail and cut the back half of the fillet free to the anal vent.

2. At the halfway point, cut the top of the fillet free along the back up to the head.

3. The belly area is bony, fatty, and has little meat. From the anal vent, angle your cut up and forward around the rib cage and gut cavity.

4. Once the fillet is removed, it should be almost triangular in shape.

5. To remove the tough, thick skin from catfish fillets, start at the tail and cut between the skin and the flesh. A pair of catfish skinning pliers gives you a good grip and makes this job much easier.

6. The side of the fillet that was attached to the skin will have a lot of dark, fatty flesh on the surface. This can give catfish a muddy, fishy taste. Take the time to trim this away from the fillet.

7. Cut each fillet in half at the line that separates the upper and lower muscle groups. Continue to trim each halved fillet until you are left with just firm white meat.

8. Now cut the fillets into nugget-size chunks that are suitable for the deep fryer. Small catfish fillets can be left whole.

9. Discard the trimmings and thoroughly rinse the fish in cold water.

GUTTING A TROUT

Cooking a freshly caught trout over a campfire is one of life's great pleasures. But first, you'll need to gut it. Gutting fish is fast and simple, and the process is the same on just about every species of fish. This process is similar for many species of fish, though you'll want to scale fish that have large scales. See page 189 on scaling panfish.

1. Start by making a gutting incision from the anal vent up to the gills.

2. Now pull the guts forward toward the gills. They should pull free by hand on smaller fish, but you may need to cut them free at the gills on large fish.

3. Most fish have a dark bloodline that runs the length of the spine. Use your thumb to scrape this away.

4. Now make a cut behind the lower jaw to loosen up the gills. Pull the gills free.

5. Give the fish a quick rinse, inside and out.

SCORING FISH

Tip: Score fish by making vertical cuts in the fillets. Cut through the skin and into the meat without cutting completely through the fillet. Scoring is a smart move if you're going to be grilling or frying whole fish. The seasonings will penetrate the fillet better and the fish will cook more evenly without curling up.

SALMON GRAVLAX

SERVES 4 TO 6

I love smoked salmon as much as the next fisherman, but it's a shame that more anglers don't experiment with other forms of cured salmon. Gravlax is a great place to start, because it's easier than making smoked salmon and the end product is entirely different. While smoked salmon can make you feel like you need to rinse with a glug of mouthwash, this gravlax tastes clean and lively. The key here is to use absolutely fresh salmon, not frozen. Pull it from the water, bleed it, put it on ice, and start making gravlax.

ALSO WORKS WITH: First choice would be either king salmon, sockeye salmon, coho salmon, or Atlantic salmon—the latter only on the condition that it's wild. Pink salmon have a different texture and don't flake as nicely as other salmon, but you can still make a good product with a fresh pink.

½ cup kosher salt

2 tablespoons sugar

4 teaspoons toasted cumin seeds

2 serrano chiles, halved, seeded, and thinly sliced

Zest of 2 limes

2 bunches fresh cilantro

1 (2-pound) salmon fillet, skin on, pinbones removed

2 tablespoons tequila

SERVE WITH

Cilantro sprigs

Crème fraîche or sour cream

Finely chopped red onion

Toasted rye bread or other variety

Mix together the salt, sugar, cumin seeds, chiles, and lime zest. Cover a baking sheet with a few layers of plastic wrap that are twice as long as the baking sheet. Arrange one of the bunches of cilantro on the plastic in roughly the space the fillet will take up. Rub the salt cure over all the fillet, flesh and skin, and place on the cilantro. Cover with the second bunch. Drizzle the tequila over the top. Fold over the plastic and tightly wrap the salmon, using more wrap if necessary. Place a casserole dish with cans (or some other weight) on top of the fish and refrigerate.

After 24 hours, remove the weight, flip the salmon, and put the weight back on again. Refrigerate for another 24 hours and repeat. Refrigerate for an additional 24 hours, then remove the plastic and herbs. Gently scrape the seeds off the flesh. Thinly slice and serve.

HOT SMOKED TROUT

SERVES 6 TO 12 AS AN APPETIZER

¾ cup kosher salt

½ cup granulated sugar

¼ cup packed brown sugar

¼ cup honey

8 cups lukewarm water

6 whole trout, up to 13 inches long, gutted, gills removed

ALSO WORKS WITH: Mountain whitefish, American eels, lake chubs, or any other small, fatty fish

SPECIAL EQUIPMENT NEEDED: Smoker or grill outfitted for smoking. If using a chamber smoker with adequate space to hang the fish, you'll need 1 (8-inch) length of cotton kitchen twine for each fish. Tie each length of twine into a loop.

SMOKED TROUT SPREAD

(See photo, page 199.) A fun and delicious preparation that uses smoked fish, especially leftover bits, is in a dip or a spread. Stir together ½ cup flaked fish (picked over to remove bones), ½ cup sour cream, 1 tablespoon minced shallot or scallion, 1 tablespoon chopped chives, dill, or other herb, the zest and juice of ½ lemon, and salt and pepper to taste. Serve with saltines.

This is by far my favorite way to prepare small trout and mountain whitefish. I've also done it successfully with a variety of other fish ranging from American eels to redhorse suckers. When I make a batch of fish like this, I eat the first few (or the whole batch) right off the bone within a day or two of smoking them. That's when they are best. If I have more than I can eat within that timeframe, I like to share them with friends or neighbors because they are so tasty and beautiful. With leftover fish, you can debone the meat and use it for smoked fish dips, mix it into omelets, or sprinkle it over a bagel that's been spread with cream cheese. A friend of mine, Chef Eduardo Garcia, uses it to fill his homemade empanadas.

FOR THE BRINE: In a nonmetallic container big enough to hold the fish, combine the salt, both sugars, the honey, and lukewarm water and whisk vigorously to dissolve the ingredients. Chill the brine. Thoroughly rinse the trout and submerge them in the brine, using a plate to weight them down beneath the surface. Brine for 6 to 8 hours in the fridge.

Discard the brine and rinse the trout again. Pat the fish dry with paper towels and place them on a wire rack in the fridge until they feel tacky to the touch. Two or 3 hours should do it.

If using a chamber smoker with adequate space, consider suspending the trout. For each fish, place the belly of a loop of twine across the back of its neck and pass the sides of the loop under the fish's gill covers and then push the knotted end out of the fish's mouth.

Prepare your smoker and preheat to a temperature of approximately 170°F. Fruit woods such as apple or cherry are ideal. If possible, suspend the trout in the smoker at least 10 inches above the heat source. If not, place them on wire racks so there's plenty of room between the fish. Begin checking the fish at around 3 hours. When done, the ends of the tail and other fins will have turned dry and crispy. The skin should peel away easily. It should seem that the flesh might easily slip away from the ribs and spine, leaving bare bones. Remove the fish from the smoker and allow to cool enough that they can be handled comfortably. These trout are best when served within a day or two, though you can wrap them in foil and store in a fridge for a week or so. For freezing, chill the fish thoroughly and vacuum seal.

PICKLED PIKE (OR SUCKER)

SERVES 6 AS AN APPETIZER

Growing up, my brothers and I fished for northern pike on the lake in front of our house. We caught them through the ice after the lake froze over, and we caught even more in the summer by trolling deep-diving crankbaits behind a rowboat powered by an ancient 10-horse Johnson outboard. Being kids, we didn't always do the best job of filleting and deboning our northerns. We each spent a fair bit of time lying on our backs on the kitchen table while our dad shined a flashlight into our mouths as he tried to remove the dastardly little Y-bones from our throats. So my family's discovery of pickled pike, with its acidic vinegar brine, was as much a medical breakthrough as a culinary one. With this recipe, it's no longer necessary to remove the bones from your northerns (or from suckers) because the bones rapidly soften and dissolve to a degree that they're no longer an issue. If that's not enough of a selling point, a jar of pickled fish is a beautifully rustic way to decorate a table with edible goods when you're having friends over for holidays or other celebrations.

- ½ cup kosher salt
- 3½ cups warm water
- Roughly 1 pound skinless northern pike fillets or other white-fleshed bony fish
- 4 cups distilled white vinegar
- ½ cup sugar
- 1 teaspoon brown mustard seeds
- 1 teaspoon yellow mustard seeds
- 1 teaspoon multicolored peppercorns
- 6 allspice berries
- 6 cloves garlic, peeled
- 1 medium red onion, sliced
- 3 lemon slices
- 2 to 3 jalapeño or dried red chiles
- 2 large bay leaves

Dissolve the salt in 3 cups of the warm water in a large glass or ceramic bowl. Place the brine in the fridge or over a bed of ice to cool.

Slice the fillets into 1-inch by 1½-inch chunks. There is no need to remove the Y-bones. When the brine is cold, submerge the fish pieces and weight them down with a plate. Leave in the fridge for 24 hours.

Pour the brine out of the bowl, then cover the fish with 3 cups of the white vinegar and let rest in the fridge for another 12 hours.

Meanwhile, make the pickling solution by combining the remaining 1 cup vinegar, the remaining ½ cup warm water, the sugar, both mustard seeds, the peppercorns, and the allspice berries in a medium saucepan. Bring to a low simmer, stir to dissolve the sugar, and then chill.

Drain the fish pieces in a colander, but do not rinse. In a clean 1-quart canning jar, layer the fish pieces, garlic, onion slices, lemon slices, chiles, and bay leaves. Leave 1 inch of empty headspace. Pour in the chilled pickling solution, making sure to get all of the peppercorns and mustard seeds into the jar even if you don't have enough space for all of the liquid. Dislodge any air bubbles by tapping the jar gently on the counter. Cap the jar and store in the fridge for a few days before eating. Enjoy over the next few weeks.

ALSO WORKS WITH: The fish here doesn't necessarily *have* to be a bony variety such as pike or suckers, though the brine's ability to dissolve pesky bones is part of what makes it such an appealing preparation. I've even pickled some delicious jars of shovelnose sturgeon using this recipe—being cartilaginous, they don't have any bones at all.

SPECIAL EQUIPMENT NEEDED:

1-quart canning jar

Tip: For more information canning fish or processing at high altitudes, go to the USDA home canning website, http://nchfp.usa.edu/, and search for the guide on preparing and canning.

PINK SALMON NUGGETS
WITH THAI SWEET CHILE DIPPING SAUCE

SERVES 4 (MAKES ABOUT 32 PIECES)

DIPPING SAUCE

5 tablespoons sugar

¼ cup rice vinegar

3 tablespoons water

1 tablespoon fresh lime juice

1 teaspoon red chile flakes

1 teaspoon chile-garlic sauce or sriracha (optional)

1 teaspoon fish sauce

2 cloves garlic, minced or grated

1 tablespoon cornstarch

Kosher salt

SALMON

½ cup cornstarch or all-purpose flour

3 large eggs, lightly beaten

2 cups panko breadcrumbs

1 pound boneless, skinless salmon fillet, patted dry, cut into 1½- to 2-inch pieces

Kosher salt

Freshly ground black pepper

About 2 cups vegetable oil

Pink salmon have a reputation as a low-grade fish, which is completely unwarranted. My brother likes to conduct blind taste tests with his fishing buddies and pinks score just as high as coho salmon. They're good grilled, they're good broiled, and they're extra-special-good when my buddy Chef Andrew Radzialowski uses them to make his revered salmon nugget recipe up at our remote fishing shack in southeast Alaska. Here's how he does it.

ALSO WORKS WITH: Any salmon. Or, really, pretty much any fish that you can get a boneless fillet from.

FOR THE DIPPING SAUCE: Combine the sugar, vinegar, 2 tablespoons of the water, the lime juice, red chile flakes, chile-garlic sauce, if using, fish sauce, and garlic in a small saucepan. Bring to a boil over medium-high heat, stirring until the sugar dissolves, about 3 minutes. Reduce the heat to medium to maintain a simmer. Mix the cornstarch with the remaining 1 tablespoon water in a small bowl until smooth. Add the slurry to the sauce and stir until it thickens, about 30 seconds. Season with salt. Transfer to a bowl and let cool.

FOR THE SALMON: Put the cornstarch, eggs, and panko in 3 separate wide shallow bowls. Sprinkle the salmon generously with salt and pepper. Working with a couple of pieces of salmon at a time, dredge in the cornstarch, shaking off any extra. Dip in the egg, then roll in the panko until evenly coated. Transfer to a baking sheet in a single layer as done.

Pour oil to a depth of 2 inches in a Dutch oven or other wide, heavy pot and heat over medium-high heat until a deep-fry thermometer reads 375°F. Place a wire rack inside a foil-lined baking sheet and set aside. Working in batches, fry the salmon, stirring gently once or twice, until golden and crisp, 1½ to 2 minutes per batch. Allow the oil to return to 375°F between batches. Transfer the fish to the wire rack as done and season with salt while still hot.

Serve the salmon with the dipping sauce.

SUCKER BALLS
WITH MAGIC SAUCE

SERVES 7 FOR APPETIZERS (MAKES 15 BALLS)

The edibility of rough fish, particularly carp and sucker species, is one of those things that fishermen never get tired of arguing about. Most everyone has an opinion about it, though most of those opinions are based on very little actual experience. Bring up the subject and you'll hear about how so-and-so heard that suckers aren't any good, or so-and-so watched his neighbor cook up some carp, and even though he didn't actually taste it himself, it sure didn't look very appealing. As someone who has a lot of experience eating a wide variety of rough fish from a handful of continents, I'd like to weigh in on the debate in a measured, reasonable way: rough fish can be good. Definitely not the best thing you ever ate, but certainly not the worst. The flesh generally *tastes* perfectly fine, but it can be mushy and, most annoyingly, full of small bones. There are plenty of things to do with rough fish, including canning and pickling, that will render the bones harmless. But fish cakes happen to be my favorite preparation. In this recipe, you bake the fillets until they're ready to fall apart. Then you debone the flesh and work up some cakes and some herbed mayonnaise. No mushiness. No bones. Just good eats.

ALSO WORKS WITH: Freshwater drum, aka sheepshead, plus gar, buffalo, common carp, silver carp, and bighead carp. This also makes an excellent crab cake, using picked crab meat. Also great for northern pike, which are bony as hell, or pretty much any leftover fish that can be crumbled up in your fingers.

HERBED MAYONNAISE (MAGIC SAUCE)

2 cups mayonnaise

2 tablespoons Dijon mustard

2 tablespoons white wine vinegar

1 teaspoon kosher salt

1 teaspoon freshly ground black pepper

6 tablespoons chopped fresh chives

6 to 8 leaves fresh basil, chopped

4 cloves garlic, minced

Zest and juice of 2 lemons

FISH

Unsalted butter, for the pan

1 pound skinless rough fish fillets (such as carp or suckers)

Pinch of kosher salt

½ cup milk

FISH CAKES

2 cups fresh breadcrumbs

½ cup thinly sliced scallions

1 teaspoon minced garlic

1½ teaspoons kosher salt

½ teaspoon freshly ground black pepper

½ red bell pepper, finely diced

½ yellow bell pepper, finely diced

¼ red onion, finely diced

2 large eggs, lightly beaten

FOR THE HERBED MAYONNAISE: Whisk the mayonnaise, mustard, vinegar, salt, pepper, chives, basil, garlic, and lemon zest and juice in a medium bowl until smooth. (This makes about 2 cups.)

FOR THE FISH: Preheat the oven to 375°F. Butter a baking dish. Sprinkle the fish fillets with salt and add to the baking dish. Pour the milk over the fish. Bake the fillets until the fish is cooked through and flakes, about 12 minutes. Pick the bones from the fillets. Once cooled, shred the fish.

FOR THE FISH CAKES: Line a baking sheet with parchment paper. Mix the fish flakes, breadcrumbs, scallions, garlic, salt, pepper, bell peppers, and onion in a large bowl until uniformly mixed. Add ½ cup of the herbed mayonnaise and the eggs and gently combine until the mixture becomes wet and sticky. Form ¼ cup of the mixture at a time into a ball. Place the balls on the prepared baking sheet, leaving space between them. Bake until the cakes turn golden brown, 18 to 20 minutes. Serve with the remaining herbed mayonnaise.

MIDWEST-STYLE FRIDAY NIGHT FISH FRY
WITH PANFISH OR SMELT

SERVES 4

PANFISH OR SMELT

About 2 pounds scaled perch, bluegill, crappie fillets, or gutted smelt, heads removed

BREADING (PANFISH OR SMELT)

1½ cups fine-ground cornmeal

2 cups all-purpose flour

3 tablespoons Creole Seasoning (page 312), or use store-bought

Peanut oil, for frying

FOR SERVING PANFISH

Lemon wedges

1 recipe Herbed Tartar Sauce (page 318)

FOR SERVING SMELT

1 bunch fresh flat-leaf parsley

Lemon wedges

Cocktail sauce

ALSO WORKS WITH: This recipe works with just about any small fish or small pieces of fish. Any boneless freshwater fish fillets, or almost any white-fleshed saltwater fish fillets, cut into panfish-size pieces will work well with this recipe. If you're working with the type of smelt known as a eulachon (sometimes spelled as hooligan, and otherwise known as candlefish), there's an added step. Before you start frying eulachons, preheat your oven to 350°F. When you remove the fish from the frying oil, lay them out on an oven-safe cooling rack and set the rack over a baking dish. Place the fish in the oven and bake for an additional 30 minutes. The oil will render out and collect in the dish. From there, pick things up from the smelt serving step.

Ever since I moved to the Pacific Northwest, where salmon and trout are king, I've suffered endless ribbing from buddies who can't believe that I spend so much time fishing for panfish that are so small that a salmon could swallow them in a single gulp. I've tried explaining by telling them of the cultural importance of panfish to the Midwesterners I grew up around, but that doesn't do much good. What does work, I've found, is inviting them to a Midwest-style fish fry. There's something about a basket containing fifty or sixty golden brown nuggets of perch, bluegill, and crappie that makes a salmon snob question their ways. With their first bite, they're curious about panfish. With their second bite, they're asking for details about where I caught them. With the third bite, they're begging me to take them out on the water. As for smelt, we always cook them the same way that we cook our panfish, except that we eat smelt bones and all.

Rinse the fillets (or whole smelt) in cold water, shake them dry, then lay them out in a single layer on top of paper towels. Pat the surface dry with additional paper towels.

Mix the cornmeal, flour, and Creole Seasoning in a shallow dish. Fill a Dutch oven with several inches of peanut oil, or a deep-fryer to the recommended fill level. Heat the oil over medium-high heat to 375°F.

Working in batches of around a dozen fillets (or whole fish), toss them in the breading mixture so they are thoroughly coated on all sides. Shake off the excess breading and drop them into the oil. The fillets will bubble aggressively when they hit the oil. Fry for just 2 to 3 minutes, until the fillets (or whole fish) float to the surface and the bubbling has slowed significantly. Remove the fillets with a slotted spoon or strainer and place on paper towels inside a Dutch oven or other heavy pot with a tight-fitting lid to keep them warm while you move on to the next batch.

TO SERVE THE PANFISH: Serve with lemon wedges and herbed tartar sauce.

TO SERVE THE SMELT: Before serving, separate a sprig or two of parsley for each serving of smelt and drop them into the hot oil. Fry the parsley just 30 seconds and use it as a garnish. Serve the smelt with a couple of wedges of the lemon and a nice dollop of cocktail sauce.

THE PERFECT FRIED CATFISH SANDWICH

SERVES 4

Every spring, I take my kids fishing for channel catfish along the lower Yellowstone River of eastern Montana. It's one of the highlights of our year. There's usually plenty of action, and catfish are a forgiving quarry. You don't need a ton of finesse to hook one, and they tend to stay on the hook once you do. It's a great way to get kids interested in fishing, and also a great way to get kids interested in eating fish. We trim the fillets of fat in order to get rid of any "muddy" flavors, and then fry up big batches of them. The kids devour the fillets as finger food (backed up by plenty of sliced pickles), while the grown-ups assemble these catfish sandwiches. I love them. The only thing better than the taste is the joy of seeing a kid take pride in the fact that he caught his family's dinner.

ALSO WORKS WITH: Smallmouth and largemouth bass, walleye, big perch, and crappie, or just about any freshwater fish with a boneless fillet that can be trimmed down or stacked up to fill a bun.

½ cup mayonnaise

1 tablespoon sriracha

½ cup all-purpose flour

2 large egg whites, beaten

½ cup cornmeal

Kosher salt

Vegetable oil, for frying

2 tablespoons bacon fat

1½ pounds catfish fillets, or about 6 ounces fish per sandwich (see Note)

Freshly ground black pepper

4 round soft buns, 3½ to 4 inches in diameter, split

Green leaf lettuce leaves, for serving

Red onion rings, for serving

4 dill pickle "stackers," halved

4 large tomato slices, for serving

Potato chips or Coleslaw (page 333), for serving

Note: If you're working with large catfish fillets that are more than 1 inch thick, lay them flat and slice in half horizontally so that you end up with two fillets that are only ½ inch thick. Trim to fit the bun. If using smaller fillets, stack them inside to fill the bun.

Mix the mayonnaise and sriracha together in a small bowl.

Put the flour, egg whites, and cornmeal in 3 separate shallow dishes and sprinkle each with some salt. Add enough oil to an 11-inch cast-iron skillet to be 1 inch deep. Heat the oil and bacon fat in the skillet over medium heat until about 350°F.

Sprinkle each fillet with some salt and pepper. Dredge first in the flour, then the egg whites, and then the cornmeal. Working with 2 or 3 fillets at a time, slip the fillets into the oil and fry until the cornmeal browns nicely, 3 to 4 minutes. Flip and fry on the other side until nicely browned, 3 to 4 more minutes. The crust should be crispy and the fillet should feel firm, not mushy. Remove to a baking sheet fitted with a wire rack. Repeat with the remaining fillets.

Divide the sriracha mayo among all bun surfaces. Place a piece of lettuce, some onion, fried fish, 1 to 2 pickle slices, and a tomato slice into each bun. Serve with potato chips or coleslaw and a chilled beverage.

PADDLEFISH OR STURGEON STEAKS
WITH TOMATOES, OLIVES, AND CAPERS

SERVES 4

¼ cup extra virgin olive oil

2 pounds paddlefish or sturgeon steaks, 1 inch thick

Kosher salt

Freshly ground black pepper

1 tablespoon white wine or vermouth

1 (14-ounce) can cherry tomatoes, drained

8 kalamata olives, pitted and quartered lengthwise

5 anchovy fillets, chopped

5 large fresh basil leaves, chopped or torn, plus additional for garnish

1 small red onion, thinly sliced

2 teaspoons capers, drained

Crusty bread, for serving

ALSO WORKS WITH: Shark, swordfish, or any other "meaty" fish that can be steaked out. You could even steak out a big catfish for this recipe, though it's essential that you trim away the fish's fat and any reddish-colored flesh.

Very few anglers target paddlefish and sturgeon, in part because of limited availability and in part because of apprehension about how to clean and prepare them. The availability issue is legitimate, though I do believe that most fishermen would be pleasantly surprised to learn just how many opportunities to chase these fish actually exist. Recently, I got a paddlefish with my bowfishing rig along the Kentucky shore of the Ohio River in the summer and then caught a handful of shovelnose sturgeon along the lower Yellowstone River the following spring. If it weren't for an ice storm that canceled a trip, I would have followed that up with a chance at a white sturgeon from Oregon's Columbia River that winter. In between those distant locations, there were plenty of opportunities that I didn't try out. So as you can see, the fish are out there. As far as the problems of handling and preparation go . . . well, that's why you bought this book.

Preheat the oven to 400°F.

Grease a 2-quart baking dish with 2 tablespoons of the oil. Sprinkle the fish with salt and pepper and arrange in a single layer in the baking dish. Drizzle a little more oil and the wine over the top of the fish. Put the canned tomatoes in a bowl and crush with your hands (or use a potato masher). Add the remaining oil, the olives, anchovies, basil, onion, capers, and salt and pepper to taste and mix well. Spread the tomato mixture evenly over the fish. Roast until the fish is cooked through and flakes easily, 20 to 25 minutes.

Serve with crusty bread.

GRILLED SALMON
WITH CLASSIC BASIL PESTO

SERVES 4 TO 6

Grilling a salmon fillet is something that most salmon fishermen can do pretty well, but it's the rare angler who can do it perfectly every time. One of those rare few is my buddy Andrew Radzialowski, a chef from the Pacific Northwest's San Juan Island. He and I have been cooking wild game together since the mid-1990s, when we stuffed a quartered-out roadkill deer into the cavity of a whole pig and roasted it inside a fifty-gallon oil drum. We've done a few things that were a tad more elegant since then, though Andy retains his pragmatic approach to cooking. Here's his take on grilled salmon.

ALSO WORKS WITH: Any salmon or steelhead, or any high-quality fish that is suitable for grilling.

CLASSIC BASIL PESTO

2 cups packed fresh basil leaves

⅓ cup pine nuts

1 clove garlic

¾ cup extra virgin olive oil

2 tablespoons fresh lemon juice

1½ teaspoons kosher salt

1 teaspoon freshly ground black pepper

½ cup grated Parmigiano-Reggiano cheese

SALMON

2 pounds salmon fillets, skin on with the pinbones removed

3 tablespoons olive oil

1 tablespoon kosher salt

1 teaspoon freshly ground black pepper

Zest of 1 lemon

SPECIAL EQUIPMENT NEEDED:

food processor

FOR THE PESTO: Pulse the basil, pine nuts, and garlic in a food processor several times, until coarsely chopped. Add 2 tablespoons of the oil and the lemon juice and process until smooth. Add the salt and pepper and, with the processor running, slowly pour in the remaining oil. Add the cheese and pulse a few more times to incorporate. (This makes 1 cup.)

FOR THE SALMON: Prepare a grill to high heat (500°F). Rinse the fish with cold running water to remove any slime or loose scales. Gently pat dry with paper towels and place on a clean plate or baking sheet skin-side down. Evenly drizzle the oil over the fish and sprinkle the salt, pepper, and lemon zest on top. Carefully oil the grill with a pair of tongs and a paper towel dipped in oil. This will help keep the fish from sticking. Once the grill is hot, carefully place the fish flesh-side down in the center of the grill. Close the lid and cook until the sides of the fillet begin to curl upward, 3 to 5 minutes. Don't move the fish until this happens or it will stick to the grill. Once a nice crust has formed on the flesh and it curls and frees from the grates, carefully flip it onto the skin side and continue cooking with the lid closed. The time will vary depending on the thickness of your fish. A good way to check for doneness is to carefully "open" the flesh by inserting the tip of the knife between the flakes on the thickest part of the fillet. Once you see the raw pink color slightly turn to light pink, remove the fillet from the grill onto a clean platter and allow the heat in the flesh to finish cooking the fish, another 3 to 4 minutes. Serve the salmon immediately with the pesto on the side or drizzled on top.

SKEWERED FIRE-ROASTED TROUT

SEE BELOW FOR YIELD

1 or 2 trout per person (depending on the size of the fish and the appetite of the angler; it works best with trout ranging from 8 to 14 inches)

Kosher salt

Freshly ground black pepper

Chermoula (page 321)

SPECIAL EQUIPMENT NEEDED: food processor; skewers of green wood, 2 to 3 feet long and ½ inch thick at the thin end; campfire

I've cooked many trout like this over the years while on river trips and mountain hikes. It fills you with backwoods pride to see a fish that you caught from the river cooking on a stick that you cut from the riverbank over a fire made from the river's own driftwood. A pinch of salt or Creole Seasoning (page 312) is all that it takes to make it pretty damn good; Chermoula, a tangy Moroccan herb sauce that is commonly paired with fish, is all that it takes to make it perfect.

ALSO WORKS WITH: Try it with other kinds of fish, especially if you're in a pinch, but it's best with trout.

Build a campfire. For each fish, find a skewer of green wood, 2 to 3 feet long and ⅓ inch thick at the thin end. The skewers need to be thin enough to go through the mouth of the fish without ripping it apart but sturdy enough to bear the fish's weight. Strip clean of leaves and smaller branches and sharpen the thin end. Also using green wood, whittle 3 or 4 pins for each fish that are about as thick as a pencil, 3 inches long, and sharp at both ends.

Sprinkle the fish with salt and pepper, inside and out, and rub it in. Run the sharpened end of the skewer into the fish's mouth and pass the end through the body cavity and then into the flesh at the base of the tail. Secure the fish to the skewer by passing the pins through the sides of the fish, crosswise to the skewer, so that the skewer is pinched between the pins and the fish's spine. Gently roast the fish over the fire, rotating every couple of minutes. You can use rocks to support the skewer in place so that you don't need to hold it the entire time. If the trout starts to curl aggressively or the fins turn black and burn, it's too close to the fire. The trout is done when the skin can easily be peeled away and the meat can be separated from the bones. Remove the fish from the skewer and serve with the Chermoula.

COCONUT CURRY FISH FILLET PACKETS

SERVES 4 (MAKES 2 FISH)

Grilling freshwater fish fillets over a fire can be tricky. A lot of the species have small fillets with lean flesh and delicate textures. It's all too easy to dry them out or have them crumble between the grates. You can solve those problems by using foil pouches and a bit of sauce—in this case, a coconut curry sauce—which make your fillets far more impervious to overcooking or other harm. This recipe is especially good for shore lunches over a campfire, but it also works well on a backyard propane or charcoal grill, or right in your kitchen's oven.

2 pounds fish fillets, boneless if possible (with freshwater fish, either scale them or remove the skin)

¼ cup green curry paste

¼ cup coconut milk, water, or Fish Stock (page 309)

¼ cup vegetable oil

4 sprigs fresh Thai basil

4 sprigs fresh cilantro

1 stalk fresh lemongrass, outer leaves discarded, halved, smashed with the back of a knife

Coconut Rice (page 330)

TO GRILL OVER A FIRE: Build a fire, preferably with hardwoods, that can accommodate a cooking grate and let the wood cook down to a bed of hot embers. While your fire burns down, prepare the fish.

If using a household grill, preheat a gas grill to medium-high heat.

Rinse the fillets and pat them dry. Stir the curry paste, coconut milk, and oil in a small bowl until smooth.

Cross two 12- by 24-inch pieces of foil. Place the fillets in the center, smear them with the curry paste, and layer them with the basil, cilantro, and lemongrass. Fold the foil around the fish and crimp to create a pouch.

Carefully lay the cooking grate 6 to 8 inches over the bed of embers. Your hand should be able to withstand only 4 seconds of time hovering over the fire. If you can hold your hand longer, add a little more fuel to the fire.

Place the packages of fish on the grates. Grill, covered, for 4 minutes; you should be able to hear the liquid inside the foil sizzling. Carefully flip the package and grill the other side, covered, for another 4 minutes, or longer for fillets that are more than ¾ inch thick. Transfer to a tray or platter and carefully open the package. Serve the fish with coconut rice.

ALSO WORKS WITH: Stick with white-fleshed fillets that can be easily deboned, such as walleye, smallmouth bass, largemouth bass, or lake whitefish. Northern pike are great like this, but be careful of those bones! It's also great with many saltwater species ranging from flounder to rockfish to snapper. (*The photograph on the opposite page features the fillets of a small saltwater flatfish.*)

30

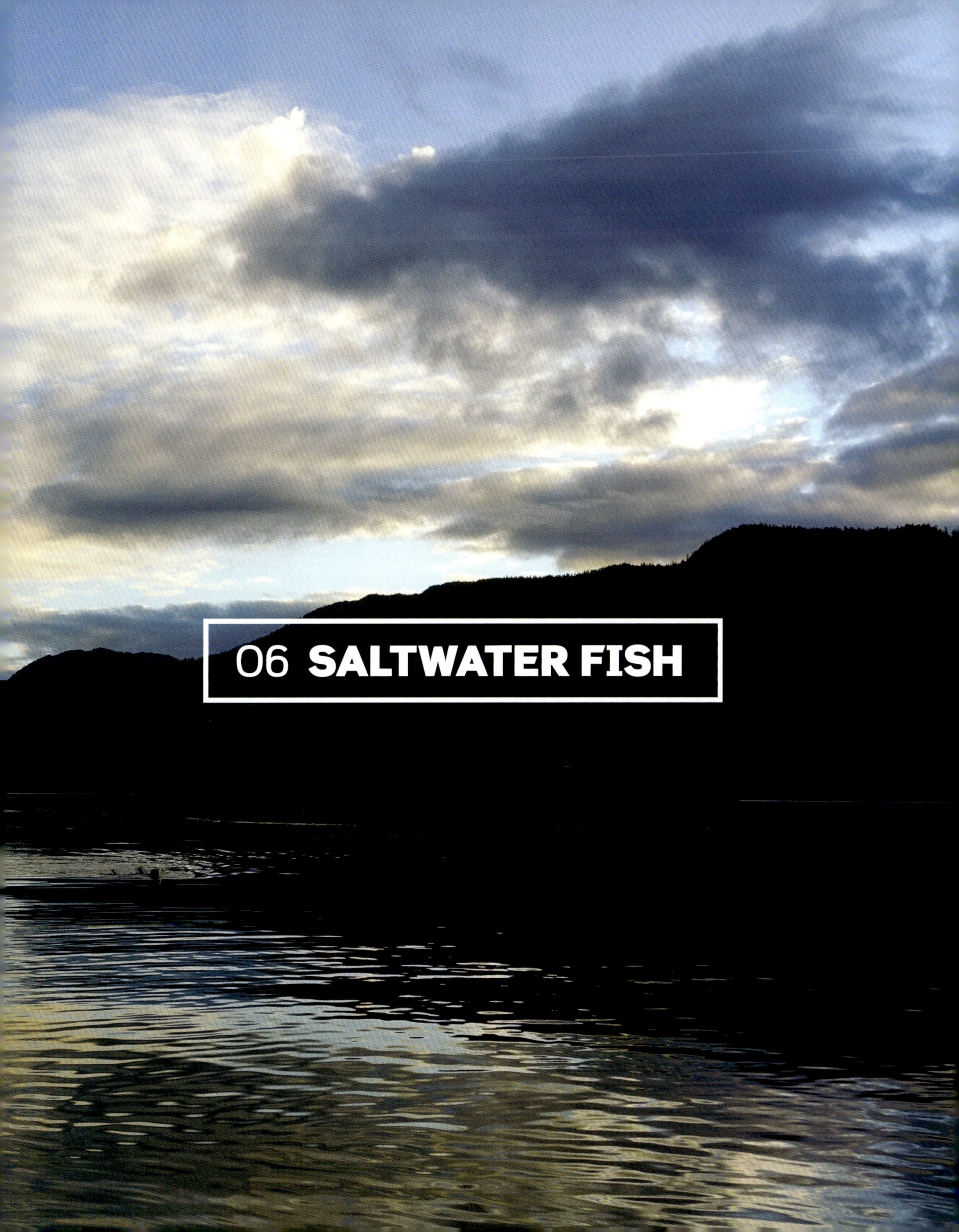

06 SALTWATER FISH

INTRODUCTION

The world's oceans, which are all connected and cover 70 percent of the Earth's surface, hold about twenty thousand species of fish. Only a fraction of those are commonly eaten, and an even smaller fraction are available to American anglers, but it's still a dizzying array of tastes and textures swimming around out there. Florida alone has a whopping ninety species that are regarded by the state's fish and game agency as "commonly caught," with plenty more that appear less regularly on the end of an angler's line. These numbers are always on my mind when I take my fishing rod and stroll down to my favorite stretch of Florida beach, which sits on the Gulf Coast side not far from Fort Myers.

My preferred setup is designed to be as appealing as possible to the greatest number of species. I use an eight-foot surf rod paired with a spinning reel that's loaded with a twenty-pound braided line. I slip a plumb sinker onto the main line and then tie on a small barrel swivel to hold it in place. To the barrel swivel I attach about thirty inches of fluorocarbon leader, and to the leader I attach a razor-sharp stainless steel hook that's big enough to hold a single live shrimp.

With that rig in one hand and a bucket of shrimp in the other, I slowly work my way down the beach as I try to read the water for clues about where the fish might be hanging out. I'm looking at a lot of things all at once, with particular focus on identifying the depths and contours of the "trough" that lies between the beach and the submerged sandbars that might sit anywhere from fifty to two hundred yards out there. This trough is like a highway for fish traffic as they travel up and down the surf in search of food.

Sunshine is helpful for reading the water, as the deeper and fishier holes inside the trough will appear to be a shade or two darker than the water around it. But even on a cloudy day you can still figure things out by watching how the waves break, which can be translated into a mental picture of the ocean's floor. Additional information can be picked up by observing the actions of seagulls and pelicans, which will betray the presence of baitfish, or by analyzing any splashes, wakes, or ripples that might be created by baitfish themselves or by bigger things that might be pursuing the bait.

All of this information, or the lack of it, goes into my head and gets processed into impulses that tell me to cast over here or cast over there. When the shrimp hits the water, I know that just about anything could happen, that there's a dozen or more kinds of fish that could take that shrimp in a gulp and then bolt for deeper water as I struggle to keep my head together and do everything necessary to keep the line from breaking. I get so pumped up with high hopes that a mermaid coming up to pluck the shrimp from the hook wouldn't be too far outside of my expectations. While I've yet to see that happen, I've seen just about everything else. To make a list of all the fish that I've ever caught from my Florida beach would be a daunting task thanks to the vagaries of memory, but I think you'll get the picture from a list of things that my buddy and I once caught there in a single long day: a southern stingray, a bunch of gulf kingfish, a redfish, a sheepshead, two spotted sea trout, a Spanish mackerel, a black drum, and several blue runners. Walking up from the beach that night, with a large cooler full of fish and ice, we had a greater assortment of tastes and textures in our personal possession than you're likely to find at even a well-stocked seafood counter in one of your local supermarkets.

No matter where you live on the nation's coasts, the saltwater world represents a nearly infinite frontier of wild game cooking that would be impossible for a single person to fully explore in a lifetime. The wild array of fishes is what excites me so much about saltwater angling. The only thing more exciting than trying to catch them is trying to cook them. Each species presents its own challenges and rewards to an adventurous cook. Sure, there really aren't any deep secrets left regarding restaurant favorites such as halibut, mahimahi, and red snapper, which are widely known thanks to their ready commercial availability and unassailable quality. But no matter how many restaurants you've been to, it's unlikely that you've ever encountered a menu featuring sea robins, monkeyface prickleback, unicorn fish, Irish lord, or the eloquently named ratfish—all of which are edible and easily obtained by a nominally outfitted angler who's willing to put in the time.

The methods and recipes in this chapter are geared toward those commonly caught species that generalist anglers are likely to encounter, but the information can be applied to just about any fish in the sea. Experienced anglers, especially the ones who know how to cook, will tell you that what happens right after you catch your fish is perhaps more important than what happens after you bring them into your kitchen. In general, I find that saltwater fish are more vulnerable to spoilage than freshwater fish. Keeping them in good condition requires constant vigilance. After catching a

fish, make sure to bleed it by cutting open its gills while it's still alive. This is especially important with fish that have lots of anaerobic muscle, such as pelagic species. You can stun the fish with a blow to the head before bleeding it; the heart will still beat for a couple of minutes.

It's smart to gut your fish. This slows down decay. Whether you gut them or not, you have to chill them as quickly as possible. Crushed ice works best, but anything is better than nothing. I've chilled a lot of fish by pouring a few gallons of seawater over a bunch of frozen gel packs to create an ice-cold bath. It's not as good as ice, but it works. If you don't have a way of icing your fish, cover it with a wet towel or even a wet jacket to protect it from the sun. As it chills, your fish will stiffen up as it enters rigor mortis. Don't overhandle the fish, and don't try bending it back straight again. That will damage the flesh and turn it to mush. Instead, let the fish relax before you fillet it. If you do all that, and then you follow the methods and recipes below, you'll be well on your way to some delicious meals. Now go. There are plenty of fish in the sea.

The following is a breakdown of some of the most commonly caught saltwater fish in five regions of the United States, including some favorite and not-so-favorite species.

Northeast

Striped bass are an absolute favorite. They are big, meaty fish with white, somewhat translucent flesh that flakes beautifully. And they are highly versatile. While often caught in tandem with striped bass, **bluefish** are far more polarizing than stripers. Their flesh is dark and somewhat oily, with a stronger flavor, but they are superb if you know how to cook them. They need to be bled and chilled immediately upon catching and preferably are eaten fresh. They are great as a smoked fish. **Porgies,** or **scup,** are a smaller species with excellent flesh that is good baked, broiled, fried, grilled, or cooked in a salt crust. Some chefs compare it to red snapper. If anything, **Atlantic cod** could be criticized for being too mild, but it is a good-tasting and versatile fish with white flesh that is suitable for people who say they "normally don't like fish." It's great for making salted cod, a fun and interesting preparation. The various flatfish species are all good, with **summer flounder,** or **fluke,** being a favorite species with a decent yield of meat. It has soft, delicate flesh with mild flavors. **Atlantic black sea bass** is firm and lean with a mild, delicate flavor—another great choice for people who are finicky when it comes to fish. **Sea robins** are much maligned by anglers targeting striped bass and other surf species, but there's no need to toss them. They make wonderful fish tacos. See also: Southeast.

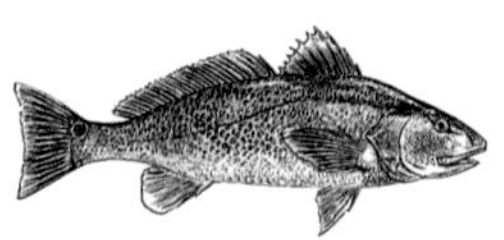

Southeast

Redfish, or **red drum,** are excellent. They are a highly versatile white-fleshed fish that flakes beautifully. **Speckled sea trout** and **gray trout, or weakfish,** are mild, delicate, and widely appreciated as a versatile fish, but they need to be handled very carefully. Chill immediately and keep cold. **Sheepshead** are also excellent. They have firm, moist flesh that is great when pan-fried, baked, broiled, and grilled. **Both gulf and southern kingfish** deserve more credit than they get. When properly chilled and handled, they are excellent frying fish that are easy and fun to catch. Like most flounders, the **southern flounder** has delicate, flaky white meat. The yield is good relative to many other small flatfish. The **spot** fish is small but fun to catch and good to eat; it is the panfish of the Atlantic. See also: Northeast and Gulf Coast.

Gulf Coast

A lot of anglers aren't crazy about them, but **Spanish mackerel** are dark, oily, and very good—they are a full-flavored fish suitable for everything from ceviche to broiling. **Snook** are one of the best fish in the ocean—they are white-fleshed and highly versatile. The various jack species, including **jack crevalle,** are often criticized as being strong-flavored and too dark, but they're good when you trim away the darkest blood-colored meat. In Mexico, they are popular for fish tacos. The **southern stingray** is a common bycatch for shore fishermen, and it's not widely utilized. Prepare according to skate recipes; a classic preparation is to serve them in browned butter with capers. Comparisons to scallops are not far off. **Pompano** are superb and flavorful with pearly white flesh and a delicious skin. **Cobia** are excellent, with a flesh that is comparable to mahimahi, a restaurant staple. They are good for sashimi. **Ladyfish** are a common annoyance to shore anglers. Their flesh is bony and mushy and hard to put to good use. There's little that needs to be said about **red snapper**. Widely regarded as one of the finest fish, they are good for just about anything that can be done with fish, including raw preparations. **Tarpon** are a popular food fish in Jamaica, but eating them in the United States is a no-no. **Tripletail** are outstanding, among the very best of all fish in the ocean. If you encounter a **lionfish** in the more southerly water, the meat is excellent—it's great for ceviche. But be careful, stings from the fish are excruciating. See also: Northeast, West Coast, and Hawaii.

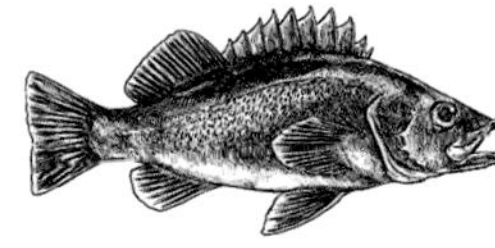

West Coast

There is boundless misinformation surrounding the edibility of **barracuda**. The meat is white and flaky and perfectly usable, though larger specimens should be avoided due to accumulations of ciguatera toxin. There are dozens of species of **rockfish**. Fisheries managers sometimes categorize them as pelagic and non-pelagic. All are excellent, with firm white flesh. Smaller specimens have a delicate flesh, while some larger rockfish have a very dense, almost "meaty" flesh. **Kelp bass,** or **calico bass,** have a mild white flesh similar to rockfish. They are very versatile. The larger species of surfperch are all fairly similar, though each species has its peculiarities. The **redtail surfperch** is a favorite, though **rubberlip, barred,** and **calico** are all good. The flesh is soft and delicate, similar to small flounder. They are great for grilling or steaming. The fillets are good when brushed with olive oil and baked in an oven until the edges begin to crisp. **White sea bass** have a firm, meaty texture with large flakes. They are similar to halibut. There are a lot of spirited debates around the food qualities of various sharks. **Blue shark** is generally unpopular and can have a strong urine flavor. **Thresher shark** and **shortfin mako** are regarded as excellent and are similar to swordfish. **Yellowtail** are one of the best fish in the ocean, with a buttery texture that is perfect for raw preparations. See also: Gulf Coast, Hawaii, and Pacific Northwest/Alaska. If you're looking for information on salmon, go to Nature of the Beast: Freshwater, on page 182.

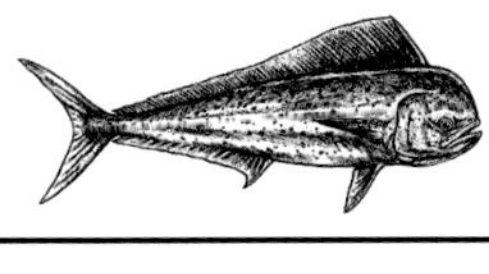

Hawaii

While killing **bonefish (o'io)** is generally frowned upon by American anglers, they are eaten in Hawaii. **Unicornfish (kala)** are excellent when grilled whole. Cook until the skin begins to crack and can be peeled away. The flesh is dense and meaty. **Striped mullet ('ama'ama)** and **sharp-nose mullet (uouoa)** are slightly oily fish that can be grilled, steamed, or smoked whole. The fillets can be pan-fried or served in raw preparations. **Mahimahi** are superb, an almost universally appreciated fish that is good for just about everything, including raw preparations. **Wahoo (ono)** are sweet-tasting and highly regarded; they have low fat content with large flakes. In Hawaiian, ono means "good to eat." **Blue line snapper** are a nonnative fish in Hawaii that are readily available in shallow waters. They are not as highly regarded as many other snapper species but are still good. **Hogfish (a'awa)** are rich and sweet-tasting—an excellent fish. **Gray snapper (uku)** have slightly pinkish flesh, similar to many other snapper species. The flavor is very good, and the fish is suitable for many applications. **Goatfish (kumu)** are a flaky, buttery fish that is excellent. **Yellowfin tuna (ahi)** is perhaps the most widely recognized and appreciated tuna species, and also one of the best. See also: Gulf Coast and West Coast.

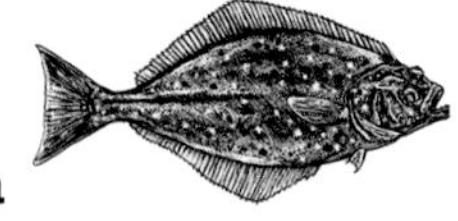

Pacific Northwest/Alaska

Kelp greenling have mild, very delicate flesh that is excellent. They must be handled carefully and kept on ice. **Yelloweye rockfish** have a white flesh that is very dense, especially on older specimens. They are excellent. Their collars invite comparisons to chicken. **Pacific halibut** are widely loved, with white, mild flesh and large flakes. Specimens in the fifty-pound range and smaller are better than larger halibut, which can be mealy and chewy. **Black cod,** or **sablefish,** are one of the best fish in the ocean from a fish lover's perspective. Its rich, oily flesh is suitable for light smoking. **Spiny dogfish** are edible and can be good, despite their rather poor reputation and sometimes off-putting odor. They need to be gutted and iced immediately. **Ling cod** are superb, far better than halibut in the opinion of many anglers. They have white, almost translucent flesh with large flakes and are highly versatile. **Pacific cod** are similar to Atlantic cod. Their mild, delicate flesh needs to be handled carefully and iced quickly. See also: West Coast. If you're looking for information on salmon, go to Nature of the Beast: Freshwater, on page 182.

FILLETING HALIBUT

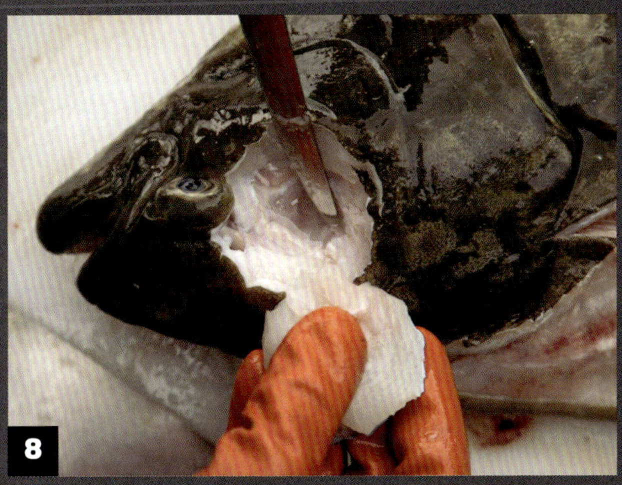
8

9

Pictured here is a Pacific halibut, which can grow to over four hundred pounds. The process used to fillet a halibut, often known as "quartering," can be used on pretty much any flatfish including fluke, flounder, and sole.

1. All flatfish have four quarters that need to be removed separately. Each side of the fish is divided into two boneless fillets, or quarters, found on either side of the spine. Start with dark side of the fish. Make an incision along the lateral line from the gill plate to the tail. Cut through the skin down to the rib cage, using the spine as a guide.

2. Along the first incision, follow the ribs outward with your knife to cut the upper quarter free from the carcass. You want to cleanly remove the entire upper fillet from the head to the tail. Use the same technique to remove the second, lower quarter on the dark side of the halibut.

3. Remove any skin from the gut cavity that is still attached to the flesh of the lower quarter.

4. The lower quarter will be shorter because you'll want to stop cutting at the beginning of the gut cavity behind the head.

5. Flip the fish over to the light side. Repeat the quartering process on this side.

6. Anchor the tail end of a fillet on the cutting board with a fork. Now, slide your knife between the skin and the flesh to cut the skin free from the fillet.

7. Take the time to remove any dark, bloody meat and interior skin from the surface of each fillet. This prevents strong, off-putting flavors and ensures better-tasting meals later.

8. Halibut have a tasty, boneless chunk of scallop-shaped cheek meat that shouldn't be wasted. Find it by feeling for the muscle behind the jaw, then make a circular cut around the cheek to remove it.

9. Flip the fish over and remove the second cheek. On large flatfish you'll also want to remove the collars. See page 231.

FILLETING MAHIMAHI

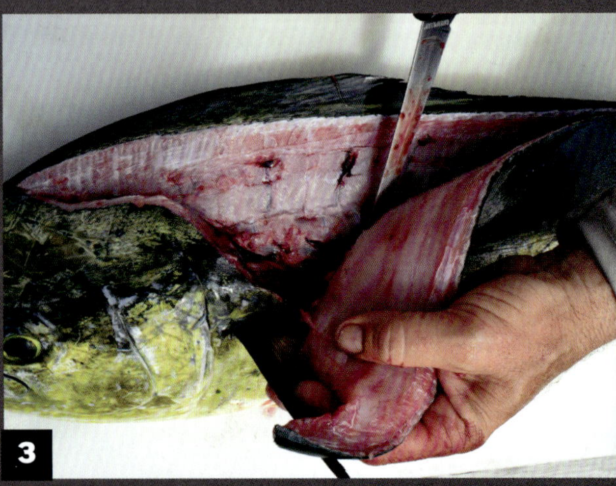

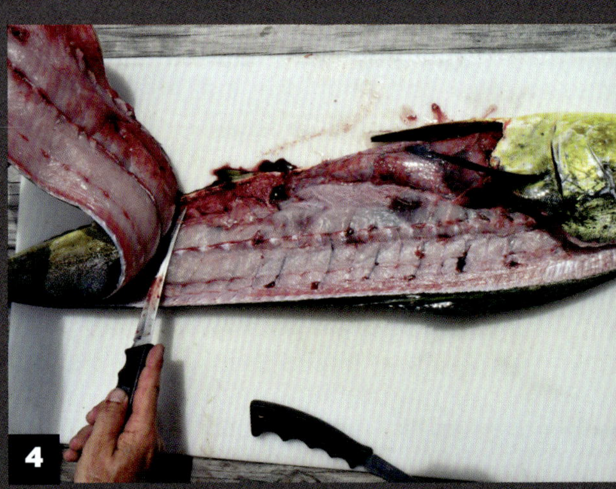

Mahimahi, whose name means "strong" in Hawaiian, are also called dorado or dolphin fish. From a butchering perspective, mahimahi fall into the general category of round fish. A similar filleting technique can be used for a wide variety of other saltwater species ranging from lingcod to redfish.

1. Make the first incision from the top of the head, down to the gill plate, and around the pectoral fin. Notice how this initial cut takes in the meat at the top of the head.

2. Where the first downward cut atop the head began, start cutting the upper portion of the fillet lengthwise toward the tail. Cut alongside the dorsal fin, following the spine, for the correct depth.

3. Following your original cut behind the gill plate and pectoral fin, continue cutting down to the belly. At the belly, you can now begin cutting back toward the tail.

4. The backbone that runs down the center of the fish is a good guide for your knife. Cut along it and continue to work toward the tail until the fillet is completely removed.

5. Now flip the fish over and repeat the process.

6. You should be able to see and feel the rib bones on the belly of each fillet. Slice the rib bones away.

7. Next, separate the skin from the fillets.

8. Here's where the process differs from many other species of fish. Mahimahi have a bloodline that separates the upper and lower muscles of the fillet. Make a lengthwise cut just above and below this line to remove the strip of dark, bloody, off-tasting meat. If you're filleting a fish that lacks this bloodline, skip this step.

9. You'll be left with two clean pieces of meat, a thick upper loin fillet and a flat, thin lower fillet. On large fillets, slice into steaks for frying, grilling, or baking.

ROCKFISH FILLETING, PINBONE REMOVAL, AND COLLARING

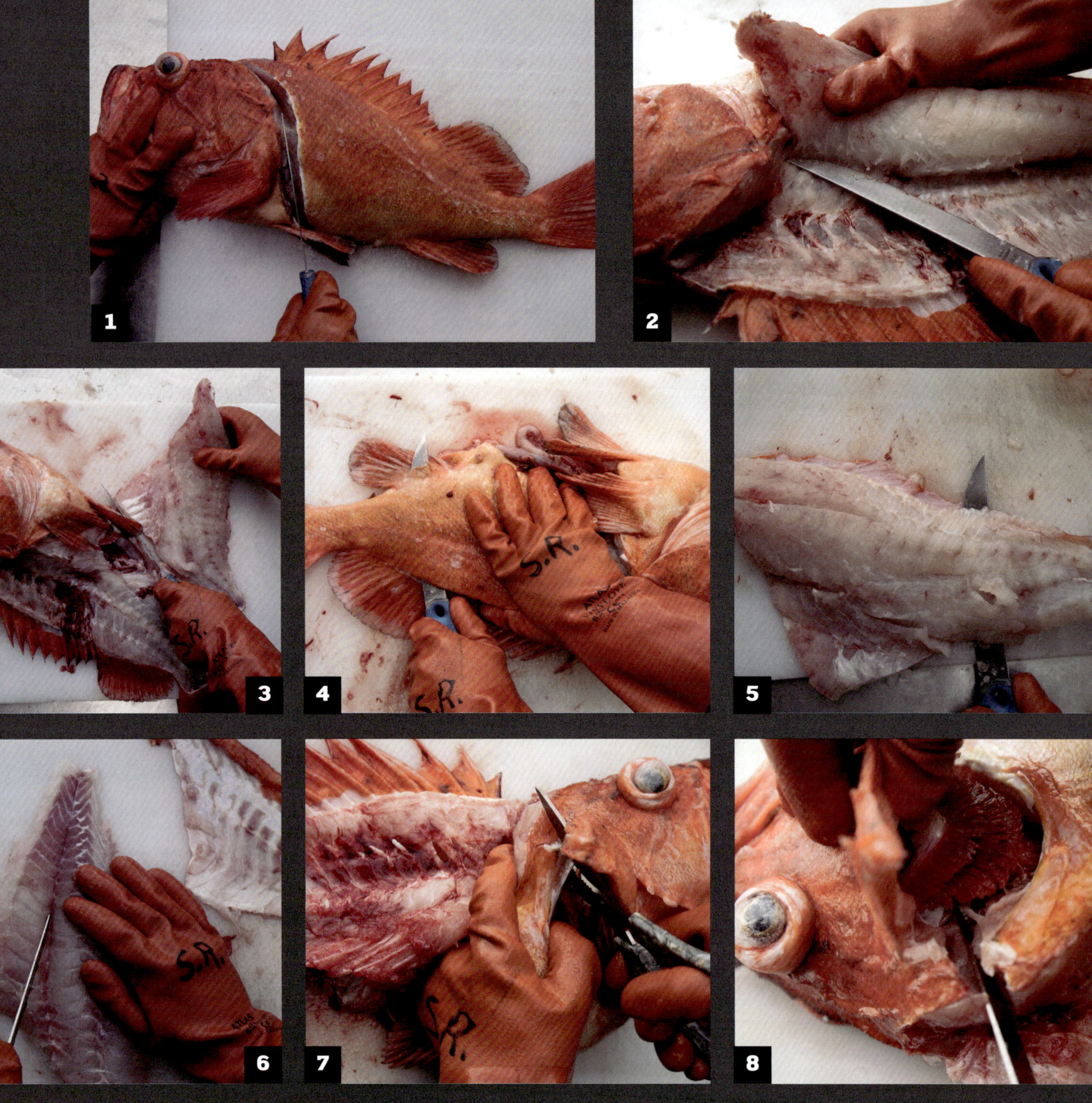

9

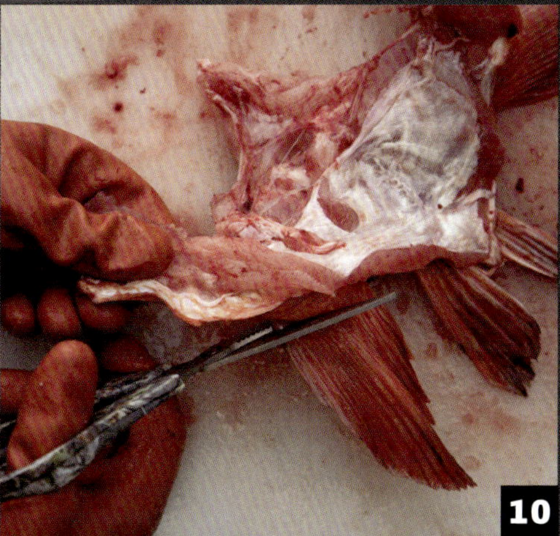
10

11

You'll need to remove the pinbones when filleting rockfish species like this yelloweye rockfish. You'll also want to save the collars on large rockfish, striped bass, salmon, and other sizable gamefish. Most anglers don't bother removing collars, but this firm meat holds together very well on the grill and breaded, fried fish collars are the seafood version of fried chicken.

1. Make the first incision from the top of the head, working down around the gill plate to the pectoral fin.

2. Next, cut the fillet free from the back down to the belly, using the spine and dorsal fin as a guide for the correct cutting depth.

3. Cut the fillet free at the belly.

4. Flip the fish over and remove the second fillet.

5. Remove the skin from each fillet.

6. Once the fillet has been skinned, rockfish, smallmouth bass, snapper, and other fish have a line of small pinbones that need to be removed. These pinbones aren't easy to see, but you'll find them by running your fingers over the center of the thickest part of the fillet. Cut away the thin strip of meat that contains the bones.

7. After you've filleted your fish, begin removing the collar by using a pair of game shears to cut through the skin and bones on the upper portion of the collar behind the gill plate. Do this on both sides of the fish.

8. Now hold the gill plate out of the way and use your fillet knife to begin cutting the collar free from the carcass where you made the initial cut with the game shears.

9. Cut the collar down and around the head. Flip the fish over and continue cutting to remove the collar in one piece. You may need to use the game shears to completely sever the collar from the bony gill and throat area.

10. Use the game shears to clip off the fins.

11. Here, you have the collar and two fillets with the pinbones removed ready to be rinsed and cooked.

MAHIMAHI CRUDO

SERVES 2

This preparation makes me think back to a simplified version that my wife and I prepared on a small island off Puerto Rico. After we polished off our catch, we waded into the water for a swim and a school of juvenile palometa attacked our fingertips to get at the fish oils. My wife had to retreat back up to the beach. I think of that experience as testament to the freshness of our meal, and also to the primal quality of eating raw fish. Here, the experience is elevated with some simple ingredients that add a zesty kick to the already lively flavors of the ocean.

ALSO WORKS WITH: Pretty much any fish that's suitable for sushi or sashimi.

---

8 ounces fresh raw mahimahi, skin removed

2 tablespoons extra virgin olive oil

4 teaspoons fresh orange juice

½ teaspoon fennel seeds, toasted and lightly crushed

½ small serrano chile, thinly sliced

2 tablespoons small fresh flat-leaf parsley leaves, torn

½ teaspoon flaky sea salt, such as Maldon

Zest of ½ orange

Very thinly slice the mahimahi on a 45-degree angle. Arrange on one or two serving plates. Drizzle the oil and orange juice over the slices. Sprinkle the fennel seeds, chile, parsley, and salt over the top. Grate the orange zest over the fish.

CEVICHE

SERVES 6 (MAKES 3 CUPS)

1 pound firm white-fleshed saltwater fish, cut into ½-inch cubes

Juice of 5 to 6 limes (1 to 1½ cups)

1 medium sweet yellow onion, finely chopped (¼ inch)

3 Roma tomatoes, seeded and finely chopped (¼ inch)

2 scallions, cut into ⅓-inch slices

1 avocado, cut into ⅓-inch cubes

1 small clove garlic, minced

1 roasted poblano chile, seeded and cut into ⅓-inch cubes (see below)

½ jalapeño chile, minced

2 tablespoons chopped fresh cilantro

¼ teaspoon kosher salt

¼ teaspoon freshly ground black pepper

Tortilla chips, for serving

Ceviche is one of my favorite preparations for saltwater fish. It's especially good as a mixed-bag dish that features a handful of different species. I've made this everywhere from a spearfishing trip in the Bahamas (grouper, snapper, lionfish, grunt) to bottom-fishing trips in southeast Alaska (rockfish, lingcod, halibut). You'll be shocked by how quickly a bowl of fish will disappear when you make this, so plan accordingly. And make sure to trim your fish, ridding it of any bones or bloodlines.

ALSO WORKS WITH: It's best with firm, white-fleshed ocean fish such as grouper, rockfish, snapper, sea bass, striped bass, and mahimahi. It can be done with select freshwater fishes, such as walleye. You can also try slightly darker and oilier fish, such as mackerel, which have a bit stronger flavor but are still excellent.

Combine the fish, lime juice, and onion in a bowl. Cover and refrigerate for 2 to 4 hours, stirring 3 or 4 times.

Remove from the fridge and drain off most of the liquid, leaving just enough to keep the fish wet. Add the tomatoes, scallions, avocado, garlic, poblano and jalapeño chiles, the cilantro, salt, and pepper and gently toss together. Serve the ceviche with your favorite tortilla chips.

TO ROAST POBLANO CHILES

Set the chiles directly on an open flame—this could be a gas stovetop, grill, or outdoor pot burner. Char the skin, turning the chiles so that all sides get directly exposed to the flame, until the entire chile is black. Place the hot chiles in a bowl and cover tightly with plastic wrap. Let the chiles steam for at least 30 minutes. Then carefully remove all the charred skin with your fingers, discarding the black flakes. Open up the chiles and remove all the seeds. This is easiest if you lay the chiles open and use the back of a knife to carefully scrape and remove the seeds. Do not rinse the chiles; it's OK if you have a few seeds and charred skin in the mix, but rinsing the chiles will remove some of the flavor. Clean your cutting board of any remaining seeds. Dice the chiles and cool.

HH

FISH CHOWDER

SERVES 4 TO 6

I tend to think of chowder and gumbo in the same way. It's not that they taste similar, but rather they share in common an ability to accommodate a wide variety of perhaps imperfect ingredients. Just as you can make a great gumbo with the mixed odds and ends found in your freezer, such as a squirrel or two, some rabbits, a pair of duck breasts, and so on, you can make a wonderful chowder with a mixed collection of fish that might not be suitable in taste, or adequate in size, for other preparations. To put it another way, I would never take a fresh piece of striped bass or halibut and whack it up for chowder. But let's say I had a few small flounder in the freezer along with the leftover tail section of a striper fillet? In that case, bust out the salt pork and fish stock. This is a Maine style fish chowder.

ALSO WORKS WITH: Virtually any white-fleshed fish, including freshwater fish. We used to make some great chowders using freshwater rock bass, which are not well-regarded as tablefare.

2 ounces salt pork, finely chopped

2 teaspoons vegetable oil

1 medium onion, chopped

1 tablespoon unsalted butter, plus more for serving (optional)

2 russet potatoes (1 to 1½ pounds), peeled and cut into ½-inch cubes

2½ cups Fish Stock (page 309)

1 teaspoon kosher salt

4 cups whole milk

2 pounds white-fleshed fish fillets (boneless, skinless, and trimmed of bloodlines; if using whole fillets, cut them down to 8-ounce portions)

Chopped fresh chives, for garnish

Oyster crackers, for serving

Put the salt pork in a large saucepan with the oil and turn the heat to medium-low. Cook until the fat renders and the bits are lightly crisped, 8 to 10 minutes. Add the onion and butter, raise the heat to medium, and cook until the onion is softened, about 5 minutes. Add the potatoes, fish stock, and ½ teaspoon of the salt, bring to a low boil, then reduce the heat and cook until the potatoes are tender, about 10 minutes. Pour in the milk and the remaining ½ teaspoon salt, raise the heat to medium-high, and bring just to a low simmer. Slip in the whole fish fillets, making sure they're covered with the milk, reduce the heat to maintain a gentle simmer, and simmer without stirring until the fish flakes easily, about 7 minutes. Remove from the heat, garnish with chives, dab a pat of butter on top, if desired, and serve with oyster crackers.

SAFFRON FISH STEW

SERVES 4

In a perfect world, you'd be able to put this stew together in a game-rich environment where it's possible to harvest your own clams and mussels and catch your own fish. I've spent some time in a number of such locations, and believe me, it's deeply rewarding. But don't worry if it's not possible for you. As long as you're starting with either your own shellfish or fish, you're well on your way to a satisfying meal that you can still call your own. So don't be ashamed if you need to round out your ingredients at a local fish shop or supermarket. Likewise, don't be ashamed if you need to cut an ingredient or get creative with substitutions. No one will be upset if your stew is graced with razor clams or quahogs in place of the littlenecks.

ALSO WORKS WITH: Because of the delicate cooking method, you want a high-quality fish that does not need a lot of dressing up to make it taste good. Skin-on fillets of smaller fish such as ocean perch or snapper work well, as do skinless portions of larger fish such as halibut and striped bass. And get creative with the shellfish. Any small hard-shell or soft-shell saltwater clam could work here.

12 littleneck clams

1 tablespoon cornmeal

3 tablespoons olive oil

2 cloves garlic, smashed

1 large leek, white and light green parts, thinly sliced

1 fennel bulb, cored and thinly sliced, fronds reserved

2 cups dry white wine or vermouth

2 cups water, plus more as needed

1 pound mussels, scrubbed and debearded

4 cups Fish Stock (page 309) or store-bought clam juice

1 tablespoon unsalted butter

1 large shallot, thinly sliced

2 bay leaves

½ cup Calvados or brandy

½ teaspoon saffron threads

Pinch of cayenne pepper

4 (3- to 4-ounce) pieces of firm, white-fleshed saltwater fish

Kosher salt

Freshly ground black pepper

½ cup crème fraîche

Toasted baguette, for serving

Chopped chives, for serving (optional)

Put the clams and cornmeal in a large bowl, cover with 1 inch of cold water plus some ice cubes, and let soak for 30 minutes. Scrub the clams and drain well.

Heat 1 tablespoon of the oil in a large Dutch oven (or other pot with a lid) over medium heat. Add the garlic and one-quarter of the leek and fennel and cook, stirring occasionally, until softened but not browned, about 5 minutes. Raise the heat to medium-high. Add 1 cup of the wine and boil until reduced to half, about 5 minutes. Add the clams and water, cover, and let steam for 4 minutes. Add the mussels and continue to steam until the shells open, about 6 more minutes. Remove the clams and mussels to a bowl, discarding any unopened shells. Strain the broth through a fine-mesh sieve into another bowl or large glass measuring cup. Discard the garlic, leek, and fennel. Add the fish stock and enough water to the strained broth to yield 8 cups.

Melt the butter with the remaining 2 tablespoons oil in a large saucepan over medium heat. Add the remaining leek and fennel, the shallot, and the bay leaves and sweat until softened, about 8 minutes. Raise the heat to medium-high, add the Calvados, and simmer until just glazing the bottom of the pot, about 1 minute. Add the remaining 1 cup wine and reduce by half, about 5 minutes. Add the stock mixture, the saffron, and the cayenne. Bring the soup to a boil, then reduce the heat to maintain a simmer and simmer until it thickens slightly and can just coat the back of a spoon. Raise the heat to medium. Sprinkle the fish generously with salt and pepper and gently slide it into the broth. Cover and poach until the fish is cooked through, 5 to 6 minutes. Discard the bay leaves.

Carefully transfer the fish to 4 bowls. Whisk the crème fraîche into the soup and adjust the seasonings. Return the clams and mussels to the soup to reheat. Then divide the clams, mussels, and soup among the bowls. Garnish with chives and serve with toasted baguette.

SALT-CRUSTED WHOLE FISH

SERVES 4

5 cups fine sea salt (see Tip below), plus more for finishing

1 (2-pound) or 2 (1-pound) whole fish, scaled and fins removed

Freshly ground black pepper

2 lemons, sliced

1 bunch fresh dill

6 cloves garlic, smashed

2 tablespoons coriander seeds, toasted, cooled, and ground

6 bay leaves, crumbled

2 tablespoons fennel seeds, toasted, cooled, and ground

6 large egg whites, lightly beaten

Olive oil, for drizzling

Lemon wedges, for serving

ALSO WORKS WITH: A wide array of fish can be used here: lake whitefish, snapper, sea bass, porgy, rockfish, black cod, large surfperch—you get the point. It's best to work with fish in the range of 1 to 4 pounds, with 2- to 3-pound fish being particularly nice.

SPECIAL EQUIPMENT NEEDED: spice grinder

Tip: Salt flavor matters. You can use kosher salt or another salt for this recipe if it's more convenient than fine sea salt, but keep in mind that the fish is essentially steaming inside the hard salt oven—so any flavor the salt carries, the fish will take on. For this reason, I don't recommend using iodized salt, as it's got a bit of a metallic aftertaste, but it would work if it's all you've got and could be disguised with some chopped rosemary or thyme mixed in with the eggs.

This process yields a tasty result and a dramatic presentation for your guests. Cracking into the crusted shell of salt to reveal a perfectly cooked fish is almost as fun as fishing. The key is to get the fish, or fishes, completely buried in the salt mixture. If your fish is larger than a couple of pounds, you might have to mix another half batch or a double batch of the salt mixture to cover it completely. Additionally, you can choose to add herbs and aromatic flavorings to the salt, or not. It adds an extra layer of complexity to your final dish if you do. I'm using lemon and dill here, but you could just as easily use orange and fresh rosemary or lemon and fresh thyme, whatever citrus/fresh herb combination makes you happy. In the end, it's the fish and the fisherman that star in this preparation.

Preheat the oven to 400°F.

Fit a baking sheet with parchment paper and sprinkle a pinch of salt onto the surface of the pan.

Sprinkle the inside of the fish well with salt and pepper. Arrange the lemon slices, dill, and smashed garlic inside the cavity (or cavities if making two fish) as evenly as possible.

Combine the remaining salt, toasted coriander, the crumbled bay leaves, toasted fennel seeds, and beaten egg whites in a medium bowl and mix well with a rubber spatula or your hands. The salt mixture should be the consistency of wet sand.

Drizzle some oil onto the parchment paper. Lay the fish down in the center of the paper. Drizzle the fish lightly with oil. Bury the fish completely in the salt mixture, covering it from head to tail. You are essentially creating a snug oven in which the fish will be happily steamed.

Bake until the salt mixture browns on the outside, about 25 minutes. Remove and let rest for 5 minutes. Then crack the hardened salt crust with a metal spoon to reveal the fish inside. Gently peel away the layer of salt and discard it. Fillet the fish as you would normally, using a knife and spoon to carefully lift the whole fillet from the spine, and transfer to a plate. Lift the head with the spine and discard to reveal the bottom fillet. (Repeat with the remaining fish if cooking more than one.) Serve with lemon wedges and finish with some sea salt.

CRISPY WHOLE THAI FISH

SERVES 2 TO 4

This is an all-time favorite of mine that I associate with beachfront vacations where I'm spending a lot of time fishing and cooking with friends and family. When you lay out a freshly caught whole fried fish on the table, you're signaling to everyone that this is a special meal that matters. While pretty much any fish is going to taste good when cooked like this, keep in mind the importance of a positive user experience. Fish that are too bony, or that yield a skimpy amount of meat, should be saved for other purposes. For this dish, you want meaty fish with stout bones that can easily be picked clean.

ALSO WORKS WITH: Stick with fish that have stout bones and lots of meat, such as snapper, rockfish, porgies, sea bass, small grouper, grunts, and black drum. It can also be prepared with freshwater species such as walleye, smallmouth bass, and even big bluegills. Keep in mind that freshwater fish, which have thinner bones, might be tougher to pick clean.

FOR THE FISH AND MARINADE: Score the sides of the fish diagonally, leaving about 1 inch between each cut.

Pick the basil, cilantro, and mint leaves from their sprigs, reserving them for the dipping sauce, and place the sprigs in a blender. Add the lemongrass, ginger, garlic, shallot, scallions, green chile, water, lime juice, palm sugar, and salt. Pulse rapidly for 30 seconds. Transfer the marinade to a container and let rest for 5 minutes.

Strain the marinade into a measuring cup and discard the solids. Place the fish in a large resealable bag and pour the marinade in the bag. Seal and refrigerate for at least 1 hour and up to 2 hours.

Remove the fish from the marinade and pat dry. Sprinkle each fish with ½ teaspoon salt. Pour the rice flour out onto a large plate. Dredge the fish in the flour, covering the entire surface, including between the score marks and the fins.

Heat the oil in a heavy pot large enough to hold one fish until the oil reaches 325°F.

Meanwhile, make the dipping sauce.

FOR THE DIPPING SAUCE: Slice 6 of the shallots and the garlic into thin rounds. Heat the oil in a medium skillet until hot. Fry the garlic and shallots until golden brown, 30 seconds to 1 minute. Drain on a paper towel. Finely chop the reserved herbs from the marinade and slice the remaining shallot. Add them to a medium bowl along with the scallions. Add the fried shallots, fried garlic, tamarind concentrate, fish sauce, soy sauce, lime juice, and palm sugar. Whisk in the warm water until the dipping sauce is smooth. Stir in the sliced chile. Transfer to a serving bowl.

FOR THE FISH: Fry one fish at a time on each side until golden brown and crispy, 6 to 7 minutes, lifting the fish occasionally with a spatula or spider to ensure it doesn't stick to the bottom of the pot. Carefully transfer the fish to a wire rack to drain excess oil. Repeat with the remaining fish.

Serve family-style with steamed rice and tamarind sauce on the side.

FISH AND MARINADE

Whole fish (Note: Ideally you'll have a fish per person, ranging in size from 1 to 2 pounds according to appetites. Larger fish can be divided at the table for two people. Fish should be scaled, gutted, and de-gilled, with the fins and head intact.)

½ cup fresh Thai basil sprigs with leaves (or substitute Italian basil)

½ cup fresh cilantro sprigs with leaves

½ cup fresh mint sprigs with leaves

1 (3-inch) piece fresh lemongrass

1 (1-inch) piece fresh ginger

6 cloves garlic

1 shallot

2 scallions, sliced

1 Thai green chile (or substitute ½ serrano chile)

3 cups water

2 tablespoons fresh lime juice

1 teaspoon palm sugar (or substitute raw sugar)

1 teaspoon fine sea salt, plus more as needed

⅔ cup white rice flour

3 quarts peanut oil

TAMARIND DIPPING SAUCE

7 shallots

14 cloves garlic

1 tablespoon peanut oil

2 scallions, thinly sliced

1½ tablespoons tamarind concentrate

1 tablespoon fish sauce

1 tablespoon soy sauce

2 tablespoons fresh lime juice

2 tablespoons palm sugar (or substitute raw sugar)

⅓ cup warm water

1 Thai green chile, sliced into rounds (or substitute ½ serrano chile)

Steamed rice, for serving

PAN-SEARED FILLETS
WITH ZUCCHINI AND SHIITAKES

SERVES 4

SAUCE

5 tablespoons unsalted butter, cut into 1-tablespoon pats

1 small shallot, finely chopped

1 clove garlic, smashed

Kosher salt

Freshly ground black pepper

1 cup dry white wine

3 tablespoons fresh lemon juice

1 tablespoon chopped fresh flat-leaf parsley

VEGETABLES AND FISH

2 tablespoons unsalted butter

¼ cup olive oil

1 clove garlic, smashed

2 small zucchini, cut into 2-inch-long baton wedges

Kosher salt

Freshly ground black pepper

4 ounces shiitake mushrooms, stemmed, halved or quartered if large

4 (5½- to 6-ounce) bluefish fillets, patted dry, skin scored 3 or 4 times on a diagonal

---

ALSO WORKS WITH: Perfect for bluefish, but can work with a wide array of fish that yield a nice thick fillet that flakes easily, such as halibut, lingcod, or striped bass.

Here's a recipe that's perfect for flavorful, dark-fleshed fish like bluefish or mackerel, but it's versatile enough that you can use it for just about any fish that yields nice thick fillets. It's convenient, too, because the addition of zucchini and shiitakes makes it a well-rounded dish that only needs some crusty bread to soak up the sauce and maybe some roasted potatoes on the side. With heavily scaled fish such as striped bass, you'll want to either remove the scales or remove the skin altogether. But with bluefish or halibut, you're better off scoring the skin and leaving it intact. Once the skin's nice and crispy, that can be the best part of the dish.

FOR THE SAUCE: Melt 1 tablespoon of the butter in a small saucepan over medium heat. Add the shallot and garlic and season with salt and pepper. Cook, stirring often, until the shallot is soft and light golden, about 5 minutes. Add the wine and lemon juice and cook until the liquid reduces by half, 6 to 8 minutes. Remove the pot from the heat and keep warm. When ready to serve, reheat until hot. Then remove from the heat and whisk in the remaining butter, one pat at a time, until the sauce thickens. Stir in the parsley and adjust the seasonings.

FOR THE VEGETABLES AND FISH: Add 1 tablespoon of the butter, 1 tablespoon of the oil, and the garlic to a large skillet over medium-high heat and cook until the butter melts and the garlic browns lightly. Add the zucchini and toss to coat well. Cook undisturbed until light golden. Stir and continue to cook until crisp-tender. Season with salt and pepper. Transfer the zucchini to a plate. Melt another tablespoon of the butter in another tablespoon of the oil in the pan. Remove the garlic and discard. Add the shiitakes and toss to coat well. Cook undisturbed for 2 to 3 minutes. Stir and continue to cook until light golden. Season with salt and pepper. Return the zucchini to the pan and toss together. Adjust the seasonings. Transfer to a plate, cover, and keep warm.

Sprinkle the fillets with salt and pepper. Heat the remaining 2 tablespoons oil in the pan. Working in batches if necessary, sear the fish skin-side down, pressing down with a spatula if they buckle up, until the skin is crisp and golden, about 5 minutes. Flip the fillets, then cook until desired doneness.

Divide the vegetables and fish among 4 plates. Serve with the sauce.

BROILED FILLET AND ASPARAGUS
WITH SAUCE VERTE

SERVES 4

An angler should regard his or her broiler as their second-best friend, next only to the tackle that they use to catch fish. I use mine for everything from walleye to salmon. It's convenient, extremely quick, and helps you get a nice crust on the fish's surface while leaving the inner flesh moist and flaky. The important thing is to stay close and pay careful attention when you're broiling fish. It's much touchier than baking fish, and you can annihilate a fillet if you let it go just a few minutes too long. During the cooking process, go ahead and crack open the oven door to keep an eye on it. While this particular recipe is tailored for halibut, which are beautiful when broiled, you can handle a wide array of fish in a similar manner.

ALSO WORKS WITH: You can broil an almost unlimited variety of fish in this manner. Any fish that could be baked or grilled would be fine to cook under a broiler. Think walleye, trout, salmon, snapper, grouper, halibut, rockfish, swordfish, and everything in between.

SAUCE VERTE (PARSLEY, CHIVE, AND CAPER SAUCE)

1 clove garlic

1 cup packed fresh flat-leaf parsley leaves

¾ cup coarsely chopped fresh chives

4 anchovies, coarsely chopped

3 tablespoons capers, drained

2 tablespoons fresh lemon juice

2 tablespoons water

¼ cup olive oil

Kosher salt

Freshly ground black pepper

FISH AND ASPARAGUS

1 (1-pound) bunch asparagus, ends trimmed

4 tablespoons olive oil

Kosher salt

Freshly ground black pepper

Grated Parmigiano-Reggiano cheese (optional)

4 (6-ounce) fish fillets, 1 to 1½ inches thick

1 tablespoon fresh lemon juice

FOR THE SAUCE VERTE: With the motor of a food processor running, drop the garlic into the food chute and process until finely chopped. Scrape down the sides. Add the parsley, chives, anchovies, and capers and process until finely chopped. With the motor running, add the lemon juice, water, and oil. Process until the liquid is incorporated. Season with salt and pepper. Transfer to a small bowl. (This makes ⅔ cup.)

FOR THE FISH AND ASPARAGUS: Preheat the broiler. Line a baking sheet with foil. Arrange the asparagus in a single layer on the pan and drizzle with 1 tablespoon of the oil. Season with salt and pepper and roll around until well coated. Broil until the asparagus are bright green and crisp tender, 3 to 4 minutes. Transfer the asparagus to a large plate, sprinkle with the cheese, if using, and cover to keep warm.

Rinse the fish under cold running water and pat dry. Place the fish skin-side down in a single layer on the same pan. Drizzle with the remaining oil and the lemon juice and sprinkle with salt and pepper. Broil until the fish is just opaque in the center, about 8 minutes for a fillet that's 1 inch thick.

Serve the fish with the sauce and asparagus.

07 REPTILES & AMPHIBIANS

INTRODUCTION

Tastes like chicken. Most hunters and anglers have heard or said that so many times it's more of a joke than an actual observation. When it is applied in a serious way, it's usually used to describe the tastes and textures of reptiles and amphibians. I'm guessing that the reason for this has more to do with the novelty of eating such things as frogs, alligators, or turtles than it does with the actual tastes of those creatures. Whoever's serving the dish might draw the comparison as a way of wooing his guests into giving such an exotic food a try. Either that or the person who's eating it for the first time is so far outside of their comfort zone that they feel the need to bring the experience around to something safer and more recognizable.

I've never been tempted to use this line myself, mostly because I love the unconventionality of wild game and I'm not inclined to make it seem any tamer than it is. Years ago, I was sitting on a riverbank with a buddy of mine trimming some deer steaks for the fire and tossing the scraps out into the water. In the morning we caught a big softshell turtle down the river and decided to have it for our evening meal. When we butchered the turtle we were surprised to find our own venison scraps inside its stomach. That meal always sticks in my head as an example of just how wild and weird the out-of-doors can be, and just how much I like it that way. Another story of another turtle occurred thousands of miles away from there, down in the jungles of South America. I was traveling with some men from the Makushi tribe when they came into camp with a turtle so big that you could fit a large American snapping turtle inside of its shell and the snapper would have room to walk around. They removed the turtle's head with a machete and then ran a long, slender stick down the inside of its spinal column in order to relax the nerves and tenderize the meat. After butchering the turtle, they placed its empty shell directly over a large bed of embers and began building a turtle stew using the same river water that the turtle was hauled out of. That was truly one of the best meals I've ever had. And yes, the turtle's meat was white. And yes, it was tender and mild. And yes, the leg bones were finger thick and you could hold them up to your mouth and gnaw off the goodness. But equating that meal to eating chicken would be like seeing the Rolling Stones in 1970 and then describing the event as being similar to your buddy's karaoke performance of "Satisfaction."

As much as I like to extol the pleasures and rewards of this esoteric category of wild game, I do so with the realization that there are firm limits to how much we can exploit the resources. Reptiles and amphibians are environmentally sensitive creatures that suffer acutely from habitat destruction and environmental pollution. In certain times and places, they have been commercially overexploited. The American alligator rebounded from such abuses in a stunning way, to the point that it went from being an almost vanished rarity to an ever-present nuisance across much of its range. The American bullfrog is actually expanding its range and is now thriving as a nonnative species in states (and even on continents) where it was historically absent. But other species have a less certain future. The diamond terrapin, a small turtle native to the coastal marshes of the eastern and southern United States, was a highly sought delicacy in the fine-dining establishments of America's large cities in the late 1800s and early 1900s. Commercial terrapin collectors, unfettered by regulations, were removing tens of thousands of pounds of

these creatures from Chesapeake Bay every year. Nowadays, the diamondback terrapin is protected across much of its range. There is no allowable harvest in Chesapeake Bay, and there are no diamondback terrapin recipes in this book.

That's not to say that the harvest of reptiles and amphibians is incompatible with long-term sustainability. Quite the opposite—small-scale recreational harvest is good for the resources. License fees from hunters and fishermen fund conservation efforts as well as the wildlife agents who enforce regulations. Plus, environmental advocacy from consumptive user groups is paramount to protecting fragile habitats. But it is important that we exercise restraint with our harvesting practices and stay well within the limits of the law when it comes to harvesting methods and bag limits. You don't need to take the maximum allowable limit of a species just because you can. Instead, take just enough to enjoy the experience and leave enough behind that you can keep coming back, year after year.

NATURE OF THE BEAST

Turtles

The **common snapping turtle** has both light and dark meat. Its meat is excellent, but it can be tough. Many people prefer to slow-cook turtle meat on the bone and then pick the meat before applying it to recipes ranging from fried turtle to turtle soup. The light meat is more tender, and on smaller turtles it can be used without slow-cooking. **Softshell turtles** (spiny and smooth) are even better than snapping turtles. The meat is more tender, though the yield isn't as high.

Frogs

Bullfrog legs are superb, with white, almost translucent flesh that is mild and very tender. It should be prepared simply in order to showcase the delicate flavor. While legal to harvest in many regions, **green frogs** are borderline too small to bother with.

Alligators

The meat from the **American alligator** is popular enough to support a thriving commercial market. The best parts are the two "tenderloins," found on the inside of the tail. The remainder of the tail is well-regarded, and there is usable meat from the legs and body as well.

Snakes

The **western diamondback rattlesnake** is the most commonly eaten snake. Specimens much smaller than 3½ feet aren't really worth messing with, because the yield of meat is minuscule. The flesh is light-colored and a tad stringy. The flavor is mild and delicate. Fried rattlesnake is by far the most common preparation.

VORTEX
Weaver Rifles

SNAPPING TURTLE

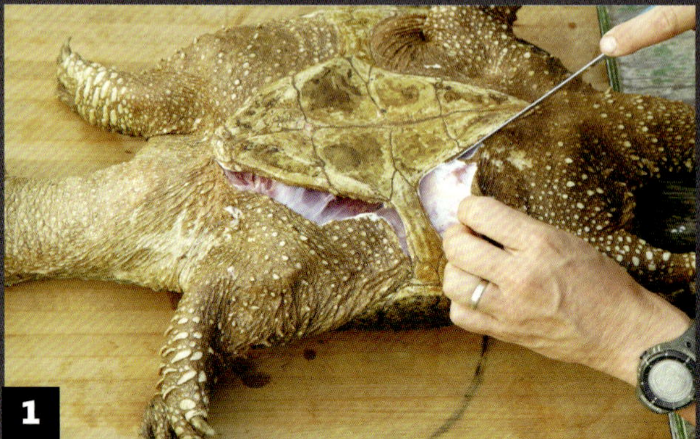

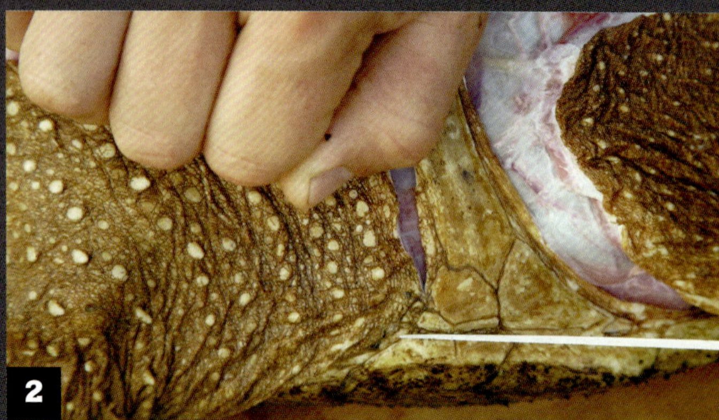

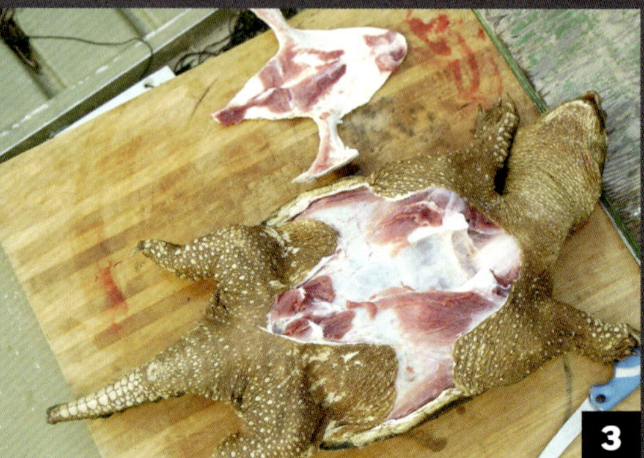

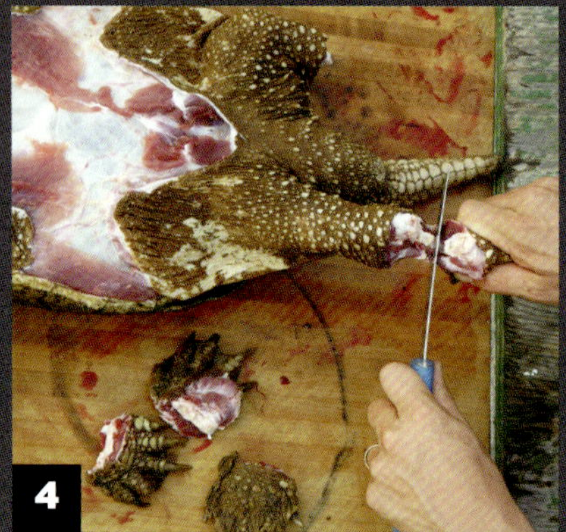

Very few hunters or anglers target turtles, despite the fact that snapping turtles and softshell turtles are common in lakes, ponds, and slow-moving rivers throughout most of the eastern half of the country, and in some areas of the West. Both species offer excellent eating for those willing to put in the work necessary to catch and butcher them. When dealing with trapped, hand-caught, and line-caught turtles, it's necessary to kill the turtle by chopping off its head with a hatchet. This turtle's head is still in place because it was killed with the arrow of a bowfishing rig. The head was later removed during the butchering process.

1. You'll need a very sharp, sturdy fillet knife and shears to cut through a turtle's tough hide, bones, and shell. With the turtle lying on its back, start cutting through the skin around the edge of the plastron, or bottom shell. Continue until the shell is completely separated from the skin.

2. Next, separate the soft abdominal shell from the hard, bony carapace by making a cut through the seam where the two shells are joined. You may need to use game shears.

3. Now you can fillet the lower shell free from the abdominal area.

4. Next, remove all four feet at the ankle joint.

5. Where the lower shell has been removed, cut the carcass free from the upper shell.

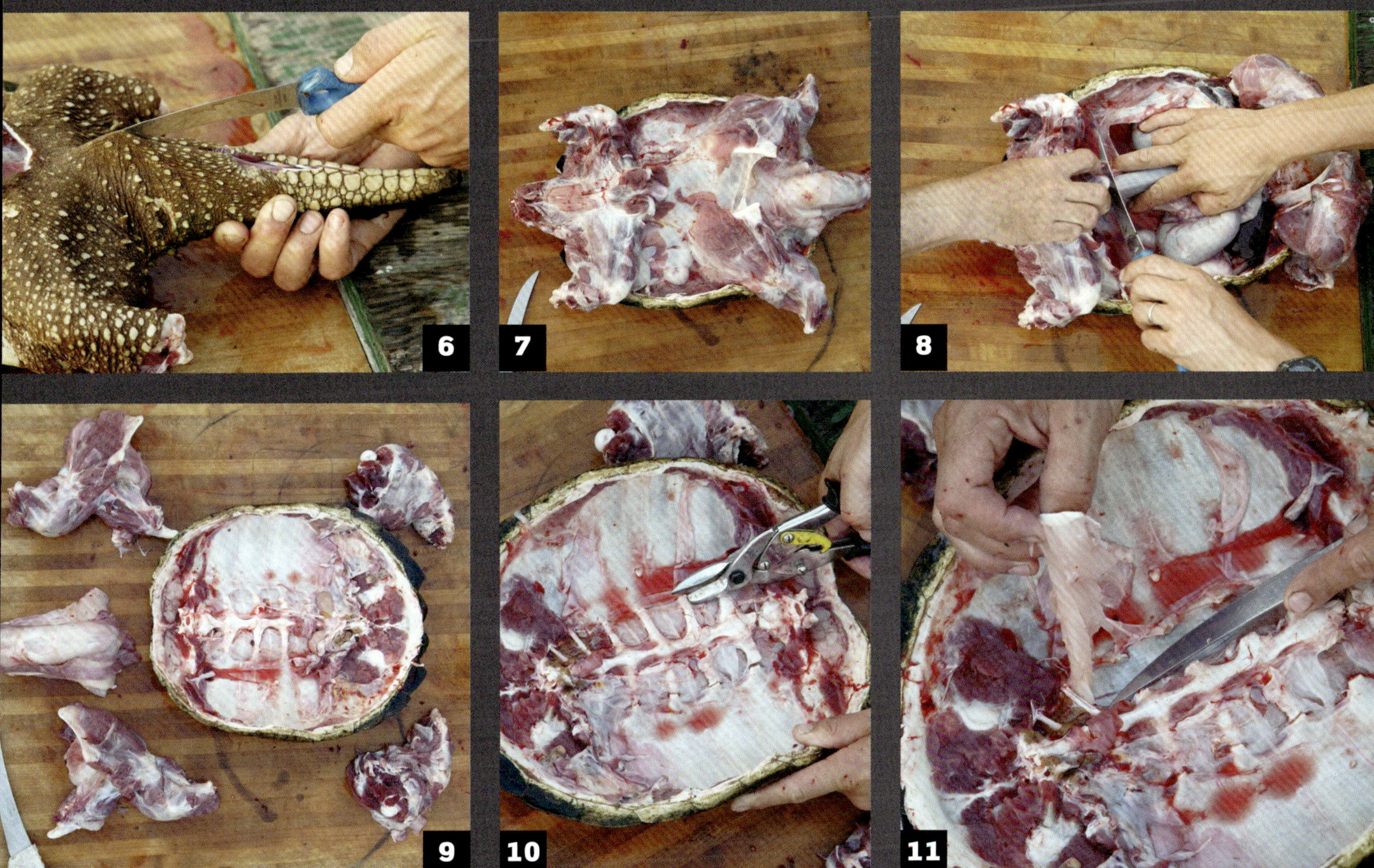

6. Make a lengthwise cut through the bottom of the tail. Now skin the turtle's tail, belly, and legs.

7. Remove the head with a hatchet, and then skin the lower neck. The entire underside of the turtle should now be free of skin.

8. Next, open up the abdomen and remove the entrails.

9. Remove the skinned front legs and shoulders by cutting them free from the interior of the carapace. Do the same with the back legs and tail.

10. The backstraps remain hidden between the ribs and the shell. Use game shears to remove the ribs.

11. Now fillet the backstraps away from the shell. Make sure to dry the shell and save it. When lacquered, they make beautiful gifts.

BULLFROG

1

2

3

4

5

6

Bullfrogs are America's largest frog species and they are found in many areas throughout the country. The availability of the frogs continues to increase as they spread into ecosystems outside of their native range thanks to ill-advised humans who turn them loose where they don't belong. In some places, introduced populations of bullfrogs have had substantial negative impacts on native amphibians. If you live in one of these areas, eat as many as you can.

1. You'll need a sharp fillet knife and a pair of catfish pliers to clean a bullfrog. Even on large bullfrogs, it's really only worth removing the muscular hind legs.

2. First, make a cut through the skin across the back, above the hips. Next, use your pliers to peel the skin downward off the hind legs.

3. Remove the feet and ankles at the second joint down the leg.

4. Now remove the hind legs at the hip.

5. Although it is not necessary, removing the femur makes eating frog legs easier. Slice the thigh muscle open and cut the bone free from the upper leg.

6. Now you've got two meaty, semi-boneless hind legs. Rinse well in cold water before cooking.

BULLFROG LEGS
WITH BUTTER AND WINE

SERVES 6 TO 8 AS APPETIZERS

Frog legs were a rare treat when I was a kid. We ate them once or twice a year, always cooked in the same way. My dad would bread 'em and fry 'em, just like he did with the vast majority of freshwater fish that we caught. There are plenty of other options for frog legs, with some of the best recipes coming from the culinary traditions of France, China, and the American South. The following recipe is a variation on a classic Louisiana preparation, though it would not be out of place in a contemporary French kitchen. This recipe is hardly elaborate, though you can simplify it by just sprinkling your frog legs with a little salt and pepper and frying them in hot butter for 4 or 5 minutes for a quick and easy appetizer. Likewise, you don't need to do anything special if you're having a fish fry with friends and someone has a few frog legs mixed in with their fish fillets. Just bread them like fish and give them a quick dip in 350°F peanut oil. You really can't go wrong, unless you overcook them to the point that they dry out.

1 pound bullfrog legs

1 tablespoon Creole Seasoning (page 312)

1 cup all-purpose flour

⅓ cup unsalted butter

¼ cup minced onion

1 tablespoon minced garlic

2 tablespoons minced fresh flat-leaf parsley, plus more for serving

Kosher salt

⅓ cup white wine

Lemon halves, for serving

ALSO WORKS WITH: The legs of green frogs are much smaller than the legs of bullfrogs, but if that's all you've got (and it's legal in your state to harvest them), go ahead and give it a try.

Work with single legs, so if your frog legs are in pairs, cut them in half. Rinse them in cold water and pat dry with paper towels. Sprinkle each leg with a small pinch of the Creole Seasoning. Add the remainder of the Creole Seasoning to the flour.

Melt the butter in a pan that's large enough to accommodate all the legs in a single layer. Use medium heat, and be careful not to burn the butter. Working in batches so that you don't overcrowd your pan, dust the legs in the seasoned flour and then add them to the melted butter. Flip the legs after 2 minutes, for a total cook time of 4 minutes per leg. Remove the legs to a plate. Add the onion, garlic, and parsley to the butter. Cook for 1 minute, then return the legs to the pan. Sprinkle the legs with salt. Add the wine and simmer until the legs are fork tender, 5 to 6 minutes. Serve with the halved lemons and additional parsley.

TURTLE SOUP

SERVES 8 TO 10 (MAKES 10 CUPS)

For reasons I don't fully understand, turtle meat has long been associated with soup. It seems to be an almost universal phenomenon. French master-chef Auguste Escoffier's 1903 magnum opus, *Le Guide Culinaire*, included a handful of variations on turtle soup. During the American Revolution, frontiersmen who raided an Indian village that was allied with the British reported finding a large kettle of broth with a boiled turtle lying in the bottom. It's also a staple of traditional Southern cooking, which is where this recipe finds its roots. Here, the turtle meat is simmered until it's tender enough to be deboned, and then it's added into a creamy, roux-thickened broth alongside seasonings, bell pepper, and chopped eggs.

TURTLE MEAT AND STOCK

2 tablespoons olive oil

1½ pounds turtle meat, cut into large pieces

2 cups water, plus more as needed

1 large carrot, cut into large chunks

1 rib celery, cut into large chunks

½ yellow onion, cut into large chunks

4 cups Blonde Game Stock (page 306) or low-sodium chicken broth

TURTLE SOUP

½ cup (1 stick) unsalted butter

1 cup all-purpose flour

1 small yellow onion, chopped

1 small green bell pepper, chopped

2 ribs celery, chopped

2 tablespoons minced garlic

½ cup Worcestershire sauce

⅓ cup dry sherry

3 tablespoons fresh lemon juice

1½ tablespoons kosher salt

1 tablespoon freshly ground black pepper

½ teaspoon cayenne pepper

¼ cup fresh flat-leaf parsley leaves, chopped

½ cup heavy cream

4 hard-boiled eggs, chopped

¼ cup chopped scallion

Buttery crackers, for serving

FOR THE TURTLE MEAT AND STOCK: Heat the oil in a large skillet over medium-high heat. Brown the turtle meat on all sides, about 8 minutes. Transfer the browned meat to a stockpot and pour in the water, making sure the meat is covered (add more water if needed). Add the carrot, celery, and onion chunks. Bring to a boil. Skim any foam or scum that rises to the surface and discard. Reduce the heat and simmer until the turtle is very tender, about 1 hour.

Remove the turtle meat from the liquid with a slotted spoon, debone the meat, and chop it into a rough medium dice. Strain the simmering liquid into a stockpot, add the stock, and keep at a simmer until needed.

FOR THE TURTLE SOUP: Melt the butter in a heavy soup pot over low heat, and then whisk in the flour, creating a roux. Cook, stirring occasionally, until it has developed a dark brown color and a nutty aroma, 15 to 20 minutes. Add the diced onion, bell pepper, and celery and cook for 4 minutes, stirring often. Add the garlic and chopped, boneless turtle meat and cook for another 4 minutes. Slowly pour in the turtle stock and whisk until incorporated. Add the Worcestershire sauce, sherry, lemon juice, salt, pepper, and cayenne and stir. Bring the soup to a boil, then reduce the heat and simmer for about 1 hour until the flavors meld.

Add the parsley, cream, half of the chopped egg, and half of the chopped scallion. Let simmer for another 15 minutes. Serve the soup hot, with buttery crackers, garnished with the remaining chopped egg and scallion.

ALSO WORKS WITH: Try this with alligator or squirrel. Or use any other critter that might prompt people to declare that classic (and somewhat annoying) assessment: "Tastes like chicken!"

FRIED ALLIGATOR
WITH TARTAR SAUCE

SERVES 4

There are currently around 1.3 million American alligators in Florida alone, up from a population of just thousands in the late 1960s. Louisiana has an alligator population approaching 2 million animals. Right now, clearly, we're living in the golden age of alligator hunting. Opportunities abound, especially for hunters who aren't too particular about whether or not they kill a gargantuan specimen. The yield on an alligator is impressive, too. Processors typically get 40 percent of the live weight in usable meat. Considering that alligators in the range of a couple hundred pounds are perfectly common, you can see why alligator hunting—and alligator meat—is growing in popularity.

ALSO WORKS WITH: Honestly, just about anything that walks, swims, or crawls.

TARTAR SAUCE

1 cup mayonnaise

⅔ cup chopped dill pickle

2 tablespoons hot sauce

ALLIGATOR

1 cup buttermilk

2 tablespoons hot sauce

1 pound alligator tenderloin, cut into ¾-inch chunks

About 5 cups vegetable oil or peanut oil (more if you're using an electric deep-fryer)

1 cup all-purpose flour

1 cup cornmeal

Kosher salt

FOR THE TARTAR SAUCE: Stir together the mayonnaise, pickle, and hot sauce in a small bowl. Refrigerate until needed.

FOR THE ALLIGATOR: Stir together the buttermilk and hot sauce. Add the alligator, cover, and refrigerate for at least 1 hour or up to 8 hours.

If using an electric deep-fryer, fill it to the maximum fill level with oil and preheat to 350°F. If not, heat 2 inches of oil in a Dutch oven or heavy 10-inch sauté pan over medium heat to 350°F. Put the flour and cornmeal in separate shallow dishes and sprinkle each with salt.

Pull out a few pieces of alligator and dredge in the flour, dip back in the buttermilk, and then dredge in the cornmeal. Slip the meat into the oil and fry, stirring once or twice, until golden brown and the chunks float, about 4 minutes. Repeat with the remaining meat, allowing the oil to come back up to temperature, for 2 to 3 batches total. Drain on a baking sheet fitted with a wire rack that's covered with paper towels. Serve with the tartar sauce for dipping.

08 SHELLFISH & CRUSTACEANS

INTRODUCTION

I can't say that everything I know about harvesting shellfish and crustaceans comes from my beloved friend Ron Leighton, though I am comfortable saying that everything I know has been *informed* by Ron. He's a lifelong resident of southeast Alaska with deep experience as both a commercial and recreational fisherman. Ron spends so much time in his boat that he looks slightly confused and out of place whenever he's walking on a surface that isn't undulating beneath him. Ron likes to express his opinions about shellfish and crustaceans in a forceful, almost pugnacious way. If you challenge his convictions about the best way to trap a Dungeness crab, he reacts similarly to how someone might respond to having their beliefs about the afterlife called into question. Some of his viewpoints are hard for me to take at face value, as they are colored by things that strike me as being borderline anthropomorphic. For instance, he's a firm believer that halibut heads are inappropriate as crab bait, owing to the fact that halibut will readily eat crabs. In Ron's assessment, the crabs hold a grudge.

"Let's just say that a crab actually watched a halibut swoop in and eat his friend," I once said to Ron. "Do you really think he's going to draw the connection between that experience and a butchered and bloody halibut head lying on the bottom of the ocean?" Ron just looked at me as though I'd never understand anything. Later that summer we were out pulling some of my crab traps and up came a trap that was loaded with Dungeness crabs packed around a halibut head that I'd wired inside for bait. Ron was so annoyed by this that his fist clenched up enough to crinkle his beer can. Gesturing to the crabs, I commented on the fact that he's clearly wrong about halibut heads. "All you proved there," he said, "is that you've got a lot of dumb crabs hanging around this place. Imagine how many you would have caught with a salmon head."

Ron does have one area of expertise that I've learned not to challenge, and that's the process of what he calls "putting up" seafood. In his vernacular, that refers to the actions that one needs to take in order to freeze or otherwise store seafood for later consumption. The reason that I maintain fidelity to Ron's guidance on putting up seafood is that I've had poor results every time I've tried to ignore it. Ron spends what used to strike me as an absurd amount of time washing his shrimp tails before bagging them for the freezer. I started taking shortcuts while washing my own shrimp tails and they came back out of the freezer looking off-color and tasting not great. Likewise, Ron insists that you should only half-cook your crab knuckles before you freeze them, and then you should do the second half of the cooking after you thaw them out. One day I decided to experiment with a batch of crab by giving them a full cooking job before freezing them. When I thawed them out, I had crab meat that was watery and difficult to pick from the shells.

"Best practices" is a good term for describing these sorts of tips and tricks, which are based more on objective reality than subjective opinion. That is, people might argue over the best bait for Dungeness crab, but there's not much room for debate when your family is all puking their brains out over some shrimp that were allowed to spoil inside a warm bucket of water left in the sun. Following best practices while dealing with shellfish can have life-and-death implications. It's generally regarded as a best practice to avoid freshwater clams and mussels. That's because bivalves are filter

feeders that accumulate environmental toxins, and freshwater clams tend to have much higher concentrations of pollutants than saltwater clams. It's also regarded as a best practice to never cook and eat a crab that was dead in your trap when you pulled it out of the water. That's because crabs deteriorate with stunning rapidity after they die, and there's no good way to know if it's still safe to eat. Finally, it was traditionally considered a best practice to only harvest bivalves during months that have an "r" in their name. That's because the dinoflagellate algae that causes paralytic shellfish poisoning is most prevalent during the warmer summer months, or the months with no "r." (Paralytic shellfish poisoning, or PSP, has been known to occur at all times of year. To play it safe, you should only harvest clams and mussels in areas where the beaches are monitored by government officials for the presence of harmful toxins.)

An awareness of the troubles that can befall a careless shellfish harvester shouldn't dissuade you from experimenting with wild-caught shellfish and crustaceans. Rather, a working knowledge of the do's and don'ts should embolden you to get out there and have a good time while making great meals without worry.

I've been targeting shellfish and crustaceans since I was a kid, when we used to gather freshwater crayfish from the lakes and rivers around our home in order to do our best Midwestern impression of a Louisiana crawdad boil. Since then, I've done everything from spearfishing lobsters in the Bahamas to "ticklesticking" octopus in Hawaii to diving for sea cucumbers along Alaska's Inside Passage. The memories and life experiences that I've accumulated through those adventures are vast. The ailments and accidents, zero. If you've had a lot of experiences with shellfish and crustaceans, I trust that you'll find some new things in this chapter that will help you improve your game as a wild game chef. If you're just starting out, the information here will get you up and running toward your next culinary adventure.

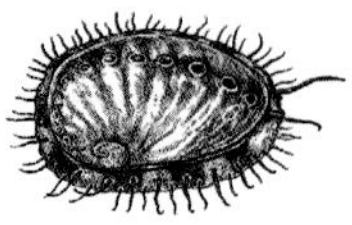

Abalone

Abalone are one of the finest delicacies that the ocean produces, and are priced accordingly in restaurants; they are similar to clam, but more buttery and with a springier texture. Any abalone preparation should be all about the abalone. Abalone flesh is often pounded gently with a mallet to tenderize it. Not to be used as filler or something that's tossed carelessly into hot oil.

Crabs

Two crab species, **blue crabs** and **Dungeness crabs,** make up the bulk of the recreational crab harvest in American waters. On the Atlantic Coast, which is blue crab country, they'll tell you that the blue crab is the best crab in the world. On the Pacific Coast, it's Dungeness. Blue crabs are the smaller of the two. Soft-shell crabs, which are regarded as a delicacy, are simply blue crabs caught while molting. These are excellent, as are hard-shell varieties. There is no soft-shell equivalent with Dungeness crabs, as Dungeness crabs have only small amounts of soggy meat during the molting process.

Squid and Octopus

The **market squid,** *Loligo opalescens*, is the squid most commonly caught by recreational fishermen, and it's also the species that's most typically served as fried calamari in restaurants. It's good for pretty much any squid preparation, as most preparations are intended for this exact same critter. The old adage about cooking for either 2 minutes or 2 hours has some truth to it, as anything in between could yield rubbery results. The **Humboldt squid** is a much larger creature that is targeted seasonally along the Pacific coast. Big specimens need to be tenderized by boiling or braising, similar to octopus.

As for **octopus,** it's astonishing how many shrimp trappers turn them loose because they're intimidated by the cooking process. It's really not hard. You can tenderize smaller specimens by placing them in a bucket with some coarse salt and then literally punching (some folks refer to it as "massaging") the legs as you rotate them around in the bucket. For bigger octopus, boil the legs in heavily salted water for thirty minutes and plunge into an ice-water bath. Peel away the outer skin, then finish according to your particular preparation.

Scallops

Scallop species are commonly divided into three classifications, **bay scallops, sea scallops,** and **rock scallops**. All are excellent. Regardless of the scallop, the edible portion that most people are after is the adductor muscle—that's the round "scallop" that shows up on your plate in restaurants. You can also eat the skirt and roe. Smaller scallops, say an inch or less in diameter, are very fragile and should be handled and cooked delicately. Big scallops can be a bit grainier and chewier. As the name implies, the Pacific rock scallop grows attached to underwater rocks or cliff faces. It has to be pried free. Their adductor muscle has different qualities than you find on bay and sea scallops. They are more watery, and are difficult to sear. They can become chewy, and even tough, from overcooking. Still, they are superb.

Mussels

Blue mussels can be found around the planet at certain latitude bands, and they are raised extensively through aquaculture. Mussels gathered in the wild are no different from commercially produced specimens, but in some areas they can be very gritty. It's a good idea to flush them in clean water (or hang them off a dock inside a mesh sack) in order to rid them of grit.

Sea Cucumber

You wouldn't guess it from looking at a **sea cucumber,** but it has a generous yield of meat inside. Each contains five long bands of muscle that look like big clam strips. It is excellent, and many regard it as preferable to clam. It can be dusted in flour and fried in butter, added to chowders, or used in a wide range of other preparations.

Crayfish and Lobsters

There's a dizzying number of crayfish species in the United States. Michigan alone has nine species. All of them are edible. If they're big enough to eat, they're good. The **red swamp crayfish** or **Louisiana crayfish** is widely available as a commercial crayfish and it's also trapped and gathered extensively by recreational harvesters. The **signal crayfish** is a large species native to the Western United States; it's often compared more closely to lobster than Louisiana crayfish. The **rusty crayfish** is a native species in the United States that has dramatically increased its range due to illegal introductions by humans. They are widely available—nowadays, *too* widely available—and good.

There's little that needs to be said about **Maine lobsters** and **spiny lobsters,** as their reputation as a high-caliber food item is well established. Maine lobster are available to recreational divers and trappers in portions of the Northeast, and various species of spiny lobsters, or rock lobsters, are available in the warmer inshore waters of California, Hawaii, Florida, the Caribbean, and elsewhere.

Clams

There are so many species of clams that it's difficult to keep them straight. Many individual species go by different names according to how big they are. Multiple clam species will sometimes be called the same thing—steamers, for example—because they're commonly cooked the same way. **Manila clams** are not native to the United States, but they're now found on the West Coast. They are sweet-tasting and commonly served either steamed or with pasta**. Hard-shell clams** are called littlenecks, top necks, cherrynecks, and chowders, depending on their size. Smaller specimens are eaten raw or steamed, while larger specimens are used in chowders. Small **soft-shell clams** are also good for

steaming, while larger specimens are used for frying or chowders.

Larger clams that need to be nominally processed before eating include **Atlantic surf clams,** which have a sweet-tasting meat that is highly versatile. They are popular as clam strips but can be used in many other preparations. **Geoducks,** from the West Coast, are one of the biggest clams in the world—wild clams weighing several pounds or more are common. The flesh is springy, even crunchy, like a cross between clam and abalone. The siphon needs to be blanched and then the rough skin can be slipped away. It is often eaten raw, including in ceviche preparations. **Razor clams** are enormously popular in the Pacific Northwest, where harvest is tightly regulated. They are good sautéed in butter, fried as clam strips, or served in chowder. **Gaper clams,** or horse clams, are another West Coast clam that is very large. The meat is tough and usually needs to be tenderized, either through grinding, mincing, or gently pounding with a mallet for use in raw preparations.

Practice caution when attempting to cook with **freshwater clams** and **freshwater mussels**. As filter feeders, bivalves readily accumulate the industrial and residential pollutants that tend to exist in higher concentrations in freshwater than they do in saltwater. They can also contain harmful bacteria. Always check your state fishing and shellfishing regulations before attempting to collect freshwater clams and mussels because many states prohibit their harvest.

KNUCKLING A CRAB

1

2

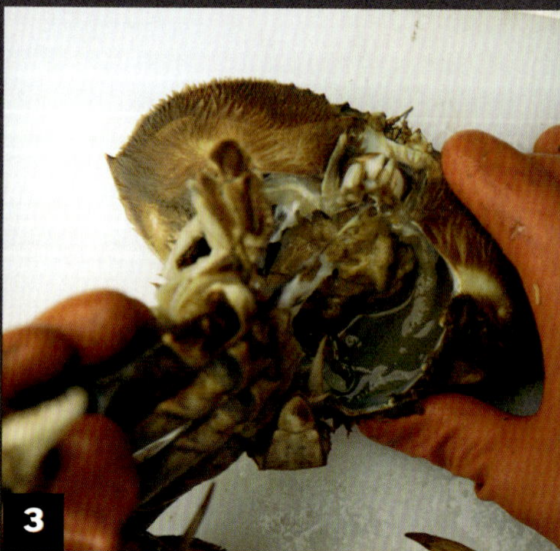
3

4

5

Dungeness crabs are one of the largest, meatiest crabs available to recreational fishermen. They are found in cold Pacific waters from California north to Alaska. Cleaning them is simple and doesn't require any special tools. Blue crabs, a common catch on the East Coast, can be cleaned in a similar fashion.

1. You always want to start with live crabs. Dead crabs deteriorate quickly and can make you very sick. Discard any dead crabs you find in your traps.

2. The edge of a table, the gunwale of a skiff, or the brim of a 5-gallon bucket will work well for breaking the underside of the crab's shell. Holding the crab with both hands, give it a sharp tap in the middle of the underside to crack it open.

3. A crab has a "knuckle" on each side consisting of the legs, the claw, and the interior meat. Remove each knuckle by firmly grasping the legs near the body and pulling them free from the outer shell.

4. Each knuckle should pull free in one piece.

5. Now pull the gills free from the meat and legs. It's important to rinse each knuckle to get rid of any broken bits of shell, grit, or guts.

SCALLOPS

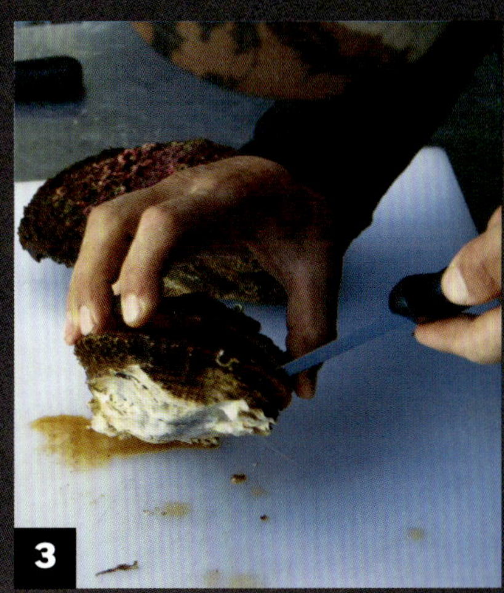

There are many species of scallops that can be collected recreationally, from small bay scallops along the Eastern seaboard to Pacific rock scallops in southeast Alaska. Cleaning them is a fairly simple process. The scallop here is a rock scallop.

1. Slip a blade or screwdriver between the two shells and pry apart.

2. Slide your knife between the two shells and cut the thin, tough outer ring of muscle that holds them together. Now you can begin opening the scallop by hand.

3. Scallops have a large, circular muscle anchored to the inside center of each half of the shell called the adductor muscle. Slice the adductor muscle free from one of the shells and open the scallop.

4. Slice the opposite end of the adductor muscle free from the other shell.

5. Pictured here are two adductor muscles from a pair of scallops. The bright orange egg sacks, or roe, can be sautéed in butter with the scallops or used to make a sauce. The remaining portions can be used to make stock.

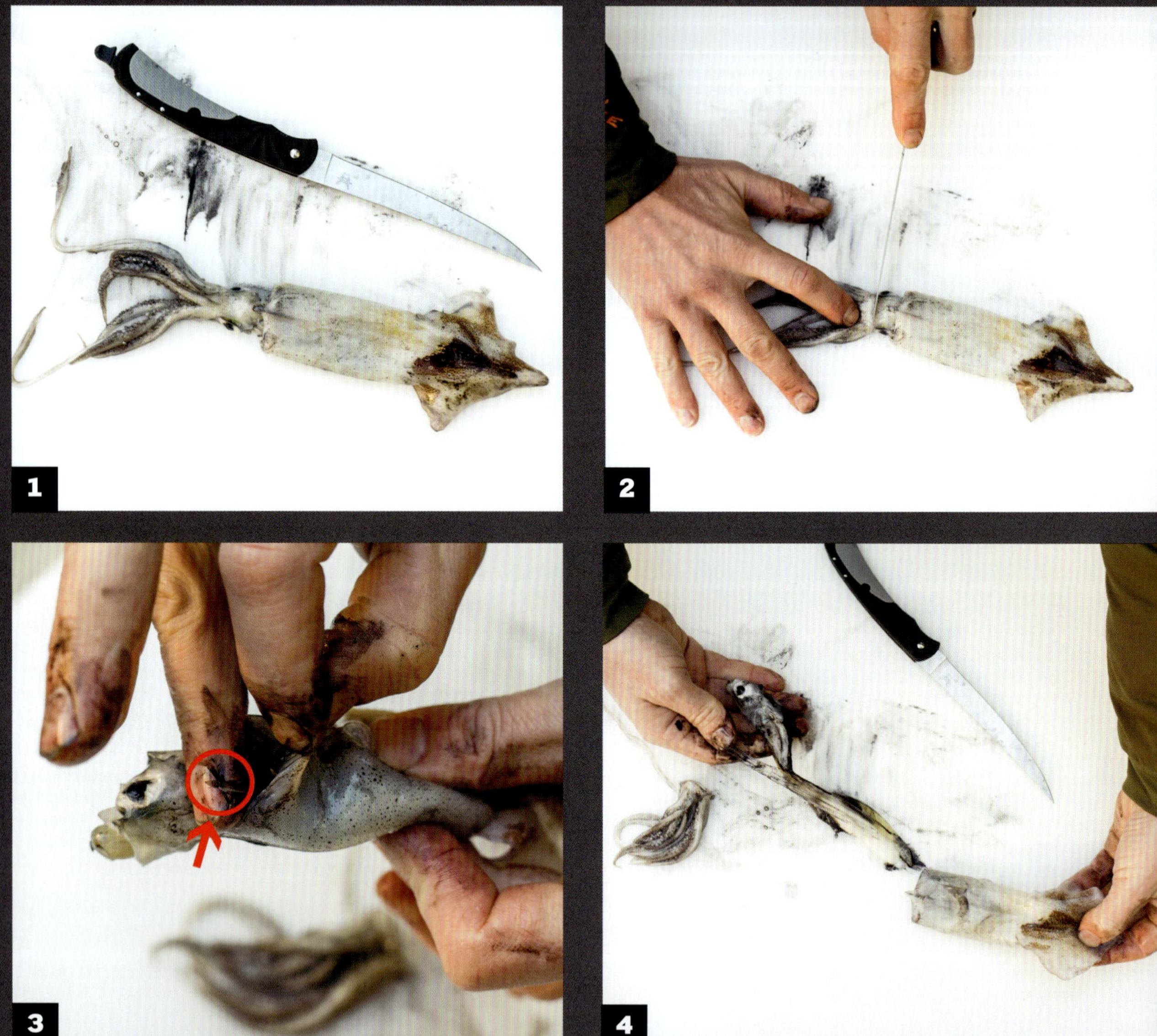

5

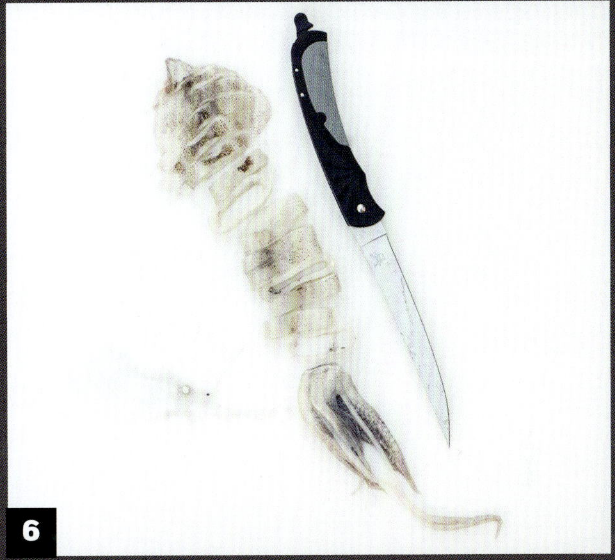
6

Many saltwater anglers regard squid as bait rather than food, but squid make excellent tablefare and they are easily targeted by anglers on both coasts. Cleaning them is easy, and the yield on a squid is high. Squid ink is used as a coloring agent in several preparations. You can recover ink from the ink sac found inside the mantle.

1. Use a fillet knife to clean squid. The edible meat comes from the arms, tentacles, fins, and the large mantle, or body. (Octopus arms can be removed pretty much the same way as squid arms.)

2. First, remove all the arms and tentacles in one bundle by making a cut just below the eyes. You'll be able to feel the hard beak at the base of the tentacles. Push it back toward the eyes as you cut, so that it stays with the head.

3. Using a fingernail, separate the squid's pen from the lip of the mantle. It looks and feels like a thin plastic blade. With your finger between the pen and mantle, slide your finger down the inside length of the mantle to completely free the pen.

4. Grabbing the top of the pen and the head, pull out the pen and the entrails.

5. The bodies are left whole for many preparations. You may want to remove the outer skin from the mantle of large squids since it can become hard and chewy once cooked. It peels away easily. On small squid it is not necessary to remove the skin.

6. For fried calamari, cut the mantle crosswise into strips. The tentacles and arms are left in a single bundle.

German
4116 Stainless

SEAFOOD FRITTATA

SERVES 6 TO 8 (MAKES ONE 10-INCH FRITTATA)

I didn't know what a frittata was until I heard the word on an episode of *The Simpsons* when I was in college. It turned out to be a formative moment in my cooking life, as I've been making these Italian omelets ever since. The beauty of frittatas is that they're pretty hard to mess up. You don't need to worry too much about your ratio of eggs to seafood, just as you don't need to worry too much about your ratio of shrimp to crab or crab to whatever the hell else you're putting in there. So rather than thinking of this recipe as a collection of rules that are chiseled in stone, think of it as a rough guideline on how to build your "egg pies," as my kids like to call them.

8 large eggs

3 tablespoons heavy cream

6 tablespoons olive oil

1 (10-ounce) Yukon gold potato, cut into ½-inch dice (about 2 cups)

1 tablespoon Creole Seasoning (page 312)

Kosher salt

Freshly ground black pepper

½ onion, diced (about ½ cup)

½ red bell pepper, diced (about ½ cup)

1 rib celery, diced (about ¼ cup)

6 ounces peeled, deveined shrimp, cut into bite-size pieces

6 small scallops, patted dry and quartered

8 ounces lump crabmeat

Preheat the oven to 400°F.

Whisk the eggs and cream together in a large bowl.

Heat 2 tablespoons of the oil in a 10-inch cast-iron skillet over medium-high heat. Add the potatoes and toss to coat evenly. Season with ½ teaspoon of the Creole Seasoning and salt and pepper to taste. Cook, stirring occasionally, until the potatoes are golden, 3 to 5 minutes. Transfer to a large plate using a slotted spoon.

Reduce the heat to medium. Add 2 tablespoons of the remaining oil to the pan, then add the onion, bell pepper, celery, ½ teaspoon of the remaining Creole Seasoning, and salt and pepper to taste. Cook until the vegetables are softened, about 8 minutes. Transfer to the plate.

Raise the heat to medium-high and add the remaining 2 tablespoons oil to the skillet. Add the shrimp and scallops and toss to coat. Sprinkle with the remaining 2 teaspoons Creole Seasoning and salt and pepper to taste. Cook until the shrimp turns slightly pink but is not opaque. Gently stir in the crab, then return the potatoes and vegetables to the pan and mix well.

Pour the egg mixture over the seafood and vegetables and stir to distribute evenly. Cook until the egg starts to set up a little around the edges of the pan, then place the pan in the oven. Bake until the eggs are puffed up and cooked through, 6 to 8 minutes.

Switch the oven to broil and run under the broiler for a minute or two to brown the top. Remove from the oven, let cool slightly, then cut into wedges and serve.

ALSO WORKS WITH: Don't feel constrained by the quantities of seafood given here. Just use what you've got. You can also substitute cooked crayfish tails or even a few ounces of cooked leftover fish that's been crumbled up.

SPICY SCALLOP AND CITRUS POKE

SERVES 6 (AS AN APPETIZER) / MAKES 4 CUPS

⅔ cup diced (¼ inch) sweet or red onion

2 scallions, thinly sliced

1 serrano or other chile, thinly sliced

2 tablespoons soy sauce, or to taste

4 teaspoons toasted sesame oil, or to taste

2 teaspoons toasted black sesame seeds

1 pound fresh scallops (the adductor muscles only), cut into ½-inch pieces

2 cups diced grapefruit segments

¼ cup diced lime segments

Cooked rice, for serving, if desired

Oftentimes, the best way to "cook" shellfish is not to actually cook them at all. Fresh shellfish taste as wild and free as the ocean itself, and heat has a way of taming that wildness and turning it into something a bit less inspiring and a bit more rubbery. Scallops are particularly vulnerable to heat. I can't think of ever eating a scallop and wishing it had been cooked longer. That's why scallops are a great choice for making poke, a raw seafood salad whose origins can be traced to Hawaii. Everything here tastes fresh and clean. If I were scallop, this is exactly where I'd want to end up.

ALSO WORKS WITH: Any scallop, regardless of whether it's classified as a sea, bay, or rock species. This is also great with abalone, though you'll want to cut the abalone into ¼-inch slices and tenderize them by hammering them gently with a meat mallet. A host of fish species can be used, in particular oily fish such as salmon and tuna. You want the fish to be fresh and firm-fleshed.

Combine the onion, scallions, chiles, soy sauce, sesame oil, and sesame seeds in a bowl. Add the scallops, grapefruit, and lime and mix well. Adjust the seasonings. Serve with rice, if you like.

Tip: Keep the scallops, grapefruit, and limes well chilled until ready to assemble and serve.

SHRIMP SCAMPI

SERVES 6 (APPETIZER)

My brothers and I do a lot of shrimp trapping near our fishing shack on southeast Alaska's Prince of Wales Island. We mainly get spot shrimp, a big and meaty species that we haul up from a depth of two hundred feet using salmon and halibut heads as bait. When they're ultra fresh I just boil them in salted water for a few minutes and eat them without butter or sauce. They're that good. I also freeze some of the tails in quart-size bags and bring them home. I'll usually handle these frozen tails differently from the fresh tails, mostly because I have more time to cook and easier access to ingredients when I'm home than I do when I'm at our shack. I'll gather up what I need to make scampi; the additional flavors of garlic, parsley, and red chile flakes, plus the crust of toasted breadcrumbs, get me excited about shrimp all over again.

1 pound shrimp, heads removed

Kosher salt

Freshly ground black pepper

3 tablespoons olive oil

6 cloves garlic, thinly sliced

Pinch of red chile flakes (optional)

1 cup white wine

Zest of 1 lemon, plus wedges for serving

1 tablespoon unsalted butter

1 bunch fresh flat-leaf parsley, finely chopped

½ cup toasted breadcrumbs, optional (see below)

Rinse the shrimp well and pat dry. Sprinkle liberally with salt and pepper.

Heat the oil in a large (14-inch-wide) sauté pan over medium-high heat. (If you don't have a pan this big, divide the ingredients in half and cook in batches.) Add the garlic and red chile flakes and cook until fragrant. Carefully lay the shrimp in the oil using tongs. Add the white wine and lemon zest and bring to a strong simmer. Cook for about 3 minutes, then flip the shrimp with the tongs to cook through; you'll know they're done when the flesh turns pink. Add the butter and swirl it into the sauce. Add the parsley and transfer to a platter. Top with the toasted breadcrumbs, if using. Serve immediately, with lemon wedges.

ALSO WORKS WITH: Spot shrimp are my absolute favorite, but they're limited to the Pacific Northwest and southeast Alaska. Substitute any wild-caught shrimp and you'll be happy.

TOASTED BREADCRUMB TOPPING

The *best* way to make seasoned breadcrumbs is to throw semi-stale bread pieces into a food processor and pulse. Then toast the crumbs with a couple of teaspoons of olive oil and a pinch of salt in a large skillet. You can also do the same thing with a cup of panko breadcrumbs.

GRILLED HEAD-ON SHRIMP

SERVES 4 AS AN APPETIZER (MAKES 10 TO 15 SHRIMP)

5 cloves garlic, minced or grated

1 small shallot, minced

3 tablespoons extra virgin olive oil

¼ to ½ teaspoon freshly ground black pepper

Pinch of sugar

1 pound large head-on shrimp, with tails peeled

Kosher salt

Lemon wedges or lemon halves (optional)

Chimichurri Butter (page 323) or

Adobada (page 314) or BBQ Sauce (page 314)

There's not a lot that needs to be said about this recipe beyond what can be ascertained from the title. These are shrimp. They are grilled. They still have their heads on. It's a beautiful and bold way to handle your wild-caught shrimp. Be mindful of freshness here. Well-rinsed shrimp tails can be successfully frozen, but frozen heads lose their magic in a hurry.

ALSO WORKS WITH: Any large shrimp

Soak 4 to 6 wooden skewers in water to cover for at least 30 minutes, or use metal skewers.

Preheat a gas grill to high heat.

Combine the garlic, shallot, oil, pepper, and sugar in a large bowl.

Wash the peeled shrimp and dry well. Add the shrimp to the garlic mixture and toss to coat. Skewer the shrimp snugly on a pair of skewers, using the skewers in a ladder formation so that the shrimp don't rotate when turned. Smear any remaining marinade on the shrimp. Sprinkle the shrimp generously with salt. Place a lemon wedge at the top of each skewer, if using.

Place lemon halves, if using, on a well-oiled grill grate cut-side down. Place the shrimp on the grates, pressing down gently to make sure they're flat. Grill, covered, turning halfway through, until the shells are pink and slightly charred and the shrimp are opaque and just cooked through, about 2 minutes per side. Carefully slide the shrimp from the hot skewers onto a plate or platter. Serve with lemon and the sauce of your choice.

MANHATTAN CLAM CHOWDER

SERVES 4 TO 6

5 to 5½ pounds small live clams (see Tip below for technique to purge clams)

2 bay leaves

1 sprig fresh thyme

2 cups water

2 strips bacon, finely chopped

1 rib celery, finely chopped

1 medium onion, finely chopped

½ teaspoon red chile flakes

¼ teaspoon kosher salt, plus more as needed

1 russet potato (about 1 pound), peeled and cut into ¼-inch cubes

1 (28-ounce) can peeled whole plum tomatoes

Saltine crackers, for serving

ALSO WORKS WITH: The diced meat of sea cucumbers and just about any clam can be put to use in a chowder. When you're dealing with small, live clams such as manila clams or young quahogs, follow the directions below. If you're dealing with larger clam species that are generally processed before cooking, such as geoducks, big razor clams, or gaper clams, plan on using 1 pound of minced clam meat for this recipe. Just sauté it in butter for a couple of minutes before adding to the pot in the final step of the recipe. In place of the 2 cups of cooking liquid that were used to steam the clams, use straight water or homemade or bottled clam juice.

If you're a clamdigger, you probably like to make chowder, and if you like to make chowder, you're probably familiar with the ancient East Coast debate over what color it should be. In New England, chowder is supposed to be creamy and cream-colored; in Manhattan, it's supposed to be thinner and redder. Both of them are good, but if I'm the one going through all the work of digging and cleaning the clams, I tend to prefer the Manhattan-style chowders because you can see and taste the fruits of your labor more clearly when they're not camouflaged by a broth that's about as thick as wood glue. Most chowder recipes take for granted that you're buying a very specific type of clam to make your chowder, but below you'll find some thoughts on how to prepare a great pot of the stuff with just about any clam.

Scrub the clam shells under cool running water. Place in a large saucepan with the bay leaves and thyme. Pour in the water, cover, and turn the heat to high. Once the water boils, reduce the heat to maintain a simmer, give the clams a stir, and continue to steam them until their shells open all the way, about 10 minutes total. Discard any that do not open. Remove open clams to a bowl to cool, while reserving the liquid in the saucepan. Shuck and coarsely chop the meat from the open clams. Line a mesh strainer with a double layer of cheesecloth, put over a bowl, and pour the liquid through the strainer. Reserve the liquid.

Rinse out the pot and return to the stove over medium heat. Add the bacon and cook, stirring, until it's crisp, about 5 minutes. Add the celery, onion, red chile flakes, and salt and cook, stirring, until the vegetables are softened, about 5 minutes. Add the potato, 2 cups of the cooking liquid, and the tomatoes, crushing them as you add them. Rinse out the can with a little water and add to the pot. Bring to a boil, then reduce the heat to maintain a medium boil and cook until the potatoes are tender, about 10 minutes. Add the clams and cook to heat through, about 2 more minutes. Taste and add salt as needed. Ladle into bowls and serve with saltines.

Tip: Purging clams helps to extract any residual sand that is left in your clams. First, tap any open clams on the countertop to be sure they're still alive. They should instantly close. If they don't, toss them. Next, add the clams to a bowl and cover with cold water along with a sprinkle of cornmeal. Let the clams sit for 20 minutes in the bowl; they will spit out the sand while you wait. Remove the clams by lifting them from the potentially sandy water. Scrub before cooking.

GRILLED LOBSTER
WITH COMPOUND BUTTER

SERVES 4

4 (1¼- to 1½-pound) live lobsters

Chimichurri Butter (page 323) or Anchovy Butter (page 323)

I thought about offering an apology here to wild game cooks who live toward the center of the country, where lobster diving opportunities are geographically prohibitive. My fear was that they'd feel left out. But then I got to thinking that most people will eventually have some sort of travel requirement, vacation or otherwise, that brings them to Florida, California, Hawaii, New England, or one of countless other locales where it's possible to dive for lobster. When that time comes, you'll be glad that you have this book. So no apologies.

ALSO WORKS WITH: American lobsters or spiny lobsters. The claws on spiny lobsters are small, with no edible meat, so disregard the below mentions of claws when dealing with those.

Cut each lobster in half lengthwise: Hold a lobster firmly by its back, stomach-side down, using a kitchen towel. Using a very sharp knife, swiftly pierce the base of the head (where it meets the abdomen) to sever the spinal cord, and push the knife down with the heel of your hand to crack the body in half lengthwise. Now continue the cut to cleave the tail in half lengthwise, repeating the pushing technique, then separate the halves. Remove the claws and give a crack in the largest part with the back of the knife. Repeat with the remaining lobsters.

Prepare a charcoal grill for direct heat. Place the claws and lobster halves shell-side down on the grill. Cut off 2 or 3 rounds of butter and put it on the tail flesh. Cover with the lid and cook until the meat is no longer translucent and the shells turn bright red, 10 to 12 minutes. The claws could take a few more minutes. Melt more of the butter and serve for dipping.

CRAB OR CRAYFISH BOIL
WITH WILD GAME SAUSAGE

SERVES 4 TO 6

- 6 to 8 quarts water
- ½ to ¾ cup Old Bay Seasoning, to taste
- 8 medium red, new, or other boiling potatoes
- 4 wild game andouille sausages, halved crosswise (see page 45)
- 2 heads garlic, halved crosswise
- 2 medium onions, peeled and halved
- 1 lemon, halved
- 12 blue crabs (3½ to 4 pounds), or 8 to 12 pounds crayfish
- 4 ears corn, shucked and snapped in half
- 2 pounds assorted shellfish (clams, mussels, shrimp, crayfish), rinsed or scrubbed if necessary
- Large loaf of bread or a couple of baguettes, sliced
- Lemon wedges
- Bottle of hot sauce
- Melted butter

I like anything that brings the woods and waters together, and this recipe does it in a big and dramatic way. It's the ultimate creation for the all-around outdoorsman. For this recipe it's OK to use some wild game andouille from your freezer (visit the chapter on big game for that), but the seafood is going to have to be so fresh that it's still crawling. Don't get overly finicky about the quantities or poundages of your crustaceans on this one. If you come up light on crayfish, or have an extra crab or two, everything will work out fine.

ALSO WORKS WITH: You can use lobster, crayfish, blue crabs, Dungeness crabs, shrimp, or pretty much any other crustacean here.

Combine 6 quarts water and Old Bay Seasoning in a lobster pot and bring to a boil over high heat. Add the potatoes, sausages, garlic, onions, and halved lemon and bring back to a boil. Reduce the heat to medium-low and slow boil until the potatoes are almost done; you should be able to start to pierce them with a fork, but don't let them get soft enough to eat, about 25 minutes.

Raise the heat to high and add the crabs and corn. If you need to add more water at this point, the ratio is 1½ teaspoons Old Bay Seasoning for each cup of water, or to taste. Bring back to a boil and cook until the crabs turn completely red, about 5 minutes. Add the shellfish, bring back to a boil, then remove from the heat and let sit until the shells open or turn completely red, about 3 minutes.

Set a strainer in the sink and pour the seafood in to drain. Spread the seafood and vegetables onto a newspaper-covered table and serve with bread, lemon wedges, hot sauce, and melted butter. No need for plates or forks, just nutcrackers or seafood crackers, maybe a small mallet, and plenty of napkins.

DUNGENESS CRAB
WITH MELTED BUTTER

SERVES 4

3 tablespoons kosher salt, or more as needed

8 knuckles from 4 Dungeness crabs (see page 278)

1 cup (2 sticks) salted butter, melted, for serving

My buddy Ron Leighton of southeast Alaska convinced me long ago that it's easier and more efficient to clean your crabs before you cook them, so that you're only boiling the legs, or knuckles, rather than the whole crab. (See page 278 for instructions for knuckling crab.) This approach especially makes sense for a crab trapper, who's likely dealing with a bigger volume of crabs than someone who goes down to the market and buys just one or two live crabs for dinner. Ron feels that the water used for boiling knuckles should be as "salty as the ocean, in order to bring out the sweetness of the crab," and I agree wholeheartedly with his assessment. Boil the knuckles for fifteen minutes. Cooked in such a way, it's easy to save any leftovers for later meals. Just pick the meat from the shells and freeze it in vacuum-sealed bags. It's not quite as good as fresh crab, but it's good enough to make you really happy that you saved some.

ALSO WORKS WITH: Any crab, but you'll need to adjust cooking times according to the size. As a point of reference, a blue crab should be cooked for about 10 minutes.

Fill a large stockpot with water and add enough salt that it tastes about as salty as seawater. Bring to a boil over high heat, and then add the crab knuckles. Boil for 15 minutes, then remove the crab knuckles and plunge them into a bath of ice water to cool. Allow them to cool to a comfortable handling temperature, then drain in a colander. Serve the knuckles alongside small bowls of melted butter for dipping.

LINGUINE
WITH CLAMS AND CHORIZO

SERVES 6

I'm always finding ways to introduce my crabs, shrimp, and clams into various concoctions that can be stirred into a pot of buttered pasta. Not only does it taste great to grown-ups, but it's a reliable way to open up your kids to the tastes and textures of seafood without camouflaging them so much that you end up hiding the very thing that you're trying to showcase. This particular seafood-and-pasta dish is for clams. I love the springy texture of the clams alongside the softer textures of pasta, and here you're adding some chorizo for a little extra kick. Recipes like this are a good reason to always freeze some of your sausage bulk (uncased, that is) in poly or vacuum-sealed bags. That way, it's quick and simple to add it to dishes without having to undo the laborious task of stuffing your sausage into natural hog casings.

ALSO WORKS WITH: Just about any clam can be put to use here. When you're dealing with small, live clams such as manila clams or littlenecks, follow the directions below. If you're dealing with larger clam species that are generally processed before cooking, such as geoducks, big razor clams, or gaper clams, plan on using a pound or so of minced clam meat for this recipe. It's fine if you're pulling already cleaned clam meat from your freezer. Stir it in after adding the garlic, and never mind the stuff about clam shells. You can also use the diced meat of sea cucumbers here.

3 tablespoons kosher salt

8 ounces Mexican chorizo (about 2 sausage links; see page 44)

¼ cup extra virgin olive oil

6 cloves garlic, minced

3 dozen littleneck or manila clams, purged (12 to 16 ounces of shucked or minced clam meat)—see page 292 for instructions on purging clams

½ teaspoon red chile flakes, or more to taste (optional)

1 cup white wine

1 pound linguine

½ cup Toasted Breadcrumb Topping (page 289)

Leaves from 1 small bunch fresh flat-leaf parsley, finely chopped

Bring a 6-quart pot of water to a boil and add the salt.

Remove the chorizo from its casing if it has one. Heat 1 teaspoon of the oil in a heavy-bottomed pot with a lid over medium heat. Cook the chorizo until it's fully cooked, about 5 minutes. If there is more than 1 tablespoon of grease in the pan, drain the excess grease and discard. Add the remaining olive oil to the pan. Add the garlic and cook for 30 seconds. Add the clams, red chile flakes, and wine. Cover and bring to a simmer over medium-high heat. After 5 minutes, remove any clams that have opened to a bowl. Cover the pot and continue to simmer for another 5 minutes; remove any more opened clams, discarding any unopened ones, as they may be dead. Remove the cooking liquid from the heat and reserve.

Set aside 12 of the clams in a bowl and cover with foil. Shuck the remaining 24 clams onto a grooved cutting board. Chop the clam meat and discard the shells, being careful not to lose any of the clam liquor. Add the chopped clams to the whole clams in the bowl, along with any liquid saved on the cutting board.

Add the linguine to the boiling salted water. Cook according to the package instructions until al dente.

Meanwhile, bring the reserved cooking liquid back up to a simmer. Reserve 1 cup of the pasta water. Drain the linguine. Add the linguine to the simmering cooking liquid, adding the pasta water ½ cup at a time as needed to make a smooth sauce. Add the reserved clams and toss to coat the pasta, adding more pasta water if needed to make a smooth, velvety sauce. Transfer to a serving platter, arranging the 12 whole clams on top. Top with the breadcrumbs and parsley. Serve immediately with additional red chile flakes, if desired.

EXTRAS

BASIC AND NOT-SO-BASIC SAUCES, SIDES, AND ACCOMPANIMENTS

GAME STOCK

STOCKS, SAUCES, BRINES, AND RUBS

BROWN GAME STOCK

MAKES 4 TO 6 QUARTS

Brown game stock (roasted game stock) can be used to enrich many of the stews, sauces, and soups in this book. An extraction of flavors housed in bones and vegetables, it's simply a ratio of game bones, aromatics, and water. A good formula to follow is to allow two pounds of bones per gallon of water. And split the ratio of your aromatics into 50 percent onions, 25 percent carrots, and 25 percent celery. In the end, stocks are really more about ratios of ingredients than a specific recipe. This recipe is a good guideline to get started and can be doubled or halved as needed. If you've got a lot of bones, scale up the recipe and use a 12- or 24-quart pot.

Note: Quantities will vary depending on the size of bones or carcasses, but more is better than less. One moose femur is plenty, while several rabbit or small game birds are necessary. A few deer leg bones or a single wild turkey carcass will do the job.

5 pounds venison or any small or large game bones (see Note)

Olive oil

2 large onions, cut into chunks

2 ribs celery, cut into chunks

1 to 2 large carrots, cut into chunks

4 ounces tomato paste

1 head garlic, top sliced off

6 sprigs fresh thyme

2 bay leaves

2 tablespoons black peppercorns

Stems from ½ bunch parsley

Preheat the oven to 400°F.

Saw the bones into 3-inch pieces or break them with a hatchet or mallet to expose the marrow. This creates a much richer stock. Place the bones on a baking sheet or roasting pan. Drizzle with oil. Roast until well browned and aromatic, about 45 minutes, stirring halfway through. Add the chopped vegetables and roast until just beginning to brown, about 10 minutes. Toss the bones and vegetables with the tomato paste and roast for another 5 minutes.

Fill a stockpot about halfway with water and turn the heat to high. Place the cooked bones with their drippings into the pot and add more water to just cover the bones. Bring to a boil over low heat and skim any foam that rises to the top. Reduce the heat to a bare simmer. Add the garlic, thyme, bay leaves, peppercorns, and half of the parsley stems. Avoid bringing the stock to a boil; a very slow simmer over low heat is best. Cook for at least 4 hours, but 8 to 12 hours is ideal to extract every bit of flavor. Some reduction is expected and intensifies flavors, but if the stock reduces too much (well below the level of the highest bones), add a little water to offset evaporation. In the last 30 minutes of cooking, add the remaining parsley stems.

After 4 to 12 hours, remove the stock from the heat, allow to cool slightly, and prepare to strain. It's safest to do the straining process on the floor or at a low table. Set a 6-quart metal pot or heavy-duty plastic container on a baking sheet on the floor or on a low table. Set a fine-mesh strainer (China cap if you have one) or a colander lined with cheesecloth in the pot. Using tongs, carefully transfer the largest solids into the strainer and allow excess liquid to drain into the empty pot. Discard the bones. Strain the remaining stock and discard the solids. If there are still a lot of particles in the stock, you can strain again and be left with a clear liquid.

TO COOL: The fastest way to cool the stock is to place the pot of strained stock in a stopped-up sink and surround the pot with ice. Fill the sink with water. Stir the stock occasionally. When completely cooled, refrigerate. After about 4 hours, the fat will rise to the top of the stock and solidify. Remove the fat and discard. Transfer the stock into quart containers and freeze until ready to use.

BLONDE GAME STOCK

MAKES ABOUT 6 QUARTS

This blonde game stock (called a "white" stock in classic French cuisine) is a stock that is not roasted. Think of it like the chicken broth your grandmother made for soup. It can help enrich lighter-colored stews, soups, and dishes when more subtle flavors are called for. A good formula to follow is to allow two pounds of bones per gallon of water. And split the ratio of your aromatics into 50 percent onions, 25 percent carrots, and 25 percent celery. This recipe is a good guideline to get started and can be doubled or halved as needed. If you've got a lot of bones, scale up the recipe and use a 12- or 24-quart pot.

3 to 5 pounds wild turkey or any small game bones (see Note)

2 large onions, cut into chunks

2 ribs celery, cut into chunks

1 to 2 large carrots, cut into chunks

1 head garlic, top sliced off

4 sprigs fresh thyme

2 bay leaves

1 tablespoon black peppercorns

Stems from ¼ bunch parsley

Note: Quantities will vary depending on the size of bones or carcasses, but more is better than less. A single wild turkey carcass will do the job, while several rabbit or small game birds are necessary.

Saw or break the bones to expose the marrow. This creates a much richer stock.

Fill a stockpot about halfway with water and turn the heat to high. Place the bones in the pot and add more water to just cover the bones. Add the onions, celery, and carrots and bring the liquid just up to a boil. Skim any foam that rises to the top (do this as needed throughout the cooking time). Reduce the heat to a bare simmer. Add the garlic, thyme, bay leaves, peppercorns, and parsley. Avoid bringing the stock to a boil; a very slow simmer over low heat is best. Cook for at least 2 hours and up to

4 hours. Some reduction is expected and intensifies flavors, but if the stock reduces too much (well below the level of the highest bones), add a little water to offset evaporation.

After 2 to 4 hours, remove the stock from the heat, allow to cool slightly, and prepare to strain. It's safest to do the straining process on the floor or at a low table. Set a 6-quart metal pot or heavy-duty plastic container on a baking sheet on the floor or a low table. Set a fine-mesh strainer (or China cap if you have one) or a colander lined with cheesecloth in the pot. Strain the stock and discard the solids. If there are still a lot of particles in the stock, you can strain again and be left with a clear liquid.

TO COOL: The fastest way to cool the stock is to place the pot of strained stock in a stopped-up sink and surround the pot with ice. Fill the sink with water. Stir the stock occasionally. When completely cooled, refrigerate. After about 4 hours, the fat will rise to the top of the stock and solidify. Remove the fat and discard. Transfer the stock into smaller containers and freeze until ready to use.

FISH STOCK (FISH FUMET)

MAKES 1 TO 2 QUARTS

Fish stock makes great use of fish carcasses that can pile up after an afternoon of filleting. Use it to enrich seafood-based stews and soups. It's a surprisingly fast stock to prepare and makes a big difference in the flavor of your dish—it's one of those tasks that's absolutely worth the effort if you're cooking a lot of fish dishes. Traditionally made with white-fleshed fish, it can also be made with salmon; it just won't be as clear. If you enjoy the flavors of dill or tarragon, feel free to add a few sprigs with the parsley.

2 pounds fish bones and heads but not gills

Kosher salt

4 ribs celery, thinly sliced

2 fennel bulbs, thinly sliced

2 medium onions, cut into chunks

1 small carrot, cut into chunks

1 medium leek, white parts only, thinly sliced (optional)

3 cloves garlic, crushed

1 bay leaf

Stems from ¼ bunch parsley

5 black or white peppercorns

Chop the fish skeletons and heads into manageable pieces if using large fish skeletons. Fill a bowl with salted water and rinse the fish bones. Drain and rinse well under fresh water.

Fill a stockpot about halfway with water and turn the heat to medium-high. Place the bones in the pot and add more water to just cover the bones. Add the celery, fennel, onions, carrot, and leek and bring up to a fast simmer. Reduce the heat to low and skim and discard any foam that rises to the top. Add the garlic, bay leaf, parsley stems, and peppercorns. Avoid bringing the stock to a boil; a very slow simmer over low heat is best. Cook for 45 minutes. Some reduction is expected and intensifies flavors, but if the stock reduces too much while cooking, you can add a little water to offset evaporation.

Remove from heat and cool slightly before straining. Set a fine-mesh strainer in a large bowl or pot and strain the stock. If there are still a lot of particles in the stock, on the second run, line the strainer with a paper towel. This will filter the stock thoroughly and you'll be left with a clear liquid. Transfer to storage containers and freeze until ready to use.

BASIC BROWN GRAVY
(AKA HUNTER'S SAUCE)

MAKES ABOUT 1 CUP

Reserved juices from pan-searing game steak or roast

Up to 2 tablespoons unsalted butter, if needed

2 tablespoons chopped shallot or scallion whites

8 ounces mushrooms (button, cremini or other mushroom), sliced

1 sprig fresh rosemary or thyme (optional)

½ teaspoon kosher salt

2 tablespoons all-purpose flour

¼ cup dry white or red wine (see Note)

1 cup Blonde Game Stock (page 306) or low-sodium chicken broth

Kosher salt

Freshly ground black pepper

Splash of Worcestershire sauce

Note: If you're out of wine, ¼ cup beer or a splash of red wine vinegar will work just as well.

This is a simple gravy recipe to make when pan-searing any kind of game steak or roast. It can be embellished with different herbs, flavored with 1 teaspoon of mustard (in with the shallots), or finished with 2 tablespoons cream or crème fraîche for extra richness (best with fowl or small game) or 2 tablespoons rinsed capers or green peppercorns. Once you've seared and cooked your piece of meat and it's safely resting, begin this gravy. It can be doubled or tripled for large roasts.

Discard all but 2 tablespoons of fat from the pan; if less than 2 tablespoons, add up to 2 tablespoons butter to make up the difference. Heat the pan over medium-high heat. When the fat is shimmering, add the shallot, mushrooms, and rosemary and cook until softened, 6 to 8 minutes. Add the salt. Reduce the heat to medium and sprinkle the flour over the mushroom mixture. Cook, stirring constantly, for 1 to 2 minutes to lightly toast the flour; be careful not to burn it or you'll ruin your sauce. Add the wine and deglaze, scraping up any caramelized bits that may have adhered to the bottom of the pan (this is where the flavor lives). Add the stock and any reserved juices released by the resting meat, raise the heat to medium-high, bring to a boil, and whisk briskly to break up any lumps. Season with salt and pepper and a splash of Worcestershire sauce. Remove from the heat.

BASIC BRINE

1 gallon water

1 cup kosher salt

1 cup packed brown sugar

10 black peppercorns

3 bay leaves

8 pounds ice (from 1 gallon water)

Good for waterfowl, upland birds, or wild hogs.

Combine the water, salt, brown sugar, peppercorns, and bay leaves in a large pot and bring to a boil over high heat. Remove from the heat and let cool to close to room temperature. Transfer the liquid to a large container with a tight-fitting lid and add the ice. Add your meat, cover, and refrigerate for the amount of time specified in your recipe.

ENRICHED BRINE

This brine is used in the Roast Pheasant recipe on page 172. It can be used for any waterfowl, upland birds, or wild hogs.

- 8 cups water
- ½ cup kosher salt
- 2 tablespoons sugar
- 1 teaspoon juniper berries, crushed
- 2 bay leaves
- 2 cloves garlic, crushed

Combine 4 cups of the water, the salt, sugar, juniper berries, bay leaves, and garlic in a large pot and bring to a boil, stirring until the salt and sugar dissolve. Remove from the heat and add the remaining 4 cups water. Set aside to cool completely. Put the meat into a container with a tight-fitting lid and pour the brine over the meat. Cover and refrigerate for the amount of time specified in your recipe.

BASIC BRINE FOR SMOKING FISH

This brine is used in the Hot Smoked Trout recipe on page 198, but it will work for just about any fish or small-size bird you plan to smoke.

- ¾ cup kosher salt
- ½ cup granulated sugar
- ¼ cup packed brown sugar
- ¼ cup honey
- 8 cups lukewarm water

In a nonmetallic container big enough to hold the fish, combine the salt, both sugars, honey, and water and whisk vigorously to dissolve the ingredients. Chill the brine. Thoroughly rinse the fish and submerge in the brine, using a plate to weight it down beneath the surface. Cover and refrigerate for the amount of time specified in your recipe.

BRINE FOR CURING A HAM

2 gallons water

2½ cups kosher salt

2 cups packed brown sugar

2 teaspoons yellow mustard seeds

20 black peppercorns

8 juniper berries

6 bay leaves

8 cloves garlic

1 tablespoon Prague Powder #1

This brine is used in the Smoked Ham recipe on page 68. It can be used for any large muscle bone-in or bone-out cuts of meat intended for smoking.

Combine the water, salt, brown sugar, mustard seeds, peppercorns, juniper berries, bay leaves, garlic, and Prague Powder #1 in a large pot and bring to a boil over high heat. Remove from the heat and let cool to room temperature, then let it chill in the refrigerator. See the recipe on pages 68–69 for how to inject the brine into a large bone-in roast and the process for brining and smoking.

CREOLE SEASONING

MAKES ABOUT ⅓ CUP

1½ tablespoons paprika

1 tablespoon garlic powder

1 tablespoon onion powder

1 teaspoon freshly ground black pepper

1 teaspoon cayenne pepper

1 teaspoon dried thyme

½ teaspoon dried oregano

This rub can be multiplied and stored for up to six months in a cool, dry place for use on grilled or smoked meats and fish, in stews (see Small Game and Sausage Gumbo on page 98), or as a seasoning for sides like roasted potatoes. Be sure to season with salt along with the rub, as this recipe doesn't include salt.

Combine the paprika, garlic powder, onion powder, black pepper, cayenne, thyme, and oregano in a small bowl. Store in an airtight container.

BBQ RUB

MAKES 3 CUPS

This rub will make just about any grilled roast or steak even tastier. You'll find it in use in the BBQ Smoked Beaver Sandwiches (page 101) and Split and Smoked Turkey with BBQ Sauce (page 169).

- ½ cup chili powder
- ½ cup kosher salt
- ½ cup packed brown sugar
- 2 tablespoons ground cumin
- 2 tablespoons granulated garlic
- 2 tablespoons dried oregano
- 2 tablespoons Hungarian paprika
- 1 tablespoon powdered mustard
- 1 tablespoon smoked paprika
- 1 tablespoon freshly ground black pepper
- 2 teaspoons onion powder
- 1 teaspoon cayenne pepper

Mix the chile powder, salt, brown sugar, cumin, granulated garlic, oregano, Hungarian paprika, powdered mustard, smoked paprika, black pepper, onion powder, and cayenne together in a bowl. Store in an airtight container. The rub will last for up to 6 months in a cool, dry place.

CLAYTON SAUNDERS'S BBQ SOP

MAKES ABOUT 1 QUART

This recipe pairs with Clayton Saunders's South Texas Wild Hog Shoulder (page 64). But this sop is too good to be kept to just one recipe. Use this to baste any game meat you throw on the grill: elk, rabbit, turkey, duck—they'd all benefit from the range of flavors here.

- 1 cup distilled white vinegar or apple cider vinegar
- 1 cup water
- ½ cup (1 stick) unsalted butter
- 1 cup ketchup
- 1 cup Worcestershire sauce
- 2 to 4 lemons, sliced
- 1 onion, sliced
- Kosher salt
- Freshly ground black pepper

Combine the vinegar, water, butter, ketchup, Worcestershire sauce, lemons, onion, and some salt and pepper in a medium saucepan and bring to a simmer. It is now ready to be applied to the cooking meat. You will need a pastry brush or kitchen rag to apply the sop.

BBQ SAUCE

MAKES 3 CUPS

2 cups ketchup

½ cup apple cider vinegar

¼ cup BBQ Rub (page 313)

¼ cup packed brown sugar

⅓ cup molasses

2 tablespoons fresh lemon juice

2 tablespoons Worcestershire sauce

1½ tablespoons liquid smoke

1 tablespoon Dijon mustard

1 tablespoon kosher salt

1 tablespoon freshly ground black pepper

Whisk together the ketchup, vinegar, BBQ rub, brown sugar, molasses, lemon juice, Worcestershire sauce, liquid smoke, mustard, salt, and pepper in a bowl. Store in an airtight container in the refrigerator, where it will keep for about 1 week, or longer if you omit the lemon juice.

ADOBADA

MAKES ABOUT 2 CUPS

8 dried guajillo chiles, wiped clean, stems and seeds removed, torn into large pieces

4 dried pasilla chiles, wiped clean, stems and seeds removed, torn into large pieces

12 cloves garlic

4 canned chipotle chiles in adobo sauce

¼ cup honey

¼ cup cider vinegar

2 teaspoons ground cinnamon

2 teaspoons ground cumin

2 teaspoons dried oregano

¼ teaspoon ground cloves

2 tablespoons kosher salt

This deep, spicy sauce is used to braise shanks (see Whole Braised Venison Shank Adobada, page 59) or any other meat from game birds to shoulder roasts. It can also be used as a basting sauce for grilled or roasted meats or seafood.

Heat a large, heavy skillet over medium heat until hot. Working in batches, toast the chiles until they blister slightly and are pliable. Transfer to a large bowl. Pour hot water over the chiles to cover them. Place a small plate on top of the chiles to keep them submerged. Soak until soft, about 1 hour.

Transfer the chiles to a blender with ½ cup of the soaking liquid. Reserve the remaining liquid. Add the garlic, chipotles, honey, vinegar, cinnamon, cumin, oregano, cloves, and salt and blend until a smooth thick paste forms. Add enough of the reserved soaking water to yield 4 cups of marinade (*adobo*) and blend until emulsified.

BASIC VINAIGRETTE

MAKES ABOUT ¼ CUP

This vinaigrette is a standard for any salad. Bump it up with herbs or swap out the vinegar for a different kind. It's one to commit to memory.

- 1 to 2 tablespoons red wine vinegar
- ½ teaspoon kosher salt
- ½ teaspoon freshly ground black pepper
- ½ teaspoon Dijon mustard
- 3 tablespoons extra virgin olive oil

Whisk the vinegar (use 1 tablespoon vinegar for a standard vinaigrette, 2 tablespoons if you like yours a little more acidic), salt, pepper, and mustard in a small bowl. Slowly whisk in the oil to emulsify. Taste and adjust the seasonings.

SPICY CITRUS DRESSING

MAKES ABOUT ¼ CUP

This is a more elaborate dressing. It's used on the salad that's paired with the Venison Carpaccio on page 34.

- 1 tablespoon fresh orange juice
- 1 teaspoon fresh lemon juice
- 1 tablespoon rice wine vinegar
- 1 teaspoon honey
- 1 teaspoon Dijon mustard
- ½ teaspoon kosher salt
- ½ teaspoon freshly ground black pepper
- Pinch of red chile flakes
- 3 tablespoons extra virgin olive oil

Whisk the orange juice, lemon juice, vinegar, honey, mustard, salt, pepper, and red chile flakes in a medium bowl. Slowly drizzle in the oil while whisking vigorously until the dressing is emulsified.

CONDIMENTS

CLASSIC GREMOLATA

MAKES ABOUT ⅓ CUP

- Zest of 2 lemons (grated on a Microplane)
- 2 cloves garlic, grated
- ⅓ cup finely chopped fresh flat-leaf parsley
- 2 teaspoons sea salt
- Freshly ground black pepper to taste

This is an excellent condiment for wild game and fish. Sometimes I like to use orange zest in place of the lemon zest, and you can play with the herbs too—parsley, mint, oregano, and basil are all possibilities. It's fantastic on Venison Carpaccio (page 34), Osso Bucco (page 60), roasted birds (pages 133, 170, and 172), and even grilled fish (page 209).

In a small bowl, combine all the ingredients. The gremolata is best if used within 24 hours.

BALSAMIC REDUCTION

MAKES ABOUT ½ CUP

- 1 cup aged balsamic vinegar

This reduction works with simply prepared meats, fish, vegetables, and cheese. It's also paired with the Grilled Venison Loin with Cauliflower Puree (page 40).

Pour the vinegar into a small, wide sauté pan and bring to a boil. Reduce the heat and gently simmer for 15 to 20 minutes, stirring occasionally, until it reduces by half and is thick enough to coat the back of a spoon. Let cool and serve at room temperature.

BLUEBERRY PORT COMPOTE

MAKES 1¼ CUPS

- 1 tablespoon vegetable oil
- 1 large shallot, finely chopped
- 2 cups (1 pint) fresh or frozen blueberries
- 2 slices fresh ginger, smashed
- 1 cinnamon stick
- 1 star anise pod
- ¼ cup sugar
- ¼ cup tawny port
- 2 tablespoons balsamic vinegar
- 1 tablespoon red wine vinegar
- 1 teaspoon finely grated orange zest
- Generous pinch of kosher salt
- Generous pinch of red chile flakes

Heat the oil in a small saucepan over medium heat. Add the shallot and cook, stirring often, until softened, 6 to 8 minutes. Add the blueberries, ginger, cinnamon, star anise, sugar, port, both vinegars, the orange zest, salt, and red chile flakes and bring to a simmer. Cook, stirring occasionally, until the blueberries start to burst and give off liquid and then slightly thicken, 8 to 10 minutes. Remove from the heat and set aside to let cool. The compote will thicken more as it cools.

Remove and discard the ginger, cinnamon, and star anise, if you like. Adjust the seasonings. Serve immediately, or transfer to a jar with a tight-fitting lid and store in the refrigerator.

APPLE, CHERRY, AND SAGE CHUTNEY

MAKES 2¼ CUPS

- 1½ pounds unpeeled Granny Smith or other tart apples, cored and chopped
- ½ cup apple juice
- ⅓ cup packed brown sugar
- ¼ cup apple cider vinegar
- ½ cup dried cherries
- ¼ cup golden raisins
- 2 tablespoons honey
- 2 tablespoons finely chopped fresh sage
- 1 tablespoon finely chopped fresh rosemary
- 1 tablespoon minced garlic
- Juice of 1 lemon
- Kosher salt

Combine the apples, apple juice, brown sugar, vinegar, dried cherries, raisins, honey, sage, rosemary, garlic, and lemon juice in a medium saucepan and cook over medium heat until the mixture starts to bubble. Add the salt. Reduce the heat to low and simmer, stirring occasionally to prevent sticking, until the fruit is soft and pulpy, the liquid is mostly absorbed, and the chutney is fairly thick, 35 to 40 minutes. Remove from the pot and let cool. Taste and add more salt if needed. The chutney will keep, covered, in the refrigerator for up to 1 week.

HERBED TARTAR SAUCE

MAKES 2½ CUPS

2 cups mayonnaise
2 tablespoons minced garlic
2 tablespoons chopped fresh chives
1 tablespoon chopped fresh rosemary
1 teaspoon freshly ground black pepper
10 fresh basil leaves, chopped
2 tablespoons chopped capers
10 cornichon pickles, chopped
Zest and juice of 2 lemons

This recipe can be quadrupled if you're feeding a crowd.

Whisk the mayonnaise, garlic, chives, rosemary, pepper, basil, capers, pickles, and lemon zest and juice in a medium bowl until incorporated.

BRANDIED CHERRIES

MAKES 3 CUPS

¾ cup water
¾ cup granulated sugar
2 juniper berries, lightly crushed (optional)
1 cinnamon stick
Pinch of kosher salt
1 cup brandy
1 pound fresh cherries, stemmed and pitted

Combine the water, sugar, juniper berries, if using, the cinnamon, and salt in a medium saucepan. Bring to a simmer over medium-high heat, stirring until the sugar dissolves, about 5 minutes. Add the brandy and cherries and stir to combine. Remove from the heat and set aside to cool. Transfer the cherries and their cooking liquid to a clean jar with a tight-fitting lid and refrigerate at least 2 days before serving. The cherries will keep in the refrigerator for at least 1 to 2 weeks.

SPICY PICKLED RED ONIONS

MAKES 1⅔ CUPS (THE ONIONS THEMSELVES MAKE 1¼ CUPS)

1 cup white wine vinegar
3 cloves garlic, smashed
1 large red onion, thinly sliced into rings
¼ cup sugar
1 teaspoon red chile flakes
1 teaspoon coriander seeds
1 teaspoon yellow mustard seeds (optional)
Generous pinch of kosher salt

Bring the vinegar to a boil in a medium saucepan over high heat. Add the garlic, onion, sugar, red chile flakes, coriander seeds, mustard seeds, if using, and salt. Cook, stirring, until the sugar dissolves and the onion wilts, about 5 minutes Remove the pot from the heat and let cool. Transfer the pickled onions to a clean jar with a tight-fitting lid and chill in the refrigerator for up to 10 days.

GREEN SAUCES I LOVE

WALNUT AND MINT PESTO

MAKES 1½ CUPS

1 cup walnuts, toasted

1 clove garlic, peeled

2 cups packed fresh flat-leaf parsley leaves

1 cup packed baby arugula

1 cup packed fresh mint leaves

Freshly grated zest from 1 lemon

¾ cup extra virgin olive oil, plus more to float on top

½ cup finely grated Parmigiano-Reggiano cheese

Juice of ½ lemon (about 2 tablespoons), or to taste

Kosher salt

Freshly ground black pepper

This recipe can be multiplied and frozen for future use. A pinch of ascorbic acid or a smashed vitamin C tablet will help to preserve the green color of the pesto. This is recommended especially if you're making a large batch.

Put the walnuts and garlic in the food processor and pulse until coarsely chopped. Add the parsley, arugula, mint, and lemon zest and process until coarsely chopped. With the motor running, drizzle in the oil through the hole in the lid. Add the cheese, lemon juice, and salt and pepper to taste and pulse until combined.

Transfer the pesto to a container with a tight-fitting lid and add a thin layer of oil to cover the top of the pesto.. Store in the refrigerator for up to 2 weeks or freezer for up to 3 months.

CLASSIC BASIL PESTO

MAKES 1 CUP

2 cups packed fresh basil leaves

⅓ cup pine nuts

1 clove garlic, peeled

¾ cup extra virgin olive oil, plus more to float on top

2 tablespoons fresh lemon juice

1½ teaspoons kosher salt

1 teaspoon freshly ground black pepper

½ cup grated Parmigiano-Reggiano cheese

This recipe can be multiplied and frozen for future use. A pinch of ascorbic acid or a smashed vitamin C tablet will help to preserve the green color of the pesto. This is recommended especially if you're making a large batch.

Pulse the basil, pine nuts, and garlic in a food processor several times, until coarsely chopped. Add 2 tablespoons of the oil and the lemon juice and process until smooth. Add the salt and pepper and, with the motor running, slowly pour in the remaining oil through the hole in the lid. Add the cheese and pulse a few more times to incorporate.

Transfer the pesto to a container with a tight-fitting lid and add a thin layer of oil to cover the top of the pesto. Store in the refrigerator for up to 2 weeks or freezer for up to 3 months.

CHERMOULA

MAKES 1 CUP

Chermoula is traditionally served with grilled fish in Morocco. But like other sauces of this type (like pesto, chimichurri, and sauce verte), it goes well with just about anything grilled, meat and fowl included.

6 cloves garlic
2 cups packed fresh cilantro leaves
2 cups packed fresh flat-leaf parsley leaves
2 teaspoons ground cumin
2 teaspoons paprika, preferably smoked
1½ teaspoons kosher salt
2 teaspoons finely grated lemon zest
1 teaspoon ground coriander
Pinch of cayenne pepper
¾ cup extra virgin olive oil
2 tablespoons fresh lemon juice

With the motor of a food processor running, drop in the garlic through the hole in the lid, one clove at a time, until chopped. Scrape down the sides with a spatula. Add the cilantro, parsley, cumin, paprika, salt, lemon zest, coriander, and cayenne and pulse to chop. With the motor running, drizzle in the oil and lemon juice and process until still slightly chunky. Transfer to a small container with a tight-fitting lid and refrigerate until ready to use.

SAUCE VERTE
(PARSLEY, CHIVE, AND CAPER SAUCE)

MAKES ⅔ CUP

Versions of this flavorful sauce are called sauce verte in France and salsa verde in Italy. It's used as a sauce for simply prepared fish and meats and as a condiment in sandwiches. The addition of anchovies and capers gives it a briny richness that makes it taste more complex than it really is.

1 clove garlic
1 cup packed fresh flat-leaf parsley leaves
¾ cup coarsely chopped fresh chives
4 anchovies, coarsely chopped
3 tablespoons capers, drained
2 tablespoons fresh lemon juice
2 tablespoons water
¼ cup olive oil
Kosher salt
Freshly ground black pepper

With the motor of a food processor running, drop in the garlic through the hole in the lid to chop it. Scrape down the sides with a spatula. Add the parsley, chives, anchovies, and capers and process until finely chopped. With the motor running, add the lemon juice, water, and oil through the hole in the lid and process until the liquid is incorporated. Season with salt and pepper. Transfer to a small bowl.

COMPOUND BUTTERS

ANCHOVY BUTTER

MAKES 2 LOGS

Put the anchovies, garlic, and Worcestershire sauce in a mini food processor and process until finely ground. Break the butter up into chunks and add it to the bowl. Process until smooth. Zest the lemon into the bowl and process again until combined. Scrape onto two pieces of parchment paper, roll into logs, and refrigerate until firm. Store in the refrigerator for up to 1 week or the freezer for up to 3 months.

10 to 12 anchovy fillets

6 cloves garlic, peeled

1 teaspoon Worcestershire sauce

1 cup (2 sticks) unsalted butter, softened

Zest of 1 lemon

CAYENNE BUTTER

MAKES 2 LOGS

Put the garlic in a mini food processor and process until chopped. Break the butter up into chunks and add to the bowl. Add the cayenne, salt, lemon zest, and lemon juice and process until smooth. Scrape onto two pieces of parchment paper, roll into logs, and refrigerate until firm. Store in the refrigerator for up to 1 week or in the freezer for up to 3 months.

2 small cloves garlic, peeled

1 cup (2 sticks) unsalted butter, softened

1½ teaspoons cayenne pepper

¼ teaspoon kosher salt

Zest of 1 small lemon (2 teaspoons)

Juice of ½ small lemon (1 tablespoon)

CHIMICHURRI BUTTER

MAKES 2 LOGS

Put the parsley, garlic, oregano, red chile flakes, salt, and vinegar in a mini food processor and process until finely ground. Break the butter up into chunks and add to the bowl. Process until smooth. Scrape onto two pieces of parchment paper, roll into logs, and refrigerate until firm. Store in the refrigerator for up to 1 week or in the freezer for up to 3 months.

2 cups packed fresh flat-leaf parsley leaves

4 cloves garlic

2 teaspoons fresh oregano leaves

½ teaspoon red chile flakes

½ teaspoon kosher salt

2 tablespoons white wine vinegar

1 cup (2 sticks) unsalted butter, softened

BREADCRUMBS, BISCUITS, AND DOUGHS

HOMEMADE BREADCRUMBS
(USING FILONE BREAD OR OTHER CRUSTY BREAD)

MAKES ABOUT 2½ CUPS

6 ounces filone (or other crusty bread)

Filone is a rustic, crusty Italian bread. Another type of crusty rustic bread may be substituted. These breadcrumbs are used in the Scotch Eggs on page 29 and the Wild Hog Milanese on page 43.

Preheat oven to 300°F.

To make coarse breadcrumbs: Cut the bread into small pieces and pulse in a food processor until they become coarse crumbs. Dry on baking sheets in the oven until dry and firm, about 20 minutes. Allow to cool before using or storing.

To make fine breadcrumbs: Return desired amount of cooled, dry breadcrumbs to the food processor and pulse until fine.

Use as recipe indicates or store in an airtight container in the freezer for up to 6 months.

BASIC PIE DOUGH

MAKES ONE 9-INCH DOUBLE CRUST

2½ cups all-purpose flour

1¼ teaspoons fine salt

1¾ sticks (14 tablespoons) unsalted butter, chilled and cut into ⅓-inch pieces

4 to 6 tablespoons ice water, or more as needed

1 teaspoon vodka or apple cider vinegar

Use this dough to turn any stew into a potpie. This recipe makes a double crust for a standard 9-inch pie dish. If rolled into a rectangle, it will make a crust large enough for a baking dish you'd use for a large potpie or enough dough to cut out a bunch of rounds for individual servings. I like to double the recipe and freeze half for future use.

In a food processor, combine the flour and salt and pulse a few times. Distribute the chilled butter pieces in the flour and toss gently with a spoon to coat each piece in a little flour. Pulse again about 20 times, until the butter pieces look like coarse meal. Remove the top and add 4 tablespoons of ice water and the vodka evenly across the crumbled butter-flour mixture. Return the lid and pulse again 2 to 4 times. Check the texture. If it's not just coming together as a dough when you give it a pinch, add 2 more tablespoons ice water and pulse again. Check the texture again. It should be crumbly but not dry.

Lay a piece of plastic wrap on a cutting board (if you can lay two pieces of plastic wrap side by side, even better). Turn the dough out onto the plastic and pat it down. It will still be crumbly. Carefully fold over the edges of the plastic wrap to make a tightly wrapped parcel, roughly ½ inch thick. Once the dough is wrapped, use a rolling pin to press the dough into a uniform thickness. Chill the dough for at least 1 hour before using. The dough will keep for up to 3 days in the refrigerator and 6 months in the freezer.

CHEDDAR CHIVE BISCUITS

MAKES EIGHT 3-INCH BISCUITS

These biscuits work as a side for just about anything. Split them in the middle, add a slice of leftover game meat, and call it a sandwich.

- 2 cups all-purpose flour, plus more for dusting
- 1 tablespoon baking powder
- 1 teaspoon fine salt
- ½ teaspoon freshly ground black pepper
- ⅓ cup finely shredded cheddar cheese (about 1 ounce)
- 1 tablespoon grated Parmigiano-Reggiano cheese
- 2 tablespoons chopped fresh chives
- ½ cup (1 stick) unsalted butter, chilled and cubed
- ¾ cup milk, plus more for brushing

Preheat the oven to 425°F and line a baking sheet with parchment paper.

Whisk the flour, baking powder, salt, and pepper in a large bowl. Add the cheeses and chives and toss gently with your fingers. Cut in the chilled butter with a pastry blender or two butter knives. When the butter is pea-size and somewhat incorporated, form a well in the shaggy dough and pour the milk in the center. Pull the sides of the well in and knead together lightly until the mixture forms a solid mass.

Sprinkle flour onto a cutting board. Pat the dough into a ½-inch-thick rectangle. Fold the dough into thirds like a letter. Pat the dough out again into a rectangle about 1 inch high. Lightly flour the top; cut biscuits with a 2¾-inch round cutter, pressing the scraps together and patting down to 1 inch, to get about 8 biscuits. Place them on the prepared baking sheet and brush the tops with milk. Bake until lightly browned on the top and bottom, about 14 minutes. Serve warm, with butter.

CORNBREAD

MAKES ONE 8 BY 8-INCH PAN

¼ cup (½ stick) unsalted butter, melted, plus more for the pan

1½ cups yellow fine cornmeal

½ cup all-purpose flour

¼ cup sugar

1½ teaspoons baking powder

½ teaspoon baking soda

1 teaspoon fine salt

2 large eggs

1½ cups milk

This is a versatile cornbread recipe. Feel free to add crumbled bacon, chopped jalapeños, or even corn kernels to jazz it up.

Preheat the oven to 425°F. Grease an 8 x 8-inch baking dish with butter.

Whisk the cornmeal, flour, sugar, baking powder, baking soda, and salt in a large bowl. In another bowl, whisk the eggs, then add the milk and melted butter. Add the wet ingredients to the dry ingredients and mix until a smooth batter forms, whisking out any lumps. Pour the batter into the prepared pan and bake on the middle rack until a toothpick comes out clean when inserted into the center of the cornbread, about 30 minutes. Let cool for 5 minutes before slicing and serving.

CATHEAD BISCUITS

MAKES 5 BISCUITS

These biscuits are intended to accompany Kevin Murphy's Kentucky-Style Squirrel Gravy (page 92). But they'd go well with just about any meal.

- 2 cups self-rising flour, plus more for sprinkling
- ¼ teaspoon kosher salt
- ½ to 1 tablespoon sugar (depending on how sweet you like them)
- 2 tablespoons lard, shortening, or unsalted butter (cut into small pieces), chilled, plus more for the pan
- 1 cup buttermilk
- 1 tablespoon unsalted butter, melted (optional)

SPECIAL EQUIPMENT: 1 mason jar (diameter of a cat head, or 3 inches)

Preheat the oven to 425°F.

Mix the flour, salt, and sugar in a large bowl. Rub the lard or shortening (or cut the butter) into the flour. When you're done, the mixture should look like coarse cornmeal.

Pour in the buttermilk and gently mix it into the flour with your hands to where it feels and looks like brick mortar (firm and wet, where it can still flow). Sprinkle in more flour as needed; the dough will be wet and sticky, but not so wet and sticky that it clings to your fingers or won't scrape off the counter. Place on a hard floured surface. Pat out into a rectangle about 7 by 9 inches. Fold into thirds like a letter. Pat the dough out again into a rectangle about 1 inch high. Lightly flour the top; cut 3 biscuits with the mason jar. Then re-form to cut out 1 more, and re-form one more time for the last biscuit. Grease up a 10-inch cast-iron skillet with lard, shortening, or butter. Arrange the biscuits around each other, leaving about a ½-inch gap between them. Brush a little melted butter on top of the biscuits, if desired (it will help with browning).

Bake until puffed and light golden brown on top, 13 to 15 minutes. Turn the oven light on to check the biscuits (don't open the door or you'll lose your heat). All ovens are different, but Kevin's takes about 13 minutes for his biscuits. If you think the bottom of the biscuits are done, you can turn your broiler on for 30 seconds or more to brown the tops.

VERSATILE SIDES

POLENTA

MAKES 4 TO 6 SERVINGS

5 cups water

Big pinch of kosher salt

1 cup polenta or yellow coarse cornmeal

½ cup grated Parmigiano-Reggiano cheese

2 tablespoons unsalted butter

Used to accompany both the Osso Bucco (page 60) and the Rabbit Cacciatore (page 103), this Italian starchy staple would pair well with any other stewy dish, especially the Whole Braised Venison Shank Adobada (page 59). This makes a very soft, creamy polenta. For a firmer polenta, use 1 cup less water for cooking and pour into an oiled 9 x 13-inch pan once cooked. Cool and refrigerate until firm.

Bring the water to a boil in a 4- to 6-quart pot. Add the salt. Whisking constantly to avoid lumps, slowly add the polenta in a thin stream. Reduce the heat to medium-low and continue to stir for 15 to 20 minutes, until the polenta becomes thick and large bubbles form (kind of like a volcano erupting). Remove from the heat and stir in the cheese and the butter until glossy and smooth. Set aside, covered, until ready to serve.

COCONUT RICE

MAKES 6 CUPS

2 cups jasmine rice

1 (13.5-ounce) can full-fat coconut milk, well shaken

½ cup water

1 tablespoon granulated sugar (optional)

1 teaspoon kosher salt

This fragrant, rich rice is a fantastic side for the Coconut Curry Fish Fillet Packets (page 213). It also works as an accompaniment for many other dishes in this book.

Put the rice in a heavy medium saucepan, add water to cover, and swish around with your fingers until the rice becomes cloudy. Drain. Repeat two more times, or until the water runs clear. Drain well. Stir in the coconut milk, water, sugar, if using, and salt and mix well. Bring to a boil. Stir the rice, scraping up any rice sticking to the bottom of the pan. Reduce the heat to low, cover, and cook, undisturbed, until the rice has absorbed the liquid and is tender, about 20 minutes. Remove from the heat and let sit undisturbed for 10 minutes. Fluff and serve.

CAULIFLOWER PUREE

MAKES ABOUT 1½ QUARTS

This recipe makes a decadent puree—great for holidays or other celebratory meals. It can be made less caloric by using solely whole milk, less cheese (6 ounces versus 8), and omitting the butter. Using a high-powered blender like a Vitamix makes the final puree velvety smooth with a texture as rich as the flavor.

- 1 medium head cauliflower, halved and cored
- 1 cup heavy cream
- 1 cup whole milk
- 1 teaspoon kosher salt, plus more for seasoning
- 8 ounces Gruyère cheese, grated
- 2 tablespoons unsalted butter
- Freshly ground black pepper

Segment and chop the cauliflower into 1-inch pieces. Put the pieces in a large saucepan and add the cream, milk (it won't completely cover the cauliflower—that's OK), and salt. Cover and bring to a gentle simmer over medium heat, being careful not to let the cream mixture boil over. Adjust the heat if necessary and simmer until knife tender, 15 to 20 minutes. Remove the cauliflower from the cream mixture with a slotted spoon, reserving the cream mixture, and put it into a blender (do this in batches if necessary). Keeping the blender lid ajar and covered with a clean kitchen towel, puree the cauliflower while hot, slowly pouring in ¼ cup of the cream mixture, until the puree becomes very smooth. While still very warm, add the cheese and butter and blend. If the mixture is lumpy, blend with a little more cream. Pour the cauliflower puree into a bowl, season with salt and pepper, and stir to fully mix. This can be made up to a day ahead of time (cool, cover, and refrigerate). Gently rewarm in a saucepan over medium-low heat when you are ready to serve.

COLESLAW

MAKES 4 TO 6 SERVINGS

This slaw accompanies the BBQ Smoked Beaver Sandwiches (page 101), but it's too good to only use when you've hunted down a beaver. Make it a go-to recipe for barbecues and picnics. It makes an excellent side.

- ½ cup mayonnaise
- ¼ cup apple cider vinegar
- 3 tablespoons sugar
- 1 tablespoon Dijon mustard
- 1 tablespoon granulated garlic
- 1 tablespoon kosher salt
- 1 teaspoon onion powder
- 1 teaspoon freshly ground black pepper
- ½ head green cabbage (about 8 ounces), cored
- 4 scallions
- 1 carrot

Whisk the mayonnaise, vinegar, sugar, mustard, granulated garlic, salt, onion powder, and pepper in a medium bowl until smooth. Slice the cabbage very thinly across the layers and add to a large bowl. Thinly slice the scallions. Shred the carrot on a box grater. Add both to the cabbage. Add the dressing to the cabbage and toss until it is completely incorporated.

ACKNOWLEDGMENTS

Many hunters, anglers, and wild-game cooks gave freely of their knowledge, recipes, techniques, and ingredients in order to make this book possible. It would be impossible to list them all, but special thanks to Ed Arnett, April Bloomfield, Ron Boehme, Ryan Callaghan, Tim Collins, Doug Duren, Shannon Harper, Jon Heindemause, James Miller, Nick Moe, Kevin Murphy, Andrew Radzialowski, Daniel Rinella, Matthew Rinella, Clayton Saunders, and Tyler Webster. Thanks also to Vivian Jao, Liz Tarpy, Stacy Basko, Jeannie Chen, and Patty Nusser for their help in testing these recipes to ensure their accuracy and ease of use.

The recipe photos in this book (as well as a lot of tweaking and refining of the recipes themselves) are the result of a great collaborative effort that took place in Bozeman, Montana. Thanks to Pancho Gatchalian, Koren Grivson, and Indra Fanuzzi for cooking. Thanks to Brian Hoffman and Jason Roehrig for dozens of other things, ranging from lighting assistance to vacuum sealing. Finally, thanks Rick Gilbert and Liz Saubuste for their work on sourcing props, and to Yeti, Weston, and Camp Chef for an array of high-quality products that made our work possible.

The imagery in this book comes from a variety of sources. Thanks to the talented John Hafner for the recipe photos in addition to a number of other beautiful images. Thanks to Garret Smith for his many contributions to this book, which were often captured under extremely difficult field conditions. Additional photography thanks to Helen Cho, Patrick Durkin, Kyle Johnson, Mahting Putelis, Daniel Rinella, Jennifer Jones, and Brian Grossenbacher. The detailed and beautiful wildlife illustrations are the work of Ryan Frost.

Many of my colleagues at Zero Point Zero Production were instrumental in the making of this book. Thanks to Joe Caterini, Lydia Tenaglia, and Chris Collins for building a company that fosters the creation of quality work. Thanks to Jared Andrukanis, Eliza Comer, Lou Festa, and Matt Gerish for general support, and to the talented team at ZPZ's graphic-design department (Mike Houston, Naoko Saito, and Dan DeGraaf) for conceptual assistance. Lastly, a huge thanks to Annie Raser and Brittany Brothers for their help and support.

Everyone at MeatEater, Inc., jumped in whenever required to make this book as good as possible. Brody Henderson provided valuable insight, research, and writing. Michelle Jorgensen provided both creative and practical support through much of the process. And, as always, Janis Putelis was involved at virtually every level of the project, ranging from photography to in-the-field expertise to core decisions around content and layout.

Thanks to my agent, Marc Gerald, for his continuing support over the last fourteen or so years, and thanks to Cindy Spiegel of Spiegel & Grau for betting on me time and again over much of that period. You guys have proven to be some of the most important people in my life. Many other folks from the S&G and Penguin Random House teams were deeply involved in this project, including Mengfei Chen, Nancy Delia, Debbie Glasserman, Mark Maguire, Greg Mollica, and Leda Scheintaub.

Lastly, thanks to my collaborator, Krista Ruane. As a writer, editor, stylist, thinker, and chef, Krista oversaw this project from inception to completion. Krista, this book is as much yours as it is mine.

ILLUSTRATION AND PHOTO CREDITS

Helen Cho 74, 220, 225, 293

Patrick Durkin 264

Ryan Frost 10,11, 80, 81, 112, 113, 148, 149, 182, 183, 184, 185, 222, 223, 224, 254, 274, 275

John Hafner vi, viii, ix, x, 28, 32, 34, 37, 38, 41, 42, 45, 46, 47, 51, 52, 55, 56, 58, 61, 66, 88, 90, 91, 93, 96, 99, 102, 104, 106, 108, 109, 122, 125, 126, 130, 134, 138, 140, 142, 144, 155, 156, 163, 164, 167, 168, 171, 172, 196, 199, 200, 205, 206, 211, 212, 234, 238, 240, 243, 244, 250, 252, 255, 260, 263, 284, 287, 288, 294, 297, 298, 300, 302, 304, 308, 315, 322, 326, 331, 334, 336, 340

Jon Heindemause 218

Kyle Johnson 191, 268, 280, 281, 282

Jennifer Jones 271, 277

Janis Putelis 216

Mahting Putelis 72, 76

Daniel Rinella 191, 237, 272, 279

Krista Ruane 246

Garret Smith xiii, xiv, 2, 3, 4, 6, 8, 9, 12, 14, 15, 16, 18, 20, 22, 23, 24, 25, 26, 27, 29, 31, 70, 75, 77, 78, 82, 83, 84, 85, 86, 87, 110, 114, 116, 117, 121, 145, 146, 150, 151, 152, 153, 154, 176, 178, 180, 181, 186, 188, 189, 190, 192, 193, 194, 195, 214, 226, 227, 228, 229, 230, 231, 232, 248, 256, 257, 258, 259, 270, 276, 278, 291, 307, 311, 319, 328, 332, 338

Yeti Coolers iv, 219

Yeti Coolers/Brian Grossenbacher 266

INDEX

Page numbers in *italics* refer to illustrations.

C

D

E

F

G

R

S

T

U

V

W

Z

ABOUT THE AUTHOR

STEVEN RINELLA is an outdoorsman, writer, wild foods enthusiast, and television and podcast personality who is a passionate advocate for conservation and the protection of public lands. Rinella is the host of the television show and podcast *MeatEater;* his most recent book is the *New York Times* bestseller *The Meateater Outdoor Cookbook*. His other titles include *American Buffalo: In Search of a Lost Icon* and *Outdoor Kids in an Inside World*. Rinella lives in Bozeman, Montana, with his wife and their three kids..

themeateater.com
Facebook.com/StevenRinellaMeateater
Instagram: @stevenrinella and @meateater